Life of Thurlow Weed

Volume I

AUTOBIOGRAPHY OF THURLOW WEED

THE LIFE OF THURLOW WEED

Volume I
  Autobiography of Thurlow Weed
                    Edited by Harriet A. Weed

Volume II
  Memoir of Thurlow Weed
                    by Thurlow Weed Barnes

Life of Thurlow Weed

Volume I

AUTOBIOGRAPHY OF THURLOW WEED

EDITED BY HARRIET A. WEED

DA CAPO PRESS • NEW YORK • 1970

A Da Capo Press Reprint Edition

This Da Capo Press edition of the
Life of Thurlow Weed
is an unabridged republication of the
first edition published in Boston in
1883 and 1884.

Library of Congress Catalog Card Number 79-87686
SBN 306-71706-9

Published by Da Capo Press
A Division of Plenum Publishing Corporation
227 West 17th Street
New York, N.Y. 10011

Manufactured in the United States of America

LIFE OF THURLOW WEED

INCLUDING

HIS AUTOBIOGRAPHY

AND

A MEMOIR

EMBELLISHED WITH

PORTRAITS AND OTHER ILLUSTRATIONS

COMPLETE IN TWO VOLUMES

VOLUME I.

J. A. J. Wilcox sculp.

AUTOBIOGRAPHY

THURLOW WEED

EDITED BY HIS DAUGHTER

HARRIET A. WEED

BOSTON
HOUGHTON, MIFFLIN AND COMPANY
New York: 11 East Seventeenth Street
The Riverside Press, Cambridge
1883

The Riverside Press, Cambridge :
Electrotyped and Printed by H. O. Houghton & Co.

PREFACE.

My father's own story of his life, so far as he committed it to paper, will be found in this volume. Written at various periods, and frequently in detached fragments, these reminiscences are sufficiently full to make, when arranged in due order of time, a connected narrative of the events and experiences of the years he deemed of chief interest or importance. Failing health prevented the accomplishment of his purpose to describe much more fully two periods, — 1842 to 1848 and 1852 to 1860, — which are but briefly alluded to.

My duties have been confined to the verification of the dates and in placing as far as was practicable the several sections of the manuscript in chronological order. I am under great obligations to my own and my father's friend, Mr. Frederick W. Seward, for the assistance he has afforded me in preparing the volume for publication.

HARRIET A. WEED.

New York, *April*, 1883.

CONTENTS.

CHAPTER I.

1797–1808.

CHAPTER II.

1808–1809.

CHAPTER III.

1809–1813.

CHAPTER IV.

1813–1815.

CHAPTER V.

1815–1816.

CHAPTER VI.

1816–1818.

CHAPTER XI.

1823–1824.

CHAPTER XII.

1824.

CHAPTER XIII.

1824.

CHAPTER XIV.

1824.

CHAPTER XV.

1824–1825.

CHAPTER XX.

1826.

CHAPTER XXI.

1826–1827.

CHAPTER XXII.

1827.

CHAPTER XXIII.

1827–1828.

CHAPTER XXIV.

1828–1829.

CHAPTER XXV.

1829.

CHAPTER XXVI.

1827–1829.

CHAPTER XLIV.

1838–1839.

CHAPTER XLV.

1837–1866.

CHAPTER XLVI.

1839.

CHAPTER XLVII.

1840–1341.

CHAPTER XLVIII.

1840.

CHAPTER LXV.

1833–1877.

CHAPTER LXVI.

1861–1880.

CHAPTER LXVII.

1861–1880.

CHAPTER LXVIII.

1861–1880.

LIST OF STEEL PLATES.

AUTOBIOGRAPHY.

CHAPTER I.

1797–1808.

SANTA CRUZ, *February* 15, 1845.

SINCE I came to this island, in December, for the benefit of a daughter's health, the idea of occupying some leisure hours in recording the events of my life has frequently occurred to me; and as such a record may at some future day interest my children, I have concluded to undertake it.

1797. — I was born at a small place called Acra, in the town of Cairo, Greene County, New York, on the 15th of November, 1797. My parents were natives of Connecticut. My father, Joel Weed, was the son of Nathan Weed, a soldier of the Revolution, who removed with a large family from Stamford, Conn., immediately after the close of that struggle, first to Dutchess and then to Greene County, New York. My mother, Mary Ells, was a native of New Haven. I am the eldest of three brothers and two sisters, of whom only one (Osborn) is now living. My sisters died early, one at Catskill and the other in Onondaga. My brother Orrin, in September, 1823, died of yellow fever in the city of New York. He was apprenticed to Henry Eckford, an eminent shipbuilder.

My father was a hard-working man, with a kind heart, and

an earnest desire to do the best he could for his children. He was withal a strictly honest man. But he was doomed to earn his bread by the sweat of his brow, in its most literal sense. He was bred a farmer, but in 1799 removed from Cairo to Catskill, and became a carman. But everything went wrong with him. Constant and hard labor failed to better his condition. If at times he succeeded in getting a little ahead, those for whom he worked would fail to pay him, or his horse would get lame, or fall sick, or back off the docks into the river. The consequence was that we were always poor, sometimes very poor. This, however, was the misfortune rather than the fault of my parents; for they were always struggling to promote the welfare of their children. They were very anxious that I should enjoy the advantages of education. I cannot ascertain how much schooling I got at Catskill, probably less than a year, certainly not a year and a half, and this when I was not more than five or six years old.

I felt the necessity, at an early age, of trying to do something for my own support.

My first employment, when about eight years old, was in blowing a blacksmith's bellows for a Mr. Reeves, who gave me six cents per day, which contributed so much towards the support of the family. I stood upon a box to enable me to reach the handle of the bellows. My next service was in the capacity of boy of all work, at a tavern in the village of Jefferson, two miles from Catskill kept by a Captain Baker, who had, I remember, made a great mistake in exchanging the command of a ship for a tavern. After the sheriff took possession of Captain Baker's wrecked hotel, I got a situation as cabin boy on board the sloop Ranger, Captain Grant. This gratified a desire I had to see the city of New York. I was then (1806) in my ninth year. I remember, as if it were but yesterday, after carrying the small hair trunk of a passenger from Coenties Slip to Broad Street, finding myself in possession of the first shilling that I could call my own. I remember, too, how joyfully I purchased with that shilling three two-penny cakes and three oranges for my brother and sister, how carefully I watched them on the passage back, and how much happiness they conferred. While on board the Ranger, we encountered a severe gale in Haverstraw Bay. The sloop's sails were blown to pieces.

The captain then let go the anchor, which was dragged a long way, but though much damage was done to other vessels, we rode it out. After the Ranger was either condemned or laid up (I don't know which), I went as cabin boy on board the sloop Jefferson, Captain Jacobus Bogardus. I believe I went one trip with Captain Bogardus in the old sloop Washington before the Jefferson was finished.

What a change has since come over the city of New York! Then it consisted mainly of what are now the first seven wards. The City Hall Park was well up town. What are now the ninth, thirteenth, fourteenth, fifteenth, sixteenth, and seventeenth wards were either waste lands, gardens, or pasturage. And what is now the twelfth ward was then "in the country." I remember that Broad Street was then built almost entirely of old-fashioned Dutch houses, with their gable ends to the street. The State Prison, now I believe a hospital for strangers, and in the heart of the city, was then out of town, and by the side of the river. There are now half a dozen streets between this old prison and the docks.

1806. — I greatly enjoyed life as a sloop's cabin boy. The trip between Catskill and New York averaged from four to ten days. When becalmed we would go ashore in a small boat to obtain vegetables, fruit, etc. I was soon familiar with all the villages and all the points of historical interest along the river. I became during that time much attached to a sailor named James Van Dervoort, a tall, handsome man, who sang "Cease, rude Boreas," and other nautical songs, with great effect. Van Dervoort, when navigation closed, shipped for a winter voyage to China, or the East Indies. In the "yarns" he used to "spin" about the wonders of the East I was greatly interested, and but for the circumstance that I could not go aloft without becoming dizzy-headed, I should have gone to sea with my friend Van Dervoort.

Thus, but for an infirmity which incapacitated me for the most essential part of a sailor's duty, my occupation would have been that of a seaman instead of a printer. Years afterwards, when a journeyman at Albany, I learned that nothing had been heard from him since the autumn of 1809, when he sailed from New York on a voyage to China. Ten years afterwards, at Rochester, I learned from Captain Trowbridge, who had been master of a vessel from New Haven, Conn., and taken prisoner at the commencement of the war of 1812, that he became well acquainted with James Van Dervoort in Dartmoor prison. He had been impressed from a merchant ship by a British man-of-war, on board of which he served as a seaman between two and three years. When our government declared war against England, mainly because six thousand of our seamen had been thus impressed, and his frigate was ordered to America, he refused to fight against his country, and with other American sailors on board the same ship was sent to Dartmoor prison, where, after enduring many hardships, he died.

About this time Catskill people were waiting with equal anxiety and incredulity for Mr. Fulton's first steamboat, that was to astonish the world by going through the water without oars or sails, and against wind and tide! There was then no wharf connecting the land at Catskill with the island in the Hudson River which is now the Landing.

I remember to have gone with other boys to the Point, where we packed our clothes in our hats, and our hats upon boards, which we pushed before us, thus swimming out to the island, where we dressed, and passed two days in succession waiting for the steamboat, which finally came, vomiting smoke and fire, and looking more like a visitor from the infernal regions than the beautiful steamers that now glide through the waters.

1807. — Governor Morgan Lewis was the first officially great man I ever saw. He came in the fall of 1807 to review a brigade of militia, as commander-in-chief, at the village of Madison, about four miles west of Catskill. It was a cold, raw, drizzling day, but I walked barefooted out and back, so happy in the privilege as not to envy the more fortunate urchins who, by holding officers' horses, were enabled to buy gingerbread.

About this time I became precociously a politician! Party lines were drawn very close. The people were much excited as Republicans or Federalists. The latter wore black cockades, with which the former were greatly exasperated, so much so, indeed, that upon one occasion, at the close of a militia review in Catskill, there was a political outbreak which threatened the most serious consequences, the belligerents having deadly weapons in their hands, which many of them were inclined to use.

My remembrance of Mr. Haight, our late State Treasurer, goes back to this period, when he was in command of a light infantry company. He was then a staunch Republican. James Powers, who is now high in the confidence of the Democratic party (as our opponents claim to be), was then a Federalist. Thomas P. Grosvenor was then a resident of Catskill, and a leading Federalist.

Among the events which made the strongest impression upon my mind were the duel between Colonel Burr and Alexander Hamilton, and the first election of Daniel D. Tompkins as Governor.

The following letter, called out, as will be seen, in 1865, by a paragraph in the Catskill paper, gives additional incidents of my Catskill life : —

ALBANY, *March* 29, 1865.

To THE EDITOR OF THE " RECORDER AND DEMOCRAT."

In your " Recorder " of the 24th inst. (which I received this morning), a writer, who recalls and describes some of the early inhabitants of your village, "remembers, as among the earliest draymen of Catskill, the two Joe Weeds (Joel and Joseph), one of whom, I do not know which, was the progenitor of Thurlow Weed. Though in humble life, both were esteemed, I believe, as honest, industrious men."

Though a matter of no possible interest to any but myself, allow me to say that Joel Weed, the younger brother, was my father. They *were* honest, industrious cartmen, my uncle Joseph being the more prosperous. Indeed, he owned a house, still standing about half-way between "Chandler's" and the bridge ; while he moved annually at least, renting apartments in the "Stone Jug," "No. 8 " (I can't remember why No. 8), Gullen's barber shop, etc., etc.

My uncle Joseph had one son, George L. Weed, a very worthy man and well-known Christian missionary. I had two brothers. One (Orrin) died in New York, and the other (Osborn) in Tennessee, in March, 1851. My father died in Onondaga, forty-six years ago ; my mother in Tennessee, in 1841. This is all — perhaps more than anybody will care to learn of my origin. But your correspondent has turned my thoughts back to the *Catskill* that I remember during the first seven years of the present century, and some of its "oldest inhabitants " may be interested in reminiscences of that period. I am not as much mistaken, probably, in the impression that Catskill was a place of more business enterprise and activity *then* than at present, as I was, after an absence of nearly twenty years, in the width of the creek, the height of the Hop-o-Nose, and the distance from Donnelly's to the court-house. At any rate, however, the Catskill of my youth was a bustling, thrifty, pleasant village, with considerable commerce, two shipyards, and in the winter a large slaughtering and packing business.

Among its inhabitants were men of decided ability; men who, in any community, would stand out prominently upon the canvas. Such, for example, were Thomas P. Grosvenor, Jacob and Samuel Haight, the Days, the Croswells, the Cookes, the Hills, etc., etc. But my mind retains most vividly incidents, rather than individuals. In those days, hard as it may seem now, poor men, however honest, lived in dread of *imprisonment!* My father was one of a class whom ill-fortune tracked through life. He worked hard, but never prospered. The debtor's prison, therefore, was ever staring us in the face. But there was one blessed mitigation of the horrors of a debtor's prison. There were "liberties" connected with the prison, of which a debtor with a reputation for honesty, and a wealthy friend who would sign his bond to remain upon the "limits," might avail himself. The limits, accurately defined, extended to business parts of the village, so that a poor man stood some chance of keeping the wolf from devouring his wife and children. This, however, was not the full measure of the law's humanity. On Sunday the debtor was free! And on these days of jubilee I used to roam with my enfranchised father down to the Point, over to the shad fishery, or up to Jefferson, with a deep sense of gratitude that he was permitted, one day in the week, to walk God's earth and breathe his atmosphere unrestrained. Creditors were always on the watch for truant debtors, who sometimes failed to return to the limits before twelve o'clock on Sunday night.

I do not remember the "Mammy Kane," whom your correspondent chronicles as the depository of boys' sixpences.

The gingerbread and spruce-beer house most resorted to sixty years ago was kept quite at the upper end of the village, near Brushingham's. There were three hotels, Donnelly's, Chandler's, and Bottsford's, in Catskill then, each, I am sure, more extensively known than any of your present hotels. The late gallant Colonel Donnelly, of Niagara County, was a grandson of the keeper of the hotel I refer to.

Among the events that impressed themselves upon my memory indelibly was the drowning of a daughter of Mr. Hill by a freshet, and the loss of a son of Mr. Donnelly, by skating into an air-hole on Moose Creek (I believe that was the name), a mile or two below the mouth of the Catskill Creek. Skating, so much the fashion now, was a favorite exercise of the grandfathers of those who so enjoy it now, though ladies did not then share the excitement.

An incident, remembered of course by but very few, was then a
" nine days' wonder." This was a personal combat between two young
gentlemen, rivals for the hand of an accomplished lady ; but, as at least
one of the parties survive (eminent and honored), perhaps even this
reference to the circumstance may be ill-timed.

The first military funeral I ever witnessed was that of Major Hale.
This was in 1803 or 1804. It was very impressive, especially in the
led horse, with the holster, boots, etc., of the deceased revolutionary
officer.

In those days there was a delusion among poor but credulous people about the buried treasure of Captain Kidd. I remember to have
been as a boy permitted to accompany a party on an expedition which
was supposed to be pregnant with golden results. Upon reaching the
mysterious locality, the throat of a black cat was cut, and the precise
spot was indicated by the direction the blood spurted. And there the
digging commenced with an energy worthy of Dousterswivel, in the
" Antiquary," but it was not rewarded by even so much as the discovery of " Search No. 1."

As boys, we used to go down to the magnificent (but even then
dilapidated and long since demolished) Livingston Manor House, at
the mouth of Johnston's Creek, to pick barberries, and get frightened
by the screeching of an insane lady confined in her apartment in the
white house upon the hill.

The *great* event, and one that excited Catskill for many months, was
a murder !

A body was discovered early one Sunday morning, on the west shore
of the creek, near Dubois farm. I forget whether the name of the
murdered man was Scott, or whether that was the name of the murderer. Soon it was ascertained that the man was last seen at Nance
McFall's, a disreputable house out of the village, but near the spot
where the body was found.

Circumstances came out which satisfied the inhabitants that he had
been murdered. Toward evening groups were seen at corners, growing more and more excited, until, Justice not yet having drawn on her
boots, the multitude pressed through the main street, strengthening in
numbers and enthusiasm, down to the dwelling of the doomed Nance,
which was demolished and scattered to the winds and waves.

Subsequently the murderer was tried, convicted, and sentenced to
be hanged ; but on the day of execution, and only an hour from the
fatal moment, when an immense concourse of people were assembled,
came a reprieve.

I wonder if any of the half dozen boys, who each, with myself, put
his clothes in his hat, and placing the hat upon a board, pushing it

ahead, swam off to the island (now steamboat landing) to await the approach of the first steamboat, still survive?

My river experience, as cabin boy and cook, was with Captains Grant and Bogardus, in the sloops Ranger and Jefferson. My inclination for the life of a sailor was always subordinate to my desire to become a printer. My great ambition was to get apprenticed to Mr. Mackay Croswell, who then (1808) published the "Recorder," but the realization of that object was postponed, though I lingered about the printing office a good deal, doing chores, and learning what I could learn as an interloper.

Your correspondent kindly refers to the circumstance that Mr. Edwin Croswell and myself "were boys together at Catskill." Though of the same age, we were not intimate as boys. He had the advantage of me in position, education, etc. Nor had he, like Jack Graham and Gil Frost, a taste for sports and adventures in which I remember to have participated. Mr. Croswell, as a boy, was noticeable for the same quiet, studious, refined habits and associations which have characterized his whole life. I left Catskill in 1808, and did not again meet Mr. Croswell for nearly twenty years.

In 1830, as editor of the " Evening Journal " (Mr. Croswell having been for several years editor of the " Argus ") I came into sharp collision with him. Albany was then, and for years before and after that period, a political centre for both the State and nation. Each party confided the duty of organization and discipline to its respective editors. A sense of responsibility stimulated both. Long years of earnest controversy and intense feeling ensued. The warfare, unhappily, assumed not only political but personal and social aspects.

The leading men of the Democratic party possessed talents, experience, and tact. The " Albany Regency," consisting as it did of such men as Van Buren, Governor Marcy, Mr. Knower, Silas Wright, Mr. Flagg, John A. Dix, S. A. Talcott, T. W. Olcott, Charles E. Dudley, James Porter, Roger Skinner, etc., etc., found in Mr. Croswell, their colleague and editor, sound judgment, untiring industry, great devotion, and rare ability.

Governor Marcy, Mr. Wright, and General Dix, distinguished for legislative and executive ability, were very able contributors to the columns of the " Argus." Mr. Flagg, himself an editor, was also a power in the " Argus." Against such men, with General Jackson as their chief, it was my privilege to contend; and now, all the bitterness engendered by such conflicts having been soothed by time, it is pleasant to remember that before the curtain fell at the closing scene of that political drama, agreeable personal relations grew up between most of those eminent men and myself.

I was introduced to Mr. Van Buren at the funeral of my intimate friend, the late Governor Marcy. This was my first and last meeting with the then ex-President.

For several years before the death of Silas Wright, we were friends. With Mr. Flagg, who survives like Belisarius with lost vision but bright intellect, I have long enjoyed common sentiments and sympathy, and my relations with General Dix, political, personal, and social, are most pleasant.

With Mr. Olcott, the able financier of the " Regency " in its palmy days, peculiar relations have ever existed. He never refused me a pecuniary favor, and for the first twenty years of my residence here I had to ask for myself and other *poor* politicians very many. He has discounted scores of notes whose maker and indorser were equally good (*for nothing*). Protests, "plenty as blackberries," never injured my credit at the " Little Belt."

I remember to have formed a high estimate of the usefulness of three citizens of Catskill, namely, Dr. Croswell, the Rev. Dr. Porter, and Jacob Haight. Perhaps I only shared the common sentiment of the village; but at any rate those gentlemen came up to my ideal of model men. Later in life, while serving with Major Haight in the legislature, my early impressions of his worth were confirmed. Your correspondent is quite right in assuming that I "cherish fond recollections " of Catskill.

In the first years of my banishment — for Catskill was an Eden to my youthful memory — my chief happiness consisted in anticipating, at some future day, a return to that charmed locality. And only last summer, moved by something like the instinct which brings " chickens home to roost," I explored the village in search of what was not to be found, a mansion with pleasant surroundings and " for sale."

The length of this letter admonishes me that it must close. In speaking or writing of things which occurred threescore years ago, old men are pretty sure to be prolix if not prosy.

Respectfully yours,   THURLOW WEED.

CHAPTER II.

1808–1809.

REMOVAL TO CORTLAND COUNTY. — LIFE IN THE FOREST. — "BLACK SALTS." — GOING TO THE STORE. — THE RATHBUNS. — THE "SAP BUSH." — MAPLE SUGAR MAKING. — SHOES AND SCHOOLING. — READING UNDER DIFFICULTIES. — LETTER TO H. C. GOODWIN. — FARMING EXPERIENCES. — CHURCHES.

IN the fall and winter of 1808, I was equivocally attached to the office of the " Catskill Recorder." I say equivocally, because I was not regularly apprenticed, and yet I carried the paper to the village subscribers, and did " chores " about the office, with a strong desire and hope that I should be received as an apprentice. But the hope was disappointed by the removal of my father, with his family, to the town of Cincinnatus, Cortland County, in March, 1808. My father had a brother residing in Cincinnatus, and three sisters in the town of Greene, Chenango County, at whose invitation he was induced to remove into the country with the hope of " bettering his condition," — a hope, however, that, go where he would, and do all in his power, was never to be realized. I bitterly lamented this change, because it cut off my cherished design of becoming either a sailor or a printer.

My uncle came with a sleigh-load of produce to Catskill, the main object being to take us back with him. Some idea of the value of our effects may be formed from the fact that a family of five, and such scanty articles of furniture as we possessed, found accommodation in an ordinary two-horse sleigh. The weather was clear and cold, and the sleighing fine. I found intense enjoyment in the novelty of new scenes and strange views. The mountains, rivers, villages, interspersed upon our route through Delaware, Otsego, and Chenango Counties, are vivid in my memory. Cincinnatus was then almost in a state of nature. Its few inhabitants were generally beginning life, with strong hands and light hearts only to rely on. Each of the families residing within a range of four or five miles from my uncle, had taken up its fifty or hundred acres of wild land, cleared away space sufficient for a log-house, and then commenced its farming operations.

The land thereabouts was heavily timbered, so much so that but for the ashes, which were then valuable for pot and pearling, the forests could not have been subdued. Indeed, for the first two or three years in Cortland County, *ashes* were silver and gold to the young or poor farmer. The first business, after getting into a log-house, was to make a clearing, in which to plant corn and potatoes.

When the trees were chopped down and into logs, and the brush piled, a "logging bee" was called. This bee was attended by all the neighboring farmers, a requisite number of whom brought their ox teams. These bees were very exciting, the more so as whiskey was in those days an indispensable beverage.

But work was never neglected. The log-heaps were then burned. The ashes were gathered, leached, and boiled into "black salts." The salts were sold to the merchant, by whom they were converted into pot or pearl ashes. With the proceeds of his "black salts," the farmer was enabled to support his family until his first crops came in. "Going to the store" was then not only a great privilege, but an affair of a high holiday and solemn responsibility.

The store was about seven miles down the river, in the town of Lisle. It was a branch of the establishment of General Ransom Rathbun, of Oxford, Chenango County, and was kept by his brother, a young man whose fine person and fashionable style of dress were the subject of remark and admiration among his wondering rural customers. Whenever a rustic matron returned from the store, her family and the nearest neighbors would assemble to listen with absorbing interest to her recital of the marvelous things she had seen and heard.

The young merchant became in after years an historical personage, being the Benjamin Rathbun whose enormous forgeries at Buffalo occasioned startling excitement throughout the State. After his conviction, a movement was made for a pardon. The feeling in his favor was so strong, that besides thousands of respectable men of Western New York who signed petitions to Governor Seward, seven distinguished citizens of Buffalo, whose names had been forged as indorsers to Rathbun's notes, wrote letters asking for the pardon. But the Governor was inflexible, and Rathbun served out his term. He was subsequently the keeper of a hotel in the city of New York. His life in all other respects was a useful and honorable one.

In 1867, Mr. Rathbun, then about eighty years old, kept the hotel corner of Broadway and Forty-second Street, where, on my way to and from the Park, I occasionally called on him. In referring, as he did without embarrassment, to the unfortunate termination of his Buffalo speculations, he commended Governor Seward warmly for his firmness in denying the strong appeal made for his (Rathbun's) pardon. Anxious as he then was to be released, time and reflection, he said, had shown him not only that his punishment was just, but that the Governor would have done wrong in showing a leniency to him which was refused to hundreds whose offenses were much lighter.

My uncle had a small clearing, with an extra log-house, into which we moved. My first employment was in sugar making, an occupation to which I became much attached. I now look with great pleasure upon the days and nights passed in the sap-bush. The want of shoes (which, as the snow was deep, was no small privation) was the only drawback upon my happiness. I used, however, to tie an old rag carpet around my feet, and get along chopping wood and gathering sap pretty well.

1809. — But when the spring advanced, and bare ground appeared in spots, I threw off the old carpet incumbrance and did my work barefooted. There is much leisure time for boys who are making maple sugar. I devoted this time to reading, when I could obtain books. But the farmers of that period had few or no books, save their Bible, for that inestimable blessing, the District School Library (in the adoption of which by the State I had some humble agency), had not then been thought of.

I borrowed books whenever and wherever I could. I remember to have heard that a neighbor, some three miles off, had borrowed from a still more distant neighbor a book of great interest, and after this book had been read by those better entitled to the privilege, I started off, barefooted, in the snow, to obtain the treasure. There were spots of bare ground, upon which I would stop to warm my feet. And there were also, along the road, occasional lengths of log fence from which the snow had melted, and upon which it was a luxury to walk. The book was at home, and the good people consented, upon my promise that it should be neither torn nor soiled, to lend it to me. In returning with the prize, I was too happy to think of the snow or my naked feet. Candles were then among the luxuries, not the necessaries, of life. If boys, instead of going to bed after dark, wanted to read, they supplied themselves with pine knots, by the light of which (in a horizontal position) they pursued their studies.

In this manner, with my body in the sugar-house, and my head out of doors where the fat pine was blazing, I read with intense interest a " History of the French Revolution."

When the sap had done running, and the other spring work commenced, I was initiated step by step into the mysteries of farming, but in its wildest and rudest state. While some of my duties were pleasant, I soon grew weary of the vocation ; and while swinging the axe or plying the hoe, my heart was upon the Hudson River. The spring, summer, and autumn passed without the occurrence of anything of particular interest. My father worked hard and continued poor, as usual. He did not take up land for himself because he had nothing to begin with! And yet, in looking back, I can see that others equally poor did purchase wild land and became independent farmers.

The experience of a young man who commences life in a wild, new country, shows how very little of the world's wealth is necessary to secure happiness. I remember a young man (Herring) who, on coming of age, married the daughter of a neighbor, and took up fifty acres of land. His entire wealth consisted of an axe and a hoe. He first cleared away a spot for a log-cabin by felling the trees outward, and then made a bee for the purpose of putting up his cabin. His wife's outfit consisted of a bed, table, two chairs, and a few pieces of crockery-ware. He then chopped two acres, and made a small logging-bee. From the ashes of the log-heaps he made black salt enough to enable him to purchase boards, nails, etc., to make a door, shelves, etc., etc., for his house. He then worked out a few days, in order to get a team to prepare his two acres for corn and potatoes. After his planting was over, he worked out again, to pay for a cow he had purchased on credit. After his corn and potatoes were hoed, he went to " slashing " for a fall crop. Slashing is a process which brings the tops of fallen trees together, so that they may be burned without the labor of cutting and piling the brush.

When the trees are slashed in the spring or summer, they get dry enough to burn early in the fall for a wheat crop. In harvest time he worked out again, for seed-wheat, and such other things as were most needed. After harvest, he prepared his own small clearing for wheat sowing, and then gathered his corn and dug his potatoes.

His wife in the mean time had borrowed a wheel, and " took in spinning," I believe, " to the halves." She was industrious, tidy, and cheerful. He was sober, honest, and affectionate. This cabin was more than a mile from any neighbor. I have seen something of the world, and its wealth and luxuries, since that period; but I have rarely, if ever, witnessed more of its real happiness than was enjoyed by that rustic pair.

I never read Moore's poem, commencing : —

> " I know by the smoke, that so gracefully curl'd
>   Above the green elms, that a cottage was near,
> And I said, ' If there 's peace to be found in the world,
>   A heart that was humble might hope for it here,' "

without thinking how truthfully and beautifully the log-cabin in the then wilderness-town of Cincinnatus was described by the sweetest of poets.

In December, a school opened for the winter about a mile from our home. I had formed high hopes of improvement from this source. The privilege, however, was only of brief duration, for in February, some six weeks after, my father moved from Cincinnatus to Onondaga, where he had great hopes of doing better.

A letter written fifty years after my removal from Cincinnatus to the author of a " History of Cortland County " will furnish the present generation with some idea of the labors, privations, and compensations of wilderness life in the early part of the present century.

Albany, *May* 16, 1858.
H. C. Goodwin, Esq.,

My Dear Sir, — Your letter of the 30th of April has remained quite too long unanswered, partly on account of severe illness in my family, but mainly because your kind and not unusual request embarrassed me. Several applications similar in character from book-makers I have simply declined, because first, there is nothing in my life entitled to historic attention; and second, if any of its events were worthy of such attention, it is neither proper nor becoming in me to furnish the materials.

So strong are my convictions of propriety in this regard, that many years ago, after refusing to furnish information relating 'to myself, asked for by the late Jabez D. Hammond, I declined also to read in manuscript what he had prepared. The consequence of that refusal is, that I go down to posterity, if Hammond's " Political History " outlives the present generation, as a " drummer in the war of 1812."

Now I am entitled to no such distinction ; for I never learned and never could learn a note or stave of music. I remember to have gone, when a boy, once or twice, to an evening singing-school, but after unavailing attempts at quavers and semi-quavers, the teacher snatched the gamut from my hand and turned me out of the class. I will, however, in this instance, depart so far from my usual practice as to furnish you the dates you desire, — though, in doing so, I feel as I suppose one should feel in robbing a hen-roost.

In the winter of 1808 we were settled in a log-cabin upon a small clearing about a mile from the Onondaga River, or, for the purpose of fixing our locality, I had better say about that distance from Brink's tavern. Cincinnatus then, whatever may be its present condition, was in its almost wilderness state. I have not been there in a half century, and am told that there are no forests or landmarks or monuments by which I could recall or identify the localities of which my mind retains familiar and distinct impressions. Inhabitants were then " few and far between." Our nearest neighbor was Mr. Gridley, a farmer rather well-to-do in the world, who would work hard through planting or hoeing or harvesting, and then seek indemnity in a week or ten days' " spree " on new raw whiskey.

The most " fore-handed " family in the neighborhood was that of Captain Carley (one member of which, Alanson, then a boy of my own age, was some years since a respected member of the legislature), among whose luxuries, as I remember, was a young apple orchard, and the only bearing orchard within a circuit of several miles.

My first employment was in attendance upon an ashery. The process of extracting lye from ashes, and of boiling the lye into black salts, was commonplace enough ; but when the melting down into potash came, all was bustle and excitement. This labor was succeeded, when the spring had advanced far enough, by the duties of the " sapbush."

This is a season to which the farmers' sons and daughters look forward with agreeable anticipations. In that employment toil is more than figuratively sweetened. The occupation and its associations are healthful and beneficial.

When your troughs were dug out of bass-wood (for there were no buckets in those days) your trees tapped, your sap gathered, your wood cut, and your fires fed, there was leisure either for reading or " sparking." And what youthful denizens of the sap-bush will ever forget their share in the transparent and delicious streaks of candy congealed and cooled in snow while " sugaring-off " ? Many a farmer's son has found his best opportunity for mental improvement in his intervals of leisure while tending sap-bush. Such, at any rate, was my own experience. At night you had only to feed the kettles and keep up your fires, the sap having been gathered and the wood cut before dark. During the day we would also lay in a good stock of " fat pine," by the light of which, blazing brightly in front of the sugar-house, in the posture the serpent was condemned to assume as a penalty for tempting our great first grandmother, I have passed many and many a delightful night in reading. I remember in this way to have read a " History of the French Revolution," and to have obtained from it a better and more enduring knowledge of the events and horrors, and of the actors in that great national tragedy, than I have received from all subsequent readings.

I remember, also, how happy I was in being able to borrow the book of a Mr. Keyes, after a two-mile tramp through the snow, shoeless.

Though but a boy, I was large, healthy, strong, not lazy, and therefore ambitious to keep up my row in planting, hilling, and hoeing potatoes and corn. The principal employment of the farmers of Cincinnatus fifty years ago was in clearing their land.

Cattle, during the winter, for want of fodder, were turned out to browse in the slashings.

As the work of clearing the land was too heavy for men singlehanded, chopping and logging " bees " were modes resorted to for aggregating labor. These seasons of hard work were rendered exciting and festive by the indispensable gallon bottle of whiskey.

There were bees also for log-house raising. After the loggings and as the spring opened came the burning of the log and brush-heaps, and the gathering of the ashes.

But little wheat was grown there then, and that little was harvested with the sickle, the ground being too rough and stumpy for cradling.

Our first acquisition in the way of live stock was a rooster and four hens; and I remember with what a gush of gladness I was awakened at break of day the next morning by the loud, defiant voice of chanticleer; and when, several days afterwards, I found a real hen's nest in a brush-heap, with eggs in it, I cackled almost as boisterously as the feathered mother whom I had surprised in the feat of parturition.

The settlers employed in clearing and bettering their land raised just enough to live on from hand to mouth. Their principal, and indeed only reliance for the purchase of necessaries from the store was upon their "black salts." For these the merchants always paid the highest price in cash or goods.

I remember the stir which a new store, established in Lisle (some seven or eight miles down the river) by the Rathbuns, from Oxford, created in our neighborhood. It was "all the talk" for several weeks, and until a party of housewives, by clubbing together their products, fitted out an expedition; vehicles and horses were scarce, but it was finally arranged; A furnishing a wagon, B a horse, C a man, and D a boy to drive.

Four matrons, with a commodity of black salts, tow cloth, flax, and maple sugar, went their way rejoicing, and returned triumphantly at sunset with fragrant bohea for themselves, plug tobacco for their husbands, flashy calico for the children, gay ribbons for the girls, jack-knives for the boys, crockery for cupboard, and snuff for "granny."

This expedition was a theme for much gossip. The wonders of the new store were described to staring eyes and open mouths. The merchant and his clerk were criticised in their deportment, manners, and dress. The former wore shiny boots with tassels, the latter a ruffle shirt, and both smelt of pomatum! I do not believe that the word "dandy" had then been invented, or it certainly would have come in play on that occasion. Thirty years afterwards I laughed over all this with my old friend General Ransom Rathbun, one of the veritable proprietors of that new store.

The grinding for our neighborhood was done at Hunt's Mill, which on one occasion was disabled by some defect in the flume or dam, and then we were compelled to go with our grist either to Homer or to Chenango Forks.

I recollect that on more than one occasion I saw boys riding with a bushel of corn (bareback, with a tow halter) to the distillery, and returning with the gallon bottle of whiskey, balanced by a stone in the other end of the bag.

In the autumn following our removal to Cincinnatus I had " worked out," and earned leather (sole and upper) enough for a pair of shoes, which were to be made by a son of Crispin (Deacon Badger, if I remember rightly) who lived on the river a mile and a half away. The deacon, I doubt not, has gone to his rest, and I forgive him the fibs he told, and the dozen journeys I made barefooted over the frozen and " hubby " road in December before the shoes were done.

I attended one regimental review, or general training, as it was called. It was an eminently primitive one. Among the officers two had chapeaux, to which Captain Carley, one of the two, added a sword and sash; four feathers stood erect upon felt hats; there were fifteen or twenty muskets, half a dozen rifles, two hoarse drums, and as many " spirit-stirring fifes." Of rank and file there were about two hundred and fifty. In the way of refreshments there was gingerbread, blackberry pie, and whiskey. But there were neither "sweat leather," " little joker," nor other institutions of that character upon the ground. Having, before leaving Catskill, seen with my own eyes a live Governor (Morgan Lewis) review a whole brigade, I regarded that training as a decided failure.

There were no events at all startling during my residence at Cincinnatus; no murders, no suicides, no drownings, no robberies, no elopements, " no babies lost in the woods," occurred to astonish the natives. A recruiting sergeant came along (it was in embargo times), and three or four idle fellows (Herring and Wilder by name, I think) 'listed and marched off.

There were neither churches nor " stated preachers " in town. A Methodist minister came occasionally and held meetings in private houses, or at the school-house.

In the winter there was a school on the river, and the master, who " boarded round," must have had a good time of it on johnny-cake for breakfast, lean salt pork for dinner, and samp and milk for supper.

There were but few amusements in those days, and but little of leisure or disposition to indulge in them. Those that I remember as most pleasant and exciting were corn huskings and coon-hunts. There was fun, too, in smoking woodchucks out of their holes.

During my residence there, Mr. Wattles and family moved into the neighborhood. He came, I think, from what was then called the " Triangle," somewhere in Chenango County, and was a sub-landagent. They were, for that region, rather stylish people, and became the subjects of a good deal of remark; one thing that excited especial indignation was, that persons going to the house were asked to clean their shoes at the door, a scraper having been placed there for that purpose.

A maiden lady (Miss Theodosia Wattles) rendered herself especially obnoxious to the spinster neighbors by "dressing up" week-day afternoons. They all agreed in saying she was "a proud, stuck-up thing," as in those days "go-to-meeting clothes" were reserved for Sundays.

Leeks were the bane of my life in Cincinnatus; they tainted everything, but especially the milk and butter. Such was my aversion to "leeky" milk, that to this day I cannot endure milk in any form.

In the fall and winter, corn-shelling furnished evening occupation. The ears were shelled either with a cob, or upon the handle of a frying-pan. There have been improvements since in that, as in other departments of agriculture.

Such are, in a crude form, some of my recollections of life in Cincinnatus half a century ago. That town, then very large, has since been subdivided into three or four towns. Upon the farm of my old friends, the Carleys, the large and flourishing village of Marathon has grown up. And there, too, a substantial bridge has taken the place of the "dug-out," in which we used to cross the river. Of the sprinkling of inhabitants who had then just commenced subduing the forests, and insinuating scanty deposits of seed between the stumps and roots, but few, of course, survive. The settlers were industrious, honest, law-abiding, and, with few exceptions, temperate citizens. The friendly neighborhood relations, so necessary in a new country, existed there.

All tried not only to take care of themselves, but to help their neighbors. Farming implements and household articles were pretty much enjoyed in common. Everybody lent what they possessed, and borrowed whatever they wanted.

You must judge whether these hastily written recollections of Cincinnatus would at all interest the few old inhabitants remaining there; and having so judged, you are at liberty to put them in your book or into the fire.	Very truly yours,

THURLOW WEED.

CHAPTER III.

1809–1813.

OUR removal from Cincinnatus was in 1809. I was then
in my twelfth year. We moved into a small log-house near
Mickle's Furnace, about one mile from Onondaga Hollow, an
equal distance from Onondaga West-Hill, where the court-house
was situated, and three miles from Onondaga Salt Springs, or
"Salt Point," as they were then called. My father found immediate employment in cutting cord-wood for the salt works, in
which employment I shared, and soon prided myself in doing
half a man's day's work. When the spring opened, we worked
out by the day among the farmers until July, when we were
brought down with fever and ague, remaining in a very helpless
situation until September. During this season of illness my
sister Mehitable, then in her seventh year, died. In the fall,
when the furnace was put in blast, I got a situation there.
My business was, after a casting, to temper and prepare the
sand for the moulders ; and I soon rose to the dignity of
moulding "dogs" (hand-irons) myself. This was night and
day work. We ate salt-pork and rye and Indian bread three
times a day, and slept on straw in bunks. I liked the excitement of a furnace life. My labor there enabled me to purchase
my first fur hat, and encouraged me to hope that I should
enjoy the further happiness of standing in boots and tassels ; I
was disappointed. The hat was bought of Reuben West, of

Onondaga, West Hill, on a furnace order. In returning with it, when no person was in sight I frequently drew off the slouching, rimless apology for a hat that I had worn a long time, to try on my new one, the possession of which afforded me great happiness. When the furnace " blew out," as was usual in warm weather, I again renewed agricultural employment with my father, who was working as usual by the day. Soon, however, I heard that Jasper Hopper, Esq., of Onondaga Hollow, who was then county clerk and postmaster, wanted a boy to work in his garden, take care of his horse, etc., etc., for which he would receive his board and schooling. I eagerly sought and obtained this situation, and it proved both an agreeable and useful one. Mr. Hopper's household consisted of himself and wife, a clerk, his son, and a colored woman servant and her son, a boy three or four years old, who some twenty years afterwards was sent to the state prison for life, having been convicted of manslaughter. This mulatto was the natural son of a lawyer residing in a neighboring county, who lived to see his illegitimate offspring arraigned for murder.

Among my school-fellows, Asher Tyler, a retired lawyer residing at Elmira, is, as far as I am informed, the only survivor. I learned much more during these few months than I had acquired in earlier life, and upon leaving Dr. Alexander's Academy (for that was its name) my school experience ended. I lived very pleasantly with Mr. Hopper about six months, when, the furnace going into blast again, I returned to my situation there, not, however, to remain long, for late that autumn I was rejoiced with the information that printing materials had arrived at Onondaga Hollow, where a newspaper was to be published. My father, anxious to see me in the way of learning a trade, gratified my own wishes by making an application in my behalf as an apprentice. But my spirit was crushed on his return, with an answer that no apprentice was wanted, one having been already engaged. I applied to Mr. Hopper, who was a leading patron of the embryo paper, for his interposition with its proprietor, who finally consented to take me on trial, remarking in no encouraging tone and manner that I was too big and clumsy for a printer, but that I could cut wood and make fires. This ungracious reception, however, did not discourage me. The ambition to be a printer was irrepressible.

My first employment as an apprentice, beside cutting wood and making fires in the printing-office, was in "treading pelts," a duty of which the present generation of printers is growing up in ignorance.

The balls, which have been succeeded by rollers, were made of green sheepskins, which had to undergo a sort of tanning process between your feet and the floor. It was a long and tedious operation, as every printer whose apprenticeship commenced previous to 1812 will attest.

In 1814 dressed deerskin began to be used instead of pelts, but it required time to induce old printers to become reconciled to this innovation.

1811. — Thomas Chittenden Fay was the name in which the editor and publisher of the "Lynx" rejoiced. He was a strange, eccentric man. The "Lynx" was established in 1811 as an organ of the Republican party. There was then one other paper in the county ; this was the "Manlius Times," a Federal journal published by Mr. Kellogg. There were then but five newspapers published west of Onondaga. There was the "Auburn Gazette," a Federal paper published by H. & J. Pace, the "Geneva Gazette," by James Bogart, also a Federalist, the "Ontario Repository," by James D. Bemis, a Federalist, the "Ontario Messenger" (Republican), by John A. Stevens, and the "Batavia Advocate," by Miller & Blodget.

In those days the mail from Albany to Buffalo passed three times a week. Its arrival by stage every other evening in our village (where passengers lodged) was quite an event, and its driver, who blew as he approached a long tin horn with the air of a man-of-war boatswain, was the tavern oracle and wag. The stage of that day was a heavy, lumbering vehicle without springs. It was five or six days going between Albany and Batavia, for that was then the end of the stage route.

It was, however, extended to Buffalo in 1812. There was then no Syracuse and no Rochester. I have frequently passed through the swamp which now constitutes a large part of Syracuse when it contained but one house.

At the creek, in the western border of the village, there was a small grist-mill and two small houses. I found the printing business all that I expected, and soon made myself useful. Every moment that could be saved I employed in reading newspapers, than which nothing afforded me more happiness.

I kept regular files of every exchange paper, with the contents of which I was perfectly familiar. I imbibed, from reading the discussions in Congress and the newspapers about the impressment of American seamen, and the Indian barbarities excited by British agents upon our western border, a deadly hatred towards England.

1812. — In the spring of 1812, when Governor Tompkins, to prevent the charter by bribery and corruption of the "Six Million Bank" (afterwards chartered as the Bank of America) prorogued the legislature, I warmly espoused the cause of the governor, though Mr. Fay, to my great grief, sustained Mr. Humphries (then in the senate from Onondaga) and other Republican members of the legislature in their votes for the bank and their denunciation of the governor. Time and the trials for bribery which ensued fully vindicated Governor Tompkins. In about a year after I came to Mr. Fay his other apprentice, Ananias Adams, left him, and I became both oldest and youngest apprentice.

Mr. Fay was a coarse, vulgar man, who used to swear and storm about the office, but, on the whole, treated me well, and rather prided himself in making a printer out of such a blockhead. By his wife, who was a patient, industrious, tidy woman, I was treated with great kindness, for which I remember her with gratitude.

In July, 1812, we were startled with the intelligence that war had been declared against England, soon after which the din of busy preparation was heard all around us. The stage came filled with officers repairing to the frontier.

My fellow apprentice had gone to live with his uncle John Adams, who kept the stage house, and had the cleaning of the passengers' boots. I went regularly evenings to assist Ananias in his boot cleaning, that I might see and perchance hear some of the epauletted gentlemen speak of the war, etc.

There was a battalion of riflemen in our county whose services had been volunteered just before the war was declared, and which was ordered into service immediately after the declaration. I was very anxious to go as a substitute for some one of the many who did not want to go, but Mr. Fay could not spare me, would not consent, and I should, they said, be rejected as too young if I obtained his consent. But the war fever was

raging in my veins and heart. Soon after the rifles marched, I
heard that troops were coming from the east. I finished my
"stent" by working most of a night, and then started off to meet
the soldiers. I reached Manlius Square (ten miles) just after
sunrise, in season to see two regiments (Colonel Thompson
Mead of Chenango, and Colonel Farrand Stranahan of Otsego) strike their tents. With these troops I trudged back to
Onondaga, where, instead of marching on with them, I was required to go back into the printing-office. Soon after this, however, I was made truly happy by the arrival of the Thirteenth
Regiment of the United States Infantry, whose tents were
pitched in a meadow near by, where the regiment lay two days.
This regiment was in a good state of discipline, had a fine band,
and made a very martial appearance. One battalion proceeded
by land to Niagara while the other marched to Oswego to embark on Lake Ontario. One battalion (that which proceeded
by land, I believe) reached the frontier in time to distinguish
itself in the battle of Queenstown. Among the officers in that
regiment "whose frown," as Counselor Phillips said of Napoleon, " terrified the glance their magnificence attracted," there
were several whom I have known intimately since. The present General John E. Wool was then a captain.

In September, 1812, Mr. Fay, who had on account of his violence of temper and in consequence of his opposition to Governor Tompkins become embroiled with his patrons and friends,
some of whom, and especially Mr. Hopper, he abused in the
"Lynx," took a single shirt, walked deliberately out of the office
through the garden into a meadow, and never returned, either
to his family or his printing-office. The creditors who took
possession of the establishment directed me to publish a half-
sheet for five or six weeks until a number of legal advertisements should run out, and then the " Lynx" closed its eyes and
doors.

I was now a half-made printer out of place. A few weeks
previous one Royal T. Chamberlin had established a paper
called the " Tocsin " at Union Springs, Cayuga County. In
that paper I saw that " *A boy who has worked some at the
business is wanted as an apprentice at this office.*" I therefore started on foot for Union Springs, and was received by
Mr. Royal T. Chamberlin as the boy who had worked some at

the business. His office was in the old town of Scipio, some
nine miles above the Cayuga bridge. We boarded with the
editor and publisher's father, who lived on a farm about two
miles from the office. We took an early breakfast, brought
our dinner with us, and returned to supper in the evening. I
enjoyed this very much, especially as it was in peach season and
Mr. Chamberlin's father had the fruit in great abundance and
perfection.

But these joys were of brief duration. Mr. Royal T. Chamberlin was desperately in love, without having, however, been so
fortunate as to have kindled a reciprocal flame in the heart of
Miss Southwick, who lived some quarter of a mile from the
printing-office. The swain grew melancholy, and passed whole
days sitting on a log, looking at the house, to catch occasional
glimpses of the object of his idolatry. Business was entirely
neglected, and the " Tocsin " soon ceased to sound its alarms.

I was again out of employment, and footed it back to Onondaga, where, though it was in October, I found the furnace in
blast, Joshua Forman (who afterwards suggested the Safety
Fund Banking System to Mr. Van Buren) having obtained
from the Secretary of War a contract for casting cannon balls.

One of the jokes of that day was an order from the Navy
Department to Lieutenant Woolsey to repair with the United
States Brig Oneida from Oswego to Onondaga to receive these
balls, overlooking the circumstance that the Oswego Fall presented a somewhat formidable obstruction to the passage of a
ship of war.

I went to work again in the furnace until December, when,
having earned some clothes and finding myself with three dollars in cash, I started on foot for Utica, where I had the good
fortune to get employment in the printing-office of Messrs.
Seward & Williams.

To my application for a situation Mr. Williams, after looking me over somewhat deliberately, replied that he had no work
for me ; but as I was leaving the office, evidently depressed and
as evidently in need of employment, he called me back, and inquired where I came from, how old I was, and why I had not
served out my apprenticeship. My answers proving satisfactory, he put a composing stick in my hand, placed some copy
before me, and in an encouraging way remarked that he would

see what I could do. When he returned two or three hours afterwards, he read over the matter that I had been "setting up," and remarked kindly that I could go with the other boys to supper. I was therefore at work in the office and domiciled in the house of a gentleman (William Williams) who became and ever remained my warm friend, and for whose memory I cherish a grateful remembrance.

In February following, an attack was apprehended from the British on Sackett's Harbor. It was supposed that the enemy would cross from Kingston on the ice. Volunteers were called for. Utica, then a small but thriving village, was strongly Federal, but though opposed to the war, the Federalists would turn out to repel invasions. Mr. Williams, one of my employers, volunteered himself and consented to my leaving the office with him. We left Utica in sleighs, and arrived at Adams — some eighty miles, and twelve miles from Sackett's Harbor — in two days. The snow was deep and the weather severe. We had good quarters, however, and passed our time pleasantly waiting until the alarm was over, when we were discharged. My company was commanded by Captain Nathan Seward, a soldier of the Revolution, and the father of one of my employers. On my return to Utica I obtained a situation in the office of the "Columbian Gazette," a Republican paper published by Thomas Walker, Esq., whose kindness and friendship during more than thirty years I hold in grateful recollection. I was much pleased with the situation, and worked hard and cheerfully until June or July, when the desire to get into the army returned with such force that I could not resist it. Every time the recruiting sergeant with drum, fife, and ragamuffins passed the office, my heart warmed and my blood coursed freely. I passed my leisure hours among the recruits and about their quarters. My first overtures to enlist were rejected on the ground of age (I was sixteen), but my importunity finally prevailed, and I one day found myself in Uncle Sam's uniform, on my way with two other recruits to be sworn in, when it occurred to me that Mr. Walker, my employer, was the magistrate before whom I was to appear.

Feeling, however, that it was too late for advice or admonition, I brushed up in the rear of my compatriots, and pulling my cap over my face placed my hand upon the book. " Take off

your cap, sir," said the magistrate. This revealed to him the face
of his whilom apprentice. " Are you going to enlist?" "I *have*
enlisted, sir." " But you had better reflect." " It is too late,
sir. I have got my bounty." " Never mind that; I will see
Lieutenant Hickox upon the subject. You had better change
your clothes and go to your work." I had too much respect for
my employer to disregard his advice, and most reluctantly doffed
the blue coat with martial buttons and returned to the " space
box." Captain Thomas M. Skinner's company of artillery
was ordered to the frontier. Of this company, Mr. Clark, our
foreman, was a member. Mr. Walker could better spare his apprentice than his foreman, and as the former did and the latter
did not want to go, I was soon dressed in Clark's uniform,
though the legs of his pantaloons and the sleeves of his coat
were sadly disproportioned to the limbs of their new occupant.
But I was far too happy to regard such things. Indeed, I have
never been fastidious in matters of dress. We were soon on
our march to the lines. Captain Skinner not going, the company
was commanded by its First Lieutenant Ells of Whitesboro.
The Second Lieutenant Rease, who has since been sheriff of
Oneida County, became and has ever since continued my warm
friend. Our regiment was commanded by Colonel Elijah H.
Metcalf of Cooperstown. During that campaign, I first saw
General Amos P. Granger and Joshua A. Spencer, Esq., who
had just commenced the practice of the law at Lenox, Madison
County.

CHAPTER IV.

1813–1815.

NEW YORK, *January* 1, 1869.

I HAD written thus far in 1845, when, for some reason that I
have forgotten, it was suspended. Within the last few years I
have been urged by friends, whose opinions and wishes are entitled to consideration, to resume, and if permitted, to complete
it. Among the prominent and most earnest of those referred
to were the late General Winfield Scott and Sir Henry Holland. I therefore, after entering upon my seventy-second year,
with impaired and uncertain health, the narrative resume.

Joshua A. Spencer, with whose name I closed the Santa
Cruz manuscript in 1845, was a Cornet in Captain Jenning's
Company of Light Artillery. That company was composed of
the most reputable young men of Madison County. Mr. Spencer subsequently became one of the most prominent lawyers
in the State, and was a member of the State Senate, residing
for many years in Utica. The late Dr. Thomas Spencer, an
eminent physician at Geneva, was a brother. And Julius A.
Spencer, for many years and still usefully connected with the
New York Central Railroad, was a nephew. An incident con-

nected with the equipment of the above-named company occasioned much merriment among them and to the citizens of Albany.

When about to enter the service, the officers met for the purpose of addressing a letter to Governor Tompkins for field-pieces. The requisition made by Captain Jennings did not suit the other officers, who in turn tried their hands at composition. But they failed to satisfy each other or even themselves; and they finally agreed to submit their productions to a village lawyer, the father of Luther R. Marsh a prominent member of the New York Bar, asking for his corrections, or if he saw fit, to prepare a letter himself for them. In due time he submitted the following: —

> "Great Daniel D., we send to thee
> For two great guns and trimmings!
> Send them to hand, or you'll be damned,
> By order of Captain Jennings."

This was adopted and immediately despatched to Albany, and accomplished its purpose. Governor Tompkins used to amuse his guests at dinners and parties with this remarkable requisition for ordnance.

Our regiment was quartered at Brownville, a few miles from Sackett's Harbor, for three months. Nothing out of the ordinary routine of camp life occurred.

Brownville derived its name from a family who owned the farm upon which the village grew up. Jacob Brown, a descendant of William Penn, removed from Pennsylvania to Jefferson County during the closing years of the last century. His sons were intelligent and enterprising merchants. The seniors were strict Quakers, educating their children in the faith and habits of that sect. But their eldest son, Jacob, developed early a strong military taste, so strong, indeed, that in disregard of the remonstrance of his father he became a militia officer, and was in consequence " read out of meeting." At the commencement of the war Jacob Brown was a brigadier-general of militia, and, residing upon the frontier, was soon called into active service, where he displayed so much ability that he was transferred with the same rank into the service of the United States, and was subsequently distinguished as a commanding general at the battles of Chippewa, Bridgewater, and Fort Erie, in Canada.

He was now (1813) in command at Sackett's Harbor, from
which post he was summoned to the funeral of his father. That
funeral was largely attended by Friends, attired in plain, simple
drab, who were sitting in silent meditation when General Brown
in full military costume dismounted at the door of the meeting-
house, and striding through the middle aisle, with the scabbard
of his heavy broadsword dangling upon the floor, took his seat
with the family. That sudden appearance of a military chief-
tain amid a congregation of demure and peaceful Quakers, to
my mind, added impressiveness to the scene. General Brown,
after accompanying the remains of his father to the burying-
ground, took leave of his relatives (including his wife and children), mounted his horse and rode back to Sackett's Harbor.

When the term of service expired I returned to Utica, and to
the printing-office of my friend Mr. Walker, devoting all my
leisure hours to newspaper and other reading. Utica, though
then in its infancy, was a thrifty village. Its elements of prosperity were found in the remarkable intelligence, enterprise,
and integrity of its mechanics. Its painters, its builders, its
hatters, its shoemakers, etc., etc., were just the men a " pent-up
Utica " then required. William Williams and Thomas Walker,
Samuel Stocking, the Danas, the Hoyts, etc., etc., are, I doubt
not, still remembered for their enterprise, public spirit, and integrity. A daughter of one of the Hoyts subsequently became
the wife of the late Friend Humphrey, of Albany, once mayor
of that city, a member of the senate, and one of the very best
men I ever knew. Among the merchants of Utica then prominent were John C. and Nicholas Devereux, Jeremiah and James.
Van Rensselaer. The two accomplished daughters of the latter
became the wives of Francis Granger and Charles H. Carroll.
James Hooker and Abram Van Santvoord, Messrs. Williams,
Walker, and Devereux, subsequently became and to the end of
their lives remained my true and sincere friends. They were
most estimable men. Mr. Van Santvoord was especially so,
being endowed and imbued with all the qualities of head and
heart that exalt and adorn mankind. John Williams, then a
clerk for James Hooker, was afterward a distinguished merchant, and was the father of Mrs. E. T. Throop Martin, of Wil-
low Brook, Cayuga County. Oneida County had at that time
a strong Bar, though its most eminent lawyers (Jonas Platt,

Thomas R. Gold, Theodore Sill, Henry R. Storrs, etc., etc.) resided at Whitesboro. General Joseph Kirkland, Nathan Williams, Francis A. Bloodgood, Morris S. Miller, and David W. Childs were then the leading lawyers residing in Utica. Greene C. Bronson, who grew up to eminence in his profession and became Attorney-General and a distinguished judge, was then a law student. Rome, then a small village, owed its prosperity in a great measure to the intelligence and enterprise of the Huntingtons (Henry and George) and the Braytons, both families of remarkable enterprise and of great public and social worth. There was also a family by the name of Hart, at Clinton, four or five of whom subsequently attained position and wealth in different parts of the State. Eli Hart, the eldest, was an eminent and wealthy flour merchant in New York. Ephraim Hart was a successful merchant and a popular politician residing at Utica. He represented that district in the Senate for four years, and was a warm political friend of Governor Clinton. Roswell Hart was a pioneer merchant in Rochester. His son was a representative in Congress from Rochester in 1866. Truman Hart, a lawyer, resides at Lyons, Wayne County, and represented that district in the State Senate in 1826. Thomas Hart was also a merchant at Rochester; he served with me in the army in 1813.

In October, 1813, I left Utica for Albany, and obtained employment in the office of Webster & Skinner, then publishers of the "Albany Gazette," and, for that period, extensive book publishers and sellers. I then attended a theatre for the first time, my previous knowledge of evening entertainments having been limited to the exhibitions of Sickles, who, during the first twelve or fifteen years of the present century, furnished middle and western New York with their whole stock of scenic wonders; and who was as famous in his day as our friend Niblo, whom he strongly resembled, became subsequently, and who was as prolific in "infant phenomena" as that inimitable provincial manager, Crummles. The war brought a large number of officers to Albany, and the theatre was consequently well attended. The company was strong, including Mr. Bernard the manager, an eminent comedian, and the Placides, the odor of whose name lingers pleasantly in the memory of old lovers of the drama.

Here and then Fanny Denny, the daughter of a revolutionary

officer, made her *début*, and became immediately popular. She soon afterwards joined a company under the management of Mr. Drake, to whom Pittsburgh, Cincinnati, and other western cities were indebted for their first dramatic entertainments. Miss Denny married a son of the manager, and as Mrs. Drake became and remained a star for more than forty years in all our Western cities, dying at her residence in Kentucky greatly respected, in 1874, at the age of eighty-four.

I was constant in my attendance, and being then not on the free list, theatre tickets and my board bill left me with nothing over; so that in December, when I found myself out of employment, I had but sixty-two cents left to bear my expenses back to Utica. Buoyant, however, with youth, health, and hope, I started on foot. At Schenectady, where for eighteen cents I dined off pork and beans in a grocery, in exchange for a "fifty cent shin-plaster" I received a counterfeit "Calvin Cheeseman" for twenty-five cents. This left me with but eighteen cents to finish my journey. I traveled till late, stopping at Conine's, a tavern well-known on the Mohawk in those days. Making frank exhibit of my pecuniary condition, the landlord in the kindest manner ordered supper for me, and in the morning, although I was ready to start at day-dawn, he would not allow me to go without breakfast; and I remember to this day the exquisite flavor of his sausages, regretting profoundly that the process of making palatable sausages is numbered among the "lost arts." Eleven years afterwards I again lodged, this time as a stage passenger, at Conine's tavern, when, recalling the circumstances under which I had made his acquaintance, I tendered him with my best thanks payment for supper, lodging, and breakfast, with interest. This, however, was declined by Mr. Conine with a playful remark that it was outlawed, to which I replied that no human law could obliterate his kindness from my memory. In 1838 I again met Mr. Conine in a Whig State Convention at Utica, where I reminded him of the early and excellent flavor of his sausages. The second day's journey brought me to East Canada Creek, where I was fortunate in meeting my friend Theodore S. Faxton, the stage driver, who not only provided me with supper and lodging, but took me to Herkimer on the box with him.

Often in later years, after the fortunes of both had changed, we have talked over this adventure. The history of Mr. Faxton shows what can be accomplished in our country by young men of industry, intelligence, and integrity. His good conduct as a driver for several years attracted the attention of Mr. Jason Parker, a principal owner in the line of stages between Utica and Albany. Before Faxton was twenty-one he was appointed superintendent of the line of which he soon afterward became a proprietor. As new modes of travel were developed, Faxton became interested in canal packet boats, express companies, railroads, and telegraphs, from the legitimate profits of which he became wealthy, and is now in his old age devoting his large income to alleviate the condition of the unfortunate and infirm. At Herkimer I obtained employment in the office of the "American," published by the late William L. Stone, then quite a young man, but subsequently prominently known as editor of the "Northern Whig," in Hudson; the "Mirror," of Hartford; the "Daily Advertiser," in Albany; and the "Commercial Advertiser," in New York. He was a zealous Federalist and I as zealous a Republican. But he was a kind-hearted, amiable man, to whom I became greatly attached. When the political campaign opened, there being no Republican press in the county, the Republican committee offered Mr. Stone the printing of their hand-bills, tickets, etc., etc., on condition that he allowed me to do their work privately. To this he assented; and I frequently, when confidentially occupied, turned the key upon my employer. When the election was over and the Republican ticket was elected, Aaron Hackley, chairman of the committee, presented me along with their thanks a five-dollar note, which at that day was munificent. Mr. Hackley, a young lawyer of much promise, was then elected to the Assembly, and four years afterwards to Congress. He was a popular man, of genial nature, who held various offices long enough to withdraw him from his profession and doom him to a fate that unhappily awaits too many successful politicians, — an old age of poverty. He died in this city five days since in his eighty-sixth year. I have always remembered him with respect and affection, and it was in my power during the last few years of his life to be of some service to him.

In Herkimer I first met a young man who, after qualifying himself for a physician and giving one day to the practice of medicine, sold his horse, gave away his saddle-bags, pill-boxes, etc., etc., entered a law-office, and commenced the study of that profession. For the law, in debating societies and in justices' courts he evinced much ability; and after his admission to the bar, had he not been drawn into public life, would have been as eminent a lawyer as he became a statesman. The gentleman to whom I refer was the late Michael Hoffman, who was for a long time equally distinguished in Congress for talents and integrity. It was to his enlightened statesmanship that New York is indebted for the financial article in the amended Constitution, which, by devoting $1,800,000 annually to the payment of the canal debt, has preserved the public credit and the public faith through every financial crisis. Here, also, I became acquainted with a bright, intelligent German boy, whose name, after a lapse of fifty-five years, is a universal household word, and whose face is familiar to every man, woman, and child in our country. He was the son of a German clergyman, who preached in that language to German congregations, and resided a couple of miles outside the village. The boy, then about twelve years old, attending an English school in the village, was very fond of newspaper reading, and came every day to the printing-office to read, and to borrow for night reading at home, our exchange papers. I was more particularly interested in him, perhaps, from the circumstance that in the mornings he brought notes from, and in the evening carried responses to, a young lady visiting a married sister who resided near his father's house, and who subsequently became my wife. That German boy afterwards represented the Herkimer district in Congress, and is now the Treasurer of the United States, Francis E. Spinner.

There came to the village two young men who entered the office of Jabez Fox as students at law. They informed me that they had been studying law and teaching school at Cherry Valley, but having purchased the exclusive right for Herkimer County of a Patent Washing Machine, they intended to give up school keeping, and support themselves as students by the sale of their machines. They accordingly published an advertisement in the village paper and in hand-bills, celebrating the merits and felicities of the invention in poetry. The doggerel jingled so humorously that I preserved the verses, and twenty years afterwards, when the two young men had become well established as lawyers, one Ira Bellows, of Pittsford, ·Monroe County, the other Alvan Stewart, of Utica, when we were attending a bar dinner at Rochester, I produced and read the patent-washing-machine poetry to the infinite enjoyment of the table, and most especially of the author, Mr. Stewart, who is remembered not only as a leading lawyer, but as the great abolitionist of his day.

In Herkimer I first became acquainted with Gerrit Smith, the handsomest, the most ˙attractive, and most intellectual young man, I then˙ thought and think now, I had ever met. He dressed *à la Byron*, and in taste and manners was instinctively perfect. He was attracted to Herkimer by Miss Wealthy Backus, daughter of Rev. Azel Backus, then President of Clinton College, a beautiful and accomplished young lady, who became his first wife. After her death Mr. Smith married a daughter of Colonel Fitzhugh, of Geneseo. Her sister was the wife of Dr. F. F. Backus (a son of President Backus), an eminent physician of Rochester, for long years our family physician and dearly loved friend.

There lived also at Herkimer a gentleman not then unknown to fame, although few I suppose will remember him. This was William Ray, who had been a prisoner in Algiers, and was released by an American fleet under the command of Commodore Preble. Mr. Ray was a poet of considerable temporary celebrity. He commemorated his sufferings in prison in a poem opening as follows : —

> "Of Litchfield County, mud and clay,
> Sprang the body of William Ray !"

Another poetical effusion from the same pen, familiar to children of that generation, found in juvenile picture-books, was a lament on the death of a canary bird, commencing : —

> "'My bird is dead,' said Nancy Ray,
> 'My bird is dead, I cannot play.'"

Herkimer, though now obscure and dilapidated, was then a flourishing village with several prominent lawyers and enterprising merchants, only two of whom, so far as I know, survive. Lauren Ford, then a talented young lawyer, now in

> "—— the sear, the yellow leaf of life,"

resides in Brooklyn, N. Y.

General George Petrie, then a clerk in Philo M. Hackley's store, is now a clerk in the General Post Office at Washington.

In April, after the election, I packed my movables in a handkerchief, and started on foot for Cooperstown, where I obtained work in the office of H. & E. Phinney. Cooperstown was then a bright, active, growing, and pleasant village. I boarded with Mrs. Ostrander, to whose daughter I became attached; but as I was only in my seventeenth year, and of unsettled and uncertain habits, and the young lady in her sixteenth year, her friends deemed it their duty to interpose, which they did *strenuously*. I did not think this unreasonable, having a distrust of my fitness for such responsibility. We agreed therefore to separate, with the understanding that if, after the lapse of three or four years, our affections remained unaltered, the engagement should be renewed.

During my residence in Cooperstown an incident occurred which, as it obtained considerable notoriety many years afterwards, requires notice here. In the company of four young men I attended a Sunday evening Methodist meeting, where, during the service, our attention was attracted to a group of girls who were by no means seriously impressed. At the close of the meeting we joined them and accompanied them to the tavern, where a conveyance awaited the party, as they resided several miles out of the village. The following day a man appeared in the village to identify the young men who, as he alleged, had committed a gross misdemeanor. And at the next session of the grand jury these young men, myself included, were indicted. The other young men, being natives of the village and reputably connected, readily obtained bail, while I, being a stranger, felt delicate about asking such a favor. While thus painfully embarrassed, my bond was unexpectedly signed by Mr. Israel W. Clark, editor of the "Watch Tower," and Ambrose L. Jordan, then a young lawyer recently from Columbia, his native county, became my volunteer counsel. Many years afterwards I was informed by those gentlemen that they were prompted by the young lady to whom I have referred, and who requested them not to let me know to whose kind offices I was indebted for bondsman and counsel. Messrs. Clark and Jordan became my warm friends, and remained so to the end of their long and useful lives. It was my privilege and pleasure in after life to reciprocate the services they rendered me at a trying moment.

Early in July of that year Mr. Stone wrote requesting me to return to Herkimer. I immediately complied with this request, footing it again from Cooperstown to Herkimer, a distance of about thirty miles, which, being a good pedestrian, I accomplished in a day. I found myself again pleasantly situated with my old employer, who, in a few weeks after my arrival, started eastward, politically and matrimonially inclined. One of his purposes was to attend a sort of Hartford Convention at Albany, and the other to visit a young lady who subsequently became his wife. I was left in charge of his newspaper. In August I received a letter from a young friend in Utica, informing me that he had received a commission from General Peter B. Porter, who was organizing " year's volunteers," and requesting me to become his orderly sergeant. This appeal was irresistible. The letter was received on Thursday, and the company was to march from Whitesboro' on the following Saturday. Mr. Stone was expected home on Wednesday. I worked night and day and up to two o'clock P. M. on Sunday to get the paper sufficiently advanced to enable Mr. Stone, on his return, to put it to press on the usual publication day. I then started on foot for Whitesboro', some nineteen miles distant, on a scorching hot day. The company had started for the Niagara frontier on Saturday morning, but I found ten or twelve stragglers, mostly Oneida and Stockbridge Indians, then sufficiently sobered to march. Of these I took command, drawing three days' rations to start with, and proceeded through Madison, Onondaga, and Cayuga counties, to Geneva, where, having no authority to draw rations, we were brought to a stand-still. My men had made sad havoc in vegetable gardens and poultry yards wherever we tarried, and they proposed to obtain further supplies by similar depredations; but this did not seem a proper or excusable mode of subsisting volunteers, and as I could find no person in Geneva to recognize me or my squad, I determined not

"—— to march through Coventry"

with them, and made my way as best I could back to Herkimer. Mr. Stone received me kindly, having in the interval avenged himself in a pleasant paragraph in his paper, saying he had left his office in charge of a young Democrat, who had followed off a strange fife and drum, leaving the paper to take care of itself.

In the following month of October my desire for military life was gratified in a more legitimate way. A brigade from Herkimer was ordered into the service. Though not liable to military duty (being under eighteen years of age), I attached myself to Captain Bellinger's company as a volunteer, and departed for Sackett's Harbor. The march in fine weather, and with good roads, was full of pleasant excitement. Quite unexpectedly, on the first day's march, Quartermaster George Petrie of our regiment (a merchant from Herkimer, subsequently a member of Congress, and now a clerk in the Post Office Department at Washington) handed me a warrant, appointing me his quartermaster-sergeant, which I still preserve, and of which the following is a copy : —

To Thurlow Weed, Greeting : —

We, reposing especial trust and confidence in your patriotism, valor, and good conduct, do hereby constitute and appoint you quartermaster-sergeant of the Fortieth Regiment N. Y. S. Militia, under my command.

You are therefore carefully and diligently to discharge the duty of quartermaster-sergeant of said regiment, and you are required strictly to obey your superior officers, and all officers and soldiers under your command are hereby required to obey you as such quartermaster-sergeant, for which this shall be your sufficient warrant.

Given under my hand and seal, this fifth day of October, 1814.

MAJOR JACOB P. WEBER, *Commandant.*

This mark of confidence was very gratifying. On three occasions, in 1840, in 1848, and in 1860, when new Postmaster Generals were appointed who were my political friends, it afforded me much pleasure to introduce my friend Petrie to them as a veteran of 1812, a meritorious, capable, and honest public servant.

Our regiment, some eight hundred strong, on reaching Sackett's Harbor was quartered in a large, vacant store in the centre of the village and directly opposite the navy yard, where several ships of war were in process of construction. Sackett's Harbor, within and around the village, was an encampment. Troops were quartered, for want of tents, in dwelling houses,

stores, shops, and barns. Here I first saw officers who afterwards became more or less distinguished, among whom were
General Jacob Brown, General Wilkinson, General Winder
(father of the Winders who were discreditably prominent as secessionists, or rebel officers), Commodore Chauncey, Captain
Jacob Jones, Captain Downs, Major Thomas L. Smith, of the
marine corps, and others. Here, too, I first met Lieutenant
Gregory, then a dashing young officer, who rose, by long and
faithful service, to be an Admiral. We were close friends, and
in the later years of his life it afforded both much pleasure to
recall the events of Sackett's Harbor and Lake Ontario. The
latter part of that season, the British, superior in naval force,
commanded Lake Ontario. Twice, while we were there, Sir
James Yeo appeared off the harbor with the British fleet, his
purpose being, as was supposed, to land troops. This caused
great excitement, and all our forces were hurried to the beach
in readiness to receive the enemy. On the first occasion, after
manœuvring his ships for two or three hours, he departed. On
the second, he appeared as the day broke, and at an early hour
sent a flag of truce demanding immediate surrender. General
Brown sent Major Laval, an officer of dragoons, to meet the
flag. Upon being informed that the officers in command of his
Majesty's army and navy demanded a surrender of Sackett's
Harbor, the major, in the strongest French accent, replied:
"Sar, you return to you *ship*, and zay to your master if he
wants *Zackett's Zarber* he must come and *take him!* *He no
run away!*" Then, turning his horse, he galloped back to headquarters. The flag-boat pulled off, and the fleet again made
sail for Kingston.

General Wilkinson assembled a large army for a descent,
through the St. Lawrence, upon Montreal. I endeavored to
join, but as his army was wholly of regular troops, that was
found impracticable. I remember an amusing incident which
occurred at General Brown's headquarters. Some of our men,
who were on picket-guard duty, brought in a man who said he
had escaped from Canada, where he had been for several
months a prisoner. Acting that day as sergeant-major, the man
was handed over to me to be taken to headquarters. General
Brown, after becoming satisfied that the man gave a true account of himself, questioned him as to what were the intentions

of the British army. He answered that it was well understood in Canada that an attack was soon to be made on Sackett's Harbor; that their intention was to land troops at Gravelly *Point*, approaching Sackett's Harbor in the rear, and not, as had been expected, in front. The general then asked him by what route they would move from Gravelly Point. He replied that he had heard they were to take Brown's smuggling road. This closed the examination; and when we got out I alarmed the poor man by telling him that he had unconsciously hit the general between wind and water. During the embargo, the Browns, who were enterprising merchants, had carried on an extensive contraband traffic with Canada by a route which came to be generally known as " Brown's smuggling road."

Late in the autumn, apprehensions of an attack having subsided, the militia was mustered out of service. During three months' service I had accumulated, as quartermaster-sergeant, a considerable amount of small rations, — salt, pepper, soap, etc., etc., — which the commissaries were frequently unable to deliver. I found myself, like other quartermasters, with fifty or sixty dollars, which, though properly belonging to the soldiers, there being no specie or small change, could not be distributed.

This, with my twelve dollars per month, enabled me to enjoy the luxury of a stage from Watertown to Utica. Among the passengers on that occasion I remember General Robert Swartwout, then a quartermaster-general in the United States Army, and the late Governor Yates, then a judge in the Supreme Court. At Lowville, where we slept, we met General Armstrong, then Secretary of War, who brought news of some success obtained by the allies over Bonaparte, which he regarded as diminishing the probability of peace with England.

When I arrived at Utica I learned that Samuel R. Brown, editor of a paper at Auburn, was about to publish a " History of the War," and wanted a journeyman. I lost no time in making my way to Auburn, and became immediately an inmate of Mr. Brown's printing-office and dwelling. Out of my seven weeks' residence there Mr. Dickens would have found characters and incidents for a novel as rich and as original as that of " David Copperfield " or " Nicholas Nickleby." Mr. Brown himself was an even-tempered, easy-going, good-natured man, who took no thought of what he should eat or what he should drink or wherewithal he should be clothed. He wrote his editorials and his " History of the War " upon his knee, with two or three children about him, playing or crying as the humor took them. Mrs. Brown was placid, emotionless, and slipshod. Both were imperturbable. Nothing disturbed either. There was no regular hour for breakfast or dinner, but meals were always under or over done. In short, like a household described by an early English author, " everything upon the table was sour, except the vinegar." The printing sympathized with the housekeeping. We worked at intervals during the day ; and while making a pretense of working in the evening, those hours were generally devoted to blind-man's buff with two or three neighboring girls, or to juvenile concerts by Richard Oliphant, an amateur vocalist and type-setter, to whom I became much attached. He afterwards served his time as an apprentice to the " art preservative of all arts," and for twenty or more years was an editor and publisher at Oswego, always sympathizing with me in politics, and remaining my warm friend to the end of his life.

I made few acquaintances then at Auburn, outside the printing house. I remember Judge Miller, — many years afterwards father-in-law of Governor Seward, — the present venerable ex-Governor Throop, John H. and Ebenezer S. Beach, as prominent citizens of an exceedingly muddy, rough-hewn, and straggling village.

Early in February it became necessary for me to reappear at Cooperstown. My trial, having been put over to the October term in consequence of my absence in the army, was to come on immediately. I therefore took leave of my good natured host and hostess, and departed on foot for Cooperstown, passing the first night with my parents, still residing at Onondaga. I stopped the following day at Cazenovia, and dined with Oran E. Baker, editor of " The Pilot." From thence I rode in a sleigh to Morrisville, where I put up for the night. Hearing that a circuit court was being held there, I went over to the court house in the evening, where I found Judge William P. Van Ness presiding. The court was engaged upon what I found to be an exceedingly interesting ejectment suit. As the amount involved was large, and the question of title complex, the array of counsel on either side was formidable. Indeed, I have never,

during the fifty-five years that have elapsed, with large opportunities, listened to the same number of really eminent lawyers.
In addition to the attorneys in the suit, Daniel Cady, Elisha
Williams, Thomas Addis Emmet, and Thomas J. Oakley appeared as counsel. I was so much interested as to remain there
two days in attendance, when, lest I should be too late for my
own trial, I started on my journey for the night, making a
forced march to Cooperstown, which place I reached just in
season, to the great disappointment of numbers who predicted
that I would forfeit my bail, and who jeered Mr. Clark for the
confidence he had reposed in me. In the long interval after the
indictment, public sentiment had pretty much fixed upon me as
the chief offender. The district attorney therefore decided to
try me first and alone. Three of the girls were called as witnesses, none of whom recollected speaking with or seeing me
after leaving the.meeting-house. The fourth witness testified
that she had been spinning at the house where I boarded for
several weeks ; that Saturday evenings she went to her home,
three or four miles out of the village, and came in to church on
Sunday evenings with the party; that in coming out of the
church she took my arm, and walked with me through the village to the road which led to her residence, where we waited till
the wagon with the other girls came up, when she bade me
good-night, got into the wagon, and drove off. This being the
testimony of one of their own witnesses, Mr. Jordan, my counsel, remarked that as the plaintiffs had failed entirely to sustain
their case, he should call no witness, and was ready to submit
the question to the jury without argument. The district attorney (General Kirkland, of Utica), father of Charles P. Kirkland, Esq., of New York, replied that if he had not relied upon
the representations of local counsel he should not have subjected the defendant to the annoyance of a trial; adding that
he would either move the court to quash the indictment, or ac-
cede to the proposition of his brother Jordan, allowing the case
to go without argument to the jury. The judge remarked that,
as a verdict of acquittal would probably be most satisfactory to
the defendant, that course would be adopted ; and the jury,
without leaving their seats, rendered such a verdict. Discouraged at this unexpected result, the pettifogger who instituted
the persecution abandoned the other indictments, so that an af-

fair which had caused me some uneasiness terminated happily
to my credit.

I was now out of employment, and uncertain which way to
look for it. A night's reflection resulted in a determination to
enlist, as I did on the following morning ; but before I had
been sworn in the news of peace was received, and as the terms
of my enlistment were "for during the war," I was again
afloat, whereupon I started for Albany. In the stage I made
the acquaintance of Captain Aaron Ward, of the Twenty-fifth
United States Infantry, subsequently General Ward, for many
years a representative in Congress from Westchester County,
of whom, should this narrative continue, I shall have further occasion to speak. I reached Albany early the following day,
stopping at a hotel in South Market Street, then kept by Ellis
Baker, an enterprising stage proprietor, who retired many years
ago with an ample fortune. Between Mr. Baker and myself a
friendship then began which has had no interval or ending. I
obtained employment within two hours after my arrival at the
office of the old "Albany Register," then the organ of the Republican party, published by Henry C. Southwick, his brother
Solomon being editor, and, until the previous year, State printer.
Possessing great talents, popular manners, and munificent in his
hospitalities and charities, he was a power in the State. He
made and unmade governors, State and judicial officers. But
in 1812 he differed with Governor Tompkins about the "Six
Million Bank," and quarreled with Judge Ambrose Spencer,
whom he denounced bitterly as a "Tyburn Hill Dictator."
Governor Tompkins had prorogued the legislature to prevent
the charter of the Six Million Bank, charging bribery and
corruption in his message. Mr. Southwick defended the legislature and denounced the governor, who was, however, sustained
by the people. The bank by another name, to wit, "The Bank
of America," was subsequently chartered. But the controversy
led to the establishment, under the management of Jesse Buel,
of the "Albany Argus," to which the State printing was transferred ; and the political sun, which had so long warmed and
brightened the pathway of Mr. Southwick, was suddenly and
forever eclipsed. In the hope of retrieving his fortunes he embarked largely in a wild real-estate speculation, which utterly
ruined him. He bore up, and struggled on with indomitable

industry and courage for more than twenty years, forgetting, as men will, that his misfortunes resulted from his own defective judgment and erroneous impulses, and complaining of the world's injustice and ingratitude. I leave him for the present, working with great industry, zeal, and usefulness upon the " Ploughboy " and the " Christian Visitant," sincerely believing himself to be both a practical farmer and a Christian, while in fact he was simply a theorist in agriculture and an enthusiast in religion.

And now, having passed my eighteenth birthday, my life as journeyman printer was fairly inaugurated. I was received cordially by the old journeymen in the office, and soon established pleasant relations with them all. Among them were some of decided literary taste and acquirements, but in too many instances their chances of rising were lost by a habit which has so often doomed the brightest intellects to toil and poverty. During the seven years that I was a journeyman printer, I am compelled in sadness to record my belief that at least one quarter of all the journeymen printers whom I knew were habitually intemperate; while more than another quarter of the number, though not inebriates, drank enough daily to keep themselves impoverished.

Of all the printers whom I knew at Albany in 1815, my venerable and respected friends, John O. Cole and Samuel Williams of Rondout, are, I believe, the only survivors. Fortunately I then had no taste but a decided distaste for liquors and wines, and to this day I have never imbibed malted liquors. While in the army, I generally found thirsty soldiers, to whom I either gave my whiskey-rations, or allowed them to do my washing in exchange for them. It is proper to say that until I was twenty-two years old I drank nothing stronger than cider, but for nearly half a century I have been an habitual wine drinker. I have also been an occasional drinker of whiskey, though always fastidious about the quality.

For fifty-four years I was an inveterate cigar smoker, though never using tobacco in any other form. During that period I learn, by a somewhat careful computation, that I must have smoked or given to friends at least eighty thousand cigars.

CHAPTER V.

1815–1816.

Aiken, S. C., *February* 2, 1869.

I RESUME the narrative which has been interrupted for a month, and the continuance of which is still dependent upon my health.

I was quite happy in my situation at Albany, animated by all the hopes that youth and health inspire. I worked diligently and cheerfully, earning from seven to nine dollars per week, as I was fully or partially employed, and boarding at two dollars and a half per week. My passion for the drama carried me almost every night into the pit of the old Green Street Theatre. This, at fifty cents a night, left but little of my earnings. That, however, caused me no anxiety. It was several years before I realized the importance of laying something by for sickness or a "rainy day." Most of my leisure hours were passed at the theatre or in reading. I went to the legislature on two or three occasions towards the close of its session, more to see the prominent members of whom I had heard than to listen to the debates. Those then most distinguished in the Senate were Martin Van Buren, Erastus Root, and Nathan Sandford, and in the Assembly, Elisha Williams of Columbia, William A. Duer and James Emott of Dutchess, Samuel Young of Saratoga, and Peter J. Monroe of Westchester. None of the members of that legislature (1815), as far as I am informed, are now living. The venerable Aaron Hackley, then a member from Herkimer, died in January of the present year, aged eighty-six. I remember nothing during the summer of 1815 worthy of further notice.

Mr Southwick was working his brain with indomitable energy on his two weekly newspapers. Much ability and zeal were evinced in both journals, but neither was adequately patronized, and in 1816 Mr. Southwick gave up both and became wholly absorbed in lotteries, opening an office for the sale of tickets, reserving numbers for himself which had been indicated in dreams or by fortune-tellers, with whom he was in frequent consultation. I became an active member of the Albany Typographical Society, and lived on friendly terms with all the journeymen printers.

My health was good and I was never idle during business hours at the commencement of 1816. I obtained a situation from Jesse Buel, editor of the "Albany Argus" and state printer. This was an advantageous change, as the state printing gave "*phat takes*" to journeymen. By working hard, as I did, or rather by working from five A. M. till nine P. M., I earned from fifteen to seventeen dollars a week. Mr. Buel himself was an example for his employees. From January till April I uniformly reached the office before daylight, and seldom failed to find Mr. Buel at his case, setting type by a tallow candle and smoking a long pipe.

At the opening of that legislature there was a memorable struggle for Speaker, which delayed for several days the organization of the House of Assembly. The contest excited general interest, and as the legislative printing was thus kept back, I had leisure to attend the sittings of the Assembly, as I did until the contest for Speaker was over. Upon calling the list of members of Assembly sixty-five Republicans and sixty-three Federal members answered. When Peter Allen of Ontario presented himself to be sworn, objection was made, that although Mr. Allen had received the certificate, Henry Fellows, having received a majority of votes, was entitled to a seat; and hereupon an issue was made and an exciting and protracted debate ensued. The facts in the case were simple and undisputed. Six votes had been cast for " Hen." Fellows instead of Henry Fellows. The county canvassers had rejected the six votes. This gave Mr. Allen a majority of *one* over Mr. Fellows. The ground taken by the Republicans was that no action could be had until the House was duly organized by the election of a speaker, when Mr. Fellows could present his claim, which would be referred to the appropriate standing committee. The Federalists maintained that as Mr. Fellows was clearly and undisputably the choice of the people, having received a majority of their votes, he could not be by an informal and unimportant abbreviation of his Christian name deprived of his seat. It was not simply who should be Speaker, but a question affecting all the political power and patronage of the State, that gave significance and intensity to the struggle. Then the Assembly named one Senator from each of the four Senate districts to constitute a "Council of Appointment," by which, on the nomination of the Governor, all the offices in the State, judicial, civil, and military, were appointed. The Federalists were ably represented in the legislature; several of our then most distinguished men, namely, Thomas J. Oakley and William A. Duer of Dutchess, Jacob Rutsen Van Rensselaer and James Vanderpoel of Columbia, John I. Ostrander of Albany, James Powers of Greene, Peter A. Jay of Westchester, and Myron Holley of Ontario, were members. On the other hand, the Republicans were comparatively weak. Their speakers, feeble and inexperienced, were overwhelmed by the Federal orators, who for three days kept the question open, "making the worse appear the better reason." Mr. Van Buren, then in the Senate, was constantly at the elbow of Mr. John H. Beach of Cayuga, Henry Leavenworth of Delaware, James Burt of Orange, and Dr. Barstow of Tioga suggesting and prompting, yet they were unable to cope with their more experienced adversaries. Finally, after three days' resistance, when the Republicans were exhausted in argument and subdued in spirit, a modest-looking young man occupying an obscure seat, evidently quite unknown to his colleagues, rose and addressed the clerk. His manner was good, his voice clear, and the first sentences he uttered riveted the attention of the House and of the crowded galleries. He first stated the question *pro* and *con* with strict fairness, and then, while maintaining that the House could only be organized by admitting Mr. Allen to the seat to which his certificate entitled him, he frankly conceded that if the facts in favor of Mr. Fellows were authenticated before a committee, he should vote in favor of giving Mr. Fellows the seat instead of Mr. Allen. In the course of his speech this gentleman successfully rebutted the argument and triumphantly answered the declamation of the distinguished Federal members. That settled the question. . His adversaries made an unsuccessful attempt to protract the struggle, but the question was demanded and taken.

Mr. Allen was sworn in. The eloquent member who had thus unexpectedly carried all before him was Henry B. Lee, a young lawyer from Putnam County, who was in April of that year elected to Congress, but died before his term of service expired. Daniel Cruger was elected Speaker, and a Republican Council of Appointment chosen. Mr. Fellows was admitted to the seat which Mr. Allen vacated on the 7th of February.

William C. Bouck, subsequently canal commissioner and Governor of the State, was a member of that Assembly, as was Herman Knickerbocker, a wit and wag who was subsequently a member of Congress, and best known as the " Prince of Schaghticoke." I knew him well; he was an amiable man and a pleasant companion. When a law student at Albany with John V. Henry, in the early part of the present century, Captain Houdin, a Frenchman who came to this country to serve in our revolutionary army, was appointed to deliver an eulogium upon Washington; whom, next to Lafayette, he idolized. His oration completed, he submitted the manuscript to his friend Knickerbocker, in whose judgment and taste the Frenchman confided. After suggesting various unimportant corrections, Mr. Knickerbocker expressed his warm approval of the effort, but remarked that he thought the closing sentence should be made more effective and dramatic. Captain Houdin asked him to help him round out the sentence, which as written was as follows: " The immortal soldier and statesman, George Washington, expired at Mt. Vernon without a sigh or a groan." Mr. Knickerbocker substituted for " a sigh or a groan " the words " a grunt or a growl," with which the Frenchman was delighted. The eulogium was actually delivered in very bad English with this ludicrous conclusion.

Of the journeymen printers then employed by Mr. Buel, there are two survivors. Samuel Williams, now eighty-two or eighty-three years old, resides at Rondout, Ulster County. Though I have not seen him for more than fifty years, our friendly relations have been preserved. Gerrit W. Ryckman, then an apprentice, worked with me at press, and when out of his time I obtained a situation for him in New York, where we again worked at the same press, becoming warm friends. In 1830, when I established the " Albany Evening Journal," Ryckman was one of the proprietors of the " Albany Daily Advertiser." Rivalry in business aggravated the differences between us occasioned by the anti-Masonic question. Alienation ensued. Mr. Ryckman soon sold his interest in the " Advertiser " to embark in other enterprises, and from that day till the present time he has fought the battle of life with varying fortune. For the last twenty years he has resided in California. After a lapse of nearly forty years of alienation a mutual friend showed me a letter from Mr. Ryckman, in which he spoke of our early friendship so kindly that I wrote him a letter, which brought back a warm response, from which the following is an extract : —

SAN FRANCISCO, *January* 29, 1866.

THURLOW WEED, ESQ. :

My very dear, good Friend, — There is no language at my command that can begin to give you an idea of the agony of joy and happiness with which my heart was overwhelmed at the perusal of your kind, generous, and noble-hearted letter to me of December 9, 1865. God in his infinite mercy bless and prosper you and yours, Thurlow Weed, friend of my early boyhood, that I love and cherish with my whole heart and soul, and which love and affection was never obliterated for a moment, although I did, in the wild, mad, persecuting spirit of former days, act toward you " many a time and oft " in the most uncalled-for and unnatural manner, although the better feelings of my nature chided me at the time being for so doing. Heaven be praised that through your magnanimity I have been forgiven, so far at least as *you* are concerned, and that I have lived to see this day and to feel and know that you and I are now the same warm-hearted, confiding, true, and sincere friends that we were in the days of lang syne.

I well remember all the much respected names you mention in your letter. Some have risen to marked eminence and great wealth, whilst others are still tugging at the oar on the frail bark of fortune. Such is life.

You tell me that you are living in Beaver Street at the present time. So you were more than fifty years ago, when I frequently used to climb upon the shed to awaken you, after you had barricaded the door that led to the entrance of your sleeping-room. Many a good, hearty laugh have I had at the idea of your endeavoring to make me believe that the fastening of the door to the wood-house was the work of that good old gentleman, Dr. Packard. . . .

The idea of your waiting, if you so please to term it, until the completion of the great railway before you think of visiting California, looks to me most passing strange and wonderful. The man who has the daring to have crossed the Atlantic as frequently as you have done should not be allowed to enter so frail an excuse as the waiting of the completion of the railway. . . . It gives my soul great joy to think and know that such a thing as your early visit to this glorious young State is within the range of human probabilities. Please, my dear friend, write me as often as your convenience will permit, and believe me now and ever,

Yours from the heart of hearts,   G. W. Ryckman.

I witnessed a street rencontre at Albany, about this time, between two young men whose names subsequently became historical. Mr. Gorham A. Worth, for many years and until his death financial officer of the City Bank, was, in 1816, teller in the Mechanics and Farmers' Bank at Albany. As in the case of Charles Lamb, Rogers, Halleck, etc., while other duties claimed his attention during the usual hours of business, his tastes were literary. All the time that could be snatched from office duties was given to the Muses. A good deal of local interest had been excited by the publication in pamphlet form of "Sketches," delineating the salient points of character of several then most prominent citizens of Albany. Chief Justice Spencer, whose character presented many strong and noticeable features, was freely sketched and universally recognized as "Saint Ambrosio." His son William, then a midshipman in the navy and at home on furlough, on learning that Mr. Worth wrote the "Sketches," met him in the street and attempted to chastise him with a rattan. A sharp rencontre ensued, but before any decisive advantage was obtained by either the combatants were separated. Mr. Spencer subsequently rose to a post-captaincy in the navy, and having married an estimable lady (Miss Lorillard) in New York, inherited a large fortune.

Mr. Worth, soon after the charter of the Bank of the United States, was appointed cashier of its branch at Cincinnati, where he became favorably known both as a banker and a man of letters. The last thirty years of his life were pleasantly passed as President of the New York City Bank, and in the occasional indulgence of his literary tastes. His son, James L. Worth, is cashier of the Park Bank. I entertained all that time a sin-

cere friendship for Mr. Worth, and had the happiness of knowing that the sentiment was reciprocated. He was a frequent
contributor to the " Evening Journal," and a familiar correspondence between us ran through his life.

During that winter, having had a good situation, I saved
money enough to improve and enlarge my previously scanty
wardrobe; and when, on the first of May, the legislative printing was finished, I started for New York, to gratify a long-cher-
ished hope of revisiting that metropolis.

There were three steamboats then running between New
York and Albany, namely, the Paragon, Car of Neptune, and
the Richmond. We left Albany at five P. M., and were in the
dock at the foot of Cortlandt Street at nine o'clock the next
morning. I was delighted with the trip, remaining on deck
nearly all night to catch glimpses of places and scenery which
had interested me when navigating the river as a sloop's cabin-
boy in 1806 and 1807.

My first situation was as a compositor in the office of Van
Winkle & Wiley, book printers, in Greenwich Street. I worked
on " Cobbett's Register," and being anxious to see the great
English radical who, when in this country in 1794, vilified
Washington almost as bitterly as he was then denouncing
George III., volunteered to carry his proof-sheets to him, at No.
8 or 10 in a basement in Wall Street, which he occupied
as a publishing office. I found him quite affable, evincing in
conversation, as in his writings, energy and will. He had served,
when a young man, in Canada, as a British soldier. Fifty-three
years afterwards, when introduced to his son in the House of
Commons, I related this incident to him. The M. P., though
bearing a physical resemblance to his father, was quiet in manner, and had evidently not inherited either the talent or the
rancor of the elder Cobbett. And here I may insert my " Reminiscences of the City of New York Half a Century Ago, by a
Journeyman Printer," given to the public at another time and
in another form : —

THE CITY OF NEW YORK FIFTY YEARS AGO.

RECOLLECTIONS OF A JOURNEYMAN PRINTER.

The New York of 1815, wonderful then as a city in eyes accustomed only to rural districts, has so changed, in aspect and habits, as to exist only in the memories of the " oldest inhabitants." Geographically, it was a compact city (saving the Rutgers mansion and grounds) as far east as Corlears' Hook. The Bowery was built up as far as Grand Street (though there was then no such street), while beyond it were pleasant country residences. About this time Eldridge and Christie streets took the names of officers of the Thirteenth United States Infantry, who distinguished themselves in the battle of Queenstown.

Brooklyn was an inconsiderable village. There was then a ferry from the Fly (now Fulton) Market, at the foot of Fair (now Fulton) Street, to Brooklyn, or rather to the navy yard, for Brooklyn was of little account; but the only mode of crossing was by row-boats. Staten Island was reached by "perryaugers" (periaguas), one of which was commanded by Captain Cornelius Vanderbilt, now a twenty-million-aire.

On the west side of Broadway, streets extended only to Lispenard, all north of which was either unsightly common or indifferently cultivated farms. There was, well out of the city, the nucleus of what became the village of Greenwich, between Seventh and Eighth Avenues, and below Fourteenth Street. When of a Sunday afternoon we wanted exercise and fresh air, we would walk up to the State Prison, then a prominent feature far away out of the city, but now standing, almost unobserved, near Christopher Street. It then looked directly upon the river ; now, several streets intercept the view.

In 1815 or 1816, the common north of Canal Street (there was neither Erie Canal nor Canal Street then) was surveyed and laid out in streets, which took the names of revolutionary officers, Green, Mercer, Sullivan, etc. I remember going, about this time, with a friend, the late George Mather, to a vacant lot situated near the now corner of Spring and Mercer streets, which he had purchased to erect an ink manufactory upon, assuming that the adjoining property would not be occupied for many years, and that he should never be disturbed by neighbors !

The erection of two basement brick dwelling-houses, the first of that class, I believe, on the east side of Broadway, between Franklin and Canal streets, caused a good deal of remark, and was regarded as gratifying evidence of architectural progress. These dwellings, considered magnificent then, were built by Messrs. Price & Simpson, managers of the Park Theatre. Whole streets of mansions, infinitely superior, go up now in a month without thought or observation.

The aristocracy of the city fifty years ago resided either in Broadway, adjacent to the Battery, or in the vicinity of Columbia College. The late Governor De Witt Clinton resided in Cherry Street.

Of what was Cortlandt Street in 1815, the only house remaining as it stood is one then occupied by the late Philip Hone. All else has been rebuilt. Cortlandt Street was rather aristocratic then. Upper-tendom had no existence even in name then. Indeed, the wealthy classes had not commenced their West-End migration until nearly twenty years later. Broadway in the mean time has, to use a familiar phrase, entirely " shed its coat." There are not, of what *was* Broadway in 1815, more than three or four spared monuments. The Prime House, opposite Bowling-Green, St. Paul's Church, and one or two more buildings, remain as they were. All else has been demolished and rebuilt, and in many cases this process has been repeated and reiterated.

In those days Hoboken was known, not because the Elysian Fields were beautiful, but mainly because it was the duelling-ground of Hamilton and Burr, and as such was much visited. Jersey City was " nowhere."

In 1815 there were no omnibus lines, no railways, and, I believe, no hacks, or if any, only a few, and those stood in front of Trinity Church. How, then, did people get to distant parts of the city? Of course, the area of the city was circumscribed, or it would have been impossible to traverse it without conveyances. But we took our time in those days. Nobody was in such a hurry to get through the world. Nobody was "fast." Business journeys to Buffalo would consume more days than hours are now required.

In 1815 the City Hotel was the only first-class public house. Washington Hall, where A. T. Stewart's store is now, opened about that time, but all the others were second-rate. Hotel fare in those days, though substantial, was plain. The culinary art among us was in its infancy. There was, indeed, a general prejudice against French cooking. Port and brown sherry (pale sherry rarely seen) wines were good. The Madeira wines were gloriously delicious. Champagne was just coming in, but comparatively little known, and was warmed before drinking ! Ice, that now domestic necessity, was then rarely seen, and used only during the "heated terms." Strawberries were never served upon hotel tables, or in private families, except at tea. The strawberry, as a hotel breakfast and dinner luxury, was first introduced by William Sykes, who opened a most luxurious " Bank Cof-

fee-house " in William Street, on the corner of William and Pine, but
who lived too fast to live long. Grapes, except those from Madeira,
were wholly unknown. None were grown except the small, sour, wild
grape. Nor was the tomato, a vegetable now found upon every table
in the city, then cultivated, or known as the esculent now so universally appreciated. I doubt whether, in 1815, a tomato was sold or
eaten in this city.

Fifty years ago, the customs and habits of New York were much
more natural and simple than they are now. There was then infinitely less wealth, less luxury, less cultivation, and less refinement.
There is, however, a cultivation and refinement in evil as in good, and
their progress, in both senses, has been coincident. We grow better
and worse. Refinement and demoralization keep about equal pace.
Such are the inevitable fruits of great prosperity. In the aggregate,
however, it is encouraging to know that there is a constantly increasing preponderance of good over evil.

There were comparatively few temptations in those days. There
were no " hells," or " gin palaces," or " saloons." There were no
clubs, though, of course, I do not confound the latter with the former. But men lived at home in those days. Perhaps I. cannot so
well illustrate my meaning as to say that the Delmonico of fifty years
ago was a colored man (" Billy "), who lived in William Street, east
of Frankfort, where it was the custom of prominent merchants, lawyers, physicians, etc., to go, winter evenings, for *buckwheat cakes*.
This was a general resort. I remember, among others, to have seen
and listened to Dr. S. L. Mitchell, Richard Riker, Pierre C. Van
Wyck, Isaac Carow, Jacob Barker, etc., taking their cakes and coffee
there socially.

Even porter-houses, as now constituted, were almost unknown then.
I believe the first introduction of newspapers for general reading was
at a porter-house on the corner of Fulton and Nassau streets. The
use of " all that intoxicates " had, of course, an earlier origin, but
most of its compound virtues were undiscovered. The " cock-tail "
and the " cobbler," now in universal request, were not then invented,
nor had the " julep " yet imparted its flavor and incense to Northern lip and nose. But, although these refinements in drinking had
not reached us, men did not lack the means of quenching thirst. The
" sling " was as potent in overthrowing Goliaths as in the days of
David.

The great, the wonderful changes wrought in fifty years relate to
daily journals. There were then two morning (the " Gazette " and
the " Mercantile ") and two evening (the " Post " and the " Commercial ") daily papers. I am not sure that the " Columbian " was not a

daily, though I believe it was only a semi-weekly. The "Gazette" was crowded with advertisements, rarely containing more than a column or a column and a half of reading matter. The "Mercantile" was not much better, — both stupid and barren of all interest, except for their ship news and advertisements. The "Post" was edited with decided, and the "Commercial" with moderate ability.

The "Mercantile" had the largest circulation, which, if I remember right, was less than 2,500. At any rate, the circulation of all the New York dailies fifty years ago did not half equal that of the "Times" now; nor was there in the whole city, then, as much press power and capacity as is now operated subterraneously under the sidewalk in front of the "Times" office. And this vast power, which furnishes political, commercial, and general intelligence for the world, is operated while thousands who pass directly over it are unconscious of its whereabouts.

The dailies I have named were all Federal in politics. The "Columbian" was then the only Republican or Democratic journal in the city. The merchants were generally Federalists, as were most of the lawyers.

Richard M. Blatchford, Esq., now one of the solid men of New York, between whom and myself there has been a lifelong, unbroken, cherished friendship, came to New York in 1815 from Union College, to seek his fortune, like the late Luther Bradish, as a schoolmaster.

Mechanics and laborers were paid, in 1815, in Jacob Barker's Washington and Warren Bank, twenty-five and fifty-cent "shinplasters." Mechanics, clerks, etc., etc., paid three dollars per week for board.

There were then several officers of the Revolution, who had served with distinction, residing in New York. Among those I remember to have seen were Colonel Marinus Willett, Colonel Nicholas Fish (Governor Fish's father), Colonel Varick, General Ebenezer Stevens, Major Z. Platt, Governor Morgan Lewis, Colonel Anthony Lamb, etc., etc. Colonel Aaron Burr, with whom I subsequently became acquainted, returned from Europe about that time.

New York was a more economically-governed city fifty years ago than it is now. There was a much higher sense of official responsibility. Municipal honors were conferred on men of high standing and character.

CHAPTER VI.

1816–1818.

A Journeyman Printer's Life in New York. — Daniel Fanshawe.
— William E. Dean. — Samuel Wood. — Mr. Gardenier. — Jona-
than Seymour. — William A. Mercien. — Peter Force. — The Old
Park Theatre. — Political Meetings. — Attending Church. —
Rev. Edward Mitchell. — Reception of President Monroe. —
Israel W. Clark and the "Register." — Going to Albany by
Sloop. — First Editorials. — The Boy and the Doctors. — Gen-
eral Montgomery. — Murder of Major Birdsall. — Hamilton's
Execution.

Retiring now from the "space box" to the "ink block," in June I obtained a situation at press with Daniel Fanshawe, in Cliff Street, where I worked on some of the first tracts printed in this country, — tract societies having then been recently organized. In a couple of months I changed to the office of George Lang, a book publisher in Pearl Street, near Coenties Slip. Here I worked at press with William E. Dean, who subsequently became a successful master printer, and is now among the few surviving friends with whom I was intimate at that early day, enjoying in retirement the fruits of early industry and frugality. I then worked a few weeks at the office of Samuel Wood & Sons, corner of Pearl and Frankfort streets. They were Quakers, and their principal business was to print and sell juvenile school-books. They were as methodical and fastidious in their printing as in the cut of their coats, but excellent people and pleasant employers. I then took a situation on the "Courier," a morning paper edited and published by Barent Gardenier, a prominent Federal lawyer, who represented the Ulster district in Congress during the war. The office was in Pearl Street, near Lang and Turner's "Gazette" office in Hanover Square.

A comparative estimate between the commerce of that and the present day may be formed, from the circumstance that, as the "Courier" had no news boat, an intelligent boy went every half hour to Mr. Lang's bulletin and brought in his memory the names of masters and consignees of all the arrivals both from foreign ports and coastwise. In this way Mr. Gardenier collected his ship news. But his paper was short-lived. It was started without capital and ran as long as it could run upon credit. Mr. Gardenier, who was practicing law, called his journeymen together and informed them that they should have their pay — requesting us to call frequently at his office in Maiden Lane and " dun " him. I, however, immediately obtained a good situation with Mr. Jonathan Seymour, a book printer, at No. 49 John Street. Not needing money as those did who had families, I concluded to wait until Mr. Gardenier should be better able to pay my bill, but in about six weeks, meeting him accidentally, he exclaimed, " Why the d—— have n't you chased me up like the rest of the pack ? I thought you had run away or were lost," fumbling meanwhile in the cuffs of his coat, where he found between three and four dollars of Jacob Barker's twenty-five and fifty cent paper currency, which he gave me, saying, " Keep dunning me till you get the balance." I mention this otherwise unimportant incident as characteristic of a man who occupied a prominent public position in his day. My situation at the office of Mr. Seymour was a very pleasant one. My press partner was James Harper, the senior of the great publishing house of Harper & Brothers, who was subsequently elected mayor of the city. We were employed upon a quarto edition of " Scott's Family Bible," and worked with a will, earning from twelve to thirteen dollars a week. We were at the office in the morning as soon as it was light, doing, in the summer months, a third of our day's work before breakfast. It was a well-regulated office and most of the journeymen were intelligent and temperate. Mr. Seymour himself was a kind-hearted man, who had an encouraging word for us all, and it afforded him evident pleasure to find his journeymen coming to him on Saturday nights to receive their wages, especially if their bills were large ones.

When James and John Harper established a small office of their own, I reluctantly left Mr. Seymour's office to take a situation in that of William A. Mercien, in Gold Street, that I might have Thomas Kennedy, who was considered the best pressman in New York, as a partner. Here, too, I found much enjoy-

ment. I soon became a favorite with Mr. Mercien, and always
had the best work in the office. Here "Captain Riley's Narrative of a Remarkable Shipwreck on the Coast of Africa" was
first printed. Making his acquaintance the day he brought the
manuscript of his book to the office, and reading the first chapter, I ventured to suggest that it was carelessly written and
needed revising, and although at first annoyed, he finally took
it away and availed himself of the services of a school-teacher,
who improved the whole narrative in its style and grammar.
The work was a great success, keeping its author before the
people for fifteen or twenty years.

I was elected a member of the New York-Typographical Society soon after I reached the city, and attended its meetings
regularly. These were occasions to me of rare interest, for
among its members were men of intellectual, moral, and social
worth. Its president was Peter Force, subsequently and for
forty years an eminent printer in Washington. Others established themselves in neighboring cities and villages, and became
influential and prosperous publishers or editors. These, however, were the exceptions, for much the largest number remained
journeymen through life. Too many of them, I regret to say,
were impoverished by habitual dram-drinking, more or less in-
temperately. The printing-house habits condemned by Dr.
Franklin had not yet been reformed. Journeymen in most of
the offices were required to pay "footing," which meant a treat
by the new comer, all the old journeymen and the masters were
required to treat the hands whenever signature "0" was put to
press. At eleven o'clock A. M. invariably, and too frequently
afterwards, journeymen would "jeff" for beer. In this way a
large share of their weekly earnings was mortgaged, each journeyman having a formidable "tick" at the grocery to be adjusted on Saturday evenings.

There was a marked difference between the journeymen who
came from Boston, Hartford, and other New England towns, and
those who came from Baltimore, Philadelphia, etc., etc., most of
the former being temperate and frugal, while most of the latter
were thriftless or dissipated. Among the journeymen from Boston was Thomas Tileston, who subsequently became a shipping
merchant, and for thirty years, as a member of the house of
Spofford & Tileston, was one of our most enterprising and es-

timable citizens. Fortunately for me, I disliked malt liquors and then drank no distilled spirits or wine. The extent of my indulgence was to repair on Saturday evenings to a porter-house in Fair (now Fulton Street) to read the newspapers and drink a glass of Newark cider. I have often reflected gratefully that my repugnance for beer and distaste for stimulating beverages in early life saved me from a fate to which different tastes and habits consigned hundreds of companions and acquaintances. But while I did not thus squander my earnings, my passion for the drama increased " with what it fed upon." I went regularly to the old Park Theatre, then in its palmy days, where I saw, with an enthusiasm that even yet fans the embers of memory, the best actors that ever graced our boards. Then the legitimate drama held possession of the stage. An occasional melo-drama like the "Forty Thieves," "Abolino," "The Dog of Montargis," "Tekeli," etc., etc., was introduced. But the plays of Shakespeare and the sterling old English comedies, with an admirable English farce, brought out almost every night such actors as Hodgekinson, Incledon, Cooper, Mr. and Mrs. Darley, Mr. and Mrs. Barnes, Hilson, Placide, Simpson, Miss Rock, Ellen Tree, Maywood, Power, and Dwyer.

In those days there came to the Park Theatre, as regularly as the actors themselves, two or three hundred New York merchants, lawyers, physicians, etc., etc., with whose faces I was forever after familiar. Among these were M. M. Noah, John Pintard, Philip Hone, Richard Hatfield, Hugh and W. H. Maxwell, G. C. Verplanck, Sylvanus Miller, Dr. Francis, and others. The omnipresence of "Old Hayes" was sufficient to preserve order.

As I had constant work and seldom lost a working hour, I knew but little of what was passing in the city outside of the printing-offices. I went occasionally to political meetings, where I heard Thomas Addis Emmet, William Samson, David B. Ogden, Peter A. Jay, Dr. S. L. Mitchell, Michael Ulshoeffer, P. C. Van Wyck, and others speak. I went also to the City Hall to see and hear the distinguished judges and lawyers of that day.

Soon after reaching New York I formed a plan of attending service at least once at all the churches of the city, commencing, I believe, with Trinity. I remember to have gone on consecu-

tive Sundays to the Methodist churches in John and Duane
streets, Rev. Dr. Phillips' in Wall Street, the two churches in
William Street (one of them now the Post Office), the church in
Beekman Street, Dr. McMurray's in Chambers Street, Dr.
Mason's in Murray Street, Rev. Mr. McClay's in Mott Street,
and from the latter I visited a little white, wooden meeting-house
in Magazine (now Pearl Street), a few doors west of Chatham.
The building stood modestly back from the street, making no
pretension to church architecture, but when seated, and the first
sentence of a prayer alike impressive and affectionate fell upon
the ear, no one could doubt that he was in the house and presence of God. This feeling deepened as the services progressed,
and at their conclusion I rose and left that place of worship
wiser and better for its instructions and associations. That was
a Universalist church under the Rev. Edward Mitchell, an eloquent man then about forty-five years of age, who labored there
and in Duane Street some twenty years afterwards, dying as he
had lived a devout Christian and greatly beloved pastor. Strong
as the sectarian feeling then was, and much as the sect to which
Mr. Mitchell belonged was disliked, all conceded piety and
purity of life to that preacher, and his congregation, it was admitted, maintained a high moral character. I became a constant attendant of Dr. Mitchell's church, and his teachings gave
a direction to my thoughts and exerted an influence which tended
to render my future life hopeful.

The following letter will give an idea of the character of that
" good pastor : " —

NEW YORK, *September* 20, 1817.

DEAR SIR, — Your letter of the 29th July, with its inclosure of the
27th, I received in due course, and can give no other sufficient reason
why they have not been sooner answered by me than this : that when
I intended to answer them I could not find them ; I looked again and
again, but to no purpose ; this morning I laid my hands on them, and
have read them with renewed pleasure ; they appear to me to contain
the warm effusions of an honest, zealous mind. I have made it a general rule to avoid hearing either the praise or censure of my official
labors, lest I should be puffed up by the one, or prevented by the
other from the discharge of a sacred duty.

Yet thus much I will own, that every instance I have that my labors
are not in vain is to me an encouragement to persevere. And I ac-

knowledge that this is to me an evidence of the weakness of human nature, for my understanding builds on an unexpressibly better foundation.   I am perfectly convinced that when God sends his laborers to sow the good word of life, he never intends that they should labor in vain ; and (to pursue the figure) though the seed may die, and rot in the ground, yet it shall produce the blade, the full ear, the glorious harvest.   The pulpit advocate is not the only laborer in this great and good work ; every believer to whom God is pleased to give the opportunity of advocating the truth, though it should be but to a single person, is then laboring for the glory of God and the happiness of man, and where is there a believer who has not this opportunity ?   I doubt if there is one so situated in the world.   Now, if every believer is thus a laborer, whose labor shall not be in vain, how great his honor, how true his happiness !   But to enjoy this happiness we must believe that our labor shall not be in vain.   I can truly assure you that this conviction has very, very often been my great support when almost every other source of support has failed me.

You ask, Is there any impropriety in making extracts for the paper from the new hymn book ?   I see none ; but I am very sure that if you tell your readers where you extract from they will not generally thank you for your pains, and yet these hymns are very generally written by those who did not believe with us.   It is a fact, though a strange one, that people who do not believe the truth will frequently express it, and so in this case.   The 468th hymn, beginning " Art Thou my Father," etc., was handed to me last summer by a dying friend.   He felt its full force, for he was the father of a numerous family who had no mother, and he himself loved God as his father.   I think he told me it was copied from a Baltimore paper into one of this city.   I am respectfully your obedient servant,

EDWARD MITCHELL.

There was another event and arrival with which I was intensely interested.   Rev. Mr. Summerfield, a youthful Methodist clergyman, came from England, and commenced preaching in New York.   He was wonderfully beautiful in the formation of his head and the features of his face, and that all these features were eloquently expressive of the purity of his life and the goodness of his nature, or the divinity of his mission, none who saw and heard him could doubt.   His voice and manner harmonized with and gave effect to his personal accomplishments. He was followed from church to church by great numbers, charming and chastening all ears and all hearts.   If any went to scoff, they inevitably " remained to pray."   If Rev. John

Summerfield had announced himself as an inspired prophet or apostle, he would have had hosts of believers. But he was himself a simple, unostentatious, "meek and lowly" believer and follower of that Saviour to whom, in person and character, he bore such striking resemblance. There are, I doubt not, old citizens who heard Mr. Summerfield, and who share in the enthusiasm of my remembrance of him.

I had the satisfaction, one summer afternoon, to witness the reception of President Monroe, who was met on the Battery by a civic and military procession under the command of Major General Morton, and escorted to the City Hall. This was the first President of the United States I had ever seen. The only one of his successors whom I never saw was General Jackson. With all the other Presidents of the United States, from James Monroe to General Grant, except President Polk, I have been personally acquainted.

1817. — In June, 1817, I received a letter from Israel W. Clark, editor of the "Watch Tower," Cooperstown, informing me that he had purchased the Albany "Register," and offering me the situation of foreman in that office. Though most reluctant to leave New York, where I was living very happily, this offer seemed too advantageous to be lost. I therefore took passage in the sloop Commerce, Captain George Monteath, left New York with a fresh breeze in our favor, and was landed at Albany in thirty-six hours. I found my new situation an extremely pleasant one. Here I was permitted to try my "'prentice hand" on editorials. I first wrote brief paragraphs upon commonplace subjects, taking occasionally great liberties with the king's English, for I was ignorant of the first principles of grammar; but Mr. Clark, the editor, would good-naturedly point to these blunders, and say encouragingly that I would improve by practice. It was not long, however, before one of my paragraphs involved Mr. Clark and myself in serious difficulty. An Irish boy, living in a garret directly opposite our office, had his leg badly injured by an explosion of powder. There came regularly to this boy's bedside three or four students of medicine, who, as I believed, were treating him unskillfully; who, indeed, were experimenting upon a poor, friendless boy. My sympathies found indignant expression in a paragraph saying that a poor boy was in danger of losing a limb, if not his life, unless an experienced physician, instead of a tyro in medicine, could be induced to visit him. This raised a storm about our ears. The young men were students of Dr. William Bay, an eminent physician, who came much excited to the editor, demanding ample and public apologies. Upon learning who the offender was, I was arraigned before Mr. Verner, a police magistrate, and reprimanded, though I did not see then, and cannot see now, by what authority. Before the next publication day (the "Register" appearing only twice a week) the boy's leg had to be amputated. This was my vindication, and the end of our trouble with the doctors. For twenty or more years afterwards the boy (Pat McAnnally), who went stumping about Albany with a wooden leg, served to remind the doctors and myself of the incident.

Soon after my arrival in Albany two events occurred which attracted general interest. On the 4th of July, the remains of General Montgomery, on their way from Quebec to New York, passed through the city. The procession, consisting of the military, civic societies, and citizens of Albany, Troy, and Schenectady, was imposing, impressive, and solemn. The Grand Marshal of the day was Major Benjamin Birdsall of the United States army, who had served gallantly in the war of 1812, and who appeared on that day for the first time without the dressing upon a severe wound in the face that he received in the sortie at Fort Erie, in 1814. On the 12th of the same month, as he was, on a Sunday afternoon, about to review his rifle battalion, he was shot by one of his soldiers. He had passed two hours of that afternoon in our office chatting with two or three friends. After he left the office, I went with a friend for a walk, and returning near sundown, between the patroon's and the old arsenal, I heard a rifle shot, and saw a commotion in the cantonment which lay between North Pearl Street and what is now known as the Little Basin. I ran to the spot, and assisted in removing the major (who was my intimate friend) on a litter to his residence in North Pearl Street, where he soon expired.

The excitement against the soldier was so intense that it was difficult to prevent the populace from lynching him. He was committed to the jail, but the feeling ran so high that the civil authorities requested the officer in command at the Greenbush cantonment to receive and protect the prisoner.

Major Birdsall at the commencement of the war resided on a farm which he rented from the patroon, near the Shaker village. He went with a volunteer rifle company, of which he was an officer, to Plattsburgh, where, in the battle that ensued, his gallantry attracted the attention of General Macomb, on whose recommendation, along with that of Governor Tompkins, he was appointed an officer in the United States Rifle Corps, and served subsequently on the Niagara frontier, again distinguishing himself in several battles, until, at the close of the campaign of 1814, he received his desperate wound in leading, under General Peter B. Porter, the assault upon Fort Erie. He had risen. against adverse circumstances, by intelligence and energy, to position and fame, and was justly appreciated by Albanians.

The prisoner, Hamilton, was soon indicted, arraigned, tried, convicted, and sentenced to be hanged. The trial (which I reported for the " Register") was in the Assembly Chamber, and although Hamilton himself always admitted the charge, and manifested no solicitude for the result of the trial, somebody (his father, it was supposed) employed counsel for him, who strenuously urged an acquittal on the ground of temporary insanity occasioned by liquor, but of course producing no effect.

After his conviction, at the request of Sheriff Hempsted, I went to Hamilton's cell, with a strong feeling of repugnance, which, however, after two or three visits, was, by a revelation of all the circumstances, changed to a sorrowful sympathy. Hamilton was the natural son of a man engaged successfully in a business that ultimately made him wealthy in the city of New York. His mother, turned adrift in disgrace and destitution, struggled as well as she could for a few years, and then left him to the world's charity.

At the commencement of the war of 1812, then about twenty years old, he enlisted, and it was shown on his trial that he served faithfully and gallantly, receiving at the close of the war an honorable discharge. He had known and greatly admired Major Birdsall during the war. After a year or two of irregularities, with uncertain and precarious employment, he sought Major Birdsall's recruiting rendezvous and reënlisted. For more than a week before the fatal rifle was fired Hamilton had been intoxicated. On Saturday, a light-colored mulatto, a fine, soldierly-looking young man, who had served during the war, also reënlisted, and was sent to camp to be mustered in; after which, the major intended to take him to his house as a waiter. At mid-day on Sunday Hamilton was told that a negro had been recruited, and as he was, like Hamilton, a tall fellow, was to be put into his platoon and mess. This, maddened as he already was with a mixture of bad whiskey and sour cider, exasperated him beyond control. He loaded his rifle, and went prowling about in search of the "negro," who, informed of Hamilton's threats, kept out of his way, — until at six o'clock Hamilton, with rifle in hand, saw him dodge behind a tent, and started after him. At this moment the major, who was approaching, called, "Hamilton, take your place!" and the rifle, which was ready to be discharged at the soldier, was instantaneously aimed and fatally discharged at the major. In his sober senses, he would have defended Major Birdsall at the risk of his own life.

As a coincidence entitled to be remembered, it is proper to say that Major Birdsall, like the man who assassinated him, was an illegitimate child, unacknowledged until after he had distinguished himself in the war. His father, Colonel Benjamin Birdsall, an officer in the revolutionary army, and an influential citizen of Columbia County, then sent for the major and acknowledged him as a son.

After Hamilton was convicted and sentenced to execution, he requested me to write his "Life and Confession." He told me that he was the natural son of a wealthy New Yorker, from whom he had received nothing, and whom he never saw; but although he owed him neither affection nor duty, he did not want his father's name made public. The day before his execution he asked permission of the sheriff to walk to the gallows instead of riding, as was usual, on a cart with his coffin. His request was granted. He then asked me to walk near him and witness his execution, that I might see and say that he died like a soldier. It was more than a mile from the jail to the place of execution. The sheriff's posse was escorted by a military company. I walked with the sheriff directly behind Hamilton, whose bearing was that of a soldier, proud of the attention he attracted. He ascended to the scaffold with a firm step, talked cheerfully with the clergyman for a few minutes, said good-bye to the multitude, and told the sheriff he was ready. At the fatal moment, when the drop fell, the rope parted, and, to the horror of all present, Hamilton lay stretched upon the ground. But instantly springing to his feet, he stood erect until the sheriff approached him and said, " This is hard, Hamilton." " Yes," he replied, " but it is my own fault ; I asked you for too much slack." The sheriff then took a cart-rope, and, handing it to Hamilton, inquired, " Do you think this strong enough ? " Hamilton replied, with a smile, " It is large enough to be strong." It was then adjusted to his neck, when he re-ascended, and placed himself upon the drop with a firm foot. Again the fatal cord was cut, and in a few seconds all was over. That was the first and last execution I ever attended.

CHAPTER VII.

1818.

IN 1818 there was a disastrous split in the Republican Party
of this State, Governor Clinton heading one faction and Mr.
Van Buren the other. A political and personal warfare of unusual virulence characterized the campaign of that year. Mr.
Clinton, an able and vituperative writer, assailed the leaders of
the opposite side through the columns of the New York " Columbian " and the Albany " Register." William L. Marcy, then
a young man, and others, replied through the columns of the
Albany " Argus." One morning a vehement article, highly denunciatory of Governor Clinton, provoked a note from the gentleman assailed to the editor of the " Argus," demanding the
name of the writer. Mr. Buel, the editor, handed the note to
Mr. Van Buren, who invited Mr. Charles E. Dudley, Mr. William L. Marcy, Mr. Benjamin Knower, and Judge Roger Skinner to his house that evening. While they were discussing the
embarrassing question which Governor Clinton's note had raised,
the servant brought Peter R. Livingston to the library. Mr.
Clinton was at the time Governor of the State, while Messrs.
Van Buren and Livingston were members of the Senate. The
conversation, as Mr. Livingston discovered, was interrupted by
his appearance. He said, in his usual brusque manner, " You
are talking secrets here, and I have interrupted you." Mr. Van
Buren replied, " Governor Clinton has demanded the name of
the writer of the article in this morning's ' Argus,' and we were
talking of the peculiar awkwardness of exposing the writer."
" There is nothing peculiar about it," responded Mr. Living-

ston, " nor need there be any embarrassment. Send my name
to Mr. Clinton." Mr. Van Buren remarked, " This is no occasion for trifling, Mr. Livingston. You know what Mr. Clinton means by his demand." " Yes, sir," replied Mr. Livingston, " I do know, and it is just what I mean ; I have long
wanted a shot at the —— rascal ! " Persisting in the avowal
that he was the writer, and in the request that his name should
be given up, they finally yielded, and Mr. Buel was instructed
accordingly. At a late hour the parties separated. Just as the
day dawned the following morning Mr. Van Buren was awakened by a violent application of his knocker, and looking out of
his bedroom window, a voice, which he recognized as Mr. Livingston's, inquired, " Is that you, Van Buren ? " On receiving
a response in the affirmative, Livingston said, " Let me in."
Mr. Van Buren threw on a wrapper, opened the door, and
showed his visitor into the cold parlor. Mr. Livingston said,
" What the devil were you talking about last night when I came
in ? " Mr. Van Buren replied, " We were talking about your
attack on Governor Clinton in the ' Argus.' " Mr. Livingston,
using a strong expletive, rejoined, " I won't stand that ! You
can't father your bantlings on me. I had been dining out, was
drunk, and you took advantage of me." This rendered it necessary to reassemble the council of the previous evening. The
real embarrassment was this : the article had been written by
James King, a young lawyer from Orange County, who had
just obtained the consent of William James, a warm personal
and political friend of Governor Clinton's, to marry his daughter, under a pledge to abstain from politics and devote himself
exclusively to his profession. And now, before the marriage
was celebrated, Mr. King had written a most abusive attack on
his intended father-in-law's intimate friend.

After much and anxious consideration, it was decided that
Mr. Knower should call on Mr. Isaiah Townsend, a mutual
friend of Mr. James and Governor Clinton, and endeavor, by
stating some extenuating circumstances, to appease Mr. James.
This, however, was no easy task, for Mr. James was of a stern
and implacable disposition. But Mr. Townsend knew his man,
drove him up to Waterford, drank two or three glasses of gin
and water, and succeeded in smoothing over the difficulty. Mr.
Townsend then proceeded to lay the whole matter frankly be-

fore Governor Clinton, whose sense of the humorous was touched by the awkward position in which Mr. Livingston's sudden belligerency had placed his friends, and by the extreme delicacy of Mr. King's domestic relations. He good-naturedly withdrew his note, and took no further notice of the subject.

In 1862, I asked the late John Van Buren if he had ever heard his father speak of this incident, which I commenced relating to him. He soon stopped me, saying that he had had many a hearty roar over the affair, and that he and his brother intended to make it the subject of a chapter in the forthcoming memoirs of his father. He expressed his surprise that I, a political opponent, should have learned the secrets of this memorable conclave. I had, however, received the accounts, more than thirty years before, from a son of Mr. James.

In 1818, the New York Typographical Society, taking advantage of my residence in Albany, applied to the legislature for a charter. I remember with what deference I then ventured into the presence of distinguished members of the legislature, and how sharply I was rebuked by two gentlemen, who were quite shocked at the idea of incorporating journeymen mechanics. The application, however, was successful, and the society was so much gratified with the result that I soon received the following manifestation of its sense of my services.

NEW YORK, May 9, 1818.

SIR, — The committee appointed by the New York Typographical Society for the purpose of procuring an act of incorporation having in their report to that institution mentioned the great assistance they had received from you during the pending of that application, the following resolution was unanimously adopted, namely, —

Resolved, That the thanks of this society be presented to Mr. Thurlow Weed, a member, for the zeal and activity with which he has exerted himself in assisting to procure the act of incorporation. And that the committee appointed for that purpose, with the addition of two other members, be authorized to carry this resolution into effect.

In conformity to the above resolution we beg leave to present you, for and on behalf of the New York Typographical Society, their sincere thanks for your voluntary exertions in their cause ; and to assure you that they shall always remember you with respect and esteem.

Permit us individually to reciprocate your congratulations, and to tender you *our* thanks.

We have the honor to be your much obliged brother members,

ADONIRAM CHANDLER,
WILLIAM GRATTAN,
JAMES R. REYNOLDS,
ICHABOD HOYT,
A. P. SEARING.

Committee on behalf of the New York Typographical Society.

For the Committee,
JAMES R. REYNOLDS.

The remainder of that year was passed pleasantly. I worked with zealous industry, anxious for the success of my employer and friend, Mr. Clark. I acquired the habit of setting up matter without manuscript. At first, I confined myself to brief news paragraphs; but finding that I could work as fast in this way as from the manuscript, I soon began to perpetrate brief editorials; and I continued this habit in Chenango, Onondaga, and Monroe counties, as long as I worked "at case." It gave simultaneous and agreeable mental and physical occupation.

Among my first elaborated articles was a defence of Pontius Pilate, who I then, as now, believed to have made earnest and fearless efforts to rescue our Saviour; and that instead of being held responsible for his crucifixion, he discharged an official duty with painful reluctance and under solemn protest. The evidence and argument in support of this view of Pilate's conduct was drawn from the scriptural history of the transaction.

(Nearly sixty years afterwards, while in attendance at the hippodrome in New York, where Moody and Sankey drew tens of thousands of hearers, I listened with much interest to an eloquent sermon from Mr. Moody, in which he vindicated the conduct and character of Pilate, taking the same line and quoting the same Scripture that I had relied on in my juvenile effort.)

Another literary effort of that day was a pamphlet of eight pica pages, which was put in type without being written.

1818. — On the 4th of July of this year ground was broken at Rome for the construction of the Erie Canal. The ceremonies attracted a large concourse of wondering, if not incredulous citizens. The idea of a direct navigable water communication between the Hudson River and Lake Erie was regarded by the masses, who had never heard of a canal, as preposterous. While the better informed were divided in opinion about its practicability, nearly all united in saying that the generation by which it was commenced would not witness its completion. I do not remember to have heard its most sanguine advocates fix upon less than twenty years, while the common remark was, " *We* shall never see it finished, but our children *may.*"

Among the distinguished people present were Governor De Witt Clinton (who removed the first shovelful of earth), Stephen Van Rensselaer, Joseph Ellicott, Samuel Young, and Myron Holley, the first commissioners, Benjamin Wright and James Geddes, the first engineers.

The first suggestion of a canal connecting the waters of Lake Erie with the Hudson River came from Joshua Forman, of Onondaga, who in 1808 introduced a resolution authorizing a survey, which passed the Assembly, but was either not acted upon or lost in the Senate. Mr. Forman, therefore, entitled himself to the credit of being, if not the original projector, at least the first mover in the enterprise which afterwards resulted so auspiciously to the State. Probably the first suggestion of such an improvement is contained in a letter written by General Washington on the occasion of his visit to Fort Schuyler, Ticonderoga, etc., in 1783. Nor was the enlightened vision of the Father of his Country limited to any one great improvement. He had even at that early day the wisdom to foresee and anticipate the connection by canals of the Delaware and Chesapeake Bays, the Ohio and the Potomac, the Lakes and the Ohio River, and Lakes Erie and Ontario with the Hudson. After speaking of the vast natural advantages for inland navigation, in a letter to the Chevalier de Chastellux, he remarked : —

" Prompted by these actual observations, I could not help taking a more extensive view of the vast inland navigation of these United States, from maps and the information of others ; and could not but be struck with the immense extent and importance of it, and with the goodness of that Providence which has dealt its favors to us with so profuse a hand. Would to God we may have wisdom enough to improve them ! " — (Writings of Washington, vol. viii., p. 489.)

Legislative action in favor of the Erie Canal was first taken in 1810, when Gouverneur Morris, Stephen Van Rensselaer, De

Witt Clinton, Simeon De Witt, William North, Thomas Eddy, and Peter B. Porter were appointed commissioners to explore a route for a canal to Lake Erie. In 1811, Robert R. Livingston and Robert Fulton were added to that commission.

One of the most remarkable features in this memorable enterprise was that the estimates for the completion of the Erie Canal from Albany to Buffalo, made by engineers wholly inexperienced, should have proven to be almost mathematically correct. The following is an extract from the commissioners' first report to the Legislature of 1812.

" The commissioners beg leave to advert to a question which comes more properly within their sphere. What will this canal cost ? An important question, but one to which they cannot give a satisfactory answer. They have taken pains to extend investigation, increased the numbers of surveyors, and accumulated the knowledge of facts. In proportion to the information acquired, is their conviction that the plan is practicable, and that the probable expense, compared with the advantage, is moderate, very moderate ; for they persist in believing that it may be accomplished for *five or six million of dollars.*"

The actual cost of the Erie Canal, when completed in 1824, was within *six million* of dollars. It is an equally remarkable, but less gratifying fact, that years afterwards, with all the advantages of experience, and all the improvements and labor-saving machinery, our engineers signally failed in their estimates to approach the actual cost of the construction of the Oswego, Chenango, and Genesee Valley Canal.

These works, together with the enlargement of the Erie Canal, cost the State three and four times more than the estimates of the engineers and commissioners, upon which the several legislatures were induced to authorize their construction.

The bill authorizing the construction of the Erie and Champlain Canal, passed in 1816, was vehemently opposed by the members from the southern and middle districts of the State. It was saved in the Senate by the vote of William Ross, a senator from Orange County, whose friendship for Mr. Clinton, it was said, led him to disregard the wishes and supposed interests of his constituents. Its most violent opponent was General Erastus Root, who stigmatized the enterprise as " Clinton's big ditch." Simultaneously with the commencement of the work a warfare against it and its author, Governor Clinton, was waged, Tammany Hall and the "New York National Advocate," edited by M. M. Noah, taking the lead. The Albany "Register" was the leading journal in favor of the canal. My own zealous support of Governor Clinton and his policy dates from 1817. As the battle waged warm during the session of 1818, when the New York city delegation attempted to repeal the law of 1816, and, as General Root expressed it, "to fill up the big ditch," Governor Clinton himself entered the arena in a series of able but bitter articles, some of which were signed "Hibernicus," and others "Heraclitus," appearing in the Albany "Register" and the New York "Columbian." As these articles strongly defended Governor Clinton's measures, and were laudatory of his Excellency, their authorship was denied by his friends. The "Register" and "Columbian" endeavored, without explicitly denying the charge, to create an impression that they were written by a distinguished friend of the governor. The dispute served to perplex the public, but although the manuscript (of which I preserved and now possess several pages) was carefully disguised, it is unmistakably the handwriting of Governor Clinton.

It will surprise the present generation to learn that after several hundred thousand dollars had been expended upon the middle section of the Erie Canal, and while operations were progressing rapidly, an effort, prompted by Tammany Hall, was made to arrest the work, and that the delegation in the assembly from the city of New York, with three exceptions, voted for it. One of that minority of three, which thus asserted its independence and intelligence, and the only survivor of the delegation, is the venerable Michael Ulshoeffer, an honorable and respected member of the New York bar. This contest was soon terminated by the overwhelming popular sentiment in favor of the canal. Brief as it was, however, it marred the fortunes of many men then occupying prominent positions, and brought to the surface others who had not hitherto found an opportunity of signalizing themselves. It was a trying question and a critical emergency for Van Buren, who was just then assuming the leadership of the Republican Party. Although understood, by his votes in 1816, to be opposed to the canal, yet he had the sagacity at an early day to discover the danger of opposing himself to a strong current of public sentiment. And here originated the term "non-committal," which for many years afterward was used to characterize his policy and action.

Governor Clinton staked his all upon the success of his canal policy, and yet, while that policy was signally vindicating itself, political power, from other causes, passed into the hands of his opponents, who took possession of and completed the work. In their day of triumph, and in the rash blindness of party animosity, they, in 1824, removed Mr. Clinton from the office of canal commissioner, — an office which he had held from the commencement of the undertaking. This occasioned great popular indignation and an entire political revolution in the State, Mr. Clinton being again called to the executive office by an overwhelming majority.

On the 26th of April, 1818, I was married at Cooperstown, Otsego County, to Miss Catherine Ostrander of that place. The engagement was entered into in 1814, when we were both, in the judgment of her relatives, too young to comprehend the responsibilities of such a step. In fact, they doubted, not without reason, the propriety of confiding the welfare and happiness of their daughter to a comparative stranger, with unsettled and roving habits. We communed together on the subject, and mutually agreed to hold no intercourse either by word or letter for two or three years, when, if her mind was unchanged, she was to write to me. I immediately left Cooperstown, and neither saw nor heard from her for more than three years, when a letter came informing me that time had made no change in her affections, to which I replied in similar terms.

We married without regard to any of the prudential considerations which restrained many then, and which restrain many more now, from contracting a similar tie. I had, when the ceremony was over, just money enough to take my young wife to Albany, where, with good health, strong hands, and hopeful hearts, we both went earnestly to work to earn a living. The value of our household goods did not exceed two hundred dollars. To this fortunate marriage I am indebted for as much happiness as usually falls to the lot of man, and very largely for whatever of personal success and pecuniary prosperity I have since enjoyed. She *more* than divided our labors, cares, and responsibilities. But for her industry, frugality, and good management, I must have been shipwrecked during the first fifteen years of trial. When from our changed circumstances and condition it was no longer necessary for her to pursue her laborious habits, she still insisted on performing many duties ordinarily transferred to servants. Economy, order, and a well-regulated system in household affairs were virtues which I did not possess, and their presence in her saved us from disaster.

After a severe illness of several months, just as the sun was rising one morning, and I sat watching by her bedside, she reminded me that it was the fortieth anniversary of our marriage, and taking from her finger the ring which I had placed on it forty years before, she put it on mine, saying, " I shall not live through the day." We had already lost our only son seven years previously, and three daughters remained to me after my wife had followed him.

CHAPTER VIII.

1818–1820.

In the autumn of 1818 an opportunity of establishing myself in business occurred. Mr. John F. Hubbard, of Norwich, Chenango County, having differed seriously with several of his leading political friends, offered his printing establishment for sale.

It was purchased by Mr. James Birdsall, David G. Bright, Obadiah German, and Nathan Chamberlain, who sold the material to me on credit for about seven hundred dollars. With this material I established a new paper entitled the "Agriculturist."

1818. — The County of Chenango, during the war with England, was pretty equally divided between Republicans and Federalists. But as the Federal Party collapsed in 1815, the Republicans had for several years almost undisputed possession of the county. As yet, the Tompkins and Clinton split had not reached Chenango. But the appearance of my paper, warmly espousing the Erie and Champlain Canal project, was the signal for a "Bucktail" organization. And as Chenango was to be taxed to construct canals which it was alleged would injure rather than benefit its farmers, the movement resulted in the formation of a strong party, led by several young lawyers, who were impatient of the influence that their seniors had so long exerted. Mr. Hubbard, whose printing establishment I had purchased, was induced to sell partly on account of personal misunderstandings with leading political friends. He had intended, I believe, to abide by his agreement with me to leave the county ; but the leaders of the new party applied to him to reëstablish his paper and become their organ. To this he consented ; and the consequence was that, while I had purchased his old press and type, Mr. Hubbard's journal soon reappeared with new material, with the further disadvantage on my part of being a stranger in the county. Mr. Hubbard had previously obtained but a bare support for his paper, and now two journals were competing for patronage which had been found scarcely sufficient for one. A very bitter warfare, personal and political, ensued. The personal wrong to me was so manifest as to raise me up warm friends, both in the village and throughout the county. The earnest and unwavering friendship, wise counsel, and important assistance I received from Mr. James Birdsall have been remembered with gratitude throughout my whole life. I formed many other friendships there which were equally enduring. Hundreds of the subscribers to my " Agriculturist " at Norwich followed me with their sympathies and their subscriptions to Onondaga, to Rochester, and to Albany.

The controversy with Mr. Hubbard and two or three of the men who induced him to violate his agreement engendered enmities which, in reference to two individuals, were quite as enduring, though between Mr. Hubbard and myself, while members of the legislature of 1830, friendly relations were reëstablished. He is still living at Norwich. His son, a highly intelligent and upright man, succeeded him as editor of the " Journal " and as a member of the last and the present Senate.

Among my political and personal friends were several who had occupied prominent public positions. James Birdsall had been a member of the Fourteenth Congress ; Obadiah German had been a United States Senator; Uri Tracy had been a Senator in Congress from the State of Connecticut, and a Representative from Chenango in the Ninth Congress.

General German was a farmer, with a common-school education. He was shrewd, active, and energetic. He was elected to the Assembly in 1818, and aspired to the speakership. I took an active part in his favor. He was chosen Speaker ; and although he had served as a member of the legislatures of 1798, 1801, 1804, 1807, and 1808, he was greatly embarrassed in taking the chair, and for several days discharged its duties in a confused and bungling manner.

In 1819 the Bucktails carried Chenango. In that year, Colonel William Munroe, a soldier of the Revolution, was a candidate for sheriff. All county officers were then appointed by the Governor and council. Colonel Munroe relied much for his success upon my acquaintance with Governor Clinton. Early in January, with good sleighing, the colonel took me into his cutter one morning before daybreak, and in this primitive mode of conveyance we started for Albany. In the box under the seat of the cutter was an ample store of baked beans and pork, bread, butter, and cheese, on which we dined sumptuously for three consecutive days. Our mission resulted in Colonel Munroe's appointment. On taking leave of Governor Clinton, he inquired how I was getting along with my paper. I replied that, with industry and economy, I hoped to keep it alive. He then handed me a sealed letter, remarking that I might find it of some service. In that letter, when I reached the hotel, I found an appointment as commissioner to take the acknowledgment of deeds, etc., etc., which proved of essential service during my residence in Chenango; for the fees, amounting to two and sometimes three dollars a week, helped to support my small family. This was the first and last appointment from a Governor or President that I ever accepted.

And here I cannot but pause a moment to contrast my expenses then and now : rent for a small house and garden, one hundred dollars a year; butter, ten cents a pound; beefsteak, eight cents a pound; eggs, six cents a dozen, with other articles produced on farms in proportion,—the whole amounting, at the close of the first year, to about five hundred dollars. Now, in 1869, we pay fifty-five cents a pound for butter, fifty-three cents a dozen for eggs, thirty cents a pound for beefsteak, and for almost everything else in proportion.

Agricultural societies were just being formed in our State, under the recommendation of Governor Clinton, in his message to the legislature in 1817. The question of scientific farming was introduced into the legislature, and elicited warm discussion. The proposition for legislative encouragement to agricultural societies was vehemently opposed by the farmers. A speech from Samuel Miles Hopkins, Esq., a distinguished lawyer, then a member of the Assembly from Ontario County, in support of the proposition, was denounced by some and ridiculed by other members, who, as farmers, scouted the idea that lawyers, doctors, or merchants could know anything about farming, or were capable of teaching others what they did not know themselves. Mr. Nye, of Madison County (father of the Honorable James W. Nye, now a Senator in Congress), closed a short but forcible speech by saying that as "a practical farmer he had witnessed a great many experiments, and heard of a great many more, intended as improvements and designed to benefit farmers, but that he never had seen or heard of a farmer who succeeded in raising a good crop of corn *with a straight back!*" But in spite of prejudices and ridicule agricultural societies and schools were established, and agricultural books were published, greatly to the improvement of agriculture and the advantage of farmers. The idea came from Berkshire, Mass., where a society was formed immediately after the war, whose annual cattle shows and fairs were occasions of great interest. Elkanah Watson, who removed from Berkshire to this State, came, apparently, to inaugurate agricultural societies. At any rate, he was the prominent feature in the earliest organizations. He claimed also to have projected the Erie and Champlain canals. He resided in Clinton County, but passed most of his time in Albany, where he is remembered by the oldest inhabitants for the tureens of oysters and the pyramids of ice cream which, as the agricultural philanthropist approached them, would disappear. General Aaron Ward, a captain in the army in the war of 1812, and for many years a member of Congress from Westchester County, married a daughter of Elkanah Watson.

Next to Mr. Birdsall, I found a warm, whole-hearted friend in David G. Bright, then clerk of the county. Mr. Bright was a German from Pennsylvania, having resided, before he came to Chenango, at Plattsburg, where, during the war, he was appointed by President Madison collector of the internal revenue. I passed many leisure hours pleasantly with Mr. Bright, who had seen a good deal of life, and was an intelligent, close observer of men and things. He resigned his office of clerk, and removed to the State of Indiana, where two of his sons became influential and prominent Democratic politicians; one of them, Jesse D. Bright, long a Senator in Congress, became during the Rebellion an active and malignant "copperhead," be-

traying the government he had sworn to support, and false to
the patriotic precepts and example of a father who was incapable of uttering or breathing a disloyal sentiment.

I frequently met the sons of my old friend, long years afterward, in New York and in Washington. They were highly
intelligent and upright men. With the Senator, until his dis-
loyalty became as unequivocal, if not as outspoken, as that of
Vallandigham, I was intimate, but during and since the Rebellion we pass each other as strangers. After an interval of nearly
thirty years I received the following letter from my old Chenango friend : —

JEFFERSONVILLE, INDIANA, *July* 26, 1848.

DEAR OLD FRIEND, — How have you been getting along since I
last saw you ? Well, I do hope. How often I think of the gone-by
days when we were living as neighbors and friends in old Chenango !
For the last five years I have been Receiver and Depositary of public
moneys at the Land Office, but I expect to resign both appointments
erelong.

My children, three sons and three daughters, all in good circumstances, desire that I should retire to private life, and spend my days
with them. I am now over seventy-three years of age ; have been a
widower for the last twelve years, and of course shall so die.

I really should be happy to hear from you. I want also to become a
subscriber to your paper. That the richest of Heaven's blessings attend you through this life, and in the world to come eternal happiness,
is the heartfelt wish of your old friend,   D. G. BRIGHT.

There were, during my residence in Chenango, few occurrences of state or national importance. Nor do I remember
occasions of any peculiar local interest. My life there was
quiet, and, with more encouragement in my business, would
have been pleasant. The Chenango County bar was then considered a strong one, but none of its members succeeded in
making enduring reputations, although several were talented
and ambitious. John C. Clark, then a young lawyer of much
promise, subsequently became a highly respected and influential
member of Congress. He was elected in 1827 as a Democrat.
In 1837 he was elected as a Whig, and was reëlected in 1839
and in 1841. During this period he was my warm friend. He
was honest, zealous, and patriotic. He coöperated with me in
several important matters, of which I shall have occasion to
speak hereafter.

James Clapp, who stood at the head of the bar, was an eloquent advocate and accomplished gentleman. Simon G. Throop, a young lawyer of much social worth, with brilliant oratorical powers, was a popular member of the legislature of 1818, is now (in 1874), though more than eighty years old, a judge in one of the northern counties of Pennsylvania.

John Birdsall, a nephew of the friend I have already spoken of, was then a student at law. When admitted to practice, he established himself at Lockport, but subsequently removed to Chautauqua County, from whence he was elected to the Assembly and the Senate of this State. In 1826 he was appointed judge of the eighth judicial district. He resigned in 1829, and removed to Texas in 1836, where he soon afterward died. He was a capable, honest, estimable man. He also was an intimate friend, of whom I shall have occasion to speak in connection with two questions of public interest.

E. P. Pellet, a son of a farmer residing a mile out of the village, then about twelve years old, passed his time between school hours in my office, sometimes reading exchange newspapers and sometimes setting type. His desire to become a printer was so strong that his father, though unwilling to lose his services on the farm, yielded to his wishes, and, after learning his trade, he became my successor as editor of a Clintonian paper at Norwich, — a paper which he conducted for many years with equal ability and fidelity. A son who bears his name is now publishing a newspaper at Baranquilla, in South America.

There was, among the boys who were in the habit of visiting the printing office in Norwich, one then not more than nine or ten years old, of uncommon intellectual promise. He was advanced far beyond his years in reading, writing, arithmetic, etc. He had great fondness for printing, and for several consecutive weeks printed with his pen a newspaper almost equal in size and typography to the seven by nine sheets of that day. He was not only a bright but a good boy, and I felt assured that he would, if his life was spared, make his mark in some useful vocation. He finally turned his attention to the cause of education, and I had the satisfaction, more than thirty years afterward, of contributing to his election as State Superintendent of Public Instruction, an office for the duties of which he was, intellectually, morally, and socially, eminently qualified. He is now Superintendent of Public Instruction in the city of New York. It is almost superfluous to add that the precocious boy, whom I remember fifty years ago, is Samuel S. Randall.

1817–1820. — In 1817, by a favorable combination of circumstances, DeWitt Clinton emerged from a political cloud which had darkened his fortunes since 1812, and was elected governor. Mr. Clinton, strong by the force of intellect and will, had a large following of party leaders, but was not popular with the people. Lacking the virtue of patience, he had committed the great error of running as an irregular candidate for President against Mr. Madison. That error was not easily condoned, for the Republicans were not inclined to forgive a man who allowed himself to be used by those who were endeavoring to embarrass and weaken the government during our war with England. Mr. Clinton's defeat was a bitter mortification. He retired from the city to a farm at Newtown, on Long Island, where he lived not only in strict seclusion, but indulging, as was alleged, too freely in strong drink. In the winter of 1817, Pierre C. Van Wyck, Sylvanus Miller, and John W. Wyman, who were among his warmest friends, went to Newtown, and succeeded in arousing Mr. Clinton from an inactivity and weakness unworthy of himself and disastrous to his party. Mr. Clinton soon reappeared in political and social circles, and again became a power in the State. He ran for governor virtually unopposed, although 1479 votes were cast for General Peter B. Porter. The whole vote of the State in 1817 for governor was considerably less than half the number of votes for governor in 1868 in the city of New York. Mr. Clinton succeeded Governor Tompkins, who had been elected Vice-President in 1816.

In 1818, the comptroller, Archibald McIntyre, in preparing his annual report to the legislature, found, in closing up the accounts of Governor Tompkins with the State, a large deficiency. This was a startling revelation. Governor Tompkins had been and was a great favorite with the Republican party. The question elicited angry discussion in the legislature, in the press, and at public meetings. The comptroller was sustained by the friends of Governor Clinton, and denounced by those of Governor Tompkins. Previously, however, Mr. McIntyre had

been long a capable and faithful public servant, and next to
Governor Tompkins was the most popular man in the State.
Many of the Republican friends of Governor Clinton believed
and maintained that Governor Tompkins had honestly expended
all the money he ever drew from the treasury, but that in the
pressure of business during the war he had failed to protect
himself with proper vouchers. With many Republicans, who
only desired to be right, there was real embarrassment. We
knew that Mr. McIntyre was an honest man, and ought not to
be sacrificed for doing his duty, — a painful duty, for he had
been more especially the friend of Governor Tompkins than
of Mr. Clinton. It was amusing also to see aspiring politicians, who were only anxious to know which would win, in a
tight place. I remember a clever dodge on the part of Nathaniel Allen, of Ontario, a candidate for reëlection to Congress,
who was appealed to at Washington both by the friends of Governor Clinton and those of Governor Tompkins. He saw the
danger of espousing the cause of either candidate, and con-
trived, by one pretext and another, to keep back his answer
until it would be too late to have an effect upon the election.

The answer, when it came, was in substance that he had seriously, impartially, and honestly looked over the whole ground;
that there was much due to Governor Clinton for his bold advocacy of the Erie Canal, an improvement of such vital importance to Western New York. On the other hand, also, much
was due to Governor Tompkins for his devotion and patriotism
during the war, and for his lifelong fidelity to the Republican
party. But while he respected and honored both, and regretted the necessity which constrained him to decide in favor of
one and against the other, he recognized the right of the electors to inquire, and of his duty to answer frankly, as he should.
" I have," he said, " made up my mind deliberately to vote for
the old governor, and I hope my friends will do the same."
Before the electors had time to ascertain which of the two political Dromios was " the old governor," the election was over,
and Mr. Allen re-chosen for Congress.

Controlled by circumstances, and ardently in favor of a system of improvement, which, it was feared, would go down with
Governor Clinton, I deemed it my duty to sustain the administration, though I never joined in or sympathized with those who

abused Governor Tompkins. The canvass was exciting and acrimonious. It was "a free fight" between Republicans, the
Federalists having no candidate. Many leading Federalists,
such as Charles King, John Sudam, Morris S. Miller, etc., etc.,
went against Governor Clinton, while most of the rank and file
Federalists either remained from the polls or voted for Clinton.
Vice-President Tompkins, though then residing on Staten Isl-
and, made a visit to Albany in February, preceding the April
election. His reception was alike imposing and enthusiastic.
Streets were crowded with people waiting his arrival. South
Market Street, now Broadway, was thronged with demonstra-
tive Republicans on their way to the ferry. In that street, Mis-
tress McHarg, who kept a thread-and-needle store, stood leaning with her elbows on the half door, looking at the crowd, when
Captain Barnum Whipple appeared, and in a jubilant voice exclaimed, "This is a proud day for Albany, Mrs. McHarg!"
"Aye, aye, my mon," the old lady replied; "but what is it all
aboot?" "Why," he said, "Governor Tompkins is coming,
and he is to have a grand reception." "Has n't he ben comin'
and going these mony years, without ony grand reception?"
"Oh, yes," replied Captain Whipple; "but now, you know, he
has stolen the hearts of the people!" "And their siller, too,"
responded the old lady, offering the captain her snuff-box, which
was declined with an imprecation.

1820. — Governor Clinton received 47,447 votes, while 45,990
were cast for Governor Tompkins.

CHAPTER IX.

1821.

1821. — SOME fourteen months' experience confirmed my early fears that two newspapers could not be supported in Norwich. It became also more and more evident that the anti-canal feeling was extending, and that the country would soon settle down with a large Bucktail or anti-Clintonian majority. I concluded late in November, 1820, to dispose of my establishment, and return to Albany as a journeyman. Though now with a wife and one child, I had no fears of my ability to support them. Most happily for me, that wife, from the day of our marriage, always contributed more than her share of the labor, care, and watchfulness incumbent upon heads of families.

I reached Albany on the second day of January, 1821, where, among the journeymen printers, I had warm friends. Daniel McGlasshon, foreman of the " Argus " office, immediately offered me a situation on the state printing. This was most gratifying and most opportune, for by working hard I could earn from fifteen to eighteen dollars a week. This, fifty years ago, was more than forty dollars a week would be now. But, unhappily for me, my good fortune was short-lived. The state printers were Messrs. Leake & Cautine. Mr. Leake was informed that a violent Clintonian, who, as publisher of a paper in Chenango, had abused Governor Tompkins, Mr. Van Buren, etc., etc., was an unsafe person to have about the office, and was not entitled to its patronage ; whereupon Mr. Leake directed McGlasshon to discharge me. I thought first of appealing to Mr. Cautine, whom I remembered during my boyhood as a resident of Catskill, but did not do so. I obtained, however, two days afterward a situation in the office of Messrs. Packard & Van Benthuysen, father of my much-valued friend Charles Van Benthuysen, now one of the oldest and best printers in the State, where all went smoothly something over a month ; when, in obedience to a resolution of the Typographical Society, the journeymen " struck," not for higher wages, but because a "rat" had been employed in our office; and now, for the first time in my life, I became seriously anxious about employment, for I was neither disposed nor could I afford to be idle. In the latter days of March my old friend Southwick, restive and impatient under his loss of power and position in the Republican party, determined to appeal directly to the people against the tyranny of leaders. He was insanely anxious to be governor, and all the more insane because of its impossibility, as it seems to me now that I look at things from a better stand-point. He had been editing with great industry and ability the " Ploughboy " and the " Christian Visitant," and beguiled himself with a confident belief that farmers and Christians, irrespective of party, would sustain him. He suggested a political visitation through the western and southwestern counties of the State, ostensibly to obtain subscribers to the " Ploughboy " and " Visitant " (to pay expenses), but really to prepare the way for his election as governor. Mr. Southwick had by his previous kindness and confidence won my friendship and gratitude. Though I did not see the way quite clear, I believed, or tried to believe, that he understood what he was doing ; though years afterwards I learned that in politics, as in almost everything else, Mr. Southwick was blinded by his enthusiasm and credulity. He provided me with a horse and wagon, and gave me a list of the names of gentlemen throughout the State on whom I was to call. I found in April "shocking bad roads," both in a material and in a political sense ; but I wended my way through Schenectady, Schoharie, Otsego, Chenango, Madison, and Onondaga counties, with reasonable encouragement so far as subscribers were concerned.

In reference to the question of governor, however, I soon discovered that my friend's hopes and chances were not worth even the services of the horse that was dragging me through the mud. At Manlius, in Onondaga County, I learned that the press and type of the Manlius " Times," a Federal paper, published by Mr. Kellogg while I was an apprentice in Onondaga Hollow, eight years earlier, were standing still in that village, Mr. Kellogg having died and his successors failed. Manlius, though years before an enterprising and flourishing village, had begun to decline, half a dozen other villages having started up around it to divide the business. The press and type were in the hands of Mr. Nicholas P. Randall, a lawyer, who had a lien upon them, and who offered them to me upon terms to be settled in accordance with the encouragement I might meet with. The business men of the village whom I consulted, while anxious to have a paper, spoke doubtfully of the prospects. With small encouragement in that quarter, I nevertheless determined to make a trial, and on the 27th day of June, 1821, the first number of the Onondaga " Republican " appeared. It was for that day a well-printed and tidy-looking sheet. I look now through its columns of selected matter with considerable interest. Under its obituary head is a notice of the death in Campbell County, Va., of Charles Lane, aged one hundred and twenty-one years, leaving a widow aged one hundred and ten years ; also in New York, of the death of Mrs. Alsop, of the Park Theatre, and a daughter of the celebrated English actress, Mrs. Jordan.

The political muddle in our State at that time may be gathered by reading an extract from my introductory editorial : —

With regard to state politics, we confess frankly that we are in a fog ! But for the fear of incurring the reproach of "trimming," a character above all others which we abhor, the subject would be passed over in silence. We are disgusted with the wayward and unprofitable contest that has existed through the last three years, — a contest which has not only sullied the character of our State, but which has vitiated the political morals of its citizens. It is time that we abandoned this warfare against reason and common sense, this crusade against an individual, and return to pursuits more salutary in their influence, more worthy of an intelligent people. In the main, then, we are friendly to the present administration of the state government, — an administration which has been prolific of great and permanent public benefit, an administration which the impartial historian will do justice to, an administration which will stand deservedly high in the estimation of posterity. When the bitter animosities which now unhappily distract our people shall have yielded to the " soft and soothing hand of Time," but few will be found unwilling to acknowledge that the administration of DeWitt Clinton was a bright era in the history of New York. That Mr. Clinton has committed errors — errors, too, which have injured himself and distracted the public mind — we are constrained to admit, but at the same time we insist that he has advanced the great and paramount interests of the State. We yield no blind attachment to Mr. Clinton, but support him because we conceive it to be an act of justice and a duty we owe to the State.

On the Saturday following the issue of the first number of my paper my family reached Manlius, finding me with an exhausted treasury, the last shilling having been that day expended. How to bridge over the coming Sunday was a question of some solicitude. This delicate matter was effected, however, by pledging with the grocer an English bank token, a silver coin nearly equivalent in value to an American half dollar. I had received this piece of money directly after the war, when coin was as scarce as it is now in 1870. Thus provisioned for Sunday, we passed that day in contentment, not doubting that we should in the future, as in the past, be provided for. On Monday morning, to my infinite relief, a man appeared who asked if I could do a job of printing for him, to which I responded affirmatively. He wanted to advertise a wool-carding machine in the paper, and to have fifty copies of the same advertisement in hand-bill form. Learning that I could deliver him the hand-bills in the course of three or four hours, he concluded to wait for them. When they were delivered, and I received a dollar and twenty-five cents in payment, I experienced a sense of relief which words would but feebly describe. I accepted and regarded it as providential. The first thing done was to redeem the bank token, which has remained ever since in the family as a cherished souvenir.

The convention for amending our state constitution convened in September of this year. The public mind was tranquil, and the time for renewing and amending the framework of a government which rose out of the chaos occasioned by the Revolution was well chosen. The people sent many of their ablest and best men as delegates to the convention. Albany County, with enlightened unanimity, elected James Kent, Ambrose Spencer, Abraham Van Vechten, and Stephen Van

Rensselaer. From Columbia County, Elisha Williams and William W. Van Ness were chosen. From Dutchess we had James Tallmadge and Peter R. Livingston. From New York came Henry Wheaton and Nathan Sanford. From Oneida, James Platt and Ezekiel Bacon. From Onondaga, Victory Birdseye. From Orange, John Duer. From Queens, Rufus King. From Richmond, Daniel D. Tompkins. From Saratoga, Samuel Young and John Cramer. From Montgomery, Alexander Sheldon. From Cortland, Samuel Nelson (present Associate Justice of the Supreme Court of the United States). From Delaware, Erastus Root. From Westchester, Peter A. Jay. Martin Van Buren, who then resided in Albany, was elected a delegate from Otsego County. Governor Tompkins was made President of the Convention. Soon after its organization it developed, under the leadership of Mr. Van Buren, strong radical tendencies. This spirit induced equally strong conservative proclivities under the lead of Chancellor Kent, Chief Justice Spencer, Elisha Williams, etc., etc. The radicals, however, were in a decided majority; though many levelling propositions, urged by extreme radicals, were defeated by the intellectual power of the conservative side. The new constitution, when framed, was obnoxious to the minority; twenty-four of whom, including the four delegates from Albany and Columbia counties, four from Montgomery, Judge Platt, of Oneida, and Peter A. Jay, of Westchester, refused to sign it. This constitution abolished the councils of appointment and of revision; abolished also the power of the governor to prorogue the legislature; also abolished the property qualification to vote for governor and senators; a large number of offices were made elective, and the elective franchise extended. It was submitted to the people in February, 1822, and adopted by a vote of 74,732 for it, with 41,402 against it. In looking over the list of delegates I find but two survivors, namely, John Cramer and Samuel Nelson. I took strong ground against the adoption of that constitution, for, while I approved of many of its provisions, I dreaded the effect of extending and cheapening suffrage. While it was evident that the constitution would be adopted, I continued my opposition to the bitter end. I had great veneration for the opinions of Mr. Jefferson, and believing with him that large cities are " ulcers on the body politic,"

I feared then, as I have ever since feared, that universal suffrage would occasion universal political demoralization, and ultimately overthrow our government. With such convictions, I
was willing to incur all the responsibility of resisting a popular
delusion.

The middle section of the Erie Canal had already been completed, and was actively in use between Utica and Montezuma.
Villages were springing up along its line, while those that had
previously arisen along the line of the turnpike, distant from
three to six miles south of the canal, were losing both their business and their business men. The newspapers, published at
Onondaga Hollow and West Hill, had both been removed to
Syracuse. With the assistance of a young man who had worked
something over a year in the office with one of my predecessors,
I got off my paper, doing most of the composition and press-
work myself. I also executed what job printing was offered.
This gave me pretty constant employment. My paper obtained
a large circulation, but received only a limited advertising patronage. My principal reliance in this respect was upon the
sheriff's office. The sheriff, H. L. Granger, was a Clintonian,
who resided at Manlius. This gave me a patronage which,
could it have been retained, would have insured the success of
my enterprise ; but the new constitution, just adopted, gave the
election of sheriffs to the people. In the election of 1822, the
struggle for sheriff, between James Webb, the Clintonian, and
Luther Marsh, the Democratic candidate, was one of great excitement and bitterness. Until the then recent division of parties, they had both been Republicans, had always been friends,
and were brothers-in-law. The Bucktail party, however, was
successful. Mr. Marsh's election took from me my most reliable means of support.

Onondaga County, even at that early day, had produced men
of considerable eminence. James Geddes, one of the three
principal engineers who constructed the Erie Canal, was a man
of great public worth and high personal character. Joshua
Forman, the founder of the city of Syracuse, and the father-in-
law of my friend General E. W. Leavenworth, was a man of
enterprise and genius. He also originated the safety-fund
banking law system. The Earles, an old and numerous Democratic family, exerted a steady and controlling political influence in that county for twenty-five years.

The Munroe family, intelligent, energetic, and wealthy farmers, exerted a still more potent and pervading financial influence throughout the county for more than forty years. They were Clintonians in 1817, Adams men in 1824, and Whigs in 1840. From the time of the patriarch Squire Munroe, through the generations succeeding down to Allen Munroe, a present representative of the family, who is every way worthy of his inheritance, the Munroes have been my political and personal friends.

Time passed pleasantly with me at Manlius. My family, with simple habits and few or no artificial wants, had all they required. We enjoyed good health, worked hard, lived frugally, and were exempt from cares and anxieties. Manlius being remote from the centre of the county and the court house, I was less than usual with public men, but I formed agreeable and enduring friendships among the villagers. There was one young gentleman, then a student at law, whose tastes and habits were peculiarly congenial. We had read Shakespeare, Burns, Scott, Johnson, Campbell, Junius, etc., etc., with kindred enthusiasm. We had read the same plays and talked about the same actors with mutual admiration, and, with the same ardent anticipation of enjoyment, we lived on the hope that at some distant day in the shadowy future we might enjoy the happiness of visiting England, to see with our own eyes what had so charmed our other senses. We then promised ourselves, and each other, that should Fortune ever favor us, the first use we should make of her smiles would be to visit Europe. In due time the efforts of both were rewarded; but while I availed myself of the first opportunity to gratify an early and earnest purpose, my friend lost his desire to see the Old World. Indeed, so indifferent had he become to what in early life had been the most cherished wish of his heart, that in 1845, when he was offered the appointment of minister to Russia, and when it was in all respects an appointment " fit to be made " and equally fit to be accepted, it was declined. That young friend was Addison Gardiner, subsequently judge of the eighth judicial circuit and of the court of appeals, lieutenant governor, and now a venerable citizen of Rochester. Of the useful and honorable career of this gentleman I shall have future occasion to speak. In 1872, when I had the pleasure of visiting my old friend at his residence in Rochester, while conversing upon bygone events, he informed

me that his chief reason for declining the mission to Russia was
his inability to speak the court language.

A village incident, although relating to private life, partakes
so much of the romantic and presents the parties connected with
it in a light so amiable, that I feel constrained to narrate it.
Two young merchants' clerks found so much of congeniality,
and possessed so many tastes, habits, and virtues in common,
that their acquaintance and intercourse ripened into a close
friendship. They were bright and cheerful, living lives of singular purity. Another villager had an only daughter, a young
lady of attractive person, agreeable manners, and estimable
character. These young men, after enjoying for three or four
years the acquaintance and society of the young lady, found
themselves mutually and devotedly in love with her. The embarrassment, one well calculated to try too severely ordinary
friendships, was frankly discussed between them, resulting in
an agreement to submit the decision of the question to the
young lady, whose regard for both was so sincere, and so evenly
balanced, that after several weeks of anxious and painful consideration she found herself unable to distress either by a choice.
If she had been poetical she might, as perhaps she did, exclaim : —

> " How happy could I be with either
> Were t' other dear charmer away ! "

Something, however, had to be done. The young men put
their heads again together. Precisely how the problem was
solved I either did not learn or have forgotten. But Charles
suddenly left the village with a letter from his employer to a
mercantile house in New York. In due time Richard married
the young lady and became a merchant in the western part of
the State. Charles soon rose to a partnership in the New York
house that first employed him as a clerk, and became a prosperous merchant. He, too, in the course of human events married an accomplished young lady of that city, with whom he
lived happily for several years, and until " consumption marked
her for its own." Subsequently Richard lost his wife by death.
When years afterwards he, from unavoidable circumstances,
encountered pecuniary disaster, Charles brought him to New
York, and succeeded after a while in reëstablishing him in business. Both preserved the highest character as merchants and

as citizens. Twenty years after the death of his wife Charles married the daughter of Richard, in whom he found reproduced the virtues and graces of her mother, his early love. I had the pleasure of a call at Albany from this happy pair, when on their bridal excursion. My friend Charles — for we have been close friends more than half a century — is now enjoying as much happiness as falls to the lot of man, with a devoted wife and affectionate children, in ease and affluence.

The anniversaries of American independence, up to and for several years after 1820, were celebrated with an enthusiasm which I then fondly believed would be as enduring as republican institutions. The day was then universally observed. Every city, village, and hamlet had its celebration, and however differing in outward show, one heart and one spirit animated the people of the whole Union. But time or other causes have, I am sorry to say, weakened the popular memory of the event which gave birth to a Republic. The Fourth of July celebrations are by no means as universal. Nor is the sense of gratitude to the fathers and founders of our government as deep and pervading as in other, and I cannot but think, better times. The feeling which inspired the following editorial, written in 1821, found response in the hearts of my readers, and it may be regarded as in accord with the general sentiment of that day : —

FOURTH OF JULY.

> "Hail, sacred day ! hail, bright, auspicious morn !
> Welcome, thrice welcome is thy glad return."

The return of that memorable day which our fathers consecrated to American liberty is connected with recollections which warm and animate the best feelings of patriotism and philanthropy. The fourth day of July, 1776, was the birthday of liberty to the United States, and its anniversary should be hailed with reverberating pæans of joy and acclamation. That American whose bosom does not glow and swell with emotions of reverence for the patriots of '76, and of gratitude to Heaven for the precious gift of liberty, whose heart is not buoyant and whose affections are not awakened on the anniversary day of our independence, is less an object of contempt than of pity. This day forty-five years ago the " Cherub-face Goddess of Liberty " erected her temple in America, and our fathers knelt at her shrine with a reverence and devotion which is scarcely surpassed by the self-immolating fanatics of Eastern idolatry. The Declaration of Independence, in a twinkling, dispelled the dark and portentous cloud which was then lowering over our country. It gave confidence to the mind, firmness to the heart, muscle to the arm, and fire to the soul of those generous spirits who were panting and burning for freedom. It kindled and renovated that flame of patriotism in the bosom of our ancestors which tyranny and oppression had long smothered, but which the fiat of Heaven alone can extinguish. It raised up chieftains whose prudence and wisdom equalled those of Fabius or Miltiades, who in moderation and self-devotedness were not inferior to Epaminondas or Regulus, and whose valor would give lustre to the laurels won by Wallace or Themistocles. It marshalled soldiers whose patriotism is without a parallel, and whose death-spurning courage ranks them with the gallant spirits whose blood flooded the fields of Bannockburn and Thermopylæ. It is a stupendous altar, consecrated to liberty by a Republican Congress, which ages can neither shake nor prostrate. It has stamped a veneration and sanctity upon the day which time will fail to obliterate. A sacred pledge was on that auspicious day sent towering to the heavens that America should be a free and independent nation. That pledge was nobly and faithfully redeemed by our forefathers. It is now our duty to maintain the rights and liberties thus secured to us, and hand them down unimpaired and unsullied to posterity.

CHAPTER X.

1822.

GOING TO ROCHESTER. — EVERARD PECK. — THE ROCHESTER "TELE-GRAPH." — DERICK SIBLEY. — COLONEL NATHANIEL ROCHESTER. — VINCENT MATHEWS. — THOMAS KEMPSHALL. — DR. BACKUS. — SAM-UEL WORKS. — THE PIONEER STAGE LINE. — ROBERT HUNTER. — THE SELDENS. — FREDERICK WHITTLESEY. — S. G. ANDREWS.

1822. — It became quite evident some months before I discontinued my paper at Manlius that I should be compelled to look elsewhere for employment and support. As the period for his admission to the bar approached, I had frequent conversations with my friend Gardiner, from whom I was unwilling to separate, about trying our futures in the Far West. Early in November, 1822, he left, with a promise to keep me advised of his whereabouts. Expecting to hear from him in Detroit, or some other far western town, a few days brought me information that he had very unexpectedly determined to try his fortune at Rochester, then the western limit of Erie Canal navigation. About the middle of November I closed my business concerns at Manlius, and departed with my family in a canal-boat for Rochester, where I was wholly unknown, and with but faint hopes of obtaining employment.

Rochester was then a new, straggling village, containing but a few hundred inhabitants. All, however, were useful, active, enterprising, and hopeful. It was a go-ahead place, and no one could for a moment doubt, from its advantages, that it was to become a large inland city. My friend Gardiner, who had opened a law office, and already rejoiced in two or three clients, welcomed me cordially. There were two printing-offices in the village. Derick Sibley printed and published the "Republican," a Bucktail paper. Everard Peck was the printer and publisher of the "Telegraph," a Clintonian paper. To the latter I applied for a situation as a journeyman. Mr. Peck replied, that though a bookseller, and prepared to print books as well as his newspaper, he had nothing then in press, and no work, consequently, for a journeyman. On learning who I was, and that I had brought my family to Rochester with the hope (a most unreasonable one, doubtless) of obtaining employment, he manifested a kind interest in my favor, expressing much regret that he was compelled to disappoint me. After some further conversation, in which his desire to serve me was very manifest, he said he would endeavor to find some work on which I could be employed for a few days. And within an hour afterwards, with coat off and sleeves rolled up, I found myself working at a press, with a comforting belief that I had found a valuable friend, and that my few days' employment would prove to be a permanent situation. And this belief, though based upon so slight a foundation, was fully realized. Mr. Peck became a warm, earnest, confiding friend, and remained such until nearly thirty years afterwards, when a good man and a true Christian was called to his final account.

That first interview with Mr. Peck was so well described twenty years afterwards in the New Haven "Palladium," by its editor, Mr. Babcock, then a clerk in Mr. Peck's bookstore, that it seems to belong properly to this narrative : —

Mr. Weed's circumstances have been as varied as those of almost any other man, — to-day upon the top of fortune's wheel, and to-morrow down again. Soon after we saw the inside of a printing-office, we also saw Thurlow Weed installed over us as editor and foreman. This was in Rochester, N. Y., some twenty years ago. Weed came penniless to the place, bringing his family with him. He asked for employment as a printer or assistant editor of the little " seven by nine " journal, then and there printed once in seven days. He was told by the worthy publisher that there was nothing for him to do. Weed thought of his family, away from their friends, and of his own impoverished condition. In spite of his efforts to prevent it, a tear was gathering in his eye, and he turned abruptly away to hide it. But the sympathizing and benevolent gentleman to whom he applied saw and *felt* it, for he called Weed back, and at once made him a liberal offer to take charge of his paper and printing-office. The proposition was accepted, and Mr. Weed gained a reputation immediately throughout the village as an able editor.

On the following morning Mr. Peck informed me that he had concluded to put a small work to press, which would, he

said, give me employment for a couple of months. On expressing the gratification I felt, I added that as I had been accustomed for several years to select copy and prepare matter for a
weekly newspaper, I would, after my day's work was over, if he
would permit it, very cheerfully take that labor off his hands.
We then conversed for some time in relation to the tone, spirit,
and general character of a newspaper adapted to the condition
of the village and county, and the tastes of the people. Evidently satisfied with my views and fitness, he frankly confided
the management of his paper to me. Assuming even then that
my situation was permanent, the sum of four hundred dollars
per annum was fixed upon as my compensation. "And then,
with a joyful heart, I commenced the world anew." Meantime
Mr. Peck went personally to the hotel and invited my family to
his own dwelling-house, where we were kindly received and
pleasantly lodged until a suitable tenement was obtained. Everything about Mr. Peck and his establishment was attractive and
cheerful. It was a privilege and a pleasure to work hard, and
to be earnest and zealous, with such surroundings. During the
winter, my wife rose long before daylight, kindled her own fire,
and prepared breakfast, of which we partook by candle-light,
and the dawning day found me at work in the office. I selected
matter and wrote editorial for the paper evenings, after my
day's work was done. And to my great satisfaction, the Rochester "Telegraph" soon became popular. Its subscribers and
its advertising largely increased. For this Mr. Peck took much
pleasure in attributing the credit to me. The success of the
"Telegraph" provoked the jealousy and ire of the "Republican," whose editor, a sharp, sarcastic paragraphist, pitched into
"Mr. Peck's hired man." The "hired man" struck back, and
a spirited war of words ensued. Mr. Peck, although quiet in
manner and equable in temperament, instead of restraining me,
quite enjoyed the tilting, so that the belligerents, who became
bitterly abusive of each other, fought it out, to the admiration of their respective friends and the amusement of general
readers.

Long years afterwards, when I was editor of the Albany
"Evening Journal," and the same Derick Sibley a *Whig* member of the legislature, we remembered how impossible it would
have been in 1822 to have imagined that an ultra-Democratic

and a rabid Clintonian editor could have become stanch friends and political co-workers.

Among the merchants and millers of Rochester at that day were many very remarkable men. Many of them were young, bold, dashing adventurers, doomed almost inevitably to pecuniary shipwreck. They were, for the most part, impulsive, liberal, energetic, and honest. Rochester was then no place for the slow, mousing, and close-fisted. Colonel Nathaniel Rochester, from whom the village derived its name, was still living. Next to him in age, influence, and standing, was Dr. Matthew Brown. The venerable Vincent Mathews, whom everybody honored, was deservedly the head of the Monroe County Bar. Among the millers of intelligence and enterprise were Harvey Ely, Ebenezer S. Beach, Wareham Whitney, and Thomas Kempshall, all differently constituted, but all men of great business talent, public spirit, and liberality. The village was fortunate in its physicians, who were not only highly educated, but were distinguished for sound judgment, practical sense, agreeable manners, and kindly sympathies. Dr. Frederick F. Backus added to his great professional attainments nearly all the various elements of usefulness which constitute the perfect man. He became a member, in the latter years of his life, of the State Senate, solely to inaugurate enactments to ameliorate the condition of suffering humanity. He was the author of the law which first extended educational relief to the idiotic. It was through his exertions and influence in the Senate that an institution for idiots was established at Syracuse, the successful working of which has fully vindicated the anticipations of its founders. Dr. Backus was related by marriage to two gentlemen distinguished for their extreme opposition to slavery. Gerrit Smith, of this State, and James G. Birney, of Ohio, married daughters of Colonel Fitzhugh, an accomplished gentleman of the old school and an officer of the revolutionary war, who removed from Maryland to Geneseo immediately after the war of 1812. Mrs. Backus was also a daughter of Colonel Fitzhugh. The first wife of Gerrit Smith was a sister of Dr. Backus. Dr. Backus, an earnest Whig, was no less earnest in his opposition to the ultra "one-idea abolitionism" of his brother-in-law. Although himself, in precept and example, a temperate man, he was warmly opposed to the Maine Law and the "prohibitory" views of Gerrit Smith, Mr. Delavan, the "Tribune," etc., etc. While zealous, untiring, and effective in maintaining political, social, moral, and religious progress, he did not sympathize with the enthusiasts who from time to time acquired a pernicious influence over the popular mind.

Two of the excellent physicians of Rochester (Drs. J. B. Elwood and George Marvin) survive. The former is still a resident of Rochester, the latter an eminent physician of Brooklyn. The merchants of the village were generally young, active, and liberal. One of the oldest, most intelligent, and best esteemed was William Pitt Shearman, one of a numerous family well known in Oneida County. He went to New York in 1825 to have a limb amputated, from the effect of which he died in that city. The Rev. Mr. Penny, a Presbyterian pastor, and the Rev. F. H. Cummings, rector of the Episcopal Church, were well educated and able preachers. Samuel Works, a tanner, from Vermont, and one of the pioneers of the village, was practically a father to all new-comers, and to all industrious, deserving mechanics and laborers. He was a plain, uneducated man, with natural ability, strong sense, clear judgment, and intuitive knowledge. I had never before and have never since known so really good and useful a citizen. Upon the appearance of Cooper's novel, "The Pioneers," the soubriquet of "Leatherstocking" was at once and universally applied to Mr. Works. Josiah Bissell, Jr., was a "make-or-break" merchant, miller, and land speculator. He was very active and ultra in religious movements. Mr. Bissell, with Aristarchus Champion, a wealthy man from Connecticut, maintaining that it was inexcusably wicked to run stages on Sunday, organized the "Pioneer," a six-day line between Rochester and Albany, which for several years was the occasion of much excitement and discord. Rochester was made up of young, dashing, generous people, attracted there from Eastern New York and New England by reports of its great and rapidly developing elements of prosperity. There were few or no idlers there. I became acquainted immediately with all the inhabitants, and formed numerous friendships, which have remained unaffected by time or absence. I renewed there my acquaintance with Robert Hunter, a very enterprising and upright man, whom I first knew as a wagoner in 1811. When the Erie Canal was completed, he converted his broad-wheeled wagons into boats, and became a forwarder, residing first at Rochester, and then at Albany, where he died in 1843, leaving a handsome estate to a wife and daughter, well worthy of the great affection he had bestowed upon them.

The brothers Samuel L. and Henry R. Selden, the former since distinguished as a judge of the Court of Appeals, and the latter as a lieutenant-governor of the State, were, when I went to Rochester, students at law. James Kane Livingston, who had just come from Dutchess County, after long years of diligent and upright business pursuits, honored and beloved by everybody, is now a venerable resident of Newark, New Jersey. Samuel G. Andrews, or, as he was best known, "George Andrews," was one of the brightest, gentlest, as well as one of the most interesting and agreeable gentlemen I have ever known. He immediately became my warm friend, and remained such with unwavering devotion to the last hour of his life. He was, at different times, member of our Assembly, clerk of our Senate, member of Congress, and mayor of the city of Rochester.

Frederick Whittlesey, who came to Rochester from Cooperstown in 1823, and commenced practice as a lawyer, was a young man of unusual talents, energy, and industry. A year afterwards he became the successor of Mr. Sibley as editor of the "Republican," and consequently my political antagonist; and although a very exciting campaign ensued, which brought us into sharp collision, our personal relations were not disturbed. Subsequently, in 1826, an event of which I shall have occasion to speak hereafter brought us together. He sold his paper, united with us politically, and from thenceforward until the day of his death, a quarter of a century afterward, "hooks of steel" could not bind friends in closer ties of mutual confidence and affection than those which united us. His manly virtues, unswerving fidelity, and great-hearted friendship still live fresh and green in my memory. My otherwise pleasant recollections of Rochester are always saddened by the remembrance that I have so often been called there to pay the last tribute to the remains of such friends. Mr. Whittlesey served several years in Congress, and was appointed vice-chancellor of the eighth judicial district by Governor Seward. I have already spoken of General Mathews, then the Nestor of the bar of Western New York. He had formerly been a member of Congress from

Tioga County. I became greatly attached to him, in whom I found a " guide, philosopher, and friend."

My first year in Mr. Peck's office was one of great contentment. My duties were always pleasant, and always cheerfully performed. In our settlement at the close of the year, Mr. Peck, in a manner which augmented the value of the money, added a hundred dollars to the amount which had been agreed upon.

CHAPTER XI.

1823–1824.

THE adoption of the new constitution in 1822 placed the political power of the State in the hands of Mr. Van Buren, the recognized representative leader of the Democratic party. Governor Clinton, as the end of his term of service approached, became as powerless as he was in 1816. Opposition to the Erie and Champlain canals had ceased. Even the guns of the "National Advocate," Major Noah's paper, were spiked. Had it been otherwise, had the partisans of Mr. Van Buren continued their hostility to the canals, Mr. Clinton could have remained strong. As it was, knowing that a reëlection was impossible, he declined the nomination, leaving the field to Judge Joseph C. Yates, the Democratic nominee, who left the bench of the Supreme Court to occupy the executive chair. My old friend Solomon Southwick, still the victim of an hallucination to which I have referred, ran for governor, receiving, however, only 2,910 votes. Mr. Southwick was always a firm believer in "Weird Sisters." He consulted such oracles on political questions concerning his own hopes, and believed implicitly in their incantations. He impoverished himself in the purchase of lottery tickets, the "fortunate" numbers of which were indicated in dreams or by fortune-tellers. There being no organized opposition to the Democratic state ticket (Yates and Root), nearly all the counties in the State elected Democratic members of the legislature. Indeed, there were not more than a dozen friends of Governor Clinton in that house of assembly.

Notwithstanding this calm, a political storm was brewing. There were four aspirants for the presidency, namely, John Quincy Adams, Henry Clay, William H. Crawford, and John C. Calhoun, all distinguished statesmen of the Republican or Democratic party. Messrs. Adams, Crawford, and Calhoun were members of Mr. Monroe's cabinet, while Mr. Clay was a member of Congress. It was soon apparent, however, that the South preferred Crawford, and Mr. Calhoun withdrew. At a congressional caucus Mr. Crawford was nominated, but the friends of neither Mr. Adams nor Mr. Clay recognized the authority of the caucus, and both refused to be bound by it. This inaugurated a free presidential fight.

William L. Marcy was then State Comptroller; Samuel L. Talcott, Attorney-General; Benjamin Knower, Treasurer; and Edwin Croswell, editor of the "Argus" and state printer. These gentlemen, with Mr. Van Buren as their chief, constituted the nucleus of what became the Albany Regency. After adding Silas Wright, Azariah C. Flagg, John A. Dix, James Porter, Thomas W. Olcott, and Charles E. Dudley to their number, I do not believe that a stronger political combination ever existed at any state capital, or even at the national capital. They were men of great ability, great industry, indomitable courage, and strict personal integrity. Their influence and power for nearly twenty years was almost as potential in national as in state politics. Of this formidable body, Messrs. Flagg, Dix, and Olcott are the only survivors. It may be questioned whether, in the annals of party, there was ever a conflict more intensely earnest, or one that for twenty years occasioned such absorbing interest, as that which was represented on the one side by the "Argus" and on the other by the "Evening Journal," whose respective editors enjoyed the confidence of the Democratic and the Whig parties. Political life, with all its responsibilities and disappointments, has its compensations. Prominent among these compensations is the circumstance that my personal relations with most of the members of the Albany Regency were pleasant, while with Governor Marcy, Comptroller Flagg, Mr. Porter, and Mr. Olcott, they became quite intimate even during the heat of the controversy. Later in life, amid the mutations of party, without any impeachment of the patriotism or consistency of these gentlemen, I found myself acting politically with General

Dix, Mr. Flagg, and Mr. Olcott. Strangely enough the law of 1840, which transferred the state printing from the " Argus " to the " Journal," led to a renewal of intercourse between the editors, who, although natives of the same place, and friends in their boyhood, had been alienated by the bitterness of party strife for twenty years. In the transfer of legal advertisements from the " Argus " to the " Journal," by a liberal rather than a literal construction of the law, an opportunity was afforded me for courtesies which Mr. Croswell deemed generous and kind. Subsequently, when a bank in which Mr. Croswell was a director failed, it was in my power to render him other services. These incidents restored the friendship which had existed between us in early life.

In 1824 an incident occurred which had an important and beneficial effect upon my future career, which, in fact, was the turning point in my " battle of life." For the three previous years the citizens of Rochester had made earnest but unavailing efforts to obtain a bank charter from the legislature. The nature of the business, milling, etc., carried on at Rochester, required banking accommodations. The merchants and millers had been compelled to go to Canandaigua, Geneva, and Auburn, for all their bank discounts. The citizens, as every year increased their embarrassments and inconvenience, determined to make a fourth and earnest effort to obtain a bank charter. The committee which had been appointed to conduct the application were divided as to a proper agent to go to Albany. Several meetings of the committee were held without being able to agree upon either of the two gentlemen urged for the appointment. In this dilemma, Mr. Works suggested that he saw no other course but to try and agree upon some third person. Whereupon George Andrews, quite to the astonishment of the older and graver men of the committee, presented my name, which, as was very natural, was not received with favor. Indeed, two or three of the committee treated the idea of appointing a comparatively unknown journeyman mechanic for such a responsible mission as preposterous, adding that such a person could exert no possible influence at Albany. Mr. Works, whose voice was always potential, intimated his approval of the suggestion of Mr. Andrews, but thought the committee had better take a day or two for consideration, which was done. On the following day, when the subject was spoken of in the village, a popular feeling manifested itself in my favor, but the judgment of a majority of the committee remained against me. As the majority was still divided on the other candidates, five out of the nine united in my favor. So little confidence, however, was felt in my appointment, that a majority of the committee declined to pay over the money contributed to defray the expenses of an agent. This, however, did not discourage my friends Works, Andrews, Peck, etc., who immediately raised three hundred dollars for my expenses, and thus fortified, in the last week of December, 1823, I started in a stage for Albany, accompanied by Enos Stone, Peter Price, and Major H. Smith, Democratic members of Assembly from Monroe County.

To make subsequent events clear, it is necessary to say here that the Rochester "Telegraph" was the first paper which placed the name of John Quincy Adams under its editorial head as a candidate for President, early in 1823, and that the first popular meeting nominating Mr. Adams was held in Rochester. These were my inspirations, and I was known throughout the State as a warm supporter of Mr. Adams. I went to Albany with the understanding that I was to report the proceedings of the legislature in letters to the Rochester "Telegraph." Mr. Bemis, of the Ontario "Repository," employed me to write letters for his paper also. At the opening of the session a reporter's seat was assigned to me in the Assembly. That legislature was to choose the presidential electors, unless an effort which we had already inaugurated, to give the choice of electors to the people, should be successful. This effort was sustained by the friends of Mr. Adams and Mr. Clay, who were in a majority in the Assembly, and opposed by the friends of Mr. Crawford, who had a majority in the Senate. I started with the political sympathies of the Adams and Clay members, all of whom soon became my personal friends. I succeeded also in establishing pleasant social relations with nearly all the Crawford members, and although the political struggle was fierce and exciting, it engendered no personal ill-will between most of the Crawford members and myself. There was scarcely an individual member of the Senate or Assembly by whom I failed on all occasions to be kindly received. I was a welcome visitor at the rooms of members, irrespective of party. I knew every member of the legislature of 1824 much better than I ever knew the members of thirty consecutive and succeeding legislatures, with whom, as is known, I was closely associated. There were three sessions of that legislature; one commencing in January, one in August, and one in November, all of which I attended, exerting, from the peculiar and fortunate combination of circumstances, an influence never before or since surpassed, and probably never equalled. Of the intensely interesting and important political events of that legislature I shall speak hereafter, confining the narrative at present to my bank mission. There were some dozen or fifteen applications for banks for other parts of the State. The strongest were those for the Commercial Bank of Albany and the Dutchess County Bank at Poughkeepsie. There were also two strong applications from the city of New York, and one from Brooklyn. I united cordially with the strong men (John Townsend, Lewis Benedict, Richard Marvin, William Cook, etc., etc.,) of Albany, Walter Cunningham and his friends of Poughkeepsie, and kept on friendly terms with the other prominent applicants for banks. Our enterprises moved along harmoniously. The bill to incorporate the Bank of Rochester was, by common consent, reported first. Several other bills were also reported favorably. Without going into a detailed account of our alternate hopes and fears during that three months' canvass, it is sufficient to say that Rochester was the only place in the State, out of the city of New York, favored with a bank charter by the legislature of 1824. Two bank applications from the city of New York were successful. One, the Fulton Bank, owed its success to a clause contributing a large amount, two hundred thousand dollars I believe, for the benefit of the then vice-president, Daniel D. Tompkins. The other, the Chemical Bank, it was alleged, purchased its charter. Such at least were the charges, and a legislative investigation showed that a large amount of money had been expended, and with a damaging effect upon several members of the legislature. The charter for the Bank of Rochester was the only one obtained upon its merits, or, as others said, on account of the close personal and social relations of its agent with the members of the legislature, and their willingness to oblige him.

With the approval of several Rochester gentlemen, then at

Albany, I made the passage of our bank bill the occasion of a
legislative supper, which was attended by all the members, and
went off very pleasantly. My return to Rochester with the
charter of the bank in my pocket secured me a cordial welcome
by the citizens generally, and was a source of peculiar gratification to the friends who had generously made themselves responsible for a journeyman mechanic. I received two hundred dollars, in addition to the three hundred with which I left Rochester,
as my compensation, the legislative banquet cost four hundred,
making in all less than a thousand dollars as the total expense
of obtaining what was so much wanted, — a bank. During the
session of the legislature I had become so intimate with all its
members, and so earnest in my support of Mr. Adams for President, that my time and efforts had become essential to my
party. The legislature, as I have previously stated, was divided
into three sections, each led by very able men. The Crawford
or Van Buren section had Silas Wright, Jr., John Sudam, Perley Keyes, Edward P. Livingston, and others, in the Senate;
Azariah C. Flagg, and others, in the Assembly. The Adams
section was still stronger, having James Burt, Isaac Ogden,
Jacob Haight, William Nelson, L. A. Burroughs, in the Senate;
with James Tallmadge, Henry Wheaton, Isaac Pierson, Samuel
J. Wilkin, Stephen Warren, G. H. Barstow, in the Assembly.
Mr. Clay's leading friends were John Cramer and Jesse Clark
in the Senate, and James Mullett, Jr., George Hosmer, Grant
B. Baldwin, and Bowen Whiting, in the Assembly. Mr. Van
Buren, Judge Skinner, Benjamin Noah, Samuel L. Tallcott,
William L. Marcy, Mr. Croswell, and other strong men, were
zealously at work for Crawford. Mr. Clinton, though gover-
nor, was much in the condition of a pastor without a congrega-
tion. Under the then new constitution, Van Buren state officers had been chosen with what was supposed to be a strong
Van Buren legislature, but to the surprise, if not dismay, of
Mr. Van Buren before its close, his party, on the presidential
question, was in a minority. Governor Clinton himself, though
hostile to Mr. Van Buren, took no decided presidential ground.
Mr. Clay was warmly supported by General Peter B. Porter,
Colonel Samuel Young, and several other distinguished politicians, some of whom were in constant attendance upon the
legislature.

Against this array of men of position and power I represented the Adams cause, outside of the legislature, single-
handed. We urged a bill through the Assembly giving the
choice of presidential electors to the people. This bill was defeated in the Senate by a vote of seventeen to fifteen. Against
the "seventeen" senators a popular sentiment of indignation
was aroused, which consigned most of them to retirement during
the remainder of their lives. Mr. Van Buren, however, remained faithful to the men who incurred popular odium for
being faithful to him. Two of those senators, Jonas Earll and
John Bowman, were appointed canal commissioners by a Van
Buren legislature. Silas Wright and Charles E. Dudley were
elected United States senators by Van Buren legislatures.
Two of those senators, Herman J. Redfield, of Genesee, and
Alvin Bronson, of Oswego, survive. They are men of high
personal character, who enjoy the confidence and regard of all
who know them. Mr. Redfield was once collector of the port
of New York.

While the defeat of the electoral law confessedly weakened
Mr. Van Buren's party with the people, it was supposed that
the legislature could be relied on for Crawford electors. And
with the vote of the State of New York in his favor, Mr. Crawford's election as President was considered certain.

In February, the division in the Democratic party on the
presidential question had assumed threatening local aspects.
The friends of Mr. Clay made arrangements to establish an
organ at Albany. In this movement Colonel Young took an
active part, and it soon became known to Mr. Van Buren that
Colonel Young had been selected by the Adams and Clay men
as a union candidate for governor. Editors had been designated for the new Clay paper, for the first number of which
Colonel Young was preparing a prospectus.

This information created much consternation in the Van
Buren camp, and a bold flank movement was immediately decided upon. Governor Yates, whose re-nomination had been
looked for as a matter of course, was unceremoniously dropped,
and the regular Democratic nomination for governor was tendered to Colonel Young, who complacently turned his back
upon his Clay friends, and returned to his allegiance to King
Caucus. Mr. Cramer, without admitting that he had aban-

doned Mr. Clay, went into the Crawford caucus and voted for his friend Colonel Young. The embryo Clay journal, which would have appeared the next week, was abandoned; and although General Porter, Senator Clark, and Messrs. Mullett and Bowen Whiting, of the Assembly remained faithful, yet the defection of Colonel Young seriously weakened the prospects of Mr. Clay. Governor Yates was equally surprised and shocked at being thus suddenly thrown overboard. Whether this movement strengthened or weakened the Crawford party, it was difficult even then to determine; but it was succeeded in a few days by a still bolder movement, and one which sealed the fate of Crawford in our State. On the last day of the session, in pursuance of a Regency fiat, John Bowman introduced a resolution in the Senate removing DeWitt Clinton from the office of canal commissioner. I had noticed a significant consultation in the Assembly chamber, and followed one of the gentlemen into the Senate chamber, who delivered a message to Senator Wright. That senator immediately opened his drawer, and handed a slip of paper to Senator Bowman. On that slip was written the resolution to which I have referred. Mr. Bowman submitted it to the Senate. The moment Mr. Bacon, the clerk, finished the reading of the resolution, I hastened back to the Assembly to inform our friends what was coming, and to prepare them for resisting it. General Tallmadge, our leader, was first appealed to. After Colonel Young's defection, it was conceded all around that General Tallmadge must be our candidate for governor. I knew how bitterly General Tallmadge hated Mr. Clinton, but in a few hurried and emphatic sentences implored him not to be caught in the trap thus baited for him. I urged him to state frankly, in a brief speech, how entirely he was estranged personally and politically from Mr. Clinton, but to denounce his removal during the successful progress of a system of improvement.which he had inaugurated, and which would confer prosperity and wealth upon the people and enrich and elevate our State, as an act of vandalism to which he could not consent to be a party. I concluded by assuring him solemnly that if he voted for that resolution he could not receive the nomination for governor. I went next to Dr. Barstow, who had been a Clintonian; but much to my surprise, instead of remaining to speak against the resolution, he walked out of the chamber. I was equally unsuccessful in an appeal to Mr. Whiting, a Clay Democrat from Ontario. In despair of finding anybody to oppose the resolution, I turned to the seat of Mr. Cunningham, of Montgomery County, which, a not unusual circumstance, was vacant; but I knew where to find him, and, just as the Speaker announced the resolution from the Senate, I entered the chamber with Mr. Cunningham, who was sufficiently posted, and who remained standing in front of the Speaker until the resolution was read, when in a loud voice and impressive manner he occupied the floor some ten minutes in eloquent and thrilling utterances against " the deep damnation of his taking off."

The following is an extract from Mr. Cunningham's speech:

When the miserable party strifes of the present day shall have passed by, and the political jugglers who now beleaguer this capitol shall be overwhelmed and forgotten, when the gentle breeze shall pass over the tomb of that great man, carrying with it the just tribute of honor and praise which is now withheld, the pen of the future historian will do him justice, and erect to his memory a monument of fame as imperishable as the splendid works that owe their origin to his genius and perseverance.

Sir, I have done; and I have only to beseech every honorable gentleman on this floor to weigh well the consequences of the vote he is about to give on this important question. It is probably the last that will be given this session, and I pray God it may be such as will not disgrace us in the eyes of our constituents.

Mr. Crary, of Washington County, also spoke against the resolution, as did Mr. Riggs, of Schenectady. General Tallmadge remained dumb. Not a word was spoken by the Democratic members. The resolution was adopted by a vote comprising nearly all the members of Democratic antecedents. Many of them, opposed to Crawford and in favor of the electoral law, voted in the affirmative, allowing themselves to be caught, as I have before remarked, in the trap successfully, if not wisely, baited for them.

Mr. Van Buren's object was, in part, to create a split among the anti-Crawford members, but mainly to place Messrs. Tallmadge, Wheaton, Pierson, Morse, Drake, Towne, etc., etc., Tammany Hall Democrats but Adams men, in a dilemma, either horn of which would prove disastrous to them. By voting for the resolution they would offend the political friends with whom they were then acting on the presidential question. By voting against the resolution, they would incur the denunciation of Tammany Hall.

CHAPTER XII.

1824.

THE intelligence of Mr. Clinton's removal spread with electric rapidity through the city. The members of the legislature had scarcely left their seats before they were occupied by the citizens of Albany. A meeting was immediately organized by the appointment of the venerable ex-Lieutenant Governor Taylor, chairman, and General John H. Wendell, a revolutionary veteran, secretary. Colonel James McKown addressed the meeting in a brief, but most eloquent and impassioned speech, concluding by submitting resolutions denouncing the act in glowingly indignant language. The following are extracts from Colonel McKown's resolutions : —

Resolved, That the removal of De Witt Clinton, confessedly without any pretence of misconduct, from the office of canal commissioner, the duties of which he had for fourteen years discharged with distinguished zeal and ability and without any pecuniary reward, is a most flagrant and wanton violation of public trust, and an act of injustice and ingratitude, revolting to the moral sense of all honorable men, and unparalleled in the political history of the State.

Resolved, That the perpetrators of this act of violence and ingratitude are utterly unworthy of public confidence, and justly deserve the reprobation of an injured community.

Resolved, That William James, Ebenezer Baldwin, Joseph Alexander, Philip L. Parker, Isaiah Townsend, Israel Smith, Samuel M. Hopkins, Chandler Starr, Elisha Jenkins, Gideon Hawley, Teunis Van Vechten, John Cassidy, Jeremiah Waterman, James McKown, Jabez D. Hammond, and Alfred Conkling, together with the chairman and secretary, be a committee to express to Mr. Clinton, in behalf of this meeting, the lively sense which we entertain of his very highly meritorious services, and to tender to him the tribute of our warmest thanks.

The resolutions were drawn by the Hon. Alfred Conkling, long a judge of the United States Court, and now closing a long life distinguished by public usefulness and private virtues at Geneseo, in Livingston County. Of the eminent and highly respected men named on that committee, Gideon Hawley, still a venerable citizen of Albany, and Chandler Starr, a retired merchant of high character, now a resident of Stamford, Conn., are the only survivors. The citizens of New York also came spontaneously together, denouncing with great severity the removal of Mr. Clinton, and appointing a committee of twenty-five of the most eminent men to make their feelings known to him. This committee, consisting of Thomas Addis Emmet, Cadwallader D. Colden, William Baird, Thomas Hertell and others, repaired to Albany and delivered their address personally to Mr. Clinton. Mr. Hammond, in his " Political History of the State," published in 1846, says : " It is a singular fact, honorable to the sense of this community, that since this transaction I have never heard a single individual of any political sect speak of it without reprobating it." I can add, with twenty-five more years of experience and observation, that I have never heard the removal of Mr. Clinton defended or excused in the halls of legislation, in the press, or by an individual. The removal of Mr. Clinton awakened a strong popular indignation throughout the State. Several members who voted for it were hissed by the people as they came out of the capitol. General Tallmadge received unmistakable evidence, on his way through State Street to his lodgings, of the great error he had committed. His hotel was filled with citizens, whose rebukes were loudly heard as he passed through the hall to his apartment. The legislature adjourned finally at mid-day. At three o'clock General Tallmadge sent for me. I found him nervously excited, pacing rapidly backwards and forwards in his parlor, " the victim of a remorse that comes too late." He perceived both the depth and the darkness of the political pit into which he had fallen. He said that he left me with the intention of first denouncing Mr. Clinton as his personal and political foe, and then, in language as indignant as he could command, denouncing the resolution and its authors, but that Messrs. Wheaton and Pierson, who occupied seats on either side of him, claimed that they were all embarked in a common cause, and that it was their duty to stand by each other, and that, thus pressed and in thus yielding, he had committed the greatest blunder of his political life.

I left Albany in the stage the next day for Rochester. The storm raged against members who had voted for the removal of Clinton with greater and still greater fury as we proceeded westward. In villages and at hotels those members were loudly denounced. At Canandaigua personal indignities were threatened. It had been arranged after the electoral law had been defeated in the Senate, and Governor Yates thrown overboard by his party, that I should go through the western and southwestern counties to inaugurate a movement through public meetings in favor of a called session of the legislature. I started early in May and labored diligently, producing satisfactory results, for a month. Governor Yates was furnished with the proceedings of well-attended village, town, and county meetings, deprecating the defeat of an electoral law, the removal of Mr. Clinton, and the ingratitude of party leaders, etc., concluding with a resolution, respectfully appealing to the governor to convene an extra session of the legislature. Simultaneously, the governor received letters from prominent men in all those counties, reflecting the spirit of various popular demonstrations. Late in May I visited Albany, and after full and free consultation with John Van Ness Yates, then Secretary of State, a nephew of the governor, who sympathized with us politically, I received an invitation to dinner at the executive mansion. Professor Yates, of Schenectady, a brother of the governor, but in political harmony with our side, John Van Ness Yates, William K. Fuller, the governor's adjutant-general, Christopher Lansing, his private secretary, and myself, were the only persons at the table. After the dessert was reached, the political questions of the day were introduced. The governor, on being informed that I had traveled a good deal through the State since the adjournment of the legislature, asked what counties I had visited; and then if I had seen many gentlemen whom he named, and what their opinions were. This led to a general discussion of the questions which occupied the public mind, coming around finally to that of the proposed recall of the legislature. John Van Ness Yates and the professor insisted that the unanimity of sentiment among the people was so pronounced as, in their judgment, to render it proper that the governor should give the subject his gravest attention. The governor asked me if I thought that the people in the country really expected that he would convene the legislature. I told him that the masses were intensely anxious, but I could not say how hopeful they were. I added that A., B., C., D., etc., etc., prominent and influential men in different parts of the State, from their knowledge of the governor's character, seemed confident that he would call an extra session. He then inquired whom I had seen in Albany, and what was thought about it by the Albany politicians. I named several leading Van Buren men with whom I had conversed, most of whom treated the subject lightly, and seemed to have no apprehension of such a step. He spoke of a meeting of the Van Buren leaders, a day or two previous, and inquired if I knew what occurred at that meeting. I was not able to answer, but Mr. John Van Ness Yates remarked that he had been informed that on Mr. Van Buren's assurance that there would be no extra session of the legislature they became quite jubilant, and separated in good spirits. I then named a gentleman who heard Attorney-General Talcott assure some people in the Mansion House bar-room that there would be no proclamation convening the legislature. On being asked why he spoke so confidently, he replied that the power to convene the legislature was a high prerogative, the exercise of which required great courage. "Very well," said his questioner, "the governor is a man of courage." "Possibly," responded the attorney-general, "but when he comes to face the question, the writing of a proclamation will require decision and nerve." Governor Yates sprang to his feet, and in a loud tone and excited manner, exclaimed, "Tallcott said dat it will require decision and nerve to write a proclamation, did he?" "That is my information," I replied. "Well, I 'll show him dat I possess decision and nerve enough to do right! John, come with me in the office." I should have said, in the proper place, that before the political conversation commenced, the governor told his adjutant, General Fuller, who was a strong Crawford man, that he could take a walk. After the governor had retired with his nephew to the library, his brother, the professor, remarked that all was right; that when the governor was stimulated to the point he had now reached, nothing could change his determination. I soon took leave in a frame of mind well calculated to assist digestion. I called in the evening upon my friend, John Van Ness Yates, who assured me that the proclamation would appear in the "Argus" on the following Tuesday, and, to the dismay of the Crawford and Van Buren men, it did so appear. The proclamation was dated June 2d, reassembling the legislature on the 2d of August.

On that day there was a very full attendance of members, and the moment the Senate convened, before the governor's message was received, Byron Green, one of the seventeen senators who had voted against the electoral law, offered a resolution, censuring the governor for calling the legislature.

The governor, in a brief message, reiterated the views contained in his proclamation, and strongly urged the passage of a law restoring the choice of presidential electors to the people. In the Assembly, immediately after the message was read, Mr. Flagg offered a concurrent resolution, stating that nothing had occurred since the adjournment of the legislature, within the letter or the spirit of the constitution, requiring an extraordinary session, and therefore that the proclamation of the governor was not warranted by the constitution, and that, therefore, if the Senate concur, the two Houses would immediately adjourn to meet again pursuant to law. Mr. Flagg's resolution, declaring the action of the governor a virtual violation of the constitution, was adopted. And yet the same House of Assembly, on the same day, adopted a resolution, by a vote of seventy-five to forty-four, that an electoral law ought to be passed. The explanation of such incongruous action is found in the fact that while Adams and Clay Democrats, who had previously voted for the electoral law, could not stultify themselves in that respect, they had not the courage or did not choose to break with their party on an independent question. The debate upon those resolutions was able and exciting. General Tallmadge was exceedingly eloquent. Mr. Wheaton and Mr. Mullett made powerful appeals. They were loudly cheered from the galleries. Very little, however, was said in reply by the Crawford members, and, after four days of wrangling, the legislature adjourned, having accomplished nothing, to reassemble on the first Monday in November, according to law, for the purpose of appointing presidential electors.

In the evening, after the adjournment, there was a consultation among the leading opponents of Mr. Crawford. The removal of Mr. Clinton gave a new phase to the campaign. It was evident that unless the popular feeling subsided, Mr. Clinton would become a formidable candidate for governor. This would distract, perhaps fatally, an organization which promised to redeem the State. The most influential and active friends of Mr. Adams, in the Senate and in the Assembly, were bitterly hostile to Mr. Clinton. This remark applies especially to senators Burt, Ogden, Burrows, Haight, and to Messrs. Tallmadge, Wheaton, Pierson, Morse, Towne, Crolius, and others of the Assembly. Without harmony upon a State ticket no hope of success could be cherished, nor would it be possible to carry the presidential electors at the November session of the legislature.

Happily, however, almost providentially, I may say, a step had been previously taken which promised the best results. It had been decided at an accidental meeting, at which General Tallmadge, Mr. Wheaton, Mr. Pierson, Mr. Haight, Mr. Nelson, Grant B. Baldwin, and myself were present, that a State convention consisting of as many delegates as there were representatives in the Assembly, to be chosen by voters opposed to Mr. Crawford for President, and in favor of restoring the choice of presidential electors to the people, should assemble at Utica for the purpose of nominating candidates for governor and lieutenant-governor. Thus, the policy of nominations, emanating directly from the people, instead of by legislative caucus, was inaugurated. The convention which met at Utica in August, 1824, was the beginning of a new political era.

My personal position now became somewhat embarrassing. I had been, as was known by our friends and alleged by our opponents, active and efficient in effecting a legislative organization ,which threatened to defeat Mr. Van Buren's electoral ticket. At least two thirds of the members, relied on for this purpose, were Democratic friends of Mr. Adams. I had been, and was then, an open and earnest Clintonian. Up to the hour of Mr. Clinton's removal, General Tallmadge had been by general consent our candidate for governor ; his friends were not

only unwilling to take Mr. Clinton, but adhered to the idea of
running General Tallmadge. Those friends asked me to make
a second pilgrimage through the State, urging all opposed to
Crawford and Van Buren to unite upon General Tallmadge for
governor. I consented to do so, not at all sanguine, however,
of being able to stem the tide setting so strongly in favor of Mr.
Clinton. I met before I started, and several times in different parts of the State, Mr. Charles G. Haines, an enthusiastic
friend of Mr. Clinton, who was actively and successfully at
work arousing the people in favor of his candidate. If I should
not have other occasions to speak of that gentleman, I have
great pleasure in saying here, that in my long life I have never
known a young man so rarely gifted and so richly endowed in
mind, character, and person, as was Charles G. Haines. He
had but recently come among us from New Hampshire, his native State, but had, by his attractive manners, generous enthusiasm, impassioned eloquence, and unmistakable fidelity and
integrity, won the regard and confidence of all who knew him.

I kept General Tallmadge advised, as I passed from county
to county, of the real state of public sentiment, not at all, as I
was compelled to admit, in accordance with his hopes; and
after being satisfied that Mr. Clinton's nomination was almost
universally demanded, I proceeded to New York and reported
the result to our friends in that city, who for a few days were
greatly discouraged. And here it may be proper to remark
that while Mr. Adams had strong friends in the legislature, it
was difficult to inspire politicians in New York or Albany with
confidence. They had been for a year or two. in the habit of
regarding Mr. Van Buren's power over the State as invincible.
I found little, therefore, to encourage me in the effort I was
making. The only prominent journal in the city of New York
warmly in favor of Mr. Adams was the "American," then
edited by Messrs. Johnston, Verplanck, and Charles King. Mr.
King, who subsequently became and ever remained my friend,
did not then like me, as I had many years previously reflected
severely upon his conduct as a commissioner in relation to the
alleged outrages committed upon Americans in Dartmoor prison.
While Mr. Crawford had the prestige of a regular Democratic
nomination, and the support of the Albany Regency, and while
Mr. Clay was sustained by warm personal friends and political

admirers who were able and influential, Mr. Adams had no personal friends, and but few acquaintances in our State. Those who supported him did so from their high estimate of his ability and patriotism.

Messrs. Wheaton, Pierson, and other Democratic supporters of Mr. Adams, were so much annoyed by the probable nomination of Mr. Clinton for governor that for a time they became almost indifferent upon the whole question. In consultation with leading friends of Mr. Clinton in the city of New York, I suggested General Tallmadge's name for lieutenant-governor, as a means of bridging over some of our difficulties. Colonel Haines and a few others approved of this suggestion, while for the most part I found the Clintonians impracticable. They would not, they said, support a man who had voted to remove Mr. Clinton as canal commissioner. Nor was the suggestion of General Tallmadge for lieutenant-governor any more acceptable to himself or his friends. The question of lieutenant-governor was left open, and I returned to Rochester. At Albany, Utica, Auburn, Geneva, Canandaigua, and Rochester, General Tallmadge's name was much better received,— so much better, a few days before the convention was to assemble, that I started for New York for the purpose of renewing the suggestion there. Time and reflection had wrought a change among the city politicians. A committee from the New York delegation had left the city, to stop at Poughkeepsie on their way to Utica, to tender to General Tallmadge the nomination for lieutenant-governor. Knowing much better than those gentlemen could know the mood in which the general would be found, I hastened to Poughkeepsie, arriving there after the New York delegation had left for Utica. General Tallmadge had peremptorily refused the use of his name as a candidate for lieutenant-governor. Believing that with "the morn and cool reflection" I should find the general in a better frame of mind, I reserved what I had to say till after breakfast the next day. I found him calm, but quite resolute. He listened attentively to a brief recital of the progress thus far of our campaign, agreeing that but for the introduction of the resolution removing Mr. Clinton all would have been harmonious and successful. I said nothing of his unfortunate vote upon that question, but endeavored to show him that, with his consent, we could carry the State ; that presidential electors in favor of Mr. Adams could be chosen by the legislature, and that in making the sacrifice, which the public sentiment and the national welfare required, even a broader field for usefulness than that of being Governor of New York would be opened to him. These and other considerations, which were leisurely presented and discussed, produced the desired effect. Before the steamboat of the next afternoon arrived, I had in my pocket a brief letter from General Tallmadge, authorizing his friends at Utica, if in their judgment the success of our cause required it, to consent to the use of his name as a candidate for lieutenant-governor, with which I arrived at Utica on the morning of the day the convention assembled.

The convention was very fully attended. Most of the delegates were men of political standing and experience. As had been assumed, there was much unanimity of sentiment in favor of Mr. Clinton for governor. Some twenty-five or thirty delegates, designated as " People's men," were loudly for General Tallmadge. Ex-Lieutenant-Governor John Taylor, of Albany, was made president of the convention, Alexander Coffin, of Hudson, vice-president, and Samuel Stevens, of Washington, secretary. The opponents of Mr. Clinton, when the convention was organized, proposed John W. Taylor, of Saratoga, then late Speaker of the United States House of Representatives, and a Clintonian, for governor. This was suggested as a compromise, and several Clintonian delegates were ready to accept it, when Mr. John L. Viele, the delegate from Saratoga, produced a letter from Mr. Taylor positively declining a nomination. Mr. Clinton was then nominated for governor by a large majority. The nomination of General Tallmadge for lieutenant-governor was made unanimously and by acclamation. When the nomination of Mr. Clinton was declared in the convention, a few of the delegates irreconcilably hostile to Mr. Clinton withdrew in a body from the convention, met at the hotel and protested against it. This, however, though causing some temporary uneasiness, amid the general and pervading enthusiasm was soon forgotten.

The election was one of the most stirring that I ever witnessed. No possible effort was omitted by either party. The utmost excitement pervaded the State till the moment of closing the polls. Mr. Clinton was elected by a majority of more than sixteen thousand (16,000) over Colonel Young; while General Tallmadge's majority over General Root was more than thirty-two thousand (32,000). Of the eight senators elected, six were Clintonians, and two Regency men; while in the House of Assembly more than three to one of the members elected were opposed to the Albany Regency. At no contested election in our State had the success of one party been so triumphant, or the defeat of the other so overwhelming.

CHAPTER XIII.

1824.

But the days of political excitement were by no means over.
The scene, however, was changed from the ballot boxes in the
respective election districts to the legislative halls.   From a
gubernatorial conflict of unprecedented interest, we turned to a
presidential contest equally exciting.   The legislature convened
on the second day of November to choose presidential electors.
The Regency, with Mr. Van Buren at its head, were alert, bold,
and confident.   General Porter, Robert Tillotson, and other
warm friends of Mr. Clay, were in attendance.   Out of the
legislature, Mr. Adams was weak.   No man of high standing
felt warmly enough in his favor to appear at Albany.   I had,
however, enlightened and sagacious men in the Senate and Assembly to consult with.   Senators David Gardiner, of Suffolk,
William Nelson, of Westchester, James Burt, of Orange, Jacob
Haight, of Greene, Archibald McIntyre, of Montgomery, Isaac
Ogden, of Delaware, James Mallory, of Rensselaer, Latham A.
Burroughs, of Broome, Jedediah Morgan, of Cayuga, Tilly
Lynde, of Chenango, and Stephen Thorne, of Dutchess, were
earnest and faithful in their support of Mr. Adams ; John
Cramer, of Saratoga, Jesse Clark, of Seneca, and Melancthon
Wheeler, of Washington, were supporters of Mr. Clay.   The
latter, however, was not considered reliable, and Mr. Cramer,
almost at the last hour, gave in his adhesion to the Regency.
In the Assembly we were ably sustained by James Mullett, of
Chautauqua, Samuel Wilkeson, of Erie, George B. R. Gove, of
Franklin, Isaac Finch, of Essex, William Furman, of Kings,

Stephen Warren, of Troy, Isaac Riggs, of Schenectady, General McClure, of Steuben, Ezra Smith, of Washington, and Henry Cunningham, of Montgomery. There were, as I have already stated, three parties in the legislature, and yet, by the constitution, only two electoral tickets could be voted for. All votes for persons not found on one or the other of the two tickets in nomination were counted as blanks. Our only chance or hope of success, therefore, was in a union upon one ticket between the friends of Mr. Adams and Mr. Clay. The great difficulty in effecting this union grew out of the circumstance that Mr. Clay's chance of becoming one of the three candidates to be voted for in the House of Representatives depended upon his receiving at least seven electoral votes from the State of New York. But that difficulty, though a very formidable one, was by prudent counsels and good temper overcome. After several anxious interviews between General Porter, Senator Clark, Mr. Mullett, and Mr. Tillotson with General Tallmadge, Mr. Ogden, Mr. Burroughs, Mr. Wheaton, Mr. Warren, and myself, a union ticket was made up by taking thirty names from the Adams and six from the Crawford ticket, thirty-six being the whole number. These six gentlemen had been placed upon the Crawford ticket, although known to have been moderate Clay men. This was done for the purpose of detaching Senators Cramer and Wheeler from the Clay side of the house. This union was effected on Saturday evening, three days before the final ballot for electors. Secrecy was solemnly enjoined upon all present. The printing was intrusted to me. The editors of the "Daily Advertiser," an anti-Regency paper, gave me possession of their office on Sunday morning, where, after locking myself in, I set up and worked off the union ballot. It was known to us that our only possible chance of success depended upon the secrecy of this movement, for with the Clay votes our ticket would be elected by two majority only. Our friends in the legislature were aware that efforts were in progress for a union, but they neither knew nor inquired for details. I delivered the ballots intended for the Clay members to General Porter for distribution at his discretion.

I must now interrupt the narrative for the purpose of introducing an incident that, but for the circumstances which I will relate, would have given Mr. Crawford the electoral col-

lege of the State of New York, and, as a corollary, would
have secured his election as President. About ten days after
the adjournment of the called session of the legislature, I left
Rochester in a canal packet-boat bound eastward. Among the
passengers I met Mr. John Stilwell, of Albany, a zealous Crawford member of the Assembly. At Palmyra, William Kibbe,
of Canandaigua, came on board, and I observed that Mr. Stilwell and Mr. Kibbe were immediately in earnest and apparently confidential conversation. Mr. Kibbe passed his winters
in Albany, and, as was alleged, was often employed about the
legislature. This circumstance, along with the fact that there
had been neither personal nor political relations between Messrs.
Stilwell and Kibbe, induced me to observe them more closely
than I otherwise should have done. At Syracuse, Mr. Kibbe
landed a letter for the Post Office, addressed to the Hon. Mr.
——, who was an Adams member of the Assembly. This confirmed suspicions, already excited, that Mr. Kibbe had been
employed to negotiate with members opposed to Crawford. The
day after I arrived at Albany, Mr. —— made his appearance,
and, with Mr. Kibbe, departed in the steamboat for New York.
I followed in the steamer next day. Among the passengers
was my old friend, James Birdsall, of Chenango, who then, as
ever, was right in his politics. I informed him what I had observed, and what I apprehended. I knew that Messrs. Kibbe
and —— would go to Moody's Hotel, in Pearl Street, because
they had boarded together during former sessions of the legislature at Moody's, before that well-known host had removed to
New York. Mr. Birdsall knew Messrs. —— and Kibbe intimately, and readily consented to take lodgings himself at
Moody's, and keep me advised if he discovered anything of
importance.

The day following our arrival in New York, Mr. Birdsall informed me that after breakfast that morning, he went with
Messrs. Kibbe and —— to their room, and while there, in a
gossiping conversation, a gentleman called, to whom he was not
introduced, but with whom they evidently had business. Mr.
Birdsall retired, but subsequently learned from Mr. —— that
the gentleman referred to was Mr. Henry Eckford, and that
although Mr. —— did not say so, he was confident that Mr.
Eckford's errand was a political one. Mr. Eckford was a warm

supporter of Mr. Crawford, and a gentleman of great wealth. I was, therefore, at no loss to conjecture the object of Messrs. Kibbe and ——'s visit to New York. On the following day, Messrs. Kibbe and —— left for Albany. At Albany they separated. I made it my business, however, to keep reasonably close in Mr. ——'s wake. He went first to Montgomery County, visiting Peter Smith and F. H. Van Buren, members of Assembly from that county, both Adams men. I knew them intimately, as I did every other member of the Assembly of 1824. I had perfect confidence in the integrity of Mr. Smith, who, when I called on him, informed me that Mr. —— had been to see him, and, after " beating the bush " for a long time, said, although he was as warm as ever for Mr. Adams, he was so sure that the Regency were too strong for them that he began to doubt whether it was wise for them to beat their brains out against a stone wall ; that if three or four Adams men would make up their mind to go for Crawford they could make any terms they chose ; that he had seen the leading men, who had, in the most liberal manner, authorized him to make the arrangement, and asked him to meet his colleague, Mr. Van Buren, and talk things over. Mr. Smith quietly replied that he had talked so strong and so much to his neighbors in favor of Mr. Adams, and had committed himself so strongly at Albany, that he could not think of changing his ground. But he thought with me that his colleague, Mr. F. H. Van Buren, who was a weak man, might not be able to resist temptation. Mr. Smith said he would take an early opportunity of talking with him, and would inform me seasonably what effect, if any, had been produced upon him. Mr. —— then proceeded to Washington County, where, as I conjectured, he visited Mr. Kellogg, another Adams member of the Assembly. I informed my friend Samuel Stevens, then a promising young lawyer, and Captain Ezra Smith, then an Adams member of the Assembly, of the purpose of Mr. ——'s interview with Mr. Kellogg, and they were to give the matter their attention and advise me in due time of the result. The information I received from Mr. Smith, of Montgomery, and from Messrs. Stevens and Smith, of Washington, rendered it quite certain that Messrs. Van Buren and Kellogg had agreed to vote for the Crawford electors. We, however, kept our information and our intentions secret.

Neither Messrs. ——, Van Buren, nor Kellogg knew that they
had been " spotted," or even that they were suspected.   On the
Sunday evening previous to the ballot for presidential electors,
General Tallmadge, Mr. Wheaton, and myself called at the
room of Mr. ——, who was then boarding at Gourley's, on
Washington Street, some distance above the Capitol.   Finding
him alone, I stated to him what is written here.   When I had
finished, without giving Mr. —— time to reply, Mr. Wheaton
said that, in view of the facts just revealed, General Tallmadge
and himself had deemed it their duty to require Messrs. Van
Buren, Kellogg, and himself to vote an electoral ballot with
their (Messrs. Tallmadge's and Wheaton's) initials indorsed.
In that way alone, he added, could they be assured of those
three votes.   Mr. —— replied that he was willing that this
course might be taken with his own ballot, and that he would
converse with his friends Van Buren and Kellogg, who, he
thought, would be willing, as they were suspected, to take the
same course.   General Tallmadge then said, " As friends of Mr.
Adams, knowing what we now know, we have a high responsibility resting upon us.   We should lose the electoral ticket if
these three votes, or even two of them, should be cast in favor
of the Crawford ticket.   In addition to what Mr. Wheaton requires, it is proper for me to say that we shall carefully examine
the ballots as they are being canvassed, and that if the three,
with our initials indorsed, appear in the box, all that has passed
here shall be regarded as confidential ; but if these ballots do
not appear, I shall, as certainly as my life is spared, rise in my
place, proclaim the facts within our knowledge, and demand a
committee of investigation."   It was then arranged that at an
hour the next day Mr. Wheaton could meet the three members
referred to, and arrange with them the time and place for the
delivery of the ballots, the time to be immediately before the
voting should commence.   We separated, with Mr. ——'s confident assurance that his two friends would act in accordance
with his advice.   Mr. Wheaton, who scrutinized every ballot,
identified the three with the proper initials.

During the counting of the ballots, when the presiding officer
of the two houses, Lieutenant-Governor Root, drew from the
box the first union ballot, he looked attentively at it, and instead of reading the names in their order, he involuntarily ex-

claimed, " A printed split ticket!" Perley Keyes, a senator
from Jefferson County, sprang to his feet, and in a loud, angry
voice, said, " Treason, by G — ! " The greatest confusion instantly ensued, and the lieutenant-governor, on hearing some
one call upon senators to return to their chamber, was about to
leave the Speaker's chair, when General Tallmadge rose, and
in a stentorian voice called for order; and after pausing until
order was partially restored, he said, " I demand, under the authority of the Constitution of the United States, under the Constitution of the State of New York, in the name of the whole
American people, that this joint meeting of the two Houses of
the Legislature shall not be interrupted in the discharge of a
high duty and a sacred trust. I demand further that the great
business of the nation shall now proceed in order to its completion."

No other word was spoken. Members resumed their seats;
the canvass proceeded, and the result was declared. Thirty-two
of the persons named on the union ticket were elected. On
one ballot four names were scratched off; Mr. Grattan H.
Wheeler, of Steuben, voted a ticket with thirty-six names of
persons friendly to General Jackson, which was not counted;
and Mr. George Hosmer, of Livingston, voted a blank. On the
second ballot four Crawford men were chosen. Had our secret
transpired before the first ballot, such was the power of the
Regency over two or three timid men, that the whole Crawford ticket would have been chosen. The result was a great
surprise to Mr. Van Buren, who to the last hour cheered his
friends by the strongest assurances that all was safe.

Many years afterward, when I became intimate with the late
Matthew L. Davis, a warm supporter of Crawford, in talking
over the secret history of this contest for presidential electors,
I was informed that Mr. Eckford's arrangement with Messrs.
Kibbe and —— contemplated the payment of a certain amount
of money for every vote cast for Mr. Crawford by an Adams
member of the legislature, and that Mr. Eckford, or some reliable friend, would be at Albany in November to carry out
that understanding; but that Mr. Van Buren and other gentlemen at Albany insisted that their electoral ticket was sure
to be chosen, and therefore that the expenditure was unnecessary. Mr. Eckford, therefore, having already advanced a con-

siderable amount, declined either to pay more or to go to Albany. Judge William P. Van Ness, who was acquainted with all the circumstances, went to Albany, where he raised a small amount, with which, together with his pledge to pay the whole sum if the Crawford electoral ticket should be chosen, he hoped to save the three votes contracted for. And it was to the circumstance that the money promised was not forthcoming, as Mr. Davis believed, we saved the votes of our three recusant friends. I have already stated that the union upon our electoral ticket was effected by an assurance from leading Adams men that seven of the thirty-six electoral votes should be given to Mr. Clay, so that he would thus be brought into the House of Representatives. In remarking upon the fact that no such votes were given in favor of Mr. Clay, Mr. Hammond, in his " Political History of the State," inquires: " Did the Adams men in the New York legislature act with good faith towards their Clay friends ? " In answer to this question, I have to say, that by a strict and literal construction of the understanding, the Adams men *did* act in good faith. The friends of Mr. Clay claimed States which they indicated as certain for their candidate. Their list included Louisiana, in relation to which State there was some doubt. It was finally settled that if Louisiana should not vote for Mr. Clay, we should not be held to make good the failure of the seven men taken from the Crawford list of candidates to vote for Mr. Clay ; in other words, if Louisiana voted for Mr. Clay, we engaged that he should have seven votes from New York; so that if neither of the seven taken from the Crawford ticket would vote for Mr. Clay, we promised that seven Adams men should do so, the object being to secure Mr. Clay's return as one of the three candidates to be voted for in Congress. But Louisiana voted for General Jackson, and that left our friends free to vote for Mr. Adams.

I am bound, however, in fairness to say that the subject gave me much solicitude and annoyance. When the electors were chosen and the legislature adjourned, I remained at Albany, at the request of our leading friends, to see the electors on their arrival, and to explain to them the circumstances to which they were indebted for their election. These circumstances were set forth in a private letter signed by the leading Adams members of the Senate and Assembly, which was placed in my hands. I

found all, or nearly all, of the Adams electors, though professing a willingness to act in good faith towards Mr. Clay, yet personally unwilling to vote for him ; so unwilling indeed, that up
to the time news was received that Louisiana had gone for Jackson, I was unable to find the first Adams elector who would
consent to vote for Mr. Clay, even to save his friends and his
party from dishonor.   And I do not believe that had the State
of Louisiana gone in favor of Mr. Clay, seven votes could have
been obtained for him from the electoral college of New York.

There was great interest manifested, and a large attendance
of politicians at the Capitol, when the electoral college met.
Pierre E. Barker, an elector from Seneca County, whose name
had been transposed from the Crawford to the Union ticket,
and whose vote was claimed both for Crawford and for Clay,
was subjected to the pressing importunities of both parties.   He
occupied a room at the City Hotel next to mine, and made me
the depository of his embarrassments, annoyances, and persecutions.   Messrs. Van Buren, Marcy, and Talcott were pressing
him hard on the one hand, while General Porter, General
Clark, Mr. Mullett, and other friends of Mr. Clay were equally
zealous on the other hand.   This continued excitement day and
night made him exceedingly nervous.   He came to me early
one morning, quite bewildered, saying that he had frankly told
me how he was situated and what his views and feelings were,
and that he desired and had made up his mind to be governed
by my advice.   I asked him if he had not some friend in the
city whom he had known longer and better, and on whose judgment he could rely.   He said he had thought it all over, and
there was nobody but me to help him.   After further conversation, he remarked that he at one time thought of applying to
Judge William A. Duer, who was, when they resided in Dutchess County, a friend of his father.   I told him that, under
such circumstances, Judge Duer was undoubtedly his best and
safest adviser.   The judge had not taken any decided part in
the election.   I advised Mr. Barker to call on him, and to say
frankly that he had come to him as an old friend of his father,
under circumstances of peculiar embarrassment, for friendly
advice.   He did so.   The judge listened to the statement of his
truly complicated condition, and then advised him to vote for
Jackson ; but by no means, if he decided to act upon that ad-

vice, to let his purpose be known. Mr. Barker returned to my room with an elastic step, and in a most jubilant spirit. I saw, before he spoke, that his mind was at ease, and, although he promised Judge Duer to be silent, he could not leave me without pretty clear indication of the nature of the advice he had received, and of the vote he should cast. I also enjoined secrecy, and enforced the injunction by telling him that if it was known that he intended to vote for Jackson both the other factions would unite in tearing him to pieces.

I omitted to say, in the proper place, that several ineffectual attempts were made to bring the two Houses into joint ballot for the choice of electors; that when one party moved a joint ballot, the other, suspecting some advantage, or not feeling safe, would resist the motion, and, as the Senate was controlled by the Crawford men, and the House by the Adams and Clay men, the consent of both was indispensable, and as both knew that the question might turn on a single vote, all were of necessity vigilant and watchful. In this critical moment I had the advantage of close and confidential relations with the Hon. Oran Follett, a member of the Assembly from Genesee County. Mr. Follett was a printer and editor, who had originally preferred Mr. Adams as a candidate for President, but had yielded his support to Mr. Crawford as the nominee of his party. But Mr. Follett remained at heart an Adams man, and he had gone very reluctantly with his party against the electoral law. We conversed frequently and freely during the sessions, and until he found himself not at all unwilling to be beaten in the choice of electors. It so happened that when we were ready to go into joint ballot, and when a motion to that effect, coming from our side of the House, would have been resisted, that motion came from Mr. Follett, an influential member on the other side, and was successful.

More than forty years afterwards, an article which I had written on the presidential election of 1824 brought Mr. Follett, who was one of the few surviving actors in that scene, out with the following letter, which, it will be seen, is a part of the history of that memorable campaign : —

THE EDITOR OF THE "TRIBUNE " : —

SIR, — I have lately received, under the Oswego post-mark (I suppose from Mr. Bronson), a copy of a New York paper containing a review of the incidents of the presidential campaign of 1824, so far as they came under Mr. Bronson's observation at Albany. This has been supplemented by a copy of the "Tribune" of January 1st, containing a letter from my old friend, Thurlow Weed, reciting his experience on the same subject. Mr. Bronson's letter appears to have been provoked by what he deemed an unjust criticism of his course on that occasion. Mr. Bronson and myself, it seems, are the two sole surviving members (he of the Senate and I of the Assembly) of the memorable legislature of 1824, — memorable as well for the great number of very able men of which it was composed, as for its political action. I retain a vivid recollection of the events of that year, though since then more than half a century of not idle time has passed. It was my first lesson on so broad a field, and its teachings have not been without their use. At this distance of time, I can comprehend some of the difficulties of Mr. Bronson's position from my own experience.

The first move on the electoral question was made in the House by Mr. Wheaton, a member from New York, afterward minister to Sweden. The House was not fully organized for business. I was sitting with A. C. Flagg at the time, drawn together, I suppose, by the similarity of our business occupations. Objections were made to the reception of Mr. Wheaton's resolution, on the ground that it was out of order. The real objection was that the movement took the question out of the hands of "our party." Flagg was indignant. What was to be done? I suggested a committee of nine, one from each senatorial district, with one extra member for chairman. Flagg had the advantage of a year's experience in the legislature, and I insisted on his offering the substitute. He did so, and it was adopted. This was the origin of the famous committee of nine that played so prominent a part in the history of the electoral question. The Regency were good drill-masters, accustomed to obedience. The question of taking the choice of presidential electors from the legislature and giving it to the people had been started by what was called "the People's Party," composed of the friends of Clay, Adams, and Jackson, as a mere party expedient. The love or rights of the "people" were secondary affairs, and this was understood fully by the Regency. Yet the proposition had the merit of being right in the abstract, and therein lay the danger of opposing it. The first move by the managers was to have the bill rejected in the Assembly. But against this so many objections were raised that doubts were entertained of success.

Then commenced the "drill." I can understand something of what others went through (and perhaps Mr. Bronson among the rest) from my own case. Mr. Marcy was comptroller, and Mr. Croswell was state printer and one of the editors of the "Argus." I was invited to spend the evening at their rooms in a house situated across the street from old Congress Hall. They were both bachelors at the time, and the conference lasted so far beyond midnight that I "bunked" with "Neddy," as Croswell was sometimes called. The operation on me was unsuccessful. My recommendation was to make the question our own, pass the bill, and go with confidence to the people. If defeated, we should stand on good ground for future operations. But no, the House must reject the bill, rejection being a point settled; and as the Assembly was the more numerous body the responsibility would be so divided that individuals would escape severe censure. Not so with the Senate, as the sequel proved, and as Mr. Bronson experienced, at least temporarily. The bill giving to the people the choice of electors passed the Assembly with but five dissenting voices, though doubtless there were many mental reservations. The Regency grew desperate. The rejection in the Senate was a labored matter. And as Mr. Bronson says he was a Clay man, he probably experienced the pressure, as I know others did. The choice of the electors resting now with the legislature, as of old, the managers stood "on their native heath." The field was familiar, and they felt sure of bagging their game.

The winter session passed without material change in the position of parties, closing with that insane blunder, the removal of Mr. Clinton as canal commissioner. Mr. Weed's use of my name in connection with that event enables me to mention a circumstance of some interest in connection with subsequent associations. After the result was declared, I passed over to General Tallmadge's chair, and kindly asked why he voted in the affirmative. Putting his arm around my neck, and drawing my head down, he whispered hoarsely in my ear, " Mr. Follett, my relations with Mr. Clinton are such that I could not help it." It was supposed that General Tallmadge had committed political suicide. The necessities of party sometimes make strange bedfellows, as in this case. Mr. Clinton was the "people's" candidate for governor at the fall election, and General Tallmadge was his lieutenant. Both were elected, — Mr. Clinton because of his vindictive removal from the supervision of a work with which his name was inseparably connected, and General Tallmadge — certainly not for helping to do it! Party necessity (the old plea) made it expedient. There was a summer session called by proclamation of Governor Yates, for the purpose of reconsidering the electoral question. It was a bootless effort, as might have been foretold. A few weeks were spent in unprofitable debate, and the session was adjourned for the fall meeting, when the choice of presidential electors would be in order.

To make this narrative intelligible, I must here state that the Regency, under the pressure of a "political necessity," operating something like that in the case of General Tallmadge, felt constrained, notwithstanding Governor Yates' contumacy in calling the extra session, to make him the party candidate for governor.   In addition, a third candidate was brought into the field.   Colonel Sam Young was nominated on an avowed Clay ticket.   The result has already been told. The triumph of the People's Party — composed of all the elements of opposition — did not tend to harmonize matters at Albany.   The principal business before the legislature at its third session was, as already stated, the choice of electors.   The Senate had no serious difficulty in making a nomination.   But as each House had to nominate before they could come together for joint ballot, it was soon discovered that there was a deadlock in the Assembly.   The Senate adopted the Crawford ticket by a vote of 17, Mr. Clay and Mr. Adams each receiving 7 votes, one not voting.   In the House, with only the variation of one vote, the result stood : Adams, 50 ; Crawford, 43 ; Clay, 32 ; Jackson, 1 vote, cast by Grattan H. Wheeler, of Steuben. The legislature then, as now, consisted of 160 members, — 32 senators, 128 assemblymen ; necessary to a choice, all present and voting, 8.   On the vote given above, only 156 responded.   So long a time has elapsed since these events occurred that I cannot recall the exact course of daily proceeding.

I have said that the Regency was a good drill-master.   As soon as the real situation was understood, a series of evening meetings was called, consisting of twenty to twenty-five members (at which the leading men of the party were usually present), for the purpose of "talking over things."   Johnny Stilwell, a member of the Assembly from Albany County, and a resident of the city, was the usual messenger of invitation.   I will here remark that Roger Skinner, United States district judge, was Mr. Van Buren's *locum tenens* while he was absent attending the United States Senate.   At one of these meetings, at which (so far as my experience went) Judge Skinner always presided, the question how to break the deadlock was discussed.   Perley Keyes, Silas Wright, A. C. Flagg, and others were present, as probably was Mr. Bronson.   It was said that as the first object was to come to a joint ballot, it was not material whether the Clay ticket or the Adams ticket was nominated ; but it was soon manifest that the leaning was decidedly in favor of the former, and the question was about being put.   (I must here remark in parenthesis that, although acting with the Regency party on general questions, I was at heart an Adams

man, as Mr. Bronson says he was a Clay man.)   As I have said, the
question was about being put, when, with my heart in my mouth, I
arose and addressed the Chair, remarking, that as the main purpose
was to bring the two Houses to a joint ballot, it would seem as a separate proposition to make small difference which of the two tickets
was nominated.   But I suggested there were considerations outside
of this object which I thought were of sufficient importance to be taken
into the account.   I then, in a hurried, and in what was doubtless a
stumbling manner, reminded the Chair that we had just passed an exciting election, and that the man, Mr. Young, whose name headed the
Clay electoral ticket, was a candidate for governor in opposition to
the regular Republican (not Democratic, as I will explain) caucus
candidate.   Would not, I asked, the nomination of the Clay ticket,
with this man's name at the head, be in a measure an indorsement of
his offence ?   When I sat down there was silence for a moment; then
the chairman was the first to speak, remarking in substance, if not
literally : " Well, gentlemen, there is something in what our young
friend says."   After a few words on the point raised, he added, " Perhaps, gentlemen, we had better postpone the question for this evening."   To this there was assent without debate, almost silently, and
the caucus adjourned without, I think, naming a time for another
meeting.   Walter Livingston, of Columbia County, and myself were
the two youngest men in the legislature, which explains the expression, "our young friend."   My position was a delicate one, and I
spent a sleepless night upon it.   The question as to which ticket
should be nominated had been postponed, but not settled.   The air
was full of rumors of bargains, plots and counterplots.   By way of
scare, the Jackson ticket had once received twenty-five votes.   What
new combination was in store, no one could tell.   At the next meeting for drill some new combination might be formed, or it might be
deemed " expedient " after all to nominate the Clay ticket.   If that
was to be done I felt quite sure that I should not be invited to the
meeting, and, if present, what could one do outside the charmed circle
to stay action on an agreed thing?   Orders were to be obeyed, not
debated.   I could not consult with party friends, there were so many
shades of opinion.   My course was determined on.   I would nominate the Adams ticket next day in open session, and thus force action
in spite of drill or adverse bargain.   Of this I could not tell an Adams
man, for he would be sure to ask his best friends to help him keep
the secret.   I was on intimate terms with many Adams men, and Mr.
Weed among the rest, who, though not a member of the legislature,
was a trusted and active agent of the party.   Thus situated, I was
forced to forego all communion, and wait the hour.   It came, and I

nominated the ticket. The nomination was rather grudgingly sustained, first by Flagg, then by Waterman, of Broome, and Ruger, of Oneida, in succession, and adopted.

I will not occupy your columns by an attempt to describe the scenes that immediately succeeded the nomination, nor those of the next two days and nights, after what Mr. Weed has said. This move narrowed the choice to two candidates, Crawford and Adams. By a union of the friends of Mr. Clay with those of Mr. Adams, as described by Mr. Weed, votes enough were secured to carry Mr. Adams into the House of Representatives as one of the highest three candidates, resulting in his election to the presidency. Mr. Weed was witness of the fact that my nomination of the Adams ticket was a surprise to all parties, but he was never informed of the secret history of the movement until within the last two or three years. He could not therefore have entered into detail, had he felt it necessary to refer to the subject at all.

Among other matters belonging to the period I have preserved the division list of the House then in use, with the proclivities of the members marked thereon. I have also preserved the original electoral tickets for each candidate, as introduced and voted during the struggle. The Crawford and Adams tickets are both headed " Republican Ticket." The ticket for Jackson electors is headed " Jackson Ticket." The Clay ticket alone is headed " Democratic Ticket." And this is the explanation in part why in caucus I used the word " Republican " when alluding to the defection of Colonel Young, who, in addition to heading a ticket against the regular Republican candidate for governor, had written an open letter to Senator Jesse Clark in favor of the "people's " movement on the electoral law, which gave additional force to my objection. The name " Democrat " was not popular, and was in especial bad odor in the Slave States. As late as 1854, when Father Ritchie resumed temporary charge of the " Richmond Enquirer," he persisted in using " Republican " as the party designation, and the Regency sympathized with this early feeling. The name " Democrat," now in use by one of the great parties North and South, was originally a term of reproach, like that of Jacobin, and subsequently like that of Locofoco, and has been freely accepted at the South only since the Rebellion.

I write this short history in compliance with requests long since preferred by valued friends, and now renewed from various quarters since the appearance of Mr. Bronson's and Mr. Weed's letters. I will add, in conclusion, that I remained nominally a member of the party until word came from Washington that the Adams administration " must be put down, though pure as the angels at the right hand of God," followed by a coalition between Mr. Clinton and the Regency, and until the "Argus" found it convenient to change its phrase of "Mister" Jackson to "General" Jackson, when I withdrew from all affiliation with a party which so uniformly accepted expediency for principle.   ORAN FOLLETT.

SANDUSKY, OHIO, *February* 10, 1881.

SANDUSKY, *April* 11, 1881.

MINE ANCIENT: — I am in receipt of your favor of the 6th inst., and take pleasure in acknowledging it.

The review of incidents in lives so long and busy as ours have been, brings in its train sad as well as pleasant recollections.

Just before the receipt of your favor I received from the family of Mr. Bronson an Oswego paper announcing the death of our old compatriot. And the day before yours came to hand I had a letter of eight pages from our old friend Lewis H. Redfield, who writes himself down eighty-eight, in which he speaks of you and Mr. Bronson very feelingly. These occurrences turn to retrospection. I am satisfied with the main incidents of my life, so far as motive was concerned ; and I look with calmness on the future. What I would change, I feel that the recording angel will in my case, as in that of my Uncle Toby, drop a tear on the record and blot it out, knowing that weakness, not wickedness, was at the bottom.

You say you did not know before reading my letter in the "Tribune" "what a narrow escape we had in adjusting the electoral ticket." We are both getting old, my friend, and our memory needs jogging occasionally. When I wrote the "Tribune" article I had in mind a slight mention of the caucus incidents, some three years ago, at your house, in the presence of Mr. Seward. Subsequently it occurred to me to look at the copy of my letter to you in 1868. By turning to your files of the "New York Commercial Advertiser," you will find under date of February 17, 1868, quite a graphic account of the whole matter. It will doubtless amuse you to read it over again.

My letter to the "Tribune" bore date January 22. It was published March 24. Wishing you peace and happiness, I remain, very truly, your friend and obedient servant,   O. FOLLETT.

THURLOW WEED, ESQ., New York.

I am tempted here to relate an incident wholly of a personal nature, containing, however, a moral, which was useful to me through life, and may possibly be of service to others. I had given nearly the whole of my time from April till December to the presidential question. I had attended two extra sessions of the legislature and a meeting of the electoral college. I had traveled twice pretty thoroughly throughout the State, and with the exception of fifty dollars contributed by Mr. Verplanck, of the " New York American," wholly at my own expense. To defray these expenses I had borrowed two hundred and fifty dollars of Mr. Lewis Benedict, of Albany, and one hundred of General Walter Cunningham, of Poughkeepsie. I paid the money borrowed of Mr. Benedict, with interest, twelve years afterwards, not being able to do so at an earlier day. For the purpose of enabling me to discharge my debt to Mr. Benedict, and to pay my board, my political friends in the legislature signed a letter, addressed to Mr. Elisha Dorr, of Albany, one of the electors, saying that it was owing to my personal zeal and efforts that an Adams organization had been effected in the State, that I had contributed largely to the union between the Adams and Clay members of the legislature, a union to which the State and the nation were indebted for the defeat of the Regency and the Crawford party, and asking the electoral college to appoint me the messenger to carry their votes to Washington. When the electors assembled, the venerable Ebenezer Sage, of Suffolk County, was absent, and ex-Lieutenant Governor John Taylor, of Albany, was appointed to supply that vacancy. Governor Taylor, always distinguished for his hospitalities, gave the electors an entertainment; and before they left his house, and while under the influence of his oysters, comfits, and champagne, Mr. John Taylor Cooper, a grandson of the lieutenant-governor, was announced as a suitable gentleman as messenger to convey the electoral vote to Washington. Governor Taylor, not originally on the electoral ticket, knew nothing of the arrangements with reference to myself. Mr. Dorr, to whom the letter of the members of the legislature had been intrusted, had left before young Mr. Cooper was announced as a candidate. Mr. Burnham, of Cayuga, informed the electors under what circumstances I was a candidate; but Governor Taylor's high standing induced the electors to disregard other considerations, and by general consent Mr. Cooper's appointment was acquiesced in. On the following day Mr. Dorr produced his letter, and endeavored to secure my appointment, but it was too late. When the question was taken, the vote of the Adams men was divided between Mr. Cooper and myself. Mr. Russell, of Niagara County, himself an elector, received the vote of the Crawford electors. As there was no choice on the first ballot, Mr. Russell succeeded, by strong personal appeals, in securing a majority on a subsequent ballot, so that the vote of the State of New York in favor of Mr. Adams was carried to Washington by a Crawford messenger.

This disappointment, more crushing to me than the loss of a much more exalted place, under other circumstances, could have been, was " a blessing in disguise." As an office-seeker thenceforward I was " discharged, cured." To the question, which has been a thousand times asked, but never before responded to, why I never accepted office, this is my answer. From the day that shameful injustice was practiced, I have had an aversion and repugnance to office, which neither time, change, nor conditions have either overcome or weakened.

The senate chamber was crowded with prominent politicians on the morning of the day that the vote was to be taken. Among others were several warm friends of General Jackson, with Samuel Swartwout at their head. Mr. Swartwout asked me what the result of the ballot would be. I replied that there would be thirty votes for Mr. Adams, five for Mr. Crawford, and one for General Jackson. Up to that moment there had been no thought or expectation of a vote in the college for General Jackson. Mr. Swartwout was incredulous, and I repeated with emphasis that there would be one vote for General Jackson. On this he offered me a bet of a basket of champagne, which I accepted. When the vote for Andrew Jackson was announced it occasioned a spontaneous cheer from the audience. Mr. Swartwout paid his champagne most cheerfully. We invited our respective friends to dine with us that day at Crittenden's. Among others at the table I remember Peter B. Porter, Francis Granger, Colonel William J. Worth, General Tallmadge, Colonel James Munroe, Henry Wheaton, Judge Duer, Senators Haight, Ogden, Burt, Nelson, Gardiner, Burrows, and especially Pierre E. Barker, the elector who had voted for Jackson. It may be well to observe here, that four years afterwards, when General Jackson became President, Mr. Barker was rewarded with the office of collector of the port of Buffalo.

CHAPTER XIV.

1824.

WHILE walking in the street at Rochester one afternoon I observed an accident to a stage-coach, and went with others to proffer assistance. It proved to be but a slight mishap, and the party, which consisted of the families of Judge Miller, of Auburn, and Judge Seward, of Orange County, who were returning from Niagara, soon proceeded on their way. The casual meeting thus made was the beginning of my acquaintance with William H. Seward. It grew rapidly on subsequent occasions, when he was called to Rochester on professional business. Our views on general politics were not dissimilar, and in regard to anti-masonry he soon became imbued with my own opinions.

Very few of our citizens possess information, other than traditional, of the mode of travel between Albany and the western part of New York, even as late as 1824. Those who step into a railway car at Albany at seven o'clock in the morning, and step out to get their dinner in Rochester at two o'clock, P. M., will find it difficult to believe that, within the memory of by no means the " oldest inhabitant," it required, in muddy seasons of the year, seven nights' and six days' constant traveling in stages to accomplish the same journey.

And yet that was my own experience in April, 1824. We left Albany at eight o'clock in the evening, and traveled diligently for seven nights and six days. The road from Albany to Schenectady, with the exception of two or three miles, was in a horrible condition; and that west of Schenectady, until we reached " Tripes " or "Tribes Hill," still worse. For a few miles, in the vicinity of the Palatine Church, there was a gravelly road, over which the driver could raise a trot; but this was a luxury experienced in but few localities, and those " far between." Passengers walked, to ease the coach, several miles each day and each night. Although they did not literally carry rails on their shoulders, to pry the coach out of ruts, they were frequently called upon to use rails for that purpose. Such snail-paced movements and such discomforts in travel would be regarded as unendurable now. And yet passengers were patient, and some of them even cheerful, under all those delays and annoyances. That, however, was an exceptional passage. It was only when we had "horrid bad" roads that stages "drew their slow lengths along."

But stage-coach traveling had its bright as well as its dark aspects. I will endeavor to reverse the scene. Take, for illustration, an early September day. The coach leaves Rochester after breakfast in the morning, if with a full complement, nine passengers inside and two on the box with the driver. At Pittsford and Mendon and Victor, where the stage stops to change the mail and water the horses, a lady or boy, but usually a lady, comes with a basket of peaches, of which the passengers are invited to partake, but for which they are not permitted to pay, except in thanks. At Canandaigua, a beautiful village, then rejoicing in a greater number of distinguished men than are now to be found in any interior city of our State, we get dinner; and the dinners at "Blossom's," as all who ate them will remember, were dinners indeed. To prove what I say in relation to the distinguished residents of Canandaigua, I will name Gideon and Francis Granger (postmasters-general under Madison, in 1812, and Harrison, in 1840), Nathaniel W. Howell, John Greig, John C. Spencer, Myron Holley, Oliver Phelps, Dudley Marvin, Henry B. Gibson, Jared Wilson, Mark H. Sibley, etc.; two or three of whom are almost certain to become our fellow passengers. Peter Townsend and Joseph Everingham are highly intelligent young merchants from New York city, who have lately established themselves there. George H. Boughton, subsequently a state senator and canal commissioner from Lockport, was then a merchant's clerk at Canandaigua. There were others, if not wits themselves, the occasion of wit in others. To this class *Spienceer Chopin*, who mawkishly affected the Scottish accent, and Judge Atwater belonged. When a prisoner was on trial for an attempt to break open Judge Atwater's mansion, the judge himself became a witness.

His manner was deliberate, and his language pedantic. He stated that he was awakened at the "witching time" of night by an unusual noise ; that on listening attentively he became satisfied that burglars were attempting to enter his castle; that he assumed an erect position on his bed, and at that particular moment "Bose" spoke. Dudley Marvin, the prisoner's counsel, rose, and with quaint solemnity said : "May it please the Court, I am not a little surprised that the witness, himself an eminent jurist, who on other occasions graces the seat which your Honor now occupies, should so far forget the law of evidence and the gravity of a charge which affects the liberty of my client, as to proceed in this most irregular manner. No person knows better than my distinguished friend, Judge Atwater, that the testimony he is giving is wholly irregular. If it is important that this court and jury should know what 'Bose' saw and heard on the night of this alleged burglary, Bose himself must take the witness's stand. Bose is no stranger ; we all know him as sagacious, observing, and vigilant." This produced an irresistible outbreak, involving the audience, the bar, the jury, and the court, in roars of laughter. And when, after an interval of several moments, order was attempted to be restored, it was found quite impracticable to proceed, and the case was actually laughed out of court. Here we find as fellow-passengers, Mr. Wadsworth or Major Spencer, of Geneseo, Mr. Ellicott or Mr. Evans, of Batavia, Mr. Coit, Major J. G. Camp, or R. B. Heacock, of Buffalo, General Porter, of Black Rock, General Paine, of Ohio, and others, who arrive in the stage from Buffalo.

Leaving Canandaigua, we are driven through a charming series of agricultural landscapes to Geneva, sixteen miles, where we have a view of its beautiful lake, a lake not unlike or unworthy of its equally beautiful namesake in Switzerland. At Geneva either Joseph Fellows, a land agent, Henry Dwight, a banker, or Mr. Prouty, a merchant, is pretty sure to join us. From Geneva to Waterloo, four miles, seems but a turn of the kaleidoscope, and the distance from Waterloo to Seneca Falls is gotten over in no time. At Seneca Falls the chances are at least one to two that we are joined by Colonel Mynderse, who is going over to Auburn to visit his friend Judge Miller.

The drive over Cayuga Bridge, more than a mile in length,

was always pleasurable and interesting. Some one would remark how much it was to be regretted that a lake so large should be of so little practical value, not being used for purposes of navigation or inhabited by fish of any value.[1] Looking north, we discern the Montezuma marshes, where Comfort Tyler failed to manufacture salt; while a southerly view, though you do not actually see, directs your attention to the beautiful village of Aurora, near the head of the lake, then the residence of Jethro Wood,[2] Humphrey Howland, Ebenezer Burnham, Ephraim Marsh, etc., and now of the Morgans, wealthy and reputable merchants; also of William H. Bogart, the veteran senate reporter, and the "Sentinel" letter-writer of the New York "Courier and Enquirer" and New York "World," a gentleman who has been for more than thirty years about the legislature without becoming obnoxious to charges of improperly interfering with legislation. Here, too, resides in palatial splendor Henry Wells, who, more than thirty-five years ago, "solitary and alone," with a single carpet-bag, founded and inaugurated what is now the American Merchants' Union Express Company. I first knew Mr. Wells more than forty years ago, teaching boys "how not" to stutter. My only son was one of his pupils. But though Mr. Wells cured others, he could not cure himself. Mr. Wells still lives to enjoy the fruits of his prosperity, and may he live long and happily, for I have known few men more worthy of prosperity. A few miles from Aurora, beautifully situated upon the lake shore, is a valuable farm, purchased many years ago by Moses H. Grinnell, one of the merchant princes of the city of New York, for some relatives, who reside there.

When finally over the long bridge, we discuss Thomas Mumford, a lawyer residing at the end of it, and Colonel Goodwin, a worthy tavern-keeper, midway between Cayuga Bridge and Auburn. And during the many years that I was accustomed to travel in stages between Cayuga and Auburn, I cannot remember the time that some one of the passengers did not amuse the coach by relating an incident that occurred to Mr. John C. Spencer several years before. The coach drove up to the hotel

---

[1] Cayuga Lake is now inhabited by excellent fish, and navigated by steam and canal boats.

[2] The inventor of the iron plow.

at the end of the bridge, to water the horses. It was a dark, rainy, cold evening. The stage was full inside and out. A lady, closely veiled, came to the steps, who was, as the keeper of the hotel said, very anxious, on account of sickness in the family where she resided, to get to Goodwin's that evening. The passengers said it was impossible, as there were already nine of them inside. But Mr. Spencer, prompted by his sympathies or his politeness, as it was but four miles, thought a lady ought not to be refused a passage, and offered, if she chose to accept it, a seat on his lap. The offer was accepted, the lady took her seat, and the stage dashed off. At Goodwin's Tavern, where the lady got out, a light was brought to enable her to find a part of her luggage, and when she removed her veil, a very ebony colored individual of the feminine gender was revealed, to the consternation of Mr. Spencer, and the amusement of the other passengers !

At Auburn we rest for the night, having made sixty-four miles. In the evening, the magnates of the village drop into the hotel bar-room to gossip with the stage passengers. There were no sitting or drawing rooms at hotels in those days; nor could a single lodging room, or even single bed, be obtained. In country inns, a traveler who objected to a stranger as a bed-fellow was regarded as unreasonably fastidious. Nothing was more common, after a passenger had retired, than to be awakened by the landlord, who appeared with a tallow candle, showing a stranger into your bed!

The leading men of Auburn were Judge Miller, George B. and E. S. Throop (since governor), Nathaniel Garrow, Parliament Bronson, etc. William H. Seward had commenced his professional and public life at Auburn one year before. Genial "Kit" Morgan was at Yale College.

In the morning, the stage was off between daylight and sunrise. The passengers refreshed themselves, enjoyed a view of refreshed and invigorated nature, to which the rising sun soon began to impart light and life. The canal was attracting business and population; the stage had just begun to run over the Northern or New Turnpike, leaving the villages of Skaneateles, Marcellus, Onondaga, West Hill, Onondaga Hollow, and Jamesville, on the line of the old turnpike, to a process of decay which has rendered them almost obsolete. I ought to have remarked that, at Auburn, passengers always dreaded an acquisition to their number in the person of Mr. Wood, who, weighing some four hundred pounds, and inconveniently broad across the shoulders and transom, made the coach every way uncomfortable. As a sleeper and snorer, he would compare favorably with any one of " the seven." For ten or fifteen miles there was little of outside interest to talk about. In passing through Camillus, the richly cultivated farms and large granaries of the brothers Squire, David and Nathan Munro, attracted attention, and some one would be pretty sure to remark that " the Munros not only owned the best farms in the town themselves, but had mortgages on all their neighbors' farms," which was true. Our approach to stage-houses and post-offices was announced by the blowing of a tin horn or trumpet, with more or less skill, by the driver. This drew together a crowd of idlers, with this difference between New York and many parts of Europe, — that instead of beleaguering the coach with imploring appeals for charity, our visitors would generally present us with some choice fruit.

At Syracuse, twenty-five miles from Auburn, we breakfasted. Syracuse then, as now, was a marvel in the suddenness and rapidity of its growth. And here, *my* story came in. I had worked in the Onondaga furnace in 1811 and 1812, and remembered having gone through what was now the flourishing village of Syracuse, with six or seven hundred inhabitants, when it was a tangled and almost impenetrable swamp, thickly inhabited by frogs and water-snakes. Indeed, the swamp foliage was so thick, and darkened the atmosphere to such an extent, that the owls, mistaking day for night, could be heard hooting. Upon the locality over which the now large and beautiful city of Syracuse has extended, there was, in 1811, but one human habitation ; that was Cossett's Tavern, on the site of the present Empire House. At the western boundary of the swamp, on the creek which empties into the lake, there was a small grist-mill and two log-cabins. In September, 1812, soon after the declaration of war with England, a letter was written by the Secretary of the Navy (Dr. Eustis), showing how lamentably that cabinet minister's geographical education had been neglected. Captain Woolsey, who commanded the United States brig Oneida, was ordered to proceed from Oswego to Onondaga, there to take on board the cannon ball manufactured at the Onondaga furnace for the government.[1]

And this incident reminds me of another, and one which at this day will be regarded almost as incredible as the order of the Secretary of the Navy; for, while ships were unable to ascend the rifts and falls of the Oswego River, salmon did make their way from Lake Ontario through the Oswego River and the Onondaga Lake into the Onondaga Creek, and were killed two miles south of the city of Syracuse. I remember well of being attracted, in the spring of 1811, to Wood's mill-dam by torches flitting below the dam in the creek. Arriving at the spot, I saw Onondaga Indians with clubs watching for and killing salmon, as they were seen making their way over the rifts. I joined in the sport, and came out with a fine salmon as my share of the spoils. I carried my salmon to Mr. Joshua Forman (then a lawyer in Onondaga Hollow, subsequently the inventor and father of Syracuse), for which he paid me a large, round, bright silver dollar; this being my exact recollection of a coin which was of more value to me then, and was a source of higher gratification, than the receipt of thousands of dollars in after years. I then spoke of Judge Asa Danforth, indicating his residence in the Hollow, who was the first white inhabitant of Onondaga County. This led me to speak of Ephraim Webster, a white boy found among the Onondaga Indians, after the Revolutionary War, in the Mohawk Valley. Young Webster, as he grew up, like Joseph among the Egyptians, grew in favor with the Indians. Before white inhabitants reached that part of the State, young Webster had been made a chief of the Onondaga nation, and had married a daughter of an Indian, and received as her bridal portion a mile square of the lands belonging to the Onondaga nation. Mr. Webster continued to reside with his Indian wife and the tribe long after the county was organized and settled by white inhabitants. In 1808 or 1809, Governor Tompkins appointed Mr. Webster agent of the State, to receive and disburse the money paid annually to the Onondaga nation. He was subsequently appointed a Justice of the Peace and Judge of the County Court. After the death of his Indian wife, in 1810

---

[1] This is paralleled by the supply of tanks for *holding fresh water*, sent from England for the English vessels of war built at Kingston during the War of 1812.

or 1811, he married an intelligent and reputable white lady, with whom he was living happily when I last heard of him, with children by both wives growing up in harmony and affection. Mr. Webster was a man of good sense, good habits, and good character, enjoying alike the respect and confidence of his white and red neighbors and acquaintances.

After breakfast, we leave Syracuse and drive rapidly on to Manlius Square, where passengers were always warmly welcomed at the stage-house by its host, Colonel Elijah Phillips, one of nine brothers, all men of mark, of whom I shall have occasion to speak hereafter. Mrs. Phillips, an estimable lady, was the granddaughter of Judge Danforth, and the first white child born in the county of Onondaga. Manlius was the residence of Azariah Smith, a merchant remarkable for his enterprise, activity, industry, and integrity. He had a greater and more varied capacity for business than any other man I have ever known. He was many years supervisor of the town, doing not only his own business thoroughly, but the business of almost every member of the Board of Supervisors. As a member of the legislature, his time and talents were severely taxed. Though chairman of the Committee on Claims, and a member of two or three other working committees, while discharging all their duties promptly, he found leisure and was always ready to do the work of fifteen or twenty idle or incompetent members from other counties. He was also an administrator or executor of such of his neighbors as left property requiring attention.

If, as the horn blew for passengers to take their seats, John Meeker did not, at the last moment, make his appearance, some one would express surprise at his absence. John Meeker was an extraordinary man. He owned and cultivated three or four of the largest farms in the towns of Pompey, Tully, and Preble. He had stores, not only in those three towns, but in Fabius, Homer, and Manlius, managed under his personal supervision by clerks. He always sold produce at the lowest prices for cash, or on approved credit. He paid the highest prices in cash or goods for black salts, and for pot and pearl ashes. He had an ashery as an appendage to each of his stores. He went frequently to Albany and New York to purchase goods. He was an uneducated man, with the appearance and in the costume of a common farmer. With all these establish-

ments, spreading over so large a surface, it will be apparent
that Mr. Meeker was a man of extraordinary business talents;
but when people have so many irons in the fire, some of them
will inevitably burn, while others as inevitably get cold ; and
in the end, like many others who over-trade, John Meeker
" came to grief."

In passing near the town of Pompey, Pompey Hill would
be suggested as the residence of Henry Seymour, a capable
canal commissioner (and father of ex-Governor Horatio Seymour). Victory Birdseye, an eminent lawyer and equally eminent statesman, also resided at Pompey Hill. There, too, Samuel S. Baldwin, a flash lawyer and fast gentleman, resided. He
married Juliana, a daughter of Judge Peter W. Yates, who
enjoyed a waxwork celebrity in Trowbridge's Museum as the
" Albany beauty." Judge Yates, when, in the early years of
the present century, he resided at Albany, occupied, if he did
not erect, the mansion subsequently owned by James Kane,
and successively occupied by Governors Tompkins, Clinton,
and Seward.

From Manlius we passed through Eagle Village to Canas-
eraga Hollow, where the chances were in favor of picking up
General J. J. M. Hurd, of Cazenovia, a merchant with agreeable manners, who went to Albany and New York to purchase
goods as often as was convenient, he evidently fancying that
part of his business. In ascending a hill, eastward, the stage
stops at the suggestion of some passenger, who invites the others
to go with him a few rods from the road and look at an immense petrified tree, lying upon the surface, and perfect, except
where it had been broken to gratify the curiosity of visitors,
each of whom, of course, carried away a specimen. A few
miles further east brought us to Quality Hill, where passengers always promised themselves enjoyment at the expense of
a most polite, obsequious, and good-natured tavern-keeper. Mr.
Webb (for that was his name) was truly an original. In deportment, if he had lived in London, and been a dancing-mas-
ter, instead of keeping a hotel on Quality Hill, he might have
rivaled Turveydrop; in his zeal to preserve the credit of his
house, and his tact in concealing the meagreness of his larder,
Caleb Balderstone might have taken lessons with advantage
from our host of Quality Hill. Here, in all probability, one of

the numerous family of Spencers would be added to our list of passengers, among the survivors of whom I know only Mr. Julius Spencer, a most worthy man and an essential fixture in the Albany office of the New York Central Railroad. Proceeding eastward, and after rising Breakneck Hill, we came to the Oneida Castle, the residence of the Oneida tribe of Indians. These Indians, long surrounded by white inhabitants, had emerged from their savage habits and customs, and were enjoying the advantages of civilization. These advantages consisted in loafing about taverns and groceries and in drinking bad whiskey. Full two thirds of the tribe had ceased to hunt, or to fish, or to cultivate their lands, than which none more fertile were to be found in the State. Large numbers of both sexes were idling about the tavern, all or nearly all of them endeavoring to sell some trinket for the purpose of buying whiskey. This process of demoralization went on until the few who did not die prematurely were induced to emigrate to Wisconsin. After leaving the Castle, the passengers would talk of the devotion of Rev. Mr. Kirkland to the Oneida Indians, of the eloquence of Skenando, one of their aged chiefs, and of a French officer, Colonel de Ferrier, who married an Indian wife at Oneida Castle, and whose sons and daughters were well educated ladies and gentlemen ; and this topic would scarcely be exhausted when we were driven into the village of Vernon, where we always changed horses.

In Vernon itself there was nothing especially remarkable. The hotel was kept by a Mr. Stuart, whose sons and grandsons were persons of more or less consideration in different parts of the State for many years afterward. From Vernon to Westmoreland was but a few miles. The hotel at Westmoreland was kept by Mrs. Cary, a widow lady with six or seven attractive and accomplished daughters, who, as far as propriety allowed, made the hotel pleasant for its guests. These young ladies, quite well known by intelligent and gentlemanly stage passengers, were sometimes irreverently designated as " Mother Cary's chickens." In this, however, no disrespect was intended, for, though chatty and agreeable, they were deservedly esteemed, and all, " in the course of human events," were advantageously married.

From Westmoreland we were driven rapidly through New

Hartford into Utica, seventy-two miles from Auburn. This was the end of our second day's journey. But, for the accommodation of those who preferred a night ride, a stage left Utica at nine P. M. Those to whom time was important took the night line. We, however, will remain over. Utica is now no " pent-up " place. But as, in an earlier part of this narrative, I have given a brief account of its highly intelligent citizens, we will pass on. And departing early the next morning, the first object that attracts the attention is the pleasantly-situated mansion and fruitful surroundings of Colonel Walker, an aide-de-camp of General Washington in the Revolutionary War. A few miles farther on, as we cross the Mohawk River, the humble farmhouse pointed out is the residence of Major-General Widrig, who was ordered, with his division, into the service during the War of 1812. But that major-general was found to be so lamentably deficient in penmanship, orthography, and arithmetic as to render his resignation as proper as it proved acceptable. Farther on, in the town of Schuyler, I pointed to a lofty, two-pronged pine tree, under which, in September, 1814, the regiment to which I belonged, commanded by Colonel Matthew Myers, of Herkimer, ate its first ration ; and where, to my great satisfaction and as grateful remembrance, the quartermaster of the regiment, George Petrie, then a merchant, subsequently a member of Congress, and now a venerable clerk in the General Post Office at Washington, appointed me his quartermaster's sergeant.

Before reaching the ancient village of Herkimer, we were driven over the fertile and celebrated German Flats, nearly a thousand acres of which were owned by Judge Jacob Weaver and Colonel Christopher Bellinger. They were neighbors, and, unless drawn into political discussion, warm friends. During a sharply contested election in the spring of 1814, while at the polls, these old gentlemen collided. The conversation waxed warmer and warmer, until they were about to engage in a personal conflict. Friends, however, interfered in season to avert what both in their cooler moments would have lamented. Subsequently they shook hands and calmly reviewed their cause of quarrel. " You ought not," said Colonel Bellinger, " to have lost your temper." " And you ought not," said Judge Weaver, " to have called me a British Tory." " I only did so," said

Colonel Bellinger, " after you called me a French Jacobin."
" And then," said Judge Weaver, " you not only called me a
British Tory again, but said that I rejoiced when Oxenburgh
was taken, and I could n't stand that." Many amusing anecdotes were told of Judge Weaver's early life, when he was a
merchant and trading with the Indians. In purchasing furs,
as the story goes, his hand, placed on the scale opposite the
fur, weighed half a pound, and his foot a pound. His accounts were kept on boards, in chalk. One of his neighbors,
Mr. Harter, in settling an account found himself charged with
a cheese. Being a farmer, and making not only cheese for his
own table, but cheese he was in the habit of selling at the store,
he asked an explanation. Judge Weaver, priding himself upon
his accuracy, was impatient with all who disputed his accounts.
But Mr. Harter appealed to his reason and common sense to
show how improbable, if not impossible, it was, that he who
made cheese for sale should have been a purchaser. This perplexed the judge, who, after thinking and talking for a long
time, was unwilling, under the circumstances, to press his neighbor to pay for a cheese, and equally unwilling to admit an inaccuracy in his bookkeeping. The question was finally laid
over till the next day, in the hope that the judge might be
able to verify the integrity of his books, or boards. On the
following day, when Mr. Harter appeared, the judge met him
in jubilant spirits, exclaiming, " It is all right ; I remember all
about it now." " But," said his neighbor, " you don't mean to
say that I bought the cheese ! " " No, no," said the merchant ;
" it was not a cheese, but a grindstone ; and I forgot to put
the hole in it ! " In Judge Weaver's mode of bookkeeping, a
circular chalk-mark represented a cheese, while the same mark,
with a dot in the centre, converted it into a grindstone. Those
two splendid farms have long since, by a very common process,
been melted into one. General Christopher P. Bellinger married the daughter of Judge Weaver, and thus inherited both
farms. General Bellinger, a very worthy man, with whom I
served in the legislature of 1830, and who has been for fifty-
seven years my intimate friend, is still living. Here resided
also Major Weber, a wealthy German farmer, who was with us
at Sackett's Harbor. Though a second officer in our regiment,
he found the service anything but pleasant. I have an order

now in my possession, directing me to take possession of a building for a regimental hospital, no word of which with more than two syllables is spelt right, and which is signed " J. P. Weber, Comadand." On one occasion, when Sir James Yeo's fleet appeared off Sackett's Harbor, for the purpose, as was supposed, of landing troops, and our regiment, with others, was ordered to a point directly opposite the fleet, Major Weber was in a greatly excited state, constantly asking subordinates and privates if they supposed the British intended to land, and complaining of the injustice of pushing militia instead of regular troops into such an exposed position. It was not, he said, on his own account that he was unwilling to be crowded into battle where he was sure to be killed, but on account of the feelings of his wife, who was in delicate health. He inquired also whether he couldn't resign his commission. Fortunately, however, for the major, after a couple of hours of trepidation and suspense the fleet made sail and soon disappeared.

From Herkimer to Little Falls, seven miles, there were no particular attractions; nor indeed was there much of interest at the Falls, a small village, with a valuable water-power, nearly unavailable on account of its being owned by Mr. Edward Ellice, a non-resident Englishman. Mr. Ellice was a large landholder in this State and in Canada. It was my privilege, in 1861 and 1862, to become well acquainted with him in London. He enjoyed the reputation of being the most influential commoner in England. He was a man of giant frame and intellect. He was one of the oldest members of Parliament, and had been once or twice a member of the British Cabinet. He died at his country-seat in Scotland in 1864, in the eighty-third year of his age. The London residence of Mr. Ellice, in Arlington Street, looking into St. James's Park, now improved and modernized, was occupied by Horace Walpole a century ago, and in it many of his celebrated letters were written.

From Little Falls we come after an hour's ride to a hill, by the bank of the river, which several years before General Scott was descending in a stage, when the driver discovered, at a sharp turn near the bottom of the hill, a Pennsylvania wagon winding its way up diagonally. The driver saw but one escape from a disastrous collision, and that, to most persons, would have appeared even more dangerous than the collision. The driver, however, having no time for reflection, instantly guided his team over the precipice and into the river, from which the horses, passengers, coach, and driver were safely extricated. The passengers, following General Scott's example, made the driver a handsome present as a reward for his courage and sagacity. We dine at East Canada Creek, where the stage-house, kept by Mr. Couch, was always to be relied on for excellent ham and eggs, and fresh brook trout. Nothing of especial interest until we reach Spraker's, a well-known tavern that neither stages nor vehicles of any description were ever known to pass. Of Mr. Spraker, senior, innumerable anecdotes were told. He was a man without education, but possessed strong good sense, considerable conversational powers, and much natural humor. Most of the stories told about him are so Joe-Millerish that I will repeat but one of them. On one occasion he had a misunderstanding with a neighbor, which provoked both to say hard things of each other. Mr. Spraker, having received a verbal hot shot from his antagonist, reflected a few moments and replied, "Ferguson, dare are worse men in hell dan you;" adding, after a pause, "but dey are chained." Mr. Spraker used to say that when his son David was a boy, he thought he would make a smart man; but he sent him to college, and when he came back from Schenectady he did n't know enough to earn his living.

At Canajoharie a tall, handsome man, with graceful manners, is added to our list of passengers. This is the Hon. Alfred Conkling, who in 1820 was elected to Congress from this district, and who has just been appointed judge of the United States District Court for the Northern District of New York by Mr. Adams. Judge Conkling is now (in 1870) the oldest surviving New York member of Congress. The late Hon. Samuel R. Betts, recently United States Judge for the Southern District of New York, was elected to Congress from Orange County in 1815. John Cramer, of Saratoga, though the senior of Judge Conkling, being over ninety, was not elected to Congress until 1833.

In passing Conine's Hotel, near the Nose, the fate of a beautiful young lady, who "loved not wisely, but too well," with an exciting trial for breach of promise, etc., would be related. Still farther east, we stop at Failing's tavern to water. Though but an ordinary tavern in the summer season, all travelers cherish a pleasant remembrance of its winter fare ; for leaving a cold stage with chilled limbs, if not frozen ears, you were sure to find in Failing's bar and dining rooms " rousing fires ; " and the remembrance of the light, lively, " hot and hot" buckwheat cakes, and the unimpeachable sausages, would renew the appetite even if you had just risen from a hearty meal.

Going some miles farther east, we come in sight of a building on the south side of the Mohawk River, and near its brink, the peculiar architecture of which attracts attention. This was formerly Charles Kane's store, or rather the store of the brothers Kane, five of whom were distinguished merchants in the early years of the present century. They were all gentlemen of education, commanding in person, accomplished and refined in manners and associations. Charles Kane resided in Schenectady, James Kane in Albany, Oliver Kane in New York, Elias Kane in Philadelphia, and Archibald Kane in the West Indies. An incident which occurred there in 1808 is remembered by some one of the passengers, who relates it. Some gentlemen, who had been invited to dine there, amused themselves after dinner with cards. In the course of the evening a dispute arose between Oliver Kane and James Wadsworth, of Geneseo, a gentleman of high intelligence, great wealth, and enlightened philanthropy, the latter years of whose life were distinguished for zeal and liberality in the cause of normal schools and school district libraries. The quarrel resulted in a challenge, and the parties met before sunrise the next morning, under a tall pine tree, on a bluff behind the store, and exchanged shots, Mr. Kane receiving a slight wound. More than thirty years afterward, I was walking with Mr. Wadsworth and his son, the late General J. S. Wadsworth, in Broadway, where he met Mr. Oliver Kane, with whom young Mr. Wadsworth exchanged salutations ; and observing that his father passed making " no sign," he said, " Don't you know Mr. Kane? " "I met him once," was the laconic reply. Supposing that James had not heard of the duel, when we were alone I mentioned it to him, to which he replied, laughing, "I knew all about that, but I wanted to draw the governor out." I had endeavored, several years earlier, to induce Mr. Wadsworth to accept a nomination for governor, and thereafter James S. was accustomed to speak to and of him as governor.

Here Commodore Charles Morris, one of the most gallant of our naval officers, who in 1812 distinguished himself on board the United States frigate Constitution in her engagement with the British frigate Guerriere, passed his boyhood. In 1841, when I visited him on board of the United States seventy-four-gunship Franklin, lying off Annapolis, he informed me that among his earliest recollections was the launching and sailing of miniature ships on the Mohawk River. On the opposite side of the river, in the town of Florida, is the residence of Dr. Alexander Sheldon, for twelve years a member of the legislature from Montgomery County, serving six years as Speaker of the House of Assembly. The last year Dr. Sheldon was in the legislature, one of his sons, Milton Sheldon, was also a member from Monroe County. Another son, Smith Sheldon, who was educated for a drygoods merchant, drifted some years ago to the city of New York, and is now the head of the extensive publishing house of Sheldon & Co., Broadway.

The next points of attraction were of much historical interest. Sir William and Guy Johnson built spacious and showy mansions a few miles west of the village of Amsterdam, long before the Revolution, in passing which interesting anecdotes, relating to the English baronet's connection with the Indians, were remembered. A few miles west of Sir William Johnson's, old stagers would look for an addition to our number of passengers, in the person of Daniel Cady, a very eminent lawyer, who resided at Johnstown, and for more than fifty years was constantly passing to and from Albany. At Amsterdam, Marcus T. Reynolds, then a rising young lawyer of that village, often took his seat in the stage, and was a most companionable traveler. He subsequently removed to Albany, where for more than a quarter of a century he held a high professional and social position.

And now, as the valley of the Mohawk spreads out more broadly, and the eye wanders over fields teeming with the bountiful products of Mother Earth, we come in view of Schenectady, first seen by a graduate of Union, who immediately becomes eloquent in his laudation of Dr. Nott, whose sermon at Albany against duelling, occasioned by the death of General Hamilton, is claimed as the greatest effort of the age. Our graduate would then enumerate the distinguished men scattered over the Union who owed their success in life to Dr. Nott's peculiar mode of lectures and training. Then, as we approached the old bridge across the Mohawk he would tell us how long it had withstood storm and tempest, and how many dark secrets it would disclose if it could talk. Next, he would have a brief history of Mr. Givens, the gentlemanly keeper of the hotel in Schenectady, and of his still more gentlemanly son, Major Givens, who brought back from West Point to Schenectady all the discipline and proprieties, physical and social, of a military education, and who vibrated for half a century between Schenectady and Saratoga, saying and doing polite and civil things to and for everybody. Perhaps allusion might be made to Mr. Given's predecessor in the hotel, only for the purpose of remarking that his daughter, a beautiful and accomplished young lady, rejected wealthy suitors for the sake of the fine person and melodious voice of a music master, preferring, it would seem, musical to circulating notes; concluding, almost certainly, with an account of a phrenological discussion, in which Governor Yates floored his antagonist by saying, " My head is not so long as Governor Clinton's, but it is a great deal *ticker*."

From Schenectady to Albany, the drive through dwarf pines and a barren soil, the turnpike road ornamented with poplar trees at uniform distances on either side, was tame, and, unless enlivened by conversation, dull. But it was an unusual circumstance to find a stage-coach, with fair weather and good roads, between Rochester and Albany, that was not enlivened by conversation, for there were almost always two or three intellectual passengers. Myron Holley, for example, with a gifted and highly-cultivated mind, had committed to memory, and would recite by the hour, gems from the British poets. Mr. Granger also had a good memory, and would often, during the evening, recite from Burns, Moore, and others. Richard L. Smith, a lawyer from Auburn, with his wit and drolleries would make hours and miles seem short. And there was an unfailing source of fun at every stopping-place in the " gibes and jokes " of the stage-drivers, who, as a class, were as peculiar, quaint, and racy as those represented by the senior and junior Weller in " Pickwick," as Samivel described them, — a class of highly-social individuals, who have been driven off the roads and compelled to earn a precarious living by tending pikes and switches, or

marrying " vidders," and whose unintellectual successors are
engine-drivers and stokers.

The stage-drivers of that day lived merry but short lives.
The exceptions were in favor of those who, after a few years'
experience, married some reputable farmer's daughter on their
route, and changed their occupation from stage-driving to farming. This must, I think, have been the case with one of my
earliest stage-driving acquaintances. It is but a few weeks
since I saw in the papers the announcement of the death, somewhere in Tompkins County, of Phineas Mapes, aged eighty
years. " Phin Mapes," a rollicking stage-driver at Catskill, is
one of my earliest remembrances. In 1803 or 1804, a stage
with four live horses was an institution, at least in the admiring
eyes of boys. I remember with what a flourish Mapes used
to dash up to the post-office door, and, while Dr. Croswell was
assorting the mail, how gracefully and gently he would throw
his long whip-lash over the backs of the leaders, and how, by
the responsive action of their fore-feet, nostrils, and ears, they
would show how well they understood that he meant it playfully. How well, too, I remember when, in 1810 or 1811, I renewed my acquaintance with this driver at Skaneateles, between
which place and Onondaga Hollow he was blowing his horn and
cracking his whip and his jokes, quite as popular here as he had
been at Catskill. The oldest inhabitants of Catskill and Skaneateles, as well as the few survivors who rode in stages upon
the great Genesee turnpike sixty years ago, will remember
Phin Mapes pleasantly, from whom, in his best days, Dickens
might have found a " jolly " original for Mark Tapley.

CHAPTER XV.

1824–1825.

HAVING given, as well as my memory serves me, a narrative of political events in this State connected with the presidential election of 1824, I will now endeavor to bring up whatever else seems of interest during the year. When not traveling on political errands through the State, I was at my work in the printing-office at Rochester, where, as often as I returned from my missions, I was warmly received by troops of friends. I greatly enjoyed at the time my Rochester residence, and look back now upon it as among the most pleasant of the many pleasant years of my life. When I returned after the adjournment of the August session of the legislature, we commenced the organization of a " People's Party " in the county, which did not at first promise success. The county, from its organization, had been Democratic. A good deal of inquiry had been aroused, but it had taken no form. We had, the year before, organized in favor of Mr. Adams in the village; but during my absence in the winter and most of the summer, little had been done. We decided, therefore, to call a mass county meeting, and took steps to secure a good attendance from the county towns. On the day of the meeting, several of us went personally about the village to rally those who sympathized with us, so that, in numbers at least, the meeting should not be a failure. But our efforts were not very encouraging. This was apparent to our

opponents.   There was, at that time, a legislative investigation
into alleged abuses in the construction of the Genesee River
Canal Aqueduct going on in the village.   The committee consisted of Azariah C. Flagg, of Clinton County, John Stilwell,
of Albany, and Grant B. Baldwin, of Tioga.   The two former
were Crawford men, and the latter an Adams man.   About an
hour before the time the meeting was to assemble at the Court
House, a colored man, employed to pass through the streets in
fantastic costume, ringing a bell and giving notice of auctions,
passed through the streets, ringing more vociferously than usual,
and in a loud voice, with vehement gestures, inviting "all good
people to attend the people's meeting at the Court House, to
hear the lion roar and see the bear dance."   This created great
amusement, and at first threatened to turn our meeting into
ridicule, but three or four quick-witted young men circulated
through the village and turned the tables by saying that the
negro Tom had been employed and paid by Messrs. Flagg and
Stilwell.   This spread with electric rapidity.   The people came
rushing towards the Court House from all quarters, denouncing
the Albany Regency, and exclaiming that the men who had refused to let the people choose presidential electors should not
overawe independent voters or throw ridicule upon a popular
movement.   The first people's meeting, therefore, in Monroe
County, owing to the fortunate turn given to a ludicrous incident, was a great success.   At least one fourth of the villagers
who attended the meeting had previously taken no part or acted
with the Democrats.   We went on from that day vigorously
with our organization.

The "Telegraph," which I continued to edit, had a large and
constantly increasing circulation.   I found earnest co-laborers
among all classes of citizens, but most especially so among the
merchants and mechanics.   How well I remember the warm-
hearted and patriotic men of that day, and how grateful to my
feelings it would be to give them by name the credit so justly
due!   But, alas! time has taken almost all of them where the
voice of praise and censure are alike unheard.   My friend, S.
G. Andrews, became an active Adams man.   General Matthews, Mr. Works, Dr. Backus, Judge Elisha B. Strong, General E. S. Beach, James K. Livingston, and others were among
our most prominent friends; while James Frazer, Gilbert Ever-

ingham, John Marchant, General Jacob Gould, the Haywoods, the Binghams, Jaspers, Danes, Ashbel Steele, Colonel A. W. Riley, Dr. Marvin, John F. Bush, Seeley Matthews, and others, were hearty, indomitable day-and-night workers. Among a class still younger were two boys so intelligent, bright, sagacious, and efficient that I do not feel at liberty to pass them without reference to their subsequent and eventful careers. One of them, Henry B. Stanton, a youth of amiable character and great promise, became, some years later, a Washington correspondent of the "New York American," distinguished as an able and interesting writer, and a fearless Whig opponent of slavery. He subsequently married Miss Elizabeth Cady, established himself at Seneca Falls, turned Democrat, and was elected to the State Senate by that party. Of an impulsive nature, he became an ultra Democrat, as he had previously been an ultra Whig. At a still later day, when the Republican party was organized, Mr. Stanton joined it.

The other, Charles F. Mitchell, was the brightest, quickest, and sharpest boy I have ever known. His watchfulness, vigilance, and tact were truly remarkable. His instincts and intuitions fitted him for politics. He would anticipate what was wanted before you had time for half an explanation, and he was as prompt to act as he was quick to comprehend. He was, when I first knew him, a miller's boy; then a journeyman miller; and afterwards in business as an enterprising miller. He was elected to Congress from Niagara County in 1839, and reëlected in 1841. While in Congress he was distinguished for his zeal and activity as a supporter of Mr. Clay; and by his agreeable manners and reckless expenses, made himself popular at Washington and at home. But there was a sad *finale* to his career. Before his term of service expired, it became known that he had for some time been in the habit of obtaining bank discounts and acceptances upon forged paper, for which he was indicted, tried, convicted, and sent to the State Prison. He was subsequently pardoned, went to Kentucky, where he resumed business as a miller, and, as I learned, obtained standing and influence. Indeed, a man so rarely gifted would be sure to make his mark wherever he went. I had several letters from him after the Rebellion broke out. He was an earnest and fearless Union man.

In October, a nominating county convention was called.   By this time, our friends were becoming hopeful.   The more sanguine believed that we could carry the county.   Two or three gentlemen were named as candidates from the village of Rochester for members of Assembly.   The name of General Gould was so well received that the other gentlemen retired.   A few days before the convention was to meet, my friend Andrews, who seemed to have my interest always in charge, began talking in my favor for a nomination to the Assembly.   The younger classes received it favorably, and it was very soon ascertained that it was still more favorably received in the county towns. This disturbed some of the older and graver people.   I was still a journeyman printer and a comparative stranger, and although I had been successful in obtaining a bank for them, that did not qualify me, in their judgment, for the higher and more responsible duties of a member of the legislature.   It became apparent, however, that if the question was left to a county convention, I should be nominated, delegates already chosen in several towns having declared themselves in my favor.   As one of the three members from the county was always taken, by common consent, from the village of Rochester, General Gould and his friends proposed that the preference of Rochester should be indicated to the county convention by a meeting of its citizens.   Accordingly a meeting of the citizens of Rochester, friendly to the election of John Quincy Adams as President, of DeWitt Clinton and James Tallmadge as governor and lieutenant-governor, and in favor also of restoring the choice of presidential electors to the people, was called at the Court House on the afternoon of the day previous to that on which the county convention was to assemble.   That meeting was largely attended.   The canvass, though animated, proceeded with order and in good temper.   No name but that of General Gould and mine was voted for.   The result was largely in my favor, and, though a good deal disappointed, the friends of General Gould acquiesced in my nomination.   On the following day Henry Fellows, of Penfield, Gustavus Clark, of Clarkson, and Thurlow Weed, of Rochester, were nominated for members of Assembly by the People's Party, of Monroe County.

The legislature was to meet early in November to choose

presidential electors. I left Rochester the latter part of October for Albany, to complete the work to which I had previously devoted so much labor and time. My friends at home regretted this necessity, as my services during the three days' election were needed; but they made up for my absence by increased zeal and diligence. The gratifying result was announced to me in the following letter from my friend Peck: —

ROCHESTER, N. Y., *November* 3, 1824.

DEAR SIR, — The election is over, and all looks fair weather. I can only give you now the result in this town on our Assembly ticket. More next mail.

H. Fellows . . . . 255.	J. Seymour . . . . 151.
T. Weed . . . . . 265.	Enos Stone . . . . 141.
G. Clark . . . . . 253.	James Smith . . . 147.
Average People's majority . . . . 111.		

Brighton gives Mr. Clinton a majority of two hundred, and about the same majority in favor of our Assembly ticket. You will lose some in Sweden, where they strike your name off and put Seymour on. But there is little or no doubt of your election.

Judge Strong and all Carthage to a man went with us. Bucktail stock is low, and faces are lengthening as the returns come in. I trust that the State is safe — the county surely is. Ever yours,

E. PECK.

In a subsequent letter, Mr. Peck gave me the full result, as follows: —

Fellows . . . . . 2,391.	Seymour . . . . 1,987.
Weed . . . . . 2,380.	Stone . . . . . 1,908.
Clark . . . . . 2,355.	Smith . . . . . 1,970.

We had anticipated a little larger majority; but it is enough. The adversary made a vigorous onset upon you in the hope of electing Seymour. [James Seymour, a very popular man, was a brother of Henry Seymour, then a canal commissioner, and an uncle of ex-Governor Horatio Seymour.] Our friends were all zealous and true to the last. Some money, coats, hats, boots, oysters, etc., etc., have been lost and won. Derick Sibley was very bitter against you personally. Dr. Elwood bet him five dollars that you would be the highest on our ticket, and lost by eleven votes only.

I congratulate you most sincerely on this result. The event will, if properly improved, be of essential service to yourself and family. I doubt not that you will do so, and that you will, in all future time,

feel that your location in Rochester was of permanent advantage to
you.   I shall be obliged to depend upon your continued assistance in
conducting the " Telegraph."   If you find time, and I think you will,
you must not only give us the legislative reports, but enrich our columns with other matters, suited to the times and the occasion.

Truly,

E. Peck.

The general result throughout the State has already been
given.   In one of the last days of December, I started with
my colleagues, Messrs. Fellows and Clark, for Albany.   Mr.
Fellows was a lawyer, with a limited practice, having more
taste for politics and gardening than for the law.   He was a
law student at Kinderhook, with Martin Van Buren and Farrand Stranahan as fellow-students.   He told us, during the winter, many characteristic anecdotes of Mr. Van Buren, all showing that Mr. Van Buren, in early youth, cherished high political
aspirations.   Mr. Stranahan established himself in his profession at Cooperstown, Otsego County.   I served under him on
the western frontier in the campaign of 1813.   He commanded
a regiment of artillery.   He was elected to the Senate of this
State in 1823, and was one of the seventeen senators who voted
against the electoral law.   Mr. Fellows had acquired much
notoriety as the " Hen." Fellows, whose seat in the Assembly
of 1813, when there was a political tie in the House, was held
by Peter Allen, until Mr. Cruger was made Speaker and a
Democratic council of appointment chosen.

Gustavus Clark, my other colleague, was a merchant of the
town of Clarkson.   He had been a clerk in his boyhood, with
James K. Gurnsey of Pittsfield, and subsequently of Bradley
Martin of Lima, an occupation in those days in which a young
man was pretty sure to obtain a good knowledge of his business.   Mr. Clark possessed that knowledge.   He was a good
merchant, a good judge of goods, and a good judge of men.
We roomed together at the City Hotel, during the session of
the legislature, where I came to know his numerous excellent
qualities, and where a mutual friendship grew up, which is as
warm now as it was when we separated at the close of the session, forty-five years ago.   Upon a political question (anti-
masonry) arising a few years later, which assumed the bitterest
aspects, setting father against son, and brother against brother,
breaking up business relations and social ties, while Mr. Clark

took one side and I the other, we met as usual, not allowing even that troublesome question to disturb our friendship. We exchange letters occasionally, and messages through mutual friends frequently.

On our way to Albany in a stage sleigh — for winters were colder and sleighing better in those days — we lodged the second night of our journey at Rust's Stage House, on Onondaga West Hill. Soon after we arrived at the hotel, I met Mr. Oliver R. Strong, whom I remembered as frequently visiting the office of the " Lynx " in Onondaga Hollow, when, in 1811, I was an apprentice there. Mr. Strong was then a deputy sheriff, and came to the office with advertisements. I recalled myself to his recollection and introduced him to my colleagues. After supper, I went into the bar-room and took up a newspaper. Several villagers dropped in, as was the custom at country inns, one of whom inquired if they remembered a boy (naming me) who used to work in Mickel's furnace, who afterwards worked in Jasper Hopper's garden, and took care of his horse, cut his fire-wood, etc., etc., mornings and evenings, to pay for his schooling, and who afterwards was in Fay's printing-office. One of the company, who dimly remembered such a boy, inquired, " What of him ? " " He came in the stage this evening, and is on his way to the legislature from Rochester," was the reply. This created a general laugh and was considered a joke. When they learned, however, that the statement was made on the authority of Mr. Strong, one of them remarked, " They must be hard run for legislative timber out West ; I believe I 'll move out there and take my chance."

1825. — The Assembly of 1825 organized by the election of Clarkson Crolius, of New York, Speaker, and Horatio Merchant, of Albany, Clerk. Mr. Crolius, with the advantage of several years' experience in the Assembly, made but an indifferent Speaker, and Mr. Merchant proved himself an inefficient Clerk. The Assembly was as remarkable for legislative inexperience as it was for real intelligence and ability. Several young men of high promise had then first been called into the public service, — men whose subsequent lives were as creditable to themselves as useful to their fellow-citizens. John W. Hulbert, of Cayuga, had been a member of Congress from Berkshire, Mass. He was a man of sprightliness and tact, without possessing, however, enlightened or enlarged views. Robert Monell, from Chenango, possessed good sense, sound judgment, and good business talent. He was subsequently a member of Congress and judge of the sixth judicial circuit. Ambrose L. Jordan, from Columbia County, was brilliant and eloquent. After several years of successful practice as a lawyer in Cooperstown, Otsego County, he returned to Hudson, his native place. In 1827 he was elected to the Senate from the third district. In 1847 he was chosen attorney-general by the legislature. Mr. Jordan was a highly honorable and upright man. His opinions, political, professional, and financial, were convictions. He was just as conscientious in his politics as in his religion. He acquired, and retained through life, a high position at the bar of our State, residing through the latter years of his life in the city of New York, where he died in 1860, leaving a good name and a good estate. John Armstrong, Jr., from Dutchess County, was a son of General John Armstrong, a revolutionary officer, and Secretary of War under Mr. Madison. He had studied law, but did not like the practice. He possessed talents and cultivation, but lacked the stimulus of both industry and ambition, and while he was much liked, his friends were constrained to admit that he did not do himself justice. Mrs. William B. Astor, the highly benevolent wife of probably the righest man in America, is a sister of Mr. Armstrong. Samuel L. Gouverneur, from the city of New York, was a ready, impassioned, and eloquent speaker. He was quite a young man, and wholly without experience. His rich voice, his happy use of language, and his effectiveness in debate were a pleasant surprise to himself and his friends. Mr. Gouverneur was a son-in-law of President Monroe, and had been his private secretary. Mr. Adams appointed him postmaster of the city of New York. He returned to Virginia, his native State, a few years before the Rebellion broke out. I met him several times at Washington during the first year of the war, and was gratified to find his sentiments and sympathies as loyal and true to the government and Union as his best friends could desire. He was a genial companion, a warm friend. James R. Lawrence, of Onondaga, was a young lawyer of decided ability in his profession, who soon acquired a habit of speaking with effect in the House. Samuel J. Wilkin, of Orange, also a young lawyer, possessed useful business talent.   He was an able, but not showy debater. Samuel Stevens, of Washington, was a young lawyer who had already attained a high professional rank in the northern counties.   He was an impulsive, but clear-headed and logical speaker. He removed soon afterwards to Albany, where he took, and held for thirty years, the highest position at the bar of the Supreme Court, the Court of Chancery, and the Court for the Correction of Errors.   William H. Adams, of Wayne County, with the advantages of a commanding person, imposing manner, and a powerful voice, was an impressive and effective speaker.   Joseph Kirkland, of Oneida, belonging to an elder class, had in former years acquired both professional and legislative reputation.   He was always a distinguished lawyer and much esteemed citizen of Utica.   His son, Charles P. Kirkland, of New York, inherited both the professional and personal qualities of his father. The gentlemen whom I have named were all, I am happy to say, my friends, remaining such through life.   Bowen Whiting, of Ontario, was also a member of the legislature of 1825. He was a man of good talents and estimable character.   He was subsequently district attorney of Ontario County.   Though opposed in politics, Mr. Whiting was always my personal friend.

There was, as I have said before, an overwelming majority of anti-Van Buren men in this Assembly.   Many and influential members had formerly been opponents of Governor Clinton, but had, in the last election, made common cause against the Albany Regency; and a decided majority, especially of the leading men, were warm supporters of John Quincy Adams, whose election as President was now confidently expected.   Governor Clinton, as I have previously stated, had not shown his hand on the presidential question.   Early in the session the governor invited me to dinner, where, instead of a large dinner party as I expected, I found Senator Silas Wright, Jr., Perley Keyes, John W. Hulbert, and myself as guests.   Ebenezer Baldwin, the governor's private secretary, was also there.   The two former gentlemen, as I need scarcely say, were prominent Democrats, and had been earnest opponents of Governor Clinton.   Mr. Hulbert was a zealous political friend of the governor, and so far as I had obtained a political status, that was my own position.   Mr. Clinton evidently regarded me as holding that confidential relation to him, or I should not have been placed in a position so embarrassing. The dinner had not proceeded very far before its object was transparent. A coalition was being formed, having for its object the support of General Jackson for President in 1828. This, it was assumed, required no compromises or abandonments on either side. It was the formation of a new party, from free, fresh elements, in favor of a candidate equally free and fresh, uncommitted to individuals and disembarrassed by associations. But while the conversation was open and the purpose avowed, the time for admitting the public into the secret had not arrived, and until all the arrangements should be perfected, it was understood that nothing occurring there should transpire ; in other words, the dinner-table conversation was to be confidential. I found myself very seriously embarrassed, and should have been much more so, if I had been called upon to take much part in the conversation. It was a relief, however, to get away from the table and out of the executive mansion, for I had mentally determined that, whatever might be the course of others, I should stand by Mr. Adams, for whose election I had been working zealously more than two years. I took an early opportunity to apprise Governor Clinton of this determination, adding that I should remain faithful to the state administration. The governor expressed, in a kind manner, his regret that I could not see my way clear to act with old political friends, expressing the hope and belief that time and reflection would bring us all together.

I was hardly free of this embarrassment before another and one still more formidable occurred. A senator in the Congress of the United States was to be chosen. But one candidate in opposition to the Regency had been named. That candidate was Chief Justice Spencer, whose age, experience, attainments, and eminent character were peculiarly adapted to that high position. The governor and chief justice, though in early life friends and brothers-in-law, became bitter enemies in 1812, and remained such for several years. ' They were now, however, warm friends, personally and politically. I knew that Governor Clinton would support General Jackson in opposition to Mr. Adams. I believed that the chief justice, like the governor, was prepared, after his election as senator, to take ground in favor of Jackson. More than half, if not two thirds, of the electors who made Mr. Clinton governor were friends of Mr. Adams. Six state senators, who reluctantly voted for Mr. Clinton for governor, were warm friends of Mr. Adams.

After much and anxious reflection, in company with Mr. Bostwick of Delaware, and Mr. St. John of Montgomery, friendly both to Governor Clinton and to Mr. Adams, we called on Judge Spencer. Our object was to ascertain whether the chief justice, if elected senator, would sustain Mr. Adams' administration. When I had made this statement, the judge rose, much excited, and in a voice and manner then well known throughout the State indignantly refused to be interrogated, adding that his character, services, and principles were well known, and that he had lived too long and labored too faithfully for the State to commence making either professions or explanations. Mr. St. John attempted to say that, as representatives, we desired information to guide our action upon the senator question. But the judge would not hear him, and continued to reprove us vehemently. Growing finally more calm, we were enabled to discover the cause of his excitement, which was the peculiar and probably conflicting views of the People's Party in the legislature. He had evidently anticipated a collision between the friends of Mr. Clinton and Mr. Adams. He asked us to reflect upon the embarrassment which would result from his submitting to be interrogated. He could not, he said, satisfy one section without offending the other, and this was a dilemma, he insisted, that his friends ought not to force upon him. But even when the storm was over, the judge said nothing and intimated nothing which led us to believe or hope that he was friendly to Mr. Adams. In now looking back upon the question, I can perceive the reasonableness and propriety of his course, although it did not then occur to me in this light. I conferred afterwards with the leading friends of Mr. Adams in the Senate, and came to the conclusion that I could not consistently vote for Judge Spencer. So strong, however, was the feeling in his favor, supported as he was by Governor Clinton, that only three " People's " men, Messrs. Bostwick of Delaware, Buck of Lewis, and Mixer of Chautauqua, consented to go with me; so that on the first day of February, when the House was called upon to vote for United States senator, in place of Rufus King, there were fifty-six votes for Judge Spencer, thirteen votes

for James Tallmadge, and four for Albert H. Tracy. I had
determined to support Mr. Tracy for the reason that, like myself, he was the political friend both of Governor Clinton and
of Mr. Adams. He had been for six years a member of Congress from Buffalo, was a gentleman of high character, great
ability, and much promise, popular alike at home and at Washington. General Tallmadge was voted for by Adams men, who
had not previously. been friends of Mr. Clinton, with the understanding, however, that they were to come to the support of Mr.
Tracy, should there be any chance for his election. The Senate,
however, as was foreseen, refused to make a nomination, a majority of its members not agreeing on any one name. On the
twenty-fifth of February, a resolution was received from the
Senate, nominating on its part Albert H. Tracy, to represent
this State in the Senate of the United States for six years, in
the place of Rufus King, whose term had expired. This resolution was rejected in the Assembly by a vote of sixty-nine to
thirty-seven. Subsequently another resolution was received from
the Senate, with the name of James Tallmadge as its candidate
for senator, which was also rejected by the House. The question returned, in one form and another, several times ; but the
session was exhausted in unavailing efforts to choose a senator.
The Democratic members of the Senate united with the Adams
men in nominating, first Mr. Tracy and then General Tallmadge,
not that they were in favor of either of those gentlemen, but
because it relieved them from the imputation of disregarding
their constitutional obligations, and because they knew that the
House would reject their nominees. Inasmuch as they could,
under no circumstances, elect a Democrat, they desired to throw
the question over to a succeeding legislature, and in this they
were successful. A few days before the adjournment I was
enabled to count fifty-four votes in the Assembly in favor of
Mr. Tracy, but as this fell eleven votes short of a majority, the
enterprise was abandoned. It was an exciting and acrimonious
struggle ; I was held responsible for the defeat of Judge Spencer,
and denounced bitterly by many of my political friends. There
was no injustice in this from the standpoint the friends of
Judge Spencer occupied, although I had, for my own satisfaction, a clear conviction that I had acted consistently and loyally.
I was an earnest friend and supporter of Mr. Adams. I be-

lieved that Judge Spencer, if elected, would oppose his administration. I knew that Mr. Tracy, who was a consistent member of our party, who had served honorably in Congress for six years, would be an able supporter of Mr. Adams' administration. Later in the session, Judge Spencer, with the consent of Mr. Clinton, wrote a letter to Mr. St. John, a member who called with me on him early in the session, saying that if elected senator, while he would not trammel himself with pledges, he should deem it his duty to give his support to all wise and just measures of the incoming administration. But this letter came after we were too fully committed to recede. Such an avowal, however, when we first called upon Judge Spencer, would have been entirely satisfactory, but I am quite certain that even that would not have changed the result. There were fifteen Van Buren or Regency senators with certainly three and probably four Adams senators, with strong Democratic antecedents, who would not in any possible contingency have voted for Judge Spencer. The Senate, therefore, would have refused or evaded a joint ballot of the two Houses. There were during the protracted canvass for senator frequent letters passing between Mr. Tracy and myself, the following extracts from which, recalling the circumstances and spirit of the contest, and showing what manner of man I had chosen to bring forward as a candidate for senator, will, I think, be read with interest : —

WASHINGTON, *February* 22, 1825.

DEAR SIR, — I have this moment received yours of the 17th, which I have read with much interest. I think I can observe from its tone that the current is setting rather adversely. But never mind, care as little for it as I do, and we shall triumph, let come what may. I am surprised that Washburne should be so pertinacious. I am sure Wilkeson and Day might put him to it if they would. But let them take their course. I might perhaps obtain some of the aid from Washington which you speak of if my health would allow of making an effort, but although decidedly better than it has been, it is still so bad as to confine me to my room ; besides, I really do not like to ask for such a favor. I live with Taylor, and know that he feels a deep interest in my success, as all Mr. Adams' real friends do, but I cannot consent to involve them in the least difficulty on my account. Storrs is frightened at his own shadow, and is disposed to conciliate his Jacksonian friends, whom he outraged by manifesting a burning zeal for the judge. I am glad they can find no worse arguments against me than youth and celibacy. These have both been urged for the last seven years. Would to God they might remain standing arguments against my holding office for half a century to come! But alas! one of them has already gone, and the other will take its flight as soon as my best friends desire. These wiseacres, however, must think they are choosing President, not senator; thirty, not thirty-five, is the requisite age for the latter office, and I think, having been in the House of Representatives six years (necessarily after twenty-five), is a tolerable certificate on this head.   Very truly yours,

Albert H. Tracy.

Washington, *March* 2, 1825.

Dear Sir, — Yours containing the proceedings on the senatorial question of the 25th was received to-day. If you have only succeeded in putting off the election till this shall reach you, I am perfectly certain all will be well. Clinton has refused the mission, and declines taking anything under the administration. His letters to me and to Mr. Adams were received to-day. I was present when Mr. A. opened his, which he read to me. There can be no doubt now what the intentions of Mr. C. and his friends are, and I am confident no one not prepared to go into a minority more abject and hopeless than Federalism in 1805 can think of putting Judge S. into the Senate. While I was with Mr. A. he received the news of my nomination by the Senate, at which he was sufficiently pleased. His remark was, "*I am in favor of the* 17*th now.*" But don't mention this circumstance, especially if the judge is elected, as it may be injurious to Mr. A. The course pursued of putting the offer of the mission into the " Daily Advertiser " before an answer was given here was grossly indelicate, and so considered universally. The object of helping the judge's election was too obvious, I think, to have any useful effect. Yours in great haste,   Albert H. Tracy.

The session of 1825 was not one of much legislative importance. All opposition to the Erie and Champlain Canals had ceased. The financial results of the Erie Canal, then navigable from Albany to Rochester, stimulated canal enterprises in other parts of the State. The Genesee Valley, Chenango, and the Chemung canals were largely petitioned for. If the introduction of the first resolution authorizing surveys, preliminary to the construction of the Oswego Canal, entitled the mover to a paternal relation to that improvement, I stand on record as the father of the Oswego Canal.

There were large numbers of applications for bank charters, among which was one covered up, as Major Noah said in his " National Advocate," " in the smoke of a Lackawanna coal pit ; " in other words, there was a bill introduced providing for the construction of a canal from the Hudson River at Kingston to the Lackawanna Coal Fields. The bill authorized the Canal and Coal Company to establish a bank in the city of New York. It was alleged that the real and only purpose of the applicants, who were strong men, was to obtain a bank charter, under the popular pretense of furnishing cheap coal to the cities of New York and Albany, and also to the intermediate villages along the river. As a member of the Bank Committee, in the belief that the canal feature of the bill was a dodge to obtain a bank, I proposed to so amend the bill which had been submitted to the committee as to ensure the construction of the canal. This was strenuously opposed by the applicants, and ruled out by a majority of the committee. But when the bill came up for consideration in committee of the whole, and when the section authorizing the company to establish a bank was reached, I offered an amendment which required a *bonâ fide* expenditure of $250,000 towards the construction of the Lackawanna Canal before the company should be allowed to commence its banking operations. This proviso, while it exasperated the friends of the bill, was received with such evident favor that the committee rose and reported, and the question laid over for several days. Several prominent men came from New York, some of whom were my personal friends, to induce me to withdraw the proviso. But they failed to satisfy me that if the real object of the bill was to provide for an important public improvement there was any injustice or hardship in making " assurance doubly sure " by the amendment which I had proposed. The bill was finally passed, thus amended. After its passage, it was understood, and admitted by many, that if the bill had passed as it was introduced the company would have immediately established their bank, but the construction of the canal would have been postponed to a more convenient season ; and for many years afterwards the citizens of Ulster County used to thank me for securing the construction of their Delaware and Hudson Canal.

I never possessed the power " to speak in public on the

stage." This defect has been the cause of frequent embarrassment and mortification, for there have been many occasions when it would have been both proper and pleasant to have been even moderately gifted with the power of speech-making. Aware of my infirmity, I of course never attempted to participate in debate; but on one occasion, when a bill which I reported myself from a standing committee of which I was a member was in committee of the whole, a member desired information in regard to the object and effect of a particular section. The information desired, though proper, was very simple; and if it had been asked for in a committee room, or informally, in the presence of a dozen or twenty persons, I should have given it without the slightest embarrassment. And, forgetting myself for a moment, I rose to reply. Before uttering a dozen words, however, I became confused, then stammered, and soon, finding myself utterly incapable of proceeding, ended in a regular muddle. This was my first and last attempt, either in that House or in the Assembly of 1830, when I was again a member.

Meantime, the city of Washington was the scene of great political anxiety and excitement. The presidential question having been removed from the States, its interest was concentrated in Congress. There Mr. Adams was situated much as he had been in the State of New York. He could be elected only by the support of Mr. Clay and his friends. As he and those friends could more readily affiliate with Mr. Adams than with Mr. Crawford, such a termination of the struggle was anticipated. Charges of coalition between Messrs. Adams and Clay were made in moderate opposition presses, while the more violent Democratic journals alleged that Mr. Clay had made a corrupt bargain with Mr. Adams. It was not quite certain, for several weeks, that the majority of the members of Congress from this State would vote for Mr. Adams, as several of them were political friends of Mr. Clinton. On the day before the election, however, the Hon. Stephen Van Rensselaer, from Albany, who had not previously avowed his purpose, declared in favor of Mr. Adams, who was duly elected by the House of Representatives. The following letters from the Hon. Albert H. Tracy, written during the pendency of the presidential question in the House, will be found interesting.

WASHINGTON, *January* 23, 1825.

THURLOW WEED, ESQ. :

Dear Sir, — Continued ill health for some days past has prevented me from acknowledging your several favors, and I fear my present feebleness will hardly admit of my now doing more than merely noticing their receipt. In addition, the incredible toil and suffering which the passage of my Niagara bill occasioned me has actually suspended, if not exhausted, all my intellectual energies in relation to other subjects. You can form no conception of the extent of exertion which the business has cost me. The triumphant majority with which it finally passed was the result of a miraculous coincidence of arrangements, which were so appropriate in character that it seemed almost impossible that anything less than a Divine interposition could produce their coöperation. The public will give me some credit for the success of the measure, but it can never appreciate the embarrassments and obstacles which I encountered and surmounted. You may form some conjecture of the peculiarities of the case from the fact that a large proportion of the friends of the bill up to the moment of its final passage considered its prospects absolutely desperate. But I forget that I am talking on a subject about which you can hardly wish to hear.

I was not surprised, and so far as my personal feelings are concerned, I can truly say I was not grieved to learn from your first letter that Judge Spencer's exertions and arrangements had been so complete as to ensure his election almost without the show of competition. Everything which I have heard on the subject since I came here convinced me that his efforts and those of his friends had been of the most unwearied nature, and I have marvelled rather that he should deem such exertions necessary than that they should have proved successful ; knowing as you do the origin and nature of my inclination on this subject, you will not disbelieve me when I say that it is of so subdued a character, that so far from feeling any painful disappointment at the cloud which has overcast our early speculations, I am really more than half pleased with the certainty that the fourth of March will terminate my long series of official cares and responsibilities. Still I would not have you think that I am disposed in the least degree to shrink from the situation in which I have consented to be placed. On the contrary, I am more than ever convinced that the election of Judge Spencer under circumstances most likely to exist will prove extensively injurious to our party at home, and politically fatal to those purposes which his elevation is particularly designed to promote. The circumstances to which I allude are those connected with the success of Mr. Adams. If, however, General Jackson shall succeed, the case may be in some degree changed, not that in this event the expectations of Mr. Clinton and his friends can be otherwise than completely disappointed, yet the unpleasant responsibility of having the failure attributed to the selection of a person not favorable to the general's views must make the office very undesirable to one standing in the complex relationship of hostility to Jackson and friendship to Clinton. At any rate, I should feel this embarrassment to such a degree as absolutely to decline the appointment in case of Jackson's success, not that I doubt my disposition to serve Mr. Clinton is equal to the judge's or my ability to do so with any administration (however vain you may think the suggestion), but I know that no man alive would so serve him with Jackson as to produce the result he anticipates, and therefore I would not for any consideration place myself in a condition to have either my skill or fidelity suspected by my friends. If Jackson becomes President, a plentiful crop of disappointments will be reaped, and I am willing that the judge should be the harvester, at any rate I will not be.

On the other hand, in case Mr. Adams is elected, no policy can be more unwise than the selection of Judge Spencer, that is, if any ulterior expectations are entertained. They stand in an attitude of direct hostility, and under circumstances that no mutual confidence can ever be created. In a word, Mr. Adams knows the judge, and comprehends all his movements and operations better than either you or I do. His information in respect to our public men is minute, and so accurate and circumstantial as to put denial to the blush ; not that he has ever acquired anything from me, for foreseeing as I have the great probability that Adams and the judge would be respectively elected, I have said and done all that policy, and perhaps some more than truth would justify, to produce with the former an impression that the latter cherished no unfriendly feelings towards him, but my efforts in this respect have had about as much effect as Phillips' letter had in persuading the King of England. In this state of things you can discover what absolute folly there will be in selecting the judge with a view of promoting any object ulterior to the gratification of his own ambition. If this alone shall be considered by the legislature a sufficient motive for the measure, I for one shall be content, as I never entertained for the judge any other feelings than those of kindness and respect. As regards the details of operations in this business I can say nothing, for in truth I know nothing. Except yourself and Carpenter, I know no one in whose judgment and sincerity I can rely. What you told me about Wilkeson, although totally inconsistent with his professions, did not surprise me, for I was aware that he had objects of his own to accomplish through J. C. Spencer. My desire for this or any other office is too little to call for any personal sacrifices in my behalf. Besides, my pretensions are too humble and my prospects too contingent to justify even a friend in making them. I have not written Carpenter for the very reason that I have delayed writing you, and because I would have you consider the present as equally for the *edification* of both. The presidential controversy is of late becoming more spirited and interesting. The development of Clay's views in favor of Adams, although perfectly understood by some of us *knowing ones* from the beginning of the session, has produced great consternation with both Jackson's and Crawford's friends. Both suffered their own unfortunate hopes to delude them to a belief that he would take ground on their side. What renders this event the more gratifying is the fact, which I know to be true, that Clay's course has not been in the slightest degree influenced by any advances or arrangements of a personal character. He and Adams are precisely in the relationship of intercourse that they have been. It is altogether the result of the public state of things. Indeed, it is hardly possible to conceive of a political man acting with that perfect independence which Mr. Adams does. I am entirely in his confidence, and I speak therefore with positive knowledge when I say that he neither has made nor has thought of making an overture to any political man living. He rests his expectations with the most composed confidence on the course of events, and turns neither to the right hand nor to the left to seek or to avoid. Gracious God, if our great man at Albany had this wisdom, how different his prospects would be! I am often struck with astonishment and disgust at the gross misconceptions which the public form of individual characters. I am crowded with letters from all quarters of the State urging me to oppose Adams and support Jackson, and the fools take it upon themselves to find reasons for my doing so. In twenty letters which I have been looking over to-day there is not a single reason suggested which I do not *know* to be founded in the grossest ignorance of the truth. The argument which I find most commonly urged is that Adams relies upon the arts of management and intrigue, while Jackson reposes in conscious dignity upon popular feeling and public services; now, the exact reverse of this I know to be the truth, and yet my friends, who know nothing personally of either, persist in endeavoring to convince me that their judgment is better than my knowledge. The attempt is as preposterous and as hopeless as the blind man's to convince one who could see well that the grass was blue and sky green. The truth is, that Jackson's friends are pushing their intrigues to as desperate an extreme as Burr's did in 1801, and the old man himself has no personal independence in the business. I could give you several illustrations of the fact; I will, however, mention only one. Jackson and Crawford, you know, have been on terms of personal ill-will, so that I believe they have not spoken to each other for years; at any rate, Jackson has indulged uniformly in expressions of the bitterest hostility, yet within three or four days "this independent old matron" has sought and had personal interviews with Crawford in order to assure him that he was, as Wilkeson would say, very much his friend. What the effect of this gratuitous profession will be remains to be seen. What its design was is perfectly obvious. I have written a great deal more than I intended, and more than the state of my health would justify, but I got a-going, and did not know where to stop. Let me hear from you frequently and particularly.

Yours truly,   ALBERT H. TRACY.

HOUSE OF REPRESENTATIVES, WASHINGTON, *February* 9, 1825.

DEAR SIR, — I have but a moment to inform you that Adams was this day elected on the first ballot, — thirteen States voting for him, of which New York was one. Jackson had seven States, and Crawford four. The votes of New York stood eighteen for Adams, fourteen for Crawford, two for Jackson. Every Van Buren man voting against us. This, indeed, is a glorious triumph of reason over passion, moral force over faction. Everything was calm and orderly.

In great haste,   ALBERT H. TRACY.

J. Q. Adams.

CHAPTER XVI.

1825.

THE MISSION TO ST. JAMES. — CLINTON AND TALLMADGE. — RUFUS KING. — A JOURNEY TO WASHINGTON. — AN INTERVIEW WITH THE PRESIDENT AND SECRETARY OF STATE. — TOBIAS WATKINS. — "THE INTELLIGENCER." — GALES AND SEATON. — HENRY CLAY. — JUDGE MCLEAN. — A WEDDING DINNER. — APPOINTMENT OF HENRY WHEATON. — THE NEW YORK POST OFFICE IN 1828. — MEETING WILLIAM KENT.

SHORTLY after the election of Mr. Adams as President, I received the following letter from Mr. Tracy : —

WASHINGTON, *February* 18, 1825.

MY DEAR SIR, — Although I am hardly able to sit up, I cannot think of going to bed without acknowledging the pleasure which your favor of the 13th has given me. As the plot develops, I feel an interest increasing far beyond any value which I place on the office. There is a boldness and independence in the whole scheme which delight me.

I was excessively pleased with the conclusion which Tallmadge arrived at in his long talk with you. His offer of the attorney-general's office makes me think of that made by a certain *gentleman* in the Scripture, who promised " all the kingdoms of the earth " for a simple genuflexion, but the title happens now, as then, to come in question. However, if he could give what he offers, I would not take it. I speak God's truth when I say I want no office. I don't value the one in question a rush, independent of circumstances at this time connected with it. I feel some better than yesterday, although I am still confined.

Truly yours,

ALBERT H. TRACY.

(CONFIDENTIAL.)

If you hear of an offer of a mission to London, advise that it be accepted, and that instantly. It is unsafe waiting for better things.

The gist of this letter was found in its postscript, which foreshadowed the appointment of Governor Clinton as minister to the Court of St. James. That appointment, a few days

afterwards, was announced.   In view of the fact that Governor
Clinton was now an avowed supporter of General Jackson, it
created much surprise, but for reasons which I will explain,
was well received by the friends of Mr. Adams in this State.
Mr. Clinton abroad, General Tallmadge, the lieutenant-governor,
would step from the Senate into the executive chamber, thus
giving our friends the State administration for nearly two
years.   But these speculations were of brief duration, for Governor Clinton declined the appointment of minister to England.   Though they were elected governor and lieutenant-governor on the same ticket, the breach between Clinton and
Tallmadge, if affected at all, was widened.   The lieutenant-
governor was constantly chafing at the idea of occupying a
subordinate and powerless position.   When Governor Clinton
declined the mission to England, Lieutenant-Governor Tallmadge decided to ask it for himself, and desired me to go immediately to Washington for that purpose.   But this involved,
in those days, the loss of a week or ten days' time, and I did
not feel at liberty to leave my seat in the Assembly so long.
His friends in the legislature, however, united in a letter to the
President, asking his appointment as minister to England.   But
the effort was unsuccessful.   Soon after the 4th of March, when
Mr. Rufus King's senatorial term expired, that gentleman received the appointment of minister to England.

Several weeks after the adjournment of the legislature, General Tallmadge requested me by letter to meet him at Albany.
In our interview, he informed me that his place had become
so irksome that he was determined to get out of it, and that
he had concluded to renew the application to Mr. Adams for a
mission, which was to be asked partly on the grounds of political
services rendered, but more especially in reference to the political future of Mr. Adams' administration.   It should be stated
here that, so far, the Adams party proper in this State, to which
Mr. Adams was indebted, first to the vote of the State in our
legislature, and next to the vote of its representatives in Congress, without which he could not have been elected, had not
been, in any political sense, " recognized."   Mr. Clay, as Secretary of State, had rewarded several of his own political friends
with desirable appointments.   Judge William B. Rochester, for
example, had been appointed minister to Panama.   I felt, there-

fore, much confidence in the success of my errand, — a confidence not diminished by the circumstance that all parties had united in attributing to me the credit, or the discredit, of carrying the State for Mr. Adams. I had never been in Washington, and had never seen the President. The journey, therefore, was one of much incidental interest. I proceeded to Philadelphia, through Newark, New Brunswick, Trenton, etc., by stage-coach; from Philadelphia to New Castle by steamboat; from New Castle across the State of Delaware by coach; from French Town to Baltimore by steamboat; from Baltimore to Washington by stage-coach. I stopped at Gadsby's, who then kept a hotel in what I think was called the "Seven Buildings," situated between the White House and Georgetown. Having heard that the President was in the habit of bathing early every morning in the Potomac, I rose before the sun, and walked down to the bank of the river, observing, as I approached it, a gentleman in nankeen pantaloons and a blue pea-jacket walking rapidly from the White House towards the river. This was John Quincy Adams, the President of the United States. I moved off to a respectful distance. The President began to disrobe before he reached a tree on the brink of the river, where he deposited his clothes, and then plunged in head first, and struck out fifteen or twenty rods, swimming rapidly and turning occasionally upon his back, seeming as much at his ease in that element as upon terra firma. Coming out, he rubbed himself thoroughly with napkins, which he had brought for that purpose in his hand. The sun had not yet risen when he had dressed himself and was returning to the presidential mansion.

The fashion of "interviewing" public men had not then obtained, or perhaps I should have taken advantage of this opportunity to state the object of my visit to Washington.

It was an exceedingly hot day in June. Immediately after breakfast I called on Dr. Tobias Watkins, who kept an apothecary store on Pennsylvania Avenue, and with whom I had corresponded during the presidential canvass. I found him a highly intelligent and accomplished gentleman. He was soon after appointed an auditor in the Treasury Department, and became, subsequently, a defaulter to the government in the sum of between six and seven thousand dollars. This defalcation was seized upon by the opposition members in Congress, and by the opposition press, as alarming evidence of the corruption of the administration and the political depravity of the times, and was so persistently and skillfully used as to awaken much popular indignation against Mr. Adams. Indeed, this defalcation, with the fact that the President, on his visit to Massachusetts, rode several miles through Rhode Island on horseback in shorts, with a jockey coat and cap, were the principal, if not the only, grounds of opposition to Mr. Adams. Something was made, or attempted to be made, by charging prodigality and wastefulness, in proof of which it was shown that the expenses of the government amounted to the enormous sum of eleven millions a year. Colonel Benton, either in a letter or a speech, and I cannot now remember which, said : " This administration, even if it be as pure as the angels in heaven, must be put down." And it was put down, — partly by the great military enthusiasm awakened for General Jackson, but mainly, as I then thought and still believe, owing to Mr. Adams' political impracticability. He was able, enlightened, patriotic, and honest ; discharging his public duties with conscientious fidelity, he disregarded or overlooked, what Monroe, Madison, and Jefferson had deemed essential, namely, political organization and personal popularity. Mr. Adams, during his administration, failed to cherish, strengthen, or even recognize the party to which he owed his election ; nor, as far as I am informed, with the great power which he possessed, did he make a single influential political friend.

Leaving Dr. Watkins, I called at the office of the " National Intelligencer," then really and truly an able, influential, independent, and patriotic journal. I had corresponded with, but had never seen its capable and estimable editors, Messrs. Gales and Seaton, who afterwards became, and remained through life, my warm friends. How well, after an almost lifelong interval, I remember their cordial welcomes, their genial conversation, and their munificent hospitalities. To Mr. Gales I explained the object of my visit. He comprehended fully its bearings and importance, and, with entire frankness, explained the political idiosyncrasy of the President, adding that if Mr. Clay, a much more practical politician, were President, he should not, for a moment, doubt the success of my mission.

Between twelve and one o'clock I repaired to the White House, and soon obtained an audience with the President. I had a brief letter of introduction from the Hon. Albert H. Tracy, which secured me a courteous reception. After some general conversation, I spoke of the political condition and aspects in New York, hoping to show him how advantageously the elements might be combined in support of his administration. As it was soon apparent that the subject did not interest him, and as the cards of two or three persons had been sent in, I took my leave, remarking that, with his permission, I would call the next day and explain the object of my visit to Washington. I then went to the State Department, and presented a letter of introduction from General Porter to Mr. Clay, whom I had not before seen. My reception was most gratifying. He led in the conversation, selecting topics that were most likely to interest me, which continued as long as I felt at liberty to occupy his time. It required but one visit to enable me to understand why Mr. Clay had won such troops of warm-hearted friends. I passed the evening where, for many succeeding years, I enjoyed delightful dinners and suppers, at the residence of Mr. Gales, who inquired how the President received me, and if I had seen the Secretary of State. My interview on the following day with Mr. Adams was embarrassing and constrained. It was evident that he failed to perceive the importance or significance of the political views which I presented. He could not, he said, give either the mission to France or to Russia to a State which had already received the mission to England; and as General Tallmadge had instructed me to say a first-class mission only would be accepted, the question, so far as it concerned him, was foreclosed. Expressing my regret at this result, I nevertheless ventured to urge the importance of a recognition of the friends of Mr. Adams by the appointment of some one of their number to a position of trust and responsibility. Mr. Adams replied that he aimed to supply vacancies in the public service by the appointment of men of character, capacity, and integrity, and that it would afford him pleasure, under that rule, to gratify his New York friends; and, finally, he went so far as to say that he would, in the distribution of diplomatic appointments, endeavor to give a second-class mission to New York. This was my last interview

with Mr. Adams, during his four years of presidential service.

I called next on the postmaster-general, Mr. John McLean,
of Ohio, to whom I had a letter of introduction from my friend,
Albert H. Tracy. He received me with great cordiality, and invited me with so much kindness to dine with him that day that
I accepted. To show that marriages in high life, forty years
ago, were much less ostentatious, gaudy, and glittering than in
these days, I will state that on the morning of that day a
daughter of the postmaster-general had been quietly married at
home, by a Methodist clergyman, to a young lieutenant in the
army, in the presence of her family, the bridesmaid, and a
brother officer of the lieutenant as groomsman. The dinner
party consisted of the persons just indicated and myself. It was
an exceedingly interesting occasion, and especially gratifying to
one whose humble origin and associations had not previously
familiarized him with such scenes. It was evident then, as I
subsequently came to know, that Judge McLean was fortunate
in his domestic relations; and this marriage also secured the
permanent welfare and happiness of the daughter and of the
gentleman to whom she had given her hand and heart. That
young lieutenant was Joseph P. Taylor (a brother of General
Zachary Taylor), an excellent officer of the army, who, as its
commissary-general, died at Washington in 1867. More than
thirty years after his marriage, I was introduced to him as Colonel Taylor of the army, and while shaking hands he recalled
the incident of my being the only stranger at his wedding dinner in 1825. To that interview, and its most important subsequent results, I shall have occasion to devote a separate
chapter.

I called again to see Mr. Clay, whose cordial manner and the
frankness with which he conversed with me attached me still
more strongly to him. Between the editors of the "National
Intelligencer" and myself a friendship sprang up, which ended
only with their lives. I also formed a high estimate of the character and capacity of the postmaster-general, and after visiting
the Patent Office and the Capitol I left Washington, in all respects but one — the disappointment in regard to General Tallmadge — highly pleased with my visit, and especially so with
the new political and personal relations established.

General Tallmadge, who awaited my return in the city of New York, was equally disappointed and annoyed at the result of my mission. He would not for a moment listen to the suggestion of accepting a second-class mission. Subsequently, in conversation with Henry Wheaton, who, next to General Tallmadge, had been as a member of the legislature of 1824 the most efficient supporter of Mr. Adams, I ascertained that he would consent to take a foreign appointment.

Before leaving New York, I wrote a letter to Mr. Adams, in which General Tallmadge and other prominent friends of the President united, and it resulted in the appointment of Mr. Wheaton, without his knowledge, as *chargé d'affaires* to Sweden; and thus commenced a diplomatic career which reflected so much honor upon Mr. Wheaton himself and upon his country.

General Tallmadge took me with him that day to dinner, with Theodorus Bailey, his relative and then postmaster of New York, where I met for the first time William Kent, only son of the eminent Chancellor Kent, then only eighteen or nineteen years of age, but giving abundant promise of a career every way worthy of his inherited talents and virtues. The building now occupied by the Farmers' Loan and Trust Company was then the post-office, in the second story of which the postmaster resided with his family.

General Tallmadge, though inordinately ambitious, with a temper easily exasperated, had many redeeming qualities. His anger could be appeased; he was hopeful and confiding; and as a politician was efficient, zealous, and popular. He would soon recover from a disappointment, however severe, and, fixing his mind upon some other position, would go to work with renewed energy.

CHAPTER XVII.

1824–1825.

LAFAYETTE'S VISIT TO THE UNITED STATES. — HIS RECEPTION IN NEW YORK. — THE EXCURSION UP THE HUDSON. — OLD FRIENDS AND COMRADES. — HIS TOUR THROUGH THE STATES.

(From the Albany Daily Advertiser, September, 1824.)

A CARD.

The undersigned take great pleasure in tendering to Commodore S. Wiswall, master of the steamboat James Kent, and Charles Rhind, Esq., agent of the North River Steamboat Company, their public acknowledgments for the active and unremitting attentions paid to General Lafayette, during his passage from New York to Albany. Commodore Wiswall and Mr. Rhind were· constant and indefatigable in facilitating the arrangements of the committees from the different villages, and in gratifying the citizens generally upon the banks of the river. The manner in which the duties of these gentlemen were discharged during this most interesting passage entitles them to this tribute; and for their polite attentions to the undersigned, individually, we beg them to accept our cordial thanks.

Morgan Lewis, Nicholas Fish, Philip Van Cortlandt, Simeon DeWitt, Matthew Gregory, Jedediah Rogers, Francis K. Huger, Henry A. Livingston, A. M. Muir, J. Taylor Cooper, Wm. L. Stone, James Stevenson, Thurlow Weed, S. Jones Mumford, Philip Hamilton.

STEAMBOAT JAMES KENT, *September* 18, 1824.

THE above card, brought accidentally to my notice, recalls an event that awakened more general and genuine joy and gratitude than any other in the history of our country. Général le Marquis de Lafayette, after an absence of thirty-nine years, revisited our country, on the invitation of Congress, as the nation's guest in 1824. He reached New York on the 15th of August, in the packet ship Cadmus, Captain Allyn, with his son and secretary. The government had tendered him a United States frigate, but always simple and unostentatious, he preferred to come as an ordinary passenger in a packet ship.

There were no wires fifty years ago over which intelligence could pass with lightning speed, but the visit of Lafayette was expected, and the pulses and hearts of the people were quickened and warmed simultaneously through some mysterious medium throughout the whole Union. Citizens rushed from neighboring cities and villages to welcome the French nobleman, who, before he was twenty-one years old, had devoted himself and his fortune to the American colonies in their wonderful conflict with the mother country for independence ; and who, after fighting gallantly by the side of Washington through the Revolutionary War, returned to France with the only reward he desired or valued, — the gratitude of a free people.

General Lafayette was now sixty-seven years of age, with some physical infirmities, but intellectually strong, and in manners and feeling cheerful, elastic, and accomplished.

The general's landing on the Battery, his reception by the military under General Martin, his triumphant progress through Broadway, his first visit to the City Hall, awakened emotions which cannot be described. I have witnessed the celebration of the completion of the Erie Canal and the mingling of the waters of Lake Erie with the Atlantic Ocean, the completion of the Croton Water Works celebration, the reception of the Prince of Wales, and other brilliant and beautiful pageants, but they all lacked the heart and soul which marked and signalized the welcome of Lafayette. The joy of our citizens was expressed more by tears than in any other way. It is impossible to imagine scenes of deeper, higher, or purer emotion than the first meeting between General Lafayette and Colonel Marinus Willett, Colonel Ebenezer Stevens, Colonel Varick, Major Platt, General Anthony, Major Popham, Major Fairlee, and other officers of the Revolution, whom he had not seen for nearly forty years, and whom without a moment's hesitation he recognized and named. But the crowning glory of that series of honors and festivities was the fête at Castle Garden on the evening of the general's departure for Albany. The Castle was expensively, elaborately, and gorgeously fitted up and adorned for the occasion. I remember that, even without the aid of gas, the illumination was exceedingly brilliant. There was a ball and supper; the occasion was graced by the intelligence, beauty, and refinement of the metropolis. How many — or rather how few — of that then youthful, joyous throng remain to recall, with memories subdued and chastened by time and change, the raptures of that enchanting scene !

The steamboat James Kent, Commodore Wiswall, chartered by the city for the occasion, dropped down the river opposite Castle Garden, brilliantly illuminated, at twelve M., where she remained until half past two A. M., when the general and his friends embarked. The party consisted of General Lafayette, George Washington Lafayette, M. Levasseur, his secretary; Generals Morgan Lewis, Simeon DeWitt, Anthony Lamb, and Philip Van Cortlandt; Colonels Marinus Willett, Richard Varick, Nicholas Fish, Robert Trout, and E. S. Duncombe; Majors Charles L. Platt, Popham, Fairlee, and Cooper; Captains Rogers and Halsey, and Lieutenant Matthew Gregory, of the Society of the Cincinnati; Major-General Morton, Recorder Riker, Alderman Hone, Colonels A. M. Muir and William L. Stone, of New York; Governor Johnston and Edward Livingston, of Louisiana; Colonel Francis E. Huger, of South Carolina; General Tallmadge, Mr. Emmet, and Mr. Oakley, of Poughkeepsie; Mrs. Lewis, granddaughter of General Washington; Mrs. Hamilton, widow of Alexander Hamilton and daughter of General Philip Schuyler; Miss Frances Wright, of England, authoress of "Manners and Society in America;" John Taylor Cooper, of Albany, and Thurlow Weed, of Rochester.

About three o'clock General Lafayette retired, and his friends were soon afterwards in their berths. I rose at five o'clock. General Lafayette came on deck before six for the purpose of showing his son and secretary where Major André was arrested; but the view was shut off by a fog, in attempting to grope through which the steamer grounded on Oyster Bank, where she lay until nearly ten o'clock; so that instead of reaching West Point at half past six, it was nearly twelve when the multitude assembled there announced our approach by a discharge of cannon. As soon as the fog lifted, General Lafayette in the most enthusiastic language and manner pointed out Stony Point, and described the manner in which the British garrison was surprised and captured by "mad Anthony Wayne." As we approached the West Point wharf, cheers of citizens lining the banks echoed and reëchoed from hill to hill, well-burnished muskets dazzled the eye, tall plumes nodded their greetings, the ear-piercing fife, the spirit-stirring drum, and the loud bugle sent forth their loftiest notes, while the reverberating cheers filled the air with welcomes. The general was received by Colonel Thayer, and ascended the hill in a landau, escorted by the officers of the Post, followed by the revolutionary officers and a long procession of citizens. He was received by the cadets from their parade ground, and escorted to his marquee, where they paid him the marching salute. From the marquee he proceeded to the quarters of Generals Brown and Scott, where he was presented to the ladies and partook of refreshments. From thence he was conducted to the library and introduced to the cadets. Dinner was served in the mess-room of the cadets, which had been splendidly decorated for the occasion. Colonel Thayer and Major Worth presided at either end of the table ; General Lafayette and General Scott were seated at the right, and General Brown and General Varick on the left, of the President ; George Washington Lafayette was seated on the right, and Colonel Huger on the left, of the Vice-President. Over the head of General Lafayette was a large eagle, with the words " September 6, 1777," on a streamer suspended from his beak, and " Yorktown " grasped by his talons.

After the removal of the cloth the customary thirteen standing toasts were drunk, the fourth of which follows : " Our guests : May the homage of a free people prove a consoling recompense for the frowns of directors, consuls, emperors, and kings." Among the volunteer toasts were the following : By General Lafayette : " The Military Academy of West Point : A school of liberty and equality, inseparable sisters ; the scientific bulwark of national defense, a happy and most precious bond of national union. An old friend of their grandfathers tenders to the cadet corps his admiration, his thanks, and his blessing." By Cadet Clay (son of Henry Clay) : " The swords which we wear : May we never draw them without being inspired by the exalted feelings which distinguish our guest, the donor." (These swords were presented to the cavalry corps by General Lafayette.) By Cadet Chase : " The noble Frenchman who placed the army of the Revolution on a new and better footing." (When the revolutionary soldiers were barefooted at Valley Forge, General Lafayette furnished them with shoes.)

At the review of the cadets, Generals Brown and Scott, in full uniform, with tall plumes in their chapeaux, stood by General Lafayette; the three, each towering up more than six feet in height, made a magnificent tableau.

The day was in all respects a happy one: it is the greenest in my memory. General Lafayette's happiness took every conceivable form of expression. He made an early visit to the ruins of old Fort Putnam, where he had been stationed. Almost every scene and object served to recall incidents of the Revolution, of which he spoke with the greatest enthusiasm. He pointed out the Robinson House, where General Washington, himself, and General Knox were breakfasting with Mrs. Arnold when the commander-in-chief received the first news of Arnold's treason. Early in the day a committee of citizens arrived from Newburg, where General Lafayette was expected to dine, and where the citizens of Orange County *en masse* anxiously awaited his arrival. But he was too much delighted with West Point to be hurried away. An early dinner had been ordered, so that the impatient thousands at Newburg might be gratified with a sight of the general before evening. The dinner, however, with the associations and remembrances it suggested, proved irresistible. Hour after hour passed, but the interest increased rather than diminished, and it was not until seven o'clock that the general could be prevailed to rise from the table. It was dark, therefore, when we reached Newburg. Upon landing, a scene of indescribable confusion ensued; troops were in line, but powerless to preserve order. The desire to see the nation's guest was uncontrollable. The huzzas of men mingled with the shrieks of women and the cries of children. All were eager to see, but everywhere good humor and kindness prevailed. The village was illuminated, and the occasion was honored by a ball and supper. The festivities of the evening, however, were saddened by the sudden death of Hector Seward (a cousin of the late Governor Seward), who received a fatal kick from an excited horse. Notwithstanding the excitement and fatigues of the day and of the preceding night, General Lafayette was as cheerful and buoyant at the ball-room and at the supper-table as the youngest and gayest of the revelers. And here again I might ask, Who of all that happy group survive? William Ross, Hector Craig, General Smith, Judge Betts, Captain Belknap, William Walsh, Gilbert O. Fowler, James Burt, General Wickham, John Duer, Ogden Hoffman, Isaac R. Van Duzer, Samuel J. Wilkin, Robert Denniston, Ward M. Gazeley, etc., then busied with the enjoyment or the aspirations of earth's honors and ambitions, now rest beneath its sod.

The general reëmbarked at one o'clock, A. M. At half past two our approach was announced by a discharge of cannon from the bluff, just below the landing at Poughkeepsie. Large piles of seasoned wood, saturated with tar and turpentine, were kindled on that bluff, fed by hundreds of boys who had been entrusted with the duty, and were kept blazing high, filling the atmosphere with lurid flame and smoke until daylight. Soon after sunrise, a large concourse of the citizens of Poughkeepsie, with a military escort, arrived at the wharf. The general, on disembarking, was shown to a splendid barouche, and the procession moved to and through the village of Poughkeepsie, where congratulatory speeches were made and reciprocated. A large party sat down to a bountiful breakfast; and here, too, death has silenced tongues that were then eloquent. Prominent among those who rendered homage to General Lafayette on that occasion were James Tallmadge, Thomas J. Oakley, James Emmett, Henry A. Livingston, Smith Thompson, Matthew Vassar, General Brush, Paraclete Potter, Nathaniel P. Tallmadge, Alexander S. Coffin, of Poughkeepsie, John Armstrong, Jr., Dr. Thomas, and that " nature's nobleman," Walter Cunningham, who acted as marshal of the day.

The party reëmbarked at ten o'clock, when the steamer proceeded up the river to the then beautiful residence of Governor Morgan Lewis, where the party landed, proceeded to his fine old mansion, and partook of a sumptuous collation. About two o'clock the steamer glided through the placid waters until between four and five o'clock, when she reached Clermont, the manor house of Chancellor Livingston, of revolutionary memory. On landing, the general was received by a large body of freemasons, and was escorted by a military company from Hudson to the beautiful lawn in front of the manor house, where the general was warmly welcomed by the master of the lodge with an appropriate speech. The afternoon was uncommonly beautiful; the scene and its associations were exceedingly impressive. Dinner was served in a greenhouse or orangery, which formed a sort of balcony to the southern exposure of the manor house. When the cloth was removed, and the evening came on, variegated lamps suspended from the orange-trees were lighted, producing a wonderfully brilliant and beautiful effect. Distinguished men from Esopus, Saugerties, Upper and Lower Red Hook, Catskill, Hudson, etc., had been invited by our host, Robert L. Livingston, to dinner. Among these, I remember Robert and John Tillotson, Walter Patterson, Peter R., Edward P., and "Oak Hill John" Livingston, Jacob Haight, Thomas B. Cook, James Powers, John Suydam, Judge William W. Van Ness, Elisha Williams, Jacob Rutsen Van Rensselaer, Ambrose L. Jordan, and Justus McKinstry, none of whom survive. But the grand event of the occasion was the ball, which was opened by General Lafayette, who gracefully led out the venerable and blind widow of General Montgomery — who fell in the assault of Quebec in 1775 — amidst the wildest enthusiasm of all present. While the festivities were progressing within, the assembled tenantry, who were "to the manor born," were feasted upon the lawn, where there was music and dancing. The party broke up and returned to the boat about three A. M. The steamer hauled out into the river, but did not get under way until sunrise.

We reached Catskill at seven o'clock. A large procession, civic and military, awaited the general's arrival at the landing. General Lafayette and the revolutionary officers were seated in open barouches, and the procession moved through the main street for more than a mile, affording the dense mass of men, women, and children the great happiness of seeing the compatriot and friend of Washington. Several beautiful arches, profusely dressed with flags, flowers, and evergreens, each one bearing the inscription, "Welcome, Lafayette," were thrown across the street. In the centre of the village a brief address was made, to which the general responded. After this he was escorted in the same order to the boat, and at eleven o'clock he reached Hudson, where a hearty welcome awaited the general. Not only the citizens of Columbia, but many of the inhabitants of Berkshire County, Mass., were present, whose acclamations, as General Lafayette was seen upon the main deck of the steamer, made the welkin ring. The ceremonies and festivities at Hudson consumed between three and four hours. A committee, consisting of the most distinguished citizens of Albany, awaited the general's arrival at Hudson, anxious that the steamer should reach Albany before dark, preparations having been made for a magnificent reception. But in this the Albanians were disappointed, for, on account of the low water above Coeyman's, the steamer's progress was so slow that it was quite dark when she reached Albany. What was lost, however, in one respect was gained in another, for between the illuminations and torches the procession, from Lydius Street landing to the Capitol, was alike brilliant and impressive. The excursion from New York to Albany occupied three days, and afforded to all who enjoyed it an interest and a happiness more complete and more touching than tongue or pen can describe. Nothing occurred to lessen or mar either that interest or that happiness. The weather was delightful, the arrangements were admirable, General Lafayette's welcome was alike hearty and joyous by all classes and all descriptions, all colors and all ages. The enthusiasm was universal and pervading. In whatever else the education of our people may have been neglected, all have been taught to honor and love Lafayette. None were too high to pay him voluntary homage, and none were so humble as to feel that they had no right to participate in the general joy which his visit occasioned.

Many delightful incidents occurred during the voyage, two or three of which I will venture to recall. As we approached Newburg, General Lafayette was on the lookout for their headquarters during the winter the army lay there. When the boat was opposite that point, the general exclaimed, "Nick" (the familiar abbreviation for Colonel Nicholas Fish in their revolutionary days), — "Nick, do you remember when we used to ride down that hill with the Newburg girls, on an ox sled?" Colonel Fish and Major Platt did remember the incident, and informed the general that some of those "Newburg girls" had married distinguished men, and were then venerable matrons.

As the steamer was approaching Esopus, on the second day, I observed a small boat pulling out from the west shore with a signal, and called the attention of Commodore Wiswall to the circumstance. The commodore immediately directed the pilot to steer in that direction. It proved to be a skiff, with an old gentleman seated in the stern, with his bandana handker-

chief fastened to his cane as a signal. As we approached the
skiff, the commodore remarked, " I know him," and then directed the steamer to be stopped, and the steps lowered. The
commodore received the old gentleman, and walked with him to
the promenade deck, where General Lafayette, surrounded by
his old comrades, was seated. No word was spoken. As we
approached, Commodore Wiswall leading the old gentleman by
the hand, General Lafayette rose, as did the other officers, but
still no word was spoken. The stranger offered both his hands,
which the general received, and each looked the other steadily
in the face. It was evident that General Lafayette was taxing
his memory severely, and, after a profound silence of more than
a minute, the general exclaimed, " My old friend, Colonel Harry
Livingston ! " and then, after a few words of mutual congratulation, he added, " Do you remember when I reviewed your
regiment of infantry on Rhode Island ? "

Soon after this incident, while we were all seated around
Lafayette, under an awning upon the main deck, Colonel Livingston asked the general a question about his imprisonment
at Olmutz, to which the general replied, " My friend and ben-
efactor, Colonel Huger, who rescued me from that prison, will
answer you that question." Until this moment, so modest and
quiet had been the bearing of Colonel Huger, that but two or
three persons present knew how honorably his name was associated with that of General Lafayette. All then listened, with
a charmed interest, to the brief narrative of Colonel Huger, to
which General Lafayette added an account of what occurred
after his recapture. I subjoin, as well as I can remember them,
the substance of these narratives.

General Lafayette, on his first visit to this country, landed
at Charleston, South Carolina. His first night in America was
passed under the roof of the father of Colonel Huger. In 1792,
young Huger, while traveling in Europe, heard of the imprisonment of Lafayette. He determined to visit Olmutz, first to
endeavor to be of some service to the general while in prison,
and next, if possible, to effect his rescue. While occupied with
this determination, he made the acquaintance of Dr. Baollmann,
a resident of Vienna, who had conceived the same design. Influenced by kindred sympathies, they soon became warm friends.
Their plans were so well laid that, after a few weeks' sojourn at

Olmutz, the officer in command of the citadel permitted General Lafayette to take exercise in the open air, guarded by two sentinels. It was arranged that they were to meet the general, and, after disarming the sentinels, the general was to mount a horse ready for the occasion, and reach the Prussian frontier. But, in the *mêlée*, General Lafayette received a severe wound in the hand, and, in the hurry to depart, mistook the direction, and lost his way. After riding several miles, he asked a peasant to guide him ; but his prison clothes and bleeding hand excited the suspicion of the peasant, who betrayed the fugitive, and he was remanded the next day to his cell at Olmutz. His imprisonment now became more rigorous, and his privations and sufferings more aggravated. He was informed that henceforth he would be known only by a number.

Dr. Baollmann and young Huger were also arrested, and consigned to eight months' imprisonment in a lonesome dungeon. Their release was effected by Count Metrowsky, an influential nobleman residing near Olmutz. Meantime, Lafayette's wife, who had been imprisoned at Paris during the Reign of Terror, was released after the downfall of Robespierre. Madame Lafayette proceeded immediately to Vienna, and obtained leave from the emperor to visit the marquis, whose imprisonment she shared until his final release. The general's protracted imprisonment and great suffering awakened attention from England and America. General Fitzpatrick brought the subject, on resolution, into the House of Commons. Colonel Tarleton, who fought against Lafayette in America, Mr. Wilberforce, and Mr. Fox spoke in favor of the resolution. President Washington wrote a letter to the emperor, asking for the release of his old friend and companion. But the Austrian despot sternly resisted every appeal, until Bonaparte, at the head of his victorious army, peremptorily demanded the release of Lafayette. The Austrians endeavored to induce the general to accept a conditional release ; but, while greatly weakened in body, his spirit was unbroken, and he refused to compromise his principles or his rights as a Frenchman and an American. His prison doors were finally thrown open on the 25th of August, 1797, after an imprisonment of five years, — one year and ten months of which had been shared by his wife. After residing two years in Holstein, he returned to his Château of

La Grange, forty miles from Paris.   Bonaparte, while first consul, made several attempts to beguile Lafayette into his service, but they were all declined.   Lafayette's vote against making Napoleon consul for life separated them forever.

In 1803, when Louisiana was purchased, President Jefferson invited Lafayette to become its territorial governor, but, unwilling to leave France while there was a hope for constitutional freedom in Europe, the offer was declined.

But delightful as it is to dwell upon the incidents connected with that memorable occasion, I will hasten to the conclusion of this chapter.

General Lafayette visited every State, and almost every city, in the Union.   His reception everywhere was distinguished by universal manifestations of mingled joy, affection, and gratitude.   His journeys displayed an unbroken series of pageants. No amount of fatigue wearied him.   His health and spirits were equal to every demand upon them.   He was always fresh, cheerful, and happy, with the magnetic power of imparting cheerfulness and happiness to others.   To the general joy, however, there was one exception.   When the bill, making provision for the payment of General Lafayette for the services he rendered our country in its struggle for independence, was under consideration in the House of Representatives, one discordant voice was heard, — a voice which sounded alike harshly and fell alike painfully upon the ears and hearts of the people and their representatives ; but that voice was heard no more in Congress, for, although a capable and growing man, he subsided into a retirement from which he never emerged.   Assuming that the representative referred to lived to deplore the error which cost him so dearly, I forbear to mention either his name or the name of the city he represented.

The triumphal tour of the nation's guest terminated at Washington, where the enthusiasm which awaited him was as fresh as that which gushed from the hearts of the people when he first landed upon our shore.   Congress voted $200,000 and a township of land in part payment, as was said, of his eminent services as a general in the army of the United States.   The United States frigate Brandywine, handsomely fitted up and supplied with every luxury, was ordered to Washington, and placed at his service.   On the 7th of September, 1825, General Lafayette, with his son and secretary, went on board, and the Brandywine, spreading her canvas to a favorable wind, departed for Havre.

General Lafayette was wholly unprepared for the reception which awaited him in America. He knew little of our estimate of his character and services, and came to revisit interesting scenes of his youth, and to enjoy a reunion with the few surviving old friends and compatriots. His once large fortune had been so diminished by confiscations that he was compelled to study economy. Making the acquaintance on board the Cadmus of a gentleman from Boston, the general inquired the expense of living at the best hotels, and the expenses of traveling by stages and steamboats, of all which his secretary made memoranda. From these data the general, aided by the Bostonian, made an estimate of what it would probably cost him to travel and reside a year in America. It is scarcely necessary to add that there was no occasion to refer to these memoranda, for his every wish was anticipated and gratified, nor was he permitted while he remained among us, unless by stealth, to expend one dollar or one dime of his own money.

CHAPTER XVIII.

1824–1825.

THE only survivors of the members of Assembly of 1825,
according to my information, are Harmon J. Quackenboss, of
Delaware, Gustavus Clark and Thurlow Weed, of Monroe,
James R. Lawrence, of Onondaga, Freeman Stanton, of Schoharie, and James De Mott, of Seneca. When I last saw Mr.
Quackenboss, at Mechanicsville, Saratoga County, he was in
high health and spirits, looking about as youthful as when I
first saw him. His legislative experience was singular, having
at intervals of five years represented three constituencies. He
was a member from Delaware in 1825, from Greene in 1830,
and from the city of New York in 1835. General Lawrence,
of Syracuse, though blind, is in good health otherwise. Gustavus Clark, my old friend and colleague, when I last heard
from him was in good health.

But few of the members of the Assembly of 1825 became
prominent in subsequent years. Ambrose L. Jordan was subsequently elected to the Senate, and many years afterwards became an attorney-general. He was a distinguished member of
the bar of this city for the twenty years preceding his death.
Gaines B. Rich, of Genesee, became a wealthy banker at Buffalo. Samuel L. Gouverneur, of New York, was a Virginian
by birth, and a truly honorable and chivalric gentleman. He
returned many years ago to Virginia, where he died during the
second year of the Rebellion. I saw him at Washington, in
1861, with a clouded brow and saddened spirit, but as true to
the government and as loyal to the Union as when his clarion
voice used to sound, clear and strong, always on the right side,

in our halls of legislation. Samuel Stevens, of Washington County, removed soon afterwards to Albany, where he became and remained for more than twenty years a distinguished member of the bar of the State.

Of the thirty-two members of the Senate of 1825, the Honorable Heman J. Redfield, of Batavia, is the only survivor. The next surviving senator is the Honorable Alvin Bronson, of Oswego, who retired in 1824, and who, like Mr. Redfield, in the enjoyment of good health, is also enjoying the rewards of an enterprising, successful, and well-spent life. Two members of the Senate of 1825, William Nelson, of Westchester, and John Cramer, of Saratoga, after turning their ninetieth year, died in 1870.

There was a remarkable breaking up or disruption of party ties in 1824. When the Senate commenced its session on the 6th of January, thirty of the thirty-two members were Democrats. Archibald McIntyre, of Montgomery, was a Clintonian, and Jedediah Morgan, of Cayuga, self-nominated, was voted for by Clintonians. William H. Crawford, of Georgia, was a congressional caucus nominee for President. John Quincy Adams and Henry Clay, although belonging to the same party that nominated Mr. Crawford, refused to go into caucus, and became independent candidates for President. At the close of a stormy and exciting session, the Senate was politically divided as follows : —

For Crawford : Messrs. Bowne, Lefferts, Ward, Sudam, Thorn, Livingston, Dudley, Wright, Bronson, Greenly, Worcester, Keyes, Stranahan, Greene, Earll, Eason, Redfield, Bowman, McCall. 19.

For Adams : Gardiner, Burt, Nelson, Mallory, Haight, McIntyre, Lynde, Ogden, Burrows, Morgan. 10.

For Clay : Wheeler, Cramer, Clark. 3.

In the final ballot, when Crawford and Adams only could be voted for, Messrs. Wheeler and Cramer voted for the Crawford, and Mr. Clark for the Adams, ticket.

It will surprise the people, if not the legislators of the present day to learn how simply and inexpensively legislation was conducted in 1825. The officers of the Assembly of that year consisted of a clerk, a deputy, and engrossing clerk, sergeant-at-arms, a doorkeeper and assistant-doorkeeper, and a fireman.

Pages had not then been invented. I will not startle readers by showing what an array of subordinates are now provided for in the Annual Supply bill. The list of messengers and pages, to say nothing of clerks of committees, postmasters, librarians, etc., etc., is fully equal in number to one third of the whole number of members. I have seen this abuse grow up from year to year on one specious pretext or another to its present enormous proportions. I do not know that one party is more to blame than another; new places are made for the relief of unfortunate and needy friends.

In showing, as I did one day, that ex-Governor Throop, of this State, as well as Chief Justice Robinson, of Kentucky, were surviving members of the Congress of 1815, I called out the fact that Hon. M. Thatcher, of Maine, now ninety-five years old, was a member of Congress in 1808, sixty-nine years ago. These instances of longevity of public men are quite interesting. I remember to have seen, two or three years ago, an article in which it was stated that Joshua Dewey, a member of our State legislature from Otsego County, in 1798, was then a resident of Brooklyn, and in the enjoyment of good health. Not being otherwise informed, I infer that he is still living. In looking through the legislative journals, I fail to recognize another survivor for twenty years, and until the session of 1818, when our respected fellow-citizen, Michael Ulshoeffer, was a member of the Assembly. David C. Judson, of St. Lawrence, was a member of that legislature, and is still living. I believe that Alexander Hamilton, a member of the Assembly from this city in 1819, is still living. Mr. Ulshoeffer was again a member in 1819. Elial P. Foote, a member of the legislature of 1820, from Chautauqua, is, I believe, now a resident of New Haven, Conn.

The legislature of 1822 was the last elected under the first State constitution. Of the delegates to the State convention of 1821, by which the second constitution was framed, the venerable Samuel Nelson, judge of the Supreme Court of the United States, is, I believe, the only survivor. Judge Nelson was a delegate from the county of Cortland. That convention met just fifty years ago. Nearly all of the delegates were men of large experience in public affairs, and, consequently, were more advanced in years than members of the legislature. The county of Albany, for example, was represented by four of the most distinguished men in the State, namely, James Kent, Ambrose Spencer, Stephen Van Rensselaer, and Abram Van Vechten, all of whom had passed their fifty-fifth birthday. Rufus King, a delegate from Queens County, himself distinguished in the annals of our country, had four almost equally distinguished sons (John A., Charles, James G., and Edward), none of whom survive.

Of the members of the legislature of 1823, the venerable Azariah C. Flagg is, as far as I am informed, the only survivor. Mr. Flagg has resided for many years in London Terrace, 23d Street; although as blind as Belisarius, with otherwise unimpaired faculties, tenderly cared for, he glides smoothly and swiftly toward " that bourne " which almost all of his colleagues have reached. Mr. Flagg will leave an unblemished record. He held high and responsible financial positions, always discharging his duties with proverbial ability and integrity.

In the memorable legislature of 1824 — memorable for its refusal to pass the law giving the choice of presidential electors to the people, and for its removal of De Witt Clinton from the office of canal commissioner — survivors visibly increased. But even now the number is " few and far between." John F. Hubbard, of Chenango, whose son is now a member of the Senate, Azariah C. Flagg, of Clinton, Oran Follett, now a resident of Sandusky, Ohio, and Samuel L. Edwards, of Onondaga, comprise the list.

Among the members of the legislature forty years ago, I recognize several whose sons have since become prominent, and who are themselves approaching " the sear, the yellow leaf " of life. Henry Seymour, member of the Assembly from Onondaga in 1820, and of the Senate in 1824, was the father of ex-Governor Horatio Seymour ; James Nye, member of the Assembly from Madison County in 1818, was the father of James W. Nye, now a United States senator from Nevada; General Joseph Kirkland, a member of the Assembly from Oneida County in 1804, 1818, 1820, and 1830, was the father of Charles P. Kirkland, Esq., now a prominent member of the bar of this city; Isaac Belknap, member of the Assembly from Orange County in 1818, was the grandfather of the present Secretary of War; Joseph D. Monell, member of the Assembly from Columbia County in 1824, was the father of Judge Monell, of this city.

Legislation, like literature, has its curiosities, such, for example, as that in the convention of 1801, by which our first State constitution was framed, Jonathan G. Tompkins was delegated from Westchester County, while his son, Daniel D. Tompkins, was a delegate from New York. Stephen Van Rensselaer and Abram Van Vechten were members from Albany of the first and second constitutional conventions. In the Assembly of 1794, the counties of Albany, Dutchess, and New York must have been about equal in population, as each sent seven members to the legislature. Josiah Ogden Hoffman, so long a distinguished member of the bar of this city, was a delegate to the first constitutional convention from the county of Albany. Colonel Aaron Burr, the president of that convention, though a resident of New York, was elected from Orange County. Martin Van Buren, a delegate to the second constitutional convention, was elected from Otsego County. Peter H. Wendover, of New York, and Henry Huntington, of Oneida, were delegates to the first and second constitutional conventions.

In primitive times people did not change their representatives merely to give A, B, C, D, etc., their turn. Under the first constitution, Matthew Adgate represented the county of Albany in the Assembly twelve consecutive years; Samuel A. Barker represented Dutchess County twelve years; Abraham Braser and his son Philip (the turtle-eating alderman) represented the city of New York eight years; Kitchell Bishop represented Washington County eight years; Aaron Burr represented the city of New York three years and the county of Orange one year; John Cantine represented the county of Ulster sixteen years; Stephen Carman represented the county of Queens twenty years, from 1798 to 1819; Jeremiah Clark represented the county of Orange eleven years; Benjamin Cole represented the county of Queens ten years; Adam Comstock represented the county of Saratoga twelve years; Clarkson Crolius represented the city of New York twelve years; Deitz, Adam, Jost, and Johannes represented the county of Albany eighteen years; Abijah Gilbert represented the county of West-

chester thirteen years ; the Havens family represented the
county of Suffolk nineteen years ; David Hopkins represented
the county of Washington eighteen years ; George Huntington
represented the county of Oneida nine years ; David Kissam
represented the county of Queens thirteen years ; the counties
of Dutchess, Columbia, Westchester, Albany, Washington, and
Montgomery had forty-seven representatives of the name of
Livingston ; Archibald McIntyre represented the county of
Montgomery eleven years ; Ebenezer Purdy represented the
county of Westchester eight years ; Erastus Root represented
the county of Delaware eleven years ; C. C. Schoonmaker represented the county of Ulster thirteen years ; Alexander Sheldon represented Montgomery County eleven years, five of which
he was Speaker of the House ; Thomas Thomas represented
Westchester County thirteen years ; Elisha Williams represented Columbia County eight years.   Between the years 1801
and 1821 there were one hundred and four representatives in
the legislature from the universal Smith family.

CHAPTER XIX.

1825.

I HAD now been away from Rochester during the winters of 1824 and 1825, most of the summer of 1824, and a part of the summer of 1825, and was anxious to get back to my duties in the printing-office, and to enjoy the society of my family and friends. I went to work with a will. I had extended my acquaintance with public men, and the "Telegraph" immediately felt the good effects by a largely extending circulation. It was already recognized as the leading administration journal in western New York. And while there necessarily was more or less of collision between the State and national administrations, I continued to support both; nor, while I refused to go with Governor Clinton for General Jackson, were my friendly relations disturbed or my influence with Governor Clinton impaired. Rochester was growing in population, business, and wealth, very rapidly. There were no necessarily idle people there, and but very few destitute of the means of support. Lands from the first settlement of the village up even to 1825 were so cheap that not only merchants, millers, and professional men, but mechanics, and even laborers, could afford to purchase and did purchase a village lot, on which they erected, at greater or less cost, a home, so that almost every family sat under and rejoiced in their "own vine and fig tree." I ought to have said before that the original proprietors, prominent among whom were Colonel Rochester, Colonel Fitzhugh, Major Carroll, and James Wadsworth, were truly enlightened men, who offered every facility for a rapid development of the resources of the place. Though an industrious and busy place, its citizens found leisure for rational and healthy recreation. A base-ball club, numbering nearly fifty members, met every afternoon during the ball-playing season. Though the members of the club embraced persons between eighteen and forty, it attracted the young and the old. The ball-ground, containing some eight or ten acres, known as Mumford's meadow, by the side of the river above the falls, is now a compact part of the city. Our best players were Addison Gardiner, Frederick Whittlesey, Samuel L. Selden, Thomas Kempshall, James K. Livingston, Dr. George Marvin, Dr. F. F. Backus, Dr. A. G. Smith and others. Messrs. E. Delafield and Augustus F. Smith, who are prominent and successful in the practice of the law in the city of New York, are the sons of Dr. A. G. Smith.

There was among the inhabitants much practical benevolence. The citizens were prompt to relieve suffering in all its accustomed phases. August and a part of September were seasons of epidemic along the lake shore, where fevers and fever and ague prevailed annually, and sometimes so pervading was the malaria that whole neighborhoods would be prostrated. I remember two such seasons, and I shall never forget the liberality with which provisions, delicacies, medicines, etc., were contributed, and the alacrity with which the attendants and nurses volunteered their services on these missions of mercy. Every house was visited throughout the infected district, extending eight or ten miles along the lake shore and between one and two miles back from the lake. I was of the party on two occasions. The visits occupied two days, and were of grateful interest.

On returning to Rochester in May (1825) I found that my friend S. G. Andrews, who was always seeking to promote my welfare, had drawn up the following recommendation, to which are appended the names of the leading and most influential citizens of Rochester. His own name does not appear, for the reason that he was then a Jackson man, although two years afterwards he, together with Mr. Whittlesey, became first anti-Masons and then Whigs, and as such Representatives in Congress : —

Hon. John McLean, Postmaster-General:

SIR,— The undersigned, citizens of the village of Rochester and its vicinity, county of Monroe, New York, respectfully recommend Thurlow Weed, Esquire, editor of the Rochester "Telegraph," for the office of postmaster in the place of Abelard Reynolds, the present incumbent.

Mr. Reynolds was appointed to the office at the first settlement of the village, when the business of the place was so trifling as to render the appointment of little importance, and the undersigned are confident that were the office now vacant, the public would not recommend the present incumbent to fill it.

Mr. Weed is a citizen of the village of Rochester, and a member of the legislature of this State from Monroe County. He would discharge the duties of the office with attention and fidelity, and his appointment would be gratifying to the citizens of the county generally.

James K. Livingston, E. B. Strong, John T. Trowbridge, Samuel Works, Ira West, Gilbert Everingham, Jr., Timothy Childs, J. W. Strong, John B. Elwood, Everard Peck.

ROCHESTER, *May* 25, 1825.

It is perhaps scarcely necessary to remark that this letter, instead of going to Washington as was contemplated in 1825, is now, in 1873, exhumed from my old papers to constitute a part of this history.

On the second day of September, 1825, the completion of the Erie and Champlain Canals was celebrated. The day was commemorated by a continuous discharge of cannon, commencing at Buffalo and extending along the whole line from Lake Erie to the Hudson River. A packet boat left Buffalo with bottles of water from Lake Erie to be mingled with the waters of the Atlantic. Canal commissioners, engineers, and invited guests, as they passed through the villages grown and growing up along the Erie Canal, were received with great rejoicing. I was earnestly invited to join them at Rochester, and though strongly tempted, I had been so much away from home that I declined. The celebrations at Albany and New York were magnificent demonstrations of popular feeling. Rarely had a people ever rejoiced so heartily, and still more rarely have there been occasions for such general joy. A fact worthy of remark in any period of history, of this or any other country, and most especially significant at the present time, is, that the original Erie and Champlain Canals were constructed and completed in accordance with the plan of the original engineers, and for the sum of money which those engineers estimated they would cost. Now the estimate of an engineer for any great public work is generally less accurate and reliable than the guess of a shrewd Yankee would be. The estimates of cost for the Chenango, Genesee, and other State canals, and for the enlargement of the Erie Canal, fell so enormously short of their actual cost as to bring a modern engineer's estimate into general contempt. The completion of these great works, while their projector was governor of the State, was a source of just pride to DeWitt Clinton, who, but for political defects and infirmities, would have risen still higher. Mr. Clinton was a great man with weak points. In his annual message to the legislature of 1826, he very unwisely charged the federal government with interfering with the state administration. The Regency Senate called upon the governor for the evidence upon which his accusation was based. That call elicited the contents of a "green bag," which, on examination, proved to be utterly insufficient to justify the governor of New York for thus arraigning the President of the United States.

Tomatoes, as a vegetable, were first grown in western New York in 1825. They were introduced by Mr. Tousey, an old gentleman retired from business, who passed his winters in Virginia and his summers in Rochester. When he came north in the spring of 1825 he brought tomato seed with him, which he planted at Rochester, and during its growth was constantly talking of its great excellence and healthfulness. When his tomatoes were ready for the table he invited several gentlemen to dine with him at Christopher's Hotel. We were quite incredulous regarding the virtues of our friend's specific. Some had known them as "love-apples," growing wild, but of no value or use. At first the tomato was found palatable to none of the party. This surprised and annoyed our host, who ate them with great gusto; but subsequently, when Mr. Tousey sent fully ripe tomatoes to his friends, our tastes changed, and before the season was over we became very fond of them. In 1830, after I removed to Albany, I inquired for tomatoes, but was told at the market that they were not produced by the vegetable gardeners, and had never been sold in that market. I induced the market gardener of whom I purchased vegetables to send to

New York for tomatoes. He did so, but found during that season but two customers, namely, the late Julius Rhoades and myself.

The whitefish, now in such general use and so highly appreciated, though abounding then as now in Lake Ontario, was then seldom seen and not generally known to exist by the inhabitants residing in its vicinity. During my long residence in Rochester I never saw a whitefish, and should not have known of their existence but for a letter written by Governor Clinton from Sodus Bay in 1817, when, as a canal commissioner, he was "prospecting" for the Erie Canal, in which he speaks of breakfasting with great satisfaction upon whitefish caught in Lake Ontario. Why so great a luxury as the whitefish inhabiting our western lakes and so easily taken, was so long in coming into general use, is a problem which I am unable to solve.

Rochester, though only a village of a few hundred inhabitants, rejoiced in a theatre which attracted dramatic celebrities, distinguished among whom was the older Kean, who was, as he rightfully claimed to be, the "proud representative of Shakespeare's heroes." He was truly the embodiment of all that was great in his profession. During the sixty years of my playgoing life I have witnessed the performances of all the eminent actors of that period in Europe and the United States. And while I remember very vividly the marvelous powers of many "bright, particular stars," Kean and Rachel stand out incomparably above and superior to all.

Maywood was an actor of much merit, but with a limited range of characters. While he played Shylock, etc., well, he was preëminent in Sir Archie MacSycophant, Rob Roy, and other Scottish characters. A pleasant and permanent friendship grew up between us, founded upon an incident which seems worth recording. During the years that the authorship of the Waverley Novels was the subject of journalistic and literary controversy, I had earnestly believed and zealously maintained that Walter Scott was the author of those universally admired romances. That, however, was not the opinion of journalists who were supposed to be better informed. An editorial in my paper discovering a remarkable peculiarity of constructing sentences both in "Waverley" and in the acknowledged writings of Scott (not yet Sir Walter), attracted the attention of Mr.

Maywood, who called to assure me that I might safely persist in claiming that Scott was really " the Great Unknown." He added that while, even in Edinburgh, and in literary circles, the authorship was denied to Scott, yet the secret was known to twenty or more persons, including the family and confidential friends. Mr. Maywood, after enjoining secrecy as long as Scott chose to maintain his *incognito*, informed me that Mr. Mackay, the Bailie Nicoll Jarvie of " Rob Roy," was his uncle, and that he heard Scott and his uncle talk and laugh on the subject without reserve. This incident occurred two years before Scott avowed the authorship, at a public dinner, in response to a toast from Lord Meadowbank.

Many years afterwards, when Lockhart's " Life of Sir Walter Scott" appeared, I was gratified to learn from it that his first clear conviction that Scott was the author of the Waverley Novels was derived from the same peculiarity in style that I had discovered twenty years earlier. Critics insisted that no man so distinguished as a poet had been or could be equally distinguished in another and opposite department of literature.

I had also, from 1819, maintained, " with more zeal than knowledge," but very confidently, that Sir Philip Francis was the author of the " Letters of Junius ; " and although Sir Philip did not, like Sir Walter, finally avow himself to be the author, his identity has been almost positively established.

Towards the close of the summer of 1825, my friend Peck, saying that it was time I was doing something better than working as a journeyman, offered to sell me the " Telegraph " establishment, having, as he said, other business enough to occupy his time ; and in September I became the proprietor, as I had for three years been the editor, of the " Telegraph." Mr. Peck thus announced his retirement : —

TO THE PATRONS OF THE " TELEGRAPH."

The arrangement in the publication of this paper, which has been several weeks contemplated, is now made. Mr. Thurlow Weed, to whose assistance in the management of the paper I have for some time past been greatly indebted, succeeds me as editor and publisher of the " Telegraph." I have known Mr. Weed intimately for the last three years, and as editor of papers in other counties much longer ; and his uniform support of correct principles through all the changes and mutations of New York politics is a satisfactory pledge (to which I can add my own assurance) that the " Telegraph " will remain true to its principles and its friends.   In his hands I trust the paper will suffer no diminution of public favor, as I am' confident it will not in its character of a public journal.

The liberal and constant encouragement and patronage which I have received during the period I have published this paper calls for my most grateful acknowledgment, and I confidently hope that the establishment, in other hands, will not be less successful.

Everard Peck.

My own introductory article follows, from which I shall content myself with brief extracts : —

In assuming the charge of the " Telegraph," newspaper usage requires an avowal of the principles which are to influence its editor. In the present instance, however, this duty seems less imperative, as the person into whose hands the establishment passes has been for some time in the employment of the late proprietor, and is not unknown to the readers and patrons of the paper.   The political character of the " Telegraph " will remain unchanged and unchangeable.

In passing, we cannot but indulge in an expression of grateful pride at the result of the late presidential election.   Recollections of the zealous though humble part which this paper sustained in that contest will be long and ardently cherished.   We declared for Mr. Adams long before the political horoscope had indicated upon whose shoulders the presidential mantle would fall.   The political head of our nation is every way worthy of the exalted station which he occupies. His ripe literary attainments, his long and faithful public services, the purity of his morals, the singleness of his patriotism, and the integrity of his character, all conspire to dignify the trust which has been committed to him, and to elevate and adorn the councils over which he presides. . . .

In turning our view to the situation of the State government, the scene is not less bright and cheering.   New York stands redeemed from the thralldom that so long enfeebled and disgraced her.   The political regeneration effected at the last election was peculiarly grateful to those who, like ourselves, had labored industriously many years for such a consummation.

In all political controversies we shall avoid, as far as possible, indulging in feelings or expressions of bitterness or acrimony.   We have seen and felt too many of the evils arising from political intemperance to be instrumental in weakening or sundering the ties which sweeten and hallow social intercourse.

> " Accursed be the verse, how smooth soe'er it flow,
> That tends to make one honest man my foe."

I felt now that the " tide in the affairs of men " had begun at last to set in my favor. With a reasonable hope that with industry and economy it would " lead on," if not " to fortune," at least to a competency, and this was all that I desired. Indeed, up to that time, I had not even desired so much, or given much thought to pecuniary considerations. I was active and zealous in the support of my party and friends, feeling more real interest in them than in what concerned myself. But I went to work now earnestly and cheerfully, confident in my ability to establish myself permanently and reputably in a pursuit congenial to my feelings, and suited to such capacity as I possessed. At any rate, I had great enthusiasm in my business of printer and editor, and liked the excitement of politics, deriving great satisfaction in being instrumental in bringing capable and good men into the public service.

About the time I became proprietor of " The Rochester Telegraph," I received the following letter from General Tallmadge : —

You will need to be in Albany most of next winter. To be there without business will impair your standing, and subject you to the charge of being a lobby man. If you were in the next Assembly, it would save your influence, protect your character, enable you to collect information and the better edit your paper, and increase your general usefulness fourfold to the public and to your friends. It is important you be on the next Assembly ticket, and that you have on it good men.

To this letter I replied that my new business responsibilities required constant attention, and that I could neither go again to the Assembly nor pass any portion of my time during the session in Albany. And then, quite to the surprise of our citizens generally, I prevailed upon the venerable Vincent Matthews, who had been twenty-five or thirty years out of the line of representative duties, to accept a nomination for the Assembly. He was elected; and although verging on seventy, repaired to Albany in good spirits, and found in legislation a pleasant interval and relief from his arduous professional labors.

CHAPTER XX.

1826.

EARLY in 1826, finding the business of the office increasing with the increasing growth of the village, and looking forward to the not distant time when a daily paper would be required, I invited Robert Martin, one of the proprietors of the Albany "Daily Advertiser," an old friend, with whom I had worked in our journeyman days, to join me in business. He came to Rochester, and after a brief examination into the condition of the establishment, became my partner; and soon afterwards, "The Rochester Daily Telegraph," published by Weed & Martin, made its appearance. All went on pleasantly and prosperously until the autumn of 1826, when an event occurred which resulted in our separation. That event was the abduction of William Morgan, — a cloud which, when it first appeared, seemed no bigger than "a man's hand," yet which spread out until it darkened the social and political horizon, occasioning a storm, which not only violently disturbed the elements in this State, but divided and distracted parties, churches, families, and friends in New England, Pennsylvania, Ohio, and Michigan. In this truly embarrassing, and as truly painful controversy, I became reluctantly involved. Though not myself a Freemason, I had all my life regarded the institution as an eminently useful one. This feeling had been inspired, probably, by the circumstance that Franklin, Washington, Lafayette, and other men distinguished by their wisdom and virtues were

WILLIAM MORGAN.

Masons. When, therefore, I saw the clouds gathering black-
ness, and felt assured that a storm of unusual severity was impending, I endeavored to escape by a withdrawal from business
and a removal from Rochester. But this purpose was overruled in ways which will be explained as this narrative progresses.

The whole history of the " Morgan affair " has never been
written. It occurred forty-four years ago. Nearly all of the
prominent actors in the scenes of 1826, 1827, 1828, and 1829,
on either side of that conflict, have been called to their final account. Of all that transpired from Morgan's abduction from
Batavia, in September, 1826, judicially and politically, I am
probably better informed than any other living witness. In
view of the fact that the importance of that event entitles it to
a place in the history of our country, it is to be regretted that
so many persons who could have contributed valuable information should have passed away, " making no sign." Several
gentlemen implicated in the abduction, and subjected to indictment, lived to look back calmly, and to converse with me with
perfect freedom and frankness. With *Colonel Simeon B. Jewett*, of Clarkson, Monroe County, who died within the last year,
my personal relations were scarcely disturbed. During the bitterest days of the controversy, when he was a defendant and I
a prosecutor, and for the last twenty years of his life, we were
close friends. With him I have gone over the whole ground
often, without the slightest disagreement about the facts. I
could name others, who, were they living, would agree with
me in all the essential facts and circumstances connected with
that extraordinary event. But, while conscious of a desire to
be just and truthful, to write without favor or prejudice, and to
deal impartially and fairly with all, I still hesitate to enter upon
a task so delicate and a responsibility so great. Twenty-five, or
twenty, or even fifteen years ago, I should have deemed it simply absurd ; for until one generation had passed away, and time
had modified the prejudices of another, it would have been idle
to expect that a person who had been prominent on either side
of the controversy should be recognized as an impartial historian. The whole question is so intimately connected, for the
next three years, with my own history ; I was so much and so
constantly occupied, first as a member of the Committee of In-

vestigation, appointed by the citizens of Rochester, and next, in judicial proceedings, that I can scarcely progress a step without stumbling over the " Morgan affair." Perhaps no one known prominently as an Anti-Mason was more obnoxious than myself. The press, far and near, was unsparing in its denunciations of me. The public judgment of my conduct was anything but flattering. It required much more than one generation to enable me to repel injurious aspersion and live down popular prejudices. It will be seen, therefore, that if I undertake the task of writing a history of the " Morgan affair," I shall do so with a due sense of its intrinsic difficulties, and a proper distrust of the propriety of asking the public to accept the testimony of a partisan who, had he written during the heat of the controversy, would have been discredited.

When it became known that I was preparing an autobiography, I was spoken to by several friends, and written to by others, all of whom urged that I should make the " Morgan affair " a part of my book. Not being able to perceive how I could ignore the subject, and hardly daring to hope for an impartial hearing, I conversed with my lamented friend, the late John A. Kennedy, and two other gentlemen, distinguished alike for their devotion to Freemasonry, their general intelligence, and their matured judgment. Those gentlemen had sought and obtained a history of the affair from Masonic sources, which, in all essential particulars, harmonized with my own recollection; and as those gentlemen united with others in expressing a desire that I should give a detailed and, as far as practicable, an authenticated history of the " Morgan excitement," I decided to undertake it, reiterating the assurance that my greatest desire, in relation to it, is to be impartial, truthful, and just.

Early in the summer of 1826 my next-door neighbor, Mr. Dyer, came in one morning desiring a private interview. He opened the conversation by asking me if I was a Freemason, and upon my informing him that I was not, he said that he had a communication of an important and confidential character to make to me, — so confidential that he desired me to take an oath that I would under no circumstances reveal the nature of it to any one. I declined to take the oath, but told him he could rely implicitly upon my promise to keep his secret. He then told me that a Captain Morgan, who had been boarding with him for several weeks, had just completed a revelation of the first three degrees of Masonry, for which they now wanted a publisher. It was necessary, he said, that the printing should be done very secretly, as, if the author became known, it would certainly be at the peril of his life. On my informing him, after some further conversation, that my partner in business was a Freemason, he said that circumstance rendered it imperative that they should seek a publisher elsewhere; and again enjoining secrecy upon me, he took his leave.

I neither heard nor thought of the incident again until, in the September following, there came a report from Batavia that a Captain Morgan, who had been residing there for several weeks, was mysteriously missing from his lodging and family. This was succeeded in a few days by an account of the seizure of the printed sheets of a book revealing the secrets of Masonry, written by Morgan, and printed by David C. Miller, editor and publisher of the " Batavia Advocate." The prolonged and unexplained absence of Morgan occasioned much inquiry, resulting in a call for a public meeting at Batavia, which was numerously attended, and presided over by the Hon. David E. Evans. A committee, consisting of the chairman, Trumbull Cary, George F. Talbot, Timothy Fitch, and other citizens, was appointed to investigate the alleged abduction of Morgan, and also an attempt which had been made to burn Miller's printing-office.

When the account of the proceedings at that meeting reached Rochester, I wrote and published the following editorial paragraph: —

EXCITEMENT AT BATAVIA.

Much excitement exists at Batavia in consequence of the mysterious and protracted absence of Captain William Morgan, who, several weeks since, seems to have been spirited away from his family and his home by Freemasons, with a view, it is alleged, of preventing his publication of the secrets of their Order. The persons engaged in this violation of law must have been over-zealous members of the fraternity. It is incumbent, however, upon better-informed Freemasons to take the laboring oar in discovering the whereabouts of the absent man, and in restoring him to his liberty.

This, as will be seen, was a reasonable and proper view of the question; but that was not the opinion formed of it by the

members of the Order, for, directly after the carriers had been
dispatched with the paper, our patrons came greatly excited to
the office, directing that their papers and their advertisements
should be discontinued.   As most of the active business men of
the village were Masons, the next twenty-four hours deprived us
of so large an amount of our best business that ruin suddenly
stared me in the face.   Nor was that all.   I had involved my
partner in a common disaster.   Inquiring of him what this extraordinary excitement meant, he handed me a book containing
an oath administered to persons joining the Masonic fraternity,
invoking retribution of the most terrible kind as the penalty
justly due to the betrayer of any Masonic secrets.

After I had read the oath, my partner, Mr. Robert Martin,
asked me what I thought of a man who, if he had taken such
an obligation, should violate it.   My answer — a very sincere,
but very superficial one — was that such a man deserved the
punishment he had called down upon his own head.   I had ever
regarded the institution of Masonry as a benevolent and useful
one, remembering how often I had heard Franklin, Lafayette,
and other eminently good men spoken of as members of the
Order.   But while I cherished these general views of Masonry,
I had never cared to become one of the brotherhood, although
suggestions to that effect had been occasionally made to me.   I
was influenced by a veneration for Washington's Farewell Address, a paper which always seemed to me to contain the
whole duty of an American citizen, and in which he warns his
countrymen against secret associations.

Soon after the publication of my obnoxious paragraph, I
turned over to my partner the printing establishment, of which
I was one half owner, with its assets, having determined to seek
employment elsewhere.   This course was induced by a desire to
protect my partner, and to avoid an angry conflict with those
who had been my best friends.   Learning, simultaneously with
this occurrence, that an editor was wanted at Utica for a journal of my own side in politics, I wrote to an intimate and influential friend, the late J. H. Ostrom, offering my services.   Much
to my surprise the offer was curtly declined.   A subsequent
effort to obtain the vacant editorial chair of the Troy "Sentinel" was attended with the same result.   I learned, years afterwards, that in both cases the Masons at Utica and Troy,

though previously my personal and political friends, were informed that I had made myself obnoxious to the Order. My position, therefore, became very embarrassing, — without employment or means, and with a wife and three children to support. It was urgently necessary that I should find something to do. There was in the village an old Ramage printing press, with a battered font of type, awaiting a purchaser. My friends, Samuel Works, Harvey Ely, and Frederick F. Backus — all since dead — bought these primitive materials, with which, thus driven to bay, I commenced the publication of an Anti-Masonic newspaper.

I have thus far anticipated events, and must now return to the investigations made by the first committee appointed by the citizens of Batavia. William Morgan was a native of Culpepper County, Virginia, and was born in 1776. He was a man of much natural ability and of fair education. He had followed the trade of stonemason, but of his early life or character little was known. After his abduction, he was represented by his Masonic brethren as intemperate and unprincipled ; while, on the other hand, his friends asserted that he was a man of good character, who had served in the army with the rank of captain in the war with England in 1812. Among other injurious charges against him, there was one of piracy, he having been, as it was alleged, one of the Lafitte gang, which infested the delta of the Mississippi. It was further represented that in 1819, with the assistance of some reckless associates, he violently abducted Lucinda Pendleton, a girl of sixteen, whom he subsequently married. It is proper to say, however, that these reports were traced to the persons who were engaged in the effort, first to suppress Morgan's book, and then in spiriting him away. Mrs. Morgan herself seemed warmly attached to her husband, and always protested that these various accusations were unfounded.

In 1821 he became a resident of York, in the Province of Upper Canada ; from whence, after the loss of his property by fire, he came to Rochester, where he worked for a year or two as a journeyman mason. In 1822 or 1823, he removed to Le Roy, in Genesee County. This village was eminently distinguished in Masonic annals, boasting even at that early day of lodges, chapters, and an encampment of knights templars, of all of which my old friend, Major James Ganson, who served with me in the legislature of 1825, was the master spirit. It was here that Morgan became an active and " a bright Mason." He devoted much of his time to the attainment of perfection in the different degrees, and he contracted then, if he had not done so previously, idle and partially intemperate habits. Misunderstandings grew up between Morgan and his Masonic friends at Le Roy, which induced his removal to Batavia, where the rupture between him and his brethren soon became an open one. The idea of revealing the secrets of the craft to the world was then conceived, and partly entered upon. Finding himself suspected, he went to Rochester, where he lay concealed, working at his book for two months. Having failed to get a publisher there, he returned to Batavia ; and now David C. Miller, an " entered apprentice Mason," concluded to take the hazard of printing the work. Other Masons soon obtained knowledge of the fact that these sheets were going through Miller's press, although the work was done at nights and on Sundays. Their first counter move was an attempt to purchase Morgan's silence, and it was alleged on their part that he consented to surrender his manuscripts and to abandon the enterprise. This, however, was denied by Miller, and Morgan's intimate friends. A few weeks before his abduction, the Canandaigua papers contained the following notice, which, however, then attracted no attention, except by those for whose eye it was especially intended :

NOTICE AND CAUTION.

If a man calling himself William Morgan should intrude himself upon the community, they should be on their guard, particularly the Masonic fraternity. Any information in relation to Morgan can be obtained by calling at the Masonic Hall in this village. Brethren and companions are particularly requested to observe, mark, and govern themselves accordingly. Morgan is considered a swindler and a dangerous man. There are people in this village who would be glad to see this Captain Morgan.

CANANDAIGUA, *August* 9, 1826.

This notice was copied into the Batavia papers, and soon afterwards a paragraph of similar import was published in a Black Rock paper, with an additional averment that the fraternity had " amply provided themselves against Morgan's impostures and swindling propensities." Things very shortly assumed a threatening aspect in Batavia. Masons from abroad were constantly in conclave with the Masons of that village. Miller was prosecuted for sundry debts and their collection harshly enforced. Menaces were heard that the publication of Morgan's book would be suppressed, and Miller, becoming alarmed, took measures for defending himself and his office in case of an assault. Morgan was also harrassed by summonses and warrants for small debts, for some of which he was committed, and subsequently bailed upon the gaol limits. He was committed to the custody of the sheriff at the suit of Nathan Follett, and was again bailed upon the limits. Other schemes were resorted to in order to arrest the publication, among which was an attempt by one Daniel Johns to get into partnership with Morgan and Miller, he to furnish all the money required to get out the book. Major Ganson was at the bottom of this fresh " dodge," which (Miller's necessities being great) was partially successful. Johns obtained and handed over to Ganson what was supposed to be the essential portion of the manuscript, but which proved to be no more than the beginning of the disclosure of the Royal Arch degree. This left Morgan and Miller free for a few days to go on with the printing of the first three degrees. It was only a brief respite, for on the 18th of August, while engaged at his employment, Johnson Goodwell, Kelsey Stone, and John Wilson, residents of Batavia, in company with Daniel H. Dana (a constable of the town of Pembroke), rushed into Morgan's apartment and seized upon his person by virtue of an execution. They also took all the papers to be found. Morgan was hurried off to prison without a moment's time being allowed him to procure bail. This happened on Saturday afternoon. As soon, however, as the prisoner's friends heard of his arrest they came forward with competent bail, but while they persevered until twelve o'clock at night, then too late to transact secular business, neither the sheriff or the jailor could be found. In the absence of these officers there was, of course, no one authorized to admit the debtor to bail. Early in the evening of the same day the constable entered the apartment of Mrs. Morgan, demanding property to satisfy the execution. Mrs. Morgan protested that they possessed nothing, but this did not satisfy either the constable or the creditor, who commenced searching trunks and boxes, pouncing upon a few manuscripts which they carried off. Morgan remained in prison until Monday, when he was admitted to bail. During Sunday he was visited by many persons, who endeavored to induce him to relinquish the publication of their mysteries. Neither entreaties nor threats were found to move him from his determination.

The next movement was a night attack upon Miller's printing-office with the design of destroying the manuscript copy, or, if printed, all the sheets of the work. Some forty men residing in different and distant towns were concerned in this incendiary movement. Supper had been provided for them at Ganson's hotel in Le Roy, where they assembled on the 8th of September. At a late hour of the night they proceeded to Batavia under the convoy of Colonel Edward Sawyer, a high Mason of Canandaigua. Before their arrival at the printing-office, however, they were informed that Miller anticipated an attack and would defend his office, and so well satisfied were the invaders that their own lives or limbs were in jeopardy that the assault was abandoned. Colonel Sawyer was bitterly reproached for the cowardice which had resulted in the entire failure of such a formidable expedition. This, however, was but a postponement of the design. A yet more atrocious crime was attempted but two days afterwards. On the night of Saturday, the 10th of September, the people of Batavia were startled from their slumbers by the cry of "Fire!" The flames were bursting from the stairway of the printing-office of Colonel Miller, but the discovery was so early, and assistance was so promptly rendered, that they were soon extinguished. Sixteen persons were sleeping in the office, so that had the stairway been burned, all these lives would have been placed in imminent peril. This calamity was averted by an apparent interference of Providence. On the evening of this memorable night a number of teamsters were stopping at the hotel opposite the printing-office. As they were not all able to obtain lodgings in the tavern, some took refuge for the night in the body of a covered stage-coach, standing in the street near the printing-office; the flames were discovered by these men, who aroused the slumbering villagers in season to avert the calamity. Cotton balls saturated with turpentine and other combustibles were found under the stairs, and moreover the building had been besmeared with the same compounds. It was immediately charged that Miller had applied the torch

with his own hands in order to increase the popular sympathy
in his own favor, and this statement was generally believed for
several months, and indeed until evidence of the most conclusive and unanswerable character vindicated him from this accusation.

On the morning of the 10th of September Nicholas G. Chesebro, a master of the lodge in Canandaigua, obtained a warrant from the magistrate of that village to apprehend William
Morgan on a charge of petty larceny. In the month of May
preceding, when on a visit to Canandaigua, Morgan had borrowed a shirt and cravat from Mr. Kingsley, the tavern-keeper
with whom he lodged, which he had not returned. This was
the alleged petty larceny for which he was to be arrested. The
warrant was issued on Sunday. Chesebro, Halloway, Hayward, Henry Howard, Harris Seymour, Moses Roberts, and
Joseph Schofield started for Batavia in an extra coach. At
Avon, Asa Nowlan, and at Caledonia, John Butterfield, and at
Le Roy, E. G. Smith joined the party. At the latter place the
warrant was endorsed by the justice of the peace of Genesee
County. While supping at Stafford, Dr. Samuel S. Butler was
dispatched in advance to Batavia with a message to William
Seaver, master of the lodge at that place. The rest of the party
left Stafford immediately, having been first joined by Major
Ganson, but were met in the vicinity of Batavia by a messenger
who informed them that their appearance in Batavia in an extra
coach would occasion fresh alarm. Cheesebro, and Hayward
the constable, then proceeded to the village on foot, and early
the following morning Hayward arrested Morgan and took him
to Daniel's tavern. An extra coach stood ready for them, but
while preparing for their departure Colonel Miller appeared and
objected to Morgan's being taken away from the limits. Ho
alleged that as he was Morgan's bail he would personally become liable for the debts. The constable answered that Morgan was now under arrest for a criminal offense, and must be
taken to Canandaigua. Miller was pushed aside by the witnesses, and Chesebro, mounting upon the box, directed the
coachman to drive fast until they should cross the county line.
Morgan himself made no objection, but remarked that once at
Canandaigua he would soon satisfy Kingsley that he had no intention of stealing the clothing. When they reached Canan-

daigua Morgan was carried before Justice Chipman, where the charge was investigated, and fell to the ground. On being discharged from this prosecution, however, he was immediately re-arrested by Chesebro for a debt of two dollars due to Aaron Ackley, another tavern-keeper, for the collection of which Chesebro produced a power of attorney. Morgan admitted this debt, for which an execution was issued on the spot. Having no money to satisfy the claim, he pulled off his coat and made a tender of that. The officer refused to take it, and Morgan was forthwith lodged in prison. On that day the sun dawned for the last time on his freedom.

Mrs. Morgan soon became alarmed by the absence of her husband, and hearing of his arrest, went to William R. Thompson, the sheriff of the county, for information of his whereabouts. Thompson gave her the particulars of his arrest and the charge against him. Mrs. Morgan inquired if his release could be effected by her giving up to the Masons the papers in her possession. Thompson thought such a surrender might effect her object, and advised Mrs. Morgan to take the papers to Canandaigua and make the attempt. He also recommended her to go in the company of a Mason, and suggested either Mr. Follett or Mr. Ketcham, but after consulting with these gentlemen, he informed her that they would not go unless they were allowed previously to examine the papers. To this demand Mrs. Morgan assented on the assurance of the sheriff that the papers should not be kept from her. Follett and Ketcham then went to Morgan's house, looked over the papers, and agreed to proceed with her to Canandaigua. At Stafford her guardians were met by Ganson and Johns, who proceeded to a reëxamination of the papers. Johns was asked if they were the same papers which he had seen while in partnership with Morgan and Miller. He replied that with the exception of one degree they were. Follett then returned to Batavia, leaving Ketcham to continue the journey with Mrs. Morgan to Canandaigua, where they arrived about noon the next day.

Ketcham, taking the papers with him, promised Mrs. Morgan to do all in his power to obtain the release of her husband. Toward evening he returned and informed the distressed woman of her husband's trial and acquittal for larceny, and of his subsequent arrest and imprisonment for debt. He added that

Morgan had subsequently been taken from the prison by a man from Pennsylvania to whom Morgan was indebted, and he was carried off in a close carriage to Pennsylvania. Ketcham then very coldly asked Mrs. Morgan when she wished to return to Batavia. The desolate woman replied that she would be glad to go immediately, as she had left a child at home but two years old and had an infant but two months old in her arms. Ketcham, it is scarcely needful to remark, was himself one of the conspirators. I knew him well, and believe that he was a kind-hearted man, and one incapable of doing any wanton wrong, but in this instance he was actuated by misguided motives of obedience and fidelity to his Order.

He now went to the stage-office and took a passage for Mrs. Morgan. Upon his return he found her in great anguish, and her sorrows awakened his sympathy, and he endeavored to soothe her by renewed assurances that he would ascertain the place of Morgan's concealment, and if possible obtain his release. He requested, however, that he should be permitted to take the papers with him to Rochester. He told her that a part of the papers which they wanted were still missing, and made liberal promises of money if she would produce it. He offered her twenty-five dollars as evidence of his sincerity, but she declined to take the money or promise her aid in obtaining the original manuscripts. Ketcham, however, upon leaving her, still solemnly promised to find Morgan and inform his wife of his condition. Mrs. Morgan returned by herself to her home in Batavia. At Le Roy Ganson again made his appearance, and told Mrs. Morgan that he was going to Batavia to make arrangements for her support, and that her husband would not be seen by her for perhaps at least a year more. He assured her at the same time that he had not been killed. In a few hours after she reached home she was visited by Thomas M'Cully, at whose suit her husband had been imprisoned in August. He informed her that the lodge had appointed him to provide for the support of herself and her children, and that he had taken lodgings for her at Daniel's tavern. All these offers were promptly rejected by Mrs. Morgan.

It is obvious that all the proceedings which had been taken against Morgan, whether by civil or criminal process, were mere pretexts to keep possession of his person until arrangements were consummated for preventing the disclosures which were so much feared. Meantime, however, the sheets revealing the first three degrees of Masonry had been printed, and were being bound.

Simultaneously with Mrs. Morgan's departure from Canandaigua, Colonel Miller received an anonymous note in an unknown hand, informing him that an attempt would that day be made to take his office by assault, for the purpose of obtaining the sheets of his supposed Masonic publication. Miller called some friends together, several of whom regarded the note as a hoax; others thought it prudent to be on their guard. Two swivels, several pistols, and twenty muskets, with clubs and other weapons, were taken into the office, and a number of citizens remained to use them if it became necessary. About twelve o'clock in the day some sixty or seventy men, armed with heavy clubs and coming apparently from different directions, entered the village. They were all strangers to the locality. The party rallied at the house of Daniel's, but made no demonstration upon the printing-office. Along with this company was French, a constable from Le Roy, and he proceeded along to the office and arrested Miller, who made no resistance. He was placed in an open wagon with seven men, strangers to him, all armed as above described, and in this manner, attended by the mob, which was increased by a number of the people of Batavia, they carried him eight miles to Stafford, where, in defiance of the remonstrance of his counsel, he was taken to the third story of a stone house, and placed under the guard of five men in a lodge-room. Miller's counsel was informed that he was arrested on a criminal process at the instance, as appeared subsequently, of his *ci-devant* partner Johns, who had succeeded in purloining a part of the Morgan manuscript, and who had charged Miller with stealing thirty or forty dollars from him. From Stafford they finally took Miller to Le Roy, not as his guards told him to be tried there, nor to appear before any ordinary tribunal; he was going, they said, where Morgan had gone. Upon arriving at Le Roy the constable proposed to take Miller to a lodge-room, but both Miller and his counsel objected to that arrangement, and insisted upon going directly before the magistrate. This course was accordingly taken. Here it appeared that the warrant was merely a civil process issued upon the application of Johns for the recovery of certain moneys advanced by him to Miller while he was acting as a counterfeit partner in what Miller supposed to be their joint speculation. After waiting half an hour, the constable not having returned himself, and no plaintiff appearing, Miller was discharged. French and his party again rallied, and made several efforts to seize Miller upon the same warrant, but his friends succeeded in placing him in a close carriage and conveying him late at night safely to his home.

On the return of Mrs. Morgan to Batavia, pecuniary assistance was offered to her by those who, she knew, were parties to the conspiracy which had deprived her of the support of her husband. Other citizens of Batavia, however, immediately provided for her and her children. Meantime, those citizens despatched an agent, Timothy Fitch, Esq., to Canandaigua. The information first procured by Mr. Fitch served only to intensify the mystery he was endeavoring to clear up. He ascertained from Hiram Hopkins that Morgan had been taken to the county prison on the evening of the 11th of September; that soon afterwards Loton Lawson hired a horse of Ackley, avowedly for the purpose of going to Rochester. Lawson returned early in the morning, informing Ackley, the innkeeper, as he was going to bed, that some gentlemen from Rochester would call for him in the course of the day. In the afternoon Burrage Smith and John Whitney, both from Rochester, did call for Lawson, who joined them, and all three left the inn together. In the evening of that day, September 12th, Lawson went to the jail, and applied to Mrs. Hall, her husband the keeper being out, for permission to see Morgan privately. This request was refused, but subsequently Morgan was called to the door, where Lawson informed him that he had come to pay the debt and costs and release him, asking him whether, on being discharged, he would go home with him and stay that night. On Morgan's replying in the affirmative, Lawson requested Mrs. Hall to let him out, saying that he would satisfy the execution; but as the jailer was not at home, and the execution being locked up, she declined to act. Lawson then said he would pay the amount of the execution when Hall came in, but Morgan replied that he was undressed and ready for bed, and might as well remain there till morning. Lawson, however, saying that he had been

running about all day for Morgan, insisted that the matter
should be arranged that night. He then left the jail to look
for Mr. Hall, but returned with another man in half an hour,
saying that Hall could not be found. He then offered to leave
with Mrs. Hall a sum larger than the amount of the execution,
but she persisted in her refusal to do anything in the absence
of her husband. Lawson became importunate, and offered to
leave one hundred dollars in pledge, but it was all of no avail.
Again Lawson left the jail, but soon returned with Colonel
Sawyer, both urging Mrs. Hall to release the prisoner. Finally
they brought Mr. Chesebro, whom Mrs. Hall knew as a plaintiff in the suit ; and on whose direction, the money having been
counted, Mrs. Hall consented to release Morgan. As Mrs.
Hall was unlocking the prison door, Lawson stepped out of the
front door, and gave a shrill whistle. When Mrs. Hall reached
the front door she saw a man coming to the steps. When
Morgan came out of the cell Lawson took him by the arm
in a friendly manner, and they departed together. Immediately afterwards Mrs. Hall heard a cry of " Murder ! " and, hur-
rying to the door, saw Morgan between Lawson and another
man, struggling and crying loudly for help. While they were
dragging him away, she saw Chesebro and Sawyer standing near
by, but taking no part. Soon afterwards a carriage, following
in the direction taken by those who had dragged Morgan away,
drove past the jail, Chesebro and Sawyer following, the latter
picking up and taking with him the hat of Morgan, which had
been lost in the affray. A neighboring woman recognized
Chesebro, Sawyer, and Coe, a stage proprietor, standing some
time near the jail before Morgan came out. This woman also
heard the cries of distress ; she also saw a carriage with Hubbard's gray horses driven by the jail, then empty ; but she soon
saw it re-pass, taking the road to Rochester, with several persons in it. These facts were corroborated by others, all sworn
to. Colonel Sawyer, on being asked what was the trouble at
the jail, replied that a man who had been lodged there on a
warrant was taken out to be tried. Hubbard said that a man
whom he did not know had engaged his carriage to take a party
to Rochester. He said that about nine o'clock in the evening
he was requested to drive down the Palmyra road, where his
passengers would overtake him. He, therefore, drove down

the road past the jail until he was requested to stop, when several men in the street got into the carriage; then he was told to turn round and drive to Rochester; that they stopped but twice on the way, and arrived in Rochester about daylight. Passing immediately through that town they proceeded to Hanford's Landing, where he understood the party expected to obtain a vessel. He left his party in the road near a piece of woods. On driving back to Rochester he met two carriages; he did not know any of the persons who had driven with him; observed no violence towards any one of the company, and had received no pay. Such, briefly, was the information elicited by Mr. Fitch, at Canandaigua.

Meantime, the protracted and mysterious absence of Morgan awakened deeper and more general feeling at Batavia. The fact that some fifteen or twenty men came from Buffalo and joined a large party at Stafford, some of whom came even from Canada on the night of the 8th of September, when Miller's office was to have been destroyed, had transpired. Several of these persons had been identified, and proved to be men of unblemished reputations. It was evident, therefore, that the conspiracy to suppress Morgan's book was widespread. In view of these fresh developments, public meetings, numerously attended, were held at Batavia on the 26th of September and on the 4th of October. The facts laid before the meetings aroused the popular indignation. It did not appear that all who belonged to the Masonic fraternity were concerned in the conspiracy. On the contrary, many highly respectable Masons were among the foremost in demanding an investigation. But it did appear that all those engaged in the conspiracy were Freemasons, generally young, but all zealous and active members of the order. A committee of ten highly respectable citizens were appointed to follow up the investigations, commencing at the point where Mr. Fitch left them. That committee was composed of such men as David E. Evans, Trumbull Cary, George F. Talbot, Harmon Holden, Timothy Fitch, etc. On the 2d of October that committee addressed a letter to Governor Clinton, enclosing a copy of the proceedings of their meeting, together with the depositions that had been taken at Canandaigua. In that letter they informed the governor that " the excitement among the people in this section of the State has assumed aspects which we think just subject of alarm, and an excitement which it will be difficult to restrain or allay, unless the cause be investigated and removed." The governor received that letter on the 6th of October, and on the following day his Excellency transmitted to Mr. Talbot, chairman of the committee, a proclamation setting forth the evils to be apprehended from such violations of the public peace as those complained of, and enjoining the State officers and ministers of justice to " pursue all just and proper measures for the apprehension of the offenders, and commanding the coöperation of the people in maintaining the ascendency of the laws."

The governor also wrote the following letter to the committee : —

ALBANY, *October* 7, 1826.

GENTLEMEN, — I received your communication yesterday by Mr. Evans, and, after mature deliberation, I have come to the conclusion that the inclosed paper, which you are authorized to publish, will answer the purpose of maintaining the peace and good order of the community. Indeed, I do not see how I can interfere to a greater extent at present. Any forcible opposition to the execution of the laws which cannot be put down by the civil authority, must be met in another shape ; but, as it does not appear that any such has been exhibited, and I trust that none will be, the magistrates of the county must proceed, in the ordinary channels of justice, to arrest the offenders, to vindicate the rights and to protect the property, liberty, and persons of individuals, and to maintain the ascendency of the laws ; and if there should prove to be any delinquency on this occasion measures suitable to such default will be promptly pursued.

As it appears that the principal offenders are known, I have not thought it necessary to offer any specific reward for their detection and apprehension ; but I am willing to pay any reasonable and necessary expenses that may be incurred for those purposes. Deeply regretting and entirely condemning the outrage of which you complain, nothing shall be wanting on my part that is due to the occasion and the emergency. Nothing can justify a resort to personal violence, or an aggression upon the peace of society, and no person can be punished for his acts, however deplorable or depraved, except by the legitimate authorities of the country.

I am, etc.,   DEWITT CLINTON.

To THEODORE F. TALBOT and others,

A committee in behalf of the citizens of Genesee County.

CHAPTER XXI.

1826–1827.

THE governor's proclamation occasioned the call of public meetings in the counties of Livingston, Ontario, Monroe, and Niagara, where committees were appointed whose combined investigations were set forth in a report prepared in convention at Lewiston, of which I shall speak hereafter. At this stage of the investigation, greatly excited as the people were, it was in the power of the Masonic fraternity to have averted most of the painful experience of the next two or three years. Most of our intelligent, enterprising citizens were Freemasons. Had prominent Masons, hundreds of whom were both innocent and ignorant of the offence, united with the people in their effort to investigate the outrage, it would have calmed the "troubled waters," for up to this period there had been no general or indiscriminate denunciations. But, unhappily, Masons generally either regarded the popular feeling as directed against their order, or were led to believe that the excitement was artificial, and that the conspiracy had for its object a crusade against Masonry. Various rumors, representing Morgan as having been seen at distant places, were circulated in the newspapers, and believed by thousands whose good opinion of Masonry prompted them to disbelieve that its members were capable of such an outrage. This general delusion on the subject was largely occasioned by the active efforts of those who were concerned in the abduction, and who deemed it essential to their own safety that their brethren should be united in their behalf. Even as late as February, 1827, at a meeting of the Grand Chapter at Albany, its charity fund was largely increased and placed at the disposal of the Masons at Rochester for the protection of " persecuted" brethren. This money was given, as I shall show hereafter, to men who took Morgan from the jail at Canandaigua and conveyed him to Fort Niagara; and with this money they fled, three to New Orleans and one to England. And yet I have information which satisfies me that a large number of the Royal Arch Masons from other parts of the State who voted in favor of that increased charity fund did so in good faith, being entirely ignorant of the facts in the case and of the motives of those who moved it.

The appointment of committees in the different counties brought several men of influence, energy, and courage into the service of the people, prominent among whom was Bates Cook, of Lewiston, Niagara County. Mr. Cook was an eminently good man. He was a lawyer in good practice, and universally esteemed. It was through his indefatigable industry and perseverance that the facts which I am about to relate were developed. Morgan had been driven, as before stated, from Canandaigua to Hanford's Landing, thirty-three miles, on the night of the 12th of September; from thence transferred to a carriage owned by Ezra Platt, of Rochester, a Royal Arch Mason, which was driven by Orson Parkhurst to the farm of Mr. Allen, two miles west of the village of Clarkson. Lawson had preceded the carriage on horseback. At Clarkson Colonel Simeon B. Jewett rode on the box with the driver to Allen's farm. After a brief conversation between Jewett and Allen, the latter took his horses from a plough, leaving it in the furrow, and attached them to the carriage in which Morgan was confined. Parkhurst returned, and Allen drove the carriage still along the Ridge Road through the village of Gaines, stopping about a mile west of it in the road by a wood, where Elihu Mather soon appeared with fresh horses. They were attached to the carriage, and Mather himself, although like Allen a man of property, mounted the box and drove to Ridgeway, where Jeremiah Brown, a wealthy farmer, supervisor of the town, and an ex-member of the legislature, took his horses from the field in which they were at work, placed them before the mysterious carriage, mounted the box and drove to Wright's Tavern, four miles north of the village of Lockport. At Wright's the carriage was driven into the barn, and, although many persons were attracted by the circumstance that Mr. Brown was seen driving a strange carriage, with curtains down, none were allowed to hold communications with its passengers or even to enter the closed barn. Some of those who stood at the barn door to keep the people away were armed, and to inquiries of citizens "what all this meant," they were informed that a prisoner, whom it was necessary to guard, was on his way to Canada. About ten o'clock that night this carriage was driven away from Wright's towards Lewiston. At Mollineaux's Tavern, four miles farther west, Eli Bruce, of Lockport, the sheriff of Niagara County, who was with it, was identified. Bruce woke up the landlord, and desired him to put a pair of fresh horses to the carriage. Mr. Mollineaux's sons opposed letting the horses go unless he drove them himself, as they were young and he was unwilling to let strangers handle them. Bruce, however, objected to this, remarking that Brown was a careful driver. Mather stopped here, but Brown drove on, returning to Mollineaux's just before daylight, on the morning of the 14th. The horses were very much jaded, having, as he admitted, been driven twenty-six miles. Arriving at Lewiston Bruce called up Major Samuel Barton, a stage proprietor, who furnished a carriage and horses for Youngstown. Corydon Fox, the driver, when his team was harnessed, was directed by Bruce to drive around into a back street, in front of Barton's dwelling-house, where he found a carriage without horses standing in the middle of the street, with its curtains closed down. Fox, who kept his place on the box, saw Bruce and a third man take some person out of the other carriage and transfer him to that which he was driving. Not a word nor a sound was spoken or heard during this transfer, nor was the silence broken during the whole drive to Youngstown, six miles. At this place the carriage stopped in front of the house of Colonel King, whom Bruce called up. While Bruce was talking with King, Fox heard some one in his carriage call for water. Bruce replied, "You shall have some," though none was brought. Colonel King entered the carriage with Bruce, and Fox was directed to drive towards Fort Niagara, about a mile distant. They stopped near the graveyard, about eighty rods from the fort. Four persons descended from the carriage and walked towards the fort. After they had proceeded a few rods, Bruce turned around and dismissed Fox, telling him, as Fox informed the committee, to "go about his business." During the following day, Fox, the stage-driver, talked freely about his previous night's work, telling two or three persons that when Colonel King looked into the carriage he understood him to say, " Are you here, Morgan ? " Colonel Barton was rebuked for having sent a driver who was not a Mason on such an errand, and in a few days afterward Fox was induced to become a Mason.

Although thrust violently into a carriage at Canandaigua, and driven through a well-settled agricultural country, lined with villages, a distance of nearly a hundred and twenty miles, to Youngstown, at the mouth of the Niagara River, it required the utmost vigilance of numerous intelligent citizens to elicit the facts here briefly narrated. The Monroe County Committee, when first appointed, consisted of prominent and influential citizens irrespective of the circumstance of their being or not being Masons. Soon after its organization, however, it was ascertained that all that transpired in the committee was communicated to the Chapter, meetings of which were held simultaneously with the meetings of the investigating committee. The subject of these disclosures having been spoken of in the committee, the Masonic members thereof quietly withdrew, and attended no subsequent meeting. The future duties and responsibilities of the committee devolved upon Samuel Works, Harvey Ely, Frederick F. Backus, Frederick Whittlesey, and (Mr. Weed) myself. These gentlemen, aided efficiently by Bates Cook, of Lewiston, and Timothy Fitch, of Batavia, continued the investigation, acquiring, in the progress of the "Morgan affair" abroad, a by no means enviable reputation.

Leaving Morgan in the hands of Sheriff Bruce and Colonel King, after which, for a long time, it was impossible to trace him, the committee turned its attention to the courts. In October bills of indictment were found against James Ganson, Jesse French, Roswell Wilcox, and James Hurlbut, for falsely imprisoning Colonel Miller. That was the first legal proceeding in the Morgan business. James Ganson, in all the Batavia and Le Roy violations of law and order, was the master spirit.

Meantime Governor Clinton, who, as I shall show hereafter, was much better informed than even the Morgan Committee, and had abundant occasion for the solicitude he evinced, wrote the following letter to the Batavia Committee : —

ALBANY, *October* 6, 1826.

GENTLEMEN, — Understanding that William Morgan is still living, I have thought it advisable to issue the inclosed proclamation, offering further rewards, which you will please to see published in the newspapers of your own and neighboring counties, and in handbills if you think it necessary, the expenses of which I will pay. I will thank you for such further advice as in your opinion may lead to a full development of the outrageous proceedings that have occurred in your vicinity.   I am, gentlemen, etc.,   DEWITT CLINTON.

T. F. TALBOT, ESQ., and others, Committee, etc.

In this second proclamation rewards were offered for the discovery of the place to which Morgan had been conveyed, in order " that the offenders may be brought to condign punishment, and the violated majesty of the law thereby effectually vindicated."

November and December were months of increasing and extending excitement among the people. In November indictments were found against Nicholas G. Chesebro, Loton Lawson, Edwin Sawyer, and John Sheldon, for a conspiracy to seize William Morgan and carry him thence to foreign parts, and to secrete and confine him there. A second indictment was found against the same parties for carrying the conspiracy into execution. These indictments were, by consent of parties, to be tried in the following January.

The committee, in continuing their investigations, learned that Hubbard's carriage, stopping ten miles west of Canandaigua, was driven into the yard of Enos Gillis, whose brother, James Gillis, now proceeded on horseback in advance of the carriage towards Rochester. James Gillis immediately disappeared, and his brother Enos soon removed out of the State.

When the connection of Bruce with the mysterious carriage became known he was, on the 29th of December, arrested and brought before a magistrate at Youngstown, on the charge of having forcibly held William Morgan in duress, and having secretly and illegally conveyed him to parts unknown. Five witnesses testified to the facts heretofore stated, but as no proof was given that William Morgan had been forcibly taken away from Canandaigua or elsewhere, or that force, violence, or restraint had been exercised upon the person of any individual in the carriage, Bruce was discharged. In Monroe County, when its court met in December, the presiding judge strongly charged the grand jury to investigate the outrage which was then the theme of universal discourse. A large number of witnesses were called and examined, but no reliable information was elicited. Edward Doyle refused to testify lest he should criminate himself. Ezra Platt, in whose carriage Morgan was conveyed to Clarkson, knew nothing. The grand jury, in its presentment, stated that "from the great caution which seems to have been observed in keeping both Morgan and the place of his destination from the view and knowledge of all such persons as may have been confidentially intrusted with the design, and who would decline giving evidence, on the ground that it might tend to criminate themselves, the grand jury have found it impossible to establish, by competent testimony, the unlawful agency of any citizen in this county in that transaction."

As the trial of Bruce and his associates was approaching in Ontario County, the district attorney, Bowen Whiting, Esq., himself a Mason, but earnestly endeavoring to do his duty, wrote a letter to Governor Clinton, asking the assistance of the attorney-general. This letter was immediately transmitted to the attorney-general with the following note : —

ALBANY, December 11, 1826.

SIR, — I inclose to you a copy of a letter from the district attorney of Ontario County, by which it appears that your attendance at the Oyer and Terminer on the first Monday in January next, in that county, is considered highly important.

Concurring with the circuit judge and the district attorney in that opinion, and hoping that you will find it not inconvenient to attend on that occasion, I consider it my duty to request it.

I am, etc.,   DEWITT CLINTON.

SAMUEL A. TALCOTT, ESQ., Attorney-General.

The attorney-general, however, found it "inconvenient," or for some other reason declined to attend the trials. The Court of Oyer and Terminer met at Canandaigua on the first day of January, 1827. Hon. Enos T. Throop, then a circuit judge, presided. The Hon. A. W. Howell, first judge of Ontario County, and Judges Younglove, Atwater, and Brooks were associated with Judge Throop. And then commenced the first of the series of extraordinary trials held in five different counties, which attracted general solicitude for the following two or

three years. Deputations from county committees were in attendance. Over one hundred witnesses, together with a large
concourse of people, pressed into the court-house. The bar was
crowded with an array of high professional experience and
talent. The prosecution was conducted by Bowen Whiting, the
district attorney, assisted by John Dixon, William H. Adams,
Jared Wilson, Theodore F. Talbot, Henry W. Taylor, Benjamin and C. Butler, who had been retained by investigating committees. The counsel for the defendants were John C. Spencer,
Mark H. Sibley, Henry F. Penfield, and W. Hubbell. The defendants, Chesebro, Lawson, and Sheldon, pleaded "Not guilty"
to the several indictments on which they were arraigned.

The first witness called was David C. Miller, who, to the
astonishment of everybody, did not answer. Having borne a
prominent part in the transactions which had agitated the community, and himself a sufferer in property and person, and subpœnaed by both parties, his absence was unaccountable. Attachments applied for by both parties were granted, and the
trials were postponed to give time for the officer to serve them
on Miller at Batavia.

On the 3d of January, when the trials were moved, Chesebro,
Sawyer, and Lawson severally withdrew their pleas of "Not
guilty" and pleaded "Guilty" to both indictments. This took
the court and the audience quite by surprise. A solemn stillness pervaded the court-room until the trial of Sheldon was
moved, whose counsel stated that he admitted that the offense
charged in the indictment had been committed, but denied having participated in it. Thus it will be seen that all the facts
and circumstances connected with Morgan's release from jail,
and his being thrust forcibly, with outcries for help, into a carriage and driven away towards Rochester, as is stated in previous pages of this narrative, is by the confession in court of the
parties implicated judicially established. This admission narrowed the scope of inquiry and diminished the interest which
the trials had awakened. The only question that remained was
one of identity. Though Mrs. Hall, the wife of the jailer, testified that she *believed* that Sheldon stood outside of the jail and
assisted in dragging Morgan away, witnesses were introduced
by Sheldon's counsel who testified that he was sitting in Kingsley's Tavern the whole evening, and that he lodged there that

night.　It was proven on the other side, however, that on the morning after Morgan was carried away, Sheldon appeared to know all about it.　Told a Mr. Prescott, "Morgan has been taken away.　I know who went to the jail after him, but shall not tell you ; he does not live in this village.　Morgan will not be seen in this country again, but if his family will accept the funds which have been provided for them, they will be well enough off."　Mr. Green, an innkeeper of Batavia, swore positively that Sheldon came to his house late in the evening of the 10th of September, lodged there, and breakfasted there the following morning ; that Sheldon said he had been suspected of kindling the fire in Miller's office, and desired him (the witness) to recollect that he had lodged in his house that night.　Sheldon said that he was a Royal Arch Mason, and that he had been in that neighborhood several days to assist in suppressing Morgan's books.　On the other hand, Kelsey Stone was introduced as a witness by the defendant's counsel, and swore that, according to his best recollection, Sheldon was not the man that he had been sent to meet at the house of Mr. Green in Batavia.

The jury, after some hours' deliberation, returned a verdict of "Guilty" against Sheldon, relying, it was said, partly upon the testimony of Mrs. Hall, and partly upon his conversations the morning after Morgan was carried off.　Sheldon made a deposition, drawn up by his counsel, and placed on record, in which he swore that he was not at the jail at the time referred to, had not been in Batavia for eight years, had not visited the jail in company with Loton Lawson, and that he had never seen or known William Morgan.　He deposed, further, that his admissions about Morgan "were made in the way of romance, and for amusement only ; " and by subsequent disclosures all this appeared to be true, and that Sheldon was in fact innocent.　The man at Green's house in Batavia was a Mr. Averill, from Orleans County, whose dress and appearance so strongly resembled those of Sheldon as to occasion the mistake.

The great significance of the facts I am now about to state will be better understood as the narrative progresses.　John Whitney and Burrage Smith, of Rochester, were called as witnesses in this trial.　Both objected to answering any questions, because in doing so they apprehended that they might criminate themselves.　They did, however, after being instructed by the court as to their privileges, testify in part. Smith admitted that he came to Canandaigua from Rochester on the 12th of September. He also admitted that he saw Lawson, but declined answering whether he had heard any conversation between Lawson and others about carrying Morgan away. The court having overruled his objection, he admitted that he did hear Lawson in conversation with three or four others upon that subject on the sidewalk near the jail. He left Canandaigua in the evening that Morgan was taken away, between six and eight o'clock. He admitted that he was at Lewiston, attending the installation of a Chapter, two or three days afterwards. Being asked if he saw Morgan at Fort Niagara, his counsel objected to the question, and the court sustained the objection.

Whitney testified to the fact of his coming to Canandaigua on the 12th of September in company with Smith, but declined telling at what time he departed on his return, lest he should criminate himself.

Corydon Fox, the Lewiston stage-driver, testified to the fact of having driven a carriage, some time in September, with closed curtains, down the river to Youngstown. Three or four persons got out of the carriage, but he did not know that either of them was Morgan, or that any person in the carriage was confined. Neither of the defendants rode with him on that occasion. On the 5th of January the counsel for the defendants moved an arrest of judgment upon one of the indictments, on the ground that the defendants could not be convicted both for a conspiracy to do an unlawful act, and also for doing that act. The court, after hearing arguments on both sides, intimated that judgments should not be pronounced upon both indictments. On the following morning the defendants appeared at the bar, where several witnesses were examined by the public prosecutor in aggravation of the offense. Among them was Mrs. Morgan, whose manner and appearance made a very favorable impression. Nothing new, however, was elicited.

Three of the defendants submitted depositions in mitigation of their offense. Chesebro knew that it was the intention to take Morgan away, but supposed that he had consented to go freely. Their object, he said, was to remove Morgan from beyond the influence of Miller, who was inducing him to publish a book disclosing the secrets of Masonry. He did not know where Morgan was, or what had been done with him. In opposition to this, Israel B. Hall, the jailer, swore that Chesebro told him, in the morning after Morgan had been taken away, that he was where Miller could not get hold of him again.

Sawyer deposed that he had never seen Morgan until the evening of the 11th of September in the justice's office; that he was not aware of any intention of taking him from the jail until Lawson met him during the evening in the street, and asked him to go and persuade the jailer's wife to release Morgan on his paying the amount of the execution. He thought that Morgan had consented to go away, until he came out into the street where the struggle ensued, at which the deponent was surprised. He deeply regretted, he said, that he did not interpose in Morgan's favor. He concurred with Chesebro as to the motives of Morgan's removal, and declared that he did not know what had become of him. A number of the most respectable citizens of Canandaigua testified to the good general habits of the defendants.

Lawson was sentenced to two years' imprisonment in the county jail; Chesebro to one year in the county jail; Sheldon to three months' imprisonment, and Sawyer to one month. Judge Throop, before pronouncing sentence upon the defendants, addressed them in remarkably effective and emphatic language, as the following extracts show : —

You have been convicted, said the judge, of a daring, wicked, and presumptuous crime, — such an one as we did hope would not in our day have polluted this land. You have robbed the State of a citizen, a citizen of his liberty, a wife of a husband, and a family of helpless children of the endearments and protecting care of a parent. And whether the unfortunate victim of your rage has been immolated, or is in the land of the living, we are ignorant, and even you do not pretend to know. It is admitted in this case, and stands proven, that Morgan was, by a hypocritical pretence of friendship and charity, and that, too, in the imposing shape of pecuniary relief to a distressed and poverty-bound prisoner, beguiled to intrust himself to one of your number, who seized him, as soon as a confederate arrived to his aid, almost at his prison door, and in the night time hurried him into a carriage and forcibly transported him out of the State. But great as are the individual wrongs which you have inflicted on these helpless and wretched human beings, they are not the heaviest part of your crime. You have disturbed the public peace, — you have dared to raise your parricidal arms against the laws and constitution of your government; you have assumed a power which is incompatible with a due subordination to the laws and public authority of your State. He was a citizen under the protection of our laws; you were citizens, and owed obedience to them. What hardihood and wickedness, then, prompted you to steel your hearts against the claims of humanity, and to dare set at defiance those laws to which you owed submission, and which cannot suffer a citizen's liberty to be restrained with impunity without violating its duties of protection, assured to every individual under the social compact? Our laws will resent such attacks as you have made upon their sovereignty. Your conduct has created, in the people of this section of the country, a strong feeling of virtuous indignation. The court rejoices to witness it, to be made sure that a citizen's person cannot be invaded by lawless violence without its being felt by every individual in the community. It is a blessed spirit, and we do hope it will not subside, — that it will be accompanied by a ceaseless vigilance and untiring activity, until every actor in this profligate conspiracy is hunted from his hiding-place and brought before the tribunals of the country, to receive the punishment merited by his crime. We think that we see in this public sensation the spirit which brought us into existence as a nation, and a pledge that our rights and liberties are destined to endure. But this is not all; your offense was not the result of passion suddenly excited, nor the deed of one individual. It was preconcerted, deliberated upon, and carried into effect by the dictates of the secret councils and conclave of many actors. It takes its deepest hues of guilt from a conspiracy, — a crime most dreaded from the depravity of heart it evinces, the power for unlawful purposes which it combines, and from its ability to defy the power of the law, and its ultimate danger to the public peace. Thence it is that the crime is considered full when the wicked purpose is proved to have been formed; and the subsequent carrying into effect the object of the conspiracy, does not, in the eye of the law, elevate the degree of the crime.

On the day before the adjournment of the court Miller was brought, under the attachments that had been issued, to answer for his contempt. It appeared by his answers that, although subpœnas had been served on Monday, he did not leave home until Wednesday, and that while on the way to Canandaigua he digressed from the direct road to another town, on his own business. He further stated that at the time the subpœnas were served no fees had been tendered him, and that he had not money to pay his expenses. This circumstance induced the court to discharge him.

CHAPTER XXII.

1827.

ON the 22d of November Governor Clinton received a long letter from Mr. Talbot of the Batavia Committee, thanking him for the interest he had already taken in the affair, and expressing confidence that, as chief magistrate of the State, everything possible would be done for the protection of its citizens and the vindication of its laws. Mr. Talbot then reported in detail the information which had been elicited by the investigating committees, adding that there were strong reasons for believing that Morgan was confined somewhere in Canada. He then spoke of the obstacles interposed by the sheriffs of Genesee and Niagara counties, — obstacles which had greatly aggravated the popular feeling in those counties. Mr. Talbot closed his letter by remarking that the committee had not yet obtained information which authorized a belief in the various reports that Morgan had been murdered. To this letter Governor Clinton replied as follows : —

ALBANY, *January* 8, 1827.

SIR, — I have received your letter of November in behalf of the Batavia Committee appointed in the case of Morgan, and I deeply regret the whole transaction, as well as the failure of the attempts to restore him to his family. I am not, however, without hopes of ultimate success. If in a state of duress, he is probably detained in one of the Canadas under false pretexts. I have written to the governor of Lower Canada, at Quebec, and of Upper Canada, at York, stating his abduction, and requesting their humane interpositions in his behalf if confined in any of the forts or prisons under their government, and I strongly anticipate favorable results. There are a number of circumstances which induce me to concur with you in the opinion you express against his being murdered. I do not think that the men engaged in the conspiracy, if as respectable as you intimate, would stain their hands with blood ; and, if bent on such a horrid crime, we can hardly suppose that they would carry Morgan to such a distance, and expose themselves so unnecessarily to detection. But, when the demon of fanaticism is at work, there is no knowing to what extent of mischief and turpitude he may lead his disciples. I am persuaded, however, that the body of Freemasons, so far from having any participation in this affair, or giving any countenance to it, reprobate it as a most unju tifiable act, repugnant to the principles, and abhorrent to the doctrines of the fraternity. I know that Freemasonry, properly understood and faithfully attended to, is friendly to religion, morality, liberty, and good government; and I shall never shrink, under any state of excitement, or any extent of misrepresentation, from bearing testimony in favor of the purity of an institution which can boast of a Washington, a Franklin, and a Lafayette as distinguished members, and which inculcates no principles, and authorizes no acts, that are not in accordance with good morals, civil liberty, and entire obedience to government and the laws. It is no more responsible for the acts of unworthy members than any other association or institution. Without intending in the remotest degree a comparison or improper allusion, I might ask whether we ought to revile our holy religion because Peter denied and Judas betrayed ?

It appears that the abduction of Morgan from Canandaigua took place on the 12th of September, and that the Batavia meeting was held on the 25th.

The affidavits published by the committee of that meeting sufficiently indicated the perpetration of the outrage, and it is to be regretted that a judicial accusation did not immediately take place, as it might at that early period have led to the discovery of Morgan.

On the 6th of October I received your communication, and on the next day issued the first proclamation. I took it for granted that the offenders would be apprehended, and that Morgan would be discovered and restored. But seeing accidentally in a Batavia newspaper that these expectations were not realized, I issued on the 25th of October another proclamation, offering specific rewards. I regret that after the first communication I did not hear from you until the 22d of November. In saying this I do not intend the least blame, — the confusion and derangement which must necessarily have grown out of such an unprecedented and abominable transaction must present a sufficient apology for any omission on the part of those who have been meritoriously engaged in detecting and punishing an outrage which would scarcely be believed were it not so well authenticated.

I observe some imputations in your letter on the conduct of the sheriffs of Genesee and Niagara. If any accusations supported by testimony are presented, I shall take due notice of them.

I pray you to accept for yourself, and to present to other members of the committee, my acknowledgments of the laudable performance of your and their duties as good and faithful citizens in a case so greatly to be deprecated, and which certainly demanded the energetic interposition of the friends of liberty and good government.

I am, etc.,   DeWitt Clinton.

Theodore F. Talbot, Esq., Batavia.

The following is a copy of the letter Governor Clinton addressed to the governors of Upper and Lower Canada : —

Albany, *January* 6, 1827.

Sir, — A person of the name of William Morgan, otherwise called Captain or Major Morgan, resided for some time with his family in Batavia, in this State. He is said to have been a native of Virginia, and to have carried on at one time the business of a brewer at York, in Upper Canada. He is described as about five feet eight inches high, well built, light complexion, and between forty-five and fifty years of age. During the last year he put a manuscript into the hands of a printer in Batavia, purporting to be a promulgation of the secrets of Freemasonry. This was passed over by the great body of that fraternity without notice, and with silent contempt; but a few desperate fanatics engaged in a plan of carrying him off, and, on the 12th of September last, they took him from Canandaigua by force, as it is understood, and conveyed him to the Niagara River, from whence it is supposed that he was taken to his Britannic Majesty's dominions. Some of the offenders have been apprehended and punished, but no intelligence has been obtained respecting Morgan since his abduction. I have, therefore, to appeal to your justice and humanity on this occasion, and to request your Excellency to cause inquiry to be made respecting him, and, if he is forcibly detained, to direct his liberation, and to communicate to me the results. It is conjectured that he is confined in some fort or prison under false pretenses.

I am persuaded that no apology is necessary for this intrusion on your time and attention ; and permit me to assure you that I shall always be happy to reciprocate your humane interposition, and to evince the high respect with which,

I have the honor to be, etc.,   DeWitt Clinton.

The Earl of Dalhousie, Quebec.

To the letter the Earl of Dalhousie replied from Quebec, January 25, 1827, that it would afford him much pleasure to comply with the wishes of Governor Clinton; that up to that time he had no information that Morgan had been in Lower Canada; and that he had immediately written to Sir Peregrine Maitland, Lieutenant-Governor of the Upper Province, on the subject.   On the 5th of February, 1827, in a letter from York, Upper Canada, Lieutenant-Governor Maitland informed Governor Clinton that he had offered a reward of fifty pounds for any satisfactory information relating to the whereabouts or fate of William Morgan.   It was subsequently ascertained, however, that several Canadian citizens were involved in the conspiracy. Bates Cook, a leading member of the investigating committee, went before a Canadian grand jury, sitting in the then village of Newark, and made complaint against residents of that village as being concerned in the conspiracy against Morgan. The foreman of the grand jury consulted with the district judge, after which the jury resolved to ignore the question.   The result of the trial of Chesebro and others disappointed everybody. Up to the moment that their plea of "Guilty" was entered, their innocence was asserted boldly by themselves and their Masonic friends.   Their good standing in the community created considerable feeling in their favor.   By pleading "Guilty," however, this impression was removed; but no additional facts were disclosed, and a general feeling of disappointment was manifested.   The conduct of Miller in absenting himself favored the impression, so industriously sought to be created, that after all it might be a mock abduction, and that Miller feared its exposure.   This, at any rate, was the aspect given to it by the press in distant parts of the country.   But the public mind in the "infected district," as it was called, underwent no change, except to deepen and strengthen the conviction that Morgan had been spirited out of the country by violence. Meetings were now held, in which Freemasonry was fiercely denounced as a dangerous institution.   This latter idea was suggested by the publications of persons, mostly clergymen, who renounced Masonry.   Prominent among these was the Rev. Mr. Barnard, a Baptist clergyman of high character and previously unquestioned veracity, who, in renouncing Masonry, stated that a Royal Arch Mason, in good standing, had declared that he

would be one of a number to put Morgan out of the way; that
God looked upon the institution with so much complacency,
that he would never punish those concerned in the disposal of
Morgan.   After the abduction, at a meeting of the Covington Lodge, Mr. Barnard said that he was violently assailed for
rebuking those who were concerned in the abduction of Morgan; that a Knight Templar present stated that if Morgan had
revealed the secrets of Masonry, and that if his throat had
been cut for it, nothing but simple justice had been done.
For denouncing this sentiment, Elder Barnard was expelled
from the Covington Lodge.   Major Ganson, who was present,
said that Morgan was not dead, but had been put where he
would " stay put till God Almighty would call for him."   In
the town of Attica, a Masonic member of the legislature said
" that the lives of half a dozen such men as Morgan, and better,
were of no consequence compared with the suppression of such
a book."   A judge of the court of Genesee County said " that
whatever Morgan's fate might have been, he deserved it."   A
Royal Arch Mason in Le Roy declared " that Morgan deserved death, and he hoped he had received it."   Gentlemen
were advised not to serve on committees of investigation, and
were told that the matter concerned none but Masons; that
they " had a right to deal with their own members according to
their own laws," etc., etc.   I have given only a few of the numerous instances of the violent and intemperate expressions of
excited members of the Order.   For the truth of these statements the public had the declarations of clergymen of various
denominations, who, until they renounced Freemasonry, were
universally esteemed.   They incurred, however, reproaches of
their adhering brethren, and were stigmatized as unprincipled
and untruthful.   In February, the people of the towns of Batavia, Bethany, and Stafford met, and resolved to withhold
their support at elections from all such men of the Masonic fraternity as countenanced the outrages against Morgan.   A similar meeting, at which a kindred resolution was adopted, was
held in the town of Wheatland, in Monroe County, about the
same time.   And immediately afterwards, at a meeting in the
town of Seneca, the people resolved that they would not vote
for Freemasons for any office whatever.   Thus was political
Anti-Masonry inaugurated.   No effort was made by the inves-

tigating committees in the different counties to restrain that movement. The Monroe County Morgan Committee made an earnest effort, seconded by prominent friends in other counties, to keep the question free from politics; and their efforts, so far as the then approaching town-meetings were concerned, were not unavailing.

Soon after the Canandaigua trial, the investigating committees reassembled at Lewiston, and resumed their labors. Simultaneously, a large number of Masons, several of whom were armed, assembled at Lewiston, and in an excited manner uttered violent threats against the members of our committee, rushing into the room, extinguishing the lights, and showering epithets upon those who were engaged in the investigation, the object being clearly to bring on a personal and physical conflict; but our committees, composed of such men as Bates Cook, Samuel Works, and their associates, remained calm, but firm, suffering nothing to divert them from their purpose. The district attorney of the county, a very zealous and excited Mason, maintained that the committees had no right to come into his county for the investigation of criminal matters.

While the committees were at Lewiston, a seemingly well-authenticated report came to us representing that an arrangement had been made between the Masons and John Brandt, son of the celebrated Mohawk Indian Chief, to take Morgan off their hands and transfer him to the British Northwestern Fur Company. In a few days, however, came an indignant denial of this impeachment from the descendant of Captain Brandt, under his own hand.

Another story was that Morgan had been taken over to Fort George and tried there by a Masonic tribunal, and executed; again, it was reported that Morgan had been taken to Quebec to be shipped on board a vessel of war; and still another report was that he was placed in a boat above the Falls, cast adrift, and thus hurried over the cataract. None of these stories were true, nor were any of them believed by the committee. Before its adjournment, however, information which they did credit they received, to the effect that when Morgan was taken from the carriage near the burying-ground in Youngstown, he was carried across the Niagara River blindfolded, pinioned, and gagged; that he had been taken into the Lodge in Newark, where, after much deliberation, the Masons had refused to incur the responsibility of disposing of or receiving him; and that he was then taken back to the American side and confined in the magazine of Fort Niagara. It was further alleged, but upon less reliable information, that Morgan was tried by a Masonic Council pursuant to an order from the Grand Chapter, and put to death by one of the methods prescribed by the Masonic penalties, namely, by having his throat cut, his tongue torn out by the roots, etc., etc. While some members of the committee now inclined to give credit to the alleged Masonic trial of Morgan, others (including myself) thought the evidence unreliable to base so serious an accusation upon.

The committee visited Fort Niagara, and satisfied themselves by careful examination that some person had been recently confined in its magazine. The Lewiston committee prepared a memorial to the legislature, praying that an additional and larger reward should be offered for the apprehension and conviction of persons engaged in the abduction and probable murder of Morgan, and for the appointment of a special commissioner to conduct the prosecutions.

The memorial was signed as follows : —

Members of the Rochester Committee: Josiah Bissell, Jr., Frederick F. Backus, Samuel Works, Frederick Whittlesey, Thurlow Weed, E. S. Beach.

Committee of Niagara County: Bates Cook, Alexander Dickerson, S. De Venux, Samuel Lacy of Chili and Wheatland Committee, William Pixley, Isaac Lacy, Benjamin Bowen, Alfred Scofield.

Batavia Committee on behalf of the Citizens of Genesee County : Freeman Edson, Clark Hall, Jonathan Lay, Timothy Fitch, Trumbull Cary, William Davis, F. Holden, Theodore F. Talbot, William Keyes, James L. Smith.

Committee of Le Roy: Edward Barnes.

Livingston County Committee: Philo C. Fuller and Jettis Clute.

Bloomfield Committee : B. Wilson, Barri Bradley, O. Benjamin, Jonathan Buell, Heman Chapin, and Josiah Porter.

Committee of Victor: James M. Wheeler, Samuel Pearson, John Sargent, Nathan Jenks, Thomas Wright, Samuel Ewing.

Committee of Canandaigua: Evan John.

Colonel King, previously spoken of, left his home in December, calling at Albany on Governor Clinton, to whom he applied for a loan of money, which was declined. He then asked Governor Clinton to recommend him for an appointment at Washington, which was also declined. At Washington, without any authority, he drew on Governor Clinton for two hundred dollars. He obtained from the War Department an appointment as sutler at Fort Towson, in Arkansas.

Early in February, John Whitney and Burrage Smith left their homes and families at Rochester. The money previously spoken of as having been devoted by the Grand Chapter to charity was paid in part to Whitney and Smith, when on their way to New Orleans. Mr. Whiting, the district attorney of Ontario County, being at Albany, obtained a warrant for the arrest of Smith, who, however, was apprised of the fact in season to enable him to effect his escape.

The Grand Royal Arch Chapter of the State met at Albany on the first Tuesday in February. This was an occasion of absorbing interest both to Masons and to Anti-Masons. The late Colonel William L. Stone, editor of the " Commercial Advertiser," who, although an adhering Mason, pursued an enlightened, impartial, truthful, and yet independent course throughout the whole affair, in speaking of that session of the Grand Chapter, says : —

The Masons were, at this time, divided into four classes. First, there were the guilty Masons and their immediate confidants, if not allies. Second, the thorough-going Masons, who, if not actually guilty, were rather disposed to think that the actors had served the traitor right. Third, retired Masons, who had resumed their aprons in consequence of the spirit of persecution that had gone abroad, and who, conscious of their own innocence, felt bound to resist the intolerant spirit of Anti-Masonry. Fourth, a much larger body of Masons than either of the preceding, having virtually retired from the institution, were now mere passive Masons, condemning the outrages as far as they believed them true, but doubting, nevertheless, whether any substantial cause existed for the excitement.

To this I may add that there were at that moment two classes of Anti-Masons : first, those who believed that the outrages perpetrated upon Morgan had the sanction of the lodges, chapters, and encampments ; second, those who believed that the outrages which had been committed by zealous and misguided members of the order had only the sanction of Masons kindred in character and spirit. This second, or latter class, now looked for some emphatic and decisive action on the part of the Grand Royal Arch Chapter in condemnation of the outrage upon Morgan, in asserting its own innocence, and in vindication of its character. I wrote an editorial article myself, stating that inasmuch as it was now well known that a citizen had been unlawfully deprived of his liberty, if not his life, by Masons in the name of Masonry, that Masons had been convicted of the offense and were then in prison, but that the local Masonic lodges and chapters to which they belonged had in no way manifested their sense of the outrages committed, it became the imperative duty of the Grand Chapter, the highest Masonic body in the State, to assume high ground, in vindication not only of the violated laws, but of its own respect for and obedience to lawful authority.

One hundred and ten subordinate chapters were represented at the session of the Grand Chapter. The Morgan matter was referred to a committee, which, previous to its adjournment, reported, —

That from the highly agitated and inflamed state of public feeling on this subject, and from the false and undeserved imputations which had been thrown upon the Masons and the Masonic order generally, your committee deem it proper that this Grand Chapter should make a public expression of its sentiments in relation to the affair alluded to. Your committee, as expressive of their views, would offer for the consideration of the Grand Chapter the following resolutions : —

Resolved, By this Grand Chapter, that we its members, individually and as a body, do disclaim all knowledge or approbation of the proceedings in relation to the abduction of the said William Morgan.

And that we disapprove of the same as a violation of the majesty of the laws, and an infringement of the rights of personal liberty secured to every citizen of our free and happy republic.

Resolved, That the foregoing report and resolution be published.

This, considered in connection with the well-known fact that a large number of " individual " Masons from Western New York, who were concerned in " the violation of the majesty of the laws," were members of the Grand Chapter present and voting for the foregoing resolution, added fuel to the flames that had been previously kindled.

Some months afterwards facts were disclosed showing that the Grand Chapter acted in a manner much more reprehensible. It appeared on the authority of General Beck, a brother of Dr. T. Romeyn Beck, and a gentleman of the highest intelligence and character, who was a member of the Grand Chapter and in attendance at its February session, that the committee to whom the Morgan question was referred reported a resolution condemnatory of the conduct of Masons engaged in the outrage, and offering a reward of one thousand dollars for the apprehension of the offenders. When the report was read, the resolution offering a reward was violently opposed by some of the New York and most of the Western members, and was rejected, as was the denunciatory preamble.

In the debate an Ontario member uttered sentiments so fanatical and fiendish as to shock the feelings of all reflecting men. And it was after that debate, and after the rejection of the resolution offering a reward, that a thousand dollars was appropriated for the relief of the " Western sufferers." The veracity of General Beck, from whom these statements were obtained, was never questioned.

Several persons who went from Canandaigua to Batavia to arrest Morgan on the trumped-up charge of larceny were tried at Canandaigua in February on the charge of falsely imprisoning Morgan; but they were acquitted on the ground that they were protected by the warrant they acted under. In Genesee County, at the February Court of General Sessions, Dr. S. S. Butler was appointed foreman. He was a Knight Templar, and two thirds of the jurors were Masons. To one of the jurymen, also a Templar, Dr. Butler said : " We have a majority of jurors, and our friends must not be indicted." This was the first direct evidence that Masonry was endeavoring to obstruct the course of justice; and this led to an investigation, which disclosed the facts that the sheriffs of all the counties of the " infected district " were Masons ; that, under the law of our State, grand jurors were then selected and summoned by the sheriffs of counties, and the further fact that on previous grand juries in these counties a majority of Masons had been summoned, and hence the impossibility up to that time of obtaining indictments against the real perpetrators of the outrage in Genesee, Monroe, Orleans, Niagara, or Erie. In Ontario Joseph Garlinghouse, although a Mason, sheriff of that county, regarded his duty to the State and to the laws as paramount to all other duties. He summoned jurors wholly irrespective of other considerations.

At the February term of the Ontario County Court, Dr. James Lakey, Chauncey H. Coe, Hiram Hubbard, John Butterfield, James Ganson, Asa Nowlan, Harris Seymour, Henry Howard, Joseph Sheffield, Moses Roberts, Holloway Hayward, James Gillis, John Whitney, Burrage Smith, Simeon B. Jewett, and Willard Eddy were indicted for a conspiracy to kidnap William Morgan and for carrying him away to parts unknown. In March some disclosures implicated Richard Howard, *alias* Chipperfield, a bookbinder at Buffalo, who had long been suspected from his conversations and admissions of being connected with the Morgan affair. The Batavia Committee, therefore, sent a messenger to Buffalo to confer with Thomas C. Love and others about the arrest of Howard. But before his arrest was effected, he obtained information of the design and suddenly disappeared. Howard went to New York, representing himself as a persecuted Mason, and received the sympathy and protection of Masons who believed him innocent, by whom money was raised to pay his expenses to Europe. Long afterwards, Avery Allen made an affidavit, stating that when attending an encampment at St. John's Hall, in the city of New York, to perfect himself in the higher orders of Masonry, he was informed by another Templar that one Howard, an Englishman from Buffalo, came to St. John's Hall in the winter of 1827, confessed himself to have been one of the persons who executed Morgan, and that he had with difficulty avoided an arrest ; and that, after consultation in the hall, money was raised, and Howard sent to Europe. Allen's affidavit was corroborated by that of a Mr. Mann, who swore that Howard had made substantially the same admissions to him before leaving Buffalo. The statements of Allen and Mann were vehemently denied and denounced by the Masons generally and by the press of the city of New York. The fact of Howard's sudden and secret escape from Buffalo, and his departure for Europe, were undeniable. Nothing was ever heard of or from him.

And now for two or three months, though the committees were diligently at work, no further developments were made. The warfare, however, grew more and more bitter and vindictive, and had by this time assumed an aspect quite as hostile to the Masonic institution as to the individual Masons implicated in the alleged outrage. It raged also with painful violence in matters of religion. Churches were distracted. Members of churches refused to listen to preachers who adhered to Masonry. The churches most affected were of the Baptist, Methodist, and Presbyterian faith. The crusade against Masonic clergymen brought troops of friends to their support and out of the " infected district " weakened the Anti-Masonic cause. Indeed, during the months of March, April, and May, in 1827, there was a popular reaction, not so much in favor of Masonry as against Anti-Masonry. Early in February Governor Clinton wrote to Mr. Talbot, chairman of the Batavia Committee, inquiring if any further authentic information had been received in relation to Morgan, and whether the executive could do anything more for the discovery and punishment of the offender. Mr. Talbot, in behalf of the committee, in reply transmitted the depositions of Trumbull Cary, Timothy Fitch, and Hinman Holden, testifying that discoveries had been made at Lewiston, affording strong reason for believing that Morgan had been put to death, and directly inculpating Bruce, sheriff of Niagara. To this letter Governor Clinton replied on the 7th of March, asking for a copy of the report of the Lewiston Convention as soon as it was printed, adding, " As the next step on my part may involve important consequences, I hope to have before me all the light that can be furnished." That letter was followed by another, from which the following is a copy : —

ALBANY, *March* 11, 1827.

SIR, — In reviewing my letter to you of the 7th of March, instant, I think it proper to avoid all ambiguity by stating explicitly that immediate measures ought to be adopted for proving and testing the allegations contained in an affidavit respecting a person criminated at Buffalo.

In the affidavit of Messrs. Cary, Holden, and Fitch, it is stated that the sheriff of Niagara County was concerned in the abduction of Morgan. I wish this charge to assume a specific shape, and to be accompanied by all the evidence that can be produced, in order that he may have a hearing, and, if guilty, be ejected from office.

I should be gratified in knowing whether any exposition of the affair is to be made by the Lewiston Convention or any other body of men. As most of the information is said to emanate from Dr. T., it would be important to have his affidavit, and such testimony as can be adduced to support his statement and character, both of which have been seriously impeached.

I have only to add, that I am determined to use every means in my power to develop all the mysterious proceedings connected with the abduction of Morgan, and to bring the offenders to condign punishment. Sooner or later this will in all probability be accomplished ; but the sooner it is done the better ; and I rely upon your continued and faithful coöperation as good citizens and useful members of society.   I am, etc.,   DeWitt Clinton.

Theodore F. Talbot, Esq.

On the 17th of March Governor Clinton sent the following message to the Assembly : —

Gentlemen, — The abduction of William Morgan, being an act of unprecedented violence, has justly excited unequivocal reprobation, and the apprehensions which are entertained of his fate have produced general alarm and anxiety. Understanding that the subject is under the consideration of your honorable body, I have thought it proper to communicate to you all the information in my power respecting it. If any future intelligence of importance should be received, I shall not fail to communicate it.

This message, and the documents accompanying it, were referred to the Judiciary Committee, to which sundry petitions and memorials on the same subject had been previously referred.

On the 19th day of March the governor issued his third proclamation, increasing the reward previously offered to any person who should restore Morgan to his family if living, or discover and bring to punishment his murderers if dead, to a thousand dollars, and offering a free pardon to any one of the accomplices in the crime who should make confession leading to the full discovery of the offense and to the conviction of the offenders.

It will be seen, by Governor Clinton's letters and proclamations, that his solicitude on the subject of Morgan had an early date, and that his convictions on the subject were clear and strong. Few if any of our public men, at a distance, manifested any such interest or anxiety on that subject. The reason for all this was simply that no other distinguished man at a distance from the theatre of action possessed the information which had been imparted, Masonically, to Governor Clinton. But while he did not feel at liberty to disclose information given to him as the highest Masonic authority in the State, he did avail himself of that information in the discharge of his official duty as chief magistrate of the State. Having said that Governor Clinton had earlier and better information, it is proper that I should state when and how he received it. Early in September of 1826 a messenger reached New York, while Governor Clinton was presiding at a meeting of the general Grand Chapter of the United States, with a manuscript purporting to expose the Royal Arch Degree in Masonry. The messenger entered the chapter at St. John's Hall, and presented the package to a gentleman from Ohio, who was temporarily occupying the chair, who, after a brief conversation with the messenger, informed the body over which he was presiding that a brother from Western New York had delivered to him the manuscript which he held in his hand, asking what disposition should be made of it. A motion was made and carried to refer it to a committee. Governor Clinton, on resuming the chair, remarked to the committee that he deemed the subject of such importance as to demand its immediate attention. The committee, in retiring, requested the attendance of the messenger, and, after a brief absence, returned and reported that the manuscript referred to them was the property of some person or persons from whom it had been surreptitiously obtained, with the recommendation that it be returned as soon as practicable to the person or persons to whom it belonged. Governor Clinton, in returning the manuscript to the messenger, remarked, with much emphasis, that it was deeply to be regretted that any such communication had been submitted; that there was too much reason to apprehend that the misguided men in the West might still further compromise themselves; that it was no justification or excuse for any violations of law that the obnoxious individual had violated his obligation as a Mason; concluding with a strong injunction to the messenger to hasten his return, and, if possible, to prevent further mischief. The chairman of the committee, who acted with so much good sense, independence, and integrity, was the late Samuel L. Knapp, of Boston.

That messenger was Robert Martin, my partner and associate as proprietor and editor of the " Rochester Telegraph." Mr. Martin's departure for New York within an hour after he informed me that he was unexpectedly called away, excited some surprise. I did not, however, suspect the nature of his errand. Some days after his return he remarked that he went to New York on some business of the chapter, and, of course, I then knew his reasons for not explaining further. But several years afterwards, when the facts above stated had been substantially obtained from a member of the committee to which the subject was referred, Mr. Martin informed me that *he* was the messenger, and that Governor Clinton did urge him to return and prevent further mischief, which he would have gladly done, but that it was too late. With this explanation, it will be seen that Governor Clinton had abundant reason, not only as the governor of the State, but as the highest Masonic authority in the Union, for the anxiety he manifested and for the prompt and bold manner in which he discharged his duties as chief magistrate.

CHAPTER XXIII.

1827–1828.

PROGRESS OF THE INVESTIGATIONS. — DIFFICULTY OF OBTAINING WITNESSES. — LEGISLATIVE ACTION. — COMMITTEE REPORT REJECTED. — FRANCIS GRANGER. — TRIAL IN GENESEE COUNTY. — THREE CONSPIRATORS CONVICTED AND SENTENCED. — KING'S FLIGHT AND RETURN. — RENUNCIATION OF MASONRY BY THOUSANDS. — CHARTERS GIVEN UP. — CONVENTION OF RENOUNCING MASONS. — DEATH OF GOVERNOR CLINTON. — ACTING GOVERNOR PITCHER'S MESSAGE. — THE NEW LAW. — JUDGE MOSELY'S APPOINTMENT. — ELISHA ADAMS' TESTIMONY. — A JOURNEY TO VERMONT. — ARREST OF ADAMS AND HIS DISCLOSURES. — GIDDINGS' EVIDENCE. — VERDICT OF "GUILTY."

THE difficulties in obtaining indictments were not lessened. Suspected persons disappeared. Witnesses were spirited away. Others brought before grand juries refused to testify on the ground that they could not do so without criminating themselves. Hiram B. Hopkins, a Mason and one of Sheriff Bruce's deputies, stated that he had directions in summoning jurors to select at least three fourths Masons. At the April session of the Niagara County court one of the grand jurors was afterwards himself indicted as an actor in the conspiracy. It was before that jury that an ineffectual effort was made to indict Bruce. One witness was excused from giving testimony because he was a poor man, and said that if he should tell what he knew it would ruin him. A witness testified that a respectable man working with him upon the Welland Canal in Canada informed him that Morgan had been taken to Fort Niagara in the night, put into the fort, and detained there three or four days ; that when the Masons in Canada refused to take him, Morgan's throat had been cut, and that his body, tied to a rope and stone, had been thrown into the lake. This witness had promised not to reveal the name of his informant, but a juror insisted that the name should be given. A large majority of the jurors present, however, sustained the witness, and he was allowed to retire without answering the question. Thirteen of the witnesses examined before that grand jury were subsequently indicted, three of whom, on the testimony of Bruce, were shown to have had a criminal agency in the abduction of Morgan. On the 6th of March, 1827, the memorials of the Lewiston Committee in relation to the abduction of Morgan were first presented to the House of Assembly. The prayer of the petitioners was for the enactment of more efficient laws for the punishment of the crime of kidnapping, and for the appointment of a special commission or tribunal of justice for the trial and punishment of the offenders. The memorials were referred to a select committee, of which Mr. Granger of Ontario was chairman. On the 4th of April the committee made a report, setting forth the extraordinary facts of the case, and arriving at a conclusion adverse to the creation of a special tribunal for that section of the country. The committee, however, reported two resolutions, the first of which authorized the governor to issue his proclamation, offering a reward of five thousand dollars for the discovery of the said William Morgan if living, and the like sum of five thousand dollars for the murderer or murderers of Morgan if dead. The second resolution proposed the appointment of a joint committee, whose duty it should be to visit the region of the excitement, now including seven counties, with power to send for persons and papers, to inquire into the facts and circumstances connected with the abduction, and to report their proceedings to the next legislature. The report and resolutions were ordered to lie on the table and be printed. On the 10th of April the subject was called up, and elicited a long debate. Mr. Granger explained the views of the committee, defending their report with earnestness and ability. While opposed to the creation of any new legal tribunals, it was believed that the appointment of a special committee to investigate the whole matter, clothed with the power of the legislature, would allay the agitation of the public mind. The resolutions were strongly opposed by Mr. Bucklin, of Jefferson, Mr. Mosely, of Onondaga, and General Root, of Delaware. They contended that the large amount of money proposed to be offered, stimulating cupidity, would expose the tribunals of justice to scenes of fraud and perjury, jeopardizing the best interests of the people and confounding the innocent with the guilty. No allusion was made in the report, or by the chairman in debate, to the institution of Masonry as being responsible for the outrage and the consequent excitement; but the institution was introduced by Mr. Bucklin and others, who appealed strongly to the sympathies of the House against the frenzied injustice and cruel persecutions of innocent Masons by an excited and reckless populace. Mr. Granger, in reply, deprecated the course of the debate. The committee had refrained from all reference to the institution, desiring only that the laws should be executed. The report was rejected by a vote of seventy-four to twenty-three. Subsequently, however, on the 16th of April, an act was passed making abduction or kidnapping felony, and punishable by imprisonment in the state prison for a term not exceeding fourteen years. Heretofore this offence had been simply a misdemeanor.

At the March term of the Court of Common Pleas in Monroe County, a majority of the grand jurors being Masons, the efforts to obtain indictments against Edward Doyle, Ezra Platt, etc., etc., were unavailing. At the May term of the Niagara Oyer and Terminer, the grand jury summoned by Bruce was so constituted that it was deemed useless to make any complaint before it. At the Court of Oyer and Terminer held in Genesee County, April, 1827, Hon. John Birdsall of the eighth circuit presiding, Jesse French, James Hurlburt, Roswell Wilcox, and James Ganson, who had been indicted for the outrage upon Colonel Miller, were tried. French, Wilcox, and Hurlburt were found guilty, and sentenced, French for one year, Wilcox for six months, and Hurlburt for three months, in the county jail. Although the testimony was clear and strong against Ganson, who was a man of wealth and influence, he was acquitted.

In the autumn of 1827, Joseph Garlinghouse, the sheriff, and Phineas Bates, the ex-sheriff of Ontario County, invested with authority to arrest Colonel King, Burrage Smith, and John Whitney, departed for New Orleans *via* Washington, where they obtained from the War Department orders to commanding officers of the army in Arkansas to furnish all needed assistance. The search for Smith and Whitney proved unsuccessful. Colonel King, however, was at Fort Towson, but the officers, who were directed by the Secretary of War to assist in his arrest, informed him of the arrival of the sheriff and connived at his escape. The messengers, therefore, after making further but fruitless searches for Smith and Whitney, returned home. Captain Hyde, the officer who enabled King to flee, was arrested and ordered to Washington for trial, but was not tried. In the latter part of May, however, Colonel King voluntarily returned to his former residence at Niagara. He immediately published a note in the Lockport paper, informing Messrs. Garlinghouse and Bates of his readiness to "transact any business" they might have with him. Having been indicted during his absence for a misdemeanor, he went before a magistrate and gave bail for his appearance at the next term of the court. King's flight and his subsequent voluntary return were among the numerous inexplicable incidents of the strange event with which he was connected.

While these investigations and trials had been in progress, public renunciations of Masonry, from professional men, from merchants, and from mechanics, were constantly and rapidly multiplying. These publications increased and intensified the popular feeling against Masonry. On the 19th of February, 1828, a convention of renouncing Masons met at Le Roy, in the county of Genesee. The convention organized by the choice of Leonard B. Rose as president, and the Rev. David Barnard, secretary. Morgan's book was declared by the convention to be a full and fair revelation of the first three degrees of Masonry. To the truth of this declaration, thirty-five seceding Masons of various degrees subscribed their names. The convention also addressed a memorial to Congress, asking the government by whose authority Fort Niagara had been converted into a prison for the incarceration of William Morgan. This memorial was presented by the Honorable Mr. Tracy, and called out remarks from Messrs. Tracy and Storrs, of New York, Barbour, of Virginia, and Wright, of Ohio, after which it was referred to the Executive Department. It was accompanied, however, by no proofs, and nothing further was heard from it. The debate indicated a general desire to get rid of the question.

On the 6th of March, 1828, another convention assembled at Le Roy, consisting of seventy-nine members, representing twelve counties. General William Wadsworth, of Geneseo, was chosen president; and Dr. Matthew Brown, of Rochester, and Colonel Robert Fleming, of Lewiston, as secretaries. The members of

this convention were leading and influential citizens, among
whom were Abner Hazeltine, of Chautauqua; Thomas C. Love,
Millard Fillmore, and Henry E. Davies, of Erie ; Bates Cook
and George H. Boughton, of Niagara ; Timothy Fitch, Harvey
Putnam, George W. Lay, and Moses Taggart, of Genesee;
Frederick Whittlesey and James R. Livingston, of Monroe.
At that convention, Samuel Works, Harvey Ely, Frederick
Whittlesey, Frederick F. Backus, and Thurlow Weed, of the
village of Rochester, were appointed a general central committee of correspondence and publication. That committee became and continued the acknowledged head of the Anti-Masonic organization. They were regarded by a large majority of
the most intelligent and reputable citizens everywhere out of
the " infected district," and by adhering Masons in that district, as five of the most unscrupulous, disreputable, and malignant men in our country, while in point of fact, than four of
the five, more conscientious, honorable, or just men could not
be found in that or any other community. Those four gentlemen have gone to their final account, each having lived upright,
useful lives, and each leaving to his family and friends an unblemished record.

The action of the convention was strong, earnest, and even
violent against Masonry. In some respects, its accusations
went farther than moderate Anti-Masons were prepared to go.
It also proposed that an Anti-Masonic State Convention should
assemble in Utica on the 4th of August following.

Governor Clinton died at Albany very suddenly on the evening of February 11, 1828. He had attended to his official
duties at the Executive Chamber during the day. He was sitting in his office, conversing, but a few minutes before his death,
with his son. Though sudden, the blow was not unexpected.
An eminent medical and intimate personal friend of Governor
Clinton (Dr. David Hosack) deemed it his duty some months
previous to admonish Governor Clinton of his liability to sudden attack ; to which, after a little reflection, and with perfect
composure, the governor replied, " I am not afraid to die."

Lieutenant-Governor Nathaniel Pitcher now assumed the duties of chief magistrate. On the 18th of March he sent a
special message to the Senate, referring to the excitement at the
West in consequence of the alleged abduction of a citizen of the

State, and the uncertainty of his fate. He suggested that while the trials and convictions which had taken place had rather increased the mystery of the transaction, the efforts of individual citizens, though stimulated by a patriotic zeal, had not always been guided by discretion, tending rather to prevent than to promote a judicial development of the truth. He therefore recommended the enactment of a law, authorizing the appointment of a competent person to investigate the alleged criminal transactions in respect to Morgan, clothed with full and ample powers to perform all duties necessary to a fair judicial determination of the whole matter. The message was referred to the committee on the judiciary, of which Mr. John C. Spencer was chairman. Three days after the receipt of the message Mr. Spencer reported a bill in compliance with the executive recommendation. This bill passed the Senate on the 25th of March, and was sent to the Assembly for concurrence. On the 15th of April this bill became a law, and Daniel Mosely, Esq., of Onondaga, was immediately appointed by the governor to fill the office thus created.

The unexpected message of acting Governor Pitcher, and the prompt response of the legislature, after its refusal a few days previously to do anything in relation to the Morgan affair, was attributed to political motives. The Democratic party, it was alleged, became alarmed at the proportions the question was assuming in the western part of the State, and intended to expose the Anti-Masonic leaders, who, it was alleged, were creating an unjust excitement for political effect; or if good grounds existed for that excitement, to arrest the tendencies of popular sentiment against the Democratic or Jackson party. Mr. Mosely was a devoted and reliable Democrat. He had expressed himself strongly against the Anti-Masonic excitement, believing, as he did in all sincerity, that it was in a great measure causeless and artificial. He entered upon the discharge of his duties with these views and impressions, — views and impressions which he was slow and reluctant to change. The members of the Morgan committee, except myself, were unknown to him. At first he was reserved, receiving information from us with evident distrust. Ere long, however, finding himself headed and thwarted at every step in his progress, Mr. Mosely's eyes began to open, and after a few weeks his intercourse with our committee became cordial, and thereafter mutual confidence existed until he resigned the office.

In view of the trial of Eli Bruce, Orsamus Turner, and Jared Darrow, at Canandaigua, in August, 1828, it was deemed important to secure the testimony of Elisha Adams, an old invalid soldier living in Fort Niagara at the time Morgan was taken there. He disappeared not long after the investigations commenced, and until within a few days no trace of him had been obtained. Acting upon information deemed reliable, I obtained a requisition from the governor of this State upon the governor of Vermont for the apprehension of Adams as a fugitive from the justice of this State, he having been indicted for a participation in the abduction of Morgan. Proceeding to Waterbury, Vermont, I obtained authority from Governor Butler to arrest Adams if he should be found within that State. At Williamstown I obtained the services of the sheriff of the county, who started with me late in the afternoon for the town of Brookfield, on the mountain, some fifteen or twenty miles distant. We arrived at a late hour (nearly twelve o'clock) at the farmhouse where it was supposed Adams was staying. Rapping loudly at the door, it was opened by a man who rose from his bed and asked us in. On inquiring if Elisha Adams was there, a voice from up stairs answered, " Yes, I'm here, and have been expecting you." And in a few minutes Elisha Adams descended a ladder by the side of the ample fire-place, saying, " I suppose I'm wanted at Lockport." The sheriff then explained the nature of his process, to which Adams replied, " I will be ready to go with you in ten minutes." He packed up a few articles of clothing in a small trunk, and bidding good-by to his brother-in-law and sister, led the way to our conveyance, and within half an hour after our arrival there we were descending the mountain on our way back to Williamstown, which place we reached before sunrise. At the hotel I was not a little surprised to find, at that early hour, quite a large number of persons, evidently excited. We passed through this crowd into a dining-room, where the landlady, calling the sheriff aside, told him that our errand had leaked out, and that word had been sent around to the Masons in and about the village, more or less of whom had been around all night. Fearing that something was wrong, she had herself gone through the village and asked those who she knew were not Masons to come there, and that as near as she could judge they were now about equally divided. She added that, expecting us back, she had breakfast ready in the kitchen. Adams and myself sat down to breakfast, while the sheriff informed his neighbors that Adams had been arrested under the authority of the governor of the State. He then ordered fresh horses to take us to Burlington. When he returned and joined us at breakfast, he informed us that there were quite a number of men in the bar-room " looking daggers " at each other, that others were constantly coming in, that those who came in last were not Masons, and that whatever might have been intended during the night, he was quite sure there would now be no attempt to rescue Adams. Adams offered to go into the bar-room and tell his friends that he was going back willingly, but the sheriff thought that was not necessary. At the county line we parted with the sheriff, an efficient officer, whom I have never since seen. At Burlington, where we arrived in the evening, we lodged at Thomas' Hotel. Colonel Thomas, whom I had previously known, was a Mason, and a most intelligent, agreeable, and highly respected citizen. We were to leave Burlington on the Lake Champlain steamboat at ten o'clock, A. M. After breakfast, Colonel Thomas expressed his regret to find me, of whom he had thought favorably, engaged in this persecution of Masons. He was, he said, like myself, a warm friend of Mr. Adams' administration, but he could not think that a good cause was to be promoted by such discreditable means, adding, " You and I know that Morgan is keeping out of the way to make money by the sale of his book." I replied that there was no time then to discuss that question, or to convince him, as I thought I could, that he knew nothing of its real merits. " But," said he, " we both know that this old man has been sent for merely to keep alive the excitement." By this time a carriage had driven up to take us to the boat, and I invited Colonel Thomas to ride with us. At the boat, I said to him, " Take Adams aside and talk with him. I will stand by the gangway ; and when you go ashore, if you still think Morgan voluntarily missing, and that no outrage was committed upon him, tell me so in as strong terms as you think proper to use. But if, on the contrary, the conversation with Adams leads your mind to a different conclusion, say nothing."

When the bell rang " All ashore," Colonel Thomas came along looking very grave, shook me by the hand, and passed off the boat without saying a word. I never saw him afterwards. Nor did I speak of him to Adams, but in the course of the day he remarked : " You sent Colonel Thomas to talk with me ! What did he say to you when he was going ashore ? " I replied that he shook hands with me without speaking. " I guess," said the old man, " that he found out that he was n't so wise as he thought himself. If he goes among his friends this evening, he could tell 'em some news." After dinner, Adams wanted to hear all that had transpired about the Morgan business. His friends at Youngstown and Lewiston had sent him a newspaper occasionally ; and once in a while, when he met Masons upon the mountain, they would undertake to tell him news about Morgan, but that their news only showed him how little they knew about it. I related in detail what our investigations had brought out, and what had been proven in court. To many of the facts that I stated he would assent ; to others, he would dissent, and occasionally he would explain circumstances or correct statements of facts ; so that, during the three days that we were together, growing more and more familiar, he revealed what he knew of the occurrences in and about Fort Niagara. His manner was cautious and his language enigmatical. He would describe persons without calling names. When he desired to inform me that Morgan frequently made loud noises in the magazine at night, he would say, " I wonder whether the people at the ferry-house heard anybody crying ' Help !' in the fort." When I informed him what Edward Giddings was ready to testify, he was much agitated, and asked quickly, " If Giddings tells all he knows, what do you want of me ? " I informed him that Giddings' testimony would be rejected on the ground of his infidelity. He replied, " I don't know but Giddings is an infidel, but I don't believe he 'd tell a lie, under oath, or not under oath." He asked me if Giddings knew anything about some gentlemen's rowing out in a boat one night towards the mouth of Niagara River. I replied that he did not. Adams added that it was necessary that some one should stand on the beach until the boat should return, so that if any strangers were around a signal could be made to prevent their landing until the coast was clear. The man who kept watch was surprised when only four persons landed, because he thought that he counted five when they went aboard of the boat ; " but perhaps I was mistaken, and there may only have been four." He spoke in a hypothetical way of several incidents known to the committee, though not yet disclosed, showing his minute knowledge of the most important features of the case.

We arrived at Canandaigua in the morning of the day that the court commenced its sitting. The newly appointed special counsel, Mr. Mosely, was present to conduct the prosecution. He was assisted by Bowen Whiting, Esq., district attorney of Ontario County. Eli Bruce, Orsamus Turner, and Jared Darrow were arraigned on an indictment of conspiracy. The testimony first introduced was similar to that given at Canandaigua on previous trials, and therefore need not be repeated. Ezra Platt testified that he was called up on the night of the 13th of September to furnish a hack. His testimony had also been anticipated on previous trials. Testimony was introduced tracing Morgan along the Ridge Road to Lewiston and Youngstown, confirmatory of what had previously been proven. Corydon Fox, who was again called as a witness, being asked whether he had not been made a Mason the day after he drove Morgan to Youngstown, refused to answer the question on the ground that it might criminate himself. The court ruled that he need not answer the question. A witness was now called whose name subsequently became a household word throughout the country. That witness was Edward Giddings. On coming to the stand, Mr. Griffen, for the defence, objected to his being sworn, on the ground of his being an unbeliever in the Christian religion, and witnesses were called to establish this position. David Morrison testified that he had often heard Giddings declare that there was no God ; that a belief in anything spiritual superior to nature was contrary to reason and philosophy ; that he had received a letter from Giddings containing the same sentiment. A witness from Canada, named Grey, who had resided a few days in the house with Giddings in 1826, swore that the latter had no belief whatever in futurity, and prided himself in his philosophy ; the Bible, he said, was a pretty story to amuse children with. In other respects Giddings was a man much respected. Another witness swore that in 1816 Giddings said that he would as soon kneel down to a cat or a dog or a horse as to the being called God. The letter addressed by Giddings to Morrison was read, and contained the following sentiment: " God has the same care of a man as of an insect ; of an insect as of a tree ; of a tree as of a stone ; with him there can be no difference or distinction between beauty and deformity, virtue and vice, perfection and imperfection. He is not susceptible of persuasion, and as relates to man he is incapable of love or hatred. This is my notion of virtue and vice, that they do not refer to any future time, but relate altogether to man in his present state." This letter was dated April 10, 1827. Witnesses were then called to counteract the preceding testimony against Giddings. One witness testified that he had known Giddings fourteen years, and had often heard him express his belief in a Supreme Being. Another witness testified that in an astronomical conversation with Giddings the latter avowed his belief in a Deity who created and superintended all things. Morrison, in his testimony, stated that he did not reply to Giddings' letter responding to the sentiments it contained. The counsel for the prosecution now introduced a letter from Morrison to Giddings, responding fully to the alleged infidel sentiments expressed by Giddings. They also introduced a letter from Giddings to his wife, dated Cincinnati, Ohio, April 19, 1818, in which he twice recognized God, and invoked his protection for health and safety to return to his family.

The prosecution then proposed to offer testimony proving the good character of Giddings. But the court remarked that moral character, however unexceptionable, would not obviate the objection ; to be a competent witness a man must believe in a Supreme Being, who holds us accountable for our conduct. No man, said Judge Howell, can be a witness who denies this accountability. The testimony of Giddings was therefore rejected.

And now my Green Mountain witness, Elisha Adams, was called to the stand. Adams did not, like other witnesses, take shelter under the law which does not compel one to criminate himself ; nor like the celebrated Italian witness, in the case of Queen Caroline, did he resort to the " non mi ricordo " dodge. His manner was calm; his answers prompt and unequivocal ; he had an emphatic negative for every question connecting the defendants in any manner with the abduction or imprisonment of Morgan. He denied having any knowledge of Morgan or any other person being confined in the magazine; denied having any charge or care of a prisoner, etc., etc. His examination was searching and protracted, but failed utterly to throw any light upon the question at issue. The next witness was John Jackson, of Lockport. His testimony, after the rejection of that which it was understood that Giddings would have given, became very important,—important to the public in clearing up the then disputed question of whether Morgan had been confined in Fort Niagara, and still more important to the defendants, as their acquittal or conviction depended upon it. Jackson, with a large number of Masons from the surrounding country, attended the installation at Lewiston, and was at the house of Giddings, his brother-in-law, the evening before the installation. The counsel for the prosecution had expected to prove by Jackson, that on the evening of the 13th of September he went with Giddings to the magazine, where Morgan was confined and making a noise, and that Jackson took with him a pistol for the purpose of intimidating him. His examination was very thorough; to every question his answers were evasive and unsatisfactory, resembling, however, the testimony of so many other witnesses who knew more than they were willing to tell. This description of testimony is so peculiar, and yet so characteristic of the Morgan trials, that I submit a full report of it, the accuracy of which was certified to by Mr. Mosely, the special counsel, in his report to the legislature.

"They were all going to the installation at Lewiston; Mr. Giddings did not go; witness did not go with the rest; Giddings went to the fort in the morning accompanied by witness; don't recollect what Giddings carried with him; it might have been provisions; Giddings had some drink, too; thinks he did take some food up; don't know whether it was in his hand, on his arm, or tied round his body; Giddings went *towards* the magazine; witness did not *see* him open it; believes he saw the door of the magazine open; supposes Giddings opened it; did not see anybody in the magazine; heard a noise; don't know what it was; it was a voice from the magazine; did not *see* anybody; don't know whether it was a man or a woman; it was the voice of a person; did not *see* Giddings leave anything in the magazine; don't know that there is any window to the magazine; witness did not stay there long; don't recollect what conversation Giddings had with the person in the magazine ; saw Giddings have a pistol at the house ; don't recollect seeing it at the magazine; Giddings presented the pistol to witness, but he declined taking it; did not see Giddings lay it down ; heard something said at the magazine about a pistol, but don't recollect certain what it was ; don't know *exactly* whether Giddings opened the door of the magazine ; thinks the door was open, and that Giddings conversed with a man who was inside ; don't know but Giddings said, ' Here is some victuals and drink for you ; ' did not stand very near the magazine door ; might have been two rods off ; don't recollect but that Giddings might have spoken to the voice within about the pistol.   When Giddings opened the door witness *might* have been looking the other way ; Giddings did not go into the magazine ; the noise was not very loud ; don't recollect any words ; heard the noise after he got away ; he was for making off when he heard the voice ; did not *see* Giddings leave anything with the man ; did not see him take anything back to the house ; if he took provisions up, he presumed that he left them ; saw Giddings take the pistol up as they started to go to the fort; witness thought it was time to be missing when he heard the noise ; Giddings did talk to the man in the magazine ; witness did not stop to see any door shut."

Jackson was a man of good habits and character, and when I last heard of him, he was a prosperous and respected citizen of Lockport.   Witnesses were instructed by eminent counsel in what way they could legally or technically rather get around embarrassing questions.   The false swearing of Elisha Adams, the rejection of Giddings as a witness, and the abortive attempt to obtain the truth from Jackson, were followed by a legal point raised by General Matthews against the validity of the indictment, although enough had been proven by other witnesses to render the guilt of the defendants morally certain. Yet when the jury retired, no one expected a verdict of " Guilty."   To the general surprise, however, after an absence of four hours, the jury returned into court with a verdict of " Guilty." The weak point in the case was, that while nobody doubted that Morgan, who was thrust into a carriage immediately after he was released from imprisonment at Canandaigua, had been traced, stage by stage, from Canandaigua to Fort Niagara, yet the fact that Morgan was in the carriage seen at Victor, Rochester, and Hanford's Landing, Clarkson, Gaines, Wright's Tavern, Mollineaux's Tavern, Lewiston, and Youngstown, *had not as yet been proven.* The jury, therefore, in finding their verdict against Bruce, Turner, and Barrow, acted without evidence in an essential particular; and yet so strong was the conviction on the public mind that Morgan was so carried from Canandaigua to Fort Niagara that no popular complaint was heard against the verdict.

When the court adjourned General Matthews, one of the counsel for Bruce, etc., walked across the Court House Green on one side of Judge Howell, and I on the other side of him. Judge Howell remarked to me, "All your time and expense in bringing the witness Adams here is lost." I simply said, " Yes," when General Matthews, with much emphasis, said, "The old rascal did not testify to a word of truth while he was on the stand." Elisha Adams, instead of going back to Vermont, as he intended, was taken by his friends to Lewiston, where they supported him. At Rochester, on his way to Lewiston, he sought an opportunity of speaking to me. Walking some rods away from the hearing of those with whom he had been talking, he said: " I suppose you was a good deal disappointed with my testimony yesterday." I assented very emphatically to this supposition. Then he continued, " I have been looking for you all the morning, because I want to explain things. That evening that we arrived at Canandaigua, Sheriff Bruce's lawyers took me into their room, and told me they wanted to let me know what the law was about a witness criminating himself. I told them I knew enough about law to know that I need not answer questions that would criminate myself. They said that by refusing to answer questions, because the answer would criminate me, I as much as confessed that I knew all about it, so that when I came to be tried in Niagara County it would all be turned against me. They then told me that, instead of refusing to answer questions, the way not to criminate myself was to say that I didn't know anything about it. They then told me what questions they supposed would be asked, and how I could answer them, and that it would be all right under the law that protects a witness from criminating himself. Now, when I talked with you on our way from Vermont, I didn't understand this so, so you see that I answered the questions just as the lawyers told me it was right to answer them."

(Of course I was bound to be satisfied with this explanation. Adams thanked me for the kindness with which I had treated him, adding that he hoped I would n't think the worse of him for not doing what he intended to do and what I expected. He very soon started for Lewiston, and I saw no more of him.)

At Rochester, some days afterwards, I told General Matthews about Adams' " explanation." The general replied that when Adams came into the room which the counsel for the defence occupied, knowing what was to be said to him, he retired, leaving that part of the business to junior counsel.

CHAPTER XXIV.

1828–1829.

MR. SPENCER, having become satisfied that after Morgan was removed from Canandaigua Rochester became the centre of the conspiracy against him, determined to make a further effort to obtain indictments against persons known to be prominently connected with it. This made it necessary, if possible, to obtain the testimony of Parkhurst, the driver, who took Morgan from Rochester to Clarkson. And I was again dispatched in search of this missing individual. I only knew that he came to Rochester from some town situated on the Connecticut River, north of Brattleboro. With this information I started, but soon discovered that the "Mingoes" (as we then called Masons) were on my trail, and it took several days to throw them off. I was compelled, therefore, to make a circuitous route through Connecticut, Massachusetts, and New Hampshire. Ascertaining in the neighborhood of the residence of Parkhurst's father that he was at work in one of the back towns of Windsor County, Vermont, I proceeded to St. Johnsbury, the residence of Governor Crafts, to obtain a requisition for the arrest of Parkhurst. At Montpelier I hired a buggy, and proceeded (unwisely, as it turned out) alone towards St. Johnsbury. In the evening, passing over a narrow, uneven road, along the side of a mountain, with few inhabitants, my path was first darkened by a thick cloud, succeeded by heavy rain, vivid lightning, and startling peals of thunder. My horse became restless, and unwilling to proceed. I got out and led him so far as I could see the way by the electric light furnished at intervals. That light, while it showed me the way, showed me also that I was on the brink of a precipice. Under these inauspicious circumstances I groped my way for more than an hour, when the storm abated, and after a while a cloudless and starlit sky appeared, and I reached St. Johnsbury at two o'clock in the morning. I called early upon the governor, who gave me my requisition promptly, and at eight o'clock I was on my way back to Montpelier. At Windsor I obtained the services of the sheriff of the county, with whom I started for the town of Wethersfield, where we found Parkhurst at work, with a dozen other men, on a factory in process of construction. He was at first much surprised and excited, taking two of his companions aside and talking earnestly with them a few minutes. These talked with some of the other men, when Parkhurst intimated to the sheriff that he was not inclined to go back to Rochester; but after ten or fifteen minutes' conversation, he expressed himself willing and ready to go with us, and in half an hour we started. Nothing occurred of any interest until we reached Albany, where the persons who had lost track of me stationed themselves, knowing that, in all probability, I would have to return through that city. They saw me with Parkhurst at the breakfast table an hour before we left Albany in the stage for Rochester. We traveled rapidly to Utica, where, Parkhurst's eyes being much inflamed by dust after several days' riding, I concluded, on that account, to take the canal packet boat. I carefully noticed, whenever the canal boat stopped, what passengers came on board. At Weedsport, which place we reached early in the evening, I was satisfied that no person on board knew Parkhurst, or suspected my business. From Montezuma through the marshes there was an interval of six hours without landing. At Weedsport but one passenger (a boy) came on board. Parkhurst had undressed himself, and was asleep in his berth. As there were five or six hours of safety, and as I had had very little rest for several nights, I concluded to avail myself of the opportunity for repose, having the promise of a friend, who was to stop at some point, to awaken me before they reached the landing. I slept, however, only about three hours, and was up about daylight. At sunrise I thought I would awaken Parkhurst; and, descending to the cabin for that purpose, I discovered, to my great consternation, that he had disappeared. Satisfied the moment I discovered his berth was vacant that my three hours' sleep had brought upon me a mortification deeper than any I had ever experienced, I was strongly tempted either to jump overboard or commit some other desperate folly. The remorse that I suffered during that miserable long day, and until we arrived at Rochester, can be more easily imagined than described.

It was believed that had the attendance of Parkhurst been secured, he would have identified several persons in Rochester as having participated in the conspiracy and abduction. The only person indicted at this term, however, was the Rev. Francis H. Cuming, then a settled clergyman in that place. Twenty years afterwards Parkhurst came to reside at Cohoes, and from that time until I left Albany, in 1865, was my warm personal and political friend. He visited me often, and we as often talked over the " Morgan affair," he frankly admitting that he drove the Morgan carriage at Ezra Platt's requisition from Rochester to Clarkson, but that Burrage Smith and John Whitney were the only persons whom he knew; that he did not know Morgan, but was told they were taking a man who had done something wrong to Canada.

The bill of exceptions taken to the Supreme Court to the indictment on which Eli Bruce, former sheriff of Niagara County, was tried and convicted in August; 1828, having been decided against him, the cause was again brought before the court in May, 1829. Hiram Hopkins, deputy sheriff of Niagara County, testified that seven or eight days before the abduction of Morgan, Bruce directed him to prepare a cell in the Niagara County jail for Morgan, who was expected there for one night. The programme, however, was subsequently changed, and Morgan was taken direct to Lewiston. The witness attended the Installation of the Chapter at Lewiston on the 14th of September, where he learned that Morgan was confined in Fort Niagara. The defendant, Eli Bruce, was sentenced to two years and four months' imprisonment in the county jail. John Whitney, as has been stated, left the State with Burrage Smith in the winter of 1827. Smith died in New Orleans. Whitney voluntarily returned to his residence in Rochester in 1829. Having been indicted during his absence, Mr. Whiting, the district attorney, had Whitney arraigned for trial at Canandaigua in May, 1829. Hiram Hubbard, of Canandaigua, and Mr. Scrantom, of Rochester, testified to the fact of Whitney's being in Canandaigua on the day of the abduction. Mrs. Hanford, wife of the innkeeper at Hanford's Landing, testified that Hiram Hubbard, who drove a carriage near their house before daylight, came in and took a decanter out to the carriage. A person got out of the carriage who resembled John Whitney, but she could not swear positively that it was he. Mr. Gregory, who lived on the Ridge Road, near Gaines, testified that he saw Burrage Smith in a sulky about the time the carriage passed. He also saw on the box of the carriage some one who strongly resembled Whitney. Levi W. Sibley, of Rochester, who attended the installation at Lewiston, saw Whitney and Smith there, both of whom returned with him on the steamboat that night. At Youngstown, Smith and Lawson went up to the fort. Mr. Whitney's partner in business testified that Whitney left Rochester in the winter after Morgan's abduction, abruptly, without arranging his business, or making any provision for the support of his family. Several other witnesses were examined, to prove Whitney's connection with the carriage in which Morgan was taken to Niagara. The first witness called by the defense was Eli Bruce, who had not yet been sentenced. Up to this moment, although Governor Clinton had removed Bruce from office, both he and his friends persistently denied that he had been in any manner connected with the abduction of Morgan. His testimony on that trial is so important that I submit a carefully prepared synopsis of it : —

He testified that he was first informed that Morgan was coming on the Ridge Road, on the evening of the 13th of September, by Burrage Smith and another person, now five hundred miles off, whose name he refused to give. About six or eight days before that time, a gentleman called and requested him to proceed to Batavia to take Morgan away. It was stated that difficulties existed between Morgan and Miller, and that the former would go away willingly. Being sheriff of the county, and not wishing to involve himself in any trouble, he declined the proposal. At about the same time, Orsamus Turner called on him, requesting that an apartment might be fitted up for the reception of Morgan in the jail. He stated that Morgan was expected there that night, on his way to Canada, and had consented cheerfully to go away.

This was on the 8th, at the time of Sawyer's expedition to Batavia, which failed. The project then was to have carried Morgan direct to Lockport. The Canandaigua movement was a distinct plot.

Witness was asked to go to Wright's Tavern, on the Ridge Road, where Morgan was said to be, — he having, as before related, been driven with the carriage into Wright's barn. Witness inquired if there was any trouble, declaring that he wished not to be involved in any. On his arrival at Wright's, which was about nine or ten o'clock, he found Morgan there. They then proceeded to Lewiston, and thence down to Niagara, David Hague, now dead, and Morgan being the only persons in the carriage from Wright's to Lewiston. He was not at the time acquainted with John Whitney. At or near the gate beyond Wright's, a person passed them on horseback whom he knew, but did not give the name. Morgan was not bound, but only a handkerchief placed over his eyes to prevent his seeing who were with him. On leaving the carriage near the Niagara burying-ground, they proceeded to the ferry near the fort, and crossed over into Canada, where Morgan was to have been put upon a farm. Morgan did not get out of the boat on the Canada side; and as the Masons there were not ready to receive him, — their arrangements for his reception not being completed, — he was brought back to the American side, and placed in the magazine of the fort to await the preparations in Canada. When Morgan got out of the carriage he locked arms with Hague and another gentleman who joined them at Youngstown (Colonel King). Morgan conversed with Hague; there was no liquor in the carriage, and he did not seem to be enfeebled. He thought he was amongst his friends. Witness left the fort before daylight on the morning of the 14th; had never seen Morgan since, and knew not what was done with him. Wright's Tavern was three miles from the residence of Bruce, at Lockport, at the intersection of a road from the latter place with the Ridge Road. Witness saw several persons whom he knew at Wright's; and at the installation, a stranger was pointed out to him as John Whitney. To a question as to whose charge Morgan had been left in at the magazine, the court would not suffer the witness to reply, upon the ground that no persons but those on trial should be implicated. For the same reason, also, the court would not allow the names of those who had crossed in the ferry-boat to be given. The project of taking Morgan away, witness said, was not concerted in the Royal Arch Chapter in Lockport, although it might have been talked over incidentally, in a desultory manner, by the members, but he could not remember specifically the time. The next day after the installation witness rode back from Lewiston to Lockport in a sulky. He knew not how Smith went to Lockport, nor how the sulky came there, but understood that it was to be sent home. He supposed it belonged eastwardly, and that the horse attached to it was owned somewhere on the Ridge; but if he had ever known, he had forgotten by whom it was owned, or whither he was to send it.

This trial lasted three days. The cause was summed up with great ability by the counsel on both sides, and went to the jury with a brief charge from Judge Howell, who, after an absence of two hours, returned with a verdict of "Guilty." Whitney was then sentenced to an imprisonment in the county jail of one year and three months.

Mr. Spencer, as I have already stated, was appointed as special counsel to continue the investigations and to prosecute the parties who stood indicted for the abduction of Morgan. He was distinguished for ability, energy, and will; he was known to be strenuously opposed to political anti-Masonry, and it was believed by the leading Democratic politicians, and by Mr. Spencer himself, that by his indomitable industry and vigor he would, in insuring the punishment of the guilty, disarm those who were perverting an honest public sentiment to promote political and selfish interests. But although he commenced his warfare against the anti-Masons with all his accustomed zeal and determination, he very soon modified his views, and long before his first year expired became an earnest political anti-Mason himself. The law under which he was acting expired one year from the date of its passage, and although it was renewed, the governor and legislature were so much dissatisfied with Mr. Spencer that they cut the salary down to a thousand dollars a year. This drew from Mr. Spencer an eloquently indignant letter, in which he stated the objects of his appointment, and maintained that instead of being supported by the government in the difficult and responsible duties he had been discharging, that he had been constantly embarrassed and frequently thwarted in his efforts to discover, arraign, and convict persons who had violated the laws, and that his official communications had been divulged, etc. For these and other reasons Mr. Spencer said that he could not, with any hope of usefulness, or any self-respect, hold the office, which he thereby resigned. Victory Birdseye, Esq., of Onondaga County, was appointed to supply the vacancy occasioned by Mr. Spencer's resignation. Mr. Birdseye's appointment gave general satisfaction. He was known to be an able, calm, clear-headed lawyer, who would discharge his duty fearlessly and faithfully, without prejudice or favor. He was not a Mason, nor was he an anti-Mason. He was opposed, however, to political anti-Masonry.

Up to this time, nearly three years after Morgan's abduction, the excitement it occasioned had been constantly increasing and extending. The leading men of the dominant party determined, if possible, to arrest its progress by a more efficient administration of justice. The Hon. William L. Marcy, then a judge of the Supreme Court, was designated by the governor to hold a special circuit in Niagara County for the trial of Ezekiel Jewett, an ex-army officer, who had charge of Fort Niagara while Morgan was confined there. Mr. Birdseye attended as public prosecutor, assisted by Mr. Ransom, the district attorney. General Matthews, Ebenezer Griffin, and Daniel D. Barnard appeared for the defendant. Mr. White, of Buffalo, announced himself as counsel for the Masonic witnesses. As this trial excited great public interest, and presented strange questions and features, a somewhat extended notice of it will, I think, be found interesting.

Jonathan Aire, whose name was first drawn as a juror, was challenged by the counsel for the government as a Mason. Judge Marcy, by consent of parties, heard the case instead of triers. Aire testified that he had taken three degrees in Masonry; he had heard that the defendant is a Mason, but should not feel bound to favor him as a juror; he did not recollect the precise words of the obligations he had taken, but he did not understand them as requiring him to show a Mason more favor than any other man; he was bound to keep the secrets of a brother Mason ; he was bound also to assist a brother Mason who was in danger of his life; there was an exception in the obligation to render assistance.   Milton W. Hopkins testified that he had taken three degrees and one or two side degrees in Masonry ; had been in many different lodges in different parts of the State, where the Masonic signs and tokens were the same. He then related the substance of a master Mason's obligation, substantially as disclosed by Morgan ; that in Jefferson County, where he was made a Mason, the obligations were rehearsed at weekly meetings ; a lecturer, he said, was sent annually from the grand lodge to see that the signs, obligations, etc., were uniform in all the lodges ; a charge is given when a member is admitted, the substance of which is to be good men, good citizens, and good Masons ; charity and obedience to the laws are inculcated, and the candidate is assured that Masonry will not interfere with his religion or his politics.   After the testimony was concluded, and the counsel on both sides heard, Judge Marcy, after recapitulating the substance of the Masonic obligations as disclosed by Hopkins, remarked : —

" That the conclusions to which he came in relation to the challenge to the juror (Jonathan Aire) were, that the oaths taken by Masons are wholly extra-judicial, and in a legal point of view are not to be regarded as binding upon the persons to whom they are administered.   If by fair construction these oaths enjoined partiality to a brother Mason, in the relation of juror and party, the engagement would not be strictly and legally obligatory.   The taking of such an oath would not, therefore, be a *principal cause* of challenge to a juror.   But if, by the fair construction of Masonic obligations and the *juror's understanding of them,* he had engaged to extend favor to a brother Mason, when that favor would be an act contrary to law, or in any respect contrary to his duty as a juror, the fact of his having placed himself under such an obligation would be a good ground of challenge for favor, and substituted as I am, by consent of parties, for the triers, I should feel it my duty to set aside a juror on such a challenge, if it was sustained.

" It is quite uncertain what were the obligations which Aire took; but assuming that they were similar to those in the oath repeated by Hopkins, most of them, it will be observed, enjoin

acts in accordance with high moral duties ; and all of them, I
think, may apply to acts which do not necessarily conflict with
the laws of the State, or any duty enjoined by those laws.

"That there are Masons so infatuated as to entertain an opinion that their Masonic obligations are paramount to the civil
laws in some instances, and that they violated the latter by
obeying the former, cannot now be doubted ; but I cannot yield
to the belief that such is the general condition of the order. I
therefore decide that Aire be admitted as a juror."

Nathaniel Denman, who was next drawn as a juror, stated
that he was a Mason, and that the obligations he had taken were
similar to those detailed by Hopkins ; that he believed Masons
had carried off Morgan, but never approved of it ; he thought,
however, that he should show all the favor he could to a brother
Mason. When questioned by the court, Denman said that he
did not know but that he should show more favor to a Mason
than to a person not a Mason, as a juror. The court then decided that he was not qualified to sit as a juror. Several other
jurors were set aside for having expressed opinions unfavorable
to the defendant, or for expressing decided opinions against the
Masonic fraternity. Orsamus Turner was the first witness
called after the jury was empanelled. He requested permission
to confer with his counsel, but this was refused, on the ground
that he had had ten days' notice, during which time he might
have consulted his counsel. Turner testified that he knew the
defendant when he resided in Fort Niagara ; that the propriety
of suppressing Morgan's book was discussed by Masons at Lockport, and measures proposed to effect that object ; witness had
heard that Morgan was coming to Lockport, but was ignorant
of the intention to lodge him in the jail : the witness declined
to answer whether the defendant, E. Jewett, was one of the
persons consulted with about suppressing Morgan's book, on
the ground that it might involve him in an indictment for murder. The court ruled, after hearing counsel, that before the
witness could avail himself of that privilege it must be shown
that Morgan had been murdered, for until that fact appeared
no indictment for murder could be had. The defendant's counsel and the witness's counsel made repeated and strong efforts
to induce the judge to modify his ruling. Judge Marcy repeated
that the witness could be in no danger of indictment for a crime

until it was known that that crime had been committed, adding
that the witness must answer the question. Turner replied
promptly, " I will not answer," and the judge responded, " Then
I shall punish you." Judge Marcy then observed that the witness was liable to indictment for every contempt, and that each
one must be entered on the record, as he should direct the district attorney to find bills for each refusal separately. The following record was then entered on the minutes of the court:
" Orsamus Turner, a witness in the cause of the People *v.* Ezekiel Jewett, having refused to answer the following question,
' Was the defendant one of the persons consulted with in relation to separating Morgan from his friends at Batavia as a
means of suppressing the contemplated publication of a book
revealing the secrets of Freemasonry?' after the court had decided that it was a legal and proper interrogatory for him to
answer, the court do adjudge that by such refusal he is guilty
of contempt in open court. It does, therefore, sentence him to
pay a fine therefor of two hundred and fifty dollars, and be imprisoned for the space of thirty days in the jail of the county of
Niagara." The examination being resumed, Turner was asked,
" Do you know that the defendant agreed to prepare the magazine at Fort Niagara for the reception and confinement of William Morgan?" The witness refused to answer this question,
on the ground that he feared it might involve him in a criminal
prosecution. The court said, " You are asked whether the defendant did agree to prepare the magazine," to which the witness replied that he could not answer it without danger. Mr.
White, the counsel for witness, requested permission to consult with him. Judge Marcy remarked that the witness had
imbibed strange and erroneous ideas; that the court wished to
preserve the rights of the witness, but that if he defiantly refused to answer questions after they had been pronounced proper
ones, the rigor of the law must be enforced.

The question, at the suggestion of the court, was varied as
follows: " Have you heard the defendant admit that he agreed
to prepare the magazine?" The witness answered that he
never heard the defendant say that the magazine should be
used for the confinement of William Morgan. To the question
whether he knew that the magazine had been prepared for that
purpose, he replied that he had no *positive* proof of it, but re-

fused to tell what or how much proof he had. The witness
was then asked, "Do you know whether the defendant was applied to for a place in or about Fort Niagara for the confinement of William Morgan?" which question he refused to answer, again claiming his privilege. The court decided that he
must answer; but, as he still refused, Judge Marcy sentenced
him to a further imprisonment of thirty days in the jail of the
county of Niagara. The witness was next asked, "Have you
ever been present at a conversation at which the defendant was
present, on the subject of confining Morgan?" But he refused
to answer the question in that and in a modified form. The
court decided the question to be a proper one, and directed the
witness to answer; but he again refused, and the court thereon
ordered another entry to be made of contempt, and sentenced
the witness to a further imprisonment of thirty days. The witness was then asked if he did not go to Fort Niagara in September of 1826 to see Jewett. But he again refused to answer, saying that it would criminate himself, and the question
was not pressed. This closed the examination of Orsamus
Turner. Mr. Turner was the editor of "The Lockport Courier," was well thought of and popular in the village and county.

Eli Bruce was then called, but refused to be sworn, adding
that he "was once sworn and examined, and no good came of
it." The court held this to be a contempt, and sentenced him
to imprisonment for thirty days in the Ontario County jail,
from which he had been taken on a writ of habeas corpus to
testify in this cause. The next witness called was John Whitney, who also refused to be sworn; for which contempt the
court sentenced him to pay a fine of two hundred and fifty dollars and to be imprisoned for thirty days.

John Jackson was the next witness called to the stand. He
was asked whether, on the morning of the 14th of September,
1826, he and Giddings, or Giddings alone, went to the magazine; but he refused to answer the question on the ground that
it might subject him to an indictment for an offence of high
magnitude. The court said that he could not now be prosecuted for the conspiracy, that offense being barred by the stat-
ute. Mr. Griffen, counsel for the defence, said that the witness
did not wish to disclose the nature of the offense for which he
fears an indictment.

By the Court: "Do you suppose it would involve you in a prosecution for murder?" Witness : "I do not know how far it would affect me." The Court: "The witness must know that a crime has been committed before he can claim the privilege. To claim the privilege on mere presumption that such a thing would occur, rendered witness guilty of perjury. If, however, the witness would brave heaven and earth and commit perjury it could not be helped. By answering, the witness need not admit that he murdered Morgan."

Mr. Barnard, of counsel for the defence, said that every man in the community believed that a murder had been committed. The witness now requested permission to confer with counsel, which was granted. On his return he still refused to answer the question. The counsel of the people asked witness if he did not testify on this point at Canandaigua. Witness replied that he answered a question of like import on the trial of Bruce. The court decided that if the witness had once waived his privilege he could not claim it now. The question being repeated, witness, after again consulting counsel, said that he did go towards the magazine in company with another person, but that person was not the defendant. To the question of, " What were your objects in going to the magazine? " witness refused to answer, and the question was waived. The next question put to Jackson was, " Was anything carried by the person that went with you to the magazine? " This question led to a long and searching examination, showing, in this case at least, that it was almost impossible to extract truth from a reluctant witness. The following synopsis of his testimony, as reported by Mr. Cadwallader, of Lockport, was certified to be correct by Judge Marcy. The object of the examination was to show that Morgan was making an outcry in the magazine, which might attract too much attention, and that Jewett, Giddings, and Jackson went to the magazine to appease or intimidate him, taking victuals and drink for him with them.

Witness thinks there was ; *don't recollect exactly what ;* thinks he had a basket in his hand ; don't recollect that he saw what was in it ; it was covered up with a cloth or brown paper ; did not see him carry a vessel with drink in it ; does not recollect that he did so at any other time ; witness thinks *he* did not carry a vessel containing drink towards the magazine ; it was a

small basket.   The other man went up to the magazine; thinks
he did not see that person go into the magazine.   Witness had
to go by the window to return; the man did not return with
him; can't say positively that he saw him come back; saw him
when he was within a few feet of the house; can't say whether
he had the basket.   At the magazine saw the man go towards
the door of it; did not see any door unlocked; the outside door
which witness saw, he thinks was down, or partly opened; the
person was a little ahead of him; did not see him enter; can't
say positively but he did enter.   Witness was next asked if
he heard the person with him speak to any person in the magazine.   He objected to answering.   The court decided that he
must answer.   Witness answered, he did; a person in the
magazine replied; thinks he did not hear a noise before or at
the time he stopped; don't recollect that the first he heard in
the magazine was the above answer; don't recollect that the
person on the outside called the one in the magazine by name;
don't recollect that he spoke to him as one he already knew.
To a question, " What was the conversation that passed between the person on the outside and the one on the inside ? "
counsel for defendant objected, on the ground that defendant
might be implicated by conversation to which he was not a
party, or which was not held in his presence.   The counsel for
the people disclaimed any such intention; they did not wish
witness to detail aught that would criminate defendant, unless
he were present; they wished justice to be done, and nothing
more.   The court then instructed the witness not to repeat any
conversation that would go to implicate defendant, unless it was
held in his presence.   Witness answers to question, that he
don't recollect; something was said; most forgets what; the
import, to the best of his recollection, was " to clear, to be off."
He took the substance to be, "Clear out!" *and he did clear out.*
Thinks the voice came from the magazine; he did not stay for
an answer to be given; he dropped what he had and ran; he
dropped a gun, a fowling-piece; got the fowling-piece from Giddings; don't know that it was loaded; the person with him requested him to take it along; *took it for the purpose of going
a-hunting;* had before concluded to go to the installation, eight
miles; put a bag on him to carry the game in; the person he
went with said, Let us go a-hunting!   This was after break-

fast. The voice witness heard caused him to run ; it "scared" him ; thinks Giddings replied to it ; don't recollect the substance of the reply, nor any part ; recollects the reply was very loud ; don't recollect that it was threatening ; the object of the reply might have been to order the man to be quiet ; can't be positive whether it was or not ; his language might have been that of a man speaking in a commanding or threatening manner ; it is his impression that it was to induce silence on the part of the man in the magazine ; heard the voice, and then told his companion he would stay no longer, thinking it best to be off ; thinks the voice was as before stated ; don't think he stayed to hear the reply of his companion ; was surprised to hear the voice from the magazine *in that manner ;* might not have been surprised if he had heard an accompanying voice ; it was the manner of the voice that induced him to run ; lodged at his friend's house the night before ; don't recollect a carriage coming to his house, nor near it, nor about it ; don't recollect *now* that any men came to the house that night ; he was told so ; had no knowledge of it. Witness before that time had been introduced to Colonel Jewett ; does not recollect that he saw him at the fort the evening previous, nor before he went to the installation ; in the morning the steamboat going to Lewiston was at the dock ; Giddings' family was going up ; Giddings was the man he went with to the magazine ; believes the fort was left in care of Giddings ; when the troops went off, Giddings was left in charge of the fort, some time before September, 1826 ; at the time of the installation, Jewett resided at the mess-house at the fort ; can't swear that he had charge of the fort at that time. Witness went to the installation in the forenoon ; thinks he saw defendant at Lewiston, and had conversation with him ; don't think he informed him of the noise ; had "special orders" when he left Giddings ; heard a noise in the magazine before he went to Lewiston ; it was a few minutes after the first time ; it was a human voice ; when he last heard the noise he was passing by the magazine to go to Lewiston ; had an errand to do there ; he was requested to inform certain persons there that the man in the magazine was making a noise ; Edward Giddings gave him the errand ; witness did not communicate it to defendant at Lewiston, nor in his presence ; don't know that it came to Jewett's ear that the man was confined in the magazine, except by hearsay; witness was requested to communicate his message to certain persons who were named; more than one or two; not to the whole installation, not to the defendant, nor to any one living at Lewiston.   Witness don't recollect that the man that went with him to the magazine had any weapon; he spoke about a pistol; he had a pistol; don't know as it was loaded; when near the magazine, the man spoke to the person in the magazine; thinks he said, "Be still, be quiet!" never recollected that anything was said to the man inside about the pistol.   Witness communicated his errand but to one person at Lewiston.   When the man in the magazine said, "Be off!" Giddings wanted witness to stop.   The man that witness communicated his errand to at Lewiston started to go to the fort. Cross-examined: Giddings at the house had a pistol; can't say he saw it after they started.   Theodore F. Talbot and Bates Cook testified that they visited the magazine in March, 1827, and discovered evidence that a person had been confined therein, and had made violent efforts to force his way out.   A number of witnesses were then introduced to prove the abduction of Morgan, and the particulars of his journey from Canandaigua to Niagara; but as no new facts were developed, it is not necessary to repeat the evidence.   William P. Daniels, when sworn, was asked if he was at the house of Solomon C. Wright, on the Ridge Road, when a close carriage was driven, guarded, into the barn; but he refused to answer the question, on the ground that it might implicate him in an indictment for murder as an accessory before the fact.   The court explained the law, as it had already done in the case of Turner; but he still refused to answer.   He also refused to say whether Eli Bruce and Jeremiah Brown were at Wright's Tavern on that occasion.   The court again explained the law, showing that the witness was in no danger of indictment for an offense not proven to have been committed, adding, "It is therefore a question of perjury or not with you; and remember that if the laws of man cannot reach you, the laws of God will." ⸱ The witness then replied that he claimed his privilege, believing that his answers to the question would implicate him in the murder of Morgan.   Daniels was then asked if he had seen Jeremiah Brown or Elihu Mather driving a close carriage along the Ridge Road on the 13th of September, 1826; which question he refused to answer.   The court decided that the question was proper, and must be answered. After consulting his counsel, the witness answered, "No." On being further pressed, however, he said he thought he did see a carriage pass that day. Being asked if he knew that Eli Bruce was in that carriage, he again consulted his counsel, and replied that he believed Bruce was in the carriage; and on being pressed, said that he had no doubt but that Bruce was in the carriage. He did not recollect seeing the defendant, Jewett, at the installation; but he *might* have talked with Jewett about the confinement of Morgan in the magazine afterwards.

A large number of witnesses were then called to prove that the defendant, Jewett, had charge of the fort and magazine while Morgan was confined there. But as they evaded some questions, and refused to answer others, the prosecution failed to obtain direct and positive proof of this fact, although it was evident that the witnesses were disregarding that part of their oath which requires them to tell the whole truth. The cause was summed up by Messrs. White and Barnard for the defendant, and Messrs. Whiting and Birdseye for the people. No evidence had been given showing that Jewett was in any way connected with the abduction of Morgan, nor in his forcible conveyance from Canandaigua to Fort Niagara. Nor was it positively proven that Morgan was the man confined in the magazine. No witness had ever seen Jewett with Morgan, although Whitney and Bruce had testified that he was taken across the Niagara River to Canada, and brought back. While, therefore, there was not a particle of doubt that Morgan was confined in the magazine of the fort, while Jewett had charge of both, the testimony relied on to establish that fact was circumstantial only.

Judge Marcy, in his charge to the jury, endeavored to present the whole question clearly and impartially, and while he did not hesitate to express his disapproval of the mode in which witnesses had evaded instead of answering questions, and while it was evident that he had himself no doubt of the guilt of the defendant, yet he was constrained to say that the jury, in finding a verdict of "Guilty," must attach more weight to circumstantial evidence than consisted with the due rights of defendant and the due administration of justice. The jury, after a brief absence, returned with a verdict of "Not guilty."

This trial lasted nearly six days. Though resulting in the

acquittal of the defendant, it went very far in the public estimation to implicate the Masonic fraternity, so many of whom, in
their desire to save a brother from punishment, either refused
to answer questions or answered them so evasively as to create
a general impression that they had committed perjury. The
developments on this trial converted Mr. Birdseye, the State
counsel, to political Anti-Masonry, and but for his high position
in and peculiar relations to the Democratic party, would have
wrought the same miracle upon Judge Marcy. The court proceeded immediately with the trial of Solomon C. Wright and
Jeremiah Brown, who were indicted for participating in the
abduction of Morgan, — Wright, for receiving and concealing
in his barn the carriage in which Morgan was confined; and
Brown for driving that carriage. Here similar scenes to those
already described with reluctant witnesses were enacted. The
testimony, for the most part, was so like that already given on
the trial of Jewett that it is unnecessary to repeat it. John
Jackson and William P. Daniels went through the same series
of "dodges." Jackson, however, now recollected that Giddings
named Morgan as the man confined in the magazine, and sent
him (the witness) to Lewiston to tell Colonel King and David
Hague that the man was making a noise in the magazine, and that
they must come down. Upon the equivocations and evasions of
the other witness, William P. Daniels, Judge Marcy remarked
that he hoped never to see another such exhibition in a court of
justice. But, notwithstanding all the equivocations and evasions, there was a positive and direct testimony, uncontradicted,
against both defendants. The cause was summed up by Messrs.
Griffen and Barnard for the defendants, Messrs. Whiting and
Birdseye for the people. Judge Marcy charged now, as in the
other case, ably and impartially, although it was evident that he
thought the testimony sufficient to call for a verdict of "Guilty."
The jury remained out thirty-six hours, and then, to the surprise of bench, bar, and people, came into court with a verdict
of "Not guilty."

Subsequently it was ascertained that ten of the jurors were
for convicting the defendants, and that two avowed their determination to hold out to the "bitter end" against such a
verdict. While the jury was out a man was detected in conveying victuals concealed in a cloak to the two recusant jurors.
He was brought before the court and promptly punished.

CHAPTER XXV.

1829.

ANOTHER special circuit was ordered in Niagara County for the trial of Elisha Adams and others. It was originally intended, inasmuch as Adams was a subordinate actor in the scenes at Fort Niagara, to use him as a witness only, but after his extraordinary testimony at Canandaigua he was indicted in Niagara County. Judge Nelson, then of the Supreme Court of this State, and now of the Supreme Court of the United States, was detailed by the governor to hold this circuit. The most important feature, and the principal interest which this trial awakened, was the introduction of Edward Giddings as a witness. Mr. Giddings held speculative or skeptical opinions on religious subjects, and while regarded as an infidel, he really believed all that was essential to qualify him as a witness, while, practically, he was a better man than those who professed much more. Orthodox people in conversing with him might fairly assume that he was an infidel ; and yet those very people, if they were well acquainted with him, would place implicit confidence in his truthfulness.

Colonel William L. Stone, in the following letter to John Quincy Adams, gave a full and reliable account of this trial. Colonel Stone's book, on which I have drawn largely in this narrative, not only contained all that the Morgan trials and the committee of investigation developed, but was written in a spirit of perfect impartiality, which in the midst of the excitement required great courage. Colonel Stone was, though not a zealous, yet an adhering Mason. In his book he commended and condemned Masons and anti-Masons, as in his conscientious judgment they deserved. Indeed, the highest evidence of the fairness of his book was found in the fact that at the time, 1832, it was rejected alike by ardent Masons and ultra Anti-Masons. I remember to have told him in what particulars I thought him unjust to Anti-Masons; but in reading it carefully now, as I have done, I do not hesitate to pronounce it a work singularly just and impartial, reflecting equal credit on the head and the heart of its author: —

NEW YORK, *March* 26, 1832.

SIR, — The fate of William Morgan, as far probably as it will ever be disclosed by human testimony, will now rapidly be developed. Another special circuit was held in the county of Niagara, commencing in February, 1831, and extending considerably into the month of March. His Honor Judge Nelson, of the Supreme Court, presiding. At this circuit all the pending indictments in the case of Morgan, which it was believed the public good required to be proceeded with, were disposed of. The two principal trials were, first, that of the People *v.* Elisha Adams; and second, The Same *v.* Parkhurst Whitney, Timothy Shaw, Noah Beach, William Miller, and Samuel Chubbuck. Both trials were severely contested and of long continuance. But as the alleged participation of the defendants in the transaction took place while Morgan was in and about Fort Niagara, and as far the greater part of the testimony was the same on both trials, I have thought it best to unite them in a single narrative. For all the necessary purposes of history this course will answer as well, if not better, than a separate outline of the respective trials, while time and labor will alike be saved both to writer and reader.

The trial of Adams commenced on the 24th of February; that of the other parties above mentioned, who were impleaded together, on the 28th. Much difficulty was experienced, on both trials, in obtaining a jury, — the greater number of the panel having been set aside for having formed opinions against the defendants. The first witness called upon both trials was Loton Lawson, who gave an account of the taking of Morgan away from the jail in Canandaigua. Before Morgan was put into the jail witness had had some conversation with him in regard to his proposed book. Morgan said he was in a scrape with Miller, and wished to get out of it. Witness went to Rochester to communicate to some Masons that Morgan was willing to be privately carried away. On his return Morgan was taken out of jail, as heretofore related. Lawson denied that he gave a signal at the door of the jail, although he heard a whistle, but did not believe it was connected with that affair. No force was used in taking him from the jail. After he had left it a few rods, another man came up, and said, " Morgan, you are my prisoner," upon which the latter cried, " Murder ! " but on being assured that he would not be hurt, he was pacified. No force was used in putting him into the carriage ; neither was he blindfolded or bound. He conversed as anybody else would, and went willingly ; sometimes the curtains were up and sometimes down ; Morgan wished them to be closed that he might travel privately, and be kept away from Miller or from his knowledge, — that he might not be followed by him. On their arrival at Hanford's, Morgan made no objection to the change of carriages ; he was not intoxicated or drowsy, and nothing was given to make him so. Witness went with the carriage to Gaines, at which place he took another conveyance, and struck off to Lockport, where he passed the night, and went into Lewiston to the installation on the following morning. He did not, while there, hear of Morgan's making any noise at the fort ; he was not himself at the fort, and had never been there. He saw Parkhurst Whitney at the installation, he being one of the officers. He believed Whitney went down to Youngstown [to the fort] in the boat, but was not certain. When Morgan was asked why he had made the noise after leaving the jail, he said he was sorry he had made such a fuss. Witness saw no restraint used upon Morgan on any subject during the day ; it was fine weather, and they had a pleasant ride. He complained much of Miller, who was to have paid him five thousand dollars, but he had not furnished money enough for the expenses of publication. He was willing to go anywhere to get away from that man.

John Whitney (tried formerly, it will be recollected, and acquitted) was sworn as a witness on the trial of Parkhurst Whitney, and others. He stated that he rode on the carriage with the driver, Hubbard, from Canandaigua to Victor. He there procured a horse, and proceeded to Rochester on horseback ; thence to Hanford's Landing ; from which place to Wright's he rode with Morgan in the carriage. Witness fully corroborated the testimony of Lawson in regard to the absence of restraint and of liquor, except two or three glasses, and also to Morgan's willingness to go. He did not recollect that any one had hold of Morgan when they got out of one carriage into another ; they got out and in like the others ; there was no scuffle, nor was any force used ; he had a talk with Morgan on the road ; he expressed a willingness to go if his situation could be made to suit him, and he was assured it should be so ; the object of keeping him secret was that Miller and those with whom he had been engaged in printing the book should not know where he had gone, so as to follow him ; he said Miller had misused him, and he did not wish him to know where he had gone ; appeared as anxious as any one to keep his journey secret; witness saw no bandage over his eyes; no threats were used; Morgan was told he could not expect friends unless he used his friends well; he said he had done wrong, and was willing to get out of the scrape; he knew they were going to Lewiston; it was the understanding that the arrangements to be made for him were to be as good in a pecuniary point of view as the speculation with Miller in publishing the book; nothing definite, however, had yet been agreed upon.

Isaac Farwell was examined on both trials. He lived near Wright's Tavern, and was there when the carriage drove to the shed, towards evening, on the 13th of September, 1826. He was requested by Wright to go into the barn, where the carriage was driven. He there got into the carriage to sit with the man whom he had been told was Morgan, while the person whom he found in the carriage with him went in to supper. He (witness) was a Mason, and, on inquiring what the disturbance was about, and who Morgan was, they told him that he had been publishing the secrets of Masonry, and gave him an account of the manner in which they had taken him away, first, from Batavia for stealing a shirt, and then from Canandaigua. He inquired what they were going to do with him, and was told that they intended to take him to Canada, where they would procure him to be sent on board of a British ship of war. Witness held no conversation with him, either by signs or words. The person in the carriage had a handkerchief drawn entirely and closely over his face. When witness entered the carriage, and the other person left it to get his supper, he said, " You d—d old hag, if you open your head while I am gone, I will smash you on my return." Morgan was helped out of the carriage, while in the barn, and soon taken in again. Witness was told that the fact of his being there was to be kept a secret. He had talked with Wright about it before the carriage came up. Wright said he did not know what the matter was, but a man came along in a sulky, and inquired if he had seen the Rev. Mr. Cummings; to which he replied that he had not. He was then directed by the man in the sulky that if a carriage should come along he must drive it into the barn and say nothing about it. Wright added that he knew not what it meant.

Eli Bruce was examined on both trials, testifying much as on his former examination, with the addition of a few particulars. Morgan's face, he said, was covered that he should not see who were with him. He talked freely, and was not bound. When asked if he knew where he was, he replied that he was passing from Rochester to Lewiston. On getting into the boat he inquired what it was. He was told, and then asked if all was safe, with which assurance he was content. He was not landed on the Canada shore. Witness supposed that Morgan was to be provided for, — that he was to be placed on a farm somewhere back in the country, away from the knowledge or influence of Miller. When the Canada people refused to receive him, witness thought it was because their arrangements were not completed. When, on coming back, Morgan was put into the magazine, he (witness) supposed he was only to be kept there until those arrangements had been settled. There was no restraint upon Morgan's limbs, — he was not bound, even in the boat. A man was left with him to keep him company at the magazine, but witness did not go into it himself. He did not previously know Morgan, but was informed that it was a voluntary proceeding on his part, or he (witness) would have had nothing to do with the affair. When he heard on the following day, at Lewiston, that Morgan was uneasy, he had some misgivings, but supposed from the character of the men who were with him that nothing dishonorable would be done, or anything that would affect his own character and standing. The last that he had ever heard upon the subject, except by rumor, was that he was quieted and contented. He had himself hoped for the best, and said nothing — being a public officer. He heard no expression from any one that Morgan had forfeited his life. He remembered of their fastening the magazine, but had not inquired into the particulars of the case.

John Jackson, the person who accompanied Giddings to the magazine on the morning of the 14th of September, 1826, and who was dispatched to Lewiston to inform Colonel King that "the man in the magazine was making a good deal of noise," was again called upon the stand. His testimony on the present occasion did not vary materially from his former statements, especially that made on the trial of Brown and Wright. In addition to his former relations, however, he now testified that he was at Batavia when Miller was arrested, on the 12th of September; and when he was first told that "there was a man in the magazine," he thought it must be Miller. He denied, however, that his business at Batavia had any connection with the proceedings against Miller. He knew not for what that individual was arrested.

There were two witnesses sworn upon the trials of Adams and Parkhurst Whitney, and those impleaded with him, whose testimony was of a peculiarly important and decisive character. The first of these was James H. Shedd, now a practicing lawyer in Ohio, whose name has not before appeared on any of the trials. He testified that he happened to be at Fort Niagara on the afternoon of September 12, 1826, when he was inquired of by Colonel Jewett, whom he previously knew, whether he was a Mason. On replying in the affirmative, he was informed that a very high-handed measure was about to be entered into by the Masons, a parallel of which could not probably be found in the history of the world, unless in the case of King Stanislaus, who was seized and carried off by the Poles ; that it was their intention to carry off Morgan for publishing the secrets of Masonry, — take him to Montreal or Quebec, and there put him on board a British vessel, if one could be found whose commander was a Mason. In the evening of that day witness, on request, assisted to row a boat over the river in which were two other persons besides himself, one of whom was Jewett. On reaching the shore, witness and Jewett went up to the village of Niagara, attended a meeting of eight or ten Masons at a lodge room, where the subject of Morgan's disposal was discussed. One proposed harsh measures, and even death ; another repelled the proposal with indignation. The meeting was broken up, nothing done, and the party returned in the boat to Fort Niagara. On Wednesday witness assisted to remove powder out of the magazine, which was said to be spoiling on account of dampness. On Thursday he was informed that Morgan had been brought to that place the night previously ; went that day to Lewiston and attended the installation. Returned the same evening. On the Monday or Tuesday morning following witness and another person met Adams coming from the magazine, who seemed to be agitated, and said he believed they had taken Morgan away. Went to the magazine ; Adams called Morgan thrice, but received no answer ; unlocked the door, entered, discovered a quantity of straw which had the appearance of having been lain upon by a man, an ammunition box, flag, silk handkerchief, pitcher, decanter, and a plank that was broken, on the floor. The straw was removed, the boxes taken out, the plank refitted to its proper place, the handkerchief destroyed, and the pitcher and decanter carried down to Giddings' house. Witness heard no explanation whether Morgan had been removed by the Canada Masons or not. He was intimately acquainted with the person who first spoke to him, and they had the sign and grip between them. Witness made no inquiries of him as to the effect of this transaction, but did make inquiries of him as to the propriety of the measure ; he said it was with extreme reluctance that he had anything to do with it, but felt himself bound as a Mason. Witness remained at Youngstown about six months afterwards, teaching school ; conversed with Mr. Shaw, one of the defendants, at Lewiston in the following January, who stated that he knew Morgan was there, and felt very bad about it. Heard Shaw endeavor to dissuade Giddings from disclosing the affair. On his cross-examination witness stated that no one was present at the time of Shaw's admissions ; never heard either of defendants acknowledge that they had had any part in the transaction ; never saw any of the persons who were present at the meeting in

Canada afterwards except Garside, who wished witness to introduce him to some Mason of high standing, that he might get his permission to put Morgan to death. Witness refused.

Orsamus Turner, whose name has become quite familiar in connection with these transactions, testified, in substance, that he was at Batavia some time before the abduction of Morgan, and heard a good many hard things said. He had learned from sheriff Thompson and others that Morgan was dissatisfied with Miller, and wished to get away, if the Masons would give him an equivalent for the book he was writing. With this view, he (witness) crossed over into Canada to complete the arrangements for taking Morgan thence, and settling him upon a farm. This farm, it was understood, was to be paid for by the Masons in Canada. It was situated near the Short Hills, and was to be given to Morgan on condition that he should take back the manuscripts already in Miller's possession, and suppress the book. Witness supposed the bargain with Morgan had been made, and that it was well understood on both sides. Four men were to be responsible : and indeed they had offered to pay Morgan an equivalent in money, should he prefer it. On his return from Canada, witness stopped at Youngstown to take tea. While tea was preparing, witness and his companion, Darrow, walked to the house of Mr. Giddings, who kept a tavern, where the subject of the removal of Morgan into Canada was talked over. It was suggested that it might be necessary for Morgan to stop there over night, and the question arose where he should be kept. Giddings proposed the magazine of the fort, and introduced witness to a person, who, he said, would make the necessary arrangements. From the rash expressions which witness had heard at Batavia, which he now mentioned to Giddings, it was feared that some violence might be offered to Morgan, and this, they thought, would have a bad effect. The arrangement for taking him into Canada was made for the double purpose of preventing violence and suppressing the book. Witness expressly told Giddings that the arrangement had been made with a full understanding that not a hair of his head should be hurt. Giddings, who felt as he did upon the subject, was charged to see that no violence should be offered to Morgan. The information had been communicated to witness by men of honor, in whom he thought he could confide, — men of character and standing. After this interview with Giddings and the other man, on the night of the 10th of September, witness had never had anything to do with the matter, directly or indirectly. He attended the installation of the Chapter, at Lewiston, but knew nothing in anywise inculpating either of the parties on trial.

The next witness called, and far the most important of any examined on either of the long chain of trials, was Edward Giddings, who had been rejected, in consequence of his alleged infidelity, on the trial of Bruce, in 1828. He was again objected to by the counsel for the defence, both on the trial of Adams, and on that of Parkhurst Whitney, and others, on the same ground as before, namely, his disbelief in a Supreme Being who will punish perjury. A long trial ensued upon this point, and the testimony taken in respect to his religious belief was, if possible, still more contradictory than before. The testimony having been closed in support of the competency of Giddings, his Honor, Judge Nelson, said that the more he reflected upon it, the more he was convinced that he ought not, upon this preliminary inquiry, to stop to weigh and canvass the facts, and see on which side the balance of proof lay. He should always hold the party objecting to make out a clear and undoubted case of disqualification before he would exclude. Doubt ought to admit. He would therefore admit the witness, allowing the counsel to urge the facts to the jury upon the question of credibility. Giddings was thereupon sworn. He testified that in September, 1826, he lived at Fort Niagara, and kept the ferry. About midnight of the 12th he was called up by Colonel King, who said he had got the d——d perjured scoundrel who had been revealing the secrets of Masonry; that he was bound, hoodwinked, and under guard; wanted witness to take them over the river and deliver him up to the Masons in Canada, for them to do with as they thought proper; went over the river with them; Morgan was sitting on a piece of timber when witness went out of the house; he had a handkerchief over his eyes; he was then led to the boat by two men; one had hold of each arm; was not intoxicated; appeared to be very weak; his legs were not bound; nothing was said to him before they got to the boat; one of the men (Eli Bruce) called for some water, and said, "The wretch is almost famished;" there were four of us with him; five in all, including Morgan, went into the boat, namely, Colonel King, Hague, Bruce, Morgan, and witness; two of the men, when we got over, went up to the town (Niagara). While they were waiting in the boat, Morgan said, "The handkerchief pains me most intolerably." The man who sat in front of him felt under the handkerchief, and said, "It is not tight; keep silent." He then said, "Gentlemen, I am your prisoner; use me with magnanimity." The man who sat before him pressed a pistol against his breast, and told him if he said anything more he would shoot him. Morgan tried to put his hands into his vest pocket, and could not; witness then saw that his hands were tied behind him. In about two hours they returned, with intelligence that the Canadians were not prepared to receive Morgan, whereupon he was brought back and put into the magazine. Witness

had the key; went up the next morning to give him food and refreshments.   They went into the porch door, and were about opening the
door leading to the magazine, when Morgan said, "You had better
not come in; for, as there are but two of you, I can defend myself
against you, as I am situated; I am determined not to be bled to
death." John Jackson then said, "Where is that pistol? Is it loaded,
is the flint in good order? for I will shoot the d——d rascal." This
was said in a loud voice, to intimidate him. Morgan then cried,
"Murder!" and made much noise. Witness requested a man (John
Jackson) who was going to Lewiston, to send somebody to still Morgan. A person (Hague) came, and in going up to the magazine, he
said, " I know Morgan, and he fears me as he does the devil; he
will make no more noise after I see him." Afterwards, thirty more
came, of whom all returned except the six defendants. The colloquies
that attended the interviews between them and their prisoner do not
seem to be material to the issue, until the evening of the 15th, when
his further disposal became a matter of deliberation, and it was at
first determined to put him to death. While they were proceeding to
the magazine for that purpose, under the direction of Colonel King,
one of them made an objection. He said he felt bound to assist, but
could not approve of the deed. They concluded, thereupon, to defer
the execution until they could send to " the Grand Lodge now sitting
at Jerusalem," for instructions. They apprised Morgan that they had
determined to send to the East for instructions what to do with him.
At this interview he said he thought that by climbing up on a frame
he could see to read, and he asked for a Bible; he also requested
permission to see his wife and children; and these indulgences were
promised to him, but not granted. After leaving the magazine they
were joined by Adams, and the manner of disposing of Morgan was
again discussed. One man said, by putting a rope round his body,
arms, and legs, and sinking him in the river, no trace of him could
ever be discovered. Miller said he could prove from Scripture that
it was right to take his life; quoted a passage, but witness don't recollect what it was; some high words passed between King and witness,
who told King he would go and release Morgan; King was in a great
passion, and told witness to do it at his peril; witness then gave him
up the key, and told King he would have no more to do with it; he
(King) took the key and gave it to another person. On the 17th witness went to York (U. C.), and returned on the 21st, when he was
told by Colonel Jewett that " they had murdered that man." The
witness also testified to murderous designs expressed by Garside (the
same person named by Shedd), but they do not seem to have pertained
to the issue.

A cross-examination followed of considerable length, one of the prominent points of which was the disclosure of terms of pecuniary advantage, upon the performance of which the witness had agreed to leave that part of the country and not appear as a witness. The Masons were very anxious to have him go off, and made him liberal offers, and he at one time agreed to go. The fact was admitted by Giddings, but as that was a matter touching his credibility only, it does not seem to be necessary to my purpose to enter into the detail. The examination and cross-examination were very long, and at times full of fearful and tragic interest.

Kneeland Townsend was next called. His testimony related principally to the proposition that had been made to silence Giddings by money. The witness (then a Mason) approved of the plan; but it was so evident, from his own confession, that the witness was so intemperate and forgetful that very little reliance, it is presumed, could have been placed upon his testimony, even if it had been important in its character.

Four witnesses, namely, Oliver Grace, Gustavus W. Pope, Loton Lawson, and Alexander Stewart, were then called to invalidate the testimony of Giddings.

The two next witnesses called by the defendants were for the purpose of impeaching the testimony of Kneeland Townsend, but their evidence was of little importance to either party.

The next and last witness, however, was called by the prosecution, and his testimony was so important that (especially as it is brief) I give it entire as reported : —

Amos Bronson : I had a conversation with Chubbuck (one of the defendants) day before yesterday (this is Saturday, 5th). We were talking about Giddings' testimony ; he said as far as he has gone he has told the truth ; this is a misfortune that has come upon us like the crash of an earthquake ; we could not avoid doing as we did, and the first we knew it was upon our shoulders ; at this time Giddings had got to where he told that quite a number had come down from Lewiston, and six stayed till after supper, and had given the names of Beach, Chubbuck, and Shaw ; I think Mr. Birdseye was examining Giddings at this time.

Cross-examined : Was here day before yesterday as a spectator ; am here to-day as a witness ; I told this conversation to several before I went home ; Chubbuck said that what Giddings had sworn to was as true as what he had sworn to himself.

The cause of Elisha Adams was ably defended by W. H. Adams, Esq., and that of the people by the special counsel, after which an elaborate charge was made to the jury by Judge Nelson. The cause was committed to the jury at about seven o'clock on Saturday evening. On Monday morning the jury came into court, and declared that they had not agreed upon a verdict, and could not agree. Eleven of them were ready to render a verdict of " Guilty," but there was one who would never agree. Such being the state of the case, the court directed the dissenting juror to stand up in the jury box. He did so, and proved to be the only Mason on the panel. The jury was then discharged.

The case of P. Whitney, Shaw, Beach, Miller, and Chubbuck was also very ably and eloquently summed up by Messrs. Griffin and Adams for the defence, and by the special counsel for the prosecution. The judge occupied an hour and a half in committing this cause to the jury, as there was a great accumulation of testimony to be analyzed and spread before them in an intelligible form. The proof of the existence of the conspiracy was established, the judge said, as had been conceded in the course of the argument on both sides. The jury, therefore, would not be under the necessity of examining that point. It was not contended, on the part of the people, that the defendants were otherwise guilty than as parties to the conspiracy, and this fact was the leading and important inquiry submitted to them. The question then arose, Were the defendants, or either of them, — for all or any of them might be convicted, — parties to the conspiracy or to the imprisonment of Morgan ? That they were was positively asserted by Giddings, under oath ; and the judge proceeded to examine the character and weight of that testimony, to enable the jury to give it its just value, retaining the ground that he was an admissible witness, and leaving it to them to judge of its credibility. The court also adverted to the testimony of Shedd, which only went to implicate Shaw, and would not of itself, conceding the truth of it, be sufficient for that. He deemed the question to rely mainly upon the credit attached to the testimony of Giddings. It was a question for the jury to decide. It was their province to pass upon the whole. If their minds were at rest on the question of guilt, they should convict regardless of consequences ; but if not, if they had any rational and conscientious doubts, their duty was to acquit.

On the morning of March 8th the jury, having been out all night, came into court with a verdict of " Not guilty " in regard to Timothy Shaw and William Miller. Not being able to agree respecting the guilt or innocence of the other defendants, the jury were discharged.

This brings us to the conclusion of the Morgan trials, or rather to the conclusion of the most important of them. I have intended, without going tediously through testimony and arguments, to show why and by whom Morgan was spirited away, and how far he had been judicially traced. It will be seen that Freemasons in the western part of the State, possessing more zeal than knowledge, conspired to suppress or destroy a book which Morgan had written and which Miller was publishing, — a book which, had it been left to depend upon its own merits, would probably have fallen still-born from the press. The Masons, when their attention was called to it, could, by remarking that it was but a reprint of " Jachin and Boaz," have effectually spoiled its market; but the concerted effort, by a large combination of Masons, first to get possession of the manuscripts, and next to destroy Miller's office, even *if* Morgan had not been *dealt* with, would have created a quick demand for the book. And we know how certainly one slip in a wrong direction leads to another. The failure to suppress the book induced the conspirators to abduct Morgan himself. Good, law-abiding men, Masons, were drawn into it by the assurance of Johns, Lawson, Ketchum, and others, that Morgan had quarrelled with Miller, and was anxious to get out of his toils. The conspiracy, rising from Morgan's arrest for debt to his rearrest for larceny, had no purpose beyond securing his separation for a year or two from his Batavia associates. Nor did the idea of taking his life occur to the most reckless until the refusal of the Masons in Canada to receive and send him to the Far West Fur Company as was expected threw him back upon their hands. Morgan had now been confined for several days in the magazine of Fort Niagara. He was becoming noisy, violent, and troublesome. The Lewiston Masons sent a messenger to Rochester to inform the persons who brought Morgan there that they must take the responsibility of disposing of him. The subject was anxiously discussed in the chapter at Rochester. Who, besides Whitney, went in consequence of this message to Niagara was not known. Simultaneously, however, the Rev. F. H. Cuming, an Episcopal clergyman, went from Rochester to Lewiston to officiate at the installation of a Knight Templars' Encampment. At the installation supper, either by design or otherwise, the zeal of those present was quickened by animated speeches and significant toasts into enthusiasm. At a late hour the chaplain, Rev. Mr. Cuming, gave the following sentiment : " *The enemies of our Order*, — may they find a grave six feet deep, six feet long, and six feet due east and west." That sentiment occasioned wild excitement. What occurred immediately afterwards was undoubtedly suggested by these speeches and toasts, acting upon temperaments more or less affected by the stimulants imbibed on such occasions. I have never believed that the men who deprived Morgan of his life were deliberately capable of so great a crime. Nothing less bewildering than the circumstances just referred to, coupled with the still more delusive idea that Morgan by violating his obligations had forfeited his life, could have so fatally misled them. Colonel Stone, writing from this standpoint, condenses into the following paragraph a confession which James A. Shedd, an unimpeached witness, examined on the trial of Elisha Adams, stated was made to him about six months after the deed was committed, by a Knight Templar: —

On the 19th of September eight Masons, having finally determined to put their prisoner to death, believing, probably, that it would be safer to have a smaller number actually concerned in the execution, held a consultation as to the best mode of proceeding. The object was to select three of their number for executioners, and to have the other five excluded, and so excluded that neither should know who else besides himself was thus released, or who were the executioners. For this purpose the following ingenious process was devised : They placed eight tickets in a hat, upon three of which were written certain marks, and it was agreed that each one of their number should simultaneously draw a ticket. They were instantly to separate before examining their tickets, and walk away in different directions until entirely out of sight of each other. They were then to stop and examine the slip of paper they had drawn, and the five drawing the blanks were to return to their own homes, taking different routes, by which means neither of them would know who had drawn the fatal numbers, and of course no one of the five could be a witness against the others. The three drawing the tickets designated were to return to the magazine at a certain hour and complete the design. The manner of his murder is believed to have been by attaching heavy weights to his body, and taking him out into the middle of the stream in a boat, where, at the black hour of midnight, he was plunged into the dark and angry torrent of the Niagara. The boat for this purpose was got in readiness by Adams, in obedience to the commands of the conspirators. The direct, positive knowledge of Edward Giddings, whose testimony was rejected on the trial of Bruce on the ground of his disbelief in a future state of punishment, but who was confessedly a truthful man,

did not go beyond the confinement of Morgan for several days and
nights in the magazine of Fort Niagara. His remonstrances and admonitions induced Colonel King and his associates to leave Giddings
out of their final programme. Mr. Giddings' own relation of what
transpired under his eye and observation is contained in his testimony
on the trial of Adams.

And here, so far as the trials of parties implicated, and so
far as the committee of investigation, of which Bates Cook was
chairman, were enabled to elicit information as to the final disposition of William Morgan, the curtain fell. Public sentiment
of the nation was divided upon the question of whether Morgan
had or had not been put to death. Not only the Masonic press,
but a majority of political journals, maintained the negative side
of the question. The statements of the Morgan Committee were
denied, while the motives and character of the individuals composing that committee were impugned and maligned. A very
large proportion of the most intelligent and reputable classes
believed that, while some few over-zealous Masons had at first
committed some vague offense towards Morgan, yet that he had
subsequently fallen into the hands of unscrupulous politicians,
who kept him concealed to create an " excitement " which would
enable them to obtain political power. Although subsequently
clear and positive information of the murder of Morgan, with
circumstances and details, came to me, I will not break the con-
tinuity of the narrative by introducing it here.

CHAPTER XXVI.

1827–1829.

Rise of Political Anti-Masonry. — A Consultation. — Renouncing Masons urge Political Action. — Votes at Town Meetings. — Dr. F. F. Backus. — Anti-Masonic Convention. — Monroe County elects Anti-Masonic Representatives. — Anti-Masons supporting John Quincy Adams. — More Renunciations. — Judge Thompson's Nomination. — Anti-Masonic State Convention at Utica. — Granger for Governor and Lieutenant Governor. — Solomon Southwick. — Van Buren's Election. — The Presidential Canvass. — The "Coffin Handbills." — Western New York. — Majorities for Adams. — Growth of Anti-Masonic Sentiment in the State. — Effect in Legislation. — The "Anti-Masonic Enquirer." — The Party in other States. — Henry Dana Ward and the Review. — Frederick Whittlesey and Rev. Mr. Cuming. — A Lifelong Friend.

I WILL now, as briefly as the nature and importance of the question will permit, give a history of political Anti-Masonry. As the town meetings in the spring of 1827 were approaching, the citizens of several towns in the county of Genesee, and of one town in the county of Monroe, of their own volition refused to vote for Masons as supervisors or justices of the peace. That circumstance occasioned a good deal of conversation and solicitude among the prominent citizens of Rochester, Canandaigua, Auburn, Geneseo, Batavia, Lewiston, and Buffalo, who had been actively engaged in the investigations concerning the abduction, the imprisonment, and probable murder of Morgan, and who yet had not contemplated political action, and who were unwilling to allow the question to assume such aspects. As soon, therefore, as it was found practicable, there was a consultation between Francis Granger, William H. Seward, James Wadsworth, Samuel Works, Harvey Ely, Frederick F. Backus, Frederic Whittlesey, Thurlow Weed, Trumbull Cary, David E. Evans, Bates Cook, George H. Boughton, Albert H. Tracy, Thomas C. Love, and George F. Talbot. Messrs. Ely, Backus, and Love were at first inclined to favor political action, but

after free and frank discussion they acquiesced in the views entertained by all the other gentlemen present, and it was therefore determined to repress, as far as we were able, the disposition
to carry the question into politics. The pressure for political
action was most earnest from seceding Masons, a large class of
influential men, who insisted that the ballot was the only weapon
that could be successfully wielded against the fraternity, and
who insisted that by no other means, and in no other way, could
they be protected from the "vengeance" of the institution
which they had renounced. We were unable, however, as the
town meetings approached, in the spring of 1827, to restrain the
citizens of Le Roy, Stafford, Elba, etc., in Genesee County, and
of Wheatland, in Monroe County, where tickets, from which
Masons were excluded, ran and were elected. Rochester had
already become the centre of Anti-Masonry. From that point
the movements, whether of a judicial or legislative character,
emanated.

We continued, in our conversations and correspondence, to
repress political agitation, until an incident occurred which
changed our views and policy. From the incorporation of Rochester as a village down to the summer of 1827, Dr. Frederick
F. Backus had been its treasurer, elected year after year without opposition. Dr. Backus having been attending a patient
until a late hour in the night of the 12th day of September,
1826, observed a carriage standing in the street surrounded by
several persons, who started off in one direction, while the carriage moved off in another as he approached it. Subsequently,
he saw those persons emerge from their hiding-places and go in
the direction the carriage had taken. After it became known
that Morgan had been taken from the Canandaigua jail in a
carriage, which was driven away in the direction of Rochester,
Dr. Backus, by comparing dates, became satisfied that Morgan
was a prisoner in the carriage whose mysterious movements he
had observed, and from that hour he took an active part in the
investigation, and became a zealous opponent of Masonry. When
the village election approached, Dr. Backus, as usual, was placed
in nomination. No person was nominated as an opposing candidate, nor was it known at the polls that any other person was
being voted for for treasurer. But upon a canvass of the votes,
it appeared that Dr. John B. Elwood was elected treasurer.

This *coup d'état*, so secretly and successfully accomplished, awakened immediate and wild excitement throughout the village. It was like a spark of fire dropped upon combustible materials. "The blow was struck but the hand concealed," according, as it was alleged, to the obligations of the Order. Dr. Elwood, like Dr. Backus, was much respected, belonged to the same political party, and was not a Freemason ; but his election, unknown even to himself until after the votes were canvassed, was attributed to the secret mandate of the village lodge ; nor in their exultations over the result did the Masons deny that "impeachment."

Our petitions for a law changing the mode of selecting grand juries having been denied by the legislature of 1827, while the portals of justice were closed against us, we now decided to appeal through the ballot-boxes to the people. Early in September of 1827 a Monroe County Convention of Anti-Masons was called for the purpose of nominating members of Assembly. Public sentiment was then divided between the friends and opponents of the administration of John Quincy Adams. As all the members of the Morgan Committee (Messrs. Works, Ely, Backus, Whittlesey, and Weed), with the exception of Mr. Whittlesey, were supporters of the administration, the Masons, irrespective of party, became identified with the Democratic, or, as it was then called, the " Jackson party." We took the field a month earlier than it was usual to make nominations. While the Anti-Masonic sentiment was strong among the farmers, it was weak in the villages, especially among the wealthy and influential classes. It was difficult, therefore, to find in the village of Rochester a well-known and prominent citizen who would take an anti-Masonic nomination. An intimate friend (Timothy Childs), who was exceedingly anxious to obtain a seat in the legislature, and to whom the nomination was offered, found it difficult to restrain his indignation at the idea of becoming the candidate of a " contemptible faction." I left him, after an excited interview, with the assurance that he would have to take the responsibility of accepting or declining our nomination. After his nomination, we had another stormy interview ; but as Messrs. Works, J. K. Livingston, Dr. Backus, and myself were his best friends, he quietly but sulkily acquiesced, regarding it, however, as fatal to all his political hopes. Two or three weeks afterwards, as the Jackson County convention was about to meet, Addison Gardiner, a Jackson man, who had the sense to discern and comprehend the significance of Anti-Masonry, endeavored to break our line by offering Mr. Childs *their* nomination for the Assembly. The Jackson men did not require Mr. Childs either to *accept* their nomination or to *decline* the Anti-Masonic one, thus making him a sort of political equestrian, riding two horses. So far, all was smooth; but when Mr. Childs reported the arrangement to our committee, he was kindly but peremptorily informed that he must immediately accept or decline our nomination. This put him in a "tight place." But in reflecting upon the fact that we were his best and only real friends, he despondingly accepted our nomination, and during the same evening he was further discomfited by hearing persons offer bets freely that the Anti-Masonic ticket would not poll five hundred votes in the county. But the result showed how little the most intelligent and influential villagers knew of the spirit abroad among the farmers. The Anti-Masonic candidates were elected by a majority of 1700. Although not nominated as such, Francis Granger and Robert C. Nicholas, of Ontario, Nathan Mixer, of Chautauqua, and Morris F. Sheppard, of Yates, acted and became identified with the Monroe County Anti-Masons.

The following year, Mr. Childs, who became an Anti-Mason so grudgingly, was elected to Congress, where he served as an Anti-Mason four years.

State and presidential elections were now approaching. The Anti-Masonic element had developed sufficient political strength to attract the attention of parties and politicians. The Masons generally, without reference to their political antecedents, sought refuge in the Jackson or Democratic party. Most of the Anti-Masonic leaders had been Clintonians, and were supporters of Mr. Adams' administration. President Adams, immediately after the abduction of Morgan was proven, wrote a letter saying that he was not, never had been, and never should be a Mason. General Jackson was known to be an adhering Mason. Hence the Anti-Masons of Western New York, though previously about equally divided in political sentiment, became early open and zealous supporters of Mr. Adams for President. The feeling of Masons, exasperated by the existence of a political organization

which made war upon the institution of Freemasonry, became
intensely so by the renunciation of Masonry by ministers, elders, and deacons of the Presbyterian, Methodist, and Baptist
churches. The conflict therefore became more embittered and
relentless, personally, politically, socially, and ecclesiastically,
than any other I have ever participated in, and more so, probably, than any ever known in our country. Thousands of Masons, innocent of any wrong, and intending to remain neutral,
were drawn into the conflict, when all were denounced who adhered to the institution. On the other hand, the Anti-Masons
maintained that the abduction and murder of Morgan resulted
legitimately from the obligations and teachings of the Order.

Meantime, the State election was approaching; and as the
Anti-Masons had extended their political organization not only
throughout all the western counties, but as it was attracting the
attention of many citizens in other sections, it became the occasion of annoyance to both of the great political parties of the
State. The Democrats saw in it an element which, if won over
to the Adams party, would constitute a majority; and while
most of the Adams politicians were anxious to conciliate the
Anti-Masons, the few adhering Masons belonging to that party
indignantly repudiated any such alliance. Masonry, as I have
before remarked, having sought and found protection in the
Jackson party, Anti-Masons naturally affiliated with the Adams
party. Having been in 1824 a zealous supporter of Mr. Adams
for President, I enjoyed in an equal degree the confidence of
the Adams men and the Anti-Masons. The policy of nominating candidates for governor and lieutenant-governor by the National Republican (Adams) Convention for whom the Anti-Masons could consistently vote, was transparent. Indeed, it was
scarcely denied that if the National Republican and Anti-Masonic vote could be united, the Jackson party would lose the
State. Francis Granger, of Ontario, a prominent National Republican, and a warm supporter of Mr. Adams before and after
his election, although he took part in the investigation which
sought a vindication of the laws against those who were connected with the conspiracy to abduct Morgan, was not as yet a
political Anti-Mason. He was well-known and popular. I spent
several weeks in visiting influential National Republicans in
different parts of the State with the hope of inducing them to

nominate Mr. Granger for governor. And when the convention met at Utica that result was confidently anticipated. Delegates from the rural districts generally were for Mr. Granger,
while those from the River Counties, Long Island, and the city
of New York were warmly in favor of Smith Thompson, a
judge of the Supreme Court of the United States, of conceded
ability and irreproachable character. The canvass, though animated, was conducted in a good spirit. All were anxious for
success, but all could not see and think alike. We assured the
convention that while two thirds or three fourths of our friends
would vote for Judge Thompson, the extreme or ultra Anti-Masons would nominate an independent ticket, for which votes
enough would be cast to secure the election of the Jackson candidates. On the other hand, it was maintained by influential
delegates that the nomination of Mr. Granger avowedly to secure the Anti-Masonic vote would offend so many National Republicans as to jeopardize not only the State, but the electoral
ticket; and this view of the question, accepted by a majority of
the delegates, finally led to the nomination, by a close vote, of
Smith Thompson for governor. Mr. Granger was then nominated by acclamation as a candidate for lieutenant-governor.

I left the convention as soon as I discovered that the nomination of Judge Thompson was inevitable, in the hope of rendering it acceptable to my Anti-Masonic friends. Two days'
observation and experience, however, satisfied me that this was
hopeless. An Anti-Masonic paper at Canandaigua, edited by
W. W. Phelps (who subsequently became a Mormon, and is
now, I understand, one of Brigham Young's elders), denounced
that nomination, and came out with a call for an Anti-Masonic
State convention. The Anti-Masonic paper at Le Roy responded
warmly. In consultation with a few discreet friends, it was
deemed advisable that Judge Thompson should be informed of
the state of feeling in the West; and the day after my return
to Rochester, I hastened eastward on this errand. A committee, consisting of John A. King, of Queens, George Tibbitts,
of Rensselaer, and Henry W. Delavan, of Albany, was appointed to wait on Judge Thompson and inform him of his
nomination. The judge was understood to be at Saratoga, and
after the adjournment of the convention, the committee left for
Saratoga; but on their arrival they learned that he had just

left for Poughkeepsie. Being at Saratoga, they remained for twenty-four hours, so that when I reached Albany I ascertained that the committee had taken the morning boat for Poughkeepsie. Leaving Albany in the afternoon boat, I encountered the committee as I landed at Poughkeepsie, waiting to take the same boat for New York. Informing them that I had important information to impart to them, they returned with me to the hotel, where I apprised them of the real condition of things in the western counties, and of the nature of my mission. They replied that even if it were desirable that Judge Thompson should decline the nomination, it was too late, for they had obtained his reluctant acceptance within the last hour. They consented, however, at that late and unpropitious time, to accompany me to his residence, where I discharged an embarrassing duty. Judge Thompson was equally embarrassed and annoyed, all the more annoyed from the circumstance that he had not desired the nomination, and after several hours' consideration had given the committee his reluctant consent to accept it. I expressed the opinion that votes enough would be thrown away upon Mr. Southwick (whom I saw in Albany, and who was more than ready to take an Anti-Masonic nomination) to defeat his election. Mr. King concurred with me in opinion. Mr. Tibbitts thought that, although it might have been wise to have nominated Mr. Granger for governor, yet the declension of Judge Thompson under the circumstances that existed would render the success of any ticket impossible. Mr. Delavan, exasperated by what he regarded as factious opposition, strongly deprecated the idea of Judge Thompson's withdrawal. The judge, therefore, a good deal disturbed by the interview, declined to withdraw his acceptance, and between twelve and one o'clock we returned to the hotel, resolved thenceforward to do our duty and hope for the best.

An Anti-Masonic State convention was immediately called, which met at Utica, and nominated Francis Granger, of Ontario, for governor, and John Crary, of Washington County, for lieutenant-governor. This placed Mr. Granger in a position of peculiar embarrassment. He had not desired, and much less had he solicited, any nomination, and yet he stood complicated by conflicting nominations from conventions with the principles of both of which he sympathized. It was difficult in accepting either or in declining either of these nominations to avoid offense, and yet this awkward responsibility was the result of circumstances entirely beyond control. Both nominations had been accorded to him in good faith by his personal and political friends. After mature deliberation he decided to decline the Anti-Masonic nomination for governor, and to accept the National Republican nomination for lieutenant-governor. His letter on that occasion, extricating himself from the false position which arbitrary circumstances placed him in, was so direct, frank, and manly as to command very general approval. The anti-Masons then nominated Solomon Southwick for governor in his stead. The election was very warmly contested. My own position was almost, if not quite, as embarrassing as that of Mr. Granger. I could not, consistently with my sense of what was due to other principles involving the welfare of the country, support the Anti-Masonic State ticket, although I knew that it would be voted for by one half or two thirds of my Anti-Masonic friends. The course which I deemed it proper to take in reference to the nomination of Southwick was briefly indicated in the following editorial in the " Anti-Masonic Enquirer," of Tuesday, September 23, 1828.

We publish to-day the proceedings of a meeting said to have been numerously attended at the capitol, in the city of Albany, where Solomon Southwick was nominated for governor of this State. This nomination, emanating from that at Le Roy, has been approved cordially, we believe, by the Ontario and. reluctantly by the Wayne County Convention. Other counties, in town and county meetings, will indicate their approbation of this measure, and Mr. Southwick will receive the divided support of the Anti-Masonic party.

This unwelcome state of things has been brought upon us by the cunning of Freemasonry. It is a crisis full of perplexing interest. Both political parties have contributed their exertions to cripple and embarrass the cause of the people. They have juggled us out of a candidate for governor. But a determination to adhere to the principles they profess now drives a large number of our friends into a measure of at least doubtful expediency.

The strongest suggestions of patriotism and the highest considerations of duty united to interest the prominent men of the State against an institution towards which Washington pointed his warning admonitions. But these high inducements failed to influence distinguished partisans. The violated laws of the country and the unavenged blood of a murdered citizen were not questions of sufficient importance to withdraw them from the pursuit of political honors. The road to office, obstructed by the power and influence of Masonry, did not appear direct enough to appease their hopes. The people were left to oppose Freemasonry without the aid of the laws and unsupported by the countenance of leading men. Indeed, so cautious were the prominent politicians, that none of them could be induced to identify their efforts and commit their political fortunes to the hands of men devoted to the cause of civil liberty. Political astrologers could not clearly discern the star by which they were to be conducted to the object of their ambition, and therefore refused to espouse the cause of truth and justice. Hence the embarrassments by which we are surrounded.

If under these multiplied difficulties the Anti-Masons incline to bestow their votes upon Mr. Southwick, though our conviction of duty will compel us to withhold our own from him, we shall by no means impugn their motives. The people are entitled to a candidate. Those Anti-Masons who believe Mr. Southwick a suitable person for governor act consistently and honorably in supporting him. We, too, shall vote for an Anti-Mason, according to the "strictest order of the sect." But we ask of our friends the same privilege which we accord to them, — the right of exercising the elective franchise independently.

The election resulted in a vote of 136,785 votes for Van Buren, 106,415 for Thompson, and 33,335 for Southwick. So that, while Mr. Van Buren was chosen, the combined vote of Thompson and Southwick left him in a minority of more than 3,000. It is possible, though not probable, that Mr. Granger's nomination by the Republican convention, supported as he would have been by the Anti-Masons, might have then overthrown the Albany Regency. As it was, Mr. Van Buren's election enabled his party to hold the State for the twelve succeeding years.

The complications in regard to our State ticket increased rather than diminished my zeal and efforts in favor of the Adams electoral ticket. Connected with the presidential canvass was an incident on which my mind always rests with satisfaction. The management of the campaign in Western New York was intrusted to me. I was known throughout this and other States to have been one of the earliest and most earnest friends of Mr. Adams in 1824. In August preceding the November election I received from the National General Committee two large dry-goods boxes containing campaign documents, upon opening which I found two pamphlets, one containing an account of the trial and execution of six militia men by General Jackson. This document was generally known, and will be better remembered, as the " Coffin Hand Bill." The other document was entitled " General Jackson's Domestic Relations," and gave an account of the general's duel with Mr. Dickinson, and his subsequent marriage with Dickinson's wife. A letter from the committee advised me that these boxes contained valuable campaign documents, the distribution of which throughout the western counties of this State was intrusted to me, adding that if more should be required, they would cheerfully furnish them. I immediately secured the boxes by additional nails, and placed them under lock and key, thenceforward doubling my diligence in the distribution of whatever else I could obtain promising to be useful among the people. Several weeks afterwards I received a letter from the national committee, saying that they were receiving applications from different villages in western New York for campaign documents, adding that if the supply was exhausted they would immediately forward others. To which I replied that I was making the best use possible of those they had forwarded to me, and that I believed I had a sufficient supply. About the middle of October, becoming uneasy from the numerous letters received, informing them that no " Domestic Relations " or " Coffin Hand Bills " could be obtained in the western counties of New York, the committee requested Mr. Joseph Blunt, of New York, to ascertain what had become of their campaign documents. Upon Mr. Blunt's arrival at Rochester I informed him that the boxes containing campaign documents were very safely and quietly reposing in the cellar of my printing office ; that not a copy had been or would be seen by an elector until the polls had closed, and that then, placing them in the square and setting the boxes on fire, we would celebrate an Adams victory in western New York by a campaign document illumination. Mr. Blunt, much excited, called upon several prominent friends of Mr. Adams, from whom, however, he obtained no sympathy, for General Matthews, Judge Strong, etc., supporters of Mr. Adams, but not Anti-Masons, were informed of and approved of my determination. Immediately after Mr. Blunt's return to

New York I was denounced in that city and in Boston as a " traitor " to the administration. Happily for me, however, my vindication followed close upon the heels of these denunciations, for while most of the southern, the eastern, the northern, and the middle counties in the State gave large majorities for Jackson, the western counties gave emphatic majorities for Adams. Monroe, for instance, gave 4,894 votes for Adams and 3,135 votes for Jackson. Livingston, an adjoining county, gave 2,183 votes for Adams and 1,304 for Jackson. Ontario, Wayne, Orleans, Genesee, Niagara, Erie, and Chautauqua gave equally decisive majorities for Adams. Had my expectations in this respect been disappointed, I should have been severely, and perhaps justly, censured, for it is doubtful whether the prominent and influential supporters of Mr. Adams ever came to the knowledge that the documents which I committed to the flames damaged the cause of Mr. Adams and strengthened that of General Jackson wherever they were circulated. The impression of the masses was that the " six militia men " deserved hanging, and I look back now with astonishment that the enlightened and able statesmen, editors, etc., etc., who supported Mr. Adams, could have believed that General Jackson could be injured with the people by ruthlessly invading the sanctuary of his home, and much less that they would permit a lady whose life had been blameless to be dragged forth into the arena of politics.

The election of 1828 imparted increased confidence, vigor, and strength to the Anti-Masonic party. It not only established itself firmly in the counties west of Cayuga Bridge, but made an important lodgment in Washington and Cortland, and revolutionized isolated towns in Madison, Onondaga, Oswego, Jefferson, Chenango, and Delaware. Wm. H. Maynard, Hiram F. Mather, George H. Boughton, Timothy H. Porter, and Moses Hayden of the Senate were political Anti-Masons. Abner Hazeltine and Nathan Mixer, of Chautauqua; David Burt and Millard Fillmore, of Erie; Calvin P. Bailey and John Haskell, of Genesee; Philo C. Fuller and Titus Goodman, of Livingston; John Garbutt, Heman Norton, and Reuben Willey, of Monroe; John Guernsey, of Niagara; John Dickson, Walter Hubbell, and Robert C. Nicholas, of Ontario; George W. Flemming, of Orleans; and Morris F. Sheppard, of Penn Yan, all Anti-Masons, were elected to the Assembly.   The practical effect of this partial triumph was the enactment of a law taking from the sheriffs of counties the selection of grand jurors.

Meanwhile my paper, the "Anti-Masonic Enquirer," with a circulation in what was known as the "infected district" quite unparalleled, had extended not only to the middle and northern counties of New York, but was being freely ordered from the Western Reserve in Ohio, from Alleghany, Somerset, Union, Lancaster, and Chester counties in Pennsylvania, and from all parts of Vermont.

The cause was being aided simultaneously by the letters of renouncing Masons, some of which, like that from Cadwallader D. Colden, a distinguished lawyer and politician of the city of New York, were very effective.   The renunciation of Elder Barnard, a talented and popular Baptist minister in Chautauqua County, was soon followed with a book from that divine, revealing the secrets of the Royal Arch Degree of Masonry.   A convention of seceding Masons, formidable in numbers and ability, met at Le Roy, by whom the truth of the revelations made by William Morgan and Elder Barnard were solemnly affirmed. Large editions of the proceedings of that convention were printed and circulated in New York, Ohio, Pennsylvania, Vermont, Connecticut, and Massachusetts, adding fuel to the flames previously kindled.   The "Anti-Masonic Review," under the auspices and management of Henry Dana Ward, a renouncing "Three Degree Mason," was about this time established in the city of New York.   Mr. Ward was a gentleman of education, refinement, and ability.   His character was unblemished.   He was impressive and earnest.   His writings carried conviction with them. His "Review" became popular, and while the excitement lasted was very influential.

The two individuals, among those prominently connected with the Morgan investigation, who most reluctantly yielded to the influences which carried the question into politics were Frederick Whittlesey and myself.   Mr. Whittlesey was the proprietor and editor of the Rochester "Republican," a Democratic journal.   He was efficient and influential, stood well with his party, and might look forward to the gratification of a reasonable ambition.   Appointed by a committee of his fellow-citizens to investigate the violation of the laws, he discharged that duty

fearlessly, but he had not contemplated the possibility of becoming alienated from his party. I in like manner held a
responsible position in the administration party, as I had enjoyed until that period the confidence of Governor Clinton,
who had himself relieved me and many other old friends by
taking ground for Jackson, while Mr. Adams had made the
path of duty smooth by becoming an Anti-Mason. While Mr.
Whittlesey was thoughtful and anxious in regard to the embarrassments of his position, an incident occurred which determined
his future course. An article signed "Vindex" appeared in a
Geneva paper, charging in bitter language a series of offenses
against me, offenses which, if true, or if half true, rendered me
unworthy of the respect of any honest or honorable citizen.
The spirit of the article was as vindictive as its language was
intemperate. Copies were gratuitously circulated in Rochester
at a moment when it was easy to add to the existing excitement.
The steps which I immediately took to ascertain who wrote
"Vindex" developed facts and circumstances which pointed so
unmistakably to the Rev. F. H. Cuming that I did not hesitate
in my reply to charge him with its authorship. This created a
new sensation. During the day the feeling grew so strong that
a prominent friend of Mr. Cuming called on him, and said that
it would be necessary to disavow the authorship of "Vindex,"
or to promptly furnish the evidence on which the accusations
rested. Mr. Cuming immediately and unequivocally denied that
he had written the article, and authorized his denial to be made
public. On renewing my inquiries, I ascertained that Mr. Cuming had been twice seen driving in a sulky in the night, between
Rochester and Geneva, only three nights before the appearance
of the offensive article. That and other circumstances occasioned so much feeling, that a meeting of the vestry of his
church was called, at the invitation of the rector, to enable him
to repel this aspersion upon his character. He appeared before
the vestry, and denied positively that he had either written the
article referred to, or was responsible for its publication. Mr.
Whittlesey was a member of that vestry. He listened attentively and silently until a resolution was about to be adopted,
not only exonerating their rector, but rebuking those who had
either recklessly or thoughtlessly made unjust accusations against
him, when he rose and stated that some ten days before "Vin-

dex" appeared in the Geneva paper, the Rev. Mr. Cuming handed him a communication for publication, which he read attentively, and which contained the same charges, and as nearly as he could remember in the same language, with the same signature as that which he subsequently found and read in the Geneva paper.

The vestry, as will be supposed, adjourned without passing their resolution or taking any action upon the subject. This most unexpected disclosure strengthened the hostility already existing from his connection with the abduction of Morgan, soon led to the withdrawal of the Rev. Mr. Cuming from the rectorship, and his removal from the State. Mr. Whittlesey, as soon as it was practicable, sold his printing establishment, ceased to be an editor, and became a zealous and influential political Anti-Mason. As soon as he would consent to be a candidate he was elected to Congress, where he served four years, usefully to his country and creditably to himself. He was among the ablest, most upright, and most reliable of all the public men I have ever known. We had been personal friends while we were political opponents, but from 1827 until the day of his death, our relations, personal, pecuniary, political, and social, were as close and cordial as mutual faith and friendship could make them.

CHAPTER XXVII.

1827.

The Dead Body at Oak Orchard Creek. — Coroner's Inquest. — Morgan or Munroe? — The Investigation. — Popular Excitement. — Mrs. Morgan's Identification of the Body. — Mrs. Munroe's Identification of the Clothing. — A Puzzle. — An Election Incident. — The "Good Enough Morgan Story."

In October, 1827, an event occurred which, from subsequent complications, roused public feeling strongly, first in the "infected district" and afterwards throughout this and other States. On the seventh day of October two men (Potter and Hoxsie), residents of Carleton, Orleans County, discovered a dead body on the beach at a point where the Oak Orchard Creek empties into Lake Ontario. Information was given to Robert M. Brown, the coroner, who summoned an inquest over the body. Nothing was found by which the body could be identified. After dismissing the inquest, the coroner caused the body to be decently interred near the spot where it was found. On the 12th of October I received the Orleans "Whig," containing the following report of the coroner: —

A coroner's inquest was held on the 7th inst. over the body of a man unknown, on the lake shore, near the mouth of the Oak Orchard Creek, in Carleton, Orleans County. Verdict of the jury, "Suffocation by Drowning." The body was discovered on the margin of the water, and was probably thrown on shore by the surf. It was in so putrid a state that it would be difficult to give a very minute description of it. It appeared, however, to be the body of a man about forty-five or fifty years of age; about five feet eight inches in height; hair about the ears considerably gray. There was apparently an old scar on the forehead, over the right eye; teeth sound excepting two missing on the lower jaw; a set of what is generally termed double teeth in front. His clothing was a frock coat of black broadcloth of a good quality; pantaloons and vest apparently the same. A white homespun flannel shirt, flag handkerchief about his neck, an almost new pair of cowhide shoes, and coarse socks. No papers were found about him to give any light; all that was found in his pocket was simply four religious tracts printed in London, a scrap of paper on which was written "September 24, 1828, Mr. James Websa," and two plugs of tobacco. R. M. BROWN, Coroner.

CARLETON, *October* 8, 1827.

Morgan had resided at Rochester most of the two years immediately preceding his abduction. Those who knew him most intimately, upon reading the foregoing description of the body found at Oak Orchard Creek, discovered so many coincidences as to convince them that it was the body of William Morgan. Dr. Ezra Strong, who had been Morgan's physician, and who had extracted a double tooth for him, remembered that all Morgan's teeth were double. He stated also that the tooth he extracted came from the *upper jaw*, while the coroner's statement represented it as being absent from the lower jaw. Mr. Russell Dyer, with whom Morgan boarded for seven months, remembered that Morgan's teeth were double all round, and that beside the missing teeth in Morgan's *upper* jaw, there was a broken tooth near the corner of the mouth, which was apparent in conversation. These and other coincidences seemed to require further investigation, and I, along with Mr. John Merchant, taking as many citizens who had known Morgan as would go with us, started for Oak Orchard Creek. Mr. Dyer was simultaneously sent to Batavia, requesting those most likely and best able to determine whether it was or was not the body of Morgan to unite with us in the investigation. In passing through the villages on my way, I gave notice of the contemplated investigation, and invited citizens generally to be in attendance. Between the village of Gaines and the lake shore nearly all the inhabitants either accompanied or followed us to the scene of the second inquest. Soon after our arrival came Messrs. Fitch, Holden, and Gibbs of Batavia, together with Mr. Dyer and Mrs. Morgan, wife or widow of William Morgan. Mr. Brown, the coroner, summoned an inquest consisting of twenty-five intelligent citizens, all residents of the town of Carleton. Before the body was exhumed Mrs. Morgan, Dr. Strong, Mr. Fitch, Mr. Gibbs, Mr. Dyer, etc., were called on to give in detail their recollection of the *personnel* and of any peculiarities by which it might be identified. These statements were written down as received, after which the rude coffin was raised and opened, when the coroner proceeded to take the testimony of all present who had anything to say. Remembering what had been said about teeth, the examination immediately took that direction. Upon opening the lips, the front teeth were found to be double, there were two missing teeth in the upper jaw, together with a broken tooth as had been described by Dr. Strong and Mr. Dyer. The face was so discolored and distorted that no feature of it was distinguishable.

The coroner then invited all persons present who had been acquainted with Morgan to step forward. Eight or nine persons, including Mrs. Lucinda Morgan, were sworn, each of whom, with one exception, after pointing out upon this body resemblances to that of Morgan, concluded by expressing the opinion and belief that the body before them was that of William Morgan. Mrs. Morgan, after identifying a scar upon the foot of this body similar to one on the foot of her husband, and describing various other coincidences, declared that she had " no doubt but that this is the body of my husband." The coroner then exhibited the clothes found upon the body to Mrs. Morgan, who testified that she had never before seen any of those articles of dress. Dr. John D. Henry testified that he attended William Morgan as a physician in Rochester. Morgan had inflamed eyes, for which Dr. Henry prescribed for several months. The teeth of this body appeared as he should have expected the teeth of Morgan would appear. The shape of the head, though much bloated, resembled that of Morgan, as did the hair. Mrs. Morgan, before she saw the body, described the place where two teeth had been taken from her husband, and she likewise described the manner in which one tooth had been broken off. She also spoke of a scar on one of his great toes. " On examining the body," said Dr. Henry, " I find two teeth gone and one broken off as she described, and also a mark on one of the great toes. The two teeth of her husband, which she had preserved, will slide into and fill the vacancies in this jaw pretty well. I should be unwilling to say that this was Morgan's body or that it was not, though the teeth, the shape of the head, and the hair, resemble Morgan's." This examination was conducted in the presence of between seventy and eighty citizens of the counties of Monroe, Orleans, and Genesee, each and all of whom had the body in view constantly from the time the rude coffin was opened until it was closed. When the testimony had all been taken, not a person present expressed a doubt but that it was the body of William Morgan. The committee, in giving their investigation to the public, closed their report as follows : —

After an examination of about four hours the testimony was closed, and the jury of inquest, consisting of twenty-three members, consulted a moment together, and agreed unanimously upon their verdict, that it was " the body of William Morgan, and that he came to his death by suffocation by drowning," which verdict was made up in the form of an inquisition, and signed by the whole panel. We have been thus particular in the statement of the facts and testimony, knowing that the subject was one of engrossing interest to the community, and that curiosity would be awakened to learn the whole circumstances, that each individual for himself might apply his own judgment to the case, and decide whether the identity had been established.

For ourselves, we do conceive that the body discovered on the shore of Lake Ontario has been identified as the body of Captain William Morgan beyond the shadow of a doubt. In this discovery we cannot but trace the hand of an overruling Providence, who, when all human efforts were found too weak effectually to penetrate the mysterious secret, has chosen his own time, and by his own means to throw a broad light upon this dark mystery. This induces us to rely with a stronger hope upon the same Providence to unravel the remainder of this entangled skein, and to provide means for bringing all the perpetrators of a daring outrage to merited punishment.

SAMUEL WORKS,
HARVEY ELY,
FREDERICK F. BACKUS,
FREDERICK WHITTLESEY,
THURLOW WEED.

ROCHESTER, *October* 17, 1827.

Morgan, it will be recollected, was taken from the jail in Canandaigua on the 12th of September. He was taken to Fort Niagara, and confined for several days in the magazine. On or about the 20th of September, according to the statement of Elisha Adams and others, he was taken in a boat to a point where the Niagara River empties itself into Lake Ontario, and there thrown overboard, heavily weighted. More than a year afterwards a body is found at the mouth of Oak Orchard Creek, forty miles from Fort Niagara, which had evidently drifted ashore from the lake. Strong as were the circumstances and coincidences which led an intelligent and impartial inquest to declare that that was the body of William Morgan, public opinion hesitated, questioned, and doubted. Was it possible, or even probable, said many presses and people, that this body could have been drifting about Lake Ontario more than a year? To these by no means unreasonable questions, it was answered that in September, 1827, under the direction of Bates Cook, persons were employed for three weeks in dragging the lake at the point at which it was supposed Morgan had been thrown into it, and that his body, thus released from its weight, might have risen and floated down to Oak Orchard Creek. While the question was being thus discussed by an excited community and in an angry spirit, information was received that in September, 1827, Timothy Munroe, a Canadian, had been drowned in the Niagara River. Messengers were dispatched to Canada, who returned in a few days with the widow and son of Munroe, and it was immediately announced that the body at Oak Orchard Creek was to be again exhumed for the purpose of identifying it as that of Timothy Munroe. Prominent Masons and Anti-Masons, therefore, repaired to the mouth of Oak Orchard Creek, near the village of Gaines, on the day designated. The occasion drew together about the same number of persons who had attended the previous examination. The clothes taken from the body found on the beach had been carefully preserved by the coroner. They had not been seen from the time of the second inquest until on the morning of the third examination they were shown by the coroner to Bates Cook, Samuel Works, Frederick Whittlesey, and myself. They were carefully examined, and a minute description of every article written down by Mr. Cook. After the parties had assembled, Mrs. Munroe was asked by Ebenezer Griffin, Esq., counsel for those who were charged with the abduction of Morgan, to describe the clothes worn by her husband when he left home on the morning of the day that he was drowned. Having done so, Mr. Cook commenced a calm, deliberate, but searching cross-examination in reference to a variety of marks and peculiarities which he had discovered in a previous examination of the coat, pantaloons, vest, shirt, and socks, of which he had a written memorandum which he held in his hand. To all these interrogatories Mrs. Munroe replied readily, confidently, and accurately. She described the rents in the pantaloons, which she had mended herself; she also stated that she had darned the heel of one of the socks with yarn differing in color from that of which the socks were knitted; indeed, her answers to all Mr. Cook's questions were so prompt and accurate as to leave no doubt in the minds of all present that she must have been familiar with every article of dress found upon that body. And yet, to render this complicated question still more deeply inexplicable, Mrs. Munroe and her son made Munroe's body four inches longer than the body found on the shore of the lake. They also testified that Munroe had a heavy black beard and coarse black hair, which had been cut short a few days before he was drowned; while the beard of the body found was grayish and the hair long, soft, and of a chestnut color, so that while the clothes were minutely and accurately described by Mrs. Munroe, the body sworn to by her and by her son was not the body upon which the clothes were found. The effect of the testimony of Mrs. Munroe and her son was subsequently further weakened by information showing that during the interval of time between the drowning of Munroe in the Niagara River and the finding of a body at Oak Orchard Creek, some thirty miles distant, the wind had been almost constantly blowing up the lake, rendering it impossible for Munroe's body to have drifted forty miles against the wind, and without any current. The question, therefore, as far as it had been settled by testimony, seemed to involve the contradiction, if not the absurdity, of proving that Munroe's clothes were found upon the body either of Morgan or of some unknown person. The political element intensified if possible the bitter feelings which were occasioned by judicial investigations. That feeling is well described in the following extract from an article written by one who observed rather than participated in the conflict:—

When the Anti-Masonic furore assumed a political aspect it is impossible for those not in the fight to conceive the deep feeling which that controversy engendered. Nothing approaching it in bitterness has marked the progress of any political contest from that day to this. It was not strange, therefore, that social ties were sundered, families divided, and law suits instituted to defend and vindicate assailed character.

The election of 1827 elicited an accusation against me which assumed proportions not dreamed of by those with whom it originated. The investigations concerning the body found on the shore of Lake Ontario occurred just previous to that election. Those who maintained that it was the body of Timothy Munroe insisted that the hair and whiskers had been pulled out or shaven. The day before the third examination was to take place at Batavia, I stopped in a billiard-room to see Mr. Gustavus Clark, of Clarkson. While talking with him, Ebenezer Griffin, Esq., one of the counsel of the " kidnappers," who was going to Batavia to conduct the examination, observed, laughingly, to me, " After we have proven that the body found at Oak Orchard is that of Timothy Munroe, what will you do for a Morgan ? " I replied in the same spirit, " That is a good-enough Morgan for us until you bring back the one you carried off." On the following day a paragraph appeared in the " Rochester Daily Advertiser," saying that in a conversation I had boasted that the body referred to, whatever might be proven to the contrary, was a " good-enough Morgan until after the election." When a few days later I appeared, as was my habit for more than forty years, at the polls of the election, a man, evidently employed for that purpose, followed me about, inquiring, " Who pulled out Timothy Munroe's whiskers? Who shaved him ? " etc. Thinking that the shortest way of disposing of the matter, I ironically assented to the accusation, and thus turned it off, with a laugh from the crowd. But there was a purpose in this manœuvre not foreseen. Our elections then ran through three days. On the morning of the second day the following affidavit appeared in the " Daily Advertiser," and, in the form of hand-bills, was circulated at the polls throughout the county : —

William C. Greene, being duly sworn, deposeth and says that he the said Greene with others did attend the poll of election held at Harvards in the town of Gates in the county of Monroe, and that there Mr. Thurlow Weed did say that he the said Thurlow did pull the whiskers from the face of the body found at Oak Orchard Creek, and that John Marchant did shave the same, he the said Thurlow being one of the Morgan committee.   WILLIAM C. GREENE.

Subscribed and sworn this 6th day of November, 1827, before me,
SAMUEL MILLER, J. P.

CHAPTER XXVIII.

1827–1829.

THE MORGAN MYSTERY. — STATEMENTS IN LATER YEARS OF SURVIVING
PARTICIPANTS. — LETTER OF FREDERICK FOLLETT. — STATEMENT OF
ORSON PARKHURST. — THE GOULD LIBEL SUIT. — CONVERSATION WITH
JEWETT AND WHITNEY. — THE STORY OF MORGAN'S DEATH AS TOLD
BY WHITNEY.

NEW YORK, *October* 20, 1873.

THURLOW WEED, ESQ. :

My Dear Sir, — I have long been aware that you had in contemplation the preparation, for publication at some future time, a history of what was termed in former days the "Anti-Masonic excitement." I am satisfied there is no man living more competent to a full, complete, and satisfactory treatment of this subject than yourself; and it is, I think, unnecessary for me to say I am rejoiced to be made aware of the fact that your labor in that direction, which has been one of years, is drawing to a close. Many of the politicians of the present day, though somewhat seared by the ravages of time, were conversant with the incidents which gave rise to the facts which you will some day give to the public, thus unsealing the mystery which has so long hung over the fate of Morgan ; others have passed away ; while it is probable, nay, almost certain, that *all* of the *immediate participants* in the tragedy that finally sealed his fate are now numbered with the dead. Who those "participants" were, until a very late period, I had no knowledge. Rumor set its seal, it is true, upon this man or that, but at the time of the outrage, and for years after, amid the whirl of excitement which pervaded all classes of community, it was difficult to say which was right or which was wrong.

The facts and incidents upon which your "History" is founded, and those which more immediately gave rise to what is termed the "Anti-Masonic excitement," transpired on the 10th day of September, 1826, at the village of Batavia, in the western part of this State. It had been rumored for some time prior to this date that William Morgan, at that time a resident of the village and a mason by trade, was engaged in writing for publication what was said to be a revelation of the secrets of Masonry. The fact that he was thus engaged, though the utmost secrecy was thought to be preserved, became known to a

portion of the members of the Masonic fraternity residents of Stafford,
Le Roy, Canandaigua, Rochester, Clarkson, Gaines, and perhaps some
other localities along the route from the latter place to Fort Niagara.
These men, it would seem, were endowed with more zeal than knowledge as to the true interests of the order, and thought they discovered
in the successful prosecution of the work of Morgan the downfall, and
in all probability the total annihilation of an institution that had successfully borne up against the opposition as well as the persecution of
centuries long past. Having arrived at this conclusion, the next question that very naturally suggested itself to these misguided and over-
zealous individuals was, no doubt, as their subsequent acts seemed to
imply (for I have no *knowledge* on this point), How is the work of
Morgan to be arrested? This question seems to have been solved in
this wise, or rather the initiatory steps to this end were thus taken :
Morgan had been a temporary resident of Canandaigua. While there
he had borrowed a shirt of one of its citizens. The first object to be
attained was to get Morgan away from Batavia, where his labor was
being prosecuted, and from the associates who surrounded and in a
great measure directed and controlled his actions. To do this the
shirt, to which allusion has been made, was to play a conspicuous
part. Having borrowed the shirt, as I suppose he did, but having
neglected to return it, the lender assumed that so long a time having
elapsed the act was to be construed as a theft, and applied for and obtained a warrant for his arrest. It is by no means a violent presumption to suppose the warrant to be placed in willing hands, — not only
willing, but anxious to see it executed. To reach Canandaigua from
Batavia it was necessary to pass through Genesee and Livingston
counties, and as the warrant was returnable at the former place, it
became necessary that the warrant should receive the indorsement of
the requisite authorities of these counties. Arrangements, as I am led
to suppose, were made in advance for this purpose. Without the
slightest premonition of the trap that had been laid for him, Morgan
was arrested at Batavia early on the morning of September 10, 1826,
and without any opportunity for consultation with his friends, hurried
off in charge of the officers to the town of Stafford. Here a halt was
made by the party in charge of Morgan, and after consultation with
others presumed to be in the secret, the prisoner in charge of the officers proceeded on to the village of Le Roy. Here, if I mistake not,
an attempt was made by the friends of Morgan to release him from
the clutches of the law. But it resulted unsuccessfully, and he was
finally confronted with his accuser before the magistrate who issued
the warrant at Canandaigua. And now commenced the trials and
tribulations of the misguided and over-zealous men who had conspired

for the abduction of Morgan. The possession of this man was the very thing they did not want, but they did desire the suppression or abandonment of the revelations he contemplated making. In this, however, they were unsuccessful. Morgan was convicted of technical theft and committed to jail. I have no means at hand wherewith to refresh my memory, and the event having occurred over forty-seven years ago, I may be at fault; but if not, Morgan was taken from the jail one dark night, placed in a close carriage, and departed on a journey from which he never returned. What his fate was, your great and persistent efforts in that behalf, I doubt not, will furnish a satisfactory solution.

I was then a Mason, and a member of the lodge and chapter at Batavia, and the encampment of Knight Templars, then located at Le Roy, but afterwards removed to the former village. I mention this fact that I may be enabled to mention another, which goes to disprove the assertion then made, and in the excitement then prevailing very generally believed, that *all Masons,* and especially of the higher order, were either concerned with or cognizant of the fact that Morgan was to be dealt with for a violation of his Masonic obligations, which is this: That although I was in the constant habit of attending every meeting of the lodge, chapter, and encampment, *I never once heard the subject of Morgan's abduction, or in any other way interfering with his personal rights, alluded to in any manner whatever.* On this point I speak confidently, for I know the fact. What may have been done outside the lodges, if anything, by individual members, looking towards such a contingency, I have no knowledge whatever, and can only speak for myself. I neither talked with any one on those points, or heard them discussed by others. And here I wish to state a fact personal to myself. I occupied a prominent position as a member and an officer in all the organizations above alluded to, notwithstanding which I was never once called upon the stand as a witness, or prosecuted as a principal, in any of the trials, and they were by no means few, growing out of the abduction of Morgan. I do not intend to convey the idea that I was wholly exempt from notice. Being at the time the editor and proprietor of a newspaper located at the village in question, young, and ardently attached to the order of Masonry, and saying hard things, probably, about those opposed to it, I was, I think, indicted for libeling somebody or something some twelve or fifteen different times. The offense was not considered of a heinous character, for if my memory serves me right my own recognizance was accepted in every instance; and I *know* I was never brought to trial on one of them, though my lawyer frequently urged the prosecuting attorney to do so.

It is now forty-seven years since the outrage that led to the excitement in question had its origin. It swept over the western portion of the State, in relation to the political standing of parties, with the devastating power of a tornado. It interfered somewhat, and in many instances wholly broke up the social relations of life. Churches became more or less involved in the controversy, and so bitter and inveterate was the feeling thus engendered that Masons were excluded from a participation in the Holy Communion; their names were thrown out of the jury box; and at the social gathering of the grave matrons of the neighborhood resolutions were, in many instances, passed, forbidding their daughters keeping company with a Mason. The old party landmarks thus swept away or swallowed up in this new element of discord and strife, it resolved itself into the fact that no member of the Masonic order was allowed to fill even the position of pound master.

I wish here to narrate a circumstance, and the incidents attending it, that transpired at Batavia on the 24th of June, 1827. I do so for the purpose of showing that the men of our country, however much they may be tempted in the hour of intense and overpowering excitement to do the very thing they are endeavoring to put their seal of condemnation upon in others, still they are not even then, when almost in the very act of committing a gross and unpardonable violation of human rights, wholly insensible to the demands of law and order. The Masons of Batavia and the surrounding towns had resolved, as was the custom of former years, to celebrate with the usual observances the day in question. This was opposed by some as injudicious, and even hazardous, in the then excited state of the public mind. Others, and by far the most numerous portion of the order, thought otherwise; and they reasoned in this way: In years gone by it has been usual for the order to celebrate this day; it is possible, nay, probable, that an outrage against law and liberty has been committed by some members of the order, but our consciences acquit us of any crime; why, then, should we be deprived of a privilege long held dear by us, because others have committed a wrong act?

This reasoning prevailed, and it was, therefore, resolved to celebrate the day. It was not intended to be done in the dark, but under the broad canopy of heaven, and the fact was published far and near. Time rolled round. The 24th of June, 1827, was ushered into the world bright, clear, and beautiful, but with it also came the deep, ominous mutterings of discontent and threatened danger. Soon after sunrise the fact was unmistakable to the residents of the village that the quiet little town was increasing in population with wonderful rapidity. At first they came singly, then by couples, and finally by companies of twenty-five and fifty, when at the time appointed for the Masons to take up their line of march for the ground where the out-door exercises of the day were to take place (which, fortunately, happened to be private property), at least *six thousand* strangers were roving through the streets of the little village. The look of things at this time was decidedly serious. In a majority of cases these men were sober and sedate farmers, mechanics, and laborers, with a sprinkling of the rougher element which pervades all society. But all were equally excited, and most of them were the dupes of bad and vicious counselors. They were too excited to reason calmly, but were ready to believe all and any rumors, even the most preposterous, that had any bearing against the members of the Masonic order, one of which was that the celebration of St. John's Day was a mere blind, while the real object in view was the destruction of Miller's printing-office, where the alleged revelations by Morgan were being published.

Colonel Johnson Goodwill and myself had been designated as marshals of the day. The Master Masons met in their room at the Eagle Hotel, the Royal Arch Masons and Knight Templars at the American Hotel, about a quarter of a mile east of the former, and both on Main Street. Receiving the Master Masons at the Eagle, we commenced the march, they keeping the sidewalk, while we, being mounted, took up our position between it and the middle of the street, without the fact ever occurring to any of us, it so happened, that this route led us directly in front of Miller's office, at which point stones and other missiles flew around our heads with a rapidity and closeness that was by no means pleasant, and was decidedly suggestive of broken heads and maimed limbs. By a judicious and active system of the "dodge game," nothing of the kind, however, occurred, though there were many narrow escapes. Arriving in front of the American Hotel, on the opposite side of the street, the procession was halted for the purpose of receiving the Royal Arch Masons and Knight Templars. When they emerged from the hotel, dressed in their rich robes of office, and were crossing the street to take their place in the line, the immense mass of human beings thus assembled broke forth in one tumultuous chorus of hatred and derision, shouting at the very top of their voices, "These are the d——d scoundrels who murdered Morgan! Down with them! Kill them!" and with this a simultaneous rush was made for them by this surging, angry, and infuriated mob, — for it now amounted to nothing else, — and the procession was broken up and scattered like chaff before the wind. Forbearance was a virtue, and in this instance a necessity also, for what could four or five hundred men do against a mad, unreasoning mob of at least six thousand ? The Masons, thus assaulted and dispersed, silently reassembled on the sidewalk in line with the Master Masons, and the march resumed amid the hooting, hallooing, and derisive and profane jeering of the mob, who followed on with frequent demonstrations of violence. Arriving in front of the office of the Hon. Phineas L. Tracy, that gentleman, seeing the imminent danger that threatened the public peace, rushed bare-headed from his office, his hair streaming in the wind, and placing himself in front of the surging mass of humanity, cried out at the top of his voice : " Men ! Fellow-citizens ! For God's sake, turn back, for you know not what you are about ! You are mad, and are about to commit a greater wrong than the one you seek to condemn ! If the rights of the citizens have been invaded, as they doubtless have, in the person of Morgan, leave it to the law and public opinion to correct the evil. I beseech you, therefore, for God's sake, for your own sake, and for the sake of humanity, turn back from your mad purpose, and permit the Masons, as they have the right, to celebrate the day in quietness and peace."

But the people were wild with excitement ; their mad passions were at fever heat, and the mild, persuasive, and entreating language of the venerable judge was almost wholly disregarded. One hundred, or perhaps one hundred and fifty or two hundred of the more thoughtful turned back ; but the great mass surged onward in their mad course.

Another event occurred soon after this, which for a time assumed a most serious and threatening aspect. Colonel Goodwill and myself, as I have already stated, were mounted ; and while he was in the middle of the street, I had posted myself on the side, and near the head of the procession. For some purpose connected with the proceedings of the day, the colonel desired to speak with me. I reined my horse alongside of his, when all at once, and with evident marks of concern visible on his countenance, he remarked, " Follett, we are gone ! " I looked around me to discover the cause which had prompted this remark. It was evident at a glance, and too threatening to admit of a doubt, for in an instant we had been surrounded by three or four hundred men, and I think I am entirely safe in saying that at least every other one grasped in his hand a newly-ground knife, with a blade not less than twelve to fifteen inches in length, glistening and sparkling in the bright rays of the sun, with the suggestive premonition that they were not made for ornament, but service. There was evidently no time for counsel or reflection. Whatever was done, must be done quickly. So I told the colonel to keep cool, and follow me. Fortunately I was mounted on a very spirited horse, and turning him suddenly to the right I attempted to force my way through the cordon that surrounded us, but my bridle reins were at once seized by four stalwart-looking ruffians, two on either side, while a fifth seized me by the right leg, shouting at the top of his voice, "Get off, you d——d scoundrel, and let Morgan ride!" I perceived the *force*, but was not strongly impressed with the *propriety* of the suggestion, and in the heat of the moment raised my sword to clear myself of his grasp. But this method was entertained only for a moment, and as speedily abandoned; for the shedding of but one drop of blood by the Masons on that day would have drenched the streets of that quiet village with that of hundreds of human beings! Resolving, therefore, not to be the immediate or the proximate cause of force myself, I immediately sunk the rowels of my spurs deep into the sides of my horse, and giving him free rein, he dashed like a thunderbolt through the mass that surrounded us, knocking down some twelve or fifteen, and thus giving us a passage out, and freeing us from immediate danger, though the volcano still kept seething and rumbling around us, ready to burst at the slightest provocation. This state of things continued until we neared the entrance to the ground in which the out-door exercises of the day were to be held, consisting of an oration by George Hosmer, Esq., at that time one of the most distinguished lawyers in the western part of the State.

Arriving at this point the procession was halted, and Colonel Goodwill, in a firm and decided voice, said : "The ground upon which we are now about to enter is my own individual property. I do not seek controversy or litigation with any of you; at the same time I shall not shrink from it if forced upon me. I am determined, however, that the first man who sets his foot unbidden on my grounds to-day shall be prosecuted for trespass." And now was witnessed a scene which went far to compensate for the trials and vexations of the day. Americans we all know are excitable, jealous of their rights, and ready to maintain them, and only in the most extreme cases can they be tempted to go so far as to trample law and order under their feet. A beautiful illustration of this trait in their character was now witnessed. These men could meet force with force, and sink beneath them the social relations of life, but when the vengeance of violated law was hurled back upon them, the silence almost of death itself pervaded this vast, excited, and tumultuous assemblage! Reason once more mounted its throne. The Masons occupied their grounds in peace, and the waves that surged and beat so madly before now rolled back in peace and quietness. And thus ended the day, the morning of which seemed pregnant with riot and bloodshed, law and order finally triumphing over the wild passions of the multitude.

Much diversity of opinion existed at the time, and the subject is not, perhaps, entirely clear to the mind of all at the present day in reference to the identity of the body found at the mouth of Oak Orchard Creek in the autumn of 1827. Many believed, and honestly, too, I have not the shadow of a doubt, that it was the body of William Morgan. Others stoutly contended, actuated doubtless by the same motives of sincerity, that it was the body of Timothy Munroe. That men at that day should have been mistaken in supposing it to be the body of Morgan is not to be wondered at, for there were many points about it indicating such to be the fact. At this late day I am not disposed to go into particulars, even were they sufficiently impressed upon my mind to enable me to do so. I will only give the impression of my mind at the time, strengthened somewhat by more recent facts, that the body thus found was not William Morgan, but Timothy Munroe. Of this I had no doubt then, neither have I now.

I have not written this long letter with the slightest idea that I have been able to throw any new light on the subject. Indeed, the great and leading facts connected with it are better known to yourself than to any other man, and for that reason I have mainly sought to treat of matters more local and personal than general, and therefore less likely to be familiar to yourself.

Respectfully yours,   Frederick Follett.

Mr. Orson Parkhurst, who, it will be remembered, was in the employment of Ezra Platt, and drove the carriage in which Morgan was confined from Rochester to Clarkson, and with whom I subsequently became well acquainted, is now a respectable manufacturer at Cohoes, and submits the following statement : —

STATEMENT OF MR. ORSON PARKHURST, MADE APRIL 11, 1870.

My name is Orson Parkhurst. I reside at Cohoes, Albany County, N. Y. I was born in the year 1804 at Weathersfield, Vt. My trade was that of a carpenter ; have been for eighteen years or about a manufacturer at Cohoes. I went to Rochester, N. Y., about February, 1826 ; arrived in Rochester in March. I had some difficulty in my lungs, and was advised by the doctors to go into some open-air employment, and I went into stage-driving from Rochester to Scottsville, right up the Genesee River. I drove only one season. I worked for Ezra Platt, who was sole proprietor of that line. I was a single man. In the month of September, I think, and also in the year 1826, I think (the month may have been October), I was called early one morning, a little before daylight, by Mr. Platt (I boarded at his house), who said that he wanted me " *to take a wedding party to Sodus Bay.*" He told me to drive down to the Eagle Hotel, I think, kept by a man by the name of Ainsworth. I got up and harnessed, and drove down to the hotel with a covered carriage. When I got down to the hotel, about daylight, there were one or two men got in. I think that Mr. Whitney was one of them. I think that Birge, or Burrage, Smith was one of the men. (He subsequently went or cleared away to New Orleans, and died.) After these men got in at the hotel I drove down to Hanford's Landing into the woods, where there was another carriage standing in the woods ; we drove within five or six feet of the carriage. Hanford's Landing was out on the Ridge Road. I think that Mr. Smith was outside on the seat with me. I think that the driver of the other carriage remained in his seat. One of the men got out of my carriage, and one or two men got out of the other carriage. They took out a man who was blindfolded with a handkerchief over his eyes and put him in my carriage. He seemed to get out willingly enough, and to get into my carriage without any compulsion. I think that two men got into my carriage, making four in all besides the blindfolded man. Smith sat on the seat with me. After the man who was blindfolded got in, and the other men, Smith, with whom I was acquainted, gave me to understand that he was the manager of the concern, and that things had got to go as he said, and he ordered me to drive slow. Smith commenced a conversation which led me to think that he was going to tell me what they were about, and I checked him, and told him I was subject to his order, but I did not want to know anything about what they were doing or what they were about. Smith then kept " mum," and we drove on to a farmer's house and stopped, and one of the men went out into the field and took the farmer's horses and put them on our carriage. It seemed to be understood that the horses were to be exchanged. On my return, I changed horses back again. This was about fifteen miles from Rochester where we changed horses, as near as I can state. When we reached Clarkson we stopped in front of the tavern. There was horse-racing that day, and a large crowd of people around that day. The men in my carriage got lunch and something to drink, which was brought out to the carriage. The man who was blindfolded did not get out. Two or three times I heard some one groan in the carriage, as if they were tired. The curtains of the carriage were down all the while. People could not look into the carriage. I think we changed horses after stopping at Clarkson, but am not certain whether it was before or after. I drove on to the town of Gaines, Mr. Smith still staying outside with me on the driver's seat. We drove under the horse-shed at the tavern at Gaines, and a man by the name of Mather hitched on to our carriage another pair of horses, — I think he took my harness. I think it was late in the afternoon when we arrived at

Gaines. Mather told me where to take my horses. I think that the change of horses was previously arranged. I took my horses into Mather's barn. I did not see the man who was blindfolded. At this place I went to a private house to stay. I don't recollect the name ; think that he kept boarders, and was under the shed, and asked me to go home with him. I did not go into the tavern at all when I was there. I got supper, and stayed there all night. This man where I stopped seemed to understand what was going on. He asked me whether I was a Royal Arch Mason, and I said that I was not ; and then he said that he supposed that no one but Royal Arch Masons knew anything about this, or were engaged in it. I told him that if there was anything which he did not want known, that he had better not say anything about it ; and he did not talk any more about it. This conversation was the same afternoon that we got there. I stayed there, I believe, only one night. The next day in the afternoon, rather late, I think, the carriage came back, and I went back with it to Rochester. None of the men that went out with me came back. I might have picked up one or two passengers on the way home. I think I reached Rochester in the night. I saw Smith and Whitney around Rochester afterwards. I was out in the city much daytimes, except Sundays. I do not recollect any conversation which I had with them on the subject. A month or so afterwards a Mr. Norton, who was engaged in the forwarding business at Rochester, called at the stable and asked me if my name was Parkhurst, and I said, " Yes." Then he wanted to know whether I drove out on the Ridge Road at a certain time. I told him I drove a "wedding party out to Sodus," and he rather ridiculed the idea, and said it would be to my advantage to tell all the facts. Norton then left, or Mr. Platt hove in sight. Norton said, " I will see you again." He left rather abruptly. Platt wanted to know of me what Norton's business was, and I told him ; and Platt said that " I had business in Michigan," and that I must go " right off." Platt settled up with me, and paid me what he owed me, and I think he advanced me twenty or twenty-five dollars, and I started right off the same day for Vermont, my old place of residence. I packed my trunk, and Platt sent it out of Rochester, and I did not find it, and had to go back to Rochester, and found it. I went by the canal. I went to my father's, at Weathersfield, Vt. My father was a carpenter. I think that I went to work at Charleston that winter, driving team for hauling grain for a distillery. Next summer I went back to Weathersfield and worked at my trade with my father. We worked at Perkinsville in the same town, Weathersfield. In September, on election day, on my way home, I met George Ketchum, of Rochester, who had come out on purpose

to see me. He came to have me go off to some other place. He was
afraid that the Anti-Masons had found out where I was. I left my
business, and started right off. I went to Norwich, Conn. He gave
me some money. I remained at Norwich that fall and winter, working at my trade. Then Ketchum came to Norwich ; he was frightened, and was afraid that they had found me, or ascertained where I
was. He wanted me to leave for some other section. I went with
him to Keeseville, N. Y., on the west side of Lake Champlain, and from
there we went out to his brother's, six or eight miles in the woods,
where his brother was carrying on the smelting business. Then Mr.
Ketchum went with me to Albany, and he went home to Rochester.
He furnished me partly with some money. I went to New York by
the river, from New York city to Boston, and from Boston to Port-
land, and came back to Boston, and got work in Boston at my trade,
and worked through the summer ; and then I went to Braintree, and
worked there at my trade about a year, and then went back to my father's in Vermont. I reached my father's in the spring, I think, of
1829. In the fall of 1829 Mr. Thurlow Weed came to Weathersfield
for me. Mr. Weed stopped at Windsor at the tavern, Pettus', I
think, and got the sheriff, Joel Lull, and they came to Weathersfield.
I was working at Perkinsville in the same town, at Samuel Downer's
Tavern, in Weathersfield. Mr. Weed inquired for the name of the
" hottest Anti-Mason in town," and Mr. Downer said that " Ira French
was hot as hell ; " he did not know whether there were any hotter
ones in town. This is as Mr. Downer told me the story. French
came with the sheriff and Mr. Weed to find me, and French skulked
around in the bushes until I was arrested by the sheriff. I did not
then know Mr. Weed personally. Mr. Weed and the sheriff came up
to me. I did not know the sheriff ; he introduced Mr. Weed of Rochester, and the sheriff said I was his prisoner. After I was arrested I
went with them to Windsor (called at my father's on the way), and
stopped over night. Next morning we started for Rochester. I consented to their taking me into the State of New Hampshire in order
to take the stage, although they had no right to go out of the State
of Vermont. We reached Albany, N. Y. The sheriff delivered
me up to Mr. Weed on the State line of Vermont and New York
State. Mr. Lull, the sheriff, however, went with me on to Albany.
At Albany, I had so gained the confidence of Mr. Weed that he allowed me to go alone to visit an uncle of mine in Hawk Street, and I
went up in the morning before the stage started, and on my return
found Mr. Weed coming after me, as the stage was waiting, and ready
for us. My uncle's name was Littimer. We rode by stage to Utica,
and we were both pretty tired, and took the packet there for Roches-

ter. The captain's name was Smith; he was a Mason. Judge Mc-
Lean was aboard. I think that he was then postmaster-general under
Jackson. He was a Mason. Jacob Graves, of Rochester, was on
board. He was a tanner, and was a peaceable and quiet sort of man.
He was a Mason also. We reached Montezuma Marshes near night-
fall. When I got on to the packet I had no intention of escaping from
Mr. Weed. I talked with Mr. Graves while I was on deck, and he
said that if I went to Rochester I would be kept until the next May;
and that if I could not get security for my appearance as a witness I
would be imprisoned, and detained in custody. This alarmed me, and
a plan was arranged for my escape, and I concluded to escape. The
captain was a Mason, and he arranged that my berth should be in the
stern and Mr. Weed's in the bow. The captain of the Geneva packet
was on board, and my trunk was placed on his packet at Montezuma.
(He did not charge me any fare to Seneca Falls. He was not a Mason,
and probably was not aware of the circumstances.) The first lock was
six miles beyond Montezuma, and I think that we went to bed before
we reached Montezuma. I was aware that my trunk was to be taken
off at Montezuma. When we reached the first lock beyond Montezuma it was about ten o'clock P. M. I was in my berth; had not been
asleep. The captain called me before I got into the lock. I stepped
into the closet, and he agreed to call me; and when the boat had
raised high enough, the captain called me. When I left the boat no
one was in sight, except the captain and bowsman. I got on to the
tow-path side and walked back to Montezuma, and got on to the Geneva packet, where my trunk was. Mr. Graves had given me some
money, and I went to Seneca Falls, Cayuga Bridge, steamboat to Ithaca, and from Ithaca I went to the town of Veteran to see an uncle of
mine, and stopped there about two weeks; and then I returned to
Montezuma and got on to the packet, and it happened to be the same
packet I had escaped from. Captain Smith knew me, and arranged
with the captain of the packet from Utica to Schenectady to take me
through to Schenectady free. The steersman saw me on the packet of
Captain Smith about as soon as I got on it at Montezuma. The
steersman said, " How do you suppose Mr. Weed felt when he knew
that you had escaped?" I said, "I did n't know; how did he feel?"
The steersman said that "if he felt as bad as he looked, he felt like
the devil;" that Mr. Weed told him that "if he would bring me
back in eight days he would give him fifty dollars." I said, "Why
did n't you let me know it? I would have gone halves with you." He
said, "Damn him! If I had known where you was, I would not have
gone an inch for you." I came on down to Albany, and saw Mr. Platt
and his wife (he had removed from Rochester to Albany). I went to

Mr. Platt's house and rang the bell; a colored servant came to the door who had lived with them in Rochester. Mrs. Platt was glad to see me, and said that if she had seen me when Mr. Weed had me in Albany that I would not have left, as she had a place to keep me. I then returned to Vermont, to Weathersfield, and went to work.

Orson Parkhurst.

In 1831 a suit for libel, commenced against me by the late General Jacob Gould, of Rochester, was tried at Albany. The alleged libel consisted of a charge in my paper that General Gould obtained money from the Grand Chapter, which he gave to Burrage Smith and John Whitney, abductors of William Morgan, to enable them to escape from justice. Among the witnesses I had subpœnaed were Simeon B. Jewett, of Clarkson, Major Samuel Barton, of Lewiston, and John Whitney, of Rochester. When the trial (a report of which will be found elsewhere) was over I invited these gentlemen to sup with me. Our conversation naturally turned upon the question which had absorbed so much of our time and thoughts for several years. Late in the evening Major Barton, addressing himself to Whitney, said, "Come, John, make a clean breast of it." Whitney looked inquiringly at Colonel Jewett, who, after a pause, added, "Free your mind." Whitney, then addressing himself to me in a manner which indicated that Colonel Jewett and Major Barton were already acquainted with the facts he was about to relate, said that it was unnecessary to go into the early circumstances of Morgan's abduction, as they were already pretty well known. "When," said Whitney, "our friends in Canada refused to take care of Morgan, the Lewiston people sent word to Rochester that he could not be kept much longer in the fort, and that we must come to Lewiston immediately." In consequence of this information Whitney, who had been with Morgan from the time he was taken out of the jail at Canandaigua until he was placed in the magazine at Fort Niagara, was again dispatched thither. He continued, "Simultaneously the installation of an encampment of Knights Templar drew together, at Lewiston, a large number of friends, of many of whom the question of what was to be done with Morgan was asked. But the matter was so perplexing that no one seemed willing to act or advise. In the evening, however, after we had been 'called from labor to refreshment,' Colonel William King asked me to step into another room, where I found Mr. Howard, of Buffalo, Mr. Chubbuck, of Lewiston, and Mr. Garside, of Youngstown. Colonel King said there was a carriage at the door ready to take us to the fort, into which we stepped and were driven hastily away. As we proceeded, Colonel King said that he had received instruction from the highest authority to deal with Morgan according to his deserts, and that having confidence in their courage and fidelity, he had chosen them as his assistants. On reaching the magazine they informed Morgan that the arrangements had been completed for his removal to the interior of Canada, where he would be settled on a farm, and that his family would follow him in accordance with the assurance previously given him by Johns. With this assurance he walked with them from the fort to the ferry, where a rowboat awaited them. The boat was then rowed in a diagonal direction to the place where the Niagara River is lost in Lake Ontario. Here, either shore being two miles distant, a rope was wound several times around Morgan's body, at either end of which a large weight was attached. Up to that time Morgan had conversed with them about his new home and the probability of being joined by his family; but when he saw the rope and the use to be made of it, he struggled desperately, and held firmly with one hand to the gunwale of the boat. Garside detached it, but as he did so Morgan caught Garside's thumb in his mouth and bit off the first joint.

"The boat was rowed back to the ferry-house, where the party landed, observed only by the old soldier Adams, who had made the boat ready for them, and who accompanied them to the carriage which stood in the road a few rods from the ferry. They reached the hotel in Lewiston about two o'clock in the morning."

This, in fewer words, is, as accurately as my memory can recall it, the statement I had from the lips of John Whitney. When Whitney concluded his narrative, Colonel Jewett said, "John, do you know that Weed can hang you now?" "Yes, but he won't," replied Whitney. I promptly responded that the confidence reposed in me would never be abused. Whitney added that it was a great relief to him to find persons with whom he could *talk* on a subject which he was always thinking about. For several years his sleep, he said, had been disturbed by horrible dreams. Slight noises in the stillness of the night would awaken him. A knock at the door, or the rattling of a window shutter, or the appearance of a stranger coming toward the house, always induced an apprehension that the sheriff was after him. He got along very well during the daytime, at his work or with company, but he dreaded the long, dark nights.

I saw no more of John Whitney until the summer of 1860, when I was in attendance upon the National Republican Convention at Chicago. Whitney called at the hotel, and after some general conversation, by which I learned he had been residing several years at Chicago, he remarked that he would like to talk with me again about the old affair, for which purpose an appointment was made. At the time fixed, however, for the interview, I was so fully occupied that we agreed to defer it until after the adjournment of the convention; and then, when Whitney called for the third time, I was on the point of leaving the hotel for an excursion into Iowa. We had a hurried conversation, in which mutual regrets were expressed that the contemplated interview must be deferred. I inquired whether, as he was the only person living who knew what had been done with Morgan, he would be willing to make a written statement to be sealed up for future use. He readily assented, and expressed a hope that I would return by way of Chicago, and write it out for his signature. But I had promised Mr. David Davis (now a judge of the United States Supreme Court) and Mr. Leonard Swett to return *via* Springfield to visit Mr. Lincoln, who had just been nominated for President. And so the last opportunity of obtaining direct knowledge of the fate of Morgan was lost. In 1868 and 1869, while occupied with this portion of my recollections, I wrote to John Whitney, renewing the suggestion made to him in 1860 : —

LONDON, *October* 10, 1868.

DEAR OLD FRIEND, — I have often thought during the last four or five years of writing to you on the subject of our conversations, first in Albany, more than thirty years ago, and then in Chicago in 1860. If I then understood your feelings, it was a relief to them to talk over the event to which I refer, in confidence, with friends.

It is forty-two years since William Morgan disappeared. You alone know all that occurred to him from the time he left Canandaigua. You alone can give to the world an authentic history of the transaction, and unless you should think proper to do so, the last scene in the last act must forever remain unwritten.

Perhaps you will remember that I stated in my paper, in 1826 and 1827, that in whatever you did, you acted from a mistaken sense of duty ; that, like a soldier on his post, or a sheriff who obeys the laws, you simply executed the orders of your superior.

NEW YORK, *July* 18, 1869.

I resume this letter, after a long interval, considerably improved in health, and hoping to be able to prepare a history of my life. If you feel at liberty to put on paper a part or all that you said to me verbally, I shall endeavor to make a proper use of it, doing justice to yourself, and being just to history. Please write to me soon.

Very truly yours,   THURLOW WEED.

12 WEST TWELFTH STREET, NEW YORK.

In two or three months afterwards the letter was returned to me through the dead-letter office. I then attempted to reach Mr. Whitney through my old friend, A. B. Williams, of Chicago, from whom I learned that Whitney died a few weeks previous to the time that my letter to him had been written. Major Barton died thirty years ago, and Colonel Jewett has been dead six or seven years. In all probability, therefore, no evidence of the fate of William Morgan more direct or reliable than that which, with an earnest desire to state the exact truth, I now record will ever be obtained.

CHAPTER XXIX.

1829–1830.

DURING the five or six years following the organization of a party opposed to Freemasonry, what was known as the Morgan Committee, of which I was a member, enjoyed its full and uninterrupted confidence. Candidates for all important offices were indicated by our committee, neither of whom would accept office themselves. As in all political organizations, there were good and bad men in our party. Those who united with us for office merely made loud professions and were temporarily successful. Of that class, however, little is remembered, while with another and larger class, influenced by higher and better motives, enduring friendships were formed. At this distant day I look back with grateful feeling to the events which brought me into personal and political relations with Samuel Works, Frederick F. Backus, Frederick Whittlesey, Everard Peck, Thomas Kempshall, Bates Cook, Millard Fillmore, Harvey Ely, E. S. Beach, Timothy Childs, Trumbull Cary, Samuel G. Andrews, James K. Livingston, Robert Hunter, Thomas C. Love, William H. Seward, Edward Dodd, Francis Granger, John C. Spencer, Albert H. Tracy, Christopher Morgan, Philo C. Fuller, William H. Maynard, Alvah Hunt, George W. Patterson, George H. Boughton, John Birdsall, Robert C. Nicholas, Luther Bradish, E. W. Leavenworth, Nicholas Devereux, Samuel Miles Hopkins, Weare C. Little, Lewis Benedict, David E. Evans, John Maynard, John W. Taylor, Rufus H. King, John A. King, Myron Holley, Gerritt Smith, etc.

It is pleasant to remember that, with one or two exceptions, common political and personal sentiments and sympathies existed between these honored and useful men and myself during life. Of those exceptions I shall have occasion to speak hereafter. Some incidents of those exciting times seem worth mentioning. In the autumn of 1827, while we were holding an inquest over the body found at the mouth of Oak Orchard Creek, then supposed to be that of William Morgan, a convention to nominate a senator for the Eighth District was held at Batavia. As I could not go to the convention, as was intended, the duty was devolved upon Mr. George H. Boughton, who went for the purpose of suggesting one of three names, either of which would have been acceptable. But after consulting with the delegates, Mr. Boughton recommended the nomination of George A. S. Crooker, of Cattaraugus. In a week or ten days afterwards our opponents produced evidence not only that Mr. Crooker was a Freemason, but that the day previous to his nomination as an Anti-Mason he had attended the Democratic senatorial convention, in the hope and expectation of receiving its nomination. This was an awkward revelation, particularly as the election was so near at hand that it would be difficult, if not impossible, to get information to the various counties composing the district in season to correct the blunder. We determined, however, upon a prompt movement. I prepared a circular letter recommending Timothy H. Porter, of Cattaraugus County, as the Anti-Masonic candidate for senator, which, signed by our committee, was dispatched by special messengers to our friends throughout the district, and Mr. Porter was elected by an emphatic majority. Mr. Crooker, notwithstanding this rebuff, remained with the Anti-Masonic party, and was subsequently elected and reëlected to the legislature.

In 1828 or 1829, Judge Birdsall, while holding a circuit in Orleans County, informed me that he intended to resign his judicial office, and that he mentioned it to me early and in confidence that I might be preparing the way for the appointment of an acceptable successor. He subsequently handed me his resignation, to take effect when a successor should be appointed, authorizing me to use it at my discretion. I then suggested to Judge Birdsall that he had better accept the Anti-Masonic nomination for Congress from the district composed of his own county, Erie, and Niagara. He replied that he would think the matter over, consult one or two friends, and inform me by letter of his determination. Two days before the Anti-Masonic congressional committee was to meet at Buffalo, I received a letter from Judge Birdsall declining its nomination, whereupon I hastened to Buffalo to participate in the deliberations of the convention. Very little was known by prominent men in cities and villages of the extent, zeal, and numerical strength of the new party. It was difficult, therefore, to induce prominent men to accept its nominations. I reached Buffalo late at night. Finding.Judge Birdsall at the hotel, he informed me that, under the advice of Albert H. Tracy, he had concluded to decline the Anti-Masonic and to accept the National Republican nomination for Congress, and that as the Jackson party, instead of presenting a candidate of their own, would concur in his nomination, success was certain. I had known Birdsall intimately from his boyhood in Chenango County. Governor Clinton had appointed him circuit judge at my request. Having much confidence in my judgment and experience, he consented, after a long and earnest conversation, to accept our nomination, provided the consent of Mr. Tracy could be obtained. Late at night, therefore, we repaired to Mr. Tracy's residence, but failed to work any change in his views. Mr. Tracy insisted that, with the National Republican nomination and the support of the Jackson party, Birdsall would be triumphantly elected, while as an Anti-Masonic candidate he would not only be disastrously beaten, but subject himself to enduring obloquy. It hence became necessary to look elsewhere for a candidate. The difficulty of this task was not diminished by the circumstance that I was compelled to leave Buffalo in the stage at nine o'clock the next morning to attend a senatorial convention at Batavia. Rising at daylight, and on my way to another hotel to find the Chautauqua and Niagara delegates, I encountered Ebenezer F. Norton in the street, and inquired whether he would accept an Anti-Masonic nomination for Congress. His reply was, "I cannot afford to decline any nomination for Congress." "If you are nominated to-day, will you stick to it?" "Do you suppose that a man who has been all his life trying to get into Congress would lose any chance of succeeding?" I then said, "Mr. Tracy will endeavor to talk you out of it." He rejoined, "Mr. Tracy can do many things, and can talk most people out of their senses, but he can't fool me, if he is my son-in-law, into declining a nomination for Congress." Thus assured of Mr. Norton's steadfastness, I found Colonel Fleming and Mr. Boughton, of Niagara, and Messrs. Mixer and Plumb, of Chautauqua, and hastily arranged with them the nomination of Mr. Norton, who, to the amazement of the wise men of the National Republican and Jackson parties, was elected by a majority of more than two thousand over Judge Birdsall.

The following year Judge Birdsall was elected to the Assembly from Chautauqua, and Mr. Tracy elected to the Senate from Erie, as Anti-Masons. The embarrassment of selecting a successor to Judge Birdsall was seriously increased by the circumstance that in that judicial district many indictments of the persons concerned in the kidnapping of Morgan were pending. We wanted an independent and impartial judge, a judge who was neither a Mason nor an Anti-Mason. There was no one, in my opinion, so free from objection as Addison Gardiner, then a young Democratic lawyer, who had taken no part in the Anti-Masonic excitement. I called late one evening at his office, and suggested the course which I believed would result in his appointment. The idea seemed to him not only impracticable but preposterous, and upon reiterating my confidence in its success, he said that if I had nothing more sensible to talk about than that, as it was late, he could dispense with my company. I told him that all that was required of him was to send to Clarkson for Colonel Simeon B. Jewett, after which, if Colonel Jewett did not concur with me in opinion, I would abandon the enterprise. Meantime, before Colonel Jewett arrived, I obtained a letter from General Vincent Matthews, a venerable citizen and distinguished lawyer, and leading counsel for the " kidnappers," warmly recommending Mr. Gardiner to the Governor; another from Hon. John C. Spencer, special counsel for the people, appointed by the Governor and Senate to conduct the prosecution, and another from Messrs. Works, Whittlesey, Backus, Ely, and myself, appointed by the people to conduct the investigations. Colonel Jewett, himself under indictment for aiding in the abduction of Morgan, entered warmly into the project in favor of Gardiner, and proceeded

with these letters to Owasco, the residence of Acting-Governor
Throop, who sent Mr. Gardiner's name to the Senate on the
first day of its session. The nomination was promptly confirmed, and the people secured the services of an eminently
enlightened and upright judge for several years in the Supreme
Court, from which he was subsequently elected to the Court of
Appeals.

Simultaneously with the news of Judge Gardiner's appointment, Albert H. Tracy arrived at Rochester in a packet-boat
from the East, calling at my house before sunrise. He was
wrapped in a long camlet cloak, and wore an air of depression that betokened some great disappointment. " You have
been East ? " I said, for I had not heard of his absence from
home. " Yes," he answered. " Then you don't know what happened at Batavia yesterday." He replied in the negative, and
I continued : " We had a convention yesterday, and nominated
a candidate for senator." When he laughingly inquired, " Who
was nominated ? " I said, " Why, we nominated you." He instantly jumped two feet from the floor and whooped like an
Indian. Then, with brightened countenance and undisguised
elation of spirit, he informed me that he had left Buffalo, simply
saying to a few friends that his health required a horseback
journey, and that he was going into western Pennsylvania ;
that, taking a circuitous route to avoid attracting attention,
he proceeded directly to Washington. Arriving there he immediately called on Mr. Van Buren, then Secretary of State,
whom he satisfied that his appointment as judge to fill the
vacancy occasioned by the resignation of Judge Birdsall would
be a wise and acceptable one. The considerations which I had
urged in favor of the appointment of Mr. Gardiner were applicable to Mr. Tracy, who was not a Freemason, and who had
not yet become a political Anti-Mason. Mr. Van Buren wrote
a letter to Judge Marcy, asking him, for the reasons already
given, to see Governor Throop on his arrival from Cayuga, and
ask for the appointment of Mr. Tracy, who arrived from Washington, with Mr. Van Buren's letter in his pocket, a few hours
after Mr. Gardiner had been nominated and confirmed ! Thus
disappointed in obtaining the judgeship, and learning that a
branch of the Bank of the United States was about to be established at Buffalo, he proceeded immediately to Philadelphia,

confident that on intimation of his willingness to accept the presidency, his friends, Messrs. Biddle and Sargent, would very cheerfully gratify him. He called first on Mr. Sargent, with whom he had served in Congress. Mr. Sargent went with him to the bank, where he was informed by Mr. Biddle that a committee of the board was about to meet for the purpose of selecting a board of directors for their Buffalo branch, asking Mr. Tracy to call again in the afternoon. Upon his second call Mr. Biddle informed him that the by-laws of the bank required that when branches were established a list of the directors should be sealed up and delivered to the cashier, to be opened on his arrival at his destination, and that the name of its president would stand at the head of the list. During Mr. Biddle's temporary absence from his room, Mr. Tracy's eye fell upon a loose sheet of paper containing a list of the directors for the embryo bank, at the head of which, instead of his own name, stood that of William B. Rochester. Thus again disappointed, Mr. Tracy turned his face homewards, arriving at Rochester to be made jubilant by the certainty that he was to have a seat in the State Senate for four years. I had the double satisfaction, therefore, not only of seeing two friends provided for, but of securing to the people, in high judicial and legislative positions, the services of two valuable public officers.

In 1828 I went to Delaware County for the purpose of organizing the Anti-Masonic party in that county, and getting delegates to the State convention. Arriving at Delhi in the stage on Saturday evening, I called on General Erastus Root after breakfast the next morning. After talking with him some time, I was about leaving, when he said to me, "No, go to church with me." I followed him into his garden, and, under the shade of a beech-tree, I found seats, and was told that that was his church, and where, in pleasant weather, he passed his Sabbaths in self-examination and self-communion. He then explained his religious views, which, though not in accordance with any orthodox creed, nevertheless were equally far from atheism. On the subject of the Anti-Masonic party he remarked that my paper had found its way into Kortright, Roxbury, and Sidney, and two or three neighboring towns, and had raised an excitement among the farmers which threatened to divide the churches and to break up political organizations in the county. He said that Colonel John F. More, a hotel keeper living in Roxbury, and a former Democrat, had become active as an Anti-Mason. Monday morning I visited Colonel More, and arranged with him for a meeting to appoint delegates. General Root, during the day, gave me a very interesting account of his service in Congress, and of the distinguished public men of that era, highest among whom he placed Jefferson and Marshall. He told me several amusing anecdotes of Mr. Knickerbacker, a representative from Rensselaer County, and formerly known as "the Prince of Scaghticoke." Mrs. Madison, on one occasion, asked him what difference there was in the creeds of the Presbyterian and the Dutch Reformed churches, to which the prince replied, that one sang long and the other short metre.

The general was familiar with the Scriptures, and fond of theological discussion. I had known General Root in 1824 as lieutenant-governor. In 1830 he was speaker of the Assembly, as a member of which I became personally intimate with him, although he was then a Democrat. Subsequently he broke with the Regency, and in 1839 was elected to the Senate as a Whig, when our acquaintance ripened into a warm friendship. To the world General Root seemed overbearing, severe, and unsocial. He was a man of large frame, hard features, and harsh voice, with a rubicund face induced by habits too frequently acquired in political and public life. These habits, however, later in life were entirely reformed. His austerity was superficial. In his family and to intimate friends he was a totally different man. His real life and nature were quiet and kindly. We were much together during his three years of service in the Senate, and I retain a fresh remembrance of his high intellectual attainments, his agreeable conversations, and his warm friendship.

From Delhi I went to Binghamton, where I called upon John A. Collier, a leading lawyer of Broome County, whose acquaintance I had made while residing in Chenango. Mr. Collier was a Federalist up to 1817, when he became a Clintonian, and subsequently an Adams man. I endeavored, by explaining to him the origin, progress, and purpose of the Anti-Masonic party, to interest him in the movement. But after listening to all I had to say, he complacently replied that men of sense in that region neither talked nor thought about Anti-Masonry. I then asked him if he could inform me who did talk or think upon the subject. He said, " There are foolish people in the country towns, and I believe that Vince Whitney has made himself busy with it." I then took leave of Mr. Collier, and found Vincent Whitney, who called an Anti-Masonic county meeting, that appointed him a delegate to the State convention, and who, in the fall, was elected to the legislature as an Anti-Masonic member. Subsequently Mr. Collier himself became an Anti-Mason, and was elected as such, first to Congress and then as a Whig state comptroller.

I made the acquaintance in 1823 or 1824 of James Wadsworth, of Geneseo, one of the earliest settlers and most distinguished men of western New York. Mr. Wadsworth was a native of Connecticut, who, after graduating at Yale College, purchased in connection with his elder brother, William Wadsworth, a large tract of land on the Genesee River during the latter part of the last century. Soon after the close of the war of 1812 Mr. Wadsworth interested himself in the subject of education, to which he devoted a large share of his thoughts during the remainder of his life. He was the father of the normal-school system in this State. One of the earliest of those schools was established at Geneseo. He subsequently inaugurated district-school libraries, and succeeded, after a few years of zealous effort, in engrafting the system upon the State, by the passage of a law authorizing the establishment of a library in every school district. In this latter work I took part, moved thereto by a remembrance of the difficulty I experienced in obtaining books while residing as a boy in a comparatively wilderness town. He devoted not only his time, but contributed largely in money, publishing at his own expense several works on education, and distributing them among the schools. I enjoyed the confidence and friendship of Mr. Wadsworth for a quarter of a century, and until his death. He was a wise and good man. Entertaining a high estimate of his wisdom and patriotism, I made several attempts to draw him into public life, all of which he firmly resisted. On one occasion in 1828 arrangements had been made to nominate him for senator, when, if he had consented to be a candidate, he would have been elected by a very large majority. The following letters will show how peremptorily Mr. Wadsworth refused office : —

GENESEO, *October*, 1828.

To THE ANTI-MASONIC CONVENTION, WHICH IS TO MEET AT RUSH
ON THE 20TH INSTANT.

Gentlemen, — I have before declined being considered as a candidate for a seat in the Senate.

In answer to a second application permit me to state that I cannot, consistently with the reasons I have before given, consent to be considered directly or indirectly a candidate for the situation referred to.

    I am, respectfully, etc.,   JAMES WADSWORTH.

October 17.

DEAR SIR, — Herewith is a copy of a letter which Mr. Wadsworth has left addressed and to be sent to the chairman of the convention to be holden at Rush, and which (copy) Mr. Wadsworth desires me to send you.   He directs me also to add that, after mature consideration, he cannot consent in any shape or manner to be brought forward as a candidate for the Senate.   He desires you to consider the letter herewith as an absolute refusal, and he hopes the convention will unite in the cordial support of Mr. Hayden.

Mr. Wadsworth has come to this conclusion after full deliberation; and he has also determined that if nominated he will immediately publish his refusal to accept.   He adds this that his acceptance may not in any manner be presumed on.

    I am very truly, your obedient servant,

                    PHILO C. FULLER.

THURLOW WEED, ESQ.

The following extracts of letters in 1838 and 1840 will show how strongly Mr. Wadsworth interested himself in the improvement of the school system : —

GENESEO, *December* 18, 1840.

DEAR SIR, — I send you an extract from a letter which was addressed to our mutual friend, Mr. Spencer; but fearing the letter might give offense, it was suppressed.   " You have permitted to slip through your fingers an opportunity to connect Whigism with the strongest passion in the human breast, that of the love of a parent for his offspring.   I refer to the miscarriage of the bill for improving our common schools.   The common-school cause ought not to be made a party question, but when the Whigs had the power, they ought to have passed the bill."

Utility is the order of the day, and the mind of the masses is already sufficiently enlightened to begin to look into and inquire as to the leading measures of different parties.   Nothing has appeared in your paper on the subject of common schools for many months. You are excusable till after the election, but not since. I submit for your consideration that you should devote a column or two very frequently to common schools. I propose that you commence with the school bill which failed to pass last winter. Get some person competent to write a critical review and analysis of this bill. Follow this with extracts from the communication made by Mr. Spencer to the legislature containing the reports of the visitors. After publishing extracts from the reports of different counties, you can, if you please, publish the report made by the committee of the board of visitors in this county. The merit of this report, if it has any, is that it points out fearlessly the defects of our school system, and offers no adulation to the legislature or the people.

The eighth district is alive on the subject of improving our common schools. It will speak in language which I think will be audible at Albany. The truth is, our representatives become so engrossed with the squabbles of party that they forget that they have the concerns of a nation to take charge of. I have taxed Governor Seward with a long letter, which I wish you to read, but I did not like to ask him to show it to you. The subject of separating the office of superintendent from that of Secretary of State is discussed by the friends of common schools. I think there will be several applications to the legislature in favor of the separation. This does not grow out of any unfriendly feelings toward the present incumbent. I am sure no one estimates his services higher than I do. But there are limits to the powers of all men. He is compelled to neglect something, and common schools are the victim. He does not travel eastward to examine the best models of schools, nor westward to witness the worthlessness of our common schools. He is not acquainted with the details of the office of superintendent. He is like a general who has not seen service, and his troops are in a most chaotic state.

Our system of normal schools as now practised is a humbug. The eighth district will do its duty, and I hope you will do yours in improving our school system. Mr. Dwight is now lecturing at Batavia, Lockport, etc. It is very important that the chairman of the committee on common schools should be a go-ahead and enlightened man. There are some excellent chapters on the Prussian and German schools in the report of the president of the Girard College, who has recently returned from Europe. Please ask some literary friend to look them up for your paper. I am truly and respectfully yours, etc.

P. S. For fear you may not find it at your bookstores, I send you a copy of Mr. Mann's lecture, and beg and entreat you to take time and read it. We are contriving ways and means to present a copy of it to every citizen of the eighth district. After reading it, please send it to Governor Seward.

Mr. Wadsworth's eldest son, the late General James S. Wadsworth, devoted himself to the cause of the government and the Union immediately on the breaking out of the Rebellion, serving efficiently and gallantly in several responsible capacities, until, at the battle of South Mountain, he lost his life. His only sister, an accomplished lady, married Mr. Murray, an English gentleman of family and distinction, who was subsequently appointed consul-general to India, where he died young. Soon after the war of 1812 Colonel William Fitzhugh and Major Carroll, both officers of the Revolutionary War, and gentlemen of education and refinement, removed from Maryland to Geneseo, and became large land-holders along the beautiful valley of the Genesee River. The presence and influence of Messrs. Wadsworth, Fitzhugh, and Carroll, liberal, enlightened, and cultivated as they were, largely promoted the general welfare and intelligence of the community in which they resided. These influences produced a salutary effect upon the inhabitants of the surrounding region, whose civilization was manifestly in advance of other agricultural communities. Henry Fitzhugh, long a prominent merchant of Oswego, and for several years an efficient canal commissioner, was a son of Colonel Fitzhugh. Dr. William Fitzhugh, now a venerable and always a genial and accomplished gentleman, still resides in the old homestead. The wife of my family physician and cherished friend, Dr. Frederick F. Backus, of Rochester, is a daughter of Colonel Fitzhugh, as is the equally accomplished wife of the now venerable Gerritt Smith.

Major Carroll was a relative of Charles Carroll of Carrollton. His son, Charles H. Carroll, was a member of our State Senate and a representative in Congress. Francis Granger and Charles H. Carroll married the accomplished daughters of James Van Rensselaer, a merchant of Utica. Colonel Nathaniel Rochester also removed from Maryland to the valley of the Genesee, and in connection with Colonel Fitzhugh and Major Carroll purchased the land upon which the large and beautiful city of Rochester has since grown up. The nucleus, a village, took the name of its founder in 1812. John H. Rochester, who served creditably in the war of 1812 as a captain, and William B.

Rochester, who was a member of Congress from Allegany County, minister to Panama, a judge of the eighth judicial district, and who as a candidate for governor in 1826 against DeWitt Clinton came within thirty-six hundred votes of being elected, were sons of Colonel Rochester. Nathaniel, Thomas H., and Henry E. Rochester, all worthy of their inheritance, still reside in the city bearing their family name.

In my visits to Mr. Wadsworth, in Geneseo, I made the acquaintance of Philo C. Fuller, a clerk of Mr. Wadsworth's land office, with whom I passed many pleasant hours, and in whom I discovered qualities which fitted him for other and higher duties. In remarking to Mr. Wadsworth that I did not think his clerk's light could be long hid under a bushel, that gentleman replied that he was quite aware of Mr. Fuller's ability, but that he was selfish enough to hope that others would not find it out. It was not long, however, before the electors of Livingston County did find out Mr. Fuller's fitness for the public service, and elected him in 1828, and again in 1829, to the Assembly; and in 1830, to the Senate; and in 1832, to Congress. In all these representative capacities Fuller was distinguished for good sense, industry, and fidelity. His services were valuable on committees; his highly intelligent views of measures and policies of government and administration were, by his popular manner and sprightly conversation, extensively impressed upon his colleagues.

After serving four years in Congress, Fuller removed to Adrian, Michigan, where, eschewing office, he took the management of a bank. But his reputation had preceded him; and almost as soon as he became a voter he was elected to the legislature, and chosen speaker of the Assembly, making himself so popular that before the adjournment his nomination for governor by the Whigs of that State was confidently anticipated. When Francis Granger accepted a seat in President Harrison's cabinet as postmaster-general, he invited Mr. Fuller to take the office of assistant postmaster-general. When Tyler's administration became unequivocally Democratic, Mr. Fuller resigned his assistant postmaster-generalship, and returned, not to Michigan, but to his old home in Livingston County. In 1850 he was appointed state comptroller in the place of Washington Hunt, who was then elected governor. That was his last

office.   In all the various and important trusts committed to
him Mr. Fuller left an unblemished record.   Indeed, his conduct and bearing were so just and fair, and the avowals of his
principles and motives were so frank and free, that he was as
highly esteemed by political opponents as he was trusted and
honored by political friends.   Between Mr. Fuller and myself
the mutual feeling of regard which our first interview inspired
grew into a friendship as tender as it was enduring.   The remembrances and associations connected with the personal, political, literary, and social friendships with men like Philo C. Fuller, of whom I have had, and shall continue to have, frequent
occasion to speak, brighten the enjoyments and solace the infirmities of my old age.

I remember, in 1850, when at my instance Mr. Fuller was
appointed state comptroller, much distrust was expressed as to
his ability; but the very able manner in which the duties were
discharged soon relieved the popular apprehension.   And here
it seems proper to say that, amid all the mutations of party, and
the liability under our form of popular government to occasionally find unworthy men elevated to high places, our State has
ever been singularly fortunate in its highest financial officer.
We have had unfaithful men in almost every other department
of the State government.   We have had, in two or three instances, comparatively weak men in the office of comptroller,
but as a rule its incumbents have been capable, firm, and incor-
ruptible.   My personal acquaintance with men who have filled
this high office commenced with Archibald McIntyre, who held
the place and discharged its duties with eminent ability and integrity from 1806 to 1821.   Among his successors, alike capable and upright, were John Savage, William L. Marcy, Silas
Wright, Azariah C. Flagg, Bates Cook, John A. Collier, Millard Fillmore, Washington Hunt, Philo C. Fuller, James M.
Cook, Sanford E. Church, Robert Denniston, Thomas Hillhouse,
William F. Allen, Asher P. Nichols, and Nelson K. Hopkins.
Of Messrs. Marcy, Wright, and Flagg it is scarcely necessary
to say that during their long terms of public service in various
responsible positions no accusation of pecuniary impropriety
was ever made and no suspicion ever existed.   The venerable
Major Flagg, now past eighty years and as blind as Belisarius,
survives.   The other Democratic comptrollers were also capable

and honest, and this is no slight praise, especially to Messrs. Allen and Nichols, who served during a period of demoralization alike discreditable and disastrous to the city of New York and to our State. Those gentlemen were succeeded by Mr. Hopkins, the present comptroller, who, with equal firmness and fidelity, has stood sentry at the treasury door, resisting rapacity and corruption.

For my direct responsibility in the selection of Bates Cook, John A. Collier, Millard Fillmore, Washington Hunt, Philo C. Fuller, James M. Cook, Robert Denniston, and Thomas Hillhouse, I look back with pardonable pride, for in few ways could better service have been rendered to the State and the people.

CHAPTER XXX.

1829–1830.

WE were now preparing for the presidential election of 1832. General Jackson had come into power upon a popular wave, and from the bold, if not reckless, policy he adopted was making warm friends and bitter enemies. The contest for the succession opened early, and promised, as it proved to be, exciting. Mr. Clay, with the support of distinguished statesmen in all parts of the Union, was, by general consent, the chosen candidate of the opponents of Jackson. But a new, and, so far as Mr. Clay was concerned, an embarrassing element entered into the canvass. Opposition to Freemasonry had assumed national proportions. The Anti-Masons generally sympathized with Mr. Clay upon questions of government policy, and especially in regard to the question of protecting American industry.

In Vermont, Massachusetts, New York, and Pennsylvania, where that sentiment had become strongest, the Anti-Masonic party was in pronounced antagonism to the Democracy. The fact, however, that Mr. Clay was an adhering Freemason rendered him an unavailable candidate. I had early conversations with Mr. Clay upon the subject. I conversed also with General Peter B. Porter, the Hon. James Clark, then a distinguished member of Congress from Kentucky, Mr. Johnson, a senator of the United States from Louisiana, and Colonel Erwin, of Tennessee, intimate personal and political friends of Mr. Clay, to whom the difficulty was frankly disclosed, and through whom an arrangement was effected with Mr. Clay, which, as was believed, would bridge over our trouble.

General Porter wrote a letter to Mr. Clay, dated in 1827, informing him that the excitement which pervaded western New York in relation to the alleged abduction and continued

absence of William Morgan, a citizen of Batavia, had induced
him to inquire into the affair. That he had learned with great
surprise and regret that over-zealous members of the Masonic
order, in their solicitude to prevent the publication of a book,
had, under various pretexts and by perversions of legal authority, spirited him away, first from Batavia to Canandaigua,
and from Canandaigua to Fort Niagara, where, after a confinement of several days, he was put to death, precisely how, or,
with one exception, by whom, he was unable to learn. The
object of this communication was to draw from Mr. Clay a
response that should place him before the country at a proper
time in the attitude in reference to Masonry occupied by J. Q.
Adams, Richard Rush, and William Wirt. Such a response
was written to General Porter, and the correspondence was to
have been made public in season to effect a union between the
National Republican and Anti-Masonic parties in favor of Mr.
Clay for the presidency. The following extract from a letter
received by me from Governor Clark of Kentucky will show
with what solicitude the friends of Mr. Clay looked forward to
the efforts making to unite the two parties : —

WINCHESTER, KY., *July* 21, 1830.

DEAR SIR, — I received your letter a few days since on my return
home from Washington. I have not yet seen Mr. Clay. He is at this
time attending the Federal Court at Columbus, Ohio. I will visit him
immediately on his return, and shall take the liberty of showing him
your letter. I am exceedingly desirous to see things restored in the
political world (America) to the state they were in when overturned
by the Jackson reformers. Nothing, in my opinion, will tend so effectually to accomplish this as success in your approaching New York
elections. There is nothing in my power within the pale of honorable political warfare that I would not do to produce this desirable
result. A visit to your State from Mr. Clay, if it should not have the
appearance of having been undertaken to further his political views,
doubtless would have great influence in your elections. The difficulty
is to find the motive for such a visit unconnected with the politics of
the day. I candidly confess I know of no particular cause he could
have for making an eastern tour apart from the approaching political
contest, and my dispassionate judgment is, his motives would be condemned. In addition to the letter you did me the honor to write, I
have received many others from almost every part of the Union.
From these, as well as from conversations held with intelligent gen-

tlemen during the winter at Washington, Mr. Clay is universally regarded as the only man that can at this time redeem the honor of the nation from the reproach cast on it by the corrupt course of the present administration. We can beat them, but it will require, as you have justly remarked, the untiring exertion of every faculty that can be brought to bear against them. Be pleased to let me hear from you frequently.

I have the honor to be, with respect and esteem, etc.,

JAMES CLARK.

P. S. Seal your letters with wax.

Meantime, however, in March, 1828, the "New York Courier," edited by M. M. Noah, contained a letter from James G. Bennett, then its Washington correspondent, from which the following are extracts: —

[From the "New York Courier."]

WASHINGTON, *March* 26.

I have already given you a few slight sketches of the uses to which the coalition have attempted to turn the Morgan excitement in the western counties of your State. But this is not all the iniquity of this business. I have heard through a channel on which I can rely, and it can be proved by respectable evidence, if gentlemen would permit their names to be used, that during the present session a check or checks for a sum of money, between two thousand and three thousand dollars, were carried out of this city for the purpose of furnishing aid directly or indirectly to keep up the Morgan excitement in the West, to spread it as far and wide in the State as possible, and by these means to give the administration of Mr. Adams a few Anti-Masonic votes at the next election. Put these questions to Mr. Weed. Ask him if he has not heard of such a check? ask him if he has not fingered it? ask him if it never reposed for a day and a night, or days and nights, in his pocket? I sincerely hope that he will say "No" to all those interrogatories, and that his conscience will echo back the monosyllable without trembling.

In reply to the challenge I responded thus: —

To the interrogatories relative to conversations with Messrs. Adams and Clay, or either of them, about converting the Morgan excitement to political purposes, or of receiving from them or their friends one thousand, two thousand, or three thousand for that or any other purpose, I do answer "No," and my "conscience echoes back the monosyllable without trembling." It is a black falsehood, basely and wantonly propagated ; for, having no existence in truth, the author must have fabricated it deliberately and willfully.

This accusation furnished material for the Jackson journals throughout the Union, as will be seen by the following extracts from different papers : —

[From the "Albany Argus."]

" In the lowest depths a lower deep " may seem somewhat paradoxical, but it is abundantly exemplified in the conduct of the political Anti-Masons. It was not believed to be an easy thing for the leaders in that congregation of malcontent and unworthy spirits to reduce themselves to a lower estimate in the public opinion than they have been, left to their course and the exposition of their characters during the past year. But they have found out the means of doing so. Thurlow Weed has been nominated by them for the Assembly from Monroe County !

[From the "Lockport Gazette."]

THURLOW WEED. We learn from the Rochester papers that this man of whisker-pulling memory has been nominated as the Anti-Masonic candidate for the Assembly in Monroe County. Whether there is any probability of his being elected we are unable to say. But this much we will say, that his election would fix an indelible stain upon the moral and political character of the county.

[From the "Batavia Press."]

" The laborer is worthy of his hire." Thurlow Weed, of Morgan manufacturing and whisker-pulling memory, has been nominated for Assembly by the Anti-Masons of Monroe County. This is only acting up to the old Bible precept, " Thou shalt not muzzle the ass that treadeth out the corn." We shall see, however, whether all the people say Amen.

[From the "Salina Herald."]

The fla-mous Thurlow Weed, editor of the " Anti-Masonic Enquirer," Rochester, is nominated for Assembly in Monroe County. Well, let Thurlow go, and make and unmake whiskers, before the Assembly, for any new ghost of Morgan that may appear there.

These charges, industriously repeated and reiterated, awakened so much feeling against Mr. Clay that they alarmed his friends to such a degree that, in reply to a letter from prominent Masonic supporters in Indiana, he disclaimed and repudiated political Anti-Masonry. This letter effectually alienated the

Anti-Masons from Mr. Clay, and consequently the correspondence between Mr. Clay and General Porter never appeared. There was good ground for believing, as many of the best-informed public men of that day did believe, that the union so anxiously looked forward to by General Porter, Governor Clark, and other friends of Mr. Clay would have secured his election. Such a union would have given him, in addition to Kentucky, North Carolina, Georgia, Louisiana, Massachusetts, etc., the States of New York, Pennsylvania, Vermont, Connecticut, and Rhode Island. If this belief was well founded, it proves that on two occasions Mr. Clay's best chances to become president were destroyed by himself, first, in writing his letter to Indiana, and again, in 1844, in writing his letter to Alabama.

CHAPTER XXXI.

1827–1829.

NIAGARA FALLS. — SENDING THE BRIG MICHIGAN OVER THE FALLS. — SAM PATCH JUMPING AT NIAGARA. — HIS FATAL LEAP AT GENESEE FALLS. — THE "PROPHET MATTHIAS." — HIS FOLLOWERS AND THEIR DELUSIONS. — THE MORMON BIBLE. — JOSEPH SMITH.

ON the 8th of September, 1827, an event occurred which created much interest in the western part of the State and in Canada. This was the sending of a condemned vessel, the brig Michigan, over the cataract of Niagara. I was one of the large concourse who went to witness that spectacle. With one or two hundred others I embarked on the steamboat Ontario, and had a delightful run to Lewiston, where we arrived early the next morning, and thence to the Falls, in time to get a " standee " at the Pavilion, rooms and beds at all the inns having already been secured by distant visitors. Stages on both sides of the river, from Buffalo, Lewiston, Queenstown, etc., swarming with passengers, continued to arrive all that day and until noon the next. The Michigan was towed by the steamboat Chippewa down to the mouth of Chippewa Creek, five miles above the Falls, in the forenoon. At precisely two o'clock P. M. they hauled out into the river, and towed her about two miles down, when the steamboat left her and made for the shore. Immediately after, Captain Rough's barge was seen pulling ahead of the brig with a line. When the steamboat left her she tacked and came on broadsides, but was headed down again by the barge, and kept steady for another mile, when Captain Rough cut loose, gave her three cheers, and pulled with a strong, steady, and fearless stroke through a torrent never before stemmed for the shore, which he made at a point about three quarters of a mile above the Falls. The interest felt for the safety of the barge was painful. Human life had never before, in that frightful manner, been voluntarily periled. All who had ever been hurried thus far into that cur-

rent went to "that bourne from whence no traveler returns."
Nothing but strong arms and steady nerves saved the barge.
Captain Rough was the oldest navigator on Lake Erie. He
was assisted by Mr. Allen, mate of the Michigan, and four
hardy, experienced oarsmen.

The Michigan was headed down stream twenty-four minutes
before three o'clock. The steamboat cut loose eighteen minutes before three ; the barge left her at thirteen minutes before
three, and reached the shore in four minutes. The Michigan
reached the first rapid at seven minutes before three, and broke
on the precipice 'at precisely three, the time appointed for the
descent.

On board the Michigan was a crew in effigy, — an old buffalo, whose period was only hastened a few days, an old and a
young bear, a fox, raccoon, eagle, two geese, and a bad dog,
that, we understood, had bit my friend Day of the "Buffalo
Journal." Either the fox or the raccoon (we could not distinguish which, but it was probably the latter) ran up the main-
mast as she went over the first reef, and Bruin mounted the
fore-top as she bounded over the second, where he was distinctly
seen by thousands clinging to the top, as she lay on her beam,
and went by the board with the mast, suspended by his paws.
The young bear reached the shore about sixty rods above the
cataract, where he was welcomed by a shouting multitude, and
carried in triumph to Forsyth's for exhibition. The other bear,
it was said, also got to shore above the Falls, but we did not see
him. We neither saw nor heard anything of the other animals.
Major Frazer recovered one of the geese. She was taken out
of the river below the Falls by the ferrymen, and was probably
the only survivor of the number that made the descent.

It is impossible to form anything like an accurate estimate
of the number of persons this spectacle called together. From
the top of Forsyth's house we could see, in every direction from
which a view of the Falls could be had, close, solid masses of
people. The banks on either side of the river, Goat Island, and
Table Rock were literally alive with spectators. Every road
and avenue leading to the Falls during the day was thronged
with vehicles of every possible description, from the "John Bull
coach and six," with its thirty passengers, down to the Canadian
pony, rode by two Indians, either of whom looked better able
to carry than to be carried by the beast.

In 1829 happened also another event of similar and more startling interest. An idle fellow, Sam Patch, who had obtained some notoriety at Providence, R. I., by jumping first from ships' bowsprits and yard-arms and main-tops, was inspired with the ambition of jumping over Niagara Falls. On his way thither he stopped at Rochester, and, to the great admiration of its citizens, jumped safely over the Genesee Falls, a distance of ninety-six feet. Here a handsome collection was taken up to reward the adventurous exploit. He then proceeded to Niagara, and leaped from a shelving rock midway between the highest point of Goat Island and the water, a distance of more than half the height of the Falls. On his return to Rochester he proposed to jump from a platform erected on the edge of the precipice, fourteen feet higher than the Falls of the Genesee. But, unfortunately for poor Sam, he had imbibed too freely during the morning. Notice had been given some days before, and an immense crowd assembled. The banks were lined with spectators for half a mile down the river on either side ; the trees and roofs of buildings were covered with them. It was evident when Sam mounted his platform and harangued the multitude that he was intoxicated, and it was plainly the duty of those nearest to him to have delayed or prevented his jumping in that condition. But after a short, incoherent speech, he threw himself forward, but instead of descending, as on the former occasion, in an erect and arrow-like position, with his arms and hands close to his body, he went down in a sprawling and limp condition. When the bubbling water closed over him the almost breathless silence and suspense of the multitude for several minutes was indescribably impressive and painful.

It was long before any one spoke or moved. But when it became too apparent that poor Sam had jumped from life into eternity all turned silently and sadly away. Several weeks afterwards his body was found at Carthage, two miles below the Falls. Sam's favorite maxim was, that " some things could be done as well as others," and this would have been true enough, even in his last leap, if he had kept sober.

And about this period still another incident happened that proved more than a " nine days' wonder," and will be remembered by the oldest inhabitants of Rochester and the surrounding villages. A journeyman carpenter by the name of Matthews, from Washington County, of more than ordinary intelligence, proclaimed himself a " prophet," changing his name to " Matthias," and allowing his beard to grow, then an unusual habit. He began to preach, uttering, as he maintained, words of inspiration as directed by the Holy Spirit. This man, like the impostors or fanatics of other days and countries, soon obtained a following. In due time he gave out that a second Saviour was, through his agency, to appear on earth. After making proclamation of this event, he waited, as he informed his followers, to be instructed who among the female believers should be the honored mother. The question was finally decided in favor of the wife of a reputable merchant, Mr. B. H. Folger, residing sometimes in New York and sometimes at Sing Sing. She was a lady of intelligence, refinement, and unblemished character, who with her husband had been converted to his doctrines. The late Colonel William L. Stone, who wrote a history of the impostor Matthias, says of Mrs. Folger that she was a young lady reared in the bosom of the Reformed Dutch Church, accustomed from her childhood to the observance of the Sabbath and the reading of the holy Scriptures, and taught to cultivate religious impressions and cherish a devoted spirit by a pious mother.

I met Mr. and Mrs. Folger about a year after they had been awakened from that dark delusion, on board of the steamboat North America, making a day passage between New York and Albany. Having known Matthews at Rochester, we had a long conversation concerning his extraordinary career. Mrs. Folger, whose manners and deportment were refined and ladylike, related step by step the progress of falsehood, imposture, and impiety, which, with the knowledge and approval of her husband, rendered her the confiding victim of his designs. So complete was the infatuation that she felt at the time a sense of Christian pride and elevation at being thus honored, believing implicitly that she was obeying a divine command. It was evident that Mr. and Mrs. Folger were equally deluded for the time being, and that subsequently, when their eyes were opened to the enormity of the imposture, the relations of confidence and affection between husband and wife remained unchanged.

About 1829 a stout, round, smooth-faced young man, between twenty-five and thirty, with the air and manners of a person

without occupation, came into the " Rochester Telegraph " office
and said he wanted a book printed, and added that he had been
directed in a vision to a place in the woods near Palmyra, where
he resided, and that he found a "golden Bible," from which he
was directed to copy the book which, he wanted published. He
then placed what he called a "tablet" in his hat, from which
he read a chapter of the " Book of Mormon," a chapter which
seemed so senseless that I thought the man either crazed or a
very shallow impostor, and therefore declined to become a publisher, thus depriving myself of whatever notoriety might have
been achieved by having my name imprinted upon the title-page
of the first Mormon Bible.

It is scarcely necessary to add that this individual was Joseph
Smith, the founder of the Mormon creed. On the day but one
following he came again, accompanied by Martin Harris, a substantial farmer residing near Palmyra, who had adopted the
Mormon faith, and who offered to become security for the expense of printing. But I again declined, and he subsequently
found a publisher in E. B. Grandin, of Palmyra, in 1830.

CHAPTER XXXII.

1829–1830.

The "Evening Journal." — Consultation with Friends. — Elected to the Assembly. — Again leaving Rochester. — The Pioneers of the Enterprise. — The Cost. — The First Editorial Article. — The Editor's Salary and Staff. — Opposing Newspapers. — Samuel Miles Hopkins.

In 1829 an enterprise began to be talked of which was destined to exert an important influence in shaping the events of my whole future life. The need of a newspaper at the capital of the State which should represent the sentiments and present the views of our political party was generally conceded, and some of the more prominent members of our organization were discussing various suggestions in regard to the establishment of such a journal. Having been again elected in the fall of that year to the Assembly, it was the expectation and wish of our friends at Rochester that I would examine the field and consult in regard to it with the Anti-Masons whom I should meet in Albany. Indeed, the real purpose of my election that year to the legislature contemplated the establishment of a journal at Albany.

This purpose, however, involved the breaking up of business and social relations at Rochester, where I had resided very happily for nine years. So strong was my attachment to Rochester, its citizens and its surroundings, that I left with the hope and determination of returning at some future day to pass the evening of my life where, in earlier years, I found so much enjoyment, and where were laid the foundations of what measure of success and prosperity attended subsequent labors.

Nor was that determination forgotten. When thirty years afterwards I retired from the "Albany Evening Journal," I returned to Rochester for the purpose of purchasing a farm on the banks of the Genesee River, in the suburbs of the city. This occurred at a time when a bitter feeling existed among

Thurlow Weed

radical Republicans against Governor Seward and such of his friends as entertained conservative views. My arrival in Rochester was announced in the Republican journal, of which I had been the first editor, in a paragraph charging me with having treacherously defeated the election of General Wadsworth, the Republican candidate for governor. A welcome so different from that which I had anticipated affected me so unpleasantly that a plan of life which I had long fondly looked forward to was abandoned.

The Albany newspaper project met with warm approval and hearty support from Messrs. Granger, Seward, Tracy, Wadsworth, Cary, Bates Cook, James K. Livingston, Timothy Childs, Thomas C. Love, and others.

It finally took the definite shape of a contribution by twenty or more of the leading Anti-Masons in the various counties, who put down their names for amounts varying from $50 to $250 each, the whole constituting a fund of about $2,500, to be devoted to the purchase of the necessary materials and payment of the expenses of commencing the publication.

One of the most active promoters of the plan for the journal was Frederick Whittlesey, as an extract from one of his letters to me will show : —

I did not get home until Sunday morning. Our court sat the next day, and I have been constantly employed in it ever since. I left some of our proposals at Utica, Auburn, Geneva, and Canandaigua, and distributed them since I have returned. The paper will be liberally supported by the West, and is looked for with deep interest. I passed through Canandaigua in the night, — therefore could not see J. C. Spencer.

You have a great responsibility resting upon your shoulders in the proposed arrangement, but I know no man who is better able to meet it than yourself, and even this responsibility has its favorable side, and brings with itself its own reward in the reflection that in assuming it you are contributing in the highest degree to effect splendid and animating results. It is a proud thing to have stood in the front of the battle, particularly when rejoicing in the victory, and they may talk what they please about humility and all that, the laurel wreath has charms which are worth the winning if won honorably. This paper will produce most excellent effects. Our friends here are satisfied and convinced that with it we are sure of the State. It will be extensively patronized. The committee here are highly gratified at the account I give of you.

It is hardly necessary to say that these pioneers of the new enterprise were my personal and political friends, with all of whom ever after I held most agreeable relations, and that a meeting with any one of them was sure to call up remembrances of the doubts and fears with which we entered upon the undertaking, and some natural pride in the thought that its success had so much more than justified our expectations.

Of the friends referred to, Weare C. Little still survives, and perhaps others, whose names I do not recall.

While these preparations were going on, letters began to come from those who wished to take the new paper. A single subscriber was a gratifying aid and encouragement, and the letters of Mr. Whittlesey and others, which often contained as a postscript the names of two or three new subscribers, were especially welcome.

The "Evening Journal" was established on the 22d of March, 1830. It was deemed, even by the warm and generous friends who suggested the effort, as a hazardous, and by all others as a wild, enterprise, several previous attempts to plant by the side of two old and well-established papers (the "Daily Advertiser" and "Argus") a third daily journal having signally failed.

The "Journal" was launched with but one hundred and seventy daily and less than three hundred semi-weekly subscribers. As soon, however, as our flag was unfurled, troops of friends rallied around it, and before the first month had expired, all doubts of the success of the undertaking had vanished. Subscribers increased daily, weekly, monthly, quarterly, and annually, until, in 1840, its circulation was larger than any other political paper in the State.

The original proprietors of the "Journal" were Benjamin D. Packard, Chauncey Webster, and Benjamin Hoffman. My salary as editor was fixed at $750 per annum.

In those days there was no "editorial staff." I not only edited the paper without assistance, but for several years reported the Assembly proceedings and personally collected all news articles and local items, read all proof, and occasionally made up the forms. These duties gave me constant but pleasant occupation.

The "Argus" and "Daily Advertiser," organs respectively

of the Jackson and National Republican parties, regarded the
" Journal " with much disfavor, and hence a warfare highly
acrimonious and personal was maintained for several years.
Ultimately, however, after the Anti-Masonic party had been
merged into the Whig organization, the " Daily Advertiser "
was discontinued.

Among the most earnest in favor of my removal from Rochester to Albany was the Hon. Samuel Miles Hopkins, then a
distinguished member of the bar, and always a gentleman eminent alike as a lawyer, a patriot, and a philanthropist.

I have seldom known a better or a purer man, or one with
whose friendship in early life I felt more honored. While the
subject of that removal was under consideration, I received the
following letter : —

ALBANY, *March* 25, 1829.

MY DEAR SIR, — I verily thought I had requested your paper to be
sent me, and have been constantly expecting it. Do me the honor to
send it, and if I did not hand you the subscription, as probably I may
not have done, though I intended it, I will remit the amount. Send
it for a month.

I understand that your answer upon a certain subject which has
been mentioned to you *puts off* the decision as *not urgent.* It *is*
urgent. We are here without counsel, — except that of the members,
— without organization, without common concert, without action. We
must have a trumpet to give some certain sound, which will be recognized. I did suppose we ought to have organized in Albany soon after
the convention. And I somehow imagined that your committee would
have given us instructions on that point. Now, however, it may probably be best to wait until after the town elections (at most of which
we should appear small), and when they are over it would be my
own opinion to call meetings and have efficient committees ; and we
must have an efficient press, and *must have it soon,* — that is if we
can. It is my own opinion, therefore, that you ought to take the subject into. early and serious consideration, and, if you agree, then to
prepare for a removal as early as you can. The other establishment
must be bought out.

It will always give me pleasure to be useful to you in all ways
within my power.

I am, dear sir, very truly yours, etc.,

SAMUEL M. HOPKINS.

T. WEED.

If your committee have any suggestions to make respecting our organizing, etc., I presume (speaking for myself only) we should be happy to receive them. It seems to me we shall be in a sad state here after the adjournment of the legislature.   H.

Mr. Hopkins was a member of the legislature of 1820-1821, where he devoted much of his time and thoughts to the improvement of agriculture, and where his voice and vote were heard and recorded upon the right side of every question of justice and humanity.

One of Mr. Hopkins's daughters married Rev. Dr. Reed, for many years professor at Union College, and now residing at Geneva. Another was Mrs. John M. Bradford, the authoress. One of his sons was a successful engineer, and another is the Rev. S. M. Hopkins, one of the professors of the Auburn Theological Seminary.

CHAPTER XXXIII.

1830.

The Rev. John N. Campbell was called this year to the First Presbyterian Church of Albany, the old brick edifice in which Dr. Nott preached his celebrated sermon on the duel between Burr and Hamilton.

Mr. Campbell had left Washington on account of the stand he had felt called upon to take upon a question which occasioned a rupture in General Jackson's cabinet. The difficulty originated in the refusal of certain ladies of the cabinet to recognize Mrs. Eaton, the wife of the newly appointed Secretary of War. General Jackson espoused the cause of Mrs. Eaton warmly. The Rev. Mr. Campbell took the other side of the question. His congregation, to which the President belonged, became so demoralized by the controversy that its pastor voluntarily withdrew.

Dr. Campbell proved not only a popular preacher, but became a highly useful and public-spirited citizen of Albany. He was a man of strong convictions, and participated actively in all movements promotive of the educational, social, moral, physical, and religious health and welfare not only of his own congregation, but of the city and the State.

He was an efficient regent of the university, and to the extent permitted to a clergyman participated in public affairs, and was frequently called into counsel by the heads of the State government. I attended his church regularly, and was fortunate in having him as a near neighbor and close friend for more than twenty years.

Mrs. Eaton is now residing in New York (1874) and our neighbor, and, although approaching fourscore, is as intellectually bright and genial as when I first saw her at Washington as Miss O'Neill, more than half a century ago, among the attractive and accomplished ladies of the metropolis. She was impoverished a few years since by an Italian adventurer, but fights the battle of life cheerfully and courageously. I had the satisfaction a few days since of accompanying her to the office of Mayor Havemeyer, who made her radiantly happy by appointing her grandson to an office worth $1,200 per annum.

William H. Seward came into public life as State senator, having been elected from the Seventh District in 1830. Mr. Seward was nominated, without his knowledge, while in attendance upon an Anti-Masonic National Convention in Philadelphia.

The canvass this year was active and exciting. The issue was between the Democratic, or Regency, and the Anti-Masonic parties, the former having the sympathies and votes of Freemasons, who under other circumstances would have been found actively opposed to the Democracy. This class was sufficiently numerous to decide the election in favor of the Regency.

The Anti-Masonic State Convention met at Utica in August. Forty counties were represented by one hundred and four delegates, among whom were William H. Seward, Obadiah German, Albert H. Tracy, Thomas C. Love, Philo C. Fuller, James K. Livingston (now in 1874 residing at Newark, N. J.), David Graham, Jr., William H. Maynard, James Geddes, Robert C. Nicholas, Thomas Clowes, and Charles Rogers, all of whom had previously or have since been prominent in public affairs.

Francis Granger was unanimously nominated for governor. The Anti-Masonic party was strong in the western and some of the northern counties, but weak in the river and southern counties. We were anxious to strengthen the ticket by the nomination of some well-known and popular citizen in the southern portion of the State. With that object in view I visited the Hon. Silas Wood, a resident of Huntington, Suffolk County, who had been for several years a popular member of Congress. Colonel William L. Stone, then editor of the "Commercial Advertiser," accompanied me to Huntington, where we passed a pleasant night with Dr. Wood. But though in political accord, we failed to obtain his consent to become a candidate. Unlike most men he preferred private life to public honors.

Returning to New York, we sought for a candidate among the prominent and influential Clay men of the metropolis, several of whom declined to accept an Anti-Masonic nomination.

A candidate, however, was finally found in Samuel Stevens, Esq., a prominent lawyer and son of a distinguished Revolutionary officer.

The nomination of Granger and Stevens was well received throughout the State, and we entered upon the canvass with sanguine hopes of success. The Democratic Convention met at Herkimer on the 8th of September, and nominated for governor Enos T. Throop, who, having been elected lieutenant-governor in 1828, was now acting governor since Mr. Van Buren's resignation in 1829 to become General Jackson's secretary of state.

Their candidate for lieutenant-governor was Edward P. Livingston, one of the "seventeen" Senators who defeated the electoral law in 1824.

Efforts were made by disaffected Anti-Masons to induce Messrs. Southwick and Crary to run for governor and lieutenant-governor, but without success. A "Workingman's" Convention met at Syracuse, and made a nomination for governor, but it failed to attract popular favor, their candidate, Mr. Ezekiel Williams, receiving less than three thousand votes.

The following extracts from Mr. Granger's letters during the varying aspects of the canvass will show something of the character and temper of our candidate for governor.

CANANDAIGUA, *August* 23, 1830.

DEAR WEED, — Will you give me a few lines stating how matters actually stand. I have read Crary's letter without any particular surprise, nor do I fear anything from it alone. . . .

I have been aware, for some time, that there were evil spirits abroad trying to make mischief, and for this reason I gave an immediate acceptance of my nomination, that it should not be suspected that I was coquetting with the Workey's Convention of the 25th. . . .

Can any mortal guess what is to be the course of the "Old Elm Tree" establishment? It seems in a more woeful quandary than I have ever seen it. Every day seems to drive it farther from the Regency, but without drawing nearer any one else. . . .

A month later he says : —

SUNDAY EVENING, *September* 26, 1830.

DEAR WEED, — I spent from two till three last night with General Root, at Geneva. He took the Ithaca road for home at four, and could not stay over, as he must be home on Friday morning to court. He will not run. . . .

He says that I stand a better chance to beat Throop with him off than on the ticket.

The election resulted in the success of Governor Throop by a majority of over eight thousand. In central New York the result was about as was expected, while in the river counties and the city of New York the majorities were overwhelming for Throop. In the eighth district, however, the vote was 26,385 for Granger to 13,433 for Throop. A letter from Whittlesey described the result in our own county : —

ROCHESTER, *November* 4, 1830.

DEAR WEED, — The result in this county goes far beyond my expectations, as you will see by the annexed canvass, namely : —

GRANGER.	MAJORITIES	THROOP.	MAJORITIES.
Gates	197	Clarkson	57
Brighton	301	Greece	4
Chili	106	Ogden	1
Henrietta	110		62
Rush	201		
Mendon	149		
Pittsford	108		
Perrinton	91		
Sweden	145		
Palmer	24		
Fenfield	289		
Riga	56		
Wheatland	149		
	1,926		
	62		

1,864 majority for Granger.

The Regency troops were disheartened and dispirited, and voted with evident reluctance; it was up-hill work to procure votes for Throop; fifty or seventy-five Masons in this village voted our ticket quietly, and they have been paid for it with unqualified abuse from the adhering *political* Masons. The election was quiet and peaceable. Don't let it mortify you that we can do so well without you; you have sown the seed and we are gathering the fruit. The whole ticket in our county is of course elected, but majorities not quite so great as on governor. I have not taken care to ascertain the amount. Barnard is now out of sight. We all feel well. Works is as happy as ever Bates Cook was. I shall walk into Congress with about three thousand majority, perhaps more.			Truly yours,

									F. WHITTLESEY.

There used to be a sharp rivalry between the " Argus " and " Evening Journal " to obtain the earliest news. The earliest copy of the President's annual message to Congress was the occasion of much solicitude. Such messages were usually received about the close of the season of navigation.

On one of these occasions I went to New York to obtain the earliest possible copy of President Jackson's message. Mr. Obadiah Van Benthuysen, one of the proprietors of the "Argus," went to New York on the same boat and on the same errand. Colonel J. Watson Webb, one of the editors of the "Courier and Enquirer," had been favored with a copy of the message in advance of its delivery to Congress. No other New York paper had it. Colonel Webb, then in political accord with the "Argus," promised Mr. Van Benthuysen the first copy printed of the "Courier," while I was to receive the second. The steamboat DeWitt Clinton, Captain Sherman, by an arrangement which Mr. Van Benthuysen had made with the agent, was to delay her departure from five o'clock P. M. until Mr. Van Benthuysen came on board, should he be able to do so by eleven o'clock.

My friend Captain Sherman advised me of this arrangement, adding that his orders were to have everything in readiness and cast off his lines the moment Mr. Van Benthuysen could get on board, expressing the hope that I might also get there before the boat was out of the dock.

We both passed the evening at the office of the " Courier and Enquirer," with hacks in waiting at the door. Towards ten o'clock the first proof impression of the message was taken and handed to Mr. Van Benthuysen, who instantly made his exit. There was a delay of nearly two minutes before I obtained my copy. In descending three flights of stairs I found the lights extinguished and was compelled to grope my way down. In this way I lost another minute, in consequence of which I reached the wharf to find the steamer under way about twenty feet from the dock. I learned from an acquaintance who was standing on the dock, that a freight steamer would leave early the next morning. Proceeding to the dock of that steamer, I induced the agent to fire up and get under-way at as early an hour as practicable. We were off in two hours after the departure of the DeWitt Clinton, and reached Poughkeepsie, where both boats were detained by the ice an hour or two, after Mr. Van Benthuysen had departed in the mail stage for Albany. I found "Bally," a well-known and active livery stable man, who assured me that he could overtake the stage before it reached Albany. In a very few minutes, therefore, I was seated in a cutter (for the sleighing was good) and off, express to Albany. "Bally" was as good as his word, for in approaching Greenbush the stage was in sight, scarcely a quarter of a mile ahead of us. Mr. Van Benthuysen and myself ran a foot race across the river on the ice, and the "Journal" and the "Argus" issued the message in an extra simultaneously.

On another of those occasions, when of a cold night the steamer was making its way with difficulty through the ice late at night, I met Governor Morgan Lewis among the passengers shivering with cold, for in those days there were no saloons, and comparatively few comforts. I had, as a friend of the captain, access to a small room in the forward part of the boat warmed by a stove, and I invited Governor Lewis thither.

After chatting with him awhile I went on deck to see what progress the steamer was making, and there I found Colonel Aaron Burr who, though protected by furs, was exposed to the wind of an intensely cold night. I told him of the warm room forward, and invited him to share in its comfort. Upon entering the room I observed that these distinguished gentlemen did not speak, although I knew that as officers in the Revolutionary War and citizens of New York they must be well acquainted. To relieve the embarrassment I seated myself between them, and for some ten minutes kept up a conversation with each, when Colonel Burr, thanking me for the invitation, and with a slight inclination of his head towards Governor Lewis, retired.

I accompanied Colonel Burr to the deck, and returning to the cabin, remarked to Governor Lewis that I should not have invited Colonel Burr there if I had known that their relations were not amicable, to which Governor Lewis replied in an excited manner, " I have not spoken to the damned reptile in twenty-five years."

CHAPTER XXXIV

1830–1831.

The United States Bank. — Mr. Webster's Speech. — Chief Justice Spencer. — The Whigs defeated on that Issue. — A Secret of the Bank Parlor. — General Jackson and Biddle and Sargent. — Clay and Webster. — McLane and Blatchford. — Van Buren's Rejection. — Silas Wright's Letter. — Rush's Letters to Livingston. — Imprisonment for Debt.

The question of a re-charter of the Bank of the United States occupied public attention as early as 1829, although the charter would not expire until 1836. The bank had so conducted its affairs for several years as to secure the confidence of the business men of the country. President Jackson, however, influenced, as it was subsequently alleged, by some of his far-seeing political friends, suggested doubts in his message of 1829 of the constitutionality of the United States Bank.

Isaac Hill, editor of the "New Hampshire Patriot," then a leading and influential journal, opened its columns against the bank, charging, among other things, that by its loans to prominent politicians it was paving the way by corrupt means for a re-charter. Other Democratic journals followed the "New Hampshire Patriot," until, in 1832, it became the leading political issue between the friends and the opponents of General Jackson.

My own sympathies were with the bank, believing that it was necessary to the commercial, manufacturing, mechanical, and agricultural interests of the country, and as a means of regulating its currency and exchanges. But I was not long in discovering that it was easy to enlist the laboring classes against a "monster bank" or "moneyed aristocracy," and that as a political issue we should lose more than we could hope to gain by it. This, however, was not the opinion of my political friends. The opponents of the administration generally accepted the issue offered by the friends of General Jackson, and I was drawn into the current, though not without serious misgivings as to the result. When, however, we were disastrously beaten, though still differing with my friends as to the cause, I determined to cut loose from the bank, and took a suitable occasion to avow that determination. This surprised most, and exasperated many of my political friends. But we finally agreed to disagree on that question, and in subsequent elections this State, out of the city of New York, was largely exempted from the odium elsewhere attached to the "United States Bank Party."

The question subjected me to frequent embarrassment, for such men as Chief Justice Spencer, Chancellor Kent, Philip Hone, David B. Ogden, R. M. Blatchford, General J. Watson Webb, Charles and John A. King, Moses H. Grinnell, Roswell L. Colt, etc., etc., my warm friends, were zealous "bank men."

On the other hand, I had been sustained by William H. Seward, Francis Granger, Millard Fillmore, Frederick Whittlesey, James Wadsworth, William H. Maynard, and other prominent western friends.

As a national party, however, we went into the presidential canvass of 1836 "with that millstone tied round our necks." Not only Mr. Clay and Mr. Webster, but all, or nearly all the leading Whig members of Congress from all parts of the Union were "bank men."

The progress, incidents, and results of the bank controversy are too well known to require recapitulation. But one or two incidents connected therewith, though occurring some years afterwards, may be properly enough recorded here.

At an immense Whig mass meeting in Massachusetts Mr. Webster made his great speech in support of the bank, and against the veto message of General Jackson. That speech was hailed throughout the country by Whig statesmen and journals as a triumphant answer and refutation of the arguments and accusations of the veto message. It did not, however, find a place in the columns of the "Albany Evening Journal." That omission occasioned remark and surprise. I received letters from prominent friends urging its publication, and finally Mr. Brooks and Joseph Blunt, of New York, accompanied by Chief Justice Spencer, of Albany, called personally at my office to insist upon the publication of Mr. Webster's speech. I urged that the issue was a dangerous and damaging one, and that the greater the efforts in favor of the bank the greater would be our losses among the "rank and file." Judge Spencer asked if I did not consider Mr. Webster's argument against the veto unanswerable? I replied that as far as justice and reason were concerned, yes; but that as a popular question, two sentences in the veto message would carry ten electors against the bank for every one that Mr. Webster's arguments and eloquence secured in favor of it. These sentences, when I was called on to point them out, were, first, that our government "was endangered by the circumstance that a large amount of the stock of the United States Bank was owned in Europe;" and second, that the bank was a contrivance "to make the rich richer and the poor poorer." Mr. Brooks confessed that these preposterous assertions were certainly having their effect in deluding the masses. Judge Spencer was annoyed, but somewhat mollified, and did not urge the publication of the speech with his usual vehemence. Mr. Blunt insisted that there was good sense enough among the people to detect the fallacies, however specious, of the veto message. I persisted, however, in withholding the speech from the readers of the "Journal." When the election was over, and we were again beaten, it was pretty generally admitted that the United States Bank, however financially useful, was not an element of political strength. There were, however, many influential Whigs so wedded to their idol that they adhered to it after it became an institution of the State of Pennsylvania.

Long after the bank was politically dead and buried, I deemed it proper to contribute something to the "truth of history" by revealing a secret of the bank parlor. Shortly before the bank applied to Congress for a re-charter, the Hon. Louis McLane, then Secretary of the Treasury, invited Mr. Biddle, the president of the United States Bank, to Washington. At their interview the Secretary informed Mr. Biddle that he was authorized by the President to say that if the proposed re-charter of the bank contained certain modifications, which Mr. McLane handed to Mr. Biddle in writing, the bill would be approved. Mr. Biddle returned to Philadelphia and submitted the proposed modifications to Mr. John Sargent, a director of the bank, and its counsel, and to one or two other confidential directors, by each of whom the modifications were accepted. But

before announcing such acquiescence to the Secretary of the
Treasury, it was deemed proper to confer·with leading friends
of the bank then in Congress. Mr. Biddle and Mr. Sargent
therefore called upon Messrs. Clay and Webster, submitting to
these gentlemen the modification required to secure the approval of the President of a re-charter of the bank. After
much discussion and consideration, Messrs. Clay and Webster
came to the conclusion that the question of a re-charter of the
bank had progressed too far, and had assumed aspects too decided in the public mind and in Congress to render any compromise or change of front expedient or desirable. Messrs.
Biddle and Sargent retired for consultation, but returned in the
evening of the same day, confirmed in their convictions that it
was wise to accept the offer of the Secretary of the Treasury.
Messrs. Clay and Webster replied that they had borne the
brunt of the battle so far, and that they were confident of their
ability to carry a bill through Congress re-chartering the bank,
even though that bill should encounter a presidential veto ; but
that they could not be responsible for the result if, in the heat
of the contest, the bank, abandoning its reliable friends, should
strike hands with its foe.

This revelation, reflecting, as was assumed, upon Mr. Clay
and Mr. Webster, provoked indignant denials and denunciations from leading Whig journals. Nor were they limited to
the Whig press. The " Evening Post " and " Journal of Commerce," both having often said many worse things against
Messrs. Clay and Webster, joined the " New York Express,"
" Times," etc., etc., in stigmatizing me with falsehood and cal-
umny.

The facts were communicated to me by Nicholas Devereux,
of Utica, a director in the Branch Bank of the United States,
of which his brother, John C. Devereux, was president. Mr.
Devereux was an intimate and confidential friend of Mr. Biddle,
who communicated this piece of secret history to Mr. Devereux
in the bank at Philadelphia while the question was pending in
Congress. Some years afterwards, on my way to Washington,
I met Mr. Devereux at the United States Hotel in Philadelphia. We had been intimate and confidential friends since
1813, and having an evening to ourselves, the information which
I subsequently felt called upon to submit as a part of the secret
history of the great bank controversy was imparted to me.

When the publication was made, however, all the gentlemen by whom it might have been denied or affirmed had passed from life. I stood alone, conscious both of the truth of what I had stated and of the propriety of its publicity.

The press, however, were united and persistent against me, and a general impression was created, that I had either misapprehended or misrepresented the case.

Fortunately one gentleman came to my relief. Mr. McLane, the Secretary of the Treasury referred to, was an intimate friend of Mr. Richard M. Blatchford, of New York, at whose house he was a guest whenever he visited the city. On one of those occasions, while at dinner with Mr. Blatchford, Mr. McLane revealed to Mr. Blatchford the same facts confided to me by Mr. Devereux relating to the interview of Messrs. Biddle and Sargent with Mr. Clay and Mr. Webster.

In 1831 General Jackson appointed his Secretary of State, Mr. Van Buren, to be minister to England. That appointment occasioned much and exciting controversy until the meeting of Congress.

As a majority of the Senate was opposed to the administration, Mr. Van Buren's rejection was demanded by the opposition press. The reasons assigned for such a demand were based upon dispatches from Mr. Van Buren, while Secretary of State, to Mr. McLane, our minister in London, in which, for the purpose of gaining a party advantage, our minister was instructed, as was alleged, to compromise the dignity and honor of his country.

Conceding, as I did, the justice of his rejection, I strongly questioned its expediency, believing, as I stated in an editorial, that now being abroad he should be permitted to remain until the people and the government were " redeemed from the condition into which they have sunk under his system of political jugglery."

The editorial referred to closed as follows : —

It would change the complexion of his prospects from despair to hope. His presses would set up a frightful howl of " proscription." He would return home as a persecuted man, throw himself upon the sympathy of the party, be nominated for vice-president, and huzzaed into office at the heels of General Jackson. Such, in our judgment, would be the effect of Mr. Van Buren's rejection.

Mr. Van Buren was rejected, and the consequences which I predicted were more than realized. His nomination and election to the vice-presidency was followed four years afterwards by his election as president.

In January, 1831, a private letter written in 1826 from Silas Wright, then a State senator, to Mr. Van Buren, then in the Senate of the United States, was found in a drawer of a bureau of Mr. Van Buren's which had been sold at auction. The letter was deemed of sufficient importance to justify its publication. As it presents in frank but forcible language the private political views of one of the ablest and shrewdest of our public men at a moment of peculiar and embarrassing interest to both of the great political parties, and subsequently became a valuable text in my conflict with the Albany Regency, liberal extracts will be found interesting and instructive.

ALBANY, *April* 4, 1826.

MY DEAR SIR, — The time for adjournment is now fixed upon, and we shall soon have done what shall at all be done to prepare for the fall contest. Much alarm and excitement is prevailing, not only here but in New York and elsewhere, from the allegations that some of us, with yourself, are inclining to join with Mr. Clinton against the administration. Many of our friends are fearful, and nearly all of them cannot under any terms be brought to join Mr. Clinton, or to consent to endeavor to sustain ourselves without running a candidate for governor against Clinton. My object, therefore, is to inform you truly what I think will be done, what course I have myself consented to, and what course will, in my opinion, alone save us from an entire division and failure at our next election.

You will readily ask what man can we offer to such a convention? If you should ask what men want to be offered, I could answer you more easily, Tallmadge, Young, etc. But it is much more difficult to say what men WE ought to offer to such a caucus and through them to the electors. Your colleague, however, is more talked of 'now by our friends than any other man. Tallmadge is the candidate of a very few of the Adams men, but they would probably be pleased to exchange him for Sanford. But my reflection and the appearances in the State have induced me to believe that no other measures will be so likely to give us the power of the State when most we shall want it. I admit if we could hold our election without any reference to the question of governor, it would probably be better for us. But it is perfectly settled that if we do not get up a candidate the great body of our political friends throughout the State would enlist themselves to support against Clinton. If, then, we should favor Clinton, there would be an effectual split produced in our ranks which could not be healed. If we should not favor Clinton our services would be required for the opposing candidate, whoever he might be, or we should be equally suspended or opposed.

In any event, then, from this state of things, it does appear to me that we should be between two fires without the least prospect of escaping the flames, instead of bringing off the spoils. We should put ourselves precisely in the situation the Federalists in this State have been in for years past, acting under colors not their own and doing journey work. But suppose we take up your colleague, and make him our own candidate. He is here considered Republican, by the Adams men he is considered an Adams man, and by us, in truth, not much different. But does not the very fact of taking him up without reference to his feelings in regard to national politics, and purely on the ground of his democracy, draw after it, as a necessary consequence, the acquisition of the administration strength of this State, while the question of national politics would not be drawn into the formation of our Congress, Senate, and Assembly tickets. Would not Clinton be looked upon not only as our State opponent, but with those who might then be disposed to involve national politics, as our national opponent, and, therefore, the only question in nominating a congressman, etc., be, is he Anti-Clintonian? If this would be the effect, the administration question would be virtually excluded from our election.

I have heard but one formidable objection to this course, which is that the Governor, if we should be successful, would have a powerful influence in giving the legislature an inclination towards administration men, and we should be stopped from resisting him. I obviate this first, by saying that now, and probably one year from now, you cannot render any question of national politics very nearly felt by the elections of this State, and if you can next year obtain such a legislature as we have elected this year, they will be equally free and willing to sustain their friends without reference to those questions.

Second, I consider Sanford different, and to be calculated upon differently from most other men. In the Senate he will be an administration man while the administration appear strong and likely to sustain themselves. As governor of the State he would be popular, and continue in that office without reference to the national politics further than should be absolutely necessary to accomplish that object.

Again, I have thought, and still think, taking the future prospect of four years of what will be the state of national politics, that I had rather have your colleague here as governor than where he is now, and should we have the power next winter I think we could better fill that place for future contest. If you can at all concur in these views, please endeavor to influence your colleague to hold himself willing to serve his friends in the way here suggested.

Do not by this letter suspect that any change in my feelings, or those with whom I have acted, has taken place favorable to the administration of Messrs. Clay, Adams & Co. It is not so.

But my own opinion is, the times of '98 are at hand, and that we should even be willing to take almost any measures which appear most likely to fortify us for the combat, that New York at that time may be found not only correct but strong in Congress. I think that Congress will commence its decisive character in the next Congress, and although we should elect an Adams governor, if a legislature elected at the same time should return to the Senate two senators of an entirely different character, the effect would be altogether obviated. You will not accuse me of an intention to flatter when I say I am strongly anxious for your reappointment, and I do not think your colleague, as governor of this State, would be as likely to defeat that object as he would in his present station.

You will consider this letter entirely confidential, but are at liberty to give our views to any friends you may think proper to communicate them to.   S. WRIGHT, JR.

Hon. M. VAN BUREN.

Mr. Sanford, so disparagingly referred to in Mr. Wright's letter, instead of flaring up, as most men would, assured Mr. Wright that there was nothing in the letter to disturb their personal relations. This evinced either less temper or more tact than is usually shown under similar circumstances. Mr. Sanford was subsequently appointed chancellor of the State. He had previously, during and after the War of 1812, served as United States district attorney, in which office he accumulated a large fortune.

A series of letters of Richard Rush " to Edward Livingston, Grand Master, &c., &c.," on account of the distinguished character of the writer, attracted much attention. Mr. Rush, though previously widely known and universally popular, now became obnoxious to severe criticism in nearly all the leading journals of the country. In early life Mr. Rush had taken three degrees in Masonry. Not caring to advance farther, he abstained from attendance in the lodges, and remained silent until his views against secret societies were called out by an appeal to him from a large number of the citizens of Pennsylvania. The testimony of one so eminent and patriotic, thrown into the scale against Freemasonry, imparted fresh zeal and confidence to the Anti-Masons, then organizing for the approaching presidential election. Although not a great, Mr. Rush was an eminently good man, and a useful public servant. He held places of distinction under the administrations of Madison, Monroe, and Adams, the duties of which were always creditably performed. None who saw or heard him in public or private life failed to discover qualities worthy of the father who bore so distinguished a part before and throughout the Revolution.

Up to this period, while philanthropists had been preparing the way for abolishing imprisonment for debt, nothing more than spasmodic efforts in that direction had been made in the legislature. Now, however, a numerously signed petition from the city of New York in favor of that reform was, on motion of Silas M. Stilwell, referred to a select committee, of which Mr. Stilwell was made chairman.

Mr. Stilwell came from the city of New York, and based his hope of political advancement upon that issue. In due time he made an elaborate report, designed to show that while the debtor always suffered, the creditor rarely, if ever, profited by the operation of an inhuman civil code. The bill abolishing imprisonment for debt elicited long and animated debate in both houses, but finally became a law, to take effect in March, 1832.

Among the members who sustained "the Stilwell Bill," as it was called, were Millard Fillmore, of Buffalo, Samuel G. Andrews, of Rochester, Charles L. Livingston and Dudley Selden, of New York, John C. Spencer, of Canandaigua, in the Assembly, and William H. Maynard and William H. Seward in the Senate.

The present generation, in looking back to the struggle of our forefathers for independence, will wonder why they did not then emancipate the country from imprisonment for debt.

And yet, up to the year 1832, hard-working men, with families dependent upon their labor, when by reverses of fortune they were unable to pay their debts, were thrown in company with felons into prison. Dickens might have found in any of our county jails materials as touching as those upon which the story of "Little Dorrit" was founded. I remember, with a shudder, a sad and sleepless night occasioned by the incarceration of my own father, who though a poor man was known to be an honest one, and for that reason was enabled to give bonds that he would remain on the "gaol liberties" until the debt (of something less than $20) was paid. The "limits," although confining debtors to circumscribed bounds in the city or village, nevertheless enabled poor men to obtain work enough to keep the family from starvation.

Creditors generally kept a vigilant eye upon debtors who were out on bail, and not infrequently beguiled them across the line long enough to enable the sheriff to serve a process upon the bondsman, and thus would secure payment of the debt.

Twenty years after imprisonment for debt was abolished, I exhumed a remonstrance against the passage of that law, signed by the merchants of Albany, and representing, among other evils, the destruction of confidence, and urging that it would be impossible for poor men to obtain credit.

Time, however, had shown the fallacy of all these reasonings. Nobody had been hurt by the abolition of imprisonment for debt, and the Townsends, the Kings, the Russells, the Cornings, the Staffords, etc., etc., to whom I showed this remonstrance, required the evidence of their own autographs to convince them that they had ever entertained views so preposterous.

CHAPTER XXXV.

1831.

JOHN RANDOLPH. — HIS APPOINTMENT TO RUSSIA. — BANK CHARTERS.
— THE SAFETY FUND SYSTEM. — HOW STOCK WAS DISTRIBUTED. —
JAMES K. PAULDING. — AN UNCONSCIOUS PLAGIARISM. — PROFESSOR
JOSEPH HENRY. — "MASTER BURKE." — EDWIN FORREST. — THE FIRST
RAILROAD. — PASSENGERS ON THE FIRST TRIP TO SCHENECTADY. —
FIRST TELEGRAPHIC EXPERIMENTS. — THE NOVELTY. — DR. NOTT. —
A SERIOUS ACCIDENT. — DAVID WILLIAMS. — NULLIFICATION. — DR.
MCILVAINE.

1831. — The appointment of the celebrated John Randolph, of Virginia, as minister to Russia, occasioned exciting debate in Congress, and elicited strong feeling in the press and among the people. Mr. Randolph's talent and temper fitted him for opposition. He had been a violent and vehement enemy of John Quincy Adams during his administration. His speeches were in the highest degree denunciatory. "There is," he said on one occasion, "no perpetuity in these Adamses: they come to the surface spasmodically; the younger is now merely serving out the term of the elder."

On the occasion of my first visit to Washington, in 1825, I was particularly anxious to see John Randolph, of whom I had heard and read so much. He came into the House of Representatives in the midst of a debate, walking to his seat without removing his hat, and, standing up with a riding-whip under his arm while drawing off his gloves, seemed to have his attention awakened by the closing remark of General Vance, of Ohio, to which he instantly replied in a twenty minutes' speech, more violent and bitter than anything I had ever heard. Mr. Randolph was tall, attenuated, and cadaverous. I learned, subsequently, that what seemed accidental and unpremeditated, was only one of his stage tricks, and that he not unfrequently came to his seat with a knowledge of what was passing and to enact a part.

The costume, manners, and caprices of Mr. Randolph at Baltimore, Philadelphia, and New York, from which port he departed for Russia, excited very general surprise. His prejudices grew more and more intense as he proceeded north. Nothing pleased him outside of Virginia. Those who saw his contemptuous manner and heard his satirical remarks readily recognized the man who had once said in Congress, replying to a speech made by General Root, of this State, on the duties on wool, that he hated sheep, " and would go a mile out of his way to kick one."

When the diplomatic appropriation bill was under consideration in the House of Representatives, a motion was made to strike out the salary for the mission to Russia, on the ground that the Secretary of State, Mr. Van Buren, had given to Mr. Randolph a roving commission, under which Mr. Randolph, on account of his seriously impaired health, was permitted to seek in other European countries a climate more congenial than that of Russia.

Most prominent in the debate against the appropriation was Tristram Burgess, of Rhode Island, who, as the leading friend of the administration of Mr. Adams, had been pitted against Mr. Randolph, its leading opponent. The ill feeling then engendered, as was alleged by Mr. Barbour, of Virginia, induced Mr. Burgess's opposition to this appropriation.

It was in one of those exciting debates that Mr. Burgess closed an eloquent speech by characterizing Randolph as a person " hated of men and scorned by women."

The dominant party in this State, after the adoption of what was known as Mr. Van Buren's Safety Fund System of Banking, committed the grave error of making that system a part of the machinery of politics.

Charters were only granted to political friends. In these charters commissioners were authorized to distribute the stock arbitrarily. At first the stock was given either to Democratic merchants or capitalists in their locality, but by degrees politicians residing at Albany began to participate, and finally, when charters were obtained for Lockport and two or three other villages, the lion's share of stock was awarded directly to prominent State officers, or indirectly for their benefit to relatives or confidential friends.

Much of this stock bore a premium of twenty to twenty-five

per cent., even before the first installment on it had been paid in. This political blunder, at a time when the public mind was much more sensitive than now, and when officials were held to a more rigid responsibility, gave us an advantage which I promptly availed myself of. Being thus enabled to show that high State officials, including judges, etc., were making money by what Mr. Leggett (then editor of the " Evening Post ") described as the " unclean drippings of venal legislation," the Albany Regency, powerful as it was, lost something of its control over the Democracy, and became still more obnoxious to Whigs.

Safety fund banking, as a system, gave the people a sound and sufficient currency, and only became unpopular when it was found that party leaders doled out charters and distributed stock with a view to their own pecuniary advantage.

After reviewing the " Dutchman's Fireside," a novel by Mr. Paulding, from the press of Harper & Brothers, I was subjected to a ludicrous and embarrassing interview with the author. Calling at the Harpers' a few days after my notice appeared, my old friend James, the senior of that house, in taking me by the hand abruptly said, " You are just in time to give an account of yourself. Here is Mr. Paulding, against whom you have brought the charge of plagiarism. We generally swear by the ' Evening Journal,' but of course you are mistaken in this case, and I have assured Mr. Paulding that you will cheerfully make an apology." Mr. Paulding very courteously remarked that he was not conscious of being obnoxious to the grave charge, but that authors not unfrequently fell into a train of thought which might subject them to criticism.

" That won't do," said Harper. " Our friend Weed has either made a great blunder, or he has found something to justify his accusation ; he must, therefore, either back out or prove his assertion." Mr. Paulding politely expressed his desire to know upon what part of his book the charge of plagiarism was founded. Harper then produced a copy of the " Dutchman's Fireside," and I turned to the following : —

" A bashful man is like a tiger ; he makes but one effort, and if that fails slinks away to his jungle and essays not another. I, myself, have my own experiences to vouch for this."

I then asked for a copy of Moore's " Life of Byron," and

turned to a letter of the latter written to Murray, in which
Byron said : —

"With regard to what you say about retouching the Juan, and the
hints, it is all very well ; but I can't *furbish*. I am like the tiger (in
poesy), if I miss the first spring I go growling back to my jungle.
'There is no second.'"

After an embarrassing pause Mr. Paulding frankly admitted
that the criticism was just, but said that, while it was quite
evident that he had used both the figure and the language, he
was oblivious while writing of the fact that he was indebted to
Lord Byron for both.

When Mr. Paulding retired, I expostulated with Mr. Harper
for placing strangers in a position of such peculiar embarrassment. He replied, laughingly, that he supposed he "was putting me in a tight place," but knew that I would work out of it
in some way, but that he regretted having " touched Mr. Paulding on the raw."

An article in " Silliman's Journal," by Professor Joseph
Henry, announced his discovery of a mode of producing " recip-
rocating motion by magnetic attraction and repulsion." While
Professor Henry and several other scientific men were pursu-
ing this line of investigation and experiment leading towards
the discovery of the electric telegraph, Professor Morse was the
fortunate one who first made practical application of the principle which has secured to the whole civilized world simultaneous intercommunication.

Professor Henry's present eminent position, in charge of the
Smithsonian Institution, induces me to refer to his early history.
I became acquainted with him at Albany in 1817. He was then
an apprentice to Mr. John F. Doty, a silversmith. As a member of an amateur theatrical company young Henry evinced so
much talent for the stage, and was so much flattered by the
applause he received, that he was strongly tempted to accept an
engagement from the manager of the Albany Theatre.

While this offer was under consideration, Dr. T. Romeyn
Beck, then principal of the Albany Academy, advised Henry to
pursue academical studies. The question was anxiously debated
between Henry and his young friends. His inclinations were
strongly in favor of the stage, but his judgment finally decided

the matter in favor of science, in which study he was also interested. Mr. Doty relinquished his indentures and Henry entered the academy, pursued his studies with diligence, and graduated with honors, which justified the hopes of a career of usefulness which have since been fully realized.

The theatrical world was a good deal moved by the appearance of Master Burke, who as an "Infant Phenomenon" had attracted crowded and admiring houses in Dublin and London. Though but twelve years of age, Master Burke played a rôle of Irish characters previously and since unequaled except by his countryman Power, who, after achieving fame and fortune in America, was lost in the ill-fated steamer President, on his return to England.

Master Burke was a great favorite in Albany, near which place, by the purchase of a farm in the vicinity, he became a resident. His father, a highly social and hospitable Irish gentleman, found it quite as easy to spend as it was for the son to make money. The consequence was that when young Burke lost his taste for theatricals, and became a professor and teacher of music, the large fortune he had made was seriously diminished. Enough, however, remained to purchase a valuable farm near Batavia, to which his widowed mother removed, and is now (in 1874) living in the enjoyment of a competency, and cheered by the annual visit from her affectionate son.

Mr. Burke, or "Jo Burke," as he is still familiarly called by his friends, is now a much-respected citizen of New York, possessing qualities of head and heart that endear him to a large circle of friends.

Edwin Forrest, a young and rising tragedian, made his appearance this year at the Albany Theatre in the character of "Spartacus," in the play of the "Gladiator," written expressly for him by Dr. Bird, of Philadelphia.

The "Evening Journal" remarked of him: "Forrest is a great favorite in Albany, and promises to become eminent as an actor. His talents are peculiarly adapted to 'Spartacus,' in which character he is truly great. He has the advantages of a fine person, genial manners, and a warm heart, qualities which will contribute largely to his professional success."

Forrest did become popular, and maintained his professional standing through life. He never possessed the genius of the

elder Booth, and failed still more signally to approach that of
the elder Kean. In truth, the criticism which made him physically, rather than intellectually, a great actor was just. My
relations with Mr. Forrest continued friendly, until his domestic difficulties culminated in a suit for divorce. With favorable
opportunities for forming opinions upon the merits of that painful question, I failed to discover truth in the accusations or justice in their prosecution.

In the summer of 1831, the great railway system of America
was inaugurated by the completion and opening of two or three
short roads, — Charleston, New Orleans, and Albany, each
claiming to have been first in the field. The point of preced-
ence, however, has been settled in favor of Albany, a portion
of whose road was then opened, and the first steam car placed
upon the " Mohawk and Hudson " track being propelled by a
locomotive from the summit of the hill at Albany to the summit
of the hill which descends into Schenectady. At either end of
the route was a stationary engine, by means of which cars were
drawn up and down the inclined plane. But even with these
drawbacks, which show how much has been since done to perfect the system, an hour was gained upon the time required by
stages between the two cities. The cars were extemporized by
placing the body of the stage-coach then in use on a simple four-
wheeled platform car.

Of my fellow-passengers in the cars of that first train I can
only identify Lewis Benedict, John Townsend, Joseph Alexander, John Meigs (high constable), John I. Boyd, and Billy
Winne (penny-post), of Albany ; and Governor Yates, John I.
DeGraff, and Hugh Robinson, of Schenectady. It was my fortune, therefore, to witness the advent of the two great material
forces which have contributed so largely to the development and
civilization of this continent. I witnessed in 1807, from an isl-
and in the Hudson River, as has been heretofore stated, the passage of the first vessel ever propelled by steam ; and I was a
passenger, in 1831, in the first car propelled by steam in the
State of New York.

I was a witness also, at a later period, of Professor Morse's
first demonstration before Congress of the working of his telegraphic invention.

A communication was made for the wires through the wall

which divided two committee rooms, in each of which members of Congress and invited guests were gathered. Professor Morse was himself the operator, with an assistant in the opposite room to receive the message. Members of Congress were requested to communicate with each other, thus preventing the possibility of collusion. The experiment was a complete success, occasioning equal astonishment and gratification; and from that beginning the whole civilized world has been spanned with wires and cables, through which Egypt, India, China, and Japan are in daily and hourly communication with Europe and America.

The arrival at Albany of the Novelty, a new steamboat, the furnaces of which were adapted to the use of coal instead of wood, created much interest along the docks. She was visited by the citizens in general. Pine wood, in consequence of the very large quantity required for steam navigation, was becoming scarce and dear. The introduction of coal, therefore, was a desideratum. But, like all radical advances, its practicability was questioned by many, and stoutly denied by others.

Time soon settled the question, and now the use of wood, except in regions where coal cannot be obtained, is an obsolete idea. Until this problem was solved, ocean steam navigation was impracticable; and for this important forward step in steam navigation the world is indebted to the genius and enterprise of the Rev. Eliphalet Nott, President of Union College, who not only conceived the idea, but, in connection with the Messrs. Brown, the New York bankers, constructed the Novelty expressly to test the principle. Dr. Nott was the inventor, early in the century, of a family stove, that came into universal use, and which was the pioneer of the base-burning stoves now so widely used.

I met with an accident in July of this year, which, while it did not incapacitate me for business, subjected me to inconvenience for several weeks. While in New York, I was invited by Mr. John F. Adriance to visit Macomb's Dam. Mr. Adriance drove a fast horse, a circumstance that I did not learn until it was too late. When clear of the city, upon the Bloomingdale Road, Mr. Adriance commenced what Commodore Vanderbilt, Mr. Bonner, and other gentlemen now call "speeding." We saw a cart some distance ahead, but, as there was plenty of roadway, nothing was apprehended until we approached within a few rods, when the cartman suddenly turned the head of his horse so as to bring the tail of his cart in contact with the wheels of our vehicle, throwing it over, and us out. I rose to find my arm seriously fractured at the wrist, with a feeling, not of regret, but of heartfelt gratitude that it was the left instead of the right arm, inasmuch as the right hand was available in editing my paper.

Being several miles away from a surgeon, the arm became so much swollen and inflamed that it was but imperfectly set, and never recovered its strength. Fortunately, however, the time when my livelihood required the use of both hands was passed, and the accident occasioned no serious consequences.

David Williams, the last survivor of the three captors of Major André, died at Rensselaerville in August of this year. I saw him on the 4th of July in Albany. He had been invited, along with other Revolutionary veterans, to grace the celebration. The soldiers of the Revolution, seated in barouches on such occasions, attracted the grateful attentions of thousands, who were enjoying the blessings which had been won by their patriotism and valor. Crowds followed Williams, anxious to hear him talk about the capture of André. I listened, with others, to his story, which he told quietly and modestly.

Vice-President Calhoun, in a letter to Mr. Symmes, of Charleston, S. C., avowed himself in favor of the right of the States to nullify the laws of the United States. This was the beginning of the end, taking successively the forms of nullification, secession, and rebellion, and finally resulting in the overthrow of slavery. Mr. Calhoun, however, did not live to reap the bitter fruit of what he had sown, or to witness the desolation which his teachings brought upon his now ruined State and its impoverished people. What form of chastisement and remorse could exceed that which Calhoun, McDuffee, Hamilton, etc., would experience, were they now permitted to revisit South Carolina!

The Rev. Charles McIlvaine, of Brooklyn, was this year unanimously chosen successor to the late Bishop Chase, of Ohio. Although a very young man, he proved himself capable of an able and faithful discharge of the duties of his high office, which he continued to occupy so many years subsequently. In 1861, Bishop McIlvaine, in company with Archbishop Hughes and myself, went upon a semi-official mission to Europe.

CHAPTER XXXVI.

1831–1832.

NATIONAL ANTI-MASONIC CONVENTION AT BALTIMORE. — JUDGE MC-
LEAN. — NOMINATION OF WILLIAM WIRT AND AMOS ELLMAKER. —
CLAY AND SARGENT NOMINATED BY NATIONAL REPUBLICANS. — THE
LEGISLATURE OF 1832. — FRANCIS GRANGER. — YOUNG ATTORNEYS IN
1832.

THE National Anti-Masonic Convention met at Baltimore on
the 26th of September. Thirteen States were represented by
one hundred and fifteen delegates, among whom were Thaddeus
Stevens, William Heister of Pennsylvania, John Rutherford of
New Jersey, Jonathan Sloan of Ohio, William Sprague of
Rhode Island, John C. Spencer, William H. Seward, James
Burt, Henry Dana Ward, Gamaliel H. Barstow, James Wads-
worth, Myron Holley, Samuel Miles Hopkins, Timothy Childs,
George H. Boughton, James Geddes, David Russell, Samuel A.
Foot, and Nicholas Devereux of New York.

The convention met with John McLean, of Ohio, in view as
its candidate for President, that gentleman having previously
intimated to Albert H. Tracy and myself his willingness to
accept our nomination, in case there should be no other candidate against General Jackson. It became known, however,
before our convention assembled, that Mr. Clay had decided to
accept a nomination from the National Republican party.

We were consequently much embarrassed by the following
letter from Mr. McLean, received at Baltimore, declining our
nomination : —

NASHVILLE, *September* 7, 1831.

DEAR SIR, — As the time for the meeting of the convention at Baltimore is near, in pursuance of my promise, I have the honor to address
you on the subject of our conversation at Columbus. There are now
three candidates for the Presidency before the people. General Jackson, Mr. Clay, and Mr. Calhoun have all been nominated by their
friends in public meetings and otherwise, and they must consequently be
considered as competitors for that distinguished station. The addition

of a fourth name to the list of candidates, and especially one as humble as mine, might lead, in so far as any influence could be attached to it, to distract still more the public mind. This I do not wish to see, as I fear it would be injurious to the best interests of the country.

If by a multiplication of candidates an election by the people should be prevented I should consider it a national misfortune. In the present agitated state of the public mind, an individual who should be elected to the chief magistracy by less than a majority of the votes of the people, could scarcely hope to conduct successfully the business of the nation. He should possess in advance the public confidence ; and a majority of the suffrages of the people is the only satisfactory evidence of that confidence. My situation on the bench imposes considerations of prudence and delicacy which do not arise, perhaps, from any other official station. Whilst no man can deny the right of the people to select their chief magistrates from any of the branches of the government, it would seem that a member of the judiciary should decline the contest, unless the use of his name would be likely to tranquilize the public mind and advance the prosperity of the country. Without presuming that my name would be favorably considered by the convention, I have to request that, if it should come under consideration, you will make known the reasons why I most respectfully decline the honor of being presented to that respectable body for nomination to the presidency.

I would do injustice to my feelings if I were not to tender to my friends in the convention my warmest gratitude for their favorable consideration, and to assure them that I shall never cease to cherish the recollection of their good opinion.

With sentiments of the highest regard, I am, dear sir, truly yours,

JOHN McLEAN.

Immediately after the organization of the convention a resolution was adopted inviting the Hon. Charles Carroll of Carrollton, signer of the Declaration of Independence, Chief Justice Marshall, and the Hon. William Wirt, to take seats in the convention. Mr. Carroll, who resided a few miles out of the city, was unable to attend, but, greatly to our gratification, the Chief Justice and the late Attorney General of the United States came into the convention, and took seats by the side of the president.

After the adjournment, accompanied by John C. Spencer, Albert H. Tracy, and Dr. Abner Phelps, of Boston, I called upon Mr. Wirt, whom we found not only in cordial sympathy with our principles, but who finally consented to the use of his name as a candidate for president. We returned in high spirits to announce the result of the visit to our anxious and impatient colleagues, most of whom rejoiced to learn that a gentleman so distinguished had consented to become our standard bearer. Thaddeus Stevens and a few others hesitated at first, but the nomination was made unanimous ; and after the nomination of Amos Ellmaker, of Pennsylvania, for vice-president, the convention adjourned, highly gratified with the result of its deliberations.

Mr. Wirt's name, as was anticipated, imparted zeal and strength to our cause, and while under the circumstances which followed no hope of success was entertained, Anti-Masons everywhere proved themselves loyal to their principles and their ticket.

The nomination of Mr. Clay, with John Sargent, of Philadelphia, for vice-president, thus dividing the opponents of the administration, rendered the reëlection of General Jackson certain.

Nothing daunted by these untoward circumstances, the respective friends of Mr. Clay and Mr. Wirt conducted the canvass with all the zeal and energy which a reasonable chance of success could have imparted. The friends of Mr. Clay, indeed, not only worked hard, but evinced their confidence by betting freely on his election.

In the legislature of 1832 there was a strong Jackson or Democratic majority in both branches. In the Senate the National Republican party had no representative, while in the Assembly the Hon. John A. King, of Queens County, as a National Republican stood " solitary and alone," as Colonel Benton said of himself when he began to roll the " expunging " ball. There were seven Anti-Masonic members of the Senate, and thirty-one Anti-Masonic members of the Assembly, whose vote Francis Granger received for speaker.

The successful candidate for that office was Charles L. Livingston, of New York, a youthful but most accomplished gentleman, who in the discharge of his duties displayed remarkable parliamentary ability. Never, during my long acquaintance with legislation, was there a more dignified, courteous, and popular presiding officer.

Mr. Granger, who commenced his legislative career in 1826,

was also, like Mr. Livingston, a gentleman of accomplished manners, genial temperament, and fine presence, with fortune, leisure, and a taste for public life. Mr. Granger looked forward with reasonable anticipations to political distinction. His eminent father, Gideon Granger, was appointed postmaster-general by Jefferson in 1802, and continued in office by Madison until 1814, when, upon leaving the cabinet, he changed his residence from Suffield in Connecticut to Canandaigua in this State. Francis Granger, therefore, had breathed a political atmosphere from his youth upward. He sought to rise by an earnest and honest discharge of the duties of the various offices which he occupied, rather than by scheming or management. My relations with Mr. Granger, personal and social, were intimate, confidential, and undisturbed for nearly half a century. Politically we differed on a single occasion, namely, in 1856, when the Republican party became a national organization. Then, declining to take part in that organization, his public life ended. He was a member of the legislature five years. In 1830 he was a candidate for governor against Enos T. Throop, and defeated by a majority of eight thousand.

In 1832 he was again a candidate against William L. Marcy, and defeated by a majority of nearly ten thousand. He was elected to Congress in 1834, and again elected in 1838, but resigned in 1841 to accept the place in General Harrison's cabinet which had been occupied by his father under Presidents Jefferson and Madison.

Mr. Granger was a man of much general intelligence and fine conversational powers. He frequented the best literary and social circles in Washington, New York, Boston, Albany, etc. He passed several weeks at Saratoga every season for more than fifty years.

At the January term of the Supreme Court, 1832, several gentlemen, who were subsequently distinguished in public life, were admitted to practice as attorneys or counselors. Prominent among them were Henry Bennett of Chenango, John V. L. Pruyn of Albany, Horatio Seymour of Oneida, and James S. Wadsworth of Geneseo, as attorneys; Amos Dean, John McKeon, and John A. Dix, among the counselors.

CHAPTER XXXVII.

1814–1839.

THE following retrospective letter, though written in 1866, seems entitled to a place with the period to which it refers : —

There is a very valuable, but little known book, entitled "The Civil List." It contains the names of all the State and county officers from the establishment of our colonial government. In looking it over, as I do very often, it occurred to me that the present citizens of New York might be interested in knowing who and what manner of men represented the city in the legislature fifty years ago. In 1814, fifty-two years ago, our senators were Peter W. Radcliffe and Nathan Sandford, the first being afterward mayor of the city, and the latter United States senator and chancellor, and both long since deceased. The Assembly delegation in 1814 was Federal in politics, and consisted of able men, the only survivor of whom is Charles King, recently president of Columbia College, and now passing the winter with his family in Rome, his son, General Rufus King, being American minister there. Mr. King was then a young, ardent, dashing member. Among his colleagues were Samuel Jones, Jr., long chief justice, Josiah Ogden Hoffman, afterwards recorder, and Richard Hatfield, Jr., a brilliant young lawyer. Mr. Hatfield was long remembered socially for his remarkably effective imitations of orators. At dinners he would repeat extracts from Bishop Hobart, Rev. John Mason, and Thomas Addis Emmett, with such perfect resemblance in voice, emphasis, and gesture as to surprise and amuse even those who were thus taken off. Among others were Jacob Lorillard, the wealthy tobacconist, David B. Ogden, a distinguished lawyer and most estimable man, Elisha W. King, a highly respectable lawyer, and Gabriel Furman. In 1815 the Republicans

carried the city, electing such men as Francis Cooper, Jacob
Drake (a wealthy butcher), Ogden Edwards (a relative of
Aaron Burr), a moderate lawyer, who obtained an unenviable
notoriety by *hissing* (I do not remember whom) while a member was speaking. This was Peter Sharpe's first year. Mr.
Sharpe was a Maiden Lane whip-maker, of the average intelligence of a mechanic, who was reëlected six successive years, and
closed his legislative career as speaker. Isaac Pierson, a most
patriotic, upright man and useful legislator, was a wealthy iron
merchant. He was to be seen every Sunday with his large family at Rev. Dr. Mitchell's Universalist Church. Peter Stagg,
of the old third ward stock, was in the House that year.
George Warner and Joseph Smith were men remarkable for
their great personal popularity. They were elected two or three
times to the legislature from the Democratic ticket when all the
others chosen were Federalists. They were well known Meth-
odists, and were voted for by that large class of electors, irrespective of party. They were constant exhorters at the Methodist Church in Division Street, Albany. In 1816 the Federalists again carried the city, electing such men as Peter A. Jay
(son of Governor John Jay), who was an enlightened but not
brilliant lawyer, mingling but little in debate, but clear and logical. He was a good rather than a great man. Philip Brasher
(better known as "Alderman Phil") was an educated and well-
informed man, with no taste for speaking, — probably because
he had no talent for it. He lost no opportunity to manifest
his contempt for buncombe speeches. He was, as Falstaff described himself, a "great fat man," who "walked as one who
had gyves between his legs." Though not a large eater, he
had the reputation of one. He was fastidious at game and
wine, but partook of neither immoderately. Edward W. Laight
was a militia general and popular with the military. Samuel
Whittemore was, I believe, a real estate man in "the village,"
as most of the ninth ward was then called. Of Joseph Bag-
ley, Augustus Wyncoop, and Andrew Morris I remember nothing. Messrs. Warner (or "Slater Warner," as some called
him) and Smith were members of this House. The House of
Assembly was organized this year, after a protracted and exciting conflict. Indeed, during the half century that I have
been familiar with legislation, on one occasion only (in 1824)

have I witnessed such a struggle. The year 1817 brought fresh elements to the Assembly. The Republican ticket, which was chosen, was headed by Henry Eckford, ship-builder. He was a man like William H. Webb, of great enterprise and public spirit. This year brought Clarkson Crolius into the House. He was a very wordy man, who seemed to think that, coming from the great metropolis, he was necessarily great himself. In speaking he had a ludicrous way of pursing and protruding his lips. He was, however, an inflexibly honest, straightforward man. Cornelius Heeny, an Irishman and a gentleman, was then a member, and one who possessed all the genial qualities of his native isle. John F. Irving, a lawyer, and brother of the late Washington Irving, was a finished gentleman, of solid rather than showy talents. John L. Lawrence, though highly respectable, did not make his mark. Of Samuel B. Romaine and Peter Sharpe I have already spoken. They, with Messrs. George Warner, Joseph Smith, and Asa Mann, a lumber merchant, I believe, made up the delegation. Mr. Heeny died twenty or more years since, leaving a large estate, principally to Catholic charities. The bulk of it was acquired in this wise. He loaned $1,000 to a mechanic, who, finding himself unable to repay the money, conveyed certain real estate to his creditor, which, though then scarcely worth the money borrowed, ultimately proved of great value, making Mr. Heeny a rich man. Mr. Heeny was a man of rare humor. His wit was remembered and talked of at Albany long years after his retirement. I remember one of his pleasant hits. He was enjoying his whisky punch (a national taste) with some of his friends when his colleague, Mr. Crolius, came in. " I was just saying, ' Croli,' " said Mr. Heeny, " that our constituents were fools to send such members as we are to legislate for them." " I do not agree with you, sir. I certainly understand the business of my constituents," replied Mr. Crolius. " No more of that nonsense, Croli. *You* a legislator! Why, man, you do not understand your own business." This piqued Mr. Crolius, who said, " Sir, I am master of my business, and have made a competency out of it." " Now," says Mr. Heeny, " I will prove that you don't know your business, and that if you have made money it was because you were born to good luck. You are a potter baker. Tell me, now, on which side of a jug would you place

the handle?" "Why," said Mr. Crolius, "that is an absurd
question. It is immaterial on which side it is placed." "There,
now!" exclaimed Mr. Heeny, triumphantly; "did n't I tell you,
Croli, you were a humbug! You would put the handle of a
jug on the *inside*, would ye?"

In 1818 the city was ably represented. The delegation was
headed by Cadwallader D. Colden, a gentleman of good talents,
fine person, and courtly manners. Robert B. Hunter was a
dapper gentleman, who was for many subsequent years, I believe, consul to Hull, in England. Henry Meigs was an aspiring politician. Isaac Pierson and Samuel Tooker, both wealthy
merchants, were excellent members. John Morse was a man of
small stature and quiet habits, possessing many elements of legislative usefulness. He was industrious, clear-headed, and honest. Messrs. Heeny, Crolius, and Sharpe were here again; and
in this Assembly a young man, whose subsequent life has fulfilled all the promises of his youth, appeared in the legislative
hall, — Michael Ulshoeffer. He was an unfrequent but effective speaker, always firm and always courteous. Few men have
discharged legislative duties more usefully to their constituents,
or more creditably to themselves. Mr. Ulshoeffer survives, respected and honored, as he deserves to be. In looking over the
list, I discover one or two more of the one hundred and twenty-
eight members now living. The Hon. Aaron Hackley, then a
member from Herkimer, now resides in this city; and I believe
that David C. Judson, of St. Lawrence, is living.

The Assembly of 1818 was full of distinguished men. Albany sent William A. Duer and Stephen Van Rensselaer;
William B. Rochester came from Steuben; Erastus Root, from
Delaware; and Thomas J. Oakley, from Dutchess County. An
incident occurred during the session which effectually squelched
a young and rising member from Seneca County. Lieutenant-
Governor Taylor invited Mr. Thompson to dinner. Mr. Thompson declined the invitation, requesting the Lieutenant-Governor
to give the value of the dinner which he declined "to the poor."
Governor Taylor sent Mr. Thompson fifty cents, requesting him
to become his own almoner. Unfortunately for Mr. Thompson,
everybody knew that Governor Taylor needed no such prompting, for, like "the fine old English gentleman" who feasted
the rich, "he ne'er forgot the poor." That letter brought As-
semblyman Thompson "to grief."

In 1819, most of the delegation of 1818 was reëlected. John F. Irving, Samuel B. Romaine, and Richard Hatfield reappeared. John I. Morgan, a man of good practical ability, was a member. Governor Dix is son-in-law to Mr. Morgan. Alexander Hamilton, son of the eminent statesman, was a member of this House. John A. King (every inch a king, and long may he live in health and happiness!) was a member from Queens. To the Assembly of 1820 the same members were reëlected, and nothing, as I remember, worthy of remark occurred in the delegation. Samuel Young, a member of that Assembly, became a distinguished man in after years, as did Judge Charles H. Ruggles, James McKown, Jonas Earll, Henry Seymour, William Nelson, etc., etc. What was intended as a passing pleasantry proved a serious annoyance to the clerk of the House (Aaron Clark) all his subsequent life. There was a sort of three-cornered canvass for speaker, General Root, Mr. Romaine, and John C. Spencer being the candidates. Mr. Clark, who had been clerk for four years previous, was an anxious candidate for reëlection. Between the three rivals for speaker the clerk was in a fix. The day before the legislature convened, what professed to be "intercepted letters" appeared in an Albany paper. They were addressed to the three candidates for speaker, proffering support to each, and giving each a dig. Mr. Clark's style was so cleverly imitated that the letters created considerable amusement. But the end of the laugh did not "trammel up" the consequences of the joke. Mr. Clark removed to this city and opened a lottery office, then a great business not unlawfully followed. Then, as now, nothing paid so well as dashing, spirited advertising. Mr. Clark saw this, and filled the newspapers, inviting attention to "Clark's Wheel of Fortune," "Clark's Lucky Star," "Clark's Golden Numbers," etc., etc. His rival lottery ticket venders exhumed his alleged Albany letters, professing devoted zeal for three candidates for speaker. This both annoyed and damaged him. But worse than this, "in the course of human events" Mr. Clark became a candidate for mayor of New York; and now the letters were brought out by the Tammany Hall Press. By this time they had become in the public mind veritable letters. And then, the joke having been carried too far, the culprit who wrote them relieved Mr. Clark from injustice and persecution by publicly confessing himself the author.

The Assembly of 1821 was honored by the election of one of New York's "favorite sons," Gulian C. Verplanck, a really great and good man. Mr. Verplanck, "a scholar and a gentleman," was eminent as a statesman and jurist, and distinguished himself in the latter capacity greatly by his opinions in the Court for the Correction of Errors. Though unknown to Mr. Verplanck then, I made his acquaintance years later, when he was in the Senate, and have sat ever since with intense edification at the feet of this literary Gamaliel, deriving instruction and strength from his thorough knowledge of books and men. Judge Ulshoeffer was a colleague of Mr. Verplanck's, as were Messrs. Heeny, Crolius, Sharpe, Romaine, etc., John Swartwout, brother of "Sam" and "Bob," as the general and collector were familiarly called. Mr. Swartwout was a large, showy man, who wore powder and limped. Mr. McDonald, the barber, furnished the hair powder, but the limp came from powder that lodged a ball in his knee from the pistol of Governor Clinton, with whom Mr. Swartwout "exchanged shots." William A. Davis and Reuben Munson were members. I believe Mr. Davis was a stationer, and brother of Matthew L. Davis. There were legislative "giants" in those days, and in this Assembly, namely, Elisha Williams, Erastus Root, John C. Spencer, Myron Holley, etc. Samuel B. Romaine was Speaker of the Assembly in 1822, Peter Sharpe, Speaker of the previous House, having been, I believe, elected to Congress. Junius M. Hatch, a young lawyer, and Jeromas Johnson, were new members. Messrs. Verplanck and Ulshoeffer were again members.

With the legislature of 1823 the Amended Constitution took effect. Its two sessions were important and exciting. The city of New York, under the new order of things, sent new men to the Assembly. Samuel S. Gardiner, who had been secretary of the constitutional convention, came to the Assembly. He was a gentleman of fair ability and refined manners. He was a younger brother of David Gardiner, a Senator from Long Island, whose daughter married "Captain Tyler." Gideon Lee, a wealthy man from the Swamp, who was subsequently mayor, was then in the Assembly. Mr. Lee removed to Geneva, where he died many years ago. Jesse Hoyt, subsequently collector, whose genial nature has not been soured either by time or adversity, made his *début* in this Assembly. John Rathbone, Jr.,

William A. Thompson (who survives), and Thomas Hyatt were members of the old régime. Messrs. Verplanck, Brasher, and Morse remained. This Assembly was distinguished for its practical good sense. It had some brilliant and many sound members. Peter R. Livingston was Speaker. Among the best practical legislators were Jesse Buel, of Albany; Victory Birdseye, of Onondaga; James Mullet, of Chautauqua; and Azariah C. Flagg (subsequently city and state comptroller), now blind, but in full possession of all his other faculties; calm under his great deprivation, even cheerful. For his affliction there is compensation, for he can turn his thoughts back upon long years of usefulness. Mr. Flagg, when elected to the Assembly, was editor of the "Republican" at Plattsburg; he now resides in London Terrace, Twenty-third Street. Eben F. Norton, of Erie, an unknown but clever lawyer, was a humorist. Early in the session, the Speaker (Peter R. Livingston), whose remarkably effective voice and manner commanded great attention, desiring to impress the House with a sense of the dignity of the constitutional convention, thus commenced speaking: "Mr. Chairman: I had the honor to preside over the solemn deliberations of the convention which amended our State Constitution. Sir, that convention was an august body." Mr. Norton rose and said, "Will the honorable Speaker allow me to correct him? The constitutional convention over which the venerable Speaker presided so ably met in *September* instead of *August*." The House was convulsed with laughter, and Mr. Livingston got no further with his speech. At the moment, Mr. Livingston attributed Mr. Norton's remark to ignorance instead of waggery.

The year 1824 produced another change in the New York delegation. Messrs. Crolius, Gardiner, Pierson, Morse, and Hyatt were reëlected. General James Benedict, a Maiden Lane jeweler and an excellent man, came in. Jacob Drake, another worthy man, was a member. Charles Town, an auctioneer and an accomplished gentleman, with David Seaman and Henry Wheaton, completed the delegation. This was a memorable legislature, in which the great struggle for president between Adams and Crawford occurred. Presidential electors were then chosen by the legislature. Three sessions were held, all exciting and stormy. Its history will be found in another chapter. On the question of restoring directly to the people the choice of electors, Messrs. Wheaton, Crolius, Pierson, Morse, Town, Seaman, Drake, and Benedict broke away from Tammany Hall and Mr. Van Buren, and went with the Adams men. General Tallmadge, of Dutchess, was the Adams leader. Mr. Flagg led the Van Buren party. The Assembly of 1824 was full of talent. The great questions which agitated it and the people brought out and tested men. Samuel J. Wilkin, then a young man of much promise, died in 1866. In looking over the list, I find but few survivors. John F. Hubbard, a printer, of Chenango County ; Oran Follett, printer, of Genesee County ; A. C. Flagg, printer, of Clinton ; C. P. Bellinger, of Herkimer, are, I believe, the only survivors.

In 1825, a political tornado swept through the State, utterly demolishing the Van Buren or Democratic party. The New York delegation consisted of James Benedict, Gilbert Coutant, Clarkson Crolius, Maltby Geltson, Samuel L. Gouverneur, John Morse, Jonathan E. Robinson, David Seaman, Ira B. Wheeler, and George Zabriskie. Mr. Gouverneur, a son-in-law of President Monroe, was a brilliant, impassioned speaker. He was upright, patriotic, genial, and popular. He was subsequently postmaster in this city, and died, where he had long resided, in Virginia ; dying as he had lived, faithful to the Union. Several members of this House (then young men) rose to eminence, among whom were Ambrose L. Jordan and Samuel Stevens, distinguished lawyers: the former residing, when he died, in this city, and the latter in Albany. Mr. Verplanck, while he was in the Court for the Correction of Errors, remarked to me that Mr. Stevens was always better prepared for the argument of his cases than any lawyer in the State. Herman J. Quackenboss, a member from Delaware County, has had the singular experience of representing three different constituencies in the Assembly : first from Delaware, then from Greene, and afterward from New York. He was also four years in the Senate from Greene and Delaware. Mr. Quackenboss, now an old man, resides in Elizabeth, N. J. In 1826 the State relapsed, the Democracy carrying the Assembly by a large majority. The city delegation was divided politically. Stephen Allen then made his first appearance in the legislature. Mr. Allen was a self-made man, with a clear head and sound heart. He brought industry, intelligence, and integrity with him into the Assembly, leaving a good record behind him. Mr. Allen, though cold and stern in look and manner, relaxed and warmed in conversation. He enjoyed quiet, cosy evenings with a friend over a single glass of toddy. How pleasantly the remembrance of those social evenings at Cruttenden's comes back over the chasm of dead and buried years! Mr. Cruttenden was of a refined, cultivated, genial nature. At his table all the intellectually great assembled. Its history — its after-dinner conversations, rich, racy, and sparkling — should have been preserved. Mr. Cruttenden himself was the impersonation of classical humor. Good things dropped from his lips without effort. One evening I was sitting with Mr. Granger and Mr. Cruttenden. The former remarked that many succeeded by using " soft soap " freely. " Yes," replied Mr. Cruttenden, " but it is in bad *taste,* — there is too much *lie* in it." Stephen Allen and his wife lost their lives by the burning of the steamer Henry Clay off Yonkers. Alderman Brasher was again at Albany, enjoying at the table of that prince of hosts, Mr. Cruttenden, his soup, his sherry, his venison, and his jokes. Elisha W. King was then in the delegation along with Francis Cooper. Aaron Vanderpoel, then of Columbia, now of this city, came into public life with this legislature. General Root was reëlected.

Alexander Sheldon, who had been speaker twenty years earlier, was also in this House. Francis Granger came also first into the legislature in 1826. He was almost the first man elected in this State after the Southern mode of self-nomination. He has since served in the legislature and in Congress. He was postmaster-general under General Harrison, as his father was under Mr. Madison. Than Francis Granger the people never had a more enlightened, upright, or patriotic representative.

In 1827 the New York delegation had quite a show of new men, such as Abraham Cargill, Jonathan I. Coddington, Gilbert Coutant, Joseph Piggot, Alpheus Sherman (afterwards Senator), and Thomas R. Smith. Major Smith was a handsome, dashing, amiable man, who has resided for more than forty-five years in Washington. I knew him first as an officer of marines at Sackett's Harbor in 1814. Alderman Brasher and Charles Town were in this House. The alderman owned land in St. Lawrence County, where a town took his name. He visited St. Lawrence in summer, and on one occasion, while driving in his gig on the Canadian shore, a rough-looking chap on a French pony, bare-back, with a rope halter, rode up by the side of the chaise, and accosted the alderman thus : " How are you, alderman ? " " Very well, sir. Good morning." " I am in no hurry. When are you going to pass a law abolishing imprisonment for stealing ? " " Why do you care about such a law ? " " Because I want to visit my friends." " Where are you from ? " " From the States." " Which State ? " - " From the State Prison in Vermont last." " Well," replied the alderman, " you are an original. But how did you know me ? " " How did I know *you*, Phil Brasher? Why I should know your hide in a tan-yard. Good-by, Phil. When you get to New York tell Old Hays I shall be down on him for injuring my character. I'm not the man to be accused of *petty* larceny."

The New York delegation was reconstructed in 1828. Two marked men came in, namely, Ogden Hoffman and Robert Emmett. We all know what an eloquent, brilliant man Ogden Hoffman was. He now sat in the seat his father occupied in 1791, and for five successive years. Mr. Emmett was a son of Thomas Addis Emmett, and a most accomplished man, — radiant, genial, and mirthful. Samuel Alley, a tall, slim man, strikingly like Henry Clay, was in this House, as was Alderman Shrivers Parker, with Messrs. Al. Burtis, Cargill, Isaac Dyckman, and Samuel Smith. Several members of this House became prominent men, namely, Benjamin F. Butler of Albany, Abijah Mann, Jr., of Herkimer, N. P. Tallmadge of Dutchess, Luther Bradish of Franklin, A. C. Paige of Schenectady, B. P. Johnson of Oneida, and Trumbull Cary of Genesee. Elisha Williams and Francis Granger were in this House. General Root was speaker.

There was a strong infusion of new elements of character in the delegation of 1829. There was more of *individuality* than usual. Mordecai Myers, who was a captain of the Thirteenth United States Infantry in the war of 1812, was a short, thickset man, reasonably capable and very complacent. Peter S. Titus, who had been an alderman, was a large bland gentleman of excellent character, with good sense and integrity. Nathan T. Arnold, a small dry-goods merchant from Greenwich Street,

was a pleasant, active, social man. Aaron O. Dayton, a lawyer, was a sort of "singed cat," worth more in ability than he
seemed. Though showing decided talent, I believe he subsided
into a department clerkship. John Van Buren (not the
"prince") was a pompous man, his speeches "full of sound
and fury, signifying nothing." On one occasion, after a flourishing preface to a resolution he was about to offer, he thus
addressed a page : "Ganymede, convey this missive to the
Speaker's rostrum." But the jewel of the delegation was Charles
L. Livingston, a frank, generous, and really chivalrous gentleman. With the advantages of an attractive person, high cultivation, and popular manners, he immediately became the favorite of the House, of which, in 1839, he was chosen speaker
(making a most capable presiding officer), from which he was
transferred to the Senate. As a legislator, politician, and
friend, Charles L. Livingston was as true as steel or flint. An
incident illustrates his character. In this House a western
member of some notoriety, of whom Mr. Livingston thought
ill, drew a seat next to him. Finding himself with an obnoxious neighbor, Mr. Livingston walked off, making propositions
to exchange with several members, who, apparently for the
same reason, declined ; but he finally found a member in an
inconvenient back seat, who for ten dollars consented to sit by
the obnoxious individual. The seat which Mr. Livingston vacated was one of the best in the House. Some days afterward
Mr. Livingston and the member referred to were placed upon
a select committee relating to "mock auctions." Mr. Livingston at first intended to decline, but as this was quite inconsistent with his sense of duty, he submitted. The committee
was called together in the evening at Mr. Livingston's apartments at "Cruttenden's." From "labor" the committee was
invited to "refreshments," always bountiful where C. L. Livingston was concerned. The obnoxious member quietly declined
the chairman's hospitalities. The committee was convened
again at Mr. Livingston's rooms, and another sumptuous board
was spread, of which *all* were so cordially urged to partake
that the invitation was accepted.

On the following day Mr. Livingston paid twenty-five dollars to get back his original seat, and a friendship grew up
between them the sweet remembrance of which brightens the

declining years of the writer of this article, who, as will be conjectured, was the member " first hated, then endured, and then embraced."

During all this period legislative action was marked, with exceptions few and far between, by honesty and integrity. The principles and habits of the earlier and better days of the government had not yet been lost or weakened by influences which subsequently obtained. Legislation was simple and inexpensive. Instead of the army of subordinates that now crowd the legislative halls, the Senate and Assembly found no difficulty in dispatching the public business in the appointment by each House of a clerk, a deputy clerk, a sergeant-at-arms, a doorkeeper, an assistant doorkeeper, and a fireman. Up to 1826 there were neither postmasters, librarians, messengers, nor pages.

The session of 1830 added two or three remarkable men to the New York delegation. Messrs. Livingston, Titus, etc., were reëlected. The delegation was divided politically, a " Workingmen's party " having helped the Whigs to elect Silas M. Stilwell, Gideon Tucker, Ebenezer Ford, and, I believe, George Curtis, a brother of Edward Curtis, who was afterward member of Congress, collector, and intimate friend of Mr. Webster. Silas M. Stilwell was an industrious, ambitious member, who spoke much and wrote more. His elaborate reports on abolishing imprisonment for debt, internal improvements, etc., were compilations evincing patient research. His manner and style of speaking and writing at first were far from faultless, but he determined to improve, and did improve. He was, in 1834, a candidate of the Whig party for lieutenant-governor. Dennis McCarty was, as his name clearly indicates, an Irishman. He was more, — he was, not merely in parliamentary language, but literally, an honorable gentleman. Like his Irish predecessor, Mr. Heeny, Mr. McCarty was genial and liked his joke at dinner, but was very grave and dignified in the Assembly. While at Albany the first idea of temperance for Irishmen was suggested, and a meeting was held to promote the object one evening in the large octagon room of the Eagle Tavern, where Mr. McCarty boarded. Several Catholic clergymen were present. The late Nicholas Devereux, of Utica, took the lead. The evils of intemperance, to which so many Irishmen fell victims, were glowingly presented. All concurred heartily in the movement; but, as they were breaking up, servants came in with a steaming bowl of hot whiskey punch. Several earnest appeals were made to Mr. McCarty to send it back; but he replied, " It's quite out of the question; you would make me commit a breach of hospitality. It's the bad liquor the poor creatures poison themselves with that should be reformed. You are forgetting that an Irishman lost his life by refusing his drink! Let us teach temperance by precept." The temptation was too strong for Irishmen. The whiskey punch conquered, and temperance was postponed for many years. Francis Granger and Luther Bradish were members of this Assembly. Philo C. Fuller, subsequently senator, member of Congress, and comptroller, came first into public life in 1830. The only changes in the New York delegation in 1831 were Nathaniel Jarvis, Dudley Selden, and Isaac L. Varian. Mr. Jarvis was a large man, with strong common sense. Mr. Selden was a brilliant man in his profession and as a legislator. He died in Paris, where his widow subsequently died. Mr. Varian was a self-made man, than whom there are none better. He had been alderman, and became mayor of New York, discharging every duty with integrity; but he had little respect for the King's English. His spelling was very arbitrary. Here is a specimen: " Mr. Varian gives notis that he will, on some futer day, introduse a bill to mend the Law relative to the Inspection of Flower in the City of New York." John C. Spencer was a member of this Assembly. The largest man in the House was Coe S. Downing, of Brooklyn. Colonel Stone of the " Commercial Advertiser " indicated him as " the gentleman with a broad transom." George R. Davis, of Troy, was a member. He had been a Federal member of a former House, and did not always work easy in his Democratic harness. One day, after *balking* a little, he came to me (I was reporting for my journal), and said: " I am losing caste with the Regency. Won't you blow me up?" I did him that favor, and the next day he came round to say that he was " all right now," but he added, " Give me another dig when you have a good opportunity." We never meet without a pleasant reminder of old times.

Several new men came to the Assembly from New York in 1832. Charles L. Livingston was speaker. Judah Hammond, a heavy-bearded, solemn man, Philip E. Mildollar, Myndert Van Schaick, a worthy Albany Dutchman of large fortune, who died recently on the corner of Fifth Avenue and Fourteenth Street, and John McKeon, a young lawyer of much promise (older now, but always buoyant and genial), were in this House. Mr. Granger was again a member. So was George W. Patterson, of Livingston, who served with honor and usefulness for several years as a member, and who presided as speaker and lieutenant-governor over both Houses. It would be well for the State if it had more representatives like George W. Patterson, or, when they find such, that they were kept constantly in the public service. Men like Lieutenant-Governor Patterson create an honest atmosphere. Their presence rebukes corruption. How legislation has degenerated!

There was a large infusion of new men from New York in 1833 and 1834. Richard Cromwell (fast Quaker, but good man), a dry goods merchant of the ninth ward ; Thomas Hertell, a worthy man, but a follower of "Tom Paine ; " Benjamin Ringgold, from Tammany Hall, and Minthorne Tompkins, a son of Governor Tompkins, were new members. Charles L. Livingston was again speaker.

In the Assembly of 1834 there was a majority of new men. Among them were Messrs. Degraw, Dusenbury, and Hone. Mr. Hertell was a teacher of atheism, but a man of integrity and good morals. His great mission was to abolish clergymen, and he finally succeeded in getting a resolution adopted refusing to pay them for opening the sessions with prayer. But the clergy beat him by officiating without pay. Mr. McKeon was a youthful, gentlemanly, useful member. " Ben " Ringgold was a burly, wolfish-looking, but a genial man, representing the " Pewter Mug." Everybody liked him. R. H. Morris was an energetic, driving member, who subsequently became recorder and mayor.

In 1835 the New York delegation was strangely constituted, men of "various colors" politically, and of diversified character, being mixed up, some of whom were elected on the Tammany, and others on the " Workingmen's Ticket." Of the latter were Thomas Hertell and Job Haskell, a carman. Job was inflated with his success, and tried to be a reformer, but failed. The Tammany men were Andrew C. Wheeler, Prosper M.

Wetmore, James I. Roosevelt, Jr., Benjamin Ringgold, Christopher C. Rice, H. I. Quackenboss, Thomas N. Carr, Charles Henry Hall, and Charles P. Clinch. The character and careers of most of these gentlemen, some of whom survive, are known; not now youthful and dashing, but with work in them yet. General Wetmore was a favorite of the late Governor Marcy. Mr. Roosevelt was often pitted in debate with Derick Sibley, a " rough hewer " from Rochester. Mr. Hall was a large real estate owner in Harlem, and brother of the late " Prescott Hall." C. C. Rice was an Irishman, with counselor Phillips' manner in a small way. He afterwards was, I believe, a purser in the navy. Charles P. Clinch, for many years deputy and acting collector of the port, was and is " a gentleman and a scholar." He was associated with Halleck, Dr. Drake, and other literary celebrities of that day. He indulged the poetic humor occasionally, when in the Assembly. Among other efforts was a dramatic description of the prominent members of the legislature. I remember the couplet for his close friend " Charlie Livingston," who was then in the Senate: —

> " Do, pray, of Charles Livingston make a *stock actor!*
> He plays ' Nature's Nobleman ' all the year round."

Tammany Hall sent a full delegation to the Assembly in 1835, headed by Mr. Clinch. Messrs. Wetmore, Ringgold, and Hertell were also reëlected. Of the new members, Francis B. Cutting, then a distinguished lawyer, was an able, eloquent, and upright legislator. (In those days, legislative integrity was the rule, — now, unfortunately, the exception.) Ezra S. Connor was a printer, type-founder, and good man; Peter A. Cowdry was a respectable lawyer; John F. Morgan, an intelligent and respected gentleman; George Sharp, a genial, good fellow; Jesse West, a cooper, and a worthy man; Luther Bradish, Preston King, Richard P. Marvin, George P. Barker, and John Stryker, were members of that House.

In the Assembly of 1837 there was an odd mingling of men and politics. Democrats, Whigs, and Workingmen were sandwiched. Messrs. Clinch, Cutting, and Hertell were reëlected. The Whigs sent Morris Franklin, an amiable gentleman; Henry Andrew, a carpet merchant and well meaning man. John I. Labagh, James W. Tucker, George Zabriskie (a worthy Knickerbocker), Anson Willis (a schoolmaster), Robert Townsend, Jr., Clinton Roosevelt, Thomas G. Tallmadge, and J. I. M. Valentine, were in the delegation.

In 1838 a political hurricane sweeping through the State overwhelmed the Democratic party. It was the first signal defeat of the old " Albany Regency " since 1824. The New York Assembly delegation was composed of able but inexperienced men, first among whom was David B. Ogden (a member twenty years earlier), distinguished in his profession, mature in years, of irreproachable character, and with the advantage of a commanding person. There was but a sprinkling of Democratic members. Mr. Ogden, with all his talents, was confiding even to credulity, and as guileless as a child, but when roused was intellectually strong. Willis Hall came into public life with this legislature. He, as is known, was subsequently attorney general, and a man of much promise ; but his career was suddenly terminated by paralysis, from the effects of which he never recovered. Adoniram Chandler was a printer, and the second president of the New York Typographical Society. He was also president of the American Institute. Noah Cooke was a thorough politician, with great power for ward organizations and of indomitable will. He was a commission merchant. Samuel B. Ruggles, then a young man with bright prospects and high cultivation, was imbued deeply with the spirit of progress and an enthusiastic Erie Canal champion. His canal reports in the House, and afterwards as a canal commissioner, constitute a valuable portion of the archives of the State. But with all his talent and genius Mr. Ruggles was no speaker, and could not, when assailed, as he was frequently, defend himself. Mr. Benjamin F. Silliman, then a member from Brooklyn, in a letter to Judge William Kent, alluded to the fact that, when Mr. Ruggles was pitched into rough shod by Abijah Mann, he could not say a word for himself, sitting " dumb before his shearers." Judge Kent in reply said : " It is too bad that ' Samivel ' (Mr. Ruggles) cannot pay back blow for blow what he gets in debate. 'But Benjie,' *you* must speak for him, as a friend like *you*, did in a memorable case reported in the Book of Numbers, xxii. 28, 29, 30." Thus the joke was turned upon " Benjie," but we all had a good laugh over it. Mr. Silliman is now United States District Attorney, and, as ever, the " right man in the right place." Mr. Ruggles goes on his mission of progress, sometimes practically, sometimes "seeing visions," but always with laudable intentions.

This brings us down to the generation still extant. I have omitted many curious legislative incidents that might wound descendants of those to whom they relate. The moral to be drawn from all this is, that legislation and legislators have within thirty years become sadly demoralized. There is not in these times that high sense of official responsibility and legislative integrity that pervaded earlier legislation. Formerly the *suspicion* of corruption in a member would have put him "into Coventry," while knowledge of such an offense would have insured the expulsion of the offender. Now "bribery and corruption" prevail to an extent greater than existed in the worst days of the Parliament of England, where, happily for England, the practice has been reformed, as it must be here, or corruption will undermine the government. No measure, however meritorious, escapes the attention of "strikers." Venal members openly solicit appointment on paying committees. In the better days of legislation, when no unlawful motive existed, it was considered *indelicate* to indicate to the Speaker any preference about committees. The evil has been growing, each year being worse than the preceding, until reform is sternly demanded. Could the secret history of the legislature be exposed to the public gaze, popular indignation would be awakened to a degree heretofore unknown. In the Assembly everything is struck at. Not even a religious charity finds exemption. That there are honest and honorable members in both houses, by whose integrity and firmness much bad legislation is arrested, is true, but there should be discrimination. The black sheep should be rejected. Districts represented on the purchasable committees at least should send better men. But a physician who describes a disease should *prescribe* a remedy. In this case it is difficult. Insufficiency of compensation is one cause of legislative dishonesty. A member who receives from this State for his services less than is absolutely necessary to pay his expenses is wronged, and therefore subject to temptation. When three dollars per day was fixed in the convention as the limit, good board was obtained for five, six, and seven dollars per week. Now it costs to live respectably twenty, twenty-five, and thirty dollars per week. This is both unjust and unwise. And what was regarded as beneficial in respect to single Assembly districts has proved the reverse. It would be better any way to return to the general ticket system. With a reasonable compensation for legislative services, and the selection of members from counties instead of districts, we should have improved Houses of Assembly. Nor has the popular idea of brief terms for senators worked well. The Senate would be stronger, and more independent and useful, by enlarging the districts and extending the term to four years.

Joshua Dewey is the oldest surviving member of the House of Assembly. He represented Otsego County in 1798 and 1799. He resided, when I last heard from him, in Brooklyn. I think that James Powers, of Catskill, is the next oldest surviving member. He was later in life a member of the Senate, and still resides where I first knew him sixty-five years ago at Catskill. Of the senators up to 1822, when the Constitution was amended, I do not know a survivor unless it be David C. Judson, of St. Lawrence. Of the Senate of 1823, Herman J. Redfield, and I believe Alvin Bronson, survive.

CHAPTER XXXVIII.

1832.

AT the close of the second year of the "Evening Journal," the success of the enterprise, as will be seen by the following editorial announcement of March 22, 1832, was assured : —

The "Journal" this day closes its second volume. We have lived out our second year and enter upon the third, cheered with the reflection that our humble labors have been most kindly rewarded, and strengthened in the assurance that our paper has become permanently and firmly established.

And now, after a lapse of more than forty years, I look back upon that crisis in my history with grateful pride. Editorial life, always congenial, then possessed a peculiar interest for me.

Every day's labor brought me nearer to the realization of hopes which rendered the active duties of my position more a pleasure than a task. I was contending almost single-handed with a powerful and popular political majority, led by men distinguished for experience, tact, and ability.

I was constantly making friends and gathering strength for my party. The duties of an editor of a daily journal then imposed upon one person the combined labor now divided and subdivided among a numerous staff. I not only edited the paper without an assistant, but reported the proceedings of the Assembly and the courts. I rose early and awaited the arrival of the steamboat from New York, to obtain newspapers two

hours earlier than they were delivered at the post office. I
also visited before breakfast the principal hotels, picking up
such items as might be found there, and regularly, before going
to my breakfast, copy was furnished for each day's journal.
After breakfast, until the publication hour, two P. M., I labored
at my editorial table. I also assisted the foreman in making
up and putting the paper to press. Afternoons and evenings
I visited friends or places of amusement, and wrote letters and
notices of new books.

I was far more concerned about the success of the cause in
which I was engaged than for things personal. My own habits
were inexpensive, and those of my family still more frugal.
My salary for the first year was $750, upon which we lived
comfortably. The success of the paper enabled the publishers
to increase my second year's salary to $1,000.

With much that was encouraging and agreeable, there was
one incident connected with my removal to Albany that dis-
quieted me. The " Albany Daily Advertiser," a journal with
which I had been in political sympathy, was published and
edited by intimate personal friends, — friends with whom I had
been many years before associated as journeymen printers.
These friends, Messrs. James Hunter, Robert Martin, and Gerritt W. Ryckman, were prominent and zealous Freemasons.
My opposition to Masonry occasioned alienation even before I
left Rochester, and the establishment of the " Evening Journal " was, in the highest degree, antagonistic to their feelings
and interest. Indeed, the " Journal " could only prosper at the
expense of the " Daily Advertiser." I would gladly have
avoided this collision with much valued friends, but that was
impossible.

The establishment of the " Evening Journal " was a political
necessity, and it happened that the same necessity required that
I should take charge of it. The warfare waged upon me was
personal and bitter, but not of long duration, for in 1833 Messrs.
Hunter, Martin, and Ryckman sold the " Daily Advertiser " establishment to Messrs. Bloodgood and Van Schaick. Messrs.
Hunter and Martin have long been at rest; but before they
departed our old relations were reëstablished, and it was in my
power to be of service to them. Mr. Ryckman went more than
twenty years ago to California. In 1864, after an estrange-

ment of thirty years, I had the happiness to receive a letter from him in which nothing was remembered but the pleasant years which preceded our rivalry, when, as journeymen in Albany and New York, we were "pulling" together at the same press.

I had in 1818 passed much of my leisure time with James Hunter, — a journeyman who was indebted wholly to the opportunities which a printing-office afforded, first, for his education, and then for the acquirement of stores of useful information. He was apprenticed in his early boyhood, and, while acquiring the knowledge of his profession, used every leisure moment for intellectual improvement. I became warmly attached to him, and retained an agreeable remembrance of the many evenings and Sundays passed in conversation with him. When separated, we kept up a correspondence. His letters were alike interesting and useful, for he never lost an opportunity to teach a lesson or point a moral.

In 1830, for reasons explained elsewhere, we came into collision. But after years of separation, and before the death of Mr. Martin, Hunter and I were friends again.

The Anti-Masonic State Convention met at Utica on the 21st of June, and was strong in the number and character of its delegates. Albert H. Tracy, of Buffalo, was its president. Francis Granger, of Ontario, and Samuel Stevens, of New York, were unanimously nominated as its candidates for governor and lieutenant-governor. The convention concurred in the nomination of Wirt and Ellmaker for president and vice-president. An electoral ticket was formed with James Kent and John C. Spencer as electors at large. We aimed, in the selection of candidates, to secure the votes of all who were opposed to the reëlection of General Jackson. The National Republican State Convention soon followed, nominating Clay for president and John Sargent for vice-president, and adopting our State and electoral ticket. This subjected us to considerable embarrassment. We were styled by the Jackson men throughout the canvass the "Siamese Twin Party." The people were told that, of necessity, somebody would be cheated. There was much difficulty experienced in arranging local nominations, — a difficulty which rendered it necessary that an influential Clay man as well as a Wirt man should attend district and county conventions. That duty devolved upon Matthew L. Davis and myself. Our peregrinations throughout the State afforded the Jackson journals much amusement, and were more or less perplexing to ourselves. However discordant the materials with which we had to deal, we generally succeeded in harmonizing conflicting interests and opinions. I remember that when the Anti-Masonic and National Republican Conventions met at Sandy Hill, to nominate a candidate for senator for the fourth district, the feeling of mutual repugnance was so great as almost to forbid the hope of amalgamation. Mr. Davis and myself labored for two days without in the least softening the asperities which divided the two conventions. Unavailing efforts were made to agree upon a number of well-known and reputable men, supposed to be acceptable to both parties. Finally, the National Republicans, despairing of a union, nominated Louis Hasbrouck, of St. Lawrence, and adjourned without knowing or even suspecting that Mr. Hasbrouck's name had been suggested to Mr. Davis by a prominent Anti-Mason from Ogdensburg. The Anti-Masonic Convention, assuming in its resolution that Mr. Hasbrouck though a National Republican was not a Freemason, concurred in his nomination. He was cordially supported at the polls by both Clay and Wirt men and elected.

The State canvass, notwithstanding the embarrassment referred to, brought out a strong vote in favor of our ticket, which, however, was defeated by a majority of about 10,000. General Jackson was reëlected, receiving 219 of the electoral votes, Mr. Clay having 49, while the State of Vermont passed its 7 electoral votes for Wirt and Ellmaker.

Matthew L. Davis was a very remarkable man. He was a politician by nature, habits, and education. His friendships, personal and political, were strong and enduring. My acquaintance with him commenced in the great presidential campaign of 1824, he being a zealous Crawford man and I an equally zealous Adams man. But although strenuously opposed, so much of common sentiment and sympathy was developed that before the conflict ended we became personal friends ; and, that campaign over, were closely united, politically and socially, during the remainder of his life. When a young man Mr. Davis became warmly attached to Aaron Burr, to whom he remained faithfully devoted during all the vicissitudes of fortune through which that extraordinary man passed. Indeed, for more than forty years Colonel Burr had scarcely any other reliable friend. During his absence in Europe he corresponded only with his daughter and Mr. Davis, the latter being the only person who welcomed the return of the once popular Vice-President. Davis informed me that Colonel Burr's first inquiry on landing was for Mrs. Eden, a widow lady once happily and prosperously situated, but who had, during Burr's absence, supported herself and two daughters as a laundress. Colonel Burr's first professional service, after his return, was in bringing the well-known ejectment suit, which, after years of litigation, resulted in favor of the Misses Eden, who, as Mr. Davis informed me confidentially, were natural daughters of Colonel Burr.

Colonel Burr made Mr. Davis his literary executor, with the understanding that from the materials bequeathed to him a history of his life should be written. The confidential female correspondence of Colonel Burr constituted a large proportion of those materials, leaving Mr. Davis, so far as he understood the views of Burr, at liberty to make such use of those letters as he might think proper. The preservation of such letters, carefully filed, and when either anonymous or with initials having the full name of the writer indorsed, was an act of deliberate treachery and baseness, of which, happily for society, few human beings have been found capable. But Burr looked upon the matter with eyes, and from a standpoint, still more unnatural; for, on the evening before his duel with General Hamilton, in a letter written to his daughter, Mrs. Theodosia Allston, he bequeathed, in the event of his fall, these confidential letters to her, indicating the boxes in which they would be found, and instructing her to read them, and to burn all such as, if made public, would injure any person.

As however Hamilton, instead of Burr, fell, those letters were preserved from 1804 to 1836, and then bequeathed, without instruction, to Mr. Davis. For two or three years before Colonel Burr's death, I occasionally visited him in company with Mr. Davis, and, although generally reticent, he was sometimes drawn into conversation about early and interesting events, always in the morbid spirit of a disappointed man. His manner was quiet and subdued. Although seldom indulging

in bitterness of language, he never spoke approvingly of any
of the distinguished men with whom he had been associated.
I went frequently to the residence of Mr. Davis, in Cherry
Street, while he was preparing his life of Burr, and had free
access to the " blue boxes " which contained the confidential
female correspondence. The letters were from ladies residing
in New York, Trenton, N. J., Philadelphia, Richmond, Va.,
New Haven, Conn., Albany, Troy, etc., and most of them from
members of well-known families. In some cases the correspondence was literary or platonic, but generally of a more ques-
tionable character.

In several instances the letters embraced a period of several
years, concluding with charges of treachery, falsehood, and desertion. Mr. Davis was particularly anxious to restore all such
letters to the persons, if living, who wrote them. Two packages were delivered by Mr. Davis personally to ladies residing
in the city of New York. One package was transmitted to a
lady in Richmond through General Scott. Mr. Davis earnestly
requested me to deliver a package to a highly respected lady
with whom I was acquainted. But when I declined that too
delicate duty he committed them to the flames.

It is due to the memory of my old friend Davis that I
should say that, although a poor man, living upon the weekly
compensation of two guineas received for letters written to the
" London Times," his honor and integrity resisted large pecuniary inducements in exchange for Colonel Burr's confidential
female correspondence. The late Major M. M. Noah was not
only liberal in his offers of money, but importunate in his appeals to Mr. Davis. All, however, proved ineffectual. Mr.
Davis made an end of the matter by consigning all the letters
that had not been restored to the writers to the flames.

I greatly fear that too many men of the present day, with a
weakened sense of what is due to society, would yield to the
temptation which Mr. Davis so creditably resisted.

CHAPTER XXXIX.

1832–1833.

The Cholera. — Its Victims in Albany. — Death of Maynard. — The Pestilence in Rochester. — A Threatened Amputation. — An Invalid Editor. — Dr. Williams. — Dr. Bushe. — Result of the Election. — Defections from the Party. — Albert H. Tracy.

1832. — In the latter part of June we were startled by information that the Asiatic cholera, which had hitherto been confined to the Old World, had reached Quebec and Montreal. Drs. DeKay and Rhinelander, of New York, and Dr. Bronson, of Albany, were dispatched to Canada for the purpose of obtaining information relating to the proper treatment of the disease. Upon their return, little was learned beyond the fact that the disease was spreading rapidly. On the 3d of July there were two fatal cases in Albany, and from that time until the 1st of September it continued its ravages. The largest number of new cases reported in one day was thirty-two, and the greatest number of deaths in one day was fourteen.

Although most of the victims of this terrible disease were persons of irregular habits, or those whose poverty drove them into unhealthy lodgings, there were exceptions enough to render all classes apprehensive and anxious. Business came almost to a stand-still. Most of those who were able left the city. I desired my wife to take the children with her into the country, but she declined to do so; and by her courage, prudence, and cheerfulness essentially aided me in the discharge of my onerous duties.

Just as the sun was rising one morning, when the cholera was at the worst, the late General James S. Wadsworth, of Geneseo, then quite a young man, having a morbid curiosity to see cholera patients, called at my house and asked me to accompany him to the cholera hospital. On our way to the hospital we encountered three hearses with the remains of as many cholera victims, who had died the preceding night. I left my friend at the hospital door, not caring to visit its patients before breakfast.

On another occasion, I met a neighbor, Deacon Dutcher, about sunrise, at the market. He was then, like myself, in perfect health. At three o'clock that afternoon I saw the hearse standing at his door, and, on inquiry, found that in his case the disease had proved fatal in eight hours.

I left Albany twice during the continuance of that pestilence. The Court for the Correction of Errors was sitting in New York when the cholera broke out, and continued in session until five of its members had premonitory symptoms of the disease.

Learning that my cherished friend, the Hon. William H. Maynard, one of the five gentlemen referred to, was unable to leave New York, I went there immediately in the hope of being useful to him. But in that hope I was disappointed. I found him in the last stage of the disease, free from pain, and fully conscious. Finding him, after sitting with him a few hours, apparently improved, I expressed the hope that he might be restored to health, to which he very calmly replied that his only concern now was about "his supreme health." He died before the next morning.

Mr. Maynard was a remarkable man. He lived exclusively, first, to acquire knowledge ; and then, by imparting that knowledge to others, to render service to his country. After attaining a high rank at the bar of Oneida, with such competitors as Green C. Bronson, Henry K. Storrs, Joseph Kirkland, and Thomas R. Gould, he became an editor, that his field of labor and sphere of usefulness might be enlarged.

The following extract from an editorial obituary notice in the " Evening Journal " will serve to mark the sense entertained of Mr. Maynard's character by one who had known him long and well : —

[From the " Evening Journal," *September* 3, 1832.]

Mr. Maynard was a native of Massachusetts, from whence he removed to Utica, where he has resided upwards of twenty years. He was for several years the editor of the " Utica Sentinel," where he acquired much of that inexhaustible fund of varied information for which he was distinguished. Retiring from his editorial labors, he applied himself with great diligence and success to the practice of the law until he had secured an adequate fortune, when he gave himself up to the service of his country. His public career has been a brief but a bright one. He was a *statesman* in the broadest and most emphatic sense of the word. His habits, his inclinations, and his acquirements all indicated the Senate as the theatre of his usefulness. As a senator his worth was fully appreciated. Not only his immediate constituents, but the whole people of this State were justly proud of the elevation and dignity which his wisdom and eloquence were reflecting upon their legislative councils.

The death of this excellent citizen and enlightened statesman will most painfully affect that portion of our State where he was best known. He will indeed be universally mourned. Even in New York, where hundreds are hurried almost daily to the tomb, his death produced a marked sensation.

Soon after the death of Mr. Maynard I was called to Rochester, and reached that city by canal packet boat about sunrise, to learn that the cholera had appeared during the night; and upon reaching the hotel learned that there were several cases, two of which had terminated fatally in a few hours. New cases were constantly being reported; dismay and gloom were depicted on every countenance. My friend, Frederick Whittlesey, was to have accompanied me to Utica, but his wife seemed so unwilling that he should leave home, that he concluded to remain. A few hours afterwards, one of his children fell a victim to the disease.

On the canal packet boat that evening I was the only passenger. If any person desires to learn what days and nights of anxiety were endured in Albany, let them read Samuel Pepy's description of the plague in London.

November and December. — At the close of this year, what at first seemed to be an attack of rheumatism in my knee developed into a white swelling, and assumed symptoms so alarming, that Dr. Williams, our family physician, advised me to visit New York and consult some of the eminent surgeons of that city. In pursuance of that advice, I went, accompanied by my wife, upon the steamboat to New York. A few hours before leaving my house Chief Justice Spencer called, and upon learning the object of my visit to the metropolis, and of my intentions to consult Dr. Mott, protested warmly against that course, and in a very earnest and emphatic manner advised me to send for Dr. Bushe, then a comparatively young, but rapidly rising physician and surgeon. Dr. Bushe, after examining my limb with much deliberation, remarked that the case was one of difficulty; that he had no doubt about the proper treatment of it, but whether the treatment would be effectual or not was a question of time. He then, by the application of lunar caustic, created a deep issue upon either side of the knee-joint, which, he said, must be kept open by the application of an unguent for five or six weeks, when, as he hoped, the progress of the inflammation would be arrested.

He had the limb placed upon a splint, enjoining upon me the importance of keeping it in repose, and further enjoining strict attention to diet, saying that I should confine myself as nearly as possible to Boston crackers, roasted apple, and cold water. On learning that I was an editor, he advised me to attend to my business as usual, taking care to keep my limb quiet, and in no case to move the knee-joint.

At the beginning of the fifth week there was an evident and gratifying improvement, of which, as requested, I informed Dr. Bushe by letter. He responded immediately, saying that the danger was over, adding, that after three or four weeks more I might move about on crutches until the limb should become strong enough to walk with the aid of a cane.

My physician and friends at Albany confidently apprehended that my visit to New York would disclose the necessity of an amputation, which I have never doubted would have been the result, had I fallen into the hands of any of the distinguished surgeons of that day. I feel that, under Providence, I am indebted to the advice of Judge Spencer, and to the skill of Dr. Bushe, for exemption from a dangerous surgical operation and the preservation of a limb.

Dr. Bushe was born and educated in Scotland. He was not long, after establishing himself in New York, in securing a large practice, but, unhappily for a city in which his skill and devotion were so highly appreciated, his life and labors terminated in the midst of his usefulness. He was overworked, and fell a victim to his desire to benefit his race.

1833.—The months of January, February, and March, 1833, although I was confined to my bed-chamber, instead of being wearisome, passed pleasantly. I sat, bolstered up in bed, reading newspapers, selecting copy, and writing editorials, from sunrise until one or two o'clock P. M.; soon after which time, Senators Albert H. Tracy, William H. Seward, and Trumbull Cary, all very dear friends, made their appearance, not unfrequently accompanied by their wives. With these cherished and intellectual friends afternoons passed delightfully. The conversation, political, literary, and social, was full of instruction and interest. Seldom, if ever, was there a more cheerful sick room.

The result of the election in 1832, when we were overwhelmed by majorities for Jackson for president and Marcy for governor, proved very disheartening. Our western counties, however, not only breasted the storm, but rode it out triumphantly, giving their accustomed majorities against the Democracy. The Regency, always disturbed by the unanimity of the west, had made previous but unsuccessful efforts to divide our friends. These efforts, now renewed under what seemed more favorable auspices for Mr. Van Buren, beguiled several leading Anti-Masons from their allegiance. Mr. Tracy, after several interviews with Mr. Van Buren, undertook to impress us not only with the idea that Anti-Masonry had accomplished all it was capable of doing, but that we could hope for nothing under Mr. Clay's banner but reiterated defeats. He succeeded in detaching Messrs. Birdsall, Childs, and several other members of the legislature; but his main mission was to win Senator Seward and the " Evening Journal," for which purpose he held long, earnest, and anxious conversations with us.

We had both been accustomed for years to allow Mr. Tracy to do our political thinking, rarely differing from him in opinion, and never doubting his fidelity. On this occasion, however, we could not see things from his standpoint, and, greatly to his annoyance, we determined to adhere to our principles. Mr. Tracy's defection made no impression upon the rank and file of our party. Mr. Seward, instead of following as before the lead of Mr. Tracy, assumed the leadership himself, and took an active and bold part in debate upon the questions of nullification and the removal of the deposits from the bank of the United States. With this separation from his party terminated, greatly to the regret of numerous friends, Mr. Tracy's public life, a life which had promised great usefulness and a brilliant career.

CHAPTER XL.

1833.

NULLIFICATION. — GENERAL JACKSON'S PROCLAMATION. — CLAY'S COM-
PROMISE. — WILLIAM H. SEWARD. — LETTERS FROM EUROPE. — RE-
MOVAL OF THE DEPOSITS. — R. B. TANEY. — FINANCIAL EMBARRASS-
MENTS. — "NO PRESSURE." — "PERISH COMMERCE." — DISSOLUTION OF
THE ANTI-MASONIC PARTY.

1833. — NULLIFICATION, one of the phases which the slave-
power assumed with a view either to force the free States into
a compliance with its exactions, or to divide the Union, had its
origin and progress in 1832, and its decline and fall in 1833.
The champions of nullification, Vice-President Calhoun, Senator
Hayne, and Representatives McDuffie and Hamilton of South
Carolina, were able in debate, bold in language, and defiant in
manner. They drew after them most of the representatives
from the Cotton States, together with a majority from Virginia.
In North Carolina Senator Mangum, Representative Edward
Stanly, with several Whig members of Congress from Tennessee, Kentucky, and Georgia, stood firmly in their utterances and
their votes with their Whig brethren of the Northern States,
against what was regarded as incipient rebellion, although spe-
ciously urged as consistent with the Jeffersonian resolutions of
1798. The question finally assumed a shape so threatening as
to call for executive interposition. South Carolina held a convention which adopted an ordinance nullifying the tariff laws.
General Jackson at once issued his proclamation declaring his
determination to enforce those and all laws of the Union, and
pronouncing resistance to them treasonable. It was a thunderbolt unexpected and effective. When, a short time after, Mr.
Clay proposed a compromise of the tariff offering a way of
escape from the dilemma into which Southern politicians had
plunged their States, it was willingly accepted, and so the danger for that time was "tided over."

The acquaintance formed at Rochester in 1824 with Mr.

Seward had been ripening into a very close friendship. Our relations, social and political, had become so intimate and our sentiments and sympathies proved so congenial, that our interests, pursuits, and hopes of promoting each other's welfare and happiness, and of being useful to our country, became identical. Our views in relation to public affairs, and our estimate of public men, rarely differed. I saw in him in a remarkable degree rapidly developing elements of character, which could not fail to render him eminently useful in public life. I discerned also unmistakable evidences of stern integrity, earnest patriotism, and unswerving fidelity. I saw also in him a rare capacity for intellectual labor, with an industry which never tired and required no relaxation ; to all which was added a purity and delicacy of habit and character almost feminine. We were now, however, about to be separated for several months, his father, Judge Samuel S. Seward of Orange County, having invited his son to accompany him upon a tour through Europe. He wrote during his absence a series of letters descriptive of places and people to Mrs. Seward which, after being read by the family, were transmitted to Albany for my perusal. Finding them very interesting I ventured, without his knowledge, to publish them in the "Evening Journal," from which they were republished in other journals, and found admiring readers throughout the country.

With the presidential election of 1832, Vermont being the only State voting for Wirt and Ellmaker, Anti-Masonry as a political organization began to subside, although as late as 1833 John Quincy Adams, Richard Rush, and Edward Everett wrote for publication letters condemnatory of the institution of Masonry. The supposed necessity for political Anti-Masonry was further weakened by a pretty general surrender of charters by the lodges in western New York, Vermont, and portions of several other States. Those surrenders, however, were soon revoked, and the institution not only recovered its status but became and remained still more attractive and popular.

In September of this year General Jackson, advised as was alleged by Mr. Van Buren, announced to his cabinet his determination to remove the deposits of the government from the bank of the United States to designated banks in the several States. The Secretary of the Treasury, William J. Duane, of

Philadelphia, declining to obey the mandate of the President, was promptly removed from office, and Roger B. Taney, of Baltimore, appointed in his place. This arbitrary act roused a storm of indignation in our commercial cities and among the friends of the United States Bank everywhere. Our statesmen and journals united in denouncing the President as a despot and usurper. Although up to this time I had thought well of the Bank of the United States, and regarded the removal of the deposits as a high-handed measure occasioned by personal resentment, I saw danger to our party in the issue our friends were making. The message of the President seemed to me well calculated to alarm and mislead the masses of our people. I therefore remonstrated earnestly with leading political friends against the evident intention of Mr. Clay, Mr. Webster, and other distinguished Whig statesmen, to make the re-charter of the Bank of the United States the leading feature in the approaching presidential election. But the sentiment and the feeling in favor of the bank, and against General Jackson for his removal of the deposits, was too general and too strong. My advice was disregarded. But while I went heartily and earnestly with my political friends upon all other questions, I steadily ignored the bank issue, insisting on all proper occasions that it "hung like a mill-stone about our necks."

The removal of the deposits necessarily constrained the bank to curtail its discounts. That created wide-spread financial embarrassment and apprehension. The friends of the bank charged that President Jackson was directly responsible for all the commercial distress that followed. His party, on the other hand, charged that the bank was curtailing its loans, not from any real necessity, but in order to produce a panic that would lead to a reversal of Jackson's policy and the restoration of the deposits.

Upon the reassembling of Congress highly influential merchants and bankers of the great commercial cities memorialized Congress for relief. The debates on the subject were protracted and exciting. Opposition members eloquently portrayed the deranged condition of the currency, the languishing condition of commerce and manufactures, and the consequent want of employment and sufferings of the people. It was during this crisis that the organ of the administration, the 'Globe," said that there was "no pressure that any honest man should regret."

It was then also alleged that General Jackson, when shown a long list of failures in the city of New York, said that " men who trade on borrowed capital ought to fail." And it was on this question, also, that Hon. Samuel Beardsley, a representative in Congress from Oneida County, in reply to a member who had dwelt upon the embarrassed condition of the country, exclaimed, " Perish commerce, perish credit, perish all rather than submit to the rule of a moneyed oligarchy."

These utterances were held as evincing a want of sympathy for the masses, and were turned by the opposition orators and journals with much effect against the administration, helping to organize and consolidate a party which ultimately overthrew the Democracy.

The election of 1833 demonstrated unmistakably not only that opposition to Masonry as a party in a political aspect had lost its hold upon the public mind, but that its leading object, namely, to awaken and perpetuate a public sentiment against secret societies, had signally failed. The Jackson party was now more powerful than ever in three fourths of the States in the Union. The National Republican party was quite as fatally demoralized as that to which I belonged. This discouraging condition of political affairs, after a consultation with W. H. Seward, Francis Granger, Trumbull Cary, Bates Cook, Millard Fillmore, Frederick Whittlesey, John C. Spencer, Philo C. Fuller, Edward Dodd, George W. Patterson, Timothy Childs, Lewis Benedict, John Townsend, Thomas Clowes, Nicholas Devereux, James Wadsworth, Thomas C. Love, and others, resulted in a virtual dissolution of the Anti-Masonic party. All or nearly all of our leading friends having no affinities of sentiment or sympathy with the Jackson party found themselves at liberty to retire from political action, or unite with the then largely disorganized elements of opposition to the national and State administrations. I had by this time become irreconcilably opposed to the Regency, and fell naturally into association with their opponents. The "Evening Journal" went diligently and zealously to work organizing the elements of opposition throughout the State into what soon became the " Whig " party.

CHAPTER XLI.

1834.

THE WHIG PARTY. — THE "JOURNAL." — SAMUEL H. DAVIS. — JACOB
BARKER. — SLAVERY DISCUSSIONS. — COLONIZATION. — ABOLITION SO-
CIETIES. — RIGHT OF PETITION. — JOHN QUINCY ADAMS. — THE " ATH-
ERTON GAG." — DOUGH-FACES. — A GRADUAL EMANCIPATION PROJECT.
— TIMOTHY PITKIN. — BRITISH EMANCIPATION. — INTERNAL IMPROVE-
MENTS. — FINANCE AND CURRENCY. — NOMINATION OF SEWARD AND
STILWELL. — UNITED STATES BANK QUESTION. — THE ELECTION AND
DEFEAT. — SEWARD'S LETTERS.

1834. — ALTHOUGH the Missouri Compromise was designed to
settle finally the slavery question, and did for a season allay the
feeling which created the necessity for such a settlement, it was
found impossible to prevent collisions, either of interest or sentiment, between the North and South. There was, as Governor
Seward described it many years afterwards, an " irrepressible
conflict" between freedom and slavery; and though it at first
only manifested itself in churches and in newspapers, it was sufficient to cause irritation, if not apprehension, among slave-hold-
ers. There was a disposition among the masses of the Northern
people to abide by the compromises of the Constitution. Meantime the Colonization Society, ostensibly rather than really an
emancipation movement, was losing its influence. Abolition societies were formed, and became, in some instances, aggressive.
Resistance to the Fugitive Slave Law was strongly urged. Those
who had, in the earlier history of the government, looked for
the ultimate abolition of slavery by the action of the several
States, now saw the fallacy of any such hopes. The institution
was constantly acquiring numerical, financial, and political
strength. It enjoyed an advantage over the Free States in the
parliamentary experience and settled purpose of its representatives. With the South, slavery absorbed all other interests and
issues, while at the North it rarely entered into our elections ;
and up to 1832 the Abolitionists had no distinctive representative in Congress.

During the last term of General Jackson's administration citizens of New England, New York, and Ohio petitioned Congress for the abolition of slavery in the District of Columbia. As this was the "beginning of the end" of a conflict which finally resulted in the overthrow of slavery, it seems proper to recall the views of our representative men of that day upon a question which so long excited, and finally involved our country in rebellion and war.

John Quincy Adams, in presenting several of these petitions, remarked that he was not in favor of the object sought, but recognized the right of petition. The petitions were referred to the Committee on the District of Columbia, whose chairman, Mr. Doddridge, reported that it was unsafe to grant the prayer of the petitioners, and wrong to move in the matter without the consent of Maryland and Virginia, by which States the territory had been ceded to the federal government. Other petitions, more numerously signed, were presented at subsequent sessions of Congress, when various propositions were made to refer, to lay on the table, and finally to reject them. On these questions, Northern members generally disclaimed any purpose or willingness to interfere with slavery, nor for a long time did the subject elicit more than brief explanations. All seemed reluctant to enter upon a debate that could not fail to prove exciting, yet this was only a question of time, — a question that could be temporarily bridged over, but which returned with increasing importunity and significance session after session. In 1838 the question had assumed an aspect so important that the Democratic members of Congress from the Northern States decided in caucus in favor of a resolution requiring all petitions, resolutions, or memorials relating to slavery, or its abolition, to be laid upon the table without being debated, printed, or referred. This was presented in the House by Mr. Atherton, of New Hampshire, and adopted by a vote of 136 to 73. Thenceforward the Democratic party identified itself with the slaveholding interest, and its northern representatives in Congress were stigmatized as " dough-faces." The Whig party, although differing widely from the anti-slavery and abolition societies and movements, was found consistently and steadily maintaining the right of petition, and the right also to use the mails and post-offices for the distribution of anti-slavery publications, —

a right which Mr. Amos Kendall, General Jackson's Postmaster-General, had refused.

The debates upon the right of petition continuing through several years, called out New York members of Congress, who became subsequently still more prominent in public affairs. Washington Hunt, subsequently governor of the State, while avowing himself in favor of the right of petition, expressed a hope that the subject would go to a committee, whose report would "put this question forever at rest, silence the fanatics on the one hand, and satisfy our brethren of the South on the other." Millard Fillmore disavowed any desire to interfere with the rights, or what was termed the property, of the citizens of other States, though he was in favor of printing the memorial. Francis Granger not only vindicated the right of petition, but warned Southern members that if they continued to deny that right, they would find enlisted under the banner of abolitionism gallant spirits of the North who would never yield.

The subject continued to attract the attention and awaken the solicitude, not only of philanthropists, but of journalists and statesmen. My own sentiments and sympathies were always strongly against slavery. I remember to have rejoiced almost as heartily as the slaves themselves upon the passage, in 1812, of the law providing for the gradual emancipation of slaves in this State.

In 1833, going from New York to New Haven by steamboat, I fell accidentally into conversation with an aged gentleman, with whose quiet manner and remarkable intelligence I was much interested. After a while, becoming known to each other, the subject of slavery was introduced. The old gentleman remarked that his thoughts had dwelt upon the future of our country, in its relations to slavery, anxiously for many years, and that he had reached in his own mind a practicable and peaceable solution of the difficulty. His programme was substantially as follows.

Inasmuch as the national debt was soon to be extinguished, and the increasing proceeds of the public domain to be released, he proposed that this large and constantly increasing fund should be devoted, with the consent of the States in which slavery existed, to gradual emancipation. He assumed that the State of Delaware, for illustration, would pass a law fixing a just valuation upon the slaves, and that one day's freedom of each slave should be purchased and paid for, every alternate year, until their entire ransom was effected. He assumed, further, that other border States, where slave property was insecure, would accept under the same provision of law a money equivalent for the labor of their slaves; and that when Maryland, Kentucky, and Tennessee should thus become free States, exposing Virginia and North Carolina to " border " depletion, those States would be constrained to " accept the situation," so that, in time, the public domain, a common inheritance, would become the instrumentality, under Providence, of securing to every human being the enjoyment of the blessings contemplated by the Declaration of Independence, " life, liberty, and the pursuit of happiness." Another advantage of this plan was that the process by which freedom was to be obtained would prepare the recipient for an intelligent use of it.

The gentleman, whose plan for the abolition of slavery I have briefly stated, was Timothy Pitkin, one of the best and ablest of the many eminent sons of the State of Connecticut. He added that his only reason for regretting his retirement from public life was that it prevented him from bringing this plan before Congress. I was so strongly impressed with its wisdom and practicability, that I entertained sanguine hopes of inducing Mr. Clay or some other influential member of Congress to make it their political " shibboleth." But in that I was disappointed; for although the time and the circumstances were propitious and favorable, I could inspire none of our statesmen with confidence in its success. It was to me for several years a source of regret and annoyance that a project of such vast national importance, and one that would have resulted in the peaceable adjustment of a difficulty that has since cost millions of treasure, rivers of blood, and almost universal demoralization, found no favor with the public men of that day.

The act of Parliament abolishing slavery in the British colonies served to stimulate movements against slavery in this country. The Colonization Society, then sending manumitted slaves to Africa, and looking forward to ultimate emancipation through this agency, came to be regarded with distrust by the more pronounced opponents of slavery. The colonization plan was regarded as a safety-valve for slavery, enabling the slave-

holders to relieve themselves from the incumbrance of free ne-
groes, a useless, if not dangerous, element. This led to the
organization of the American Anti-Slavery Society, under the
auspices of Arthur and Lewis Tappan, with William Lloyd
Garrison at the head of an anti-slavery paper. This antagonism occasioned serious riots in Philadelphia and other places,
where anti-slavery meetings were held. So strongly conservative were the Northern people at that time, that a school, established in Connecticut for the education of colored children, was
broken up, and those children were not permitted to attend
church with white people.

The policy and measures of the Federal and State administrations were regarded by the enterprising portion of our citizens as destructive to the various business interests of the State.
In inaugurating the Whig party, therefore, we took issue with
the Democracy on the questions of internal improvement, protection, and finance. This rendered our party popular in the
city of New York, where, at the charter election, a majority of
Whig aldermen were chosen, and the Whig candidate for mayor
lost his election by only a few votes. That result, and the partial success of the Whig ticket at the Albany charter election,
encouraged our friends to enter upon a vigorous canvass for
governor. Several able and well-known Democrats, dissatisfied
with the destructive policy of the administration, had become
Whigs. Prominent among these were Gulian C. Verplanck and
Jesse Buel. In looking around for gubernatorial candidates,
the names of both of these gentlemen were suggested. They
were visited by Messrs. Seward, Whittlesey, and myself, but for
reasons deemed wise by us all they declined the nomination.
Mr. Granger, who had been a candidate in 1830 and 1832, now
preferred to run for Congress, with the certainty of an election.
When the State convention met in September, William H.
Seward was with entire unanimity nominated for governor, and
Silas M. Stilwell for lieutenant-governor. The venerable Peter
R. Livingston, who presided over the deliberations of the convention, made an eloquent and thrilling speech upon what he
regarded as an auspicious result, and the delegates departed in
high spirits.

The canvass was a very spirited one. Our candidate for
governor, by his ability, courage, and fidelity during his four

years' service in the Senate, proved strong and popular throughout the State, and especially so among its young men. Confident expectations of success were cherished, but enthusiasm was mistaken for strength. The aggressions and abuses of the Regency party had not yet culminated. We made a gallant canvass, but our ticket was beaten by a majority of over 12,000. That disappointment occasioned temporary depression, from which, however, we soon rallied. The victory of our opponents served only to render them more aggressive and reckless.

Having always deprecated the United States Bank question as a political issue, I found, as will be seen by the following editorial in the " Evening Journal," one source of consolation in the defeat we had just sustained.

[From the "Albany Evening Journal," Saturday Evening, November 15, 1834.]

There is one cause of congratulation connected with the result of the recent election in which even *we* can participate. It has terminated the United States Bank war. It will not be in the power of its enemies to perpetuate its existence. None will regret its death more sincerely than the Regency, for, with that in the field, the reign of demagogues would be perpetual.

We have from the beginning deprecated the successive conflicts in defense of the bank. No matter how ill the bank was used, or how profligate the motives of those who waged war upon it, they were sure to be " *victors.*" But we have gone with our friends through three campaigns, under a strong and settled conviction that, in every issue to be tried by the people to which the bank was a party, we must be beaten. After staggering along from year to year with a doomed bank upon our shoulders, both the bank and our party are finally overwhelmed. The burden, however, is now removed, and we hope to see the efforts of a great and patriotic party directed, with better chances of success, to the ultimate restoration of the rights of the people and the honor of the country.

The following extracts from letters written by Mr. Seward immediately after his defeat show something of the character and spirit of the young statesman destined to render signal services to his country : —

AUBURN, *November* 6, Thursday.

The election returns already received conclusively prove that we have all been deceived in our calculations, and that our opponents have been again signally successful. Evil tidings fly fast enough. I shall not trouble myself to give them speed. You will hear all from those to whom they bring joy. So far as I have heard I give you the reported majorities in this county. Do not take any grief for this result on account of my feelings. Be assured that it has not found me unprepared. I shall not suffer any unhappiness in returning to private life, except that which I shall feel with all our political friends. Believe me, there is no affectation in my saying that I would not now exchange the feelings and associations of the vanquished William H. Seward for the victory and " spoils " of William L. Marcy. If I live, and such principles and opinions as I entertain ever find favor with the people, I shall not be without their respect. If they do not, I shall be content with enjoyments that politicians cannot take from me.

Remember me with expressions of gratitude to all our friends who may take so much personal interest in me as to inquire how the defeat of our just cause is borne by him who they were willing should enjoy the best fruits of its success.

A week later he wrote : —

I have cleared away the ground since the action. After a brief visit to Albany I shall be ready with a good heart in the labors of my profession, and devote myself to them and to the cultivation of what taste I have for study. Let me have your assurance that you have acquired the same philosophy. . . . Granger spent a day with me. He has had a fortunate escape from his dilemma, and I am rejoiced at it. He is a noble fellow, and I am glad that, if we could not make him what we wished, we have been able to put him into a career of honor and usefulness.

CHAPTER XLII.

1835–1836.

EDITORIAL LIFE. — LIFE INSURANCE. — OLD FRIENDS. — THEODORE S. FAXTON. — ADDISON GARDINER. — CHAPMAN. — PATTERSON. — LEAVENWORTH. — VIVUS W. SMITH. — EDWARD DODD. — STEPHENS, THE TRAVELER. — SAMUEL P. LYMAN. — A. B. DICKINSON. — NOMINATION OF VAN BUREN. — JESSE BUEL. — GOVERNOR MARCY. — PRESIDENTIAL ELECTION. — "HARD MONEY" POLICY. — SAFETY FUND BANKS. — "SMALL BILL" LAW. — LAWRENCE AND TAYLOR.

1835–1836. — THE years 1834, 1835, and 1836 were less eventful politically than those which preceded and followed. My time was during those years occupied diligently and pleasantly in extending the circulation and influence of the "Evening Journal," in strengthening and encouraging the Whig party, and in agreeable association with a constantly widening circle of personal, political, and literary friends.

Although the "Evening Journal" had been financially as well as politically successful, I was quite satisfied with a sort of sliding scale salary, which had been augmented at the annual rate of $250 from $750 in 1830 to $2,000 in 1835. Up to this period, at the age of thirty-eight, I had laid nothing aside in view of contingencies for which most thoughtful men are anxious to provide. My solicitude on that subject had been quieted with a policy for $5,000, which I had taken in 1836 from the New York Life and Trust Company. I remember the emotion which the possession of that policy awakened in my heart. To have secured, in the event of my being called suddenly away, $5,000 for my wife and children, was an event which afforded me much consolation. I have paid in premiums and interest more than four times the amount of the policy, but there is no pecuniary claim that I meet more cheerfully.

I had become personally acquainted with nearly all the active, intelligent, enterprising citizens of Albany. The merchants, the river and canal forwarders, almost without exception, were warm friends. With the eminent divines, the distinguished physicians, and most of the leading lawyers, I had formed pleasant relations. There were, however, exceptions occasioned by sharp and exciting political conflicts, although then, as before and since, I was privileged to recognize many personal friends among my political opponents. The friendships formed at Utica, Herkimer, Cooperstown, Norwich, Manlius, Rochester, and Albany, embracing a period of fifty years, were for the most part as enduring as life. And, while the grave has closed over the remains of nearly all these cherished friends, a very few have been spared.

George Petrie, a young merchant at Herkimer, who appointed me his quartermaster-sergeant while on our march to the frontier in 1814, is now, in his eighty-second year, a clerk in the General Post Office at Washington. Theodore S. Faxton, Augustin G. Dauby, and Samuel Farwell, for whom my regard dates back full sixty years, are closing out useful and honored lives at Utica. Benjamin Chapman, an enterprising and estimable merchant of Norwich, who has been my close friend since 1818, still lives in the enjoyment of an honestly acquired estate, solaced by the affectionate attentions of those whom he loves and for whom he labored. Addison Gardiner, between whom and myself there have ever been common sentiments and sympathies, and with whom in literary and social communings many of the pleasantest hours of my life were passed, after a long and brilliant judicial career, voluntarily retired from the public service, and is passing the evening of life tranquilly surrounded by its compensations and refinements, upon a beautiful farm adjoining the city of Rochester. But while visiting, as I recently did, the villages and cities in which I formerly resided, where I was permitted to cross palms with these few old friends, my thoughts were saddened by the reflection that the cemeteries contained hundreds whom I had left in high health, fighting the battle of life with energy, zeal, and confidence, and it is anything but flattering to human pride to reflect and realize that men of talent and worth, who had acquired a reasonable share of distinction, die and are so soon forgotten. Friendships alike enduring and endearing were formed at Albany with men residing not only in different parts of this State, but in other States, — men distinguished alike for their personal worth and their public services; men about whose views and votes, however far and long we might have been separated, I was never in doubt, as we were sure to think and act alike. For example, there has not been during the last forty years a question of principle or policy in the management of public affairs about which such men as George W. Patterson, of Chautauqua, Edward Dodd, of Washington, Christopher Morgan, of Cayuga, Elias W. Leavenworth, Vivus W. Smith, and Julius J. Wood, of Onondaga, with many others, held opinions in the slightest degree differing from those which I entertained. I could, therefore, always and confidently rely upon the active coöperation of a numerous and influential class of men throughout the State in carrying forward measures designed to promote the public welfare. This, in later years, was observable in the confidence with which the "Evening Journal" had inspired the Whig journals of this State, and, to some extent, those of other States.

I found, amid my active and laborious occupations, several hours every day for reading. Appropriate notices of new books, copies of which I received from all the leading publishers in New York, Boston, and Philadelphia, proved an agreeable occupation. The books published by the Harpers, who worked with me as journeymen printers in 1816, were sure to receive prompt and cheerful attention. They were in the habit of sending me copies several days in advance of their publication. This afforded time for careful reading and thoughtful notices of such as were most meritorious. Greatly interested in a book entitled "Incidents of Travel in Egypt, Arabia Petræa, and the Holy Land," I wrote an elaborate and glowing review, predicting an extended sale of the book, and bestowing high praise upon its unknown author. Towards the close of a pleasant summer's day, while the family of the "patroon" (General Van Rensselaer) were seated at the dinner table, with a young gentleman from New York as the only guest, a servant brought in the "Evening Journal," which was opened by one of the young ladies, who, after reading a few lines, was asked by her father "if there was any news." She replied, "Yes, sir, there is a *new* book, which the 'Journal' thinks is very charming, and I suppose it must be, for ma believes everything the 'Journal' says." The young lady was then called on to read the article, with which they were all so much delighted that a servant was immediately dispatched to "Little's" for a copy of the book. To one listener the reading of that article awakened emotions that cannot be described. That listener was John L. Stephens, the then unknown author of the book. He retired without acknowledging himself, and came directly to my house, introducing himself, and related the incident which had afforded him so much pleasure. He left New York, he said, nervously anxious and doubtful about the reception of his book, the publication of which had been urged by those whose affection he feared had misled their judgments. The book in money and fame produced and realized all I had anticipated. Mr. Stephens was encouraged to travel again and again, first in Northern Europe and subsequently in Central America, giving, as the result of his observation and researches, those admirable works entitled "Incidents of Travel in Greece, Turkey, and Northern Europe," and "Central America, Chiapas, and Yucatan."

The public was indebted for these interesting works of an enterprising and enthusiastic traveler to the accidental circumstance that when he left college, enfeebled and jaded by confinement and study, the family physician deemed it essential for the renovation of his constitution that he should devote a year or two to foreign travel. He left New York in a packet ship for Liverpool with a promise to keep his family advised of his whereabouts in letters addressed to his sister. These letters were written without a thought of their being read outside of the family circle, and this circumstance imparted a freshness and freedom to his letters which constitutes the peculiar charm of his books. Mr. Stephens was not less interesting in conversation than as a writer. We became close friends. I enjoyed much of his society for several years. He was the only son of a wealthy citizen of New York, but his health was always delicate, and after a few years of literary occupation amid home associations and refinements, he found rest in an early grave, a grave hallowed by the memory of his virtues.

Among the active, zealous, and rising politicians of that day was Samuel P. Lyman, an intelligent and popular young lawyer of Utica. In one respect Mr. Lyman belonged to my school or class of politicians, — a school or class not likely to become too numerous. He never sought or seemed to desire office. The devotion of his time and talents to politics found compensation in the elevation of his friends. He had especial regard for, and confidence in me, acting with alacrity upon any and every suggestion concerning party organizations and nominations. He became an early admirer of Daniel Webster, to the advancement of whose political fortunes he devoted himself, with unwavering fidelity, to the end of that great statesman's career. The practice of law was too monotonous and its rewards too slow to satisfy Lyman's temperament and nature, nor could his active mind find sufficient occupation in any " pent up Utica." Among other enterprises he became connected at an early day with the Erie Railroad, and was prominently influential, first, in inducing the legislature to authorize a loan of $3,000,000 to that company, and subsequently in obtaining a law converting the loan into a gift. He embarked simultaneously in various other speculative enterprises with such success, that after a few years he regarded himself and was regarded by others as a man of large wealth. Meantime our intimacy continued, and his friendship for me prompted a generous desire that I should share in his prosperity. He endeavored to remove any scruple that I might have by urging that my friendship, advice, and influence had contributed to his success, and that inasmuch as I devoted myself wholly to the success of our party and the advancement of political friends, it was right and proper that those friends should take an interest in my welfare. And although this reasoning did not satisfy my doubts or remove my objections, General Lyman sent me deeds for six lots and two dwelling-houses in the city of Utica, eight lots in the city of Brooklyn, and a hundred acres of pine lands in the county of Allegany. There having been no consideration paid for these deeds, I did not think the property belonged to me, and determined to exercise no act of ownership over.it. The deeds were consequently not recorded, but my friend, Mr. Lewis Benedict, upon being informed by General Lyman that I owned two houses and six vacant lots at Utica, assumed the management of them, and for several years received the rents. Twenty years afterwards, through the vicissitudes in life which so often bring the most fortunate and successful as well as the most enterprising men to pecuniary grief, General Lyman found himself first embarrassed, then crippled, and finally impoverished. Meantime my lots in Brooklyn and my land in Allegany, not having been claimed, by lapse of title or through tax sales passed into other hands, whose hands I never knew or inquired. But I do know that the Brooklyn lots, my deed for which is preserved among other valueless securities, are now worth more than $200,000. When I learned that General Lyman's affairs were embarrassed, regretting that the Brooklyn and Allegany lots and lands had been lost, I reconveyed the Utica property to Mrs. Lyman with the accrued rents, in acknowledgment for which I received the following letter : —

NEW YORK, June 21, 1850.

THURLOW WEED, ESQ.

My Dear Sir, — By the inclosed you will see I have done your bidding, and have made out a simple deed for you and Mrs. Weed to execute to Julia Lyman. If you please you may send it to me, and I will attend to its being put on the record. A judge will take the acknowledgment.

With respect to the other part of the matter, you have only to give her an order on Mr. Sanger, or Benedict & Sanger, and she will go to him or them for the accrued rents, and whatever they say to her will be satisfactory.

God bless you. I am, dear, etc., yours, etc.,

S. P. LYMAN.

General Lyman's regard for Mr. Webster was warmly reciprocated. Next to Edward Curtis and Peter Harvey, General Lyman was Mr. Webster's most confidential political friend. While Mr. Webster was Secretary of State, General Lyman passed much of his time in Washington, possessing a good knowledge of what was going on, of all of which he kept me advised. The following letter furnishes a key to what was passing at the capital among the political leaders of that day : —

WASHINGTON, December 15, 1850.

MY DEAR WEED, — The pressure on the administration is now very hard. I have the good luck to know something of the details.

Mr. Hoxie, of New York, is here, and advocates the claims of several, yea many, suffering Whigs to some of the offices. He says they are good Union men, friendly to the administration, and thoroughly opposed to the whole Seward clique.

I learn from reliable authority that Mr. Ketchum is highly offended at the bare idea that you and Mr. Seward are likely to be friendly to

Mr. Webster and the administration. It is a wrong for you to be using what he claims the exclusive right to do. This reminds me of what Curtis told me, which was that he thought Ketchum's ideas were, that it was best for half a dozen men to get together confidentially, give Mr. Webster a dinner, and then at dinner elect him president before anybody else had a chance to do it. Indeed, the Union committee-men, some of them, threaten to quit if all the Whigs are going in for the administration. Mr. Brooks insists upon it that Governor Seward intends to be a candidate in 1852.

Mr. Duer, Mr. Phœnix, Mr. Brooks, and their friends here in and out of Congress, openly aver that Governor Seward and yourself are "laying low" just now for the sole and express purpose of retaining all the fat offices of the government, that you and he are not to be trusted, etc., etc. Last night Mr. Conrad, Secretary of War, asked me what all this meant? I told him. He says they are confused.

Mr. Duer says (yesterday and to-day) he will be d——d if he don't give it all up, it don't pay. He came to see Mr. Webster last night while I was there. Mr. Webster treated him very kindly and received him with marked attention. I left them sitting on the sofa and Mr. Webster saying civil things to him.

Mr. Brooks told a friend of mine yesterday, that the only way was to cut you all off, have nothing to do with you and Seward; that was the way he did with your friends in his district. But he added, that you and Seward *would succeed " in pulling the wool over Fillmore's eyes ; his mind was made up on that point."*

Fuller, of the " Mirror," and Schermerhorn, of Rochester, thought that it was best to put you all down at once, and have nothing to do with any Free-Soiler. Mr. Fuller told Schermerhorn it was best to from a union with the Hunkers of the Democrats and lick you all out, and that would be the end of you all. However, I persuaded Schermerhorn afterwards to admit that your votes might be of some use to the Whig party next fall. These are specimens.

Now don't let one of these dying throes disturb you in the least. I hope every paper that they charge with the vice of being in the interest of Governor Seward will be more zealous than ever in showing themselves the friends of the Union and of the Whig party. If we are only patient and forbearing a while the Whig party will be as firmly united as any party ever can be. Let us keep this object steadily in view.

Sitting where you are, you can almost see how these men are operating on the minds of the President and his cabinet by this incessant fire. Mr. Schoolcraft told me last night that Governor Seward called on Mr. Corwin day before yesterday, and that they both " kept up a

sort of armed neutrality," and that Mr. Corwin did not come out to
Mr. Seward as frankly as he did to Mr. Schoolcraft. Mr. Schoolcraft
will call on the Secretary of the Treasury again to-morrow. Mr. Webster told me Corwin would do what he had said.

I saw the President on Friday night. I had a few words with him.
He expressed his pleasure at what I told him; he asked me to come
to see him some evening this week. I am to dine with him on Thursday. I feel satisfied that all is right so far. What these men in their
madness will do remains to be seen, but if attended to, and all our
friends in New York city and the State act well their part, and like
good men occupy at once the vantage ground, all that was lost will be
fully regained. Urge them to do it.

I hope the tone of the "Journal" will be favorable to the perfect
union of the party in the State ; that it will express the hope that de-
signing men will not have the power to disturb by any suggestions the
harmony that seems to prevail. Don't for anything let these dying
men have an ounce of food to save their lives for a single day. Let
these men here do the grumbling.

I don't permit myself to say one word about any office in behalf of
any human being, no matter how strongly pressed. I urge on the
administration the policy of letting everything stand as General Taylor did it, as the best platform that can be erected in that respect,
and that in making other appointments, if there is occasion for it, the
departments should do the most they can to promote harmony. *I tell
them this is the way to make peace in New York.*

I am yours, etc.,   S. P. LYMAN.

Every year brought to Albany, as members of the Assembly
or the Senate, men whose personal worth, political fidelity, and
social qualities, added to their practical knowledge of the re-
quirements of the people, rendered their services as valuable
as their society was agreeable. Between such representatives
and myself enduring friendships were formed. Among the
earliest of these friends was Andrew B. Dickinson, a member
of the Assembly from Steuben County in 1830. He was a
farmer, whose early education was entirely neglected. Marrying early, he fortunately found a teacher in his wife, who found
a willing and diligent pupil in her husband. Dickinson was
intellectually strong by nature. His perceptions and intuitions
were clear and ready. On questions which interested him he
took part in the debates of the House, and while "the King's
English" suffered, he never failed to make himself understood

and felt. Dickinson's seat was near my own, and although differing politically, he being a Democrat and I a Clintonian, I saw that he was an honest man, sure to become a prominent politician. I cultivated his acquaintance, and won his confidence, believing that with so much of common sentiment and sympathy we should not be long politically separated. Nor was that anticipation disappointed, for Mr. Dickinson, two or three years afterward, became an earnest Whig, and as such was elected to the Senate in 1839, where for four years he was able, fearless, faithful, and inflexibly honest. While a candidate for the Senate, one of Mr. Dickinson's private political letters fell into the hands of a political opponent, by whom it was sent to Colonel Young, a Democratic senator, whose patience was severely tried by Mr. Dickinson's frequent rough-hewn assaults. The spelling in the letter referred to was equally ingenious and arbitrary, while all the rules of grammar were set at defiance. Under strong provocation Colonel Young took the letter from his drawer with the avowed intention of reading it to the Senate, when Mr. Dickinson expressed the hope that Colonel Young would carry out his threat by violating a principle which he had been told was held sacred by men of education. He had been quite anxious, he said, to read a letter written by Colonel Young in 1824, which, although well spelled and perfectly grammatical, would amuse the Senate and the people. But inasmuch as that letter was a confidential one, and had been surreptitiously obtained, he did not feel at liberty to violate a rule applicable to such things until the example had been set him by an honorable senator who rejoiced in a college education. Colonel Young, without a word of reply, restored the letter to his desk.

On another occasion, Mr. Hunter, a senator from Westchester County, in replying to some remarks made by Dickinson, criticised and ridiculed his language and style. Mr. Dickinson immediately rejoined, saying that the difference between the senator from Westchester and himself was so marked that it must be apparent to those who were familiar with both, — that while his difficulty consisted in a want of suitable language with which to express his ideas, his colleague was troubled with a flood of words without any ideas to express.

With the disadvantages to which I have referred, Mr. Dickinson's independence, consistency, practical good sense, evident and uncompromising fidelity to his party, welfare of the State and interest of the people, won for him long before he left the Senate the affection of his friends and the respect of his opponents.

" Bray Dickinson," as he was generally and familiarly called, was an enterprising farmer, — too enterprising, indeed, for he undertook more than he could accomplish. His ambition was to be the largest cattle and produce grower in his county. If his whole time and thoughts had been given to farming, his anticipations might have been realized, but, as it was, he experienced the fate of those who keep too many irons in the fire. He struggled on, however, with indomitable industry and iron will, having reliable friends, like Charles Cook, of Chemung, on whom he could rely for loans in cases of emergency.

Mr. Dickinson was an early, ardent, and influential political and personal friend of Governor Seward, on whose recommendation Mr. Lincoln, in 1862, appointed him minister to Nicaragua. Finding, soon after his arrival at his post, that his diplomatic duties were insufficient to occupy his time and thoughts, the " ruling passion " prompted the purchase of a coffee plantation.

We were now approaching another presidential election. The nomination of Vice-President Van Buren as General Jackson's successor was everywhere anticipated. The slavery question during the year 1835 occasioned renewed agitation, which had resulted in augmenting the political power of the Democratic party. The Southern section of the Whig party was embarrassed and weakened by those agitations, and yet the leading Whigs of the South, with such men as Willie P. Mangum, Edward Stanly, and Lewis Williams, of North Carolina, John M. Botts and John Taliaferro, of Virginia, John Bell and Meredith P. Gentry, of Tennessee, Charles S. Morehead and John White, of Kentucky, were fearless and uncompromising. Mr. Van Buren, a " Northern man with Southern principles," entered the canvass enjoying the confidence and support of at least three fourths of the slave-holding States, without losing his hold upon the Democracy of the free States, and having pledged himself to " follow in the footsteps of his illustrious predecessor," inherited a large share of General Jackson's strength.

These advantages rendered his success more than probable. They did not, however, serve to relax the efforts and zeal of the Whig party. The prospects were not sufficiently encouraging to tempt Mr. Clay to accept a nomination. The Southern Whigs urged the Hon. Hugh L. White, of Tennessee, as a candidate. Senator Mangum was named by North Carolina and Mr. Webster by Massachusetts, while the Middle and Western States supported General Harrison and Francis Granger for president and vice-president. Mr. Van Buren's election being a foregone conclusion, the Whigs conducted the presidential canvass with a view to strengthening their State and congressional organizations.

Jesse Buel, of Albany, and Gamaliel H. Barstow, of Tioga, were nominated by the Whig State Convention for governor and lieutenant-governor. They were men of recognized ability and irreproachable character. Governor Marcy and Lieutenant-Governor Tracy were renominated by the Democratic State Convention and reëlected.

With Mr. Van Buren's advent to the presidency an opposition was inaugurated which " meant mischief." We found in the " hard money " policy of the administration a salient point of attack. Contractions of the currency produced financial derangement, paralyzing the various industrial interests of the country. The safety fund banking system, of which Mr. Van Buren was the acknowledged father, became an essential part of the political machinery of the Regency. Colonel Samuel Young, Michael Hoffman, and other leading Democrats, took strong ground in the legislature against any enlargement of the Erie Canal, and against the construction of lateral canals. These questions, antagonizing the Whig and Democratic parties, became prominent and absorbing political issues. From the start, therefore, President Van Buren encountered the opposition of a formidable and homogeneous party. Responding to the demands of Colonel Benton and other " hard money " advocates in Congress, Governor Marcy recommended the passage of a law prohibiting banks from issuing notes under the denomination of five dollars. The recommendation was carried into effect by a legislature in both houses of which there was more than a two thirds Democratic majority. This was done under Colonel Benton's pleasant but delusive promise that when bank notes went out of use we should all rejoice in a silken purse through the interstices of which "yellow boys" would glisten. But the bank notes disappeared without making either gold or silver as plentiful as had been promised. In fact the suppression of small bills proved not only a serious inconvenience, but occasioned much positive loss, for in place of the small notes of our own banks, instantly redeemable in coin, the State was flooded with irredeemable and too often worthless small bills of banks of other States and from Canada. We were not slow in availing ourselves of the popular advantage which this financial blunder offered. The Democratic Federal and State administrations were, however, so strongly wedded to their "hard money" policy that the legislatures of 1836 and 1837 refused to repeal the law of 1835. In 1838, although the Whig party found many other weak points to assail, they made the "small bill" question their principal issue in this State. Early in the session of 1838 a bill was introduced repealing the "small bill law," for which many Democratic members avowed their determination to vote. The Regency, acting, as was supposed, under instructions from Washington, took decided ground against the repeal. But they could not control members from the rural districts whose constituents were clamorously demanding "small bills." It was evident, as things stood, that the bill would pass both houses. It was equally evident that its passage would, by relieving the Regency from the odium its operation occasioned, diminish our chances of success in the approaching State election. In other words, it was "stealing the thunder" upon which we were confidently relying for a victory. In this critical emergency I called upon my friend, the late James R. Lawrence, then a member of the Assembly from Onondaga, who was to speak on the question, and suggested a line of argument to which, after listening attentively, he replied, "Such a speech would defeat the bill." I asked him if he did not think we could afford to endure the existing evils·a few months longer in view of the complete overthrow of the Regency in the approaching election. But neither this view of the question, nor the other idea that the evil which produces good may be temporarily tolerated, prevailed with the general, who regarded my programme as highly exceptionable. I admitted that the views I urged him to adopt would unite the Democratic party and

constrain a solid vote against the bill. But he was too direct
and straightforward to act upon them. I then called upon
Henry W. Taylor, a member of the House from Ontario County,
an able man, who always spoke with animation and energy.
He, like General Lawrence, listened attentively to the brief
which I submitted to him. He did not, however, need to be
told either the object or the effect of such a speech, for he instantly comprehended both. The Whig party having been politically shipwrecked by its unfortunate advocacy of and complications with the Bank of the United States, we felt that it
was legitimate party warfare to turn the tables upon the Regency by showing that the safety fund banking system was a
part of their machinery of politics, and in making them as
odious as they had made us by an issue which gave us the benefit of the popular sentiment and sympathy against the bank
party.

When the bill came up in the Assembly several speeches
were made, showing how greatly the business of the State, commercial, manufacturing, and mechanical, were suffering from
the withdrawal of the safety fund bank notes of the denominations under five dollars from circulation. It was urged, also,
that the laboring and poorer classes were subjected to serious
loss by the introduction of the depreciated and sometimes worthless small notes that had rushed in from other States to take the
place of the notes of our own sound banks. Mr. Taylor finally
obtained the floor, arraigning and denouncing the Albany Regency for all the evils, mischiefs, inconveniences, and losses
from which the State and the people were suffering. He
charged that the safety fund banking system was an engine of
party ; that charters were doled out by the Regency to their political friends, among whom the stock was distributed by party
commissioners, and immediately sold out to capitalists at a premium of from twenty to twenty-five per cent. He read the
names of a large number of Democratic politicians throughout
the State to whom the stock of several banks had been given.
He charged that the order for striking our small bills out of
circulation came from Washington, and was designed to enable
Mr. Van Buren and Colonel Benton to carry out their "hard
money" policy. He closed by denouncing the safety fund system as a scheme to combine all the banks of the State, or "lit-

tle monsters," as he styled them, into a State " monster " infinitely more fraudulent and dangerous than the United States "monster," against which the Jackson and Van Buren party had aroused popular indignation. He closed by demanding the repeal of the law striking our small bank notes out of circulation, saying that no member except those wearing a " Regency collar " would vote against it, and that none who did so vote would ever find their way back to the capitol.

This speech, bitter and defiant in language and manner, coming from an Anti-Mason and Federalist (as Mr. Taylor was classified), enabled Speaker Humphrey, John Wilkinson, George P. Barker, Lemuel Stetson, etc., prominent Democratic speakers, to " whip in " their wavering and weak-kneed friends, thus securing by a party vote the rejection of the bill. That rejection, prolonging for another year the inconvenience and loss consequent upon the lack of reliable currency, increased the popular exasperation against the Regency, enabling us, in the election which followed, to overthrow a party that had held the State government and the legislature for ten years.

CHAPTER XLIII.

1837–1838.

1837. — UNTIL 1834 or 1835 Albany was distinguished for the intelligence and enterprise of its merchants, its physicians, its lawyers, its bankers, its clergy, and its politicians. Then in these various callings men stood out prominently in contrast with the middle and subordinate classes. If the same distinctions exist now, I am unable to discover them. By some process, during the last twenty-five years, there has been a levelling, either up or down. Intelligence, by means of improvement and progress, intellectual and material, has been diffused and equalized. As jurists, there are at Albany no successors to Chancellor Kent, Chief Justice Spencer, Abram Van Vechten, John V. Henry, Samuel Stevens, Marcus T. Reynolds, etc. The widely-known and conceded ability of Isaiah and John Townsend, William James, Lewis Benedict, Rufus H. King, Erastus Corning, Friend Humphrey, and the Marvins, as merchants, is now probably divided between twenty merchants of equal intelligence, but who, since canals, railways, and telegraph wires came into use, stand on a level with others, enjoying but a local reputation. There is, I doubt not, corresponding intelligence and ability in the medical and clerical departments, but a few men do not now, as formerly, enjoy a monopoly of distinction in their professions. Among the eminent men who made a residence at Albany so desirable forty years ago, Thomas W. Olcott is the most distinguished survivor. Among the eminent merchants referred to, my cherished friend, Ezra P. Prentice, president of the Commercial Bank, was for many years, I believe, the only survivor.

My residence in Albany as the editor of an Anti-Masonic journal promised small social enjoyment. There had been, up to this time, scarcely a dozen reputable citizens who openly avowed themselves political Anti-Masons. Of that very limited number, Weare C. Little and William White alone survive. While, therefore, the Anti-Masonic idea was decidedly distasteful, the " Evening Journal," even with that drawback, was made first endurable, and afterwards popular, especially in families. And while the paper was growing in favor I was personally wearing out the prejudices encountered at the beginning. Friendships, alike enduring and endearing, were formed. Business men, who had previously taken no active part in politics, became and ever after remained zealous and influential politicians. Lewis Benedict was for more than twenty years a member of the Whig State committee, and one of its most earnest and efficient workers. Merchants and business men, who had previously contented themselves with simply depositing their ballots on election days, now taking a broader view of the question, saw that something more was due and expected from them, and it was largely due to the zeal and liberality of that class that, after a long struggle, we were enabled to overthrow Regency rule, first in Albany, then in the State, and in 1840 to elect a Whig President. The scene of most exciting action in our early struggle with the Regency was the fourth ward of the city of Albany. That ward was the residence of Captain James Maher, a popular, adroit, and clear-headed Democratic leader, and myself, who were respectively charged with the organization and conduct of the elections, then occupying three days. I had known Captain Maher in command of a company of " Irish Greens " at Sackett's Harbor in 1813. Though politically opposed, a warm personal friendship existed between us, a circumstance which, in the most exciting fourth ward elections, on more than one occasion prevented violent outbreaks. There was a large number of canal and river men always drifting about the poll of the fourth ward, whose votes gave the ward to the party that succeeded in obtaining them. For many years the Regency, physically too strong for us, carried the ward by a decisive majority. That physical superiority not only gave them "the drift-wood," as it was called, but by violence and intimidation kept quiet and infirm Whig electors from the polls. To obviate this difficulty, it became necessary to meet force by force. I therefore, in 1835, organized a force, avowedly to preserve order, and enable all peaceable electors to reach the ballot-boxes. I apprised Captain Maher of our intention to protect our electors, " peaceably if we could, forcibly if we must." He approved of this determination, and endeavored to induce his hard-fisted men to act with ours in preserving order. But that was impossible ; and soon after the polls were opened a collision occurred, in which our man, " Bob Chesebro," a stage-driver, was victor. That quieted things for several hours, when another fight came off between a Democratic bully and George W. Daly, which resulted in favor of Daly. The first day of the election, therefore, closed auspiciously. This so much exasperated our opponents, that a large number of them appeared the next morning with concealed weapons, and bent upon mischief. Captain Maher, however, was enabled to control his followers, and the second day passed off quietly. But on the third and last day, an hour or two after the polls opened there was a violent outbreak, in which twenty or thirty men with clubs were engaged, and in which Bob Chesebro, Henry Y. Webb, George W. Daly, Samuel Strong, and other Whigs, not only stood their ground, but bore themselves, as Polonius advised Laertes, " so that the opposer ' might ' beware of them." That election resulted in a handsome Whig gain. Our physical force was therefore maintained and augmented, and in 1837, after a desperate struggle, we carried the ward, as we did the State. Thenceforward the fourth ward became a sort of political barometer, both parties accepting the idea that " as goes the fourth ward so goes the State." To the men whom I have named, and other devoted workers in the fourth ward, including James Weldon, Chauncey Dexter, Thomas Hillson, David Nelligan, Stephen Thorn, Shepard, the Winnes, Stillman Witt, now a millionaire of Cleveland, Ohio, Provost Vesey, the Whelpleys, and others, I became much attached. Most of these men were dependent upon their labor for the support of their families, but such was their zeal for the Whig cause that all other considerations became secondary, and, with one exception, they have remained faithful through life.

George Daly, from his great activity, became conspicuously obnoxious to the Regency, and was frequently assailed in the

" Argus " as " one-eyed Daly," " Weed's henchman," etc.   He was a man of much brightness, with a fair common-school education, with a character made up of good and bad elements, the bad preponderating in the estimation of his enemies, and the good in the opinion of his friends.   As a runner, first for stages, and then for canal boats, his associations subjected him to pecuniary and social temptations.   When successful in business, he left his savings with me until he was enabled to invest $5,000 in a house and lot, thus providing a home for his family, to whom he was always tenderly attached.

At the commencement of the Rebellion he went into the army, and served with credit during the war as an officer in General James Bowen's brigade.

The financial crisis, or what Governor Marcy in his message to the legislature described as the " unregulated spirit of speculation," reached its culminating point in 1837.   Commercial pressure was first apparent in numerous failures at New Orleans, which were soon followed by similar disasters in Charleston, Savannah, Baltimore, Philadelphia, and New York, when the panic became general.   Our banks suspended specie payments, fortunately while the legislature was in session, for by a provision of law the failure to pay specie worked a forfeiture of their charter.   The idea of legalizing the suspension of specie payments was at first denounced and resisted by the " Albany Argus " and leading Democratic politicians.   Such a step by the legislature of New York would conflict with the " hard money " policy of the federal administration.   But the necessity was an overwhelming one, and the Democratic Senate concurred with the Whig Assembly in the passage of a bill rescuing our bank charters from forfeiture, and Governor Marcy signed it.

The pressure was occasioned by a policy on the part of the general government designed to arrest land speculations.   The national debt had been paid off, and the national treasury was burdened with a surplus of more than forty millions.   The country, as a result of the wisdom and honesty of the administrations of James Monroe and John Quincy Adams, had reached the condition of high and palmy prosperity.   In all this the Democratic leaders saw evil and danger.   Speculation, they said, was stimulated by paper currency, for which they resolved to substitute gold and silver.   The President pronounced the banks unsafe depositories for the public funds. Congress carried out an executive recommendation by the establishment of sub-treasuries. Committees of merchants from our principal cities visited Washington, asking from the government some relaxation in its rigorous "hard money" policy, but were unsuccessful. The Washington "Globe," then Mr. Van Buren's organ, had added fuel to the flame by saying that there "was no pressure that any honest man need regret." And here, upon this question, a political campaign was inaugurated which revolutionized New York in 1838, and overwhelmed the Democracy of the nation in 1840.

1838. — The success of the Whig party in 1837 occasioned well-founded hopes of the final overthrow of the "Albany Regency" in 1838. During the ten years of struggle against the Democratic party, a considerable number of Whigs had worked themselves into prominence and were enjoying the confidence of their party. With a reasonable assurance that their political labors were to be rewarded in the approaching election, six or seven gentlemen were named by their friends as candidates for governor. Most prominent among these were Francis Granger, Luther Bradish, and William H. Seward. As the canvass progressed my own position was one of much embarrassment. My relations, personal and political, with each of these gentlemen were intimate and confidential. I knew them to be alike capable, honest, and patriotic, and that each had rendered good and faithful service to the State and to the Whig party. I had known Mr. Granger longer and had been more intimate with him than with either of the other candidates. But I did not feel at liberty, upon a question involving so much of public interest, to allow myself to be controlled by personal friendship. I determined, inasmuch as either of the gentlemen named were equally well qualified and deserving, to take no part in the choice of delegates.

But I was not long permitted to remain non-committal. The friends who had been so long accustomed to confide in me insisted upon knowing who, in my judgment, ought to be nominated. Mr. Seward, during his four years' service in the Senate, had been found strong and earnest in exposing and denouncing misrule, while upon every question of public improvement and popular reform he had placed himself in sympathy with the

masses. Believing that his nomination, by awakening enthusiasm especially among the young men of the State, would give
our ticket its best chance of success, I declared in favor of his
nomination.

The State Convention met at Utica on the 12th of September.
It was largely composed of men of great intelligence, nearly all
of whom had occupied seats in the national or state legislature,
or held important county or city offices. The following well-
remembered names will show that the people appreciated the
importance of the occasion and selected their best men to repre-
sent them: Samuel Stevens, Friend Humphrey, and Joel B.
Nott from Albany, Luther Badger of Broome, Asher Tyler of
Cattaraugus, John H. Beach of Cayuga, Alvah Hunt of Che-
nango, John Miller of Cortland, Millard Fillmore of Erie,
Charles E. Clark of Jefferson, Hugh Maxwell and Chandler
Starr of New York, Fortune C. White and John H. Ostrom of
Oneida, Victory Birdseye, John G. Forbes, Chauncey Betts, and
James R. Lawrence of Onondaga, Robert C. Nicholas and H.
W. Taylor of Ontario, George M. Grier of Orange, Henry Fitz-
hugh of Oswego, Henry Van Rensselaer of St. Lawrence, John
Maynard of Seneca, Martin Lee of Washington, and John M.
Holley of Wayne.

The deliberations of the convention, though earnest and exciting, occasioned no ill feeling. The friends of each candidate
acted upon their best convictions, and it was evident from the
beginning that, result as it might, the nominee would be cheerfully and heartily accepted by the whole convention. Hugh
Maxwell, of New York, was made president of the convention.
Four informal ballots were taken, the first showing 52 votes for
Mr. Seward, to 39 for Mr. Granger, 29 for Mr. Bradish, and
4 for Judge Edwards. The second ballot resulted, Seward 60,
Granger 52, Bradish 10, and Edwards 3. The third ballot,
eight of Mr. Bradish's friends going over to Mr. Granger, resulted Granger 60, Seward 59, Bradish 8. The convention then
adjourned. During the evening and until the convention met
the following day, the canvass between the friends of Mr.
Granger and Mr. Seward was active and spirited, but in good
temper. The formal and final ballot resulted, Seward 121,
Granger 1, Bradish 1, blank 1, when, on motion of Mr. Stevens,
of Albany, a warm supporter of Mr. Granger, the nomination

of Mr. Seward was declared unanimous. Mr. Bradish was nominated by a unanimous vote for lieutenant-governor.

The Democratic State Convention met on the same day at Herkimer, and renominated Governor Marcy and Lieutenant-Governor Tracy, a ticket which united and brought out the whole strength of the Democratic party. The issues, state and national, were clearly defined; both parties had confessedly nominated their strongest men, and each entered upon the canvass with zeal and confidence. We, however, had our opponents on two or three questions at a disadvantage. President Van Buren's policy and measures had deranged financial matters, embarrassed commerce, and crippled manufactures. In obedience to instructions from Washington, Governor Marcy had reluctantly favored the law which prohibited the circulation of safety fund bank notes under the denomination of five dollars. This had substituted for the small bills of our own specie-paying banks the irredeemable currency of other States and Canada. This proved to be our most effective weapon. Auxiliary to our efficient Whig organization, there was a popular under-current among the masses setting strongly in favor of "Small Bill Seward." I had not before, nor have I since, seen a canvass in which the principles of the two parties were more squarely and frankly avowed and maintained, or one which was more fairly conducted. It was a contest which tried the fidelity and tested the strength of two great parties asking a verdict after a full and free hearing from the people.

An incident, not at first deemed of importance, became unexpectedly an element in several elections alike vexatious and mortifying to Governor Marcy and his friends. Governor Marcy while judge of the Supreme Court held, under a special act in 1829, the Niagara circuit, at which several of the men indicted for the abduction of William Morgan were tried. The act provided for the payment by the State of the judge's traveling and hotel expenses. Judge Marcy kept an account of his expenses, and on his return to Albany received payment from the comptroller, to whose annual printed report it was appended. I remember that that account contained the following item: "For mending my pantaloons, 50 cents."

To what I regarded as an unjustifiable personal attack in the "Argus," I retorted the fifty cent account against the State for

mending Governor Marcy's pantaloons. This paragraph was
republished and severely commented upon by Whig journals
throughout the State. It was served up also upon the stump.
Unfortunately for the Democracy, their journals denied the
truth of the statement. When the account duly authenticated
appeared, explanations were attempted, but under the circumstances they proved unsatisfactory. Letters were received from
friends in different parts of the State, saying that unless the
accusation could be disproved it would cost the Governor many
votes. Years afterwards I learned from Governor Marcy himself, and from members of his family, that nothing during his
political life had so much disturbed and annoyed him.

In looking back, after an interval of nearly forty years, and
with a perfect knowledge of Governor Marcy's character, I
cheerfully accept the justification then offered. It was that, instead of aggregating his hotel expenses, including that with
other charges in one item, Judge Marcy conscientiously enumer-
ated every article, thus proving his honesty, for nothing would
have been easier than to have included the tailor's bill under
an item of "incidental expenses." But during one of the later
canvasses Governor Marcy avenged himself at my expense.
Soon after the Morgan affair reached the courts, Governor
Throop appointed John C. Spencer special counsel to investigate the charges against persons accused of the abduction of
Morgan, and to act upon all trials as counsel for the State. In
the progress of his investigation the testimony of a witness supposed to be in Vermont or New Hampshire became indispensable. I was a member of what was known and styled the "Morgan Committee," taking an active part in the investigations and
trials. With the approval of that committee I was dispatched
by Mr. Spencer in pursuit of Adams, the absent witness. The
first step was to obtain a requisition from Governor Throop
upon the Governor of Vermont. The Governor was at his residence near Auburn, and as time was important I was driven to
Auburn that night in a buggy, so that I might get my requisition and take the stage east the following morning. My expenses and those of the witness who returned with me to
Canandaigua were paid by Mr. Spencer from a legislative appropriation. Mr. Spencer's accounts and vouchers were rendered to the comptroller's office, the incumbent then being

William L. Marcy. Governor Marcy ten years afterwards, brushing up his memory and repairing to the comptroller's office, detected there the following item: " For transporting Thurlow Weed to Auburn, $7." This item, in a paragraph written in Governor Marcy's happiest vein, appeared in the " Albany Argus." That paragraph, while conceding the propriety of "transporting" me to Auburn, and admitting the reasonableness of the price paid, concluded by remarking that the State could well have afforded to pay a much larger sum, if the individual thus "transported to Auburn" had been detained there.

This retort went much farther to relieve Governor Marcy from the obnoxious "patch" than all the grave explanations and arguments of the Democratic press.

CHAPTER XLIV.

1838–1839.

THE canvass resulted in the election of Mr. Seward to be governor, and Mr. Bradish lieutenant-governor, by a majority of over 10,000. There was also a decided majority of Whig members of the Assembly elected, of which George W. Patterson was chosen speaker. Of the eight senators elected, six were Whigs and two Democrats. The Senate, however, even with this gain, was Democratic by a majority of four. As no appointments could be made without the consent of the Senate to the Governor's nominations, so far as party patronage was concerned this was a barren victory. The first duty of the Governor elect was equally delicate and difficult. A large number of highly intelligent and meritorious Whig friends intimated their willingness to accept positions upon the Governor's staff. It was embarrassing, where all the candidates were alike meritorious, to make a selection. For the office of adjutant-general there · were three candidates, standing equally high, equally well qualified, with equally strong political claims. This so perplexed the Governor that he delayed his decision until the appointments became absolutely necessary, and then, at a late hour of the night, several hours having been spent in considering and reconsidering the question, the name of a gentleman, not a candidate and not before thought of, was suggested and instantly accepted. That gentleman was Lieutenant Rufus King of the United States army, then on a visit to Albany. As it was known that Lieutenant King was to leave the

William H. Seward

city for his post early the next morning, I was deputed to inform the young lieutenant that he had been promoted to the
office of adjutant-general. I found him at the house of his
father-in-law, Colonel Elliott, packing his trunk. It is scarcely
necessary to add that the trunk packing was suspended, and
an amiable family were made quite happy by a surprise, which
entirely changed the fortunes of the young lieutenant. General King discharged for four years the duties of his office faithfully and creditably, after which he became my associate in editing the " Evening Journal," removing subsequently to Milwau-
kee as editor and proprietor of the " Sentinel." Early in the
Rebellion, in 1861, General King was appointed brigadier-general by President Lincoln, and served honorably in the Army of
the Potomac until, in 1863, he was appointed minister to Rome,
where he remained until the papal court was superseded by the
coming of Victor Emmanuel. General King was a graduate of
West Point ; he was amiable, refined, and popular. I took an
early interest in him, and a mutual friendship existed between
us until his death. He was a son of my greatly esteemed friend,
the late Charles King, for many years editor of the " New York
American," and subsequently president of Columbia College.

   1839. — Governor Seward was equally fortunate in the selection of other members of his staff. Samuel Blatchford, a son
of the late Richard M. Blatchford, of New York, though but
nineteen years old, was appointed private secretary. Upon the
fitness of a secretary to the Governor of our Empire State very
much depends. The relation to the Governor is constant, close,
and confidential. Governors of our State have frequently been
seriously embarrassed by failing to appreciate these considerations in the selection of a private secretary. In young Blatchford Governor Seward found remarkable ability, untiring industry, tact, and discretion. The relation was so mutually
pleasant that when Governor Seward returned to his profession in 1843, and his secretary had been admitted to the bar,
he became a member of the law firm of Seward, Morgan, and
Blatchford.

   Among the other members of the staff were Jonathan Amory,
Le Grand Cannon, and James Bowen, now residents of the city
of New York, and Robert H. Pruyn, of Albany. Between
these gentlemen and Governor Seward endearing and enduring

social, political, and official relations grew up and existed until his decease. It was through Governor Seward's knowledge and appreciation of their ability and worth that General Bowen was appointed brigadier-general, and assigned to the duties of provost marshal general of the Department of the Gulf States, and Robert H. Pruyn sent as minister to Japan. The Governor remembered his devoted friend, Colonel Amory, who had removed to Boston, by designating him as dispatch agent at Boston during the war.

The inauguration on the 1st of January, 1839, was an occasion of much interest. There had not been until now, since the death of Governor Clinton in 1828, a governor whose opinions and sentiments harmonized with that distinguished statesman. Democratic chief magistrates had contented themselves with looking after things as they existed, rather than undertaking to advance public interests. Governor Seward struck out boldly for improvements and reforms. He urged mental and physical development as a duty of government, and held that by utilizing emigration, capital, and credit, the resources and happiness of the commonwealth and the people would be developed, promoted, and perpetuated. Regarding the judicial machinery of the State as unnecessarily complex and onerous, he recommended simple and economic reforms.

A report from the Committee of Ways and Means, of which Samuel B. Ruggles was chairman, was earnestly in favor of internal improvements, and especially urging the enlargement of the Erie Canal, accompanied by statistics showing that the net revenue from canal tolls would not only pay interest on the amount of money required for such enlargement, but furnish a sinking fund sufficient to retire the canal debt in a few years. The Governor approved the policy recommended by that report. Upon this approval, the " Albany Argus," responsive to the views of " Regency " State officers, took issue. The " Argus" assumed and asserted that Governor Seward was in favor of a " forty million debt." This constituted the prominent point of attack upon Governor Seward's administration. The Democracy proclaimed itself in favor of the " pay as you go" policy, charging its opponents with improvidence in expenditures and recklessness in the creation of debt, predicting bankruptcy and ruin to the State and the people. We maintained, on the other hand, that the canals had enriched both the people and State, and that their future prosperity depended upon the enlargement of the Erie Canal, so that its capacity would meet the increasing demands of business.

State officers were then appointed by the legislature on joint ballot. This furnished a long wished-for opportunity of placing eminent and deserving Whigs at the head of the different State departments. John C. Spencer was elected secretary of state, Bates Cook, comptroller, Willis Hall, attorney general, Jacob Haight, treasurer, and Orville L. Holley, surveyor general. The canvass for attorney general was very spirited, Joshua A. Spencer, of Oneida, and Samuel Stevens, of Albany, being the most prominent candidates. These gentlemen were urged on the ground of being older and better lawyers than Mr. Hall, as they undoubtedly were, who was better known on the stump than at the bar. Mr. Hall was supported by the New York delegation, whose zeal in his favor proved irresistible, although his opponents finally united in favor of Mr. Stevens. Bates Cook, of Lewiston, Niagara County, had but a local reputation, and it required the strongest assurances from Governor Seward and myself that he was abundantly qualified to discharge the duties of the office creditably to secure his nomination. We could safely give such assurances, for we knew him to be what he proved himself, capable and honest. The nomination of Jacob Haight for treasurer afforded me great satisfaction. I had learned in my boyhood at Catskill, where from 1800 he had been a much respected merchant, to esteem and honor him. In 1824, when as a Democratic senator he along with James Burt, of Orange, David Gardiner, of Suffolk, William Nelson, of Westchester, Isaac Ogden, of Delaware, James Mallory, of Rensselaer, Latham A. Burrows, of Broome, and Jesse Clark, of Seneca, he arrayed himself against William H. Crawford, of Georgia, the "caucus candidate" for president, zealously supporting John Quincy Adams, and as zealously supporting the bill taking away the choice of presidential electors from the legislature and restoring it to the people, my early remembrances of him grew into a warm personal friendship. It was, therefore, peculiarly gratifying to me that an opportunity occurred not only to oblige an intimate friend but to recognize and mark the public sense of his patriotism in an important crisis as a member of the State Senate. Orville L. Holley commenced life in this State in 1817 or 1818 as editor of a literary review. He subsequently was for many years editor of the "Troy Sentinel." He belonged to a remarkably gifted Connecticut family. His eldest brother, Smith Holley, was at the head of a large iron foundry in Salisbury, Conn. Myron Holley, another brother, established himself at Canandaigua as a lawyer, was a member of the Assembly from Ontario County in 1816, 1820, and 1821, and was one of the original canal commissioners under whom the western section of the Erie Canal was constructed. His tastes were all and always literary. Horace Holley, another brother, was a Unitarian clergyman, who was known during his brief ministry as one of the most attractive and impressive orators that have graced the American pulpit.

The " Argus," and other Democratic journals, were especially hostile to Willis Hall, the new attorney general, whose zeal, energy, and tact had been conspicuous and effective in overthrowing their party in the city of New York.

The choice of a senator in Congress devolved upon the legislature. Hon. Nathaniel P. Tallmadge had been elected by the Democrats in 1833. During the " sub-treasury " and "hard money" crusades under the auspices of Jackson and Van Buren, prominent Democrats, who opposed those measures without intending to break with their friends, finding that such differences could not be tolerated, were driven out of the party. Most prominent among these were Messrs. Nathaniel P. Tallmadge of the Senate and John C. Clark of the House of Representatives. These gentlemen, with other members of Congress, were styled " Conservatives." The Sub-Treasury Bill, in 1837, on motion of John C. Clark in the House of Representatives, was laid upon the table by a union of " Conservative " and Whig votes. In 1838 Messrs. Tallmadge, Clark, and others, with their political friends, supported the Whig State ticket. It was deemed, therefore, both just and expedient that the Whig party should adopt Mr. Tallmadge as their candidate for United States Senator. This, in view of the fact that several prominent Whigs had been looking forward to the expiration of Mr. Tallmadge's term with not unreasonable hopes of becoming his successor, was an equally delicate and difficult task. Among the senatorial aspirants were John C. Spencer, Millard Fillmore (then in the House of Representatives), John A. Collier, and Joshua A. Spencer. Mr. Fillmore's solicitude was intense. He protested earnestly against the policy of discarding tried and faithful friends, and of conferring the highest and most important place in our gift upon a new recruit, on whose fidelity we could not rely. Mr. Collier and the Messrs. Spencer were at Albany personally urging the same considerations against Mr. Tallmadge. But, strong as those gentlemen were in the Whig party, they were unable to overcome a conviction in the minds of the Whig members of the legislature that in view of the approaching presidential election Mr. Tallmadge was entitled to their support for reëlection to the Senate. He was, therefore, with considerable unanimity, nominated in the Whig legislative caucus. The Senate, however, which consisted of nineteen Democrats to thirteen Whigs, in voting as they did for nineteen different individuals, prevented a nomination, and defeated an election for senator. The same thing was done in 1825, when there was a large " People's " majority in the Assembly with a Democratic majority in the Senate. The late Chief Justice Spencer was the " People's," or Clintonian, candidate for senator. The Democratic senators voted for seventeen different candidates, thus preventing a nomination and avoiding a joint ballot.

In January of this year the Hon. Stephen Van Rensselaer, the well-known and greatly beloved "patroon" of Albany, died. I may not have another opportunity of paying a tribute to the character, services, and memory of that truly good man. Of his estimable private character, and of the bounties and blessings he scattered in all directions, or of the pervading atmosphere of happiness and gratitude that his life-long goodness created, I need not speak, for they are widely known and well remembered.

The " patroon " was a Federalist during the lifetime of that party, and though always decided was never ultra. He was a member of both branches of our legislature, and Lieutenant-Governor of the State. In 1812, as major-general of a division of militia, he repaired to the Niagara frontier, where he served creditably until the close of the campaign. He was a Federal candidate for governor in 1813, and, though far the strongest man of his party, was beaten by Governor Tompkins. He was

appointed canal commissioner in 1816, and was president of the
board at the time of his death. In 1824 he was a member of
Congress. The memorable presidential campaign in that year
twice depended upon the vote of the State of New York. Our
legislative session commenced with a decided majority in favor
of Mr. Crawford, who, with the vote of this State, as was known
and admitted, would have been elected. But after a long, sharp,
and most warmly contested fight, Mr. Adams received twenty-
six votes, Mr. Crawford five, Clay four, with one cast by Pierre
A. Barker claimed both by the Crawford and Clay men, but
who, when the electoral college met, voted for Jackson. This
result threw the election of president into Congress, when New
York again became a pivot State. General Van Rensselaer's
preference had not been expressed, and was unknown. His reticence for several weeks occasioned much solicitude, for on his
vote the question turned. It was believed by Mr. Van Buren,
and feared by the friends of Mr. Adams, that of the three between whom the choice was to be made (Jackson, Adams, and
Crawford), General Van Rensselaer had thought favorably of
Crawford. It was alleged, further, that if Mr. Clay had been
one of the three from whom the choice was to be made, General
Van Rensselaer would have voted for him. A few days before
the question was decided I received a letter from Hon. Albert
H. Tracy, then in Congress, informing me confidentially that
General Van Rensselaer had decided to vote for Mr. Adams, as
he did. General Van Rensselaer was a member of the Consti-
tutional Convention of 1821.

Among the best known and most respected citizens of Albany, from the beginning of the present century until he died,
in 1851, was James Kane. He was, until the great commercial
crisis of 1815, an enterprising and prosperous merchant. Making an honorable surrender of all his property to his creditors, he
lived for more than thirty years in a garret, subsisting upon the
simplest and cheapest food, dividing his time between reading
and visiting friends. His mind was stored with all that is valuable in science and literature. His manners were polished, his
conversation rich, his temperament cheerful, and his nature genial. He was a welcome visitor everywhere. A large number
of families (ours included) expected and welcomed him at regular intervals at their tea-table. In this respect we were partic-

ularly favored, always deriving information and interest from him. He was connected by marriage with Chancellor Kent, with whom he was intimate, and with whose characteristics he was better acquainted than any other man.

Among the many incidents related to me by Mr. Kane, that which I will endeavor to repeat displays the Chancellor's real character in a light equally natural, frank, simple, and amiable. In the first year of the war with England, a distinguished judicial friend from Philadelphia was dining with Chancellor Kent, who resided in Columbia Street, then an aristocratic quarter. When the dessert was served, his son William, since an eminent New York judge, then a boy of three or four years old, was called in; but before the party rose from the table the youngster grew fretful, and after several unsuccessful efforts to appease him, the Chancellor rose hastily from the table, taking his " son and heir " in his arms, left the dining-room, and while ascending the hall stairs was distinctly heard resorting to that mode of chastisement more frequently applied in the nursery by mothers and nurses. On returning, the Chancellor very gravely said, " Mrs. Kent, how long have we been married?" Receiving from Mrs. K. an answer to that question, he added, " I desire that you should say, for the information of our friend and guest, and in justice to me, whether during our married life you have ever known me guilty of committing so gross an act of impropriety as that of which I have just now been guilty?" Receiving from Mrs. Kent an assurance that this was his first offense, the Chancellor's equanimity was restored, and, taking his seat, the conversation was resumed as pleasantly as if nothing had occurred. When the stranger retired, the Chancellor turned to Mr. Kane saying, " Cousin James, everything has gone wrong with me to-day. When I went into Johnny Cooke's this morning to get my bottle of Ballston water and be shaved, the little man handed me a subscription paper for the relief of the sufferers at Buffalo [that village having just been burned by the British], asking me to put down my name for the same amount as that given by Lieutenant-Governor Taylor. I refused flatly, saying that the idea was preposterous, Governor Taylor being a rich man, and I dependent upon my salary. But he insisted that if the Federalists refused to come forward and subscribe as liberally as the Republicans, the patroon, General Stephen Van Rensselaer, the Federal candidate for governor, would certainly be defeated. I was finally cajoled into putting my name next to that of Lieutenant-Governor Taylor for the same amount that he subscribed. But I was annoyed all day by thus exposing myself to ridicule, for everybody in Albany knows that I am opposed to the war, and rejoiced when Buffalo was burnt. But my vexation did not end there. On coming home to dinner, after a weary day's labor, through a cold, drizzling storm, and as I had just hung up my overcoat and hat in the hall, the knocker [there were no door-bells then] was heard. On opening the door, a thinly clad, shivering woman applied for relief, saying that her husband had enlisted and gone to the war, leaving her and her children without support. I replied that her husband was a fool, and that she must look for support from those who supported the war, and then shut the door in her face. I had scarcely got seated at a warm fire before it occurred to me that I had treated this unfortunate woman very brutally, and, seizing my hat, hastened out, in the hope of repairing my error. But the search was unavailing, and, without her name, I had no clew to her residence."

Those who knew the Chancellor well will recognize him in these successive incidents. He was impulsive, but always quick to correct and repair an error or an injury. In all his relations to and intercourse with society he was the simplest and the frankest of men. When, forty years afterwards, I related this incident to Judge William Kent, he laughed heartily at, and vainly endeavored to remember the paternal castigation. From him, and from my friend Benjamin D. Silliman, who studied law in the Chancellor's office, I have heard incidents and anecdotes enough to make an interesting volume, and which, if Mr. Silliman fulfills his promise and purpose, will make such a volume.

In 1839, calling early of a winter evening at the executive mansion, the residence of James Kane in his prosperous days, Governor Seward informed me that an office had just become vacant which could be filled without the consent of the senate, adding, " Let us put on our thinking caps and find some meritorious friend who is worthy of, and needs the place." Isaac Dennison had been the agent of the State for paying annuities to the Six Nations of Indians for many years, and until from age and infirmity his family had induced him to resign. We were not long in remembering that James Kane was, of all living men, fitted to be the agent for paying annuities to Indians with whom he had traded long before they migrated to their reservations at Green Bay, and by whom, as by their descendants, he was affectionately remembered as an adopted chief, bearing an Indian name. The appointment having been promptly made, not a moment was lost in communicating the gratifying information to our mutual and much valued friend. On my way to Columbia Street I stopped at the Eagle Hotel, that another intimate friend of Mr. Kane (John I. Boyd) might share in the anticipated pleasure. It was now between nine and ten o'clock. We found Mr. Kane in his garret, reading by the light of a tallow candle. Upon handing the commission to him, which he read twice, slowly and attentively, his astonishment could not have been greater if it had come to him through the window or the ceiling. If there was a man in the whole city of Albany to whom the idea of an office had never occurred, that man was James Kane. And if the idea of an office had been suggested to him, and he had been asked what office he would prefer, that which had now come to him, unexpectedly and providentially, was the very one that he would have selected. But there was room in his heart for one emotion only, — gratitude. When the time came, in the following month of June, to depart for the far west with money to pay the Indians, accompanied by a nephew and a niece, the cup of Mr. Kane's happiness was full to overflowing.

When the appointment appeared in the "Journal" the next day, it was hailed throughout the city as one of the best that had been, or could have been made.

CHAPTER XLV.

1837–1866.

THE political success in the election of 1837 encouraged the hope that the Whig party of the Union might carry the presidential election of 1840. We therefore determined upon inaugurating a vigorous campaign. With that view a cheap weekly paper for extended circulation was suggested. In casting about for an editor it occurred to me that there was some person connected with the "New Yorker," a literary journal published in that city, possessing the qualities needed for our new enterprise. In reading the "New Yorker" attentively, as I had done, I felt sure that its editor was a strong tariff man, and probably an equally strong Whig. The chairman of our State committee, Mr. Lewis Benedict, accompanied me to New York. I repaired to the office in Ann Street, where the "New Yorker" was published, and inquired for its editor. A young man with light hair and blonde complexion, with coat off and sleeves rolled up, standing at the "case" "stick" in hand, replied that he was the editor, and this youth was Horace Greeley. We sat down in the composing room, when I informed him of the object of my visit. He of course was surprised, but evidently gratified. Nor were his surprise and gratification diminished to learn that I was drawn to him without any other reason or information, but such as I had derived from the columns of the "New Yorker." He accepted an invitation to dine with Mr. Benedict and myself at the City Hotel, where it was arranged that Mr. Greeley should, in case he could either sell his "New Yorker," or make some arrangement that would enable him to pass two days in each week at Albany, accept our invitation. Mr. Greeley suggested and we adopted the "Jeffersonian" as the name for the new paper.

The first number of the "Jeffersonian" appeared in February, 1838. That was the opening of a career in which during the ensuing thirty-four years he was so eminently distinguished. The "Jeffersonian." was conducted with marked ability. It discussed measures clearly, calmly, and forcibly, exerting during the year of its existence a wide and beneficial influence. As the canvass proceeded a more pronounced party paper for popular circulation was needed, and in 1840, under the auspices of the Whig State Committee, Mr. Greeley started the "Log Cabin." The "Log Cabin" was zealous, spirited, and became universally popular. The singing of patriotic songs at political meetings had its origin in that year, which was long, and is even yet, remembered as the "Tippecanoe and Tyler too Campaign."

It has been stated that I differed with Mr. Greeley about the new political element, he being in favor and I against the songs. This misapprehension was caused by my objection to the publication in the "Log Cabin," not of the songs, but of the words elaborately set to music, the plates taking up too much room. I saw that the songs attracted large meetings everywhere, and awakened much enthusiasm.

While at Albany during the year he was editing the "Jeffersonian," Mr. Greeley was our guest, and we became not only intimate politically but socially. I formed a high estimate of his ability and character, confidently anticipating for him a career alike honorable and useful to himself and his country. He was unselfish, conscientious, public spirited, and patriotic. He had no habits or tastes but for work, steady, indomitable work. Our sentiments and opinions of public measures and public men harmonized perfectly; our only difference was, that upon the temperance, slavery, and labor questions he was more ardent and hopeful. In this I gave him credit for fresher and less disciplined feelings.

The year following the presidential election of 1840 found Mr. Greeley at the head of a highly influential journal, "The Tribune," and possessing the friendship and confidence of the strong men of his party. Next to Hezekiah Niles, of "Niles's Register," Mr. Greeley was recognized as the best informed and most efficient tariff man in the country. After President

Harrison's death, and while the Whig party was demoralized by Tylerism, the "Tribune" avowed itself in favor of Mr. Clay's nomination for the presidency in 1844, exerting an influence which contributed largely to an almost unanimous nomination of Mr. Clay by the Whig National Convention. Mr. Greeley, as its editor, by his industry, zeal, and enthusiasm extended the "Tribune" and its influence throughout the Union. We were in constant communication, and concurred heartily in the mode and manner of conducting the campaign. Time served to confirm and strengthen my early impressions of his single-eyed and single-hearted devotion to his country and his countrymen. Occasionally, when some of the "isms" which subsequently became chronic cropped out, I was enabled to repress them.

Mr. Greeley's sympathy with and friendship for the "toiling millions" led him to favor "associations" and "unions" of laborers and journeymen, — organizations which, countenanced by the widely circulating "Tribune," became as formidable as they were mischievous. But his peculiarities in this respect never turned him away from or impaired his consistent and hearty efforts in the Whig cause. Our first radical difference was after he had established the "Tribune," when under the influence of Albert Brisbane, a young man from Batavia, who returned from France with a "mission." That mission was to unsettle and remodel our social system, establishing "Fourierism" in its place. Finding Greeley imbued with that heresy, I remonstrated earnestly against his determination to espouse it in the "Tribune." Many other friends labored to change his purpose, but all was in vain. Mr. Greeley in that matter, as in the temperance and other questions of reform, was inflexible. We differed, however, as friends, and he lived to see, though I believe in that as in other things he made no admissions, that "Fourierism" was among the plausible but fallacious theories the impracticability of which time explodes. His letters show some of the obstacles Mr. Greeley encountered in the early history of the "Tribune."

New York, *December* 7, 1841.

Friend Weed, — I am in sore perplexity. I have this morning letters from high sources, representing that I *must* come to Washington and take charge of "The Madisonian;" that I can thereby save the Whig party, reconcile our disgraceful factions, etc., etc. I fear it is *too late* for any one to do this, and that I should only expose myself to suspicion and odium from old friends ; and yet it seems to me that I must go there and look over the ground, anyhow.   Is it not best ?   It is safe to do it, for the " Tribune " is just beginning to draw ahead in spite of the absence of all party or mercantile advertising from its columns.   We have about two hundred and fifty subscribers for the weekly in the last three days, and are a little more than paying our expenses in this dullest month.   I had just begun to feel that things would be easier with me by and by, so that I could indulge in the luxury of a leisure occasionally, and live less like a miser than I have always been obliged to do.   Besides, Mrs. Greeley is in most critical health, so that I dread to be absent from New York even a week.

Yet I think I shall go to Washington to-morrow, and look over the ground.   If the New York delegation second the plan heartily, I think I shall take hold of "The Madisonian" and try it a few months.   But I won't live there, anyhow ; and I hate to be away from my paper now that it has just been raised into promise.   I wish I could consult you five minutes.

Write me a line by return to Washington, and a word on the subject to Fillmore, if you think it worth while.

Yours,   H. GREELEY.

P. S. We shall try to send our message type to-morrow night.

Greatly as Mr. Greeley was needed in the " Madisonian," he was much more needed in the "Tribune," and I wrote strongly protesting against the change.   The following refers to a very important crisis in the history of the Whig party.

While at Washington, looking actively over the political field, Mr. Greeley wrote me as follows ; the "Fiscality" spoken of was a bill establishing a " Fiscal Agency," designed to take the place of the Bank of the United States, which encountered President Tyler's veto : —

NEW YORK, *December* 15, 1841.

FRIEND WEED, — I came here yesterday, and drop you a line, to add a little to the light you already possess on matters at Washington.

I think some Fiscality will be adopted, though it goes hard ; most of our shrewd men go it decidedly, even those who have most of private feeling against Tyler, — such as Tallmadge, Granger, John C. Clark, etc.   New England, pretty generally, and Pennsylvania will support it, with a majority of the Southern Whigs.

On the other hand, Clay says little, but is savage for a national bank, and says *the West is unanimous for it!* He will say just so when we get beat in two thirds of the West next summer. Many of the Western men are ferocious and ugly, — witness Tom Marshall's gratuitous insult to Gilmer.

Cost Johnson is ugly ; Truman Smith is ditto, and I fear will influence a part of the Connecticut delegation. Maynard is very warlike, and *will vote against the bill,* unless influences are brought to bear upon him from home. Think of it, Fillmore is also crooked, on account of the appointments in Buffalo, but he will come right.

If Clay chooses to kill the measure he can do it, but it will kill himself ; let it pass, and John Tyler sinks into his primitive insignificance ; defeat it, and you give him a giant weapon, and in time a powerful party. But I have no hope that Clay can be made to see this ; I more expect he will resign, and then all can be arranged.

Tyler's Virginia animals don't want the Fiscality passed ; they want it defeated, and have it to fight Clay upon against a national bank. Of course, Clay, Cost Johnson, Botts, Maynard, etc., will walk right into the trap. Has Morgan gone on ? write him, so that he shall see what ought to be done.

I have great hopes of some real retrenchments this winter, — something that will tell for us. I worked very hard for this in Washington to give it a lift. If we could only get the pay of members cut down, the rest would be easy. If this is neglected, all that is done will amount to little.

I went on to Washington, as I wrote you I would, and reported myself to Spencer and Allen, ready to edit the "Madisonian" for any length of time, and charge nothing, making only the condition that I should have the chief control of the paper.

I stayed long enough to be satisfied that Tyler and his nether cabinet (Allen has seceded) *do not want to harmonize with the Whig party,* do not want peace, or to carry their measures, but mean to keep up the quarrel as long as possible, with a view to the succession. They were, therefore, very clear of letting *me* have hold of the "Madisonian ;" they want that wherewith to flash "the light of burning effigies" in the eyes of the people. So I thought it not best to expose the cabinet proper to the mortification of a direct defeat in a collision with the President, but crept out and came away as soon as possible, promising to come back when wanted, which I trust will not be this winter. The fact is, the "Madisonian" can do no good, and reflect credit on no conductor, after what it has been, and is ; all that is wanted is that it be knocked in the head. No management would be so good as this. I dread a summons to have anything to do with it.

The editor is one of those cattle that Solomon says might be brayed in a mortar without taking the folly out of them. He is ridiculously unfit for his business. Cushing told me, the last word he said to me, in answer to my earnest entreaties, that no more provocation should be given, nor ever made by it. Yet, look at Wise's letter in the paper you will get with this. Look at the editorial drivel, to identify this scheme with General Jackson's ; we are an unfortunate party.

There is no mistake in this, that the Southern and Western Locos mean to throw Van overboard. There is music ahead. Yours,

H. GREELEY.

During 1837 and 1838 what was known as the "Patriot War" broke out on the Canadian frontier. Citizens of St. Lawrence, Jefferson, Erie, Chautauqua, and other counties, under the auspices of Preston King, and other influential men, enrolled themselves in the "Patriot Army," to be commanded by a son of Colonel Solomon Van Rensselaer, who, in the war of 1812, led the assault on Queenstown Heights, where he was badly wounded. Canada was to be invaded from two points, namely, Fort Schlosser, on the Niagara River, and Ogdensburg, on the St. Lawrence. The steamboat Caroline, while at anchor in our waters, was captured by the British, set on fire and adrift, to go over the Falls. The force, which crossed from a point near Ogdensburg, landing at Windmill Point, near Prescott, encountered a superior force, and were, after a brief resistance, beaten and dispersed, some escaping in their boats, while others were taken prisoners, and, after trial and conviction, transported to Van Dieman's Land. This failure, alike signal and mortifying, resulting in the banishment for life of several young men of intelligence and character, so preyed upon the sensitive and peculiar mind of Preston King, as to occasion deep sorrow for several months, terminating in a mental aberration requiring treatment at an asylum in New England, from which, however, he in a few months recovered. I had known Preston King as a member of the Assembly for four successive years, commencing in 1835. He was a Democrat from principle and from prejudice. He had grown up hostile, not only to canals, but to improvements of every description ; the world, he said, was good enough for him as it stood, and would progress quite fast enough without the aid of legislation. He considered the Whig as the Federal party with another name. If he was sometimes forced to admit that the Democratic party could, and possibly had erred, yet at the same time he insisted that the Whig party could not, and never had done any good thing. In truth, I think I never knew a more dogged, obstinate, and uncompromising Democrat than Preston King; and yet, while as wide apart as the poles, politically, and during his first year in the Assembly looking daggers at each other, we gradually relaxed, and long before his legislative career closed we became warm personal friends, and ceased to differ so widely in our estimate of public men, and in our views upon some of the public questions of the day.

Mr. King was transferred by his constituents from the State to the national capital, where he was soon disturbed by the aggressive spirit and encroaching designs of slavery. Nor was he long in making up his mind that, with all his devotion to and affection for the Democratic party, he could not go with that party in its avowed purpose of extending slavery into the territory acquired from Mexico. In 1846 he united with General Brinckerhoff of Ohio, Hamlin of Maine, and Wilmot of Pennsylvania, in favor of a proviso to be attached to bills appropriating money to organize the territory obtained from Mexico, excluding " slavery or involuntary servitude except for crime." This, while it did not yet separate him from the Democratic party, was followed by his opposition to the Fugitive Slave Law of 1850, and to the efforts of the Pierce and Buchanan administrations to extend slavery into Kansas and Nebraska. In 1855 he took an active part in the inauguration of the Republican party.

In 1856, when John A. King was nominated for governor, there was an understanding between leading Republicans that the United States Senator, to be chosen by the legislature in the following February, should come from the Democratic section of the party. Even before the legislature met, it being known that there was a large Republican majority in both branches, an active canvass for senator commenced. Prominent among the aspirants were the late James S. Wadsworth, Ward Hunt, and David Dudley Field. Soon after the legislature convened Mr. Wadsworth and one or two other gentlemen withdrew in favor of Mr. Field, who personally pressed his claim with characteristic earnestness. Some days before the legislative caucus was to be held, Messrs. Wadsworth, Ward Hunt, and one or two other friends of Mr. Field called to confer with me on the subject. I admitted that it was distinctly understood at our State convention that the United States senator was to be a man of Democratic antecedents. But when they urged Mr. Field as the candidate, I replied that there was a pretty general understanding in the State convention that Preston King should be the senator. In this they differed widely from my impressions, saying that, so far as they knew, there was no such understanding or expectation. They then proposed that inasmuch as the senator was conceded to their section of the party, the designation should be left to the Republican members of the legislature who formerly belonged to the Democratic party. I objected to this as a step calculated to prevent homogeneousness between the two sections in the new party. But at their earnest request I yielded to their view. Meantime Mr. King remained at his residence in Ogdensburg, taking no part personally in the canvass. The Democratic Republican members were confidentially invited to indicate their wishes in relation to senator. At that meeting, after free discussion, when the result of a ballot was announced, the friends of Mr. Field were found to be in a minority! As I had confidently believed all along, there was quiet but determined sentiment in favor of Preston King, who more than any other Democratic member of the Republican party had contributed to its rise and progress, and who, during his services in the House of Representatives, had done so much to resist the aggressions of the slave power. His election to the United States Senate was therefore a just recognition of his services and patriotism. During the eventful six years which ensued, and through an ordeal which tested both the strength of the government and the courage and fidelity of its representatives, Preston King was fearless and faithful. He never, however, appeared as a debater, nor has he left any written evidence of the remarkable wisdom he always displayed in council. His judgment upon questions of government policy, his advice in political emergencies, and his knowledge of men, might be and was safely trusted. His term expired in 1863.

I reached Washington the day after Mr. Lincoln was assassinated, and found Governor Seward and his son Frederick in what was supposed to be a dying condition. Vice-President

Johnson became president. He had served in Congress with Preston King, between whom and himself common sentiments and warm friendship existed. I asked Mr. King by telegraph to come immediately to Washington. On his arrival two days afterwards he stopped at the Kirkwood House, where the Vice-President lodged, and where, but for an accident, he too would have been assassinated. There I was introduced to the new President, breakfasting with him and Mr. King. As was hoped, Mr. Johnson received Mr. King warmly, and consulted him freely and fully in reference to the important and responsible duties which had been so suddenly devolved upon him. All looked right and promised well. Mr. Lincoln's general policy and views were to be adopted, and subject to such modifications as circumstances required to be carried out. President Johnson's administration was to be what Mr. Lincoln's had been, inflexibly and unchangeably Republican. The war was to be prosecuted vigorously for the maintenance of the government and the preservation of the Union. " Treason " was pronounced " a crime," and "traitors" were to " be punished." When these essential objects had been secured, and the new administration fairly under way, Preston King returned to his home in St. Lawrence. I then firmly believed, and strangely as things happened afterwards I now believe, that Mr. Johnson entered upon his duties as President with a sincere and honest intention to serve out Mr. Lincoln's term adhering to his principles and policy as nearly as Mr. Lincoln himself would have done, had his life been spared. In 1865 Governor Seward informed me that a successor to Mr. Barney as collector of the port of New York was wanted. Several names had been suggested. The relative fitness and claims of each having been discussed, the subject was laid over for further consideration. When the matter came up again I suggested the name of Preston King, first because he was eminently worthy of the office, and next, because it was not quite certain that among the city candidates the best man would be selected. Governor Seward heartily approved of this suggestion, and Mr. King's name was sent to the Senate without his knowledge. His appointment equally surprised and alarmed him. When I met him in New York, so strongly was he impressed with the idea of his unfitness for the duties of the office, that he expressed an earnest desire that we should consent to his declining it. But yielding to the solicitation of friends he accepted and entered upon the duties of his office with apparent cheerfulness. He, however, attempted too much. He thought it incumbent upon him to sanction nothing and sign nothing which he did not personally examine and understand. That involved too much labor and thought for any man, the more especially with one of his sensitive organization. He became nervously apprehensive that by some fault or misfortune his bondsmen might suffer. I discovered in conversation with him that he was ill at ease, and that he judged more wisely than his friends in distrusting his fitness for the onerous duties of collector. Finally, becoming anxious about his health, I yielded to his frequently expressed desire to resign, after which he recovered his spirits and we talked pleasantly until twelve o'clock at night, when I left him with the understanding that he was to forward his resignation to Washington the next day. Unhappily that conclusion had been reached too late. The strain upon his excitable temperament had been too severe. He rose before sunrise, and saying to his attendant (a relative) that he would take a walk before breakfast, left the Astor House unaccompanied. On his way to the Jersey City ferry he purchased a bag containing several pounds of shot, with which he went on board the ferry-boat, and when about half way over to Jersey City he deliberately walked overboard and immediately disappeared.

CHAPTER XLVI.

1839.

THE State election this year was only important in its bearing upon the Senate, where a Democratic majority not only
refused to confirm Governor Seward's nominations for State
officers, but obstructed the passage of bills deemed essential to
the public welfare. By reason of two unexpected vacancies,
three senators were to be chosen in the third (Albany) district.
The political complexion of the Senate depended, therefore,
upon the result in that district.

The district had heretofore been Democratic, but we had
for two or three years been diminishing the majority against
us, and on this occasion had determined to make a very spirited
canvass. A week before the election I became satisfied that the
chances of success were against us, and so reported to my political friends in New York. This stimulated them to renewed
efforts. On the Saturday morning previous to the election some
Whig merchants and bankers met hastily, and appointed a
committee to visit Albany. On Sunday morning early, while
dressing, I was summoned to the Eagle Tavern, where I found
in the parlor Messrs. Robert B. Minturn, Moses H. Grinnell,
Simeon Draper, R. M. Blatchford, and James Bowen. They
had arrived about daylight in the steamboat Columbia, especially
chartered by them. They took a large bandana handkerchief
from a trunk, which they opened and spread upon a centre-
table. It contained packages of bank notes of various denominations, amounting to $8,000. My friends remarked that no
possible effort must be spared to carry the district, and desired
me to take as much of this fund as could be advantageously
disbursed, adding that if more were needed they would draw
checks for it.

The election was to commence on Monday morning and to terminate on Wednesday evening. I informed them that it would be quite impossible in so short a time to use any such amount of money, and, after explaining what I thought might be accomplished in the brief interval before the election, took $3,000, $1,500 of which was immediately dispatched by messengers to Columbia, Greene, Delaware, and Rensselaer counties; $1,500 was reserved for Albany.

A question of much embarrassment occurred to us, namely, how the unusual circumstance of the arrival of a strange steamer could be explained without exciting suspicions as to the real object of its visit. Governor Seward was sent for, and joined in the consultation. It was decided that all the New York gentlemen named, with one exception, should remain incog. at the hotel. Mr. Minturn, whose father-in-law, Judge Wendell, resided in Albany, went to his relatives' house, and from thence to church. Still, we were very apprehensive that the " Argus " might get some inkling or clew to the business in hand, and this, we knew, would have been fatal to our plans. So it was arranged that G. W. Daly, then known as an efficient fighting Whig at the polls, should see " Abe Vanderzee," a journeyman in the " Argus " office and a Democratic pugilist. Except when excited at the polls these two men were friends, though one was a zealous Whig and the other an equally enthusiastic Democrat. Daly took Vanderzee a stroll along the docks, and said to him with apparent surprise, " Here is a strange steamer. What can she have come for ? " They made inquiry, and found that she had arrived there at daylight, without passengers and without apparent object. Daly said, " Well, never mind ; I 'll find out in the course of the day what this means. There 's a nigger in the fence somewhere." After dropping in a grocery or two, and " smiling " once or twice, they separated. Early in the evening Daly went to the " Argus " office, accidentally fell in with Abe, and told him he had found out the whole story of the steamer, adding that, on Saturday evening after the mails had left New York (this being before telegraphs), a steamer had arrived from England, bringing information that the crops had been destroyed, and some flour speculators had chartered the boat to come to Albany, and had immediately upon their arrival started off in different directions to buy up flour, so as to secure a monopoly.

Meanwhile, the steamer dropped down to Van Wie's Point. At sundown the New York·gentlemen were driven to that place in close carriages, taken on board, and returned to New York in safety.

That day and most of the night were spent in active preparations for the next three days' battle. Springsted, Beardsley, and Van Schaick were hastily dispatched to the county towns with additional material aid. G. W. Daly, H. Y. Webb, Sam Strong, Bob Chesebro, John Ross, etc., were to organize a physical force sufficient to clear a passage to the polls. Chauncey Dexter, Stillman Witt (then an employee of the People's Line of steamboats, now an Ohio millionaire), Rans Van Valkenburg, James Weldon, Tom Hillson (now in the custom house), Provost Vesey, the brothers Young, etc., were to look after the canal boatmen. The brothers Benedict, I. N. Comstock (now in the appraiser's office), Drs. Kane and Grant, the Fredenrichs, etc., were to look after the "drift" voters in the Texas portion of the ninth and tenth wards. George Cuyler, and others of his tact and vigilance, were to act as challengers. Captain L. W. Brainard (now in the custom house), Rufus Rhoades, and Tommy Cowell were to bring all the Whig steamboat and sloop hands from New York and alongshore between New York and Albany. David Nelligan, Mike Clark, Pat. Murphy, and Michael O'Sullivan (then a Catholic schoolteacher, afterwards a Union officer through the Rebellion) were to look after the "few and far between" Irish voters. Tom Kirkpatrick and Hugh J. Hastings were to swing around the various polls and ascertain where screws were loose or machinery required oiling.

The flour "blind" served to bridge over the danger for one day, Monday morning's "Argus" appearing, to our great relief, without any reference to the arrival of the steamer. The mail of that day brought news from England by the Great Western, announcing among other things the arrival, late on Saturday night, of over $2,000,000 "for British service in Canada." In this circumstance the "Argus" was convinced that it had discovered the whole secret of the sudden appearance of the Columbia, and on Tuesday morning it contained the following editorial : —

A MYSTERY, AND ITS EXPLANATION.

Our city was not a little excited on Sunday by the mysterious arrival, about noon, of the steamboat Columbia from New York, which place she left at twelve the previous night, with only four or five persons on board, one of whom started express to the north, and the others returned in the Columbia at two P. M. All the afternoon groups were inquiring, " What's in the wind ? " Numerous were the conjectures, and rumors, and surmises which the quidnuncs started to solve the mystery.

The explanation doubtless is, that as the Great Western brought over $2,000,000 for Canada, preparatory to the resumption of specie payments by the provincial banks, an agent was dispatched express to advise of its arrival ; and as there is no day boat on Sunday, and as the loss of a day would have ensued by waiting until the afternoon of that day, the Columbia was dispatched specially for the purpose.

The election occupied three days of extraordinary interest and excitement, each party doing its utmost. A great deal of bitter feeling was necessarily provoked on the other side by our boldness and confidence. The result was a signal triumph, our three senators, Erastus Root, Friend Humphrey, and Mitchell Sanford, being chosen by an average majority of one hundred and thirty-three. General Root, however, had a narrow escape, obnoxious as he was to the extreme abolitionists. He was elected by a majority of only two. This victory changed, as was anticipated, the political character of the Senate, giving effect to the nominations of Governor Seward, sustaining the general banking law, and upholding the canal policy of the Whig party.

Thus a memorable *coup d'état*, completely revolutionizing the State, was effected, on the very verge of the election, by the thoughtfulness and liberality of a few zealous politicians in the city of New York. The secret was well kept, for until now no whisper of it has ever been heard.

It may be added, that soon after this event Vanderzee became a Whig, and, like Daly, and a battalion of other stalwart fellows, remained faithful during their lives. Vanderzee was well known and well thought of for twenty years, and until his death at quarantine, Staten Island. Daly served gallantly in the war, under General Bowen.

The gratification experienced at the time by our political
friends in New York may be judged by the following short extracts from letters of Mr. R. M. Blatchford : —

November 8.— After our sad disaster here, your good news is
cheering beyond measure. I thank you from the bottom of my heart
for all that you and our good friends have accomplished throughout
the State. . . . You never witnessed such wild exultation as there is
here to-day.

Again : —

November 11. — Fairly afloat at last, friend Weed. It is a triumph indeed. I want words to express my joyful feelings. The dismay of our enemies is dreadful. . . . It is you who have saved the
State.

After the adjournment of the legislature in May, the public
mind had been turned to the approaching presidential election.
President Van Buren's visit was the occasion of popular demonstrations in New York, Albany, etc., and served to awaken the
zeal of his political friends. Mr. Clay, then a prominent candidate for the presidency, who was warmly supported by nearly
all of our influential and leading Whigs, visited Saratoga
Springs. Though warmly attached to Mr. Clay, and preferring
him over all others for president, I did not believe that he could
be elected. I was influenced by two considerations : first, that
Mr. Clay himself should not be subjected to the mortification
of defeat ; and second, that the Whig party should not lose its
opportunity. Those with whom I acted entertained a confident
belief that a nomination combining all the elements of opposition would result auspiciously. The difficult and delicate task
of presenting these views and considerations to Mr. Clay devolved upon me. I repaired to Saratoga, where the subject was
under earnest but calm consideration for two days. Nothing
could be more courteous and kind than Mr. Clay's bearing
throughout the conversations. He thought that we attached too
much importance to the United States Bank controversy, and
that our apprehensions in other respects would disappear when
the national convention should have placed its ticket in the
field. In conclusion, Mr. Clay said that while he could not, in
view of the earnest wishes of troops of friends throughout the
Union, refuse them the use of his name, he would await the ac-

tion of the convention, and cheerfully and heartily acquiesce in the result of its deliberations. Without accomplishing the object of my visit, I left Mr. Clay on that, as on other occasions, with a high sense of his devotion to principles and friends.

The canvass, as it progressed, developed great zeal and unanimity in favor of Mr. Clay in the city of New York and along the river counties. General Harrison, who had been brought forward by the Whigs of Ohio and Pennsylvania as the " hero of Tippecanoe," was popular in the central parts of our State, while the west was strong for General Scott. The delegates to the Whig National Convention were chosen by congressional districts. Mr. Clay was supported by Colonel Webb of the " Courier and Enquirer," and by Colonel Stone of the " Commercial Advertiser;" Charles King of the " New York American" supported General Scott; while the " New York Express," then a Whig paper, supported General Harrison.

The convention met at Harrisburg in December. Kentucky, with most of the Southern States, and three fourths of the delegates from Eastern States, supported Mr. Clay warmly. Ohio, Indiana, and Pennsylvania were for Harrison. Of the New York delegation, twenty were for Scott, ten for Clay, and two for Harrison. At the Astor House, on my way to Harrisburg, I met George Ashmun and General James R. Wilson, of New Hampshire, devoted friends of Mr. Webster ; but as that gentleman was not a candidate, they were free to support the candidate most likely to strengthen the ticket. Before reaching Harrisburg we agreed to act together. We found a decided " plurality " in favor of Mr. Clay, whose friends were zealous and influential. In the opinion of a large majority of the delegates from Pennsylvania and New York, Mr. Clay could not carry either of those States, and without them he could not be elected. After full and free discussion and deliberation between the delegates friendly to Generals Harrison and Scott, it was deemed best to unite in favor of the former. The organization of the convention and the mode of proceeding occasioned much solicitude among the friends of different candidates. Governor Barbour, of Virginia, was chosen president with entire unanimity. After much discussion, and several ballotings, the final one resulted as follows : Harrison, one hundred and forty-eight ; Clay, ninety ; Scott, sixteen. The final vote was

intentionally delayed by the friends of the stronger candidate
twenty-four hours. During this interval earnest efforts were
made to reconcile the ardent friends of Mr. Clay, whose disappointment and vexation found excited expression ; and although
General Harrison's nomination was finally made unanimous,
that unanimity was anything but cordial. With a view to union
and zeal in the canvass, it was deemed vitally important that
some prominent friend of Mr. Clay should be nominated for
vice-president. For this purpose the convention adjourned immediately after the nomination of General Harrison was announced. The task was difficult, and until late the following
day seemed impossible. The prominent Clay men persistently
repudiated the suggestion. The "grand committee" finally
presented the name of B. Watkins Leigh, of Virginia, a warm
friend of Mr. Clay, as the candidate for vice-president. But
that gentleman immediately rose in the convention and declined
the nomination. My candidate for vice-president from the beginning had been John M. Clayton, of Delaware ; and after
Mr. Leigh's declension, with the coöperation of General Wilson
and Mr. Ashmun, the grand committee was induced to present
his name ; whereupon Reverdy Johnson, of Baltimore, rose and
read a letter from Mr. Clayton, authorizing him to withdraw
that gentleman's name should it be presented to the convention.
To this we replied, that the instruction to Mr. Johnson only referred to the presidency, it being well known that Mr. Clayton,
a devoted friend of Mr. Clay, would not permit himself to be a
candidate against him. But Mr. Johnson persisted in saying
that Mr. Clayton's name could not be used either as a candidate
for president or vice-president. Finally, all other efforts failing,
John Tyler, a delegate from Virginia, who had voted for Mr.
Clay, consented to take the nomination. Efforts were made during the last hours of the convention to awaken some enthusiasm
for the ticket. But the deep mortification of the friends of Mr.
Clay rendered those efforts but partially successful. The delegates separated, less sanguine than usual of a united and zealous effort to elect the ticket. But the aspect of affairs was soon
changed.

CHAPTER XLVII.

1840-1841.

A WHIG LEGISLATURE. — THE NEW YORK SCHOOL QUESTION. — DR. NOTT AND DR. LUCKEY. — BISHOP HUGHES. — HIRAM KETCHUM. — WILLIAM KENT. — LEGAL REMINISCENCES. — WADSWORTH AND THE SCHOOLS. — THE HARPERS' SCHOOL LIBRARY.

IN 1840 both branches of the legislature were Whig, and as the executive departments had been previously filled by Whigs, we became wholly responsible to the people for the protection of their interests and the promotion of the public welfare. In the Assembly George W. Patterson (elected to Congress from the Chautauqua district in 1876) was chosen speaker over Levi S. Chatfield, the Democratic nominee, by a vote of 68 to 56. Governor Seward's second message, like his first, was able, progressive, and suggestive. He had become even more solicitous for the improvement and extension of public schools. The attention which he had given to the subject during the recess had shown him that the public schools in the city of New York, excellent in most respects, failed to reach a very numerous class of citizens whose children were growing up in ignorance. That class consisted largely of the children of foreign parents, whose condition was aggravated in most instances by the misfortunes or infirmities and neglect of such parents. The public school system of the city differed from the common school system of the State. The city schools were placed in charge of highly reputable, intelligent, and philanthropic citizens, representing the various Protestant denominations. It was claimed to be unsectarian, and this, so far as Protestantism was concerned, was true. Catholics were excluded but not proscribed. Their exclusion was voluntary, the Romish priesthood, up to that period, taking upon themselves the duty of educating the children of Catholics. After much and anxious reflection upon this subject, the Governor said : [1] —

---

[1] Seward, vol. ii. p. 215.

The advantages of education ought to be secured to many, especially in our large cities, whom orphanage, the depravity of parents, or other forms of accident or misfortune seem to have doomed to hopeless poverty and ignorance. Their intellects are as susceptible of expansion, of improvement, of refinement, of elevation, and of direction, as those minds which, through the favor of Providence, are permitted to develop themselves under the influence of better fortunes; they inherit the common lot to struggle against temptations, necessities, and vices; they are to assume the same domestic, social, and political relations; and they are born to the same ultimate destiny.

The children of foreigners, found in great numbers in our populous cities and towns, and in the vicinity of our public works, are too often deprived of the advantages of our system of public education in consequence of prejudices arising from difference of language and religion. It ought never to be forgotten that the public welfare is as deeply concerned in their education as in that of our own children. I do not hesitate, therefore, to recommend the establishment of schools in which they may be instructed by teachers speaking the same language with themselves and professing the same faith.

This created an unexpected storm. The Governor became obnoxious to influential journals of both parties. Zealous Protestants saw in the recommendation a desire to win Catholic favor by pandering to the power of the Romish Church. It was alleged, and generally believed by excited Protestants, that the obnoxious recommendation in the message was an inspiration of Bishop Hughes, who was believed to have been in communication with the Governor. Nothing was or could be farther from the truth than all these accusations and assumptions. Governor Seward had not been influenced in the slightest degree by the motives attributed to him. He was then unacquainted with Bishop Hughes, and had never communicated with him on that or any other subject. And while he had no thought, purpose, or wish but to confer the blessings of education upon all the poor and neglected children of the State, he was not insensible of, or oblivious to, the fact that children being taught to read and write would be more likely to form their own religious opinions than those who were left in ignorance. Instead, therefore, of conferring with Bishop Hughes, whom he did not know, he invited the Rev. Dr. Nott, an eminent Presbyterian, and the Rev. Dr. Luckey, a distinguished Methodist divine, into consultation. After a long discussion with those gentlemen the extract we have quoted was with their approval adopted.

But Governor Seward, conscious of the rectitude of his course, quietly and silently bided his time. Experience of the beneficial effects of his recommendations has abundantly vindicated the wisdom of his action. The law subsequently enacted under his auspices is still in operation, and not the first voice has been for many years raised against it.

Early in the session of 1841, yielding to a strong pressure from the New York bar, Governor Seward nominated Hiram Ketchum for judge of the Supreme Court. That nomination, in view of the active and marked hostility of Mr. Ketchum to the Governor upon the school and law reform questions, was a concession which less magnanimous men would have been incapable of. But Mr. Ketchum showed himself a man of very different mould. While his nomination was pending in the Senate, but feeling assured of its confirmation, Mr. Ketchum came to Albany at the head of a committee appointed to oppose the School Bill, before a Senate committee to which that bill had been referred, when, in the course of a violent harangue against the bill, he charged unworthy motives and discreditable conduct to the Governor. This was going even beyond the point where forbearance ceases to be a virtue. The Governor, though rarely disturbed by personal accusations, and always tolerating the largest liberty of speech, felt that in this case a rebuke was demanded. The moment Mr. Ketchum's speech was published, and in anticipation of an executive session of the Senate, the Governor sent a message withdrawing the name of Hiram Ketchum, supplemented by another nominating William Kent for the same office. The nomination of Mr. Kent, promptly confirmed by the Senate, was received with equal satisfaction by the bench, the bar, and the citizens of New York. The ermine of his illustrious father rested as gracefully upon the young judge as it had upon the venerable chancellor.

Until he had an opportunity of distinguishing himself upon the bench, William Kent had been overshadowed by the fame of his father. Now all saw and acknowledged his great ability. It was, however, the privilege of a few chosen friends only to see how his mind and character were graced and adorned by social and literary attractions and attainments. Among those friends were Benjamin D. Silliman, Samuel B. Ruggles, and myself. I remember a summer excursion in 1839, with Kent and Silliman, from which I derived more intellectual enjoyment than any other ten days of my life afforded. We had the companionship as far as Niagara Falls of George Wood, then the leading member of the New York bar. Mr. Wood stood in the foremost rank of his profession, but socially was what is known as a "heavy weight." In our progress Kent was buoyant and vivacious, while Mr. Wood remained impassive, preferring to converse upon grave rather than lighter topics. Mr. Wood had never visited the Falls, and Kent was curious to learn what impression a first view of the great cataract would make upon the great lawyer. The moment we reached the hotel, Kent, Silliman, and myself were on the "*qui vive*" to see the Falls. Mr. Wood had seated himself at the table in the reading-room, and upon being invited to accompany us he declined, saying that he had found in a New York paper a law opinion which he preferred to read!

The hotel or tavern at the then embryo village of Silver Creek, in Chautauqua County, was no more or less primitive than other country inns. But, contrasted with those in cities, it was sadly deficient in luxuries and comforts. The day's experience, however, was instructive and amusing. But when we were shown, by the light of a tallow candle, our sleeping apartment, with two beds for three guests, things assumed a different aspect. The weather was extremely hot, and the windows of the apartment had been closed during the day and evening. To remedy this, however, the windows were immediately thrown up. Other and worse horrors were soon revealed. Upon opening the beds, my companions discovered, from the soiled sheets, that they had been occupied by predecessors. This was bad enough for my fastidious friends, but worse things were in store. It required but little scrutiny to justify more than a suspicion of fleas and bed-bugs. My friends turned away with disgust, to pass the night in sleeping upon chairs in the bar-room or "baying the moon," comforting themselves with the thought that the night at that season of the year would soon be succeeded by daylight. I, however, called the hostler from the buffalo robe upon which he was snoring, and asked him to get a lantern and show me into the barn, where I found in the hayloft plenty of fresh, sweet clover. Returning to the bar-room, I found my friends endeavoring to reconcile themselves to their fate, and surprised them with the information that I had found charming lodgings for us all. They accompanied me cheerfully until I turned into the barn, and announced that we were to lodge there. From this suggestion they recoiled with a look of surprise and disgust. But I insisted on their accompanying me to the haymow, where they greatly enjoyed the perfume of the clover ; and after being assured by the hostler that they should not be stirred up in the morning with a pitchfork, we composed ourselves to rest, and enjoyed a refreshing night's sleep. That adventure afforded pleasant remembrances in all after years.

In his conversations and correspondence William Kent evinced culture and refinement, humor and genius, which constantly reminded his friends of what they had heard and read of Charles Lamb.

Another of my most pleasant remembrances is a day steamboat passage from New York to Albany with Captain Marryatt and William Kent. For ten hours nothing could exceed the brilliancy of their conversation, — conversation enriched by recitation and anecdotes of literary people, and enlivened by wit and humor. Several of Kent's American stories were utilized in Marryatt's subsequent novels.

The judge related several peculiarities of manner in one of his legal friends, with which I was greatly amused. When the judge was at his summer residence at Fishkill, the friend referred to was his guest from Saturday evening until Monday morning. At the morning service of the Episcopal Church the responses of his friend were so audible and prolonged as to attract observation. After the service, and on their way from church, Kent said to him, " In the afternoon, I hope you will ' descend into hell ' with the rest of the congregation ; I don't care how or when you get out."

The fondness of a New York gentleman for handshaking was well known, and often the subject of remark by acquaintances. Kent said of him that he frequently woke his wife up in the night to shake hands with her.

I remember a judicial incident which occurred at Albany that convulsed a densely filled court-room with laughter. A young man, whose name I cannot now remember, was on trial for secreting himself in the house of Mr. Knowlson, and snapping a pistol at Miss Knowlson. The prisoner was a discarded suitor of Miss Knowlson, and a comparative stranger in the city, but was represented by the few who knew him as an amiable, inoffensive young man. And although the evidence was very direct against him, his appearance and manner excited much sympathy. He was defended by Samuel A. Foote, Esq., then a promising young lawyer. The district attorney was assisted by Elisha Williams, a giant (for there were legal giants in those days). Mr. Foote, as was well known, though symmetrical and finely proportioned, was small, almost diminutive, indeed, in stature. It was alleged that the prisoner, in concealing himself in a closet, upon the basement floor of the house, had made a noise heard by Mrs. Knowlson, who desired her daughter to see what the occasion of it was. Miss Knowlson took a candle, and, followed by a younger sister, went down-stairs, where the prisoner, concealed in the closet, struck the candle from her hand and snapped a pistol at her. The girl screamed, and the prisoner fled. Such was the testimony. Mr. Foote, for the prisoner, attempted to prove an alibi; but his testimony, though uncontradicted and reliable, as far as it went, left a gap of more than half an hour open and unexplained, and this half hour was about the time that he was charged with being at Mr. Knowlson's house.

In his opening for the defence, Mr. Foote argued strongly that the witness must have labored under some strange hallucination in regard to the prisoner being concealed in the pantry, for, although but a small man, he should be able to satisfy the court and jury that the pantry was too small, that it was impossible that he should have been concealed in it. Mr. Williams, when he came to reply to that part of Mr. Foote's argument, with great earnestness and emphasis, said that he was much surprised that the able counsel for the prisoner had attempted to rest his client's case upon the weakest point in it; that instead of being too small to hold the prisoner, he should be able to satisfy the court and the jury, and the large and intelligent audience present, beyond the shade or the shadow of a doubt, that the pantry was large enough to hold both the prisoner and his counsel. This occasioned an outbreak of laughter in the audience, which extended, first to the bar, then to the jury, and finally to the court. It was some time before order could be restored, and during the remainder of the trial things continued to look worse and worse for the prisoner. Fortunately, however, for the young man, Judge W. W. Van Ness, who was holding the circuit, had become impressed with the idea of his innocence, and in his charge to the jury, while giving full credit to the high character and honest belief of the young ladies, he suggested so many reasons for supposing that they were nervous and excited, and might therefore have been mistaken, that the jury, after several hours' absence, returned with a verdict of "not guilty," for which they were warmly cheered by the audience. Subsequently it was ascertained, and admitted by the family, that a cat, who was foraging in the pantry, alarmed by the appearance of the young ladies with the light, in jumping from the shelf knocked the candlestick from the young lady's hand and put out the light.

After giving this ludicrous incident, it is due to Mr. Foote that I should say that he was an able, upright, and much respected member of the bar of our State, and that during the years 1856 and 1857 he represented Ontario County in the Assembly with distinguished ability. His whole life, public and private, was without reproach.

The project of libraries for the district schools, urged so many years before by James Wadsworth, had now received legislative sanction. My old friends, the Harpers, prepared an excellent collection of volumes, which was adopted by the State, and in due time distributed to the schools. An article in the "Evening Journal" brought from them the following letter: —

NEW YORK, *January* 2, 1841.

THURLOW WEED, ESQ. :

Dear Friend, — Your gratifying letter of the 31st ult. came to hand this moment.

You have indeed made us very happy. This is a glorious beginning for us, for which we beg you to accept our unbounded and inexpressible thanks. We feel better and more thankful than though we had been presented with the sum of $5,000.

The "Brothers Cheeryble" (if we may be allowed for once to apply your beautiful compliment to ourselves) will ever remember your kindness. Individually and collectively wishing "a happy New Year" to the "Dictator," we remain,

Your obliged friends,   HARPER & BROTHERS.

CHAPTER XLVIII.

1840.

THE PRESIDENTIAL CAMPAIGN. — "TIPPECANOE AND TYLER TOO." — GEN-
ERAL OGLE. — COLONEL BOND. — SPEECHES. — SONGS. — MASS MEET-
INGS. — "LOG CABINS." — THE ELECTORAL TICKET. — POLITICAL TOUR
IN WESTERN COUNTIES. — THE SYRACUSE BET. — DEAN RICHMOND. —
THE GLENTWORTH EXCITEMENT. — A DEAD-LOCK IN THE STATE BOARD
OF CANVASSERS. — CUSTOM HOUSE LITERATURE.

THE enthusiasm of the people in favor of the ticket nominated at Harrisburg in December soon inspired general confidence. The Whig party throughout the Union went to work
with a will. A canvass never surpassed, never equaled in zeal,
was spontaneously inaugurated. The friends of Mr. Clay everywhere were conspicuously active. The speeches of Gen. Ogle
of Pennsylvania, and Colonel Bond from Ohio, in the House
of Representatives, showing the extravagant expenditures and
the anti-republican habits in and around the White House,
adopted as campaign documents, were scattered in pamphlet
form broadcast over the Union. They proved as effective as
they were unanswerable. The "first gun," as the election in
Maine was styled, was fired in September, announcing a decisive
Whig victory. That campaign inspired and was celebrated by
the following song : —

> "What has caused this great commotion — motion — motion,
> Our country through,
> It is the ball a-rolling on
> For Tippecanoe and Tyler, too,
> For Tippecanoe and Tyler, too.
> And with them we'll beat little Van,
> Van, Van, is a used up man."

Immediately after the Maine election mass meetings were
held in other New England States, in New York, in New Jersey, in Pennsylvania, in Ohio, etc., etc. These meetings were
attended by unprecedented numbers and distinguished by equally

W. H. Harrison

unprecedented enthusiasm. At all meetings, great or small, singing proved an element of great strength. "Tippecanoe and Tyler, too," with other popular songs, formed an essential part of the programme. The most memorable meeting of that campaign was held at Syracuse, which was attended by distinguished orators from our own and other States. The people came singly, in pairs, by dozens, by hundreds, and by thousands. Canal boats from all points along the Oswego, the Chenango, the Seneca, the Genesee Valley, and the Erie Canal, alive with people, began to arrive at sunrise, and continued arriving until two o'clock P. M., many of them with bands, and all with glee clubs, making the air melodious. It was altogether the most exciting scene I ever witnessed. "Log cabins," emblematic of our candidates' rustic origin and habits, were erected in the principal cities and villages, in all of which enthusiastic meetings were held.

At the Whig State Convention, which met at Utica in the latter part of September, Governor Seward and Lieutenant-Governor Bradish were re-nominated without opposition and by acclamation. Those nominations were enthusiastically ratified by a mass meeting, which was held simultaneously. A popular electoral ticket was headed by the venerable James Burt, of Orange, with Pierre Van Cortlandt, of Westchester, Archibald McIntyre, of Albany, Gideon Lee, formerly mayor of New York, then of Ontario, B. Davis Noxon, of Onondaga, and Peter B. Porter, of Niagara.

Governor Seward encountered the opposition (more or less active) of lawyers whose interests were unfavorably affected by the reforms in practice recommended in his messages. He was also opposed by many zealous Protestants on account of his school recommendations. In consequence of these defections, while General Harrison received a majority of over thirteen thousand, Governor Seward's majority was reduced to five thousand. William C. Bouck, of Schoharie, was the Democratic candidate for governor, and Daniel S. Dickinson, of Broome, for lieutenant-governor.

In July and August I made an extensive electioneering tour through the middle and western counties, distributing Colonel Bond's speeches, organizing glee clubs, and urging the erection of "log cabins." At Rust's Hotel in Syracuse, while in

conversation with a large number of political friends who had
called to see me, Dr. Colvin, a zealous Democrat, asked very
audibly whether I was ready to " back the opinions " I had so
confidently expressed. Seeing that this question was asked for
a purpose, and that in declining to bet I would be giving our
adversaries an advantage, I replied, that although I was not in
the habit of betting on elections, I was ready to prove my confidence in General Harrison's strength. " Very well," said the
doctor, " I offer you a bet of a thousand dollars that Harrison
will not be elected president." Of course I had no such amount
of money with me. But I asked the doctor to accompany me
to the bank of which my friend Hamilton White was president,
of whom I presumed the money could be borrowed. Explaining the matter to Mr. White he readily counted out the money,
whereupon Dr. Colvin, instead of producing his thousand, proposed to bind the bet by each depositing two hundred dollars,
which was done. But after election Dr. Colvin's eight hundred
dollars was not forthcoming, and his loss was two hundred dollars instead of a thousand.

Some years afterwards, when Dean Richmond became, as he
remained during life, my warm friend, he reminded me of this
incident at Syracuse in 1840, adding that he asked Colvin to
make the bet for him, with no idea that it would be taken, and
that by keeping in the background he heard the conversation,
and as I took the bet so promptly he thought that if I was
willing to risk one thousand dollars, there must be something in
the " hard cider " and "log cabin " talk. On that account, when
we were going across the street to the bank, he told Colvin to
put up the two hundred instead of the thousand dollars.

The real element of strength in that presidential canvass was
opposition to the financial policy of Mr. Van Buren's administration, a policy which paralyzed all the industries of the
country.

But wide-spread enthusiasm was awakened by the singing of
popular political songs at public meetings, and by turning a
paragraph in a Democratic journal to excellent account. A
Richmond paper manifested its contempt for General Harrison
in the following paragraph: " Give him a barrel of hard cider,
and a pension of two thousand dollars, and our word for it, he
will sit the remainder of his days contented in a ' log cabin.' "

Immediately Whig journals and speakers inaugurated a "hard cider" and "log cabin" canvass. Log cabins were erected in cities and villages, the "latch strings" of which were always "out." To most of the present generation the "latch string" in the door of a log cabin requires explanation. In the primitive and almost wilderness days of our country, admittance to the log cabin was obtained by pulling the string attached to the latch on the inside of the door. At night the latch string was pulled in. During the campaign the Whigs boasted that the "latch string was always out," hospitably inviting all who appreciated "hard cider" as a beverage. Log cabins were impressed upon medals and badges. To appeals of this character there was no answer, and for two or three weeks before the election intelligent Democrats saw that songs, log cabins, and hard cider were carrying the masses against Van Buren.

A few weeks before the presidential election of 1840, the canvass was enlivened by a charge that one Glentworth had been furnished with money by Moses H. Grinnell, Simeon Draper, R. M. Blatchford, James Bowen, and Robert C. Wetmore, to bring illegal voters from Philadelphia to elect Governor Seward in 1838, for which he had been rewarded with the office of tobacco inspector. The newspaper accusations were followed by a charge to the grand jury by Recorder Robert H. Morris. Glentworth's private papers were simultaneously seized by the recorder. The facts in this case were, that the gentlemen before named were informed by Glentworth, a former resident of Philadelphia, that arrangements had been made to bring a large number of men from Philadelphia to vote the Democratic ticket. Glentworth, at his own suggestion, was furnished by those gentlemen with money to head off that movement. The positive assurance of Messrs. Grinnell, Blatchford, Draper, Bowen, and Wetmore, that they had paid their money, not to bring illegal voters from Philadelphia but to prevent such frauds, satisfied not only their political friends but all unprejudiced citizens. Mr. Grinnell, who had previously and peremptorily declined a reëlection, now accepted a nomination for Congress. Among the Glentworth papers was a letter in which he said that the men sent from Philadelphia were to be employed in laying the pipes for the introduction of Croton water. The Whig leaders were immediately stigmatized as "pipe layers," a term persistently applied to them for several years. Their vindication, however, came first, in the fact that Mr. Grinnell ran ahead of all the other candidates on the Whig ticket, and next in the presentment of the grand jury, censuring not the gentlemen accused by the recorder, but the recorder himself.

The election of 1840 resulted in a great triumph of the Whig party. General Harrison received a very emphatic majority for president. Governor Seward, though falling several thousand votes behind General Harrison, was still reëlected by a handsome majority. The State canvassers, consisting of the Secretary of State, Comptroller, Attorney General, Treasurer, and Surveyor General, all Whigs, discovered a defect or irregularity in the return of votes from the County of St. Lawrence, which, if regarded as fatal, deprived Governor Seward of all the votes (some twenty-seven hundred) cast for him in that county. The Secretary of State, Mr. John C. Spencer, regarded the return as fatally defective. The other members of the board asked for time to examine precedents, and the question was laid over until the canvass in other respects should have been completed. When, finally, that question came up, Mr. Spencer found himself opposed by Bates Cook, the Comptroller; Willis Hall, the Attorney General; Jacob Haight, Treasurer; and Orville Holley, the Surveyor General. An evening's discussion resulted in nothing but to confirm all in the correctness of their views. On the following day the board was required by law to complete their canvass. The morning and afternoon of that day were devoted to an exciting and acrimonious discussion, without producing any change. The board adjourned at four o'clock P. M., to meet again and finally at seven P. M. Up to this time their proceedings had been private. After the four o'clock adjournment, Messrs. Cook and Hall waited upon the Governor and informed him of the muddle in which they were involved. This not only surprised, but exasperated Governor Seward, whose patience had been a good deal tried by the loss of votes for other causes. He had, in his first and second messages to the legislature, urged a reduction of lawyers' fees; he had also encountered the serious opposition of sectarians upon the school question. Though popular in other respects with his party, he lost from these two interests some three thousand votes. The determination, therefore, of the Secretary of State, his political and personal friend, to deprive him of the Whig vote of St. Lawrence County, was regarded as the " unkindest cut of all." But the Governor knew that Mr. Spencer would resent any interference from him ; he knew also with what tenacity Mr. Spencer adhered to his opinions, — a tenacity which any collision of opinions with colleagues served to confirm and strengthen. A remark which Sir Walter Scott applied to a Scotch judge, who could never relieve a case of an embarrassment, and " especially if it was an embarrassment of his own creation," applies with great force to Mr. Spencer. The Governor knew that neither arguments, nor precedents, nor authorities would weigh a feather with the Secretary. I was immediately advised of this dead-lock in the board of canvassers. I had something more than an hour for reflection. It was a cold, dreary December evening. I waited until the board had reassembled in the old state hall, and then passed into an ante-room, where I knew I should find the deputy secretary, Mr. Archibald Campbell, who was quite as reliable as any fixture in the department. I inquired for Mr. Spencer. " He is," replied Mr. Campbell, " engaged with the other State canvassers, and told me not to call him." I remarked that my business was important, and desired him to say so to Mr. Spencer, and to add that I would detain him but a moment. Mr. Spencer left the board, and came rapidly toward me with a look which no one who knew him could misunderstand. His countenance said, as plainly as words could have expressed it, " You will make nothing by this visit." I apologized earnestly for intruding, adding that a question of considerable importance had suddenly arisen, upon which I was unwilling to act without his advice, adding that if he could not give me five minutes of his time I must do the best I could without his counsel, which I felt would be of the utmost importance. This relieved him of the suspicion that I had come to interfere with the canvass. His features relaxed, and taking a chair, he listened attentively to my hypothetical case; a case sufficiently sophistical and abstruse to interest him. After a few moment's reflection, he briefly stated the ground of his opinion, an opinion which I accepted with all the gravity that the occasion demanded ; and after thanking him for it, and again apologizing for my intrusion, I rose to depart. After bidding him good-night, he said, "I suppose you know what detains me here?" To which I replied, "I suppose you are afraid the people won't get the worth of their money unless you work nights for them." "It's not that," said Mr. Spencer. "This is the last day for completing the State canvass, and the Attorney General has wasted the whole day in an effort to count votes for Governor Seward which are irregularly returned." I inquired how many votes were thus irregularly returned, and on being informed, added, "Why, that does not affect the result; without these votes, Governor Seward has more than two thousand majority. It's a shame to waste time, when nothing but the Governor's pride is concerned." "So I have told them," said Mr. Spencer, "but it is of no use." "But," said I, "though Holley is impracticable, Cook and Haight have sense, and ought to go with you, and I would tell them so if I could see them." Mr. Spencer mused briefly, and then invited me into the room, saying to his colleagues that I had called to see him on other business, and that since, as State printer, I was in some sense officially connected with them, he would, if there was no objection, explain to me the cause of delay in completing the canvass, and thus obtain the views of an outside friend. Mr. Spencer then stated the case, as he understood it. It was that the Whig vote for governor in St. Lawrence County had been returned by the county board of canvassers to the State canvassers "For William Henry Seward," instead of "For William H. Seward." Mr. Spencer insisted that the substitution of "Henry" for the initial "H." was a fatal defect. Mr. Hall, the Attorney General, then gave his version. He maintained that inasmuch as the Governor's name was really and truly William Henry Seward, although usually known and addressed as William H. Seward, and inasmuch as it was not only an evident but undisputed fact that the votes in question were intended for "William H. Seward," the inaccuracy, even if it were one, which he denied, was wholly non-essential, and immaterial. Mr. Spencer replied briefly, but with animation, and Mr. Hall rejoined in a corresponding spirit. Then came a pause. I broke the silence by expressing deep regret that Governor Seward, after the mortification of finding himself several thousand votes behind General Harrison on account of the school question and the opposition of the lawyers, should now be further annoyed by the loss of two or three thousand votes more, but that I could see no help for it; that the State canvassers, in my judgment, had no right to allow these votes to Governor Seward; that if the St. Lawrence County return was right, then the returns of all the other counties were wrong; that, on the other hand, if all the other counties in the State had made proper returns, then it was certain that the St. Lawrence return was defective. But, I added, however much we might all desire to spare the feelings of the Governor, yet practically the loss of a few hundred votes was of no real importance. His election, as their canvass would show, was safe by a handsome majority, and that was all the welfare of our party and the interests of the State required. Mr. Spencer was radiant, while the other members of the board "looked daggers," but nothing was said. I made my bow and retired. But, after opening the door, I turned, saying that the Governor would of course be vexed at the loss of these votes, but that it was no fault of the board of canvassers; that I was myself responsible for the error of the St. Lawrence board of canvassers; that I had misled them by an act of stupidity, and that I should take the whole blame upon myself; and again started for the door. Mr. Spencer instantly inquired, " How did you mislead them? " I replied, that after our nomination for governor, in placing the name of the candidate in the usual way under the editorial head of the " Evening Journal," instead of contenting myself with plain " William H. Seward," I flaunted it forth as " William Henry Seward," so that it might harmonize with " William Henry Harrison," whose name stood immediately over it as our candidate for president. The other Whig papers in the State, including that of St. Lawrence County, followed this lead, having under their editorial head the names of " William Henry Harrison" for president, and " William Henry Seward " for governor. This alliteration, as it seemed to me, gave a poetic, if not a popular effect to the eye and ear. It was not only very foolish, but, as it proved, mischievous; and I was very much ashamed of it. Mr. Spencer rose, opened the door, and asked Mr. Campbell for the file of the " Evening Journal," which was brought to him; and turning back the files of September, October, and until the day of election in November, he found the names of " William Henry Harrison" and " William Henry Seward" in garnished capitals under the editorial head of the paper. Handing the paper round to the other members of the board, "This," said Mr. Spencer, "is important; and if the Whig paper in St. Lawrence County placed these names under its editorial head, the fact would justify the return of the St. Lawrence County board." I stated that the St. Lawrence County paper was on file at the reading-room of the Young Men's Association, and volunteered to produce it. Upon this authority, proving, as Mr. Spencer assumed, that the electors of St. Lawrence County were informed that the Governor's name was "William Henry Seward," and voted understandingly, he withdrew his objection to the return, and cheerfully united with the other members of the board in receiving the St. Lawrence County vote for Governor Seward. The State canvass was completed and signed within fifteen minutes, when the board adjourned as harmoniously as if nothing had happened to disturb its deliberations.

Had Mr. Spencer known or suspected that I had been informed of their disagreement, and came with the idea of inducing him to change his views, my errand would have proved abortive. All the arguments that human wisdom or ingenuity could urge or suggest went for nothing with Mr. Spencer, after he had on such occasions locked the door and put the key to his mind in his pocket. He could neither be persuaded nor driven to change. But those who knew him well could sometimes beguile him.

In looking through old manuscripts, one of an ancient date, but in a familiar hand, turned up. This manuscript shows that in former times custom house officers relieved the monotony of their duties by conducting their correspondence in poetry instead of prose. Since my friend, Charles P. Clinch, has been a deputy collector of customs for the port of New York, "the memory of man runneth not to the contrary." Some thirty years ago Mr. Barker was an officer of customs for the port of Philadelphia. Both gentlemen were more than suspected of poetic indulgences. Under a former tariff, a question of whether an article then being imported from Greece was subject to duty, occasioned a collision of opinions between importers and officials. Mr. Clinch, who desired the opinion of Mr. Barker, his Philadelphia friend, submitted the question thus: —

The oils of Grease, the oils of Grease,
Were burning shames to Goths and Vandals,
Where grew no arts of war or peace
By which to mould it into candles.
The mountains look on Marathon,
And Marathon looks on the sea ;
And musing there an hour alone,
I dreamed that Grease might still be free.
" But the collector says it *pays* as tallow."

The return mail carried back this answer : —

Oh, tho' you say that Greece is free,
That lovely land of bards and beauty,   C.
Yet Otho there exacts his fee,
And dares to subject Greece to duty.
The appraisers look on Marrow-bones
For Marrow-bones once tallow bore ;
Report, and spare importers' groans,
" 'T is Grease, but living Grease no more! "   B.

CHAPTER XLIX.

1841–1842.

Meanwhile the school question lost none of its interest or bitterness. The opponents of the Governor's recommendation, under the auspices of two or three religious journals, carried it into the city nominating conventions. Pledges were required from legislative nominees. Bishop Hughes, who, as I have before said, had no participation in or knowledge of the Governor's school reform programme, saw that it was both wise and beneficent, and came to its support. His determination brought Governor Seward and myself to acquaintance with the bishop, and was the basis of a friendship alike endearing and enduring. After the Whig and Democratic parties had made their nominations for the Assembly, it was ascertained that a majority of the candidates on both tickets were committed against us on the school question. In view of this fact Bishop Hughes called a meeting at Carroll Hall. I dined with the bishop that day, but did not think it expedient to accompany him to the hall. I went however, unobserved, into the gallery, where I listened with intense interest to his bold and telling speech to a crowded and enthusiastic auditory. After explaining clearly and forcibly the truly enlightened and philanthropic recommendations of Governor Seward, and dwelling eloquently upon the blessings which it was designed to extend to poor neglected and orphan children, he told his hearers that most of the candidates in nomination by both the Whig and the Democratic convention were opposed to school reform. He then said he had endeavored to ascertain the opinions of all the nominees, and had selected from both tickets names which he in consultation with well informed friends thought could be trusted, and that he was about to submit for their consideration a ticket which, thus made up, he believed worthy of confidence, and that he hoped and believed would receive their united and zealous support. The ticket thus selected contained ten of the Tammany Hall nominees with five of the nominees of the Whig party. He also took one candidate for senator (Morris Franklin) from the Whig ticket and one (Isaac L. Varian) from the Democratic ticket. That ticket, when read, was received with tremendous cheering, and when the question was put by the bishop, the responsive "aye" was loud, emphatic, and unanimous. The bishop then remarked that success depended upon their industry, zeal, and courage ; that efforts would be made by both parties to beguile or intimidate them. "You have unanimously," said the bishop, " adopted this ticket. You are pledged to its support. *Will you stick?*" The responsive "Yes" to this question seemed to shake the hall, and then with three ringing cheers the meeting was adjourned. The Carroll Hall ticket, greatly to the disappointment and indignation of the Democracy, was elected.

The "New Era," a Democratic paper, bewailed the inroad made upon Tammany Hall in the following paragraph : —

THE WHIG BISHOP *vs.* THE DEMOCRATIC MEMBERS.

Bishop Hughes thought proper, in nominating his ticket, to select ten from among the candidates of our party. His reason for doing this, he intimates, was that they were favorable to a distribution of the school fund as recommended by Governor Seward and Thurlow Weed. The true reason, in our opinion, was to insure their defeat. This was the move — this the understanding of Bishop Hughes, Thurlow Weed, and William H. Seward. Our candidates, however, have "headed the Junto" by an open avowal of their opinions on the school question, and an emphatic disclaimer of any intention or desire to support Seward, Weed & Co. in their project!

The school bill, embodying the recommendations of the Governor, carefully prepared by the Hon. John C. Spencer, with the cordial approval of Bishop Hughes, became a law in 1842. That bill extended the provisions of the common school law of the State to the city of New York. Under that law the present admirable school system of our city has grown up to its present proportions and perfections. It has fully realized the anticipations of its projectors. Large and commodious schools have

been erected throughout the city. Their doors are open to all
its children. What was denounced as the scheme of a dema-
gogue to promote his political fortunes is now universally acknowledged as eminently useful. Our schools are not only
sources of pride to our own citizens, but attract the attention
and approbation of strangers interested in education at home
and abroad.

Among the Democratic young men of political promise thus
elected to the Assembly was William B. Maclay, a lawyer, and
son of the Rev. Dr. Maclay, a popular Baptist clergyman. The
opponents of the school bill, counting upon his descent and
religious education, brought a strong pressure to bear upon him.
Leading Democrats told him that in voting for the bill he would
ruin his political prospects. I knew Mr. Maclay very well, and
conversed freely and frankly with him on the subject. I told
him that so far as my political experience and observation went,
men who, in the discharge of representative duties, acted upon
their convictions, rarely suffered for it ; that, believing as he
did that the school bill was right and would prove beneficial to
his constituents, in voting for it, however obnoxious that vote
would render him temporarily, his vindication would be sure
and early. He made up his mind to support the bill and did
so manfully, for which his reward came in his nomination and
election to Congress the same year.

My residence at Albany, as editor of the " Evening Journal,"
brought me into acquaintance, from time to time, with the leading merchants of the city of New York — a class to whose intelligence, enterprise, and integrity that metropolis is largely
indebted for its high commercial character and great prosperity.

Prominent among the gentlemen referred to as distinguished
merchants forty years ago with whom I became pleasantly acquainted were Philip Hone, Eli Hart, Stephen Whitney, Isaac
Carew, George and Nathaniel T. Griswold, Grinnell, Minturn
& Co., Simeon Draper, Charles H. Russell, Jonathan Sturgis,
Spofford & Tileston, John C. Green, Charles H. Marshall, Robert Jaffray, Moses Taylor, Wilson G. Hunt, Aymar & Co.,
Howland & Aspinwall, Roswell L. Colt, Pelatiah Perit, Jonathan Goodhue, John Ward, and George Curtis, bankers, of all
of whom my friends Charles H. Russell and Moses Taylor are
the only survivors.

In my visits to New York I was a guest at the tables, and greatly enjoyed the refined hospitalities, of these "merchant princes." From year to year questions affecting the commercial interests of New York were introduced into the legislature. I made it my business to see that while wholesome laws were enacted, unjust or oppressive ones should be defeated, and ere long New York merchants, who never asked for anything that was wrong or opposed anything that was right, advised me of their wishes in reference to legislation, giving themselves no further trouble about it. Occasionally after the adjournment of a legislature during whose session New York interests were supposed to have required a good deal of my time and attention, suggestions of compensation were made and declined. The late Robert B. Minturn, one of the best and purest men I ever knew, after one of these interviews, wrote me the following letter: —

TUESDAY EVENING.

MY DEAR SIR, — An impression remained on my mind, after leaving you this evening, that the suggestion which I made in regard to your agency for the merchants of this city might have contravened your sense of delicacy and propriety, although unconscious myself how such could be the case, and feeling as I do under great obligations for the many friendly services which I have received at your hands, and deeply sensible as I am of your generous readiness at all times to promote the wishes of your friends here, I cannot bear the thought that you should suppose me insensible to these sentiments, or that you should feel that I had made a proposal which would be unbecoming. Pray let me know if anything I said conveyed such impression to your mind, as, if so, I must see you before you leave the city.

I beg you to believe me, with the greatest respect and sincerity, your friend,   ROBERT B. MINTURN.

Meeting Mr. Minturn and other friends soon afterwards at dinner with Mr. Grinnell, referring to Mr. Minturn's letter, I remarked that I had already been handsomely paid for all the services I had rendered New York merchants, and in reply to the question of "How?" or "When?" I reminded them that in important State and national elections I came, as they would remember, to New York for campaign funds, and that on all such occasions they had responded liberally and cheerfully. With that explanation my friends were content to let me go on serving them until, in 1854, my cherished friend, General Bowen, handed me the following letter: —

DEAR WEED, — You will receive in the course of a day or two a very flattering evidence of the high appreciation in which your services in behalf of the commercial interests of this city are held by its most important and respectable houses, and the compliment is very greatly enhanced by the cordial manner, and by the expressions of personal regard, which accompanied the assent of the several gentlemen who have joined in this testimonial.

The present itself is worthy of the merchant princes of New York. As a work of artistic merit, I suppose nothing in its department has hitherto been produced in this country that can compare with it.

Yours sincerely,   JAMES BOWEN.

NEW YORK, *April 25*, 1854.

NEW YORK, *April 21*, 1854.

THURLOW WEED, ESQ., ALBANY.

Dear Sir, — We desire to express to you our sense of the important services which you have many times rendered to the mercantile interests of the city, by the exertion of your great influence in resisting objectionable measures and promoting those which are beneficial; and, in order to give an enduring form to this sentiment, we beg you to accept the testimonial which we present herewith, and with the assurance of our sincere personal regard.

We are, dear sir, yours very faithfully,

NATHANIEL L. GRISWOLD,
BROWN BROTHERS & CO.,
HOWLAND & ASPINWALL,
GOODHUE & CO.,
JOHN C. GREEN,
GRINNELL, MINTURN & CO.

Though the massive silver thus presented, with its beautiful chasings, is intrinsically valuable, the feelings which inspired the letter, with the autographs of merchants equally distinguished at home and abroad for their public spirit and private virtues, are in my estimation more precious.

As a class, during the half century of my intimacy with them, it would be difficult to find one more intelligent, liberal, or patriotic. Always ready with their influence, their means, and their votes in carrying out their political principles, they rarely desired to participate in the results of political success. Prominent among those who did so much to promote the welfare of the city, and to extend its commerce throughout the world, was Mr. Minturn. He earned and was justly entitled to the reputation of being a "merchant prince." It has been my good fortune to make the acquaintance and to enjoy the friendship of very many of the best men of our country. In looking back among those whom I remember with affection, Minturn stands in the foremost rank. It would be difficult to find a better balanced mind, a truer sense of the duties of life, or a man more earnest and enlightened in the discharge of those duties than Robert B. Minturn. While diligently, actively, and constantly engaged in large and world-wide commercial enterprises, he found time and availed himself of opportunities to be useful in all charitable, religious, and educational missions. In whatever concerned the health, happiness, and prosperity of his fellow-citizens he took an active interest. His desire for good government induced a zealous discharge of his political duties, and while he persistently refused to accept office, his advice was frequently sought in shaping the action of his party and of the government. In person and manner he was attractive and accomplished. In the formation of his character, the strength and firmness of his own sex were blended with the gentleness and refinement of the other. But Mr. Minturn's character, the objects which engrossed his thoughts, the aspirations which guided him, and the enterprises which he promoted, will be best understood by reference to his own letters.

CHAPTER L.

1841–1842.

GENERAL HARRISON immediately after his inauguration
called the following gentlemen into his cabinet: Daniel Webster, Secretary of State; Thomas Ewing, Secretary of the Treasury; John Bell, Secretary of War; George E. Badger, Secretary of the Navy; Francis Granger, Postmaster General; and
John J. Crittenden, Attorney General.

This selection evinced great wisdom in the President. He
could not have chosen a stronger or a better cabinet. Its members added to marked ability and high personal character large
experience in public affairs. General Harrison, therefore, commenced his administration under the most auspicious circumstances. It was, however, unhappily for the country, of short
duration. One month from the day of his inauguration President Harrison died. This was the first death of a President
during his term of service. One of his last acts was a proclamation convening the Twenty-seventh Congress in extra session
on the 3d of May. The deranged financial and embarrassed
commercial condition of the country was deemed a sufficient justification for an extraordinary session of Congress. General
Harrison's cabinet was continued by his successor, and all went
smoothly for several weeks. The President's message reflected
the opinions of his predecessor upon the leading questions then
affecting the public welfare, and was well received by Whig
members of Congress and Whig journals. Bills were introduced in the House of Representatives to repeal the sub-treasury law, to establish a Bank of the United States, to distribute
the proceeds of the public lands, to enact a bankrupt law, and

to amend the tariff. All, it was understood, with the approval of President Tyler. While these measures were maturing mischiefs were brewing. Mr. Clay, with a degree of unanimity heretofore unknown, had already been designated as the Whig candidate for president in 1844. It was suggested, first in whispers, but soon afterwards audibly, that Mr. Tyler aspired to the presidency; and ere long it was charged that Democratic members of Congress, in their frequent visits to the White House, were more cordially received than Whig members. At this crisis, at the request of Whig friends, I went to Washington, and was for several weeks laboring to pour oil upon the troubled waters. I soon discovered faults on both sides. President Tyler, while unmistakably hoping to become the *actual*, as he then was the *accidental* President, had yet no thought or intention of abandoning the Whig party. Mr. Clay, for whose nomination Mr. Tyler had labored in the Harrisburg convention, in his interviews with the now President was exacting and dictatorial, and feelings of mutual distrust and ill-will soon grew up between them. With a view of testing his fidelity, the United States Bank bill was hurriedly passed, and encountered a veto ; after which, John Sergeant, an eminent Whig member from the city of Philadelphia, had an interview with President Tylor on the bank question. Mr. Sergeant was induced, from that interview, to believe that a modified bank bill would be signed.

Simultaneously, Hon. John M. Botts, of Virginia, had a long conversation with the President. He concurred with Mr. Sergeant in assuring his friends that a bill changing the name, and in other respects meeting the views of the President, would receive his signature. Such a bill was prepared, and promptly passed through both houses of Congress. But things had gone too far. "Captain" Tyler, as he now began to be called, had gone over to the Democracy. He not only vetoed the bill prepared to obviate his objections to a former one, but vetoed the tariff, land distribution, and bankrupts' bill. The end of the session now approached. Finding the Whig party in and out of Congress powerless, as was feared, to carry out the reforms promised during the election and greatly needed by all the paralyzed and languishing industries of the country, nothing saved the party in and out of Congress from despondency but the strong and almost universal feeling of indignation against the recreant

President. If, however, Congress should adjourn, as then
seemed inevitable, without the relief so confidently promised and
anticipated, all the fruits of a victory which placed the Whig
party in possession of the executive and legislative departments
of the government would be lost.

In this emergency the Whig members of Congress were called
together for consultation. The attendance was general. The
Secretary of State, Secretary of War, and Attorney General
also attended. For nearly an hour the conversation was carried on in groups, all seeking for encouragement, but little or
none was found. Supper was then announced, and all gathered
around a long table, furnished with the delicacies of the season, which, moistened with champagne, produced an enlivening
effect, yet nobody spoke and nobody seemed to know what to
say or what to expect.

Finally Mr. Webster appeared at the head of the table in
buff vest and blue coat with metal buttons. All eyes were turned
toward him, and, after a lengthened pause, amid profound silence, I listened to a most effective, conclusive, and irresistible
appeal to the patriotism of Congress. Mr. Webster commenced
with subdued voice and in a quiet manner, but, as he proceeded,
became more earnest and eloquent than I had ever heard him,
or than those who had known him best and longest had ever
heard equaled. He explained the necessity and importance of
the Tariff, Public Lands, and Bankrupt bills, and then reminded members of Congress that they were elected expressly
to furnish the relief which these measures contemplated, and
concluded by indicating parliamentary methods by which salutary results could be reached. He showed that union and harmony, although requiring sacrifices of opinion and feeling, would
insure the passage of laws which, while promoting the public
welfare, would restore and invigorate the Whig party. Mr.
Webster spoke for three quarters of an hour, and was rewarded,
in conclusion, with three ringing cheers. Hope and confidence
returned. It was the only speech of the evening. All were
happy, and all became hilarious. Senator Morehead, of Kentucky, sang "Rosin the Bow." At twelve o'clock Christopher
Morgan, then a member of Congress, prevailed upon Attorney
General Crittenden and John Bell, Secretary of War, who had
no idea of going home "till morning," to take seats in our car-

riage. If Mr. Webster's speech had been reported I am confident that it would have been regarded as one of the ablest and happiest efforts of his life. His appeal was not made in vain. The Whig members took their seats the next day, determined that the expectations of the people should not be disappointed. And they were not, for all the measures essential to the public welfare became laws within ten days.

But no reconciliation between Mr. Clay and "Captain Tyler" was possible, and, as the Whig party was almost a unit in favor of Mr. Clay, President Tyler drifted away to the Democracy, but found himself in a party to which he did not rightly belong; a party which, after obtaining what patronage they could, threw him off, and, after serving out his accidental term, no man of either party was found willing to do him reverence.

Before the meeting of members of Congress just referred to, an excursion was arranged under the auspices of the Secretary of the Navy, which, as was hoped, might by its social influences win the President back to his political allegiance. Members of Congress were invited to join the President and his cabinet in a visit to the United States seventy-four-gun ship Delaware, then ready for sea at Annapolis under the command of Commodore Morris. But, to the great disappointment of those who proposed in a political sense to play "Hamlet," the part of Hamlet was omitted. In other words, though the excursion came off, and was an exceedingly pleasant one, President Tyler did not put in an appearance.

During the exciting month which I then passed in Washington an incident occurred which is entitled to a place here. Early one Sunday evening Christopher Morgan went with me to call on Senators Mangum of North Carolina and Morehead of Kentucky, with whom we were politically and socially intimate. When, after a pleasant hour had been whiled away, we took our leave, Governor Morehead accompanied us to the door, saying, as we stood outside, that he had been very much disturbed all the evening by a conflict of honor with duty, but he could not let us go without imparting to us a secret. He then stated that a secret understanding existed to reject the nomination of Edward Everett as minister to England. The opposition originated with South Carolina senators, who had obtained a copy of a letter from Mr. Everett, written a few years earlier, to an anti-slavery society. Upon this letter senators enough had been secretly committed to vote against Mr. Everett to insure his rejection. The list included all the senators from slave States. Mr. Clay had at first made up his mind to speak against the confirmation of Mr. Everett; but at the request of friends he was to content himself with a silent vote against the confirmation. On reflection, however, Governor Morehead, who also was committed to vote for the rejection, discovered and realized not only that injustice would be done to Mr. Everett, but that the Whig party would be greatly wronged. I then asked him how Mr. Mangum felt about it. He replied that Mangum felt as he did, but was hampered by his pledge of secrecy. Governor Morehead, then inviting us back, informed Mr. Mangum that he had "peached." Both senators then became disembarrassed, and a plan to avert this evil was arranged. Messrs. Mangum and Morehead said that they would either prevent an executive session on Wednesday, or, failing to do so, would get the question on Mr. Everett's confirmation postponed for a week. Meantime Morgan and myself were to arouse a strong popular sentiment against the "deep damnation" of rejecting the nomination of the most distinguished citizen for a position to which his eminent talents and character entitled him.

We repaired to Morgan's apartment and set ourselves to work writing "correspondence" for Whig journals in Raleigh, N. C., Richmond and Winchester, Va., Wilmington, Del., Louisville, Ky., Baltimore, Philadelphia, Trenton, New York, New Haven, Providence, Boston, Albany, etc., followed by brief letters to influential Whigs asking them to write to all Whig members of Congress with whom they were acquainted, protesting against the contemplated rejection. This labor was completed at sunrise, just in season to get our letters off by the morning mails. The question of Mr. Everett's rejection was laid over for a week. Meantime indignant "public opinion" poured in through journals and letters from so many quarters, and with such telling effect, that Mr. Everett's nomination was confirmed, nearly all the Whig and two or three Northern Democratic senators voting for it. No one except Messrs. Morehead, Mangum, Morgan, and myself knew how or what had caused that "great commotion."

A year afterwards I went to Europe, and being personally unacquainted with our minister, Mr. Everett, I was furnished with cordial letters of introduction to him from Mr. Webster and Daniel D. Barnard, who had served in Congress with Mr. Everett, and lived " in the same mess." From the character of my letters, both of which stated that I was particularly anxious to hear the debates in Parliament, I anticipated a kindly reception. Mr. Everett received me in a courtly manner, remarking, as he took my letters, that it being " packet day " he was occupied with his correspondence. I replied that I would not trespass farther upon his time than to say, as he would find' in the letters I had handed him, that I desired to hear the debates in Parliament, and that as it was stated in the morning papers that Mr. O'Connell had the floor, I hoped to get admission that night. The minister replied that his power of admission to the House was limited, and that he could not conveniently oblige me in that respect, but that his official card would admit me to the House of Lords. Thanking him for so much courtesy, I took leave; but while upon the threshold he remarked that Americans visiting London called without formality at his house on Sunday evenings.

Presenting the minister's card that evening to an usher at the door of the House of Lords, I was shown into a dark gallery where, as they say at an over-crowded theatre, there was "standing room only." I remained there for half an hour, when, finding that the strangers standing next to me knew as little as I did of " who is who " among the lords, and unable to extract any information from surly officials, I left the House of Lords very little wiser than I was upon entering it, and not in the best of humor towards Mr. Everett. I learned subsequently, when in Paris, that Mr. Everett's card for admission to the " stand up gallery " was given so indiscriminately that doorkeepers felt at liberty to be uncivil to those who were dependent upon it.

Although construing Mr. Everett's mention of Sunday evening reunions at his house into an invitation, I made up my mind not to accept it. Two of my companions, however, who were anxious to go, induced me to accompany them. Our names were announced by a footman in the hall, another at the head of the stairs, and a third as we entered the drawing-room. Not seeing Mr. Everett, and being unknown to his lady, we wandered about the room looking for acquaintances. This second rebuff was anything but pleasant. When, a fortnight afterwards, I reached Paris, I gave the American legation a wide berth. A few days after my arrival, Henry Ledyard, then chargé d'affaires (Governor Cass, the minister, having returned to America), called at my lodgings, and in a friendly way complained that I had not let him know that I was in the city, and invited me so cordially to dinner that day that I could not decline. While at dinner, he inquired again why I had kept away from him, when I frankly related to him my London experience. He remarked that there were a great many Americans abroad, most or all of whom expected attentions from their ministers, who were frequently annoyed by unreasonable requests. He was surprised that Mr. Everett should have ignored me, even if I had presented myself to him without letters. This did not diminish my own annoyance, and when I returned to London I was by no means amicably disposed to Mr. Everett.

Two days after I reached London, Parliament was to be prorogued by the Queen in person. I should have been much gratified to have seen and heard her majesty on such an occasion. But, discouraged by the reception given me by our own minister, I had withheld letters of introduction to Lord Stanley, then the premier, Lord Ashburton, and Sir Henry Holland, either of whom, as I subsequently learned, would have given me admission to the House of Lords, where the Queen read her speech. As it was, I hired a chair on a balcony by which the royal procession passed on its way to Westminster. The occasion furnished me an opportunity of revenging myself upon Mr. Everett, as will be seen by the following extract then written for the Albany " Evening Journal " : —

I observed our minister, Hon. Mr. Everett, with his daughter, in a bright yellow coach, with coachman and outriders in rich livery, and Mr. E. himself (instead of the plain republican garb with which Benjamin Franklin, John Adams, and John Jay used to appear on such occasions) in full court dress, with gold and embroidery. I don't half like this departure from the simplicity which distinguishes our form of government, though it is certain that the American minister has acquired great popularity here, and perhaps augments his influence by his conformity in matters of display and etiquette.

Mr. Everett, as I knew, was exceedingly sensitive to criticism of any kind, and I felt sure that in contrasting his bearing as an American minister to a foreign court with that of his early predecessors, I should touch him on his tenderest point. Nor was I disappointed. The letter was republished, not alone by many American papers, but in London. Mr. Everett was so disturbed by it that he wrote our mutual friend, Hon. Robert C. Winthrop, a confidential letter, proving that my shaft had been well aimed, and that its barb had left its sting. To Mr. Winthrop, when he called to talk with me on the subject, I admitted that I had written the paragraph in question in the hope that it would annoy Mr. Everett, and then related the circumstance which provoked it. Mr. Winthrop, after saying that he had hoped to have been able to make explanations which would induce a willingness on my part, by a friendly reference to Mr. Everett, to quiet his uneasiness, frankly added that he could neither suggest nor see any possible way of doing so. And with his consent the matter was dropped.

In 1863 my warm friend, Sir Henry Holland, visited America, and after passing some days at Washington visited several friends in New York and Montreal, and proceeded to Boston, where, until the sailing of the Cunard steamer, he was the guest of his intimate friend Mr. Everett. In making a list of gentlemen to be invited to meet Sir Henry the following day, the latter, assuming that Mr. Everett and myself were friends, remarked that I was coming to Boston to take leave of him on board the steamer, and expressed his regret that I would arrive too late for the dinner. Instantly Mr. Everett dispatched a telegram to Albany, inviting me to dinner the following day to meet Sir Henry Holland. The invitation, which was promptly accepted, reached me in season for the afternoon train to Boston, sleeping at Springfield, I reached Boston at eleven o'clock A. M. Mr. Everett's carriage was at the station, from whence I was driven to his house and very cordially welcomed. I met there such guests as Mr. Everett was accustomed to bring to his table, and the dinner was in every sense very enjoyable. I surprised Sir Henry when we were left alone, by telling him that he had been the means of healing an old "unpleasantness." A friendship immediately grew up between Mr. Everett and myself which lasted during the remainder of his life. I had always cherished a high appreciation of his great ability, of the value of his services, and the purity of his character. Sir Henry Holland, in his "Recollections of Past Life" (page 173), refers as follows to his agency in bringing Mr. Everett and myself together : —

"I may mention here as an interesting recollection to myself, that on two different occasions in one of my visits to the United States (in 1863), I became the medium, without any direct intervention on my part, of reconciliation between persons of much political influence, who had in each case been separated by the heat of party conflicts."

CHAPTER LI.

1842.

IN 1842 Captain Mackenzie, on his return from the coast of
Africa in the United States brig Somers, discovered a mutiny
headed by Midshipman Spencer, who with two seamen was arrested and put in irons. A court was immediately organized
for their trial, which resulted in their conviction, and their execution immediately followed. The Somers arrived in New York
about the 20th of December. I reached New York on my way
to Washington on Sunday morning, the Somers having arrived
on Saturday. There was a midshipman on board whose warrant I had obtained, and who was a sort of protégé of mine.
Immediately after breakfast I went to the navy yard to see him.
Commodore Perry informed me that Captain Mackenzie had
gone with his officers to church, but that as soon as they returned he would ask Captain Mackenzie to give Midshipman
Tillotson leave to come to the Astor House. As I was leaving
the hotel on my way to dinner with my friend Moses H. Grinnell, the young man joined us, and I took him with me to
dinner. He was instructed by Captain Mackenzie not to converse on the subject of the mutiny until after the captain's official report had been made. He remarked, however, before he
left me, that it required all the officers of the vessel except
Captain Mackenzie and himself, the junior midshipman, to constitute a court. He, therefore, was officer of the deck, where
Captain Mackenzie remained during the trial. Lieutenant
Gansevoort, who presided, came on deck twice during the trial
and conferred with Captain Mackenzie. He also stated that
the arrest of the accused parties took them all by surprise.
Midshipman Spencer was very unpopular with the officers, while
Small, one of the sailors who was executed, was greatly liked

by officers and crew. After the arrest everything was quiet on board, and there were no signs of insubordination among the crew when their comrades were run up to the yard arm.

On Sunday evening I left New York for Washington, stopping over night at Philadelphia, where I met Passed Midshipman Gansevoort, a cousin of Lieutenant Gansevoort, who was first officer on board the Somers. Both of these officers were from Albany, where I had known them in their boyhood. Of course the Somers affair formed the staple of our conversation. He informed me that his cousin, on his way to Washington with the official dispatch, passed the previous evening with him at that hotel, and at a late hour, and after much hesitation, he had made a revelation to him which he thought proper to make to me as a friend of them and their families. That revelation, as literally as I can remember it, was as follows : —

After the witnesses had all been examined, " I," said Lieutenant Gansevoort to Midshipman Gansevoort, " went on deck and informed Captain Mackenzie that the testimony was not as strong as had been represented to him, and that I thought from the indications the court did not attach much importance to it. Captain Mackenzie replied that the witnesses had not been thoroughly examined, and directed me to recall them, and put certain interrogations to them, a copy of which he handed to me. I returned and complied with this request, but elicited nothing more specific than the first examination had brought out. Some general conversation after the conclusion of the testimony satisfied me that the court was not prepared to convict the accused. I again repaired to the deck, and expressed my opinion to Captain Mackenzie, who replied that it was evident these young men had wholly misapprehended the nature of the evidence, if they had not also misapprehended the aggravated character of the offense, and that there would be no security for the lives of officers or protection to commerce if an example was not made in a case so flagrant as this. It was my duty, he urged, to impress these views upon the court. I returned and did, by impressing these considerations, obtain a reluctant conviction of the accused." Passed Midshipman Gansevoort, who gave me this startling narrative, sailed the next day in a United States brig, which, with all on board, was engulfed at sea.

I was greatly disturbed as to the course I ought to pursue in reference to this painful revelation. The father of Midshipman Spencer, Hon. J. C. Spencer, was then Secretary of War. We had been for several years intimately associated in public life, and were warm personal friends. I was to meet him in Washington, and the question with me was whether the above statement ought or ought not to be laid before him. I called at his house, undetermined how to act. The servant, who took my card, returned, saying that Mr. Spencer was engaged. I then asked for Mrs. Spencer, a lady whom I had long esteemed, and from whom it required a strong mental effort to conceal information so important, especially as the conversation turned upon her great bereavement.

It is proper to explain here why Mr. Spencer declined to see me. While Secretary of State of New York, in the preceding month of September, Mr. Spencer received a letter from President John Tyler, inviting him to become his Secretary of War. Mr. Spencer brought the letter directly to me, saying that it was a delicate question, on which he wanted advice. I suggested a consultation with his colleagues in the State administration, to which he assented. I therefore invited Governor Seward and such other Whig State officers as were in the city to dinner that day. Vice-President John Tyler, who had succeeded to the presidency on the death of General Harrison, was in collision with the Whig Congress, and was rapidly incurring the displeasure of the Whig party. Mr. Spencer expressed the hope that he would be able, with a seat in the cabinet, to reconcile these differences, or at least, as he phrased it, " bridge over" the breach between the President and the Whigs of this State. In this Mr. Spencer was perfectly sincere, though with our knowledge of his political eccentricity of character none of us doubted that from the moment he entered Mr. Tyler's cabinet he would zealously espouse and warmly defend Mr. Tyler's views and policy. Knowing that Mr. Spencer could not resist the temptation of a cabinet office, our advice was of course in accordance with his wishes. Mr. Spencer, whose trunk was already packed, started for Washington that evening in the steamer. I accompanied him, at his request, to New York, sitting till a late hour in his state room listening to his programme for the political regeneration at Washington.

In October, 1842, Mr. Spencer appeared unexpectedly at Albany. Summoning me to his apartment, he astonished me with the outline of a speech which he had come to deliver at a Whig meeting in Schoharie County. He was evidently quite as much astonished when I informed him that whilst his speech would be accepted by a Democratic audience, it would be indignantly repudiated by Whigs. Of course we separated, after some further conversation, " agreeing to disagree," and Mr. Spencer's contemplated speech took the form of a letter, and appeared in a Tyler organ. Soon after his return to Washington he requested my friend, Christopher Morgan, then a member of Congress from Cayuga County, to write to me, saying that I had " become so obnoxious to the President that my appearance in Washington would seriously embarrass him (Spencer), and to request me not to come there." But notwithstanding this, I had occasion to visit Washington in December, when Mr. Spencer declined to see me, thus depriving himself of the opportunity of proving at the court of inquiry, subsequently held on Captain Mackenzie, that his son had been unjustly executed.

While the court was holding its sittings at the Brooklyn Navy Yard, a sense of justice involuntarily drew me thither, intending either to offer myself as a witness to Mr. Morris, the son-in-law of Mr. Spencer, who was managing the prosecution, or to suggest questions to be put to other witnesses. But Mr. Morris, whom I had known intimately, understanding, if not sharing in Mr. Spencer's feelings of hostility, declined to recognize me, and I returned again disappointed. In the following summer, at Boston, in visiting the United States seventy-four-gun ship Ohio, I encountered Lieutenant Gansevoort, and invited him to dine with me at the Tremont House. At dinner the sad fate of his kinsman was spoken of, when I remarked that I had passed the evening with him previous to his sailing from Philadelphia, adding that we sat gossiping over our hot whiskey punch into the small hours. The lieutenant, with evident surprise, asked, with emphasis, " Did he tell you that I passed the previous night with him?" I answered in the affirmative. He said, " What else did he tell you?" I replied, with equal emphasis, " He told me all that you said to him about the trial of Spencer." Whereupon he looked thoughtfully a moment, then drank off his champagne, seized or raised the bottle, again filled his glass and emptied it, and, without further remark, left the table.

I did not see him again for seven years, — seven years which had told fearfully upon his health and habits. In the last years of his life, when he was stationed at the Brooklyn Navy Yard, then a sad wreck of his former self, he came frequently to see me, but was always moody, taciturn, and restless. In my conversations with him I never again referred to this affair, nor do I know that he ever spoke of it to others. But I do know that a bright, intelligent, high principled, and sensitive gentleman, and a most promising officer of the navy, spent the best part of his life a prey to unavailing remorse for an act the responsibility of which belonged to a superior officer.

Public opinion was at the time, and has always remained, much perplexed with regard to the motives which prompted Captain Mackenzie to this unusual act of severity, and, although acquitted by a naval court of inquiry, that lenient judgment was never quite in accordance with popular feeling. It is obvious, from the narrative which I have now given, that there was no necessity for or justice in the execution of the alleged mutineers, one of whom, Small, a great favorite with the crew, exclaimed, " God bless the flag ! " at the moment he was run up to the yard-arm. I never coincided in the opinion which attributed the execution to cowardice on the part of Captain Mackenzie. I could not then and cannot now resist the belief that he was influenced by ambition for the *éclat* which would follow the hanging of a son of the Secretary of War as a pirate. Captain Mackenzie was Alexander Slidell, a brother of John Slidell, United States senator from Louisiana. He appended the surname of Mackenzie to his own for the purpose of availing himself of a legacy bequeathed on that consideration by a relative.

CHAPTER LII.

1841–1866.

The publication of " Home as Found," by Mr. J. Fenimore Cooper on his return from a prolonged visit in Europe, was the occasion of general and sharp criticism. Mr. Cooper " found " nothing in the "home" to which he returned to commend or approve. Even in the place of his birth and the scenes of his boyhood, where most people after a long absence find friends and associations whose welcome and remembrances constitute sources of high enjoyment, Mr. Cooper " found " everything so changed as to provoke severe reproof. One of his first acts was to prohibit the citizens of Cooperstown from enjoying picnic excursions at a point on Otsego Lake which had been set apart for that purpose by his father, and had been a favorite summer resort for all classes of citizens for nearly forty years. This called out a denunciatory article against Mr. Cooper from Mr. E. D. Barber, the editor of the "Otsego Republican." Having passed while a journeyman printer more than a year very pleasantly at Cooperstown, and remembering the attractions of "Fish House Point," I copied Mr. Barber's article supplementing it with some approving remarks. General J. Watson Webb, then editor of the "New York Courier and Enquirer," who had resided for some time in his youthful days at Cooperstown, also sympathized with its citizens, and was severe in his remarks upon Mr. Cooper's conduct. Mr. Cooper procured an indictment against General Webb in Montgomery County, simultaneously commencing a suit against me for libel in Otsego. The "New York Tribune," responsive to a pretty general public sentiment, joined in what Mr. Cooper denounced as " a conspiracy of the press " against him, for which Mr. Cooper proceeded against

Mr. Greeley for a libel in Saratoga County. His libel suits against Mr. Barber were tried at Cooperstown before Judge Gridley, who construed the law of libel in accordance with the English doctrine and decisions, which denied to defendants the right to justify by proving the truth of the statements, and charged the jury to find a verdict for the plaintiff. Mr. Barber, unable to stand up against Mr. Cooper and the court, was driven from the county.

The first of Mr. Cooper's libel suits against me stood at the head of the calendar in the Montgomery Circuit in October, 1841. I was prepared with my counsel, Marcus F. Reynolds, Esq., to leave Albany on the morning of the day that the court convened. But, on account of the sudden and alarming illness of a daughter whose physician assured me that I could not safely leave home, a messenger was sent to Fonda, stating the reason of my absence, and asking that the cause might be put over till the next day. When the case was called, Mr. Sacia moved for a day's delay, appealing to Mr. Cooper for that measure of indulgence, under an agreement that if I did not appear on Tuesday, Mr. Cooper might take his judgment by default. I repaired on Tuesday morning with my counsel to the depot, but before the train started a hurried message was sent informing me that my daughter's illness had suddenly assumed an alarming aspect, when, after writing a hurried note to General Webb at Fonda, I immediately returned home. When the case was again called, Mr. Sacia assuring the court of my attendance the moment that on the advice of the family physician I could leave home, appealed to Mr. Cooper for another day's delay. This was peremptorily and angrily denied by Mr. Cooper in person, who, in accordance with the previous day's agreement, demanded his default. The case was called, no defence was made, and the jury under the direction of the court returned a verdict for the plaintiff for four hundred dollars damages.

General Webb, who had been indicted for a libel similar or more aggravated than mine, was then tried. The distinction then taken by judges enabled indicted persons to offer the truth in justification, while in civil suits judges were at liberty to hold with Lord Mansfield, that "the greater the truth the greater the libel." In General Webb's case, although Judge Willard charged strongly against him, the jury stood eleven for acquittal and one for conviction, and as an agreement could not be reached the jurors were discharged. Satisfied with this experience, Mr. Cooper procured no more indictments, but thenceforward preferred the civil to the criminal side of the calendar.

The press commented severely upon Mr. Cooper's conduct in taking advantage of my constrained absence, to obtain a verdict which could in no way or manner benefit him except in the few hundred dollars it enabled him to put in his pocket. Several editorials thus elicited were copied in the "Evening Journal," for each of which Mr. Cooper commenced a fresh libel suit against me. One of those suits was based upon the following paragraph from the "New World," a literary paper : —

[From the " New World."]

MR. COOPER AND HIS LIBEL SUITS. — We approach this subject with a serious reluctance. No single reader of this journal can be more weary than we are with "the mild and handsome Mr. Effingham." Yet, justice to our contemporaries demands some notice of the issue of the two libel suits which have just been tried in Montgomery County in this State. In the case of James Fenimore Cooper *vs.* Thurlow Weed, the defendant did not appear, and judgment went by default. The jury gave a verdict against Mr. Weed of $400. The reason of the defendant's non-appearance at the trial was the serious indisposition of his wife and the dangerous illness of his daughter. This fact was stated to the court by the defendant's counsel, but as the day of trial had been agreed upon, the court could not interfere. The counsel then appealed to Mr. Cooper's humanity, but he might as well have appealed to the reddest of the great novelist's Indians when the war-paint was on him, and the scalps of the pale faces hung reeking at his belt.

This trial came on at Cooperstown before Judge Gridley, in September, 1842. I appeared with my witnesses, and Willis Hall, Henry G. Wheaton, and Levi S. Chatfield as counsel. Messrs. Samuel S. Bowne and Richard Cooper appeared as counsel on the other side. The libel consisted in re-publishing what appears above, from a literary journal. My counsel offered to prove facts and circumstances tending to justify the accusation or inference of the writer of the article in the "New World." But the court decided that no evidence of that kind was admissible. All my testimony, therefore, being thus ex-

cluded, I was compelled to go before the jury utterly defense-
less. In the same case Mr. Cooper claimed damages for an
article copied from the Buffalo " Commercial Advertiser " containing the following paragraph: —

[From the Buffalo " Commercial Advertiser."]

J. FENIMORE COOPER. — We have never joined in the cry against
this gentleman. He has written some very foolish things, has shown
bad temper and worse taste, has made himself ridiculous by setting up
as the arbiter of the conventionalities of social life, and, more than all,
has been guilty of the folly of decrying and defying the whole newspaper press of the country, and prosecuting sundry prominent gentlemen connected with it for the offense of severely criticising some of
his last literary productions. For all these things he deserved a rasp-
ing, but for the whole press to open upon him was almost too much.
The battle was too unequal, and besides, Cooper had made too many
and valuable contributions to our national literature to be put down
for a few foolish ebullitions of spleen and ill-temper. Much can be
forgiven the man for the good he has done. But the worst enemy of
Mr. Cooper could not wish him in a more discreditable position than
the one in which he is now placed by his own act. If the account of
the " Courier and Enquirer " is true, Mr. Cooper has exhibited a
want of manhood and feeling alike disgraceful to him as a man and
gentleman."

The court having decided that this article, the republication
of which was admitted, was libelous, my counsel offered to
prove the truth of the statement by submitting Mr. Cooper's
book entitled " Home as Found " to the jury. But Judge Gridley rejected the offer on the ground that it did not specify the
portions of the book relied on as justification. My counsel,
though insisting upon their right to read the whole book, so
that the jury might render their verdict understandingly, submitted, under protest, to the ruling of the court, and subsequently selected, and offered to read to the jury such extracts
as would in their judgment amount to a justification. But this
offer was also rejected, and the case was given to the jury, de-
nuded of all the testimony offered and relied upon by the defendant. Judge Gridley, in his charge to the jury, amid
much else showing a strong bias in favor of the plaintiff, said:

It is my duty to tell you that you have heard from counsel a great
many matters that have nothing to do with this case. So far, then,

the plaintiff has established the fact that the alleged libelous matter was published by the defendants. The question then arises, Is the publication complained of libelous ? The court have passed upon that question. We believed that that was not a matter for your consideration, but one exclusively the province of the court. We have adjudged that the publication is libelous. We believed the law required such a decision.

The libel is contained in a paragraph which, after setting forth the conduct of Mr. Cooper at the taking of the inquest on a former trial at Fonda, goes on to say that an appeal was made to his humanity for a short postponement, in order that the defendant might appear and answer, but that it might as well have been made to one of the reddest of his Indians, etc., thus charging him in effect with being as inhuman as one of the wild savages of the forest. Now, it is impossible not to see that this comment upon Mr. Cooper has a direct tendency to bring him into disrepute. This charge we have pronounced to be libelous, and that question, therefore, is not left for your consideration.

The next question submitted by counsel was, that they might be permitted to prove certain facts, which they alleged would show the truth of the charge which had been made by the defendants. In obedience to another rule of law, which requires the judge to determine whether the evidence which is offered will cover the charge made, I have excluded the testimony which is offered. From that decision there is no appeal to the jury.

Here the decision of the circuit judge is final. I have excluded the evidence which was offered. You are therefore to bear in mind that there has been no evidence given, no witness sworn, no paper read, no fact before you as jurors in this cause, except the evidences of the publication of the libel. You have nothing to do with the supposed facts presented to you by counsel. I say to you that there is no evidence before you of the matters which have been thus irregularly discussed by counsel.

Having decided that the publication is libelous, the action is maintained. To this action there is no defence. As to any facts in the publication, or inference legitimately to be drawn from it, you are at liberty to deliberate upon them in coming to a conclusion as to the amount of damages which you are to render to the plaintiff. But in relation to this point you are to be confined to the evidence before you. Here is the libelous matter. You are to deliberate upon it, and determine what amount of damages you will give. When, therefore, you find out what amount of damages is really and honestly due to the plaintiff, you will give it unhesitatingly, and then your duty will be accomplished.

The jury, thus instructed, had no alternative but to find a verdict for the plaintiff. They marked their sense, however, of the merits of the case, by a verdict for $200, which was anything but complimentary or gratifying to Mr. Cooper.

In the trial of two other libel cases against me, jurors rendered still smaller verdicts. While six or seven other suits were pending against me, Mr. Greeley's trial came off before Judge Willard. He made a vigorous defense, but, like Judge Gridley, Judge Willard ruled out his testimony, and a verdict was rendered against him. On a report of this trial in the " Tribune " Mr. Cooper based another suit for libel. The pleadings in this second suit brought the parties before the Supreme Court, where the question was argued by the late Governor Seward for the defendant.

SEWARD. — I will not detain the court with further reply to the criticism on the pleas. They will be found fully answered in the points submitted to the court.

In conclusion, I have shown, in the first place, that certain departures as to the law of pleading, which took place long ago in this court, before any of its members had seats on the bench, have rendered the defense in actions of libel complicated, dangerous, and difficult. Secondly, that *obiter dicta* which have fallen from the bench have extended still wider the broad and dangerous definitions of libel which in an unfortunate age were adopted in England, and have rendered it next to impossible to justify any libel, however true.

The conductors of the press have legitimate functions to perform, and if they perform them honestly, fairly, and faithfully, they ought to be upheld, favored, and protected, rather than discouraged, embarrassed, and oppressed.

Under such circumstances, it is neither wise, nor will it be successful, to enforce on an honest, enlightened, and patriotic journal the rules of libel established in the worst times of England, — that if a publication reflect upon any man or magistrate, it shall be presumed without proof and against all rational presumption of candor and fairness that the error was intentional, malicious, and malignant, and that vindictive damages shall be awarded where an honest but unsuccessful effort to justify is made. Far wiser and better would it be to open the doors wider to defense in such cases, and to restore the ancient English law which distinguished harmless invective, or that temperate and discreet censure or ridicule which promoted public morals, from vicious and licentious defamation. If this course is not taken, but we shall still adhere to the dictum that any censorious or ridiculing writings shall be deemed malicious, and therefore libelous, the law cannot be executed, because not sustained by a sound public opinion. The action of libel will more and more be relinquished by good men, for whom it was designed, and be left to fall more completely into the hands of litigious and corrupt men as an engine of extortion and oppression. The judgments of a court will be but *brutum fulmen* if they be not sustained by the candid judgment of society, and will have no power to arrest the evil of licentiousness. Whatever may be the course of courts of justice, the press will go on to perform its high and imperative duties, sustained by the free people, whose liberties it maintains and defends. To fetter it with the star chamber rescripts of libel will be an effort as vain as would be an attempt to graduate and control by the ancient laws of the highway the velocity of the newly-discovered and all-revolutionizing magnetic telegraph.

Mr. Cooper's libel suits had all been commenced in counties where the circuit courts were held by Judges Gridley and Willard, both of whom had assumed to decide what was libelous, and to exclude testimony offered in justification. Enough has been shown to prove that Mr. Cooper could rely upon both those judges for verdicts in all his libel suits; but, thanks to the intelligence and independence of jurors, in the sums recovered Mr. Cooper scarcely got hundreds for the thousands claimed. But when the expenses incidental to such litigation were added, the amount became onerous. While many suits were pending, and after consultation with eminent counsel, editors who were being victimized by Judges Gridley and Willard determined to seek relief by legislative and constitutional modifications of the law of libel, modifications which deprived judges of the power to oppress obnoxious defendants, and permitted defendants upon trial for libel to prove the truth of their accusations, and show that their motives were justifiable. In an effort so manifestly just and wise we were successful, both by wholesome legislative enactment and by a constitutional amendment. It is scarcely necessary to add that after these modifications of the law of libel Mr. Cooper's pending libel suits were never brought to trial.

Until the publication of "Home as Found," I had been an enthusiastic admirer of Mr. Cooper and his novels, all of which with one exception ("The Monikins") I had praised to the

.echo. With an elaborate and exceptionally unfavorable review of that work in the " Evening Journal " Mr. Cooper was greatly exasperated. I was informed by those who were most intimate with Mr. Cooper, that criticisms upon " The Monikins" so ex‑ cited the author as to provoke vehement denunciations of the whole American press.

Several years after these trials Mr. Paul Cooper, the novel‑ ist's son, removed to Albany. Here I not only became acquainted with that gentleman, but formed agreeable social relations with him. In conversation relative to the libel suits, I related an incident which he regretted had not come to the knowledge of his father. It was this : On my way to the depot to attend one of Mr. Cooper's libel trials, I stopped at Little's bookstore to avail myself of some new book with which to while away leisure hours pending the trial. The new book proved to be Mr. Cooper's " Two Admirals," received from New York that morn‑ ing. I commenced reading it in the cars, and became so charmed with it that I took it with me into the court-room, and occupied every interval that my attention could be with‑ drawn from the trial in its perusal.

During my fifty years of editorial life it was my lot to be chosen defendant in more libel suits than I can remember or enumerate. There was, or seemed to be, something in my manner or style of writing to " make the galled jades wince." My opponents, instead of contenting themselves with replies, frequently resorted to libel suits. On the other hand, though provoking much and severe denunciations, I but once in my life was plaintiff in a libel suit. The " Albany Argus," during an exciting canvass, charged distinctly that I had escaped convic‑ tion upon a criminal offense by a technicality. When the cause was ready for trial, Mr. Croswell sent an attorney to Coopers‑ town to collect the testimony in support of the charge, who on his return reported that he was unable to find anything on which the defense could rely. The Hon. Benjamin F. But‑ ler, an eminent counselor, then visited Cooperstown on the same errand. Mr. Butler learned from the old citizens of the village, that in the affair out of which the accusation had grown I was in no way or manner culpable. The origin and result of that affair I have given in a previous chapter. Messrs. B. F. Butler and A. L. Jordan, counsel respectively for Mr. Croswell and myself, prepared a full and frank retraction, which was published in the " Argus."

Of all my other libels I remember but one in which great and inexcusable injustice was done. During an animated and stirring charter election campaign at Albany, the late Erastus Corning being the Democratic candidate for mayor, Lewis Benedict, Jr., and I. N. Comstock came hurriedly into the "Evening Journal" office with a letter, the publication of which it was believed would prove very damaging to the Democratic candidate for mayor. The letter was written by Mr. Corning to Hiram Perry, overseer of the poor.

The following is a copy : —

ALBANY.

DEAR SIR, — David Jones wants some wood. If he is right, please let him have a load.   Yours, truly,   ERASTUS CORNING.
HIRAM PERRY, Poor Master.

This letter with some stinging comments immediately appeared in the "Journal," and, as was expected, raised a storm against Mr. Corning. The "Argus" of the following morning denounced the letter as a forgery. On the same day Mr. Corning commenced a suit for libel. Mr. Corning's handwriting was too well known to allow any one to doubt the genuineness of the letter. But upon a closer examination it was ascertained that the word " it " had been erased and the word " he" substituted. This made all the difference in the world. The letter as written was an entirely proper one, but as printed as highly improper. I promptly made the explanation, accompanied with an expression of deep regret that I had unintentionally done Mr. Corning great injustice. This, however, did not appease Mr. Corning. He expressed his determination to pursue the matter to the bitter end. Nor was the matter adjusted until the morning of the day set down for the trial, when my counsel, Samuel Stevens, succeeded in a settlement by the payment of costs, the payment of a liberal counsel fee to John Van Buren, and the publication of a second retraction drawn up by that gentleman.

My last and culminating libel suit was a memorable one. There had been for several years growing ill-will between Mr. George Opdyke and myself. Feeling that that gentleman on several occasions had done me great injustice, I prepared with much care an article so direct and severe in accusation and comment as to induce Mr. Opdyke, under the advice of his counsel, David Dudley Field, to commence a suit for libel. The cause came on for trial in New York, before Judge Mason of the fifth judicial district, attracting for nineteen days a crowded and attentive auditory. Judge Emott was associated with Mr. Field as counsel for the plaintiff. Messrs. Blatchford, Seward, and Griswold were my attorneys. They retained William M. Evarts and Edwards Pierrepont as counsel. During this protracted and exciting trial Judge Mason held the scales of justice with an even balance. The jury disagreed.

Returning from court quite satisfied with the result of the trial, I drew three checks of $2,500 each, payable to the order of Messrs. Blatchford & Co., Mr. Evarts, and Mr. Pierrepont. Handing them to Mr. Blatchford, I requested him to make a bill for the whole expense of the trial as soon as practicable, that it might be paid before I left the city. I called at Mr. Blatchford's office the following day, but was told that the account was not yet ready. But on the succeeding or third day after the trial I received a letter from General James Bowen, containing the bill of items covering the whole expenses of the trial, amounting to over seventeen thousand dollars, my three unused checks, together with the names of friends who had voluntarily contributed and paid the whole amount. I had received no intimation of this movement, nor had such a thought entered my mind. But its delicacy served to increase my sense of its generosity. It is gratefully remembered among the many evidences of devoted friendship which, through a long life, has strewn my pathway with flowers.

CHAPTER LIII.

1842.

THE State of Rhode Island was the scene of a popular movement in 1842 which assumed a serious aspect. There had been
agitation for several years in favor of a constitutional government, Rhode Island having been content so far to live under
the provisions of a royal charter giving a colonial government
to "Rhode Island and Providence Plantations." Impatient of
delay, Thomas W. Dorr put himself at the head of a revolutionary faction. The Governor, by proclamation, called upon
the law-abiding citizens of Rhode Island to aid him in maintaining the authority of the government. The "Free Suffrage"
men held a convention and adopted a constitution, under which
an election was held, Dorr receiving all their votes for governor. He issued a proclamation, inviting citizens of other
States to unite with the "oppressed" citizens of Rhode Island
in an effort to overthrow the "royal charter government."
The chief ground of complaint was that the charter required
a property qualification for voters. The real difficulty in the
case was, that "Governor Dorr" attempted to do the right
thing in the wrong way. At that juncture Governor Seward
deemed it proper to tender the support of New York to the
Governor of Rhode Island, if, in the judgment of the latter,
such aid was needed. His private secretary, the present Judge
Blatchford of the United States court, with one of his aides-
de-camp, Colonel James Bowen, subsequently, during the war
for the Union, a general and provost marshal of New Orleans,
and for many years president of the Board of Charities and
Correction in the city of New York, were dispatched to Rhode
Island with Governor Seward's letter to Governor King.

On that occasion, at the suggestion of the Governor, I accompanied Messrs. Blatchford and Bowen in my usual capacity as an "unofficial" or "outsider." We reached Providence before sunrise, and were presented, at that early hour, to Governor King, who was holding council with the civil and military authorities at the State House. The din of arms was heard throughout the city. Among prominent citizens of Providence doing duty as privates, with muskets upon their shoulders, was my greatly esteemed friend, Charles H. Russell, who though a resident of New York, and one of its "merchant princes," hastened on the first alarm to the defense of the government of his native State. Among those also most earnest in their support of the government were the father, brother, and brother-in-law of Dorr. Troops were moving towards the scene of expected battle, some sixteen miles from Providence, where, on Acot Hill, Dorr was encamped. General McNeil, an officer of the United States Engineer Corps, commanded the State troops, with Colonel Bankhead, distinguished in the War of 1812, in command of a detachment of United States troops from Fort Adams.

Having determined to accompany the troops to the field, General McNeil invited us to join his staff. Vehicles of all descriptions, from the coach to the cart, were in such request that with difficulty we succeeded in getting a gig in which but two could be accommodated, and, although my young companions insisted upon taking their turn on foot, I entered so much into the spirit of the march and the music that I attached myself to a company commanded by Captain Greene, a grandson of General Greene of the Revolutionary army. The day was exceedingly hot, and, while I felt no fatigue or inconvenience from the march, I found on my return to Albany that the sixteen miles, which had been accomplished in less than five hours, had developed varicose veins in a form so serious as to occasion much solicitude. My family physician, the late Dr. Platt Williams (to whose memory in the double relation of friend and physician for more than fifty years I desire to pay a tribute of affection and gratitude), after a careful examination, decided that the only remedy was in surgery. Before deciding upon the surgeon to be employed, I met at the Astor House Dr. Alexander H. Watson, a young physician just from Edinburgh, who

subsequently married an accomplished daughter of Elisha W.
King, a long time ago an eminent lawyer in New York. Informing Dr. Watson that I was about to submit to an operation
for varicose veins, he remarked that he believed a remedy had
been discovered which would change the practice in relation
thereto. He had seen in London a compress stocking, which it
was believed would obviate the necessity for cutting and tying
up veins. Finding, upon consultation with friends, that I could
spare two or three months from my duties, and that so much of
relaxation was needed, I decided to go to England. On reaching London, guided by Dr. Watson's memoranda, I found the
compress stocking manufactory, where I tried on and purchased
the article. While it did not sit pleasantly, and was not all I
had expected, yet it enabled me to walk a mile or two a day,
and, on the whole, was a great relief. After passing a month
in England and Scotland, I went to Paris, where, on the morning of my arrival, I found an advertisement in "Galignani"
which promised perfect and permanent relief to all who suffered from varicose veins. Repairing immediately to the street
and number indicated, I found M. Flamet, with his wife, in a
garret, diligently knitting stockings with yarn saturated in India rubber. Monsieur Flamet took my measure, and two days
afterwards brought the stocking to my hotel. It fitted exactly,
and, in walking about the apartment, I experienced a sensation
of happiness and gratitude to which language can give no adequate expression. I learned from M. Flamet that he had been
several years in the French army, from which, being disabled
by varicose veins, he was discharged. Upon the principle that
" necessity is the mother of invention," feeling sure that there
must be some better relief than was obtained by bandaging, he
went on with experiments until India rubber, which has been
found universally valuable, could be utilized so perfectly as
to change the entire practice in the treatment of varicose veins,
thus conferring upon the human race a boon as precious, though
not of such universal application, as that conferred upon mankind by Dr. Jenner.

On my return to America I suggested names of druggists
in New York, Albany, and other cities, for the sole agents for
the sale of M. Flamet's India rubber stockings. Ten years
afterwards, when I visited Paris, M. Flamet occupied a large

house, and employed between fifty and sixty women in his manufactory, and had become wealthy. He informed me that the demand for his stockings in America was quite equal to the demand on the Continent. While, therefore, M. Flamet, in seeking personal relief, was the means of rendering great service to his race, my visit abroad to obtain personal relief was the means of introducing a beneficent remedial invention to Americans several years earlier than it would otherwise have found its way here.

After this long digression let us return to the closing scenes of the " Dorr war." When the advance guard of State troops reached the foot of Acot Hill the adjutant dashed up the steep hill, every one expecting when he reached the summit to see him fall. But of this there was no danger. Dorr had broken up his camp, and, with his routed followers, was in rapid retreat. One or two hundred stragglers were captured, among whom were fifteen or twenty of " Subterraneans " from New York. He himself was reported among the prisoners, but this proved not true. I found among the prisoners two newspaper reporters, who, when the facts were made known to General McNeil, were discharged. The duties and excitement of the day being over, General McNeil's headquarters were established in a pleasant grove, where hampers of cold meats, poultry, game, etc., etc., with baskets of champagne, soon appeared. The spread was a bountiful one, the repast was animated by patriotic toasts and speeches, and was not concluded until near six o'clock, when the general, with his suite and guests, departed in hilarious spirits for Providence, reaching that city about midnight.

Thus ended the " Dorr war," leaving in the history of our country the remembrance of a political spasm, kindred to " Shays's " rebellion in Massachusetts.

Having sustained the State government, and vindicated their " law and order " character, the good citizens of Rhode Island met in convention and formed and adopted a Constitution free from the objections which time and progress had disclosed, and in harmony with the Constitutions of sister States and the spirit of the age.

The following letter may appropriately find a place here : —

[Letter to George W. Curtis.]

December 16, 1873.

MY DEAR SIR, — I have received your note of Saturday, making inquiry as to the origin of the term " Barn-burner," formerly applied to one wing of the Democratic party.

Without undertaking to positively guarantee the correctness of my memory on that point, I give you the facts as I now recall them in regard to its derivation.

About the year 1842 a popular movement in Rhode Island, for a change of the State Constitution, finally took the shape of an insurrection, named, from its leader, " the Dorr Rebellion." Among the acts incident to that time of public disorder, were highway robberies and the burning of farmers' well-stored barns. These acts the " law and order party " charged upon their radical opponents, whom they stigmatized as "robbers," " rioters," " incendiaries," and " barn-burners."

A few years later, when discords arose in the Democratic party in the State of New York in regard to canal policy and other subjects, the radical wing advocated a change of the Constitution. They bestowed upon the conservative portion of the party the nickname of " Old Hunkers," implying their stubborn resistance to reforms. The latter retorted by saying the so-called constitutional reformers were " barn-burners," like their Rhode Island prototypes. It added point to the charge that some of the " barn-burner " presses and politicians were remembered as having encouraged the " Dorr Rebellion." But Colonel Samuel Young, who presided at one of the first State conventions held by the radical faction, accepted the title. " Gentlemen," said he, " they call us Barn-burners. Thunder and lightning are barn-burners sometimes ; but they greatly purify the whole atmosphere, and that, gentlemen, is what we propose to do." During the agitation of the slavery question, which followed, the Old Hunkers maintained a conservative attitude, while the more radical " Barn-burners " became the nucleus of the Free Soil party of 1848.

CHAPTER LIV.

1826–1862.

Some Dinner Experiences and Incidents. — Mr. Clay's Dinner. — Samuel L. Southard. — The Gadsby House. — Matthew St. Clair Clark. — Why I did not dine with the Duke of Wellington. — Guests but no Dinner.

In 1826, while at Washington, I received an invitation from Mr. Clay to dinner. The day after, the porter of Gadsby's Hotel, where I was staying, said to me, "I hope you will accept Mr. Clay's invitation, sir." I said, "How did you know I had an invitation from Mr. Clay?" "Oh, sir; the letter came through the office, and we all know Mr. Clay's handwriting." He repeated his hope that I would go, and added, "Gentlemen sometimes come to Washington on business without bringing their dress coats with them; possibly you may have forgotten yours; if you did, you would do me a great favor by accepting one that I have n't worn, and which would fit you nicely." The porter, who was evidently an observing and sagacious man, had divined the truth. I not only had not brought a dress coat, but I did not possess one to bring, and was really regretting the necessity of declining the invitation for that reason. But the porter urged his offer with such kindness and delicacy that I accepted both the coat and the invitation.

General Jackson in 1828 succeeded Mr. Adams as president. From that time until 1840, during the administrations of Jackson and Van Buren, a period of twelve years, I was not again in Washington. In the latter year, after the election of General Harrison, I again visited the city, and in passing through the Treasury Department I encountered my old friend Brady, the thoughtful porter whose coat I had worn to Mr. Clay's dinner, and with whom I exchanged a very hearty greeting. He informed me that he had received a clerkship in the department from General Jackson, but as the "spoils belonged to the victors," he now expected to lose his place. After parting with him I went to the Secretary of the Treasury, Mr. Ewing, and related to him the peculiar obligation under which I had formerly placed myself to the friendly porter, adding what I was quite sure he would find true, that he was a very capable and faithful clerk. The Secretary was amused at the nature of the obligation I had incurred years before, and cheerfully consented to retain my friend in his situation.

In 1843, while again at Washington, the Hon. D. D. Barnard, our representative from Albany, invited me to dinner. His "mess" consisted of the Hon. John Greig of Canandaigua, the Hon. Henry Van Rensselaer of Ogdensburgh, and the Hon. Jared Ingersoll of Philadelphia, — a very select and refined circle, all being gentlemen of high social position. When the dessert was about to be brought on, it being an exceedingly hot day, Mr. Greig suggested that we should move to the veranda, where we could enjoy the cool breeze from the river. In going from the dining-room to the veranda, I discovered in the person arranging the table my old friend Brady, the porter, with whom I cordially shook hands. I learned, from the brief questions I put to him, that he was the host of that house, and that these members of Congress were his guests. As soon as he retired, I commenced relating the story of the coat, which my fastidious friend Mr. Barnard attempted to interrupt, from a sense of horror that a friend whom he had honored with an invitation to dinner should voluntarily confess that he had worn a porter's coat to a dinner with the Secretary of State. Mr. Ingersoll's susceptibilities seemed also to be disturbed; but Mr. Greig, one of "Nature's noblemen," and Mr. Van Rensselaer, an accomplished son of the old patroon, and son-in-law of the late John A. King, enjoyed the story immensely, and insisted upon having Brady called in to give his version of the incident. My old friend remained through several administrations in the treasury department, and died years ago, extensively known and greatly respected among the citizens of Washington.

Another incident of that visit in 1826 to Washington was a dinner at Mr. Southard's, who was then the Secretary of the Navy. Among the guests were two gentlemen, who subsequently became Whig presidential candidates, Mr. Clay, then Secretary of State, and General Harrison, at that time senator in Congress. Another guest was Mr. Joseph Gales of the "National Intelligencer." The old mansion which our host occupied, known for many years in Washington as the " Gadsby " House, became subsequently the residence of Mr. Gales, and later of John A. and James G. King, of New York, when they were in Congress in 1850, at whose hospitable table I was again a guest, and at the time of the secession of Louisiana, in 1861, was occupied by Senator Benjamin.

Another dinner was at Hyatt's well-known boarding-house. At this were present many whose names are readily remembered: among them Michael Hoffman, Henry R. Storrs, John G. Stower, Nathaniel Garrow, and Matthew St. Clair Clarke, who, for many years clerk of the House of Representatives, held that position in 1826. He was one of the most agreeable dinner-table companions, with an infinite stock of amusing anecdotes, especially of members of the House of Representatives who were noted for eccentricities or eloquence. His stories and imitations of some of the members, senators and representatives, who at one time or another represented New Orleans, Detroit, or St. Louis, always " set the table in a roar."

" Why I did not dine with the Duke of Wellington " may be narrated next.

We reached London on Saturday afternoon, November —, 1852, and took lodgings at Christie's Hotel, in Regent Street. I had brought with me three barrels of very large and excellent American apples, ten pair of prairie chickens, and ten brace of canvas-back ducks. I divided the game, etc., and sent it that afternoon to my friends, the Hon. Abbott Lawrence, our minister to England ; Mr. Peabody, the eminent American banker ; and Mr. Joseph Parkes, a distinguished barrister of London. The next morning (Sunday) Mr. Lawrence sent his son James, who had been our fellow-passenger in the Baltic, to ask us (my daughter and myself) to dine with him that day. My daughter, having just left the ship, declined, but I accepted the invitation. On my way from Regent Street to Piccadilly, I passed the residence of my friend Parkes in Saville Row, and rang his bell, with an intention of paying my respects and passing on. I found my friend, with his wife and daughter, seated at the dinner-table. After a cordial greeting, he remarked, " You are just in time to take some of your own medicine. We are dining upon your American grouse." I replied that I was then on my

way to dinner with Mr. Lawrence, whose invitation I had accepted in the morning. The servant in the mean time had
placed a chair at the table, into which I was beguiled, as I supposed, for a few moments only. But that beguilement or fas-
cination, in spite of several attempts to rise, kept me seated
until it was more than half an hour late; and then, on the assurance of my friend that no person in London allowed a guest
more than fifteen minutes' grace, I "gave it up." Mr. Parkes
remarked that there was an American gentleman of distinction
at the Albany, for whom he would send; and a few minutes afterward the servant returned with Mr. Robert J. Walker, then
in Europe for the purpose, as was said, of promoting free trade.
We discussed the tariff question somewhat warmly, sitting until
nearly twelve o'clock. The evening would have passed pleasantly if I could have divested myself of the sense of the impropriety I had committed. Early the following day, embarrassed
and mortified, I called on Mr. Lawrence to make the best apology in my power for that indecorum. Mr. Lawrence heard
me in his usually bland manner, and then in a pleasant way
remarked that improprieties of this nature, like all others,
brought their own punishment, as it had in this case, for he had
invited his neighbor, the Duke of Wellington, to meet me at
dinner, and that I had lost three hours of familiar conversation
with the conqueror of Napoleon. I felt and acknowledged that
my disregard of a dinner obligation had been severely but justly
punished.

Nearly ten years after this incident, I was guilty of a still
greater and more inexcusable dinner impropriety.

In the winter of 1862, the most critical and trying period of
the rebellion, I occupied a semi-official position in London,
where I met, either at the American legation, or at the mansions of those who sympathized with the North, friends who
came to London from other parts of the kingdom. Distinguished among these friends were Mr. Ashworth, the Mayor of
Manchester, and Mr. Pendar, a wealthy and influential manufacturer of that city. Although prominent in a class whose interests were unfavorably affected by the war, Messrs. Ashworth
and Pendar were warmly and generously the friends of our
government. Anxious to become better acquainted with them,
and to obtain what information and aid I could, while passing

an evening with them at the residence of Mr. Adams, our minister to the court of St. James, I invited those gentlemen to dine with me the following day. The invitation was accepted. When I returned that evening to my lodgings, I received information which caused much anxiety, and required immediate attention. My time and thoughts that night and the next day were so engrossed that the invitation to Messrs. Ashworth and Pendar was driven from my mind; nor did it occur to me until, at seven o'clock in the afternoon, to my consternation and horror, my guests appeared. No dinner had been ordered. Feelings of mortification and remorse almost deprived me of utterance. I was incapable of making explanations or apologies, for my conduct admitted of neither. I think the gentlemen discovered my embarrassment, for, after a few minutes' conversation, — confused and incoherent on my part, — they took their leave. I made an attempt afterwards to write an apologetic letter to them, but broke down with the first sentence. The only atonement I can ever hope to make them will be found in this public acknowledgment of an act of great discourtesy, occasioned by unpardonable forgetfulness.

CHAPTER LV.

1843.

My first voyage to Europe in 1843 was described in letters to the "Evening Journal." They are given just as they were hastily written and originally published : —

Packet Ship George Washington,
At Sea, *June* 21, 1843.

Having paid the landsman's tribute (sea-sickness) to Neptune, I am now sufficiently recovered to get on deck in pleasant weather, and enjoy fresh air and sea views. We have been "afloat" fourteen days, with light but favorable winds. We are about 2,400 miles from New York, and only some 800 miles from Liverpool! This enumeration of miles seems formidable to one who has been accustomed to run either to New York with Captains McLean or Brainerd, or to Utica, Auburn, or Rochester upon the railroad. The passage so far has been auspicious. The ship has been headed directly to Liverpool from the moment she was put upon her course, and, except for two or three hours in what threatened to be a gale, the large sails have not been taken in.

When the kind and beloved friends who accompanied us down the bay had, on their return to the city, passed out of the reach of my strained vision, we fixed our eyes upon the receding shores until object after object grew first indistinct and then disappeared. Long before twilight all the traces of land had faded away. We continued to cast long, lingering, last looks homeward until night let down her curtain. And then, separated for the first time by a liquid element from family, friends, home, and country, came a sense of loneliness to which my soul had been a stranger. Anxious to be alone to indulge " thick coming fancies," I lighted my cigar, went forward and seated myself upon the windlass for a long, quiet self-communion, which, however, was almost abruptly terminated by a wave that, dashing over the bows, gave me the ill-timed luxury of a shower-bath, and drove me dripping wet back to the quarter-deck. During the night the wind lulled, and soon after sunrise, when I came on deck, the captain pointed me to the land-shade of Montauk Point, within about twelve miles of which we could see. Our course had been parallel with Long Island, keeping about twenty-five miles from shore. We were forty-five miles from Sandy Hook at sunset of the first day. I happened to be forward when the mates were dividing the crew into " watches," the first and second mates choosing (as we choose sides at ball play) the best sailors for their respective watches. It was a novel and amusing scene. The sailors gave their names, " Dick," " Bob," " Bill," " Charlie," " Tom," " Jack," as they were asked. One gave the name of " Howard." The mate replied, " your other name." " Zeb, sir," was the response. The mate, shaking his head, said, " Zeb is not a ship-shape name, let it be Howard." Another gave the name of Van Schoonhoven. " Oh," says the mate, " belay that long name and unship your short one." The boy then gave " George," which proved more satisfactory. After a brief outline of duty, announced in a seaman's manner and language, from the chief mate (Mr. Gibbs), the second mate's watch was sent below. Among the duties enjoined upon the crew were " strict obedience to orders, a bright lookout, no swearing in the tops, and no bawdy songs when ladies or gentlemen are on deck." The ship's crew consists of the captain, three mates, seventeen able seamen, a carpenter, three boys, a steward, cook, and three waiters and a stewardess. Our crew seems an excellent one. Two of the sailors have been former mates of vessels, but for want of such situations, and rather than be idle, ship on board the Liverpool packets. These lines of packets, by the way, are nurseries for American shipmasters. The captains of all these noble vessels, like Bonaparte's best generals, have risen by merit from before the mast to the quarter-deck. Captain Burrows, who commands our ship, first came on board the Silas Richards, Captain Holdridge, as a " boy," and passed from step to step through the grades of ordinary seaman, able seaman, third, second, and first mate, to the high and responsible station he now occupies so honorably to himself and usefully to the owners of his ship. His predecessor, Captain Holdridge, who came from the same town (Groton) in Connecticut, rose in the same way, and is now fitting out the Victoria, a magnificent new ship to be placed in the same line. Captain Burrows succeeds, in turn, to the next new ship, though he will leave with regret, as did Captain Holdridge, his favorite George Washington, a ship that has done her work so far faithfully and gallantly, and that has been the scene of so many of their trials and achievements. It is a very remarkable fact, and one of which Connecticut and Massachusetts may be justly proud, that almost all of the packet ships belonging to the several lines running between New York and Liverpool and New York and London are commanded by natives of those States. Indeed, most of the captains of the London "liners" are natives of the same town (Lyme) in Connecticut! this fact shows that, with the advantages of a common-school education, fortified by "steady habits," a New England boy will carve out his fortune even in a profession where humble merit encounters the most formidable obstacles to advancement. For the first ten days our ship bounded gayly over the billows with fair and fresh winds. But we have been becalmed for two days, and at this moment the mighty elements, that may be so soon lashed into terrific rage, sleep as sweetly and breathe as gently as an infant or a zephyr. Yesterday large schools of porpoises disported themselves around us for hours. To-day the marine visitors of yesterday are succeeded by whales, real whales, though I cannot vouch for their being "right" or "sperm." The first one "spouted" within a hundred yards of the ship, passing along lazily astern. Another soon appeared on the starboard side of the ship and still nearer, which was followed by two others, all continuing spouting and sporting for two hours. This display of Neptune's curiosities was crowned, after tea, by the appearance of a huge· shark in the ship's wake and but a few feet astern.

We are a large, but exceedingly harmonious community. The steerage passengers number over one hundred and fifty, most of whom are disappointed emigrants returning to the Old World, without having found in the new the "ready dug" gold that seduced them across the Atlantic. In talking with some of

these people, I find that they return more because they cannot
reconcile themselves to our " social reforms " than for the want
of employment. Some, it is true, are unfortunate, as some always must be in a world of vicissitudes. The returning English emigrants go home in great disgust with Brother Jonathan.
They concentrated all their hatred of our country by saying
that " everything in America stinks, but the vinegar, and that
is sweet." But even this picture has its bright hues as well as
its dark shades. There are, among the steerage passengers, an
old Irish lady and gentleman of the name of Tobin, from Cincinnati, who go back to the " Green Isle " to die where they were
born, that their dust may rest where rests the dust of their fathers. They have lived prosperously in America, but they could
die happy only in Ireland. Six children are left in America, and
one daughter, with that filial devotion which hallows a daughter's affection, accompanies her parents on this sepulchral pilgrimage. Noticing an intelligent looking Scotchman forward,
I inquired if he too was tired of America? " Na, na, friend.
It 's no that way wi' me. I 'm but running o'er on a matter o'
bisiness, and to make a short visit. From the first day I set
foot in Oneida County, Mr. Wolcott—a vara nice man he is
(perhaps you ken something of the Wolcotts—they are manufacturers at York Mills)—gave me employment, and I have not
seen an idle hour, or lacked any of the enjoyments of life since.
The last winter I purchased a farm in Clinton. The crops are
a' in and growing, and wi' God's blessin' I will be back to the
harvesting o' them. I have help enough in my own family to
work my farm. Three sons are well grown up lads, and others
are coming up after them. The gude wife has fourteen bairns."
Much agreeable conversation passed with this industrious, thriving, cheerful Scotchman, Mr. Bryden, who represents a numerous and valuable class of our emigrant citizens, with the
habits, principles, and temperament of the Bailie Nicol Jarvies
who are to be met in our " Saut Markets," and the " Dandie
Dinmots " who fertilize our soil. No stranger need turn hun-
gry or naked from our shores. There are, by the way, two
classes of steerage passengers. My Scotch friend, and several
others, have large rooms partitioned off from the steerage
proper, with the benefit of good air and light. They, however,
" eat themselves," as Pat says, and pay fifty dollars for their

passage. A second-class steerage passage is but ten dollars. Among the first-class steerage passengers I was not a little surprised to find the "Columbian Minstrels," for whose high vocal powers our friend Meech of the Museum has so often made the "Evening Journal" voucher. They are on a professional visit to England, where Mr. Rice, the original "Wirginny Nigger," was eminently successful. As these vocalists can out-"jump Jim Crow," and give ten songs to his one, I hope their success may be in proportion. We are indebted largely to Europe for her Fanny Ellslers, Mad. Celestes, Mons. Adriens, etc., etc. It is a pleasure, therefore, to send abroad, in return, these "Columbian Minstrels," whose success, if there is taste and sentiment in England to enjoy the music of nature, will be more than triumphant. Nor are these Yankee minstrels the only national novelty the ship George Washington is wafting to England. We have two thousand wooden clocks on board! These "notions" are of Massachusetts fabrication, and find, I am informed, a ready market with John Bull. The purchasers are among the humblest of the middling classes, who form clubs of twelve, fifteen, or twenty, paying sixpence a week into a purse for the purchase of clocks, which are drawn for by lottery, the contribution and the drawings continuing until each member of the club rejoices in a wooden clock. This is one of the triumphs of American manufacturers.

WEDNESDAY.

Our good ship George Washington has always been a favorite packet. On her June passage of last year Charles Dickens returned in her to England. Captain Burrows informs me that he made himself extremely popular with all on board. In his "Notes" he speaks in highly complimentary terms of the ship and her commander. Grant Thorburn, the well-known seedsman and florist, returned to America in this ship, and I make the following extract from his book for the purpose of saying that every word of it is as applicable to her present captain and crew as to her former excellent commander: "If you have a friend in the world to whom you wish well, and that friend wants to cross the Atlantic, tell him to wait for the George Washington, Captain Holdridge and crew. We have been nine days out, and have not heard an oath from an officer or a sailor;

sometimes making twelve knots an hour, with the waves as high
as Snake Hill in Jersey, and neither a sigh nor a groan has escaped the ship's timbers. Her sheets of canvas, swelling in the
breeze, are moved by her steady and willing crew without noise
or confusion, — all as if impelled by the god of order." The
same spirit of order, and the same proprieties of language and
temper, reigned throughout the vessel during the twenty-one
days we were on board of her. But enough for this writing.
So, adieu for the present.

PACKET SHIP GEORGE WASHINGTON, ⎰
AT SEA, June 23, 1843. ⎱

Our noble ship has been reposing for three days upon the
unruffled bosom of a slumbering ocean, and, although we number more than two hundred souls, all is quietness and tranquil-
lity on board. The captain and mates pace the quarter-deck,
looking and whistling rather impatiently for wind. The passengers, at their books, shuffle-board, back-gammon, chess, or
checkers, seem alike content with wind or calm. Much of our
conversation, however, consists in discussing the probabilities of
our arrival at Liverpool before the steamer that left Boston
nine days after us, and the Akbar, a fast sailing ship that left
New York thirty hours before us. The first predictions of those
who have "crossed before" were for a passage of nineteen days,
but since the calm they are willing to compound for a twenty-
one, twenty-two, or twenty-three days' run. Our ship has passed
everything she has encountered so far, but without wind the
steamer will pass us the day after to-morrow. The sea, like
politics, makes "strange bed-fellows." Our cabin passengers
have been drawn from nearly all the different points of the
compass on the globe, and are as diverse in characters and pursuits as in birth and language. But we all affiliate and harmonize wonderfully. There is not an ill-natured or querulous
spirit among us. This, I am told, is unusual, and my own
slight experience in traveling has shown a "black sheep" in
almost every flock. In addition to our own party of four, we
have a quiet Englishman, who is returning from a visit to a
sister residing in Canada, surprised and gratified to have found
a large and flourishing town (New York) between London and
Montreal. There is an affable, talkative old gentleman from
Sheffield (a razor manufacturer, I believe), returning from a

visit to New York. He went out in the packet ship North
America last spring, and was beached near Sandy Hook. There
are two young officers of the British army returning home with
chilling recollections of a Canadian winter; a Scotchman and
his niece from Terre Haute, Indiana; a Pennsylvanian and his
sister, from the good Whig county of Somerset, going to Ireland after a legacy, I infer, their father having been an Irishman and their mother Scotch; an Englishman from Boston;
a partner in an extensive merchant tailor's establishment in
Park Place, who goes to London and Paris to purchase clothes
and "catch the fashions as they change;" a dry-goods dealer in
Broadway, who, though born in Holland, persists in claiming
America as his native country; a young gentleman who, though
born in Baltimore, gives himself out as an Englishman. He
was left with a fortune, partly on this and partly on the other
side of the Atlantic. His habits, in some respects, are most
thoroughly English, for he sits up until four o'clock in the
morning, rises at one P. M., breakfasts and drinks porter inordinately. But he is intelligent and agreeable. We have a gentlemanly English merchant and his accomplished lady, changing
their residence from New York to Liverpool, the tariff having
destroyed his business in America; a companionable, frank,
honest Yorkshireman, connected with a cloth house in New
York, and residing in Brooklyn, who is going to Leeds for his
wife and child; a retiring partner in the great iron house of
Sanderson and Brothers, Sheffield, who, after a residence of
fourteen years in New York, goes to the Island of Jersey to
enjoy the fruits of his enterprise and industry. This gentleman
is one of John Bull's legitimate sons, — his aversion for Brother
Jonathan is purely national. His most formidable charge against
republican institutions is their relaxing influence upon domestic
discipline. He attributed the recusancy of a son and the elope-
ment of a daughter wholly to these causes, and will never learn
that the "iron rule" in the government of children is quite as
likely to have occasioned the disappointment of his parental hopes.
This gentleman is, however, an agreeable companion with kindly
feelings, and, I doubt not, a worthy man. He has an inexhaustible fund of cheerful conversation. We have a young German
gentleman, who has passed four years in the commercial cities
of England, France, and America, and is now returning to

Hamburg to commence his own commercial career. He is very generally informed, and has, in the broadest sense of the term, completed his education. We have also a Catholic priest (a native of Bavaria), who was some time at Detroit, but now from Cincinnati, returning home out of health.

Father De Smet, a native of Belgium and a missionary of the Jesuits, is returning from a four years' residence among the Indians beyond the Rocky Mountains. His errand was one of true Christian benevolence, and, in searching the wide world, few men could be found so richly endowed with the qualities and so deeply imbued with the principles of that divine missionary who was sent to proclaim peace and good will to man. Father De Smet belongs to a family possessing rank and wealth. He gave his fortune to his brothers (reserving only what was necessary to defray his expenses), and departed for the New World and its wilderness, giving up the remainder of his life to the improvement and the amelioration of the condition of the poor Indian. He went among the most savage of the tribes, with no defense but the cross, and though constantly passing through scenes of violence and outrage, and living amid slaughter and rapine, not a hair of his head has been injured. We have been delighted, during the passage, with his recitals of Indian habits, customs, wars, worship, etc., etc.

This reminds me of an adventure of Father De Smet. On one occasion, when several thousand miles from the habitations of white men, he reached a strange and evidently savage tribe of Indians. He was accompanied by a wandering half-breed, who had been in the service of the fur traders, and who acted as his guide and interpreter. The Indians were seated in a circle on the ground. A chief was proceeding with a talk, which the interpreter was rendering into English, when suddenly an Indian sprang to his feet, approached the missionary, and exclaimed in a broad, rich, Irish brogue, " This blackguard, bad luck to him, is lying to your reverence ! " And then, taking the office of interpreter upon himself, Paddy gave a true version of his chief's talk. Upon inquiry, the missionary learned that the Irishman, whose habits and disposition were of a migratory character, had worked his way westward, until he found himself among the Indians; and having adopted as a rule of action never to look or turn back, he finally brought up among this remote tribe, with whom he had lived for thirteen years.

On his recent return to St. Louis, where he contributed largely, by his efforts in Europe, to endow a college, Father De Smet traveled, with an Indian companion, three thousand miles through the wilderness by a pocket-compass. His letters to the Superior of his Order, recently published, make a volume of exceeding interest. He is laboring with intelligence and zeal to introduce the virtues of civilization, without its vices, among the Indians. He first impresses the truths of revelation upon their minds, and then instructs them in the pursuit of agriculture. His present visit to the Old World is connected with his philanthropic duties. He returns to the Rocky Mountains in November by the way of the Columbia River. My traveling companions have made a donation to the good father for the benefit of his Indians. We have also as *compagnons du voyage*, Bishop Hughes, of New York, and Bishop Purcell, of Ohio, two eminent and excellent ecclesiastics of the Catholic church. As educated and enlightened men, they have been conversed with and listened to by us all with pleasure and advantage. But as ministers of the gospel, their presence has imparted a still higher interest. On the first Sabbath out, Bishop Hughes preached a sermon, standing at the step of the mizzen-mast, which was most attentively listened to by a congregation of over two hundred. The subject (St. Paul's Epistle to the Romans, 11th chapter, from the 22d to the last verse) was appropriate, and his commentary truly impressive. He made the ocean a witness in favor of the truth of revelation ; he spoke of it, too, as a glorious page in the great book of nature, which could not be contemplated without exciting more of admiration than of awe. Man, he said, may boast of his power and wisdom, as displayed in the construction of this strong and beautiful ship ; but how impotent is man's power, and how fruitless his wisdom, until God in his abounding goodness fills our canvas with his winds! On the following Sabbath the same community reassembled for divine worship. Bishop Purcell officiated. His sermon was designed as a vindication of the truths of revelation, and to enforce the duties of faith and obedience. His language and manner were fervent and affectionate. He entered upon a train of argument to show how reason and philosophy expose and confound their teachers, in which he was truly impressive and conclusive. Not a word was uttered by either of these good bishops to which all Christians would not heartily respond. I had often heard of Bishop Purcell, of Cincinnati, as a man much beloved by his own people, and as much respected by all others. He is worthy of affection and regard, for all the kindliest elements are mixed up in his character. Of Bishop Hughes, from whose enlightened conversations upon various subjects I derive much instruction, I shall speak in another letter.

Sunday afternoon, June 25. — The calm was broken yesterday by a fresh southeasterly wind, which compelled us, about three o'clock P. M., to shorten sail. I lay on deck — it blew rather too hard for landsmen to stand — while the sailors were taking in, first the light sails, and then reefing the larger sheets, and can now sympathize understandingly with those who admire and celebrate the sailor's enthusiasm and gallantry. The wind seems *their* element. The men, who had been lounging lazily about the ship during the calm, when a young tempest came, sprang lightly into the tops, some laying out upon the yards, and others ascending higher to furl the maintop gallant-sail, the ship in the mean time bounding over billows that made her bow and stern alternately describe angles of forty-five degrees. The easterly wind is driving us off our course. The captain's observation and reckoning at twelve o'clock to-day brought us within an hundred miles of land, and about thirty miles northward of Cape Clear, the entrance to the British Channel. With the wind as it is now, we expect to make the land to-morrow morning, and then to decide whether it is best to attempt the south, or take the north channel. I have been struck with the variations in time as we have been running down from a longitude of 59 into one of 14. Bishop Hughes, who has a truth-telling watch, has kept his New York time. By ship time it is now nine o'clock P. M. And yet you at Albany are just coming from the afternoon churches at five. When we were at breakfast this morning at eight, few, if any, of you had opened your eyes ; and before the sentinel in sheriff Adams's belfry sings " Past eleven o'clock, and all is well," it will be daylight here.

Monday morning, June 26. — We went on deck this morning expecting to be greeted with a view of land, but were sadly disappointed. The wind came off dead ahead about midnight, since which time we have been heading to windward, and are yet some forty miles from land, without any hope of getting into the Channel until the wind changes.

12 *o'clock M.* — The captain, who was intent yesterday and to-day upon his charts, etc., has just taken an observation. His reckoning shows us about twenty-five miles from land, and about thirty-five from Valentia, a small port on the northwest coast of Ireland, to which he has concluded to run, and where many of us intend to land, and make an excursion through the Green Isle.

4 *o'clock P. M.* — The wind has baffled us. By drawing round two points to the north and east we are defeated in our intention of making the harbor of Valentia. She has been put about, and is now running south along the coast, with the hope of such a change of wind as will enable us to get into the British Channel.

7 *o'clock P. M.* — We are just called on deck from the tea-table to see land. The outline of what seems a high mountain was first discovered. High, bold headlands in the County Kerry were soon distinctly seen. Then came the Skellig rocks, looming up like " Butter Hill " at the entrance of our own Highlands. One of these high promontories, in the distance we are viewing it, assumes the form of a majestic mansion, of fine architectural proportions, with roof, chimneys, etc.

Tuesday morning, June 27. — We have been all night struggling with a head wind, and find ourselves this morning more than twenty miles from Cape Clear. The Irish shore is but ten miles off, and its mountains of rocks, with their Druidical towers, are in full view. The coast is barren and frowning.

5 *o'clock P. M.* — We have been all " dragging our slow length along " the coast of Ireland, and the most of our passengers have been restless and impatient. To me it has been a day of interest and enjoyment. We have passed the Bay of Bantry, and several bold headlands, of which the steerage passengers who are going back to " sweet Ireland " have been giving me traditions and legends. A bright sun and balmy atmosphere have enabled me to remain all day on deck, enjoying those rugged views.

At three o'clock the steamer Acadia, from Boston, came in sight, pushing directly for Cape Clear, the point at which we are aiming. Her appearance was indicated long before the vessel could be seen by a black column of smoke streaking the horizon. She passed within about seven miles of us, and pushed up the Channel. The Acadia left Boston on the 16th inst.; she will, therefore, make a twelve days' passage. But for head winds and calms we should have been in Liverpool on Saturday last.

6 *o'clock P. M.* — We are at last opposite Cape Clear, with the ship's head to the channel; but there is only a breath of wind; this comes, however, from the right quarter. If we should get becalmed off the Cove of Cork, which is some sixty miles from here, we go ashore there with the bishops.

Wednesday morning, June 28. — We have been three weeks at sea, and are still becalmed in the British Channel, two hundred and ninety miles from Liverpool. Last evening, an hour before sunset, a small boat from Crook Haven Harbor came alongside us, with fresh fish, as we supposed, but, as it turned out, with potatoes only. They offered to take passengers ashore, and Mr. Tobin, the old gentleman referred to in another letter, with his wife and daughter, finding themselves within a few miles of their native town, left the ship. In reply to our questions for news, they said that troops had arrived at Dublin, and that O'Connell was at Skibbereen, his place in the mountains, where he had made a speech to 300,000 people.

12 *o'clock M.* — An Irish "hooker" came alongside after breakfast, with whom fifteen emigrants concluded to land. The captain of the "hooker" informed us that there was a tremendous and destructive gale here on the 7th of June, the day we left New York. Much shipping was lost, and, among other vessels, one American, but of all this you will have accounts.

The captain of the "hooker" informed us that O'Connell is to address a mass meeting at Kinsale on Monday. My desire to see him is so great that I went below to pack a few changes in my carpet-bag, and go ashore, but while we were getting ready the "hooker" was cast off, at the instance of the friends who were unwilling to let us go off with "wild Irishmen" in a crazy craft. We intend, nevertheless, to avail ourselves of the next opportunity for landing.

5 *o'clock P. M.* — A rowboat has just come alongside, and I close the letter to get a few "traps" ready for a descent

upon Ireland. The boatmen are to row nine of us ashore for ten shillings sterling each. So good-by to the George Washington!

[During this visit to Europe, the following letter was written, in answer to a request from home.]

LONDON, *August* 18, 1843,

MY DEAR JAMES, — The girls write me that you are about to commence business in company with Mr. Parsons, of whose character and capacity I think favorably ; and that Mr. White went to New York with you to purchase materials.

This is a very important step in your life. Your future happiness, and the hopes of your parents and sisters, hang upon this enterprise. Much depends upon yourself. With industry and economy, I entertain strong confidence that you will succeed ; but indolence or inattention will be sure to bring ruin and disgrace. I beseech you, therefore, to give your whole attention to your business. Industry and economy in early life, unless some peculiar misfortune overtake you, will secure you the means of support and enjoyment when old age or sickness comes. And what is equally important, industry and enterprise insures the respect of your fellow-citizens, without which life is scarcely worth preserving.

But prosperity must be earned. You should rise early, and, if necessary, work late ; and above all things, be prompt and punctual in doing whatever you have in hand.

Deal justly and honestly with everybody. Money costs too much if it be not honestly acquired.

Don't incur any unnecessary expense, or run into debt. Consult Mr. White and Mr. Benedict in all matters of business which are difficult or embarrassing.

Treat everybody with whom you have business with civility and attention. Kind words and courteous deportment are essential to success in business.

Make my respects to Mr. Parsons, accompanied with my earnest prayers for the health and prosperity of both of you. Affectionately,

YOUR FATHER.

The following letter, written, as it will be seen, after passing a social evening with my family, and received in London, will, I think, give the reader a good idea of the real character of my old friend, General Erastus Root : —

ALBANY, *Sunday, September* 10, 1843.

MY DEAR FRIEND, — On Friday evening Mrs. R. and myself called at your house to take leave of your good wife and daughters on our being about to journey to Delhi upon the adjournment of our court for the term. After an agreeable chit-chat, yourself and the rapidity of your movements, the agreeable sprightliness of your interesting letters, published in the " Evening Journal," furnishing the chief topic of our conversation, Mrs. Weed handed me this broad sheet for me to pack my Sunday meditations for exportation to Europe. An ordinary sheet, she gave me to understand, is insufficient under the revenue laws of her excellent majesty's Post Office Department, to wrap all the varied and various commodities of little value I might wish to envelop. My wife took the sheet, rolled in a scroll, as you may well perceive by its rumpled condition. We took leave for four or five weeks, when the court will resume its sitting. Yes, sir, we took leave, — my wife with a kiss, — I barely looked a kiss. Not as closely, I imagine, as you looked at the young lady you handed into the coach when beset by the Drogheda " widows " " your honor " so liberally coppered. We go this evening to Catskill and to-morrow to Delaware, — to that not *fairy* but *dairy* land, — to a land that flows with milk and honey, — not unlike the ancient promised land, beyond Jordan, in many respects. Its people have formerly been fed with the political manna of righteousness shed from the heavenly firmament of freedom, but latterly they have bowed the knee to Baal, — have followed after strange gods to worship, — have followed in the ways of Jeroboam, the son of Nebat, that made Israel to sin. But I believe there is balm in Gilead, that there is a physician there. Yes, the temples of the ungodly will be prostrated, the workers of iniquity will be scattered abroad. The political saviour of his country, with healing in his wings, will make his advent at Washington on the 4th of March, 1845.

You will have seen by the papers that there has been a strong push, chiefly editorial, I imagine, in the first place, to set up a State convention and organize for a regular field fight at this fall election. I think I had some influence in dissuading the central committee from the measure. I thought it folly, partaking in some measure of madness, to organize as a great national party and engage with the whole army in a general field fight under the banner of Henry Clay. We have no national officers to elect. There are many county officers, besides members of the legislature, to elect. State and county politics and feelings should be allowed full swing, and without external and over-bearing restraint. Especially since the seeds of strife have been sown, and already germinated among our triumphing foes. Let the " Hunkers " and " Barn-burners " contend. Instead of hushing their disquiet, it might be made the rather to fan the flame. By pressing their wounds while fresh we shall cause them to heal. Let them become callous and seared by hot counteraction and they cannot become united. Next year, when the House of Representatives shall have attempted to destroy our renovating prosperity, and it shall be seen that naught could have stayed the hand of destruction but patriotic Tennessee, then let us arouse with renovated vigor. Go into the battle confident of success and determined to conquer, and we shall be victorious.

The bells begin to summon us to church. I think I will go, leaving Mrs. R. to finish picking up and packing away the duds, and leaving you in anxious waiting for my report on my return. . . . I have just returned from church, Mr. Kip's, — the clock striking twelve while on my way. Mr. Kip was present and read part of the service, but did not preach the sermon. That was done by a pretty good-looking and well-spoken man. I did not learn his name. He preached from one of Isaiah's prophecies of the Messiah. From it he undertook to show the truth of our religion. He proved the position he has taken, as all others do, — you and I have heard it over and over again.

State Street looks quite ragged and stony, especially from Pearl Street up nearly to the Franklin, where I stay. They are re-paving and changing its grade, especially as respects the gutters and centre. Where it is down it looks very nice. The workmen appear to me in better employ than those I saw engaged in shoveling the snow in Maiden Lane the day before your corporation election. Perhaps, however, it will not equally swell the Loco-foco vote at the coming election. The *coming election!* In writing the word, a thought rushed upon my mind which nearly paralyzed my hand! Poor Willis Hall! I had joyed on the prospect of having him again in the Assembly, and the hope and the rallying point of all our hopes, and at no distant day the chief executive of all our desires in this State. That he would be to this State what we hope and believe *Harry* of the *West* will be to the Union. But alas! how are our hopes prostrate? Although he is getting better, yet we cannot expect a consummation of our late hopes.

Governor Seward appeared before us the other day, and moved to open a cause for argument which had early in the term been defaulted. He was evidently embarrassed, and more so when he ran foul of an unexpected snag. It is an embarrassing situation in which he is placed. Returned to the bar less fit for its duties, and, when compared with his former contemporaries, far less than when he left, and still every one looking upon him as a far greater man, and he aware of their high expectations must necessarily feel embarrassed. It will take him some time to regain his former comparative standing at the bar.

I had written thus far, and finding no *material* at hand wherewith to fill the sheet, as by commandment I felt bound to do, I called on my wife to supply the defect. She observed that she did not know what I had written, and, as all prudent and discreet women are wont to do, requested me to read ; I began, but soon found that what I had written before I went to church was hardly legible even by him who perpetrated the scrawl. In the mean time the rap came for dinner. At one o'clock we dine on Sunday. How that must sound to an *Anglicized* ear, and I suppose yours are already *Anglicized*, or are they rather *Hibernianized*, and you wish to eat your potato at an earlier hour than allowed on the banks of the Thames, and therefore you urge a repeal of the Union. Well, as I was going to say, we were rapped down to the dinner, a little prior to the bell-call of the *canaille*. We had dinner, — roast beef as good as old England can afford, pudding and pastry as good, and fruit a great deal better. The water and musk melon delicious, the pears and peaches in no wise behind, and the plums and grapes I shall not attempt to describe, for we had none on the table. We had them the other day, and in high perfection.

My wife has gone out of the room, and I have not read to her this interesting and highly scientific essay, nor have I yet read it myself. If I should happen to send it all the way to Europe without even a reading or correction, I beg you will not show it to any of the Oxonians when you visit that venerated university. Speaking of that university, reminds me of the *Puseyism* imported thence and implanted in the city of New York. I wish you to inquire when you go there whether tapping so many scions to graft in this country has injured the parent stock. If so, tell them to get some Virginia *abstractions* and ingraft upon the Oxonian tree ; and I have no doubt it will bear the most luscious fruit.

My sheet is filled ! God bless you and preserve you to a safe and happy return to your family and friends. Mrs. R. remembers you with high esteem and regard. Adieu.   Erastus Root.

Thurlow Weed, Esq.

CHAPTER LVI.

1844.

A YEAR later another sea voyage was taken, which is described in the following letter : —

SHIP CORNELIA, AT SEA, }
November 27, 1844. }

We left New York, as you know, on the 25th instant, with a cracking northwester, which stiffened during the afternoon, and gave us a fine offing. In looking around, when we were fairly outside, I found myself one of thirty passengers, all but seven of whom were seeking, in a milder climate, that boon without which life is bereft of its chief enjoyments. Those of us who were in health (a blessing too lightly appreciated until lost) accompanied invalid wives, husbands, sisters, or daughters. Separation from home and families, under such circumstances, awakens emotions peculiarly their own. We go abroad, when in high health, without realizing that we are liable to be struck down at any moment, and buoyant with the hopes of a reunion. But the patient goes, with hopes to be sure, but hopes chilled by apprehensions, leaving friends at home to wear out weeks and months of painful suspense and solicitude.

Our ship, as you will imagine, was at best but a marine hospital. Only a few hours elapsed before she became such in the strongest sense of the term, for a rolling sea soon added its discomforts to the horrors of seated disease. From almost every state-room and berth the inmates were heard unburdening their nauseated stomachs. Steward, stewardess, and waiters were in constant requisition. Every attention, however, was paid to them, and thus the situation of the sufferers rendered as tolerable as might be ; and, after the first twenty-four hours, convalescents began to emerge, some with good appetites, and others to be driven back to panada, arrow-root, and gruel.

Our friend, Dr. Van Alstyne, who came very ill and greatly exhausted on board, has had two most distressing days and nights. His symptoms are all alarming, but he is stout-hearted, and says that if he can survive the voyage he is sure that the climate of St. Croix will build him up.

Friday, November 29th. — The last twenty-four hours a heavy, rolling sea has given the ship (comparatively light) an uneasy motion, very painful to invalids. Dr. Van Alstyne suffers most, and doubts whether he can reach his haven of hope. In anticipation of his decease, after asking me to take possession of his effects, he expressed a wish that his remains should be taken to St. Croix, instead of being cast, as is generally deemed necessary in tropical climates, into the deep. Captain French, who came to his state-room, assured him that his wishes in this respect should be faithfully carried out. With his mind at ease upon this subject, he very calmly explained the course of treatment best calculated to sustain him through the voyage. But his cough increases while his strength fails. After crossing the Gulf Stream, where the weather is always " dirty," as the sailors describe it, we may look for a pleasant passage, — so at least says the captain, who knows these seas most familiarly, having been upon them most of his time these eighteen years.

Sunday, December 1st. — Wind fair and fresh ; soft, balmy, refreshing atmosphere. Passengers on deck enjoying their transition from the cold, piercing winds of our own climate to the gentle and healthful breathings of " the trades." What a phenomenon, by the way, these " trade winds " are. How strange it is that while the oceans elsewhere are subject to the common laws of nature, here, for thousands of miles, the wind blows for ever and ever from the same points.

The Sabbath, always a day of peculiar solemnity at sea, became, from several causes, eminently so with those on board the Cornelia to-day. Most of the passengers are in a precarious state of health, and at least one of our number is rapidly approaching the end of the voyage of life. We assembled for divine service at eleven o'clock. The Rev. Mr. Clark, of Skaneateles, who with his wife, accompanied by Mrs. Horton, of that village, are going to the island of Jamaica, officiated. The Episcopal service was read impressively, and an appropriate

sermon preached to a most attentive audience, made up of passengers, officers, and crew. After the services were over, Dr.
Van Alstyne expressed a strong desire to be carried on deck,
that he might gratify a long cherished desire to look upon the
vast ocean; but, in making the attempt, he was found to be so
weak that it was thought prudent to remove him only to the
door of the forward cabin, where he could inhale the fresh air.

We have now been six days at sea, and have made over nine
hundred miles' progress, one hundred and seventy of which
were run the last twenty-four hours. Our ship is one of the
largest that sails from New York, and, with her canvas all
spread, as it now is, she makes a lofty and noble appearance.

Monday, December 2d. — Oh, what a sun rose this morning
to cheer and animate the pilgrims of the deep! And what a
friendly, refreshing wind is wafting us (almost too rapidly) onward to our destination! This day realizes all that the imagination has conceived of the deliciousness of a southern ocean
and a tropical climate. It presents all the bright, without any
of the dark, features in a beautiful picture of life. The passengers were on deck early, drinking an atmosphere with " healing upon its wings." Its reviving and benign influences are
apparent upon almost every patient. The ship in full dress
has a majestic appearance, and glides almost noiselessly along
at the rate of eight miles an hour. And the crew, for once
having nothing to do, are at repose, some with books and others
at their " yarns." Poor Dr. Van Alstyne is fast sinking, though
his mind is clear and his nerves strong. He continues to prescribe stimulants, in the hope that they will prolong life until
the ship arrives at St. Croix.

6 *o'clock P. M.* — All is over with Dr. Van Alstyne. He
expired in possession of all his faculties, and without a struggle,
having prescribed with a perfect knowledge of what was necessary to spin out the already attenuated thread of life till within
five minutes of the time that his last breath was drawn! Such
firmness, under circumstances so trying, has rarely been exhibited. But for the sufferings occasioned by the rough weather
and high sea during the first three days out, it is thought he
would have survived the voyage. His remains, to be preserved
with salt, and inclosed in a coffin which the carpenter is making, will be taken to St. Croix. Dr. Marsh, of Chester, Pa.,

and the Rev. Mr. Clark were constant in their attentions to the deceased, as also was Captain French, who in this, as in all other cases, manifested his kindness and generosity.

Wednesday, December 4th. — We are enjoying, in its highest perfection, the poetry of the ocean. We have a bright sun, whose genial heat is fanned by the more genial winds, and an atmosphere too ethereal for earth. And oh, how gorgeously the sun took its leave of us last night! Its rays, gilding the clouds, enabled the imagination to fashion castles, battlements, columns, temples, and chariots of surprising magnificence, out of aerial elements. How ardently I wished that the devoted friends whose loved forms I could almost distinguish in the clouds were here to enjoy these delightful scenes. My friends Chancellor Whittlesey and Lieutenant-Governor Gardiner, if they remember a sunset we witnessed on Lake Ontario, in returning from a fishing excursion, can form a very faint idea of this magnificent view.

I went again on deck late at night. Here was another view to awaken admiration. The mate walked the quarter-deck; the man at the wheel, and two men looking out, were alone to be seen; all else were at their repose. The ship, trimmed so as to catch every breath of wind, and looking like a belle in full ball dress, literally danced through the sparkling waters, whose gems were brilliantly reflected by a radiant moon. Those only who have seen a noble ship, with all her white, flowing canvas spread, and each sheet doing its share in driving her onward, with the broad heavens above, and the mighty waters beneath, can appreciate this beautifully sublime scene. I have rarely, indeed, passed an hour of more exquisite enjoyment.

We have now come to know each other quite well, and are upon the best terms. The invalids, for the most part, are patient sufferers. This virtue invests itself with a peculiar charm when displayed in sickness or in affliction. Mrs. Kernochan and Mrs. Pierson, the wives of two most esteemed New York merchants, who cherish but feeble hopes of recovering, have, by their cheerfulness and amiability, created a warm sympathy among their fellow passengers. May a kind Providence restore them in health to the families and friends to whom they must be very dear, and to circles which their virtues are so eminently calculated to adorn. Stephen Whitney, Jr., son of an esteemed and wealthy New Yorker, who is also in delicate health, is an intelligent traveler and agreeable companion. It is pleasant to meet, as we too seldom do, in one of the heirs to an estate of millions, a quiet, unostentatious gentleman.

The delightful weather of the last two days has brought all of us upon deck, the invalid portion having been placed upon their mattresses, where, under the shade of a grateful awning, they enjoy pure air, and are fanned by the genial winds, from immediately after breakfast until tea time, the waiter bringing their dinners to them. This change is doing wonders for them. Harriet, who was very ill for seven days, and unable to take any nourishment, now listens attentively for the sound of the steward's bell, and even talks of disputing my claim to the sole possession of the dish of baked pork and beans.

Thursday, December 5th. — We came, as our captain predicted last night, in sight of land this morning. The Virgin Gorda, a comparatively barren island, appears to windward. We then entered the Sombrero Channel, and soon afterwards the Tortola Islands appeared in sight. These were succeeded by a view of St. John's, after passing which the far more important island of St. Thomas lifted itself to view in the distance. We are now in the Caribbean Sea, an apochryphal island of which Miss Porter has invested with all the charms that genius lends to imagination. So truthful and life-like is her " Sir Edward Seaward's Narrative," that many well-informed readers, and even reviewers, mistook it for veritable history. It is a delightful book, in which interest, instruction, and morality are most happily blended. Let me commend it to all who have not enjoyed the luxury which its pages afford. It has recently been republished by the Harpers, to whose teeming press the intellectual community is so largely indebted.

At four o'clock P. M. the men at mast-head descried the island of St. Croix, and half an hour afterwards our Patmos was in full view from the deck. As we approach, its deep green verdure contrasts strangely with the leafless trees and frosted shores we left but ten days ago. So sudden a transition from a land of snows and ice to one of luxuriant fruits and foliage seems like an exchange of worlds. We all remained admiring this scene until the steward summoned us to our last dinner on board the Cornelia. This repast, like those which preceded it, was excellent and bountiful. Before rising from the table, a letter to Captain French, of which the following is a copy, was very cheerfully signed by the passengers : —

> ON BOARD SHIP CORNELIA, }
> *December 5, 1844.* }

To CAPTAIN FRENCH : —

Dear Sir, — We cannot consent to leave your noble ship, at the termination of a voyage from New York to St. Croix without tendering to you, and through you to your lady and officers, our grateful acknowledgments for the attentions and kindnesses which have rendered that voyage safe, pleasant, and short, — too short, indeed, for many of us, whose only regret is that we are so soon to separate. Nor are we willing that this should be regarded as a mere commonplace acknowledgment ; for your constant, unremitted, and untiring watchfulness, first to your ship and then to the numerous calls and wants of your passengers (most of them being invalids), entitles you to our unfeigned and heartfelt gratitude.

Please to communicate an expression of our thanks to your officers, and accept for yourself and lady assurances of our sincere regard.

> H. M. Pierson, Laura Horton, Anna W. Scovel, Jane Hammond, Sarah E. Clark, Eliza Davis, Harriet A. Weed, M. E. Kernochan, J. G. Gregory, Hiram Upson, Joseph T. Clark, Archibald Campbell, Stephen Whitney, Jr., W. J. Wilcox, William Hammond, L. Davis, Louis Butterfield, John Strachan, Joseph Kernochan, Thurlow Weed, Henry L. Pierson, J. C. Dodge, J. H. Marsh, P. H. Gowen, Angelo Ames, Daniel Austin, A. R. Diets.

At eight o'clock we cast anchor in the West End harbor, opposite the Danish fort, and abreast the town. I went ashore with Captain French and the letter-bag. We were received by Mr. Walker (son of our fellow-citizen, Mr. Willard Walker), who came over here seven years ago so ill as to forbid any hope of recovery, but who was almost miraculously restored. He is now the owner of a plantation here, and the agent of several non-resident planters. Having secured pleasant lodgings with a very kind hostess, I returned to the ship for the night.

Friday morning. — Before leaving the Cornelia we had a solemn duty to perform. The necessary arrangements having been made by our vice-consul, Captain Codwise, for the interment of Dr. Van Alstyne, the remains were brought upon deck, where, in the presence of the passengers and crew, the funeral service of the Episcopal Church was read by the Rev. Mr.

Clark.   The remains were then taken ashore in a small boat, preceded by another with the captain, clergyman, and passengers.   At the wharf they were received by the Rev. Mr. Mines, the resident clergyman, the vice-consul, and several citizens of St. Croix, and conveyed in procession to the Episcopal burying-ground, where the Rev. Mr. Mines officiated in returning " dust to dust, ashes to ashes."

The Cornelia leaves here for the island of Jamaica, where she lands the Rev. Mr. Clark and family, and goes from thence to Mobile, to take in a cargo of cotton for Liverpool.   She has made three remarkably short passages from New York to this island.   The first was performed in nine, and the two last in ten days.   She has accommodations for fifty passengers.   Captain French and his lady (who always accompanies him) are very excellent, kind people, from whom invalids receive every possible attention.

There are two regular packets running between this island and New York.   The ship Emily, Captain Davis, owned, I believe, by Aymar & Co., of New York, and Mr. A. H. Hill, a highly esteemed citizen of this place, who is gratefully remembered for his kindness to Americans sojourning upon the island.   The brig Eliza, Captain Lockwood, is owned by De Forest & Co., who are owners also of two valuable plantations.   These vessels have good accommodations for passengers, and Captains Davis and Lockwood are spoken of as excellent officers.

I will give you some notion of how things are going on in this out-of-the-way portion of man's heritage in another letter, and close this by saying that there is good reason for supposing that the sugar crop will be unusually large, and that the planters are very anxious for the " repeal of the tariff of 1842."

CHAPTER LVII.

1846.

ONE cold, drizzling, cheerless evening in the latter part of the winter of 1846, while sitting in a barber's chair enjoying tonsorial manipulations, I listened to a conversation which in its results added something to my domestic responsibilities, but much more to my domestic enjoyment. The incident itself, and the revelations which during the succeeding fourteen years it occasioned, possess, as I believe, sufficient interest to constitute a chapter in this work. Indeed, the intimate friends to whom they have been occasionally related, would usually exclaim, " Truth is stranger than fiction."

A barber's shop, as everybody knows, is the place for city or village news. From those who sat gossiping on this occasion I learned that one Chapman, a writing-master of intemperate habits, had died that day of delirium tremens in his school-room, and that late in the afternoon the cries of a small child had attracted the attention of persons living in the same building. This child had evidently been for several hours in a cold room with the remains of its deceased father. I learned, further, that George Jenkins, a city constable, had raised by subscription money to bury Chapman, and that he would take the child to the almshouse in the morning. At the tea-table, fifteen minutes after I had left the barber's shop, I repeated to my wife and children, without manifesting either interest or sympathy, the conversation I had overheard. We had all seen Chapman, but neither of us had ever heard that he had either a wife or child. My wife inquired where the child was, and on being informed that I did not know, expressed surprise that I had not ascertained. My son (James), rising from the table, asked if he should not find out what had been done with the child. It was quite evident that a common feeling of sympathy had been awakened. My eldest daughter, who left the table before I did, met me at the front door, saying that she would accompany me in pursuit of this orphan. Now, all this was what I hoped, but fearing that others might not share in the spontaneous sympathy which I felt for the offspring of a hateful dwarf, an offspring which, for aught we knew, might inherit his deformities, I imparted the information to my family with apparent indifference.

Mr. Jenkins informed me that he had left the child for the night with Mrs. Woolley, a milliner, living in South Pearl Street. The child, as I was shown into Mrs. Woolley's room, was sitting on a stool in a dark corner, alone. "Mary," said Mrs. W., "this gentleman wants to see you," whereupon a delicate mite of a girl came over where I was seated and extended her hand to me with a look of confidence and reliance which will never be forgotten. To my question, "Will you go home with me?" she replied promptly, "Yes, sir." Mrs. Woolley, to whom I then made myself known, complied very cheerfully with my request that she would take Mary to my house, adding "that she was glad enough to cry, to think that the child would have such a home." My family, although I had not intimated any such purpose, were waiting impatiently, and gave the newcomer as hearty a welcome as if she had been a lost and recovered member of the household, and with that slight, frail creature, as she crossed our threshhold, came a joy which grew brighter and higher year after year, as her beauties and graces of person and mind were unfolding, until, like others too good for this world, she was removed to another.

We subsequently learned that the mother of our adopted daughter died; that she was in person and manners attractive and ladylike, and that she had evidently been accustomed to good society. The ladies of the hotel in which she had boarded during her last illness became much interested in her. To one of them, Mrs. Lyman, she, just before her death, gave little Mary, then an infant. Mrs. Lyman, who accepted the trust, died herself soon afterward, leaving the infant to a second orphanage. Two months afterwards, and soon after we adopted the child, Mrs. Wood, the mother of the deceased Mrs. Lyman, brought a small trunk to us containing articles that had been carefully preserved by Mary's mother, who had committed the trunk to Mrs. Lyman with a request that it should be kept until Mary should be old enough to appreciate a mother's gift. The trunk contained a miniature of Mary's mother, and some jewelry belonging to and worn by her in her English home, in earlier and better and happier days. It contained, also, two marriage certificates, the earliest one giving her family name. It contained, also, an article which subsequently led to her identification.

The child when brought to us was subjected to the discipline which that " remarkable man, Mr. Dick," suggested in the case of David Copperfield, the evening of the day that he arrived at his aunt's cottage near Dover. Most of the night was consumed in preparing a temporary wardrobe, in which Mary was arrayed, appearing at the breakfast-table in the morning as much at ease as the other children. And long before that day closed she seemed as really one of the household as if she had been " native and to the manor born." And from that time forward she was never the occasion, to my wife or myself, of an impatient word or an anxious thought; nor between her and her new sisters and brother was there anything but mutual, uninterrupted, and growing affection. She was remarkable for an early and intuitive sense of propriety. Habits of order and system were immediately noticeable. Before she was four years old she watched for opportunities to be useful, and was always anticipating what many other children would require to be told. Long before other children think of such things, she was thoughtfully and ambitiously occupied with little household duties. She soon became known in the neighborhood, and was a favorite among the children of refined and cultivated people. She was always cheerful, and sometimes joyous. She derived pleasure from dolls, toys, pictures, and flowers, at intervals; but her constant study was to be diligently useful, to learn household duties, and to help her mother and sister. Before she was six years old, her wardrobe, library, and play-room, where perfect order and neatness reigned, attracted visitors and admiration. In her seventh year she made a shirt for me, which was exhibited at the American Institute in New York, to which a silver medal was awarded as the best specimen of plain sewing. At school, though not brilliant, she made satisfactory proficiency in all her classes, and was remarkable there, as elsewhere, for the unerring propriety of her conduct.

In November, 1851, accompanied by my daughter Harriet and our friends Mrs. and Miss Hunter, I departed in the steamer Baltic for England. On our way to Paris we reached Boulogne on Saturday afternoon, where we concluded to remain until Monday morning. At the table d'hote dinner we fell into an easy conversation with Captain Paget of the British navy, the only other guest at the table, who was residing there temporarily with his family. Before separating, he invited us to attend the English chapel on Sunday, adding that he would call for us at the proper time. At the close of the second service, Captain Paget invited us to tea at his apartments. There we found in Mrs. Paget an equally agreeable acquaintance. Harriet becoming interested with a daughter about Mary's age, and as she fancied resembling her sister, gave Mrs. Paget an account of Mary. Coming on Monday morning to take leave of us, he remarked that his wife had interested him in the character and history of our adopted daughter, and inquired whether we had found the family of her mother in England? I replied that our inquiries had been ineffectual. He remarked that the records of families throughout England were very perfect, indicating the proper sources of information, and then inquired how much we knew of the mother; and upon hearing her name, and such a description of her appearance as we could give, he recognized her as an acquaintance, her family, a highly respectable one, residing near his own. He added that she was well educated and attractive. Left friendless in India, she became an inmate of the family of a Danish merchant, and went, not long afterward, with that family to Copenhagen. A year later, she accompanied Governor Van Scholten as his housekeeper to Santa Cruz, a Danish West India island. That, Captain Paget said, was the last reliable information concerning her that reached her family in England. He had heard, without knowing how reliable the information was, that after remaining a year or two with Governor Van Scholten, she married and went to America. The accuracy of Captain Paget's information was confirmed by an incident, furnishing "proof strong as holy writ," that Isabella Shore, whom he traced from her parental abode through India and Denmark to the West Indies, was the mother of our Mary. I passed the winter of 1845 with my daughter Harriet in Santa Cruz, where we became well acquainted with Governor Van Scholten, and were guests at the executive plantation. We heard during the winter of an accomplished English lady who had formerly resided there. In the trunk given by Mary's mother to Mrs. Wood, and which subsequently came into our possession, was a Danish linen sheet with the name of Governor Van Scholten. Recognizing this sheet as belonging to the household of the Governor of the Danish West India Islands, we wondered how it found its way into a trunk belonging to Mary's mother. This, however, was made plain by Captain Paget's revelation.

On our return from Europe in the following July, Mary stood with her adopted mother upon the wharf to welcome us. From that time until the autumn of 1855, her life was one of uninterrupted enjoyment, always diligent, considerate, and cheerful. In the autumn of 1854 a severe cold settled upon her lungs, from which, after months of patient suffering, she died. Two days before her death, up to which time she had been very hopeful, she expressed a desire to sit in the rocking-chair, and, turning her feet out of bed, discovered that they were swollen. Lifting her eyes to mine with an expression which I too well remember, she quietly said, "Has it come to this?" Young as she was, she instantly comprehended the fatal significance of her discovery.

In May, 1857, I was called to Brunswick, Georgia, on business. My wife and daughter, ever since Mary's death, had been anxious to learn whether, as we had heard, twin brothers had been left at Charleston. They accompanied me thither. We left New York for Savannah by steamer. After attending to my business in Brunswick we came to Charleston, arriving on Sunday morning, and taking apartments at the Mills House. After breakfast I repaired to the reading-room, where a group of gentlemen engaged in conversation, casting frequent and furtive glances at me, seated some distance from them with a newspaper. After some ten minutes had elapsed, they were joined by another gentleman, who, after exchanging a few words, came over, offering me his hand, remarking that his name was Beach, then a merchant in Charleston, but a native of Marcellus, Onondaga County, and the son of one of my old Onondaga friends. Mr. Beach informed me that my appearance in Charleston, where so much excitement upon the slavery question existed,

was the subject of conversation among the gentlemen whom I
had noticed, but that his assurance would be sufficient to quiet
their apprehensions.

The gentlemen soon dispersed, and I went with my family to
church. Finding the name of Mr. Henry DeSaussure associated with the charities of the city, I drove to his residence, but
was informed that he went from church to the "Orphan House,"
and would not be at home until after the second service. Driving thence to the Orphan House, and finding Mr. D., I informed him that I was in pursuit of knowledge under difficulties. He replied courteously that if it was in his power to aid
me, he would do so cheerfully. I told him that I had reason to
believe that some eighteen or nineteen years before twin brothers were left to the charities of Charleston, adding that the
name of their mother was the only information I could give.
Mr. DeSaussure then, observing that I was a stranger, asked
where I resided, and what interest I had in the inquiry; and
on learning that I had adopted a sister, he replied with a smile
that I had sought for information from the right source, he having adopted the surviving brother of the twin orphans referred
to. Presently a young man came in, whose remarkable resemblance to his sister could leave no doubt of their relationship.
Mr. D. and his adopted son accompanied me to the Mills
House, where, if he had entered the parlor alone, he would have
instantly been recognized by my wife and daughter from his
face, expression, and manner, as a brother of Mary. Henry
DeSaussure Gray was then nineteen years old. His father died
of cholera a few weeks before his birth. Mrs. DeSaussure, and
other ladies of Charleston, finding in Mrs. Gray qualities which
interested them, provided a pleasant apartment for her, where
she remained until after her confinement. Subsequently she
found employment, the twins meanwhile remaining in the Orphan House. Under these circumstances she made the acquaintance of Chapman, a dwarf writing-master, who, representing
himself as wealthy, with a plantation in Missouri, offered marriage. Expecting to find a comfortable home for herself and
children, this destitute and lonely woman, whose life had been
so eventful, married a man from whom, under other circumstances, a refined nature would have shrunk. Some months
afterwards he prevailed upon her to come North upon a summer

excursion, with a promise to return to Charleston in the autumn, and then remove with the children to his plantation in Missouri. But none of these promises were kept. Mrs. Chapman died at Albany, leaving the infant daughter, who providentially fell into our hands. The twin brothers grew up in the Charleston Orphan House. Both were intelligent, studious, well-mannered, and popular. One was adopted by Mr. DeSaussure, while the other found a home in the family of a Charleston bookseller, dying at the age of sixteen.

The Charleston Orphan House, among its other laudable regulations, sends its most meritorious orphan boy annually to college. Several useful and one or two distinguished citizens of South Carolina are indebted to the Charleston Orphan House for their support and education. Captain Gedny, a distinguished officer in the revenue and coast survey service, belonged to the same class of orphans. Henry D. Gray, as the most meritorious orphan of his class, was now in his third year in college. Before leaving Charleston, it was arranged that the young man should pass his approaching vacation with us at Albany. He left Charleston by steamer immediately after Commencement. We found in this amiable young man much to console us for the loss of his sister.

In September he went to Niagara, returning *via* Montreal and Saratoga. In passing under the sheet of water at Niagara he took a severe cold, which, settling upon his lungs, terminated fatally in November. Instead of returning, therefore, with expanded views and agreeable remembrances and fresh hopes to resume his college course, we discharged the sad duty of depositing his remains by his sister's side in the Rural Cemetery at Albany.

CHAPTER LVIII.

1848.

GENERAL TAYLOR. — EARLY ACQUAINTANCE WITH COLONEL JOSEPH TAYLOR. — THE MEXICAN WAR. — CORRESPONDENCE WITH COLONEL TAYLOR. — THE GENERAL'S LETTERS. — THE ALLISON LETTER. — HIS NOMINATION AT PHILADELPHIA. — THE "FREE SOIL" PARTY. — THE ELECTION.

MY relations with General Taylor originated in circumstances so peculiar, and became so intimate and confidential, that I feel quite certain a full narrative would be found interesting; and, as he sustained a distinguished part in the military and civil history and councils of the country, I shall refer briefly to his early life. He was born in Orange County, Virginia, November 24, 1784, and died in Washington, D. C., July 9, 1850. His father, Colonel Richard Taylor, who served throughout the Revolutionary War, moved to Kentucky early in the present century. Zachary Taylor was employed upon his father's plantation until he was twenty-four years old, when his elder brother, a lieutenant in the United States army, died, and he became his brother's successor as lieutenant in the seventh regiment infantry. In 1810 he was promoted to a captaincy, and in 1812, after the war with England broke out, he was stationed with his company at Fort Harrison, on the Wabash River. It was an advanced post, and the first object of attack by the Indians led by Tecumseh, who invested the fort in large numbers, and, after repeated efforts to beguile Captain Taylor with professions of peace and friendship, made a furious night attack, setting fire to the fort at several points. One half of Captain Taylor's company were ill with fever, but with twenty-five effective troops he repelled several assaults, and finally extinguished the flames, when they abandoned the siege. For his gallantry on that occasion he was promoted to a majority. The war with England over, he became an efficient and gallant officer throughout our Indian troubles, and had risen at the commencement of the Mexican

Zachary Taylor —

war to the rank of general. His gallant and distinguished career throughout that war is too familiar to require a recital. Two or three weeks after the battle of Resaca de la Palma, his second victory over the Mexicans, I was coming to New York on board the steamboat, where I was introduced by the late Cornelius W. Lawrence to Colonel Taylor of the army, Mr. Lawrence remarking that he was a brother of the general who had so distinguished himself in Mexico. On expressing my gratification with his acquaintance, Colonel Taylor remarked that our acquaintance had a much earlier date, and although I had naturally forgotten it, the occasion was one likely to live in his memory. Unable myself to recall the occasion, the colonel said that when he was a young lieutenant I dined with his father-in-law the day of his marriage, adding that his wife was a daughter of the late John McLean, Postmaster General under John Quincy Adams. This occurred in 1825. I now fell into conversation with Colonel Taylor in relation to his brother. To my inquiry about his political opinions, the reply was that he had no politics; that he neither knew nor cared anything about parties. I said that for a man of his high position this was remarkable. The colonel then said, that while his brother had never attached himself to either party, and had seldom if ever voted, he had strong prejudices. I inquired what they were. He replied that the general was a warm admirer of Mr. Clay, and was strongly prejudiced against General Jackson, and that his prejudices were so strong against foreign manufactures that he would not wear a coat except made from American cloth, nor a button upon his coat that had been imported. On replying that I was not sure but that his *prejudices* were quite as important and practical as *principles*, Colonel Taylor asked why I was so curious about his brother's politics. " Because," I replied, " your brother is to be our next President." The colonel with a most incredulous look and air said, " That is a preposterous idea. General Taylor's habits and tastes are purely military. He knows nothing of political or civil affairs. When I tell you he is not as fit to be president as I am, you will see the absurdity of your suggestion." "Nevertheless," I responded, " if your brother goes through the Mexican war as he has commenced it he will be the next President of the United States." Colonel Taylor was then on his way from Detroit to Mexico.

I informed him that my object in drawing him aside was to ask him to deliver a message to his brother. He reiterated the remark that the whole thing was preposterous, but said that he would deliver the message. I asked him to say to General Taylor that it would not be long before numerous letters from men of all political stripes, offering him their support for the presidency, would pour in upon him; that no such letters needed a reply; that if the General kept his eyes toward Mexico, closing them and his ears to all that was passing behind him, the presidential question would take care of itself and of him; that until Mr. Clay wrote his letter to Alabama in 1844 his election as president was certain ; and that, finally, if General Taylor himself left the question entirely to the people they would certainly elect him. While all this made no impression upon Colonel Taylor's mind, and would as he believed be looked upon as visionary by his brother, he promised to deliver my message. As he was to leave New York for the South by an early train he bade me good-by. On the following morning, however, while in the breakfast room at the Astor House, Colonel Taylor quite unexpectedly seated himself by my side. He had been reflecting, he said, upon our conversation the evening previous, and, instead of leaving as he intended by an early train, he remained over to request me to put my message to his brother upon paper, with which request I complied. On my return to Albany, after that conversation with Colonel Taylor, I wrote the following editorial paragraph : —

[From the " Albany Evening Journal " of June 18, 1846.]

Battles afford generals an opportunity to distinguish themselves. General Jackson and General Harrison have been elected to the presidency. General Taylor is in the minds of many, and in the hearts of many more, for the same high place. One or two more successful conflicts would bring him in triumph to the White House in 1848.

The ground was thus publicly broken for General Taylor as a candidate for president two years before the Whig National Convention met at Philadelphia. The "one or two more successful conflicts " anticipated in the above paragraph soon followed, bringing General Taylor prominently before the people, and challenging their admiration and gratitude.

Several weeks afterwards I received a letter from Colonel

Taylor, dated at Matamoras, informing me that before he reached that post General Taylor had moved on towards Monterey, that remaining there to gather supplies for the army, he had taken advantage of a train going to headquarters to inclose my memoranda in a letter which he had written to his brother. Not long afterwards I received another letter from Colonel Taylor, informing me that he had his brother's answer, which contained a postscript that he detached and inclosed to me, of which the following is a copy: —

Memoranda of the conversation you had with an Albany editor, and to which you request a reply, seems to me too visionary to require a serious answer. Such an idea never entered my head, nor is it likely to enter the head of any sane person. I shall be well satisfied to get creditably through this campaign. For your friend's confidence in me, however, you will make my acknowledgments. Z. T.

The capture of Monterey, succeeded in due time by the great battle and brilliant victory at Buena Vista, closed General Taylor's campaign, not only " creditably " as he hoped, but in a manner which won the admiration and gratitude of his countrymen.

Even before the battle of Buena Vista General Taylor received evidence, by letters and in newspapers, that many "sane" people were thinking of him for president, and after his crowning victory his name became a political " household word." About that period I received another letter from Colonel Taylor, of which the following is a copy: —

Matamoras, Mexico, *April* 24, 1847.

Dear Sir, — I have just received yours of the 3d inst., and noted the contents. For the kind allusion you have been pleased to make to the services of my brother, General Taylor, be pleased to accept my sincere thanks.

It cannot be disguised that General Taylor, with his command, was lately in a most perilous position, and I consider it almost a miracle that he was able to sustain himself under the trying and most extraordinary position in which Major-General Scott, in his wisdom, thought proper to place him and his command. Indeed, we are at a loss to account for the course pursued by General Scott in withdrawing so large a force from General Taylor's command, and leaving him so weak, — say only some 7,500 troops to oppose General Santa Anna in front with some 25,000 well appointed troops, and defend many important depots and keep open and defend our long line of operations, from Brazos Island to Saltillo, a distance by water and land upwards of 500 miles. It really seems to me that it was nothing more or less than an invitation to Santa Anna to come and retake all that we had acquired since the commencement of hostilities.

Indeed, had General Scott been sent to Mexico for the avowed and express purpose of playing the part of an executioner, by having General Taylor and his command destroyed, he could not have taken a wiser and surer plan to effect the object than the one he adopted; as, I feel convinced, had General Taylor been defeated, or fallen back on Monterey, as advised to do by General Scott, *all* and *everything* would have been lost and our glorious flag tarnished; but, thanks to a kind Providence, General Taylor took the bold and *only* course to stay the impending danger, by fighting Santa Anna at Buena Vista, and driving him back or perish in the attempt.

Now, my dear sir, as regards General Taylor being brought forward as a candidate for the presidency, I am free to say to you that I really do not believe the subject for a moment occupies his thoughts, and that, if he is ever elevated to that high and distinguished office, it will be by no seeking of his, and he must reach it, if at all, by the spontaneous wishes of his fellow-citizens, and without promises, pledges, or bargain.

I agree with you most fully that General Taylor should pursue the "even tenor of his way," and, as long as he remains in this country, devote himself *solely* to the duties of his station, and let the presidential question take care of itself.

From information just received from Washington city I expect, in a few weeks, to be ordered to New York on duty, where I hope to have the pleasure of meeting you frequently.

I am, very respectfully, your obedient servant,

J. T. TAYLOR.

Mr. THURLOW WEED, Albany, N. Y.

Mexico was entered at three different points by armies respectively of Generals Scott, Wool, and Taylor. General Scott, the commander-in-chief, moved upon the city of Mexico, that being the objective point. Naturally supposing that Generals Taylor and Wool were to play subordinate parts, he recruited his own army by depleting theirs. Of this Generals Taylor and Wool complained bitterly, both to General Scott and the War Department. How keenly General Taylor resented the loss of his regular troops, will be seen by Colonel Taylor's letter.

General Scott himself, in the following letter to General Taylor, seems conscious of the injustice of depriving him of his regular troops : —

> I shall be obliged to take from you most of the gallant officers and men, regulars and volunteers, whom you have so long and so nobly commanded.

General Taylor's force was thus diminished to 5,000 troops, only 500 of which were regulars. Nevertheless, he moved his army forward several miles, and, selecting vantage ground, awaited the approach of General Santa Anna's army, consisting of 21,000 disciplined troops. Here the battle of Buena Vista was fought and won, and here, after faithful, gallant, and continuous service for thirty-nine years, General Taylor's military career closed in a blaze of glory.

The Mexican war, immediately after the capture of Mexico by General Scott, terminated, and in November, 1847, General Taylor reached his plantation near Baton Rouge. The presidential canvass had been already inaugurated. Henry Clay and Daniel Webster were urged by their respective friends for the Whig nomination. General Taylor's name soon loomed up in the political horizon. Nothing being known of his political sentiments or sympathies, "rank and file" Democrats as well as Whigs were found favoring his nomination. Leading politicians endeavored to repress the movement. It was easy, however, for those who were accustomed to consult upon popular feeling to perceive that the movement in favor of General Taylor was irrepressible. Early in the winter of 1848 those only who were blinded by their zeal in favor of other candidates failed to see that General Taylor would be nominated and elected, for it was quite evident that if the Whig National Convention, as was generally expected, should nominate Mr. Clay, the Democrats would nominate and elect General Taylor.

Thus impressed, I went zealously but quietly to work, first through the metropolitan and rural Whig press to incline the public mind towards General Taylor, and next to secure a delegation to the National Convention in favor of his nomination. This required extreme caution. Mr. Clay was the choice of at least three fourths of the Whigs of our State. Many leading and influential Whigs were devoted to Mr. Webster. While careful not to offend, I labored to persuade, and, before the National Convention met, did persuade, many of our intelligent political friends that Mr. Clay's nomination would result in his and our defeat.

The presidential campaign of 1848 opened and was prosecuted up to the last hour preceding the nomination by the Whig National Convention under circumstances more embarrassing than I had before experienced. My own position was alike responsible and difficult. The claims of Mr. Clay, who was in 1840 the choice of the Whigs, had been ignored in favor of General Harrison, " an available candidate." In 1844 Mr. Clay was nominated with great unanimity, and, until the publication of his letter to an Alabamian concerning the annexation of Texas, no doubt was entertained of his election. That letter, arousing and uniting the abolitionists against Mr. Clay, cost him the presidency. But the result strengthened rather than weakened the devotion of his friends. Early in 1848 it was apparent that Mr. Clay was the choice of a large portion of the Whigs of the Union. Mr. Webster, who had left the field open to Mr. Clay in 1844, now reappeared as a candidate. He had many warm and influential friends in the city of New York, prominent among whom were Moses H. Grinnell, R. M. Blatchford, Simeon Draper, Edward Curtis, and Hiram Ketchum. General Scott, who was supported by the Whig delegation of New York in 1840, was again a candidate. My relations with Mr. Clay, Mr. Webster, and General Scott were equally intimate and agreeable. All had been very kind to me. I would cheerfully have supported either, if my judgment had accorded with my feelings. But I entertained from the beginning of the canvass an unwavering belief that General Taylor, if not nominated by the Whigs, would be taken up and elected by the Democrats. I knew him to be an honest man, and I had learned enough from his brother, Colonel Taylor, to be entirely satisfied that his " prejudices " in favor of domestic manufactures, against the annexation of Texas, his life-long admiration of Mr. Clay, together with the legacy of patriotism inherited from a Whig father, were sufficient guaranties for a Whig administration. The impatient friends of Mr. Clay, anticipating the usual call of a State convention, moved spontaneously in their congressional districts, where the delegates chosen to the

Whig National Convention were instructed to vote for Mr. Clay. The first and most influential Whig journal that came out boldly for General Taylor was the " New York Courier and Enquirer." General James Watson Webb, who wrote the article, believing that the true interest of the Whig party and the country would be promoted by the nomination of General Taylor, had his editorial article set up and placed in the paper without the knowledge of his associate editors; who, on the morning it appeared, were alike surprised and annoyed, but were not long in discovering that General Webb had sounded a key-note. Thenceforth the " Courier and Enquirer " zealously urged the nomination of General Taylor. Soon after that paper broke ground, a Taylor committee was formed in the city of New York, consisting of General Webb, Moses H. Grinnell, Simeon Draper, Prescott Hall, Charles King, Edward Curtis, Hugh Maxwell, Richard M. Blatchford, and several other leading Whigs. Mr. Maxwell was made chairman of the committee. An active organization was now pushed forward. Abbott Lawrence, of Boston, was designated for nomination as vice-president. In the Whig National Convention, that met in Philadelphia on the 8th day of June, 1848, the several States were represented by their ablest and strongest men. The friends of Mr. Clay, remembering that his claims had been ignored in 1840, were determined upon his nomination. They were aided materially by the late Vice-President Henry Wilson and other influential New England Whigs, who could not be persuaded that General Taylor, a native of Virginia, a resident of Louisiana, and a slave-holder, could be relied on in an emergency which approached, and which would determine the question whether slavery should be extended into the territory devoted to freedom by the Missouri Compromise, and whether California should be admitted into the Union as a free State. Some of these gentlemen were satisfied with the assurances of General Taylor's brother, Colonel Joseph P. Taylor, who, at my request, became the guest of the late Josiah Randall, a distinguished Pennsylvania Whig, who did not survive to endure the mortification of seeing his son recreant to the teachings and principles of his Whig father and grandfather. I had at no time doubted our ability to nominate General Taylor, but the danger I had foreseen now assumed a threatening aspect. Several prominent delegates threatened to bolt. Some of my friends, alarmed by the excitement of the canvass, urged me to consent to the nomination of Mr. Clay. Two of them insisted that I should be held responsible for a split in the convention, and, consequently, the ruin of the Whig party. My convictions, however, of what was both wise and right, were too strong to be shaken. When the convention resolved to go into a ballot the names of Henry Clay, Daniel Webster, Winfield Scott, John M. Clayton, and Zachary Taylor were presented as candidates by their respective friends. Upon the fourth ballot General Taylor was nominated. Although the result was hailed with great enthusiasm by the citizens in attendance, it was openly denounced by many delegates, and regarded with apprehension by many others. The opponents of General Taylor manifested immediate and active opposition to the nomination of Abbott Lawrence for vice-president. They would not, they said, "have King Cotton both ends of the ticket." General Taylor was represented as a grower and Mr. Lawrence as a manufacturer of cotton. John A. Collier, of this State, took the convention by surprise by nominating Millard Fillmore for vice-president. He was nominated on the first ballot. Mr. Fillmore, then comptroller of this State, united with me in a letter to Mr. Lawrence, requesting him to allow his name to be presented to the National Convention as a candidate for vice-president. His own nomination, however, under changed circumstances, served to unite the party and strengthen the ticket. I will not now anticipate events by referring to the disastrous effects of that nomination. The history of Mr. Fillmore's rise and downfall will constitute another chapter. Several delegates, led by Henry Wilson, withdrew from the convention, all of whom, however, subsequently supported and voted for General Taylor.

The nominations inspired confidence throughout the Union. The canvass was progressing favorably until several letters, written by General Taylor in reply to letters asking his opinion upon various subjects, appeared in different parts of the country. When it is remembered that Mr. Clay ruined himself as a candidate in 1844 by writing a letter to Alabama, it will not appear strange that General Taylor's letters embarrassed his friends and encouraged his opponents. Some of them were

written with no thought of their publication, and all unconscious of the facility with which they could be misconstrued
and perverted. I hastily prepared a letter to General Taylor,
apprising him of the use our opponents were making of his
letters, and suggesting the form of one which I thought would
disembarrass us. Mr. Fillmore adopted this letter as his own.
General Taylor replied promptly, thanking Mr. Fillmore for
his suggestions, adding that he would immediately write a final
letter to his kinsman, Captain Allison, in which he would review his political correspondence. That letter, written on the
4th of September, soon appeared in a Baton Rouge Whig
paper, and had the effect anticipated. It inspired the confidence
and awakened the zeal of the now united Whig party. Constituting, as that letter does, an interesting link in the political
history of our country, it seems entitled to a place in this volume : —

A " ROUGH AND READY " LETTER FROM GENERAL TAYLOR.

EAST PASCAGOULA, *September* 4, 1848.

DEAR SIR, — On the 22d of May last I addressed you a letter explaining my views in regard to various matters of public policy, lest
my fellow-citizens might be misled by the many contradictory and
conflicting statements in respect to them which appeared in the journals of the day, and were circulated throughout the country. I now
find myself misrepresented and misunderstood upon another point, of
such importance to myself personally, if not to the country at large, as
to claim from me a candid and connected exposition of my relations to
the public in regard to the pending presidential canvass. The utmost
ingenuity has been expended upon several letters, and detached sentences of letters, which have recently appeared over my signature, to
show that I occupy an equivocal attitude towards the various parties
into which the people are divided, and especially towards the Whig
party as represented by the national convention which assembled in
Philadelphia in June last. Had these letters, and scraps of letters,
been published or construed in connection with what I have heretofore said upon this subject, I should not now have to complain of the
speed with which my answers to isolated questions have been given
up to the captious criticism of those who have been made my enemies
by a nomination which has been tendered to me without solicitation or
arrangement of mine ; or of the manner in which selected passages in
some of my letters, written in the freedom and carelessness of a confidential correspondence, have been communicated to the public press.

But riven from the context, and separated from a series of explanatory facts and circumstances which are, in so far as this canvass is concerned, historical, they are as deceptive as though they were positive fabrications. I address you this letter to correct the injustice that has been done me and the public, to the extent that I am an object of interest to them by this illiberal process. I shall not weary you by an elaborate recital of every incident connected with the first presentation of my name as a candidate for the presidency. I was then at the head of the American army at the Valley of the Rio Grande. I was surrounded by Whigs and Democrats, who had stood by me in the trying hours of my life, and whom it was my destiny to conduct through scenes of still greater trial. My duty to that army, and to the republic, whose battles we were waging, forbade my assuming a position of seeming hostility to any portion of the brave men under my command, all of whom knew I was a Whig in principles, for I made no concealment of my political sentiments or predilections. Such had been the violence of party struggle during our late presidential election, that the acceptance of a nomination under the various interpretations given to the obligation of a candidate presented to the public with a formulary of political principles, was equivalent almost to a declaration of uncompromising enmity to all who did not subscribe to its tenets. I was unwilling to hazard the effect of such relationship towards any of the soldiers under my command when in front of an enemy common to us all. It would have been unjust in itself, and it was as repugnant to my own feelings as it was to my duty. I wanted unity in the army, and forbore any act that might sow the seeds of distrust and discord in its ranks. I have not my letters written at the time before me, but they are all of one import, and in conformity with the views herein expressed. Meanwhile I was solicited by my personal friends and by strangers, by Whigs and Democrats, to consent to become a candidate. I was nominated by the people in primary assemblies, — by Whigs, Democrats, and Natives, in separate and mixed meetings. I resisted them all, and continued to do so till led to believe that my opposition was assuming the aspect of defiance of the popular wishes. I yielded only when it looked like presumption to resist longer ; and even then I should not have done so had not the nomination been presented to me in a form unlikely to awaken acrimony or reproduce the bitterness of feeling which attends popular elections. I say it in sincerity and truth, that a part of the inducements to my consent was the hope that by going into the canvass it would be conducted with candor, if not with kindness. It has been no fault of mine that this anticipation has proved a vain one. After I permitted myself to be announced for the presidency, under the circumstances above noticed, I accepted nomination after nomination in the spirit in which they were tendered. They were made irrespective of party, and so acknowledged. No one who joined in those nominations could have been deceived as to my political views. From the beginning until now I have declared myself to be a Whig on all proper occasions. With this distinct avowal published to the world, I did not think that I had a right to repel nominations from political opponents any more than I had a right to refuse the vote of a Democrat at the polls; and I proclaimed it abroad that I should not reject the proffered support of any body of my fellow-citizens. This was my position when in November last I returned to the United States, long before either of the great divisions of the people had held a national convention, and when it was thought doubtful if one of them would hold any.

Matters stood in this attitude till spring, when there were so many statements in circulation concerning my views upon questions of national policy, that I felt constrained to correct the errors into which the public mind was falling by a more explicit enunciation of principles, which I did in my letter to you in April last. That letter, and the facts which I have detailed as briefly as a proper understanding of them would permit, developed my whole position in relation to the presidency at the time.

The Democratic convention met in May, and composed their ticket to suit them. This they had a right to do. The national Whig convention met in June, and selected me as their candidate. I accepted the nomination with gratitude and with pride. I was proud of the confidence of such a body of men representing such a constituency as the Whig party of the United States, a manifestation the more grateful because it was not cumbered with exactions incompatible with the dignity of the presidential office, and the responsibilities of its incumbent to the whole people of the nation. And I may add that these emotions were increased by associating my name with that of the distinguished citizen of New York, whose acknowledged ability and sound conservative opinion might have justly entitled him to the first place on the ticket. The convention adopted me as it found me, — a Whig, — decided, but not ultra in my opinions; and I would be without excuse if I were to shift the relationships which subsisted at the time. They took me with the declaration of principles I had published to the world, and I would be without defense if I were to say or do anything to impair the force of that declaration.

I have said that I would accept the nomination from Democrats, but in so doing I would not abate one jot or tittle of my opinions as written down. Such a nomination, as indicating a coincidence of opinion on the part of those making it, should not be regarded with disfavor by those who think with me, as a compliment personal to my-self, it should not be expected that I would repulse them with insult. I shall not modify my views to entice them to my side, I shall not re-gret their aid when they join my friends voluntarily.

I have said I was not a party candidate, nor am I in that straight-ened and sectarian sense which would prevent my being the president of the whole people, in case of my election. I did not regard myself as one before the convention met, and that body did not seek to make me different from what I was. They did not fetter me down to a se-ries of pledges which were to be an iron rule of action in all, and in despite of all, the contingencies that might arise in the course of a pres-idential term. I am not engaged to lay violent hands indiscriminately upon public officers, good or bad, who may differ in opinion with me ; I am not expected to force Congress, by the coercion of the veto, to pass laws to suit me or pass none. This is what I mean by not being a party candidate. And I understand this is good Whig doctrine, — I would not be a *partisan* president, and hence should not be a party candidate in the sense that would make one. This is the sum and sub-stance of my meaning, and this is the purport of the facts and circum-stances attending my nomination, when considered in their connection with, and dependence upon, one another.

I refer all persons, who are anxious on the subject, to this statement for the proper understanding of my position towards the presidency and the people. If it is not intelligible, I cannot make it so, and shall cease to attempt it.

In taking leave of the subject, I have only to add that my two let-ters to you embrace all the topics I design to speak of pending this canvass. If I am elected, I shall do all that an honest zeal may effect to cement the bonds of our Union, and establish the happiness of my countrymen upon an enduring basis.   Z. TAYLOR.

To CAPTAIN J. S. ALLISON.

To this letter I appended the following editorial : —

This frank, manly, independent letter from General Taylor, vindi-cating and explaining his principles and positions, will be read with deep and grateful emotions by all true and good men. General Tay-lor, like good metal, rings clearest when most severely tested. We have been perplexed and annoyed by some of General Taylor's letters, but now that he has reviewed them all, and boldly (as is his habit) planted himself upon independent Whig ground, we are constrained to say that he is a wise as well as a good man. He is, we are sure, the man whom the country wants at the head of its officers. He is the pilot that will take our national ship through all its perils. All that we see and hear of him adds to our admiration of his character and principles.

With this letter, thousands of alienated Whigs will warm back to General Taylor. He is all truth and honesty and patriotism. The country and the crisis demand such a man.

We shall have him for president; and the people, with hand and heart, will be grateful to a beneficent Providence for raising so great and good a man to be their ruler.

The result of the election vindicated the wisdom of General Taylor's nomination, while the purity and patriotism of his administration fulfilled the assurances and expectations of his friends. He was elected by a vote of 163 against 127 for General Cass. New York then, as on other occasions, was the pivot upon which the general result would depend. Early in the canvass it was charged that by defeating the nomination of Mr. Clay I had thrown away the State. Soon, however, an element cropped out which entirely changed the aspect.

The friends of Mr. Van Buren, exasperated by the refusal of the Democratic National Convention to nominate that gentleman, determined to run him as a " Free-Soil " candidate. That movement was encouraged by the dissatisfaction in the Whig party with the nomination of General Taylor. It was believed that a large Whig vote, especially in the New England States, would be cast for the " Free-Soil " candidates, Charles Francis Adams, of Boston, being on that ticket for vice-president. The Free-Soil organization was for several weeks the occasion for anxiety and apprehension, but as the election approached confidence was reëstablished ; and while a few local leaders dropped out of line, the Whig masses became united and zealous, and the campaign ended in victory.

CHAPTER LIX.

1828–1852.

There are few, if any, occupations better calculated to make
us acquainted with the virtues and vices of men with whom we
are associated than politics. My experience in this respect has
been both pleasant and painful. I have seen the best and the
worst aspects of human nature, and I have lived long enough to
understand the workings and influences which occasionally per-
vert the judgments and stifle the convictions of aspirants for
high political honors. My opportunities in this respect have
been larger than those of others differently situated. Enjoying,
as I did for many years, not only the confidence of my political
friends, but the reputation of shaping the action of conventions,
candidates for office naturally sought my support. Had I exercised my influence capriciously, or failed to respond to the popular sentiment of my party in the selection of candidates, my
influence would have been short-lived. It was my good fortune,
therefore, as was conceded by our friends, and alleged by our
opponents, to be recognized in county, district, state, and even
national conventions from 1824 to 1872. I was first seriously
embarrassed in 1838, when Messrs. Granger, Bradish, Seward,
Collier, Stevens, Kirkland, and Noxon were candidates for governor. Messrs. Granger and Bradish were the seniors of Mr.
Seward in years and in political service. The other gentlemen were also his seniors at the bar, and felt that they were
quite as well, if not better, entitled to the nomination for governor. These gentlemen were all my personal and political
friends. I believed that Mr. Seward was our strongest candi-

date, and after a very sharp and exciting canvass secured his nomination. Messrs. Collier and Noxon felt their disappointment keenly. The former, however, became reconciled when a few years later he was made comptroller. But Mr. Noxon never forgave me.

I first met Millard Fillmore in a convention at Buffalo in 1828. He had then been recently admitted to the bar. Although passing but a few hours with him, I was so favorably impressed as in the following year to suggest his nomination for the Assembly. In 1830, while serving with him in the Assembly, my favorable impressions of his ability and fitness for public life were much strengthened, and we became warm personal and political friends. In 1832 he was elected to Congress, where he soon acquired the reputation he enjoyed in our State legislature of being able in debate, wise in council, and inflexible in his political sentiments. He served eight years in Congress, and during a protracted and exciting tariff struggle he sustained himself as chairman of the ways and means committee with marked ability. He was our candidate for governor in 1844, and would have been elected but for the unfortunate letter that Mr. Clay wrote to a friend in Alabama—a letter which enabled the abolitionists to beguile from the Whig party in Oneida, Madison, Oswego, Cayuga, Wayne, Ontario, Monroe, Genesee, and Chautauqua, votes enough to defeat the Clay electoral ticket in this State, and to elect Silas Wright governor over Millard Fillmore, Alvan Stewart, the Abolition candidate for governor, receiving 15,000 votes. Until the appearance of Mr. Clay's letter, in which he remarked that he did not consider it a matter of any consequence whether Texas came into the Union as a State with or without slavery, the abolitionists had acquiesced in the nomination, and had intended to vote for Mr. Fillmore. In 1847 Mr. Fillmore was elected State comptroller. During these twenty years my intimacy with and friendship for Mr. Fillmore was not only uninterrupted but constantly strengthening. In the then approaching presidential campaign he was the first person to whom I suggested General Taylor as an available candidate for president. He cheerfully acquiesced, and we conferred together constantly up to the time that I left Albany to attend the national convention at Philadelphia. Concurring with me in the opinion that Abbott Lawrence of

Boston would be our best candidate for vice-president, he accompanied me to New York for a consultation with Mr. Lawrence at the Astor House. At the national convention where, after an exciting and bitter canvass, so bitter indeed as to threaten a serious division in the party, General Taylor was nominated, the friends of Mr. Clay broke ground fiercely against a New England candidate for vice-president, declaring vehemently that they would not "have cotton at both ends of the ticket." When the convention after a stormy recess assembled, Mr. John A. Collier, in a speech eloquently portraying the feelings of sorrow and disappointment felt by the friends of Mr. Clay, said that he rose with a peace-offering which, if accepted, would go far to reconcile those friends and to prevent a fatal breach in the party, and then, to the general astonishment, appealed to the convention for a unanimous response to his nomination of Millard Fillmore for vice-president. This *coup d'état* was a success, and while the friends of Mr. Lawrence were greatly disappointed, they gave an immediate and hearty support to the ticket. From that day till the election Mr. Fillmore and I were in constant communication. During the canvass we became a good deal alarmed about a matter which seemed to require an explanation from General Taylor. With this view I wrote what seemed to be required, which was adopted by Mr. Fillmore, and went to General Taylor as a letter from his associate on the ticket. In response to that letter General Taylor immediately wrote and published one which satisfactorily relieved all our apprehensions. Between Vice-President Fillmore and Senator Seward there had been no political differences, but each had their friends and supporters between whom difficulties might arise in the distribution of patronage under the new administration. To avoid such a possibility the Vice-President and Senator dined with me at Albany when on their way to Washington. Here everything was pleasantly arranged. The Vice-President and Senator were to consult from time to time, as should become necessary, and agree upon the important appointments to be made in our State. General Taylor after his election, conscious of his own want of experience in civil affairs, supposed, until otherwise advised by Hon. John J. Crittenden, that the Vice-President could be *ex-officio* a member of his cabinet. Expressing in a letter to Mr. Fillmore his regret that he could not have the benefit of his presence and advice in the cabinet, he added that he should rely upon his experience and ask his advice upon all important questions. Soon after this, in the hope of serving two meritorious political friends I went to Washington. I met the Vice-President at Willard's Hotel. My reception was more courteous than cordial. It was soon apparent that Mr. Fillmore's feelings towards me had undergone a strange and unaccountable change. After a brief interview upon commonplace topics I withdrew. From Senator Seward, upon whom I next called, I learned that the appointments for our State, so far as they had been made, were upon Mr. Fillmore's recommendation and of his particular friends. I then called upon the Attorney General, Reverdy Johnson, with whom I had long been intimate, who received me so coldly that I did not even sit down. I next repaired to the Post-Office Department, confidently anticipating a different reception from my old Vermont friend, Collamer. But that gentleman, whose feelings toward me had not changed, frankly informed me that he could make no New York appointment without the approval of the Vice-President. Mr. Seward, when informed of these rebuffs, said that the understanding between himself and the Vice-President about appointments had been disregarded. The first knowledge he had of the New York custom-house appointments was when their names were read in executive session. I then returned to Albany with the unpleasant feeling of being "left out in the cold" by a President from whom I was entitled to very different treatment. In a subsequent visit to Washington my relations with the President and his cabinet, as has been explained elsewhere, became and remained friendly and confidential, and though much at Washington while General Taylor lived I did not again meet the Vice-President, who, now aspiring to the presidency, saw in Mr. Seward a formidable rival, and assuming that he could not rely upon me as against the Senator severed ties which I had supposed would never be broken. This, however, was but the first of a series of sacrifices, involving on the part of Mr. Fillmore, not merely old and cherished friends, but older and even more devotedly cherished principles.

Upon the slavery question, which had for many years entered more or less intensely into our political action, Mr. Fillmore was always more pronounced and aggressive than Mr. Granger, Governor Seward, or myself, and had in the legislature and in Congress sympathized and acted, whenever he could do so without losing caste as a Whig, with Giddings of Ohio and John P. Hale of New Hampshire. He had uniformly opposed compromises with slavery. At that time the question of the admission of California as a State into the Union engrossed the attention of Congress and of the people. The slave States, through their representatives in Congress, threatened resistance to the admission of California with a constitution prohibiting slavery. President Taylor informed those representatives that if the people of California adopted a constitution prohibiting slavery, and Congress passed the bill, he should approve and sign it. On the eve of the passage of that bill President Taylor died. Compromise measures, comprehensive in scope and extraordinary in character, were promptly introduced and passed through Congress. Those measures included a fugitive slave bill, so revolting to every sentiment of justice and humanity that it was thought impossible to find approval with the President, who could not sign it without violation of principles and feelings which had been proclaimed and reiterated publicly and privately from the time of his entrance into public life up to his latest utterances. But the promise and hope of being rewarded for a sacrifice of all that he had held most sacred with the presidency was strong enough to command his approval of the Fugitive Slave Law. In signing a bill even yet remembered with popular indignation, Mr. Fillmore signed his political death-warrant. Having served out President Taylor's term, Mr. Fillmore passed into retirement, from which he never emerged. Mr. Fillmore's public life up to the time of his temptation had been so consistent, he had always adhered so firmly to his political convictions, and was in all respects so reliable, that my regard for and confidence in him had been unbounded. Mr. Fillmore might have exclaimed with Cardinal Wolsey : —

> "Fling away ambition,
> By that sin fell the angels. How can man then,
> The image of his Maker, hope to win by it ?"

CHAPTER LX.

1849–1850.

GENERAL TAYLOR'S CABINET. — THE GALPHIN CLAIM. — PROPOSED CHANGE OF CABINET OFFICERS. — GOVERNOR FISH. — EDWARD STANLY. — DEATH OF THE PRESIDENT.

IN the winter of 1849 and 1850 the payment by the Secretary of the Treasury of the old and long disputed " Galphin claim " was the subject of assault, both in the Democratic journals and in Congress, upon General Taylor's administration. It was a Georgia claim, and, among the parties interested, was Mr. Crawford, then Secretary of War. As the investigation and discussion progressed, General Taylor became more and more disturbed. No man entertained a higher sense of official integrity than General Taylor. He not only intended that his administration should be an inflexibly honest one, but hoped to guard it against suspicion. After a careful examination of the nature of the claim, and the law of Congress referring it for adjustment to the Treasury Department, he very reluctantly came to the conclusion, not only that his Secretary of War had used his influence in favor of a claim in which he had a pecuniary interest, but that the Secretary of the Treasury had paid it without personal examination into its merits, on an opinion given by the Attorney General, who, it was alleged, had been of counsel in the case before he was called into the cabinet. Three members of his cabinet, therefore, were compromised. Under these accusations, affecting the purity of his administration, the President chafed for several weeks, and until he came to the conclusion to make a new cabinet. To Mr. Meredith, the Secretary of the Treasury, General Taylor had become warmly attached, while his relations with the other members had been pleasant. But he could not endure the idea of going on while his administration rested under such imputations. In announcing this purpose to me he said that he came to Washington wholly unacquainted with civil affairs, and painfully distrustful of his fitness for the high duties that had been imposed upon him. He called to his aid several statesmen, Hon. John J. Crittenden, of Kentucky, being one of them, upon whose knowledge and experience he felt that he could rely, and in consultation with whom his cabinet officers were selected. He now had learned enough to know that with the wisest and purest men in public life their choice would be influenced more or less by their personal if not political preferences and aspirations. And with this knowledge, inasmuch as the responsibility rested with him, he should now exercise his own judgment in the formation of a new cabinet. He should, he said, consult no other person, and his only purpose in conferring with me was to avail himself of such information as I possessed of the character and qualifications of the men whom he might think of for the cabinet. He then produced a memorandum with the names of prominent statesmen in different parts of the Union, with the remark that, as the free States contained much the larger population, with interests more diverse than the interests of the Southern people, in changing his cabinet, instead of giving the Southern States a majority, as he had done in forming his present cabinet, he intended to select a majority from the free States. The cabinet, as it then stood, consisted of Clayton, of Delaware, Secretary of State, Meredith, of Pennsylvania, Secretary of the Treasury, Crawford, of Georgia, Secretary of War, Preston, of Virginia, Secretary of the Navy, Ewing, of Ohio, Secretary of the Interior, Johnson, of Maryland, Attorney General, and Collamer, of Vermont, Postmaster General. There was no reason for changing Mr. Ewing or Mr. Collamer, and the President expressed a determination, as soon as opportunity offered, of tendering diplomatic appointments to those gentlemen. He had decided, in asking for the resignation of Mr. Meredith, to offer him the mission to France.

The first question settled was that of a successor to Mr. Crawford, the Secretary of War. For that position he selected Edward Stanly, then a representative in Congress from North Carolina. He then took up the question of the secretary of the treasury, about which he expressed much solicitude, deeming it far the most important department of the government. He was particularly anxious, he said, to find a secretary of the treasury of inflexible and proverbial firmness and integrity, and one sound and reliable in reference to the protective tariff. He spoke of several able and earnest Whigs from Southern States, either of whom he would be willing to trust on every question but the tariff. Among the Northern men he spoke of were Governor John Davis, of Massachusetts, Horace Everett, of Vermont, Cooper and McKennan, of Pennsylvania, and Vinton, of Ohio, all perfectly competent and reliable. After considering these names for more than half an hour, without deciding which to adopt, I asked and obtained his permission to suggest the name of Hamilton Fish, then Governor of New York. This struck him with much favor. After several minutes' reflection, he inquired whether Governor Fish was sufficiently acquainted with financial affairs to enable him to manage the Treasury Department. I replied that if that question was put to our prominent public men they would generally answer in the negative. I remarked, further, that my own knowledge of financial questions being but limited and superficial, I ought to distrust my own judgment, and that I certainly had no right to expect him to rely on it. I then gave him my reasons for believing Governor Fish remarkably well qualified to discharge all the duties of the Treasury Department understandingly, assuring the President that if this were not so Governor Fish himself would be sure to know it, and equally sure to say so, and decline the appointment. After going over the ground again, the President decided in favor of Governor Fish for the treasury. Having fixed upon the secretary of war from a Southern State, he intimated his intention to find a secretary of the navy from an Eastern State, and an attorney general from Tennessee or Kentucky; but nothing farther was settled. This was late in June, and, as Congress was expected to adjourn in July, the President intended to call an extra session of the Senate the day after the adjournment, when his new cabinet would be nominated. The subject was laid over until the 6th or 7th of July, when I was to return to Washington and aid the President with such information as I could impart in the completion of his new cabinet. But most unhappily for the American people, the fatigue and exposure of that 4th of July bereaved the country of the services of one of its most upright and patriotic presidents. I had observed, two or three days before leaving Washington, that General Taylor's nervous system, on account of the congressional impugnment of the integrity of his cabinet, was greatly disturbed. Before leaving the White House I informed Colonel Bliss, his son-in-law and private secretary, that General Taylor was excited and feverish, and ought, if possible, to get a few days' repose. Colonel Bliss replied that the general was strong, and had gone safely through a good many worse trials. On my way home I stopped at Baltimore to reiterate my apprehensions about General Taylor's health to Dr. Wood, another son-in-law, who said he would take the next train to Washington, and pass a day or two with the President. The cabinet-making business was to be kept profoundly secret. The President, however, allowed me to ask my friend Stanly, in the event of an early adjournment of Congress, to remain in Washington until I could see him, but without telling him why. Nor did Mr. Stanly know the President's intention to call him to the War Department until I met him some two years afterwards. I was permitted, also, inasmuch as Governor Fish would necessarily need a few days to put his gubernatorial house in order, to intimate that his services might be required at Washington. My last interviews with General Taylor would be remembered most pleasantly, if I could dissociate them from the sudden and sad bereavement which deprived the country of the services of this great and good President. He had, as it will have been observed in previous references to him, given me in the fullest and frankest manner his entire confidence upon every subject affecting his personal and political feelings, his views in regard to measures before Congress, and of the policy of his administration spoken without reserve or restraint. He had reflected much and earnestly upon the question which in one form or another had seriously disturbed the country and the government for a quarter of a century; a question which, for a brief season, was appeased by the Missouri Compromise, but which, in the form of "nullification," reappeared during General Jackson's administration, and which now returned "to plague" the government upon the admission of California into the Union. He saw in the minds of influential and reckless Southern leaders a determined hostility to the Union, and he seriously apprehended an effort to disrupt it. He saw, also, in Northern political leaders a disposition to encourage, if not to sustain the extreme South in its threatened raid upon the government.

Determined that the authority of the government and the integrity of the Union should be maintained and preserved during his administration, he was most anxious to secure for his administration the confidence and support of Congress and the people, and this, in his judgment, could only be accomplished by great uprightness and integrity in the discharge of public duties, and by being just and faithful to the party by which he had been elected. General Taylor insisted that it was not only the right, but it was the duty, of the press and the people to hold him responsible for an economical and honest administration of the government. He was sensitively alive to the importance of official integrity, believing that high officials should not only be honest but above suspicion. With these convictions, it did not surprise those who knew him best that when a question was brought before Congress arraigning the action of the government and impugning the conduct of at least one member of his cabinet, no breath of suspicion attached to the President.

CHAPTER LXI.

1850–1861.

Diplomatic Incidents. — Mr. Barnard and Governor Fish. — John M. Clayton. — George P. Fisher. — President Fillmore. — A Foreign Mission, or the " Evening Journal." — Hugh Maxwell's Recollections. — An Adventure at Vienna. — At an Imperial Meeting. — An Incident of 1861. — Mr. Hunter and the Consul at Falmouth.

Some six weeks or two months before the death of President Taylor, Governor Fish informed me that the Hon. Daniel D. Barnard desired a foreign mission; that an application, accompanied with letters from several distinguished statesmen, had been some time pending; that Mr. Barnard, who, as I knew, was in a delicate state of health, had become morbidly impatient to go abroad. Governor Fish was aware that my relations with Mr. Barnard were not then friendly, although both at Rochester in 1825, and at Albany twenty years afterward, I had been very intimate with Mr. Barnard, who was a gentleman of ability, cultivation, and integrity, with peculiarities which I have had occasion to speak of in a former chapter. The relations between Governor Fish and Mr. Barnard, political, personal, and social, were very close. They were near neighbors, and much together. Mr. Barnard's nervous importunities for a mission finally induced the Governor to ask me, first as an act of justice to a zealous friend of the administration, and next as a favor to himself, to go to Washington and obtain the desired appointment. I readily consented, and started immediately for Washington.

After assuring the President of Mr. Barnard's high personal character, his eminent ability, and his fitness for the diplomatic service, I informed him that the appointment would be particularly gratifying to Governor Fish. He replied that Governor Fish's friend should be gratified, and authorized me to call on Mr. Clayton, Secretary of State, and ascertain what missions

were available. I called upon Mr. Clayton, as was my habit,
in the evening, at his lodgings, where I usually met Mr. Fisher,
— now Judge Fisher of the United States Court for the District
of Columbia, then Mr. Clayton's private secretary, — and where,
with agreeable conversation and excellent old " Bourbon," I
passed many delightful hours. Mr. Clayton, who had served
in Congress with Mr. Barnard and knew him well, indicated
Austria or Naples as courts likely to suit his tastes, adding that
either, if the President approved, was open for him.

In the morning I reported to General Taylor, who said,
"Very well; let Mr. Barnard take which he pleases, though it
would please me better to give the mission to you. You have
been working hard for your friends a good many years, and are
entitled to repose." I thanked him gratefully for his kindness,
and took my leave, much gratified with what I regarded as an
auspicious result of my journey.

Arriving in Albany early in the evening, I called upon Governor Fish at his house to announce the result of my visit to
Washington. He also was manifestly gratified and relieved ;
and while talking to him about the President, for whom he entertained a warm friendship, Mrs. Fish put on her hat and
shawl and hastened to inform the Barnards of the good news;
news which proved, however, anything but good or satisfactory
to Mr. Barnard, who instantly rejected both places, nothing but
a first-class mission being worthy of his acceptance. Austria
and Naples were not then in this category. When I reported
Mr. Barnard's refusal to General Taylor, he again renewed
his offer to me, kindly urging its acceptance ; and although the
temptation was very great, and Italy, above all other countries,
one I desired to visit, yet I adhered to my determination of declining all offices.

Mr. Barnard, though disappointed for the moment, was soon
gratified in the object of his ambition. Providence bereaved
the country of its President. One of the earliest diplomatic
appointments of Mr. Fillmore, who, as Vice-President, became
General Taylor's successor, was that of the Hon. Mr. Barnard
as Minister to Prussia ; and strangely enough, a few months
afterward, the mission to Austria was offered for a second time,
by another President, to myself. And as this statement, unexplained, will occasion surprise, if not incredulity, I will proceed

to show how and why President Fillmore tendered me a mission.

The country had every appearance of being on the eve of a revolution, from the meeting of Congress in 1849 until July, 1850, when General Taylor died. The language and spirit of the representatives of the States of North and South Carolina, Georgia, Virginia, Mississippi, etc., were quite as violent and defiant as they were in 1860. Those representatives, sustained by the Southern press, threatened to go out of the Union if California was admitted into it with a constitution prohibiting slavery. The ruling party of the North was united and firm in its determination to admit California under the constitution which its citizens had adopted. Vice-President Fillmore had been, through his public life, distinguished for nothing more than his earnest opposition to slavery. Though always a Whig, his opinions on that subject were always in advance of Francis Granger, Albert H. Tracy, Luther Bradish, Charles P. Kirkland, and other prominent gentlemen with whom he was politically associated. The Whig party, therefore, was startled, first by rumors, and then by trustworthy information, that in assuming the executive department of government he would back down from the high position which President Taylor, a Southern man and a slave-holder, had taken. He formed a very able cabinet, with Mr. Webster at its head, and had decided to approve a series of pro-slavery or compromise measures (including a stringent Fugitive Slave Law) repugnant to the principles and sympathies of the Whig party. Against these measures, and consequently against Mr. Fillmore's administration, I took strong ground, denouncing the President and his policy in no measured language. This, of course, divided the Whig party, and occasioned an exciting and bitter conflict. I will not here discuss its merits.

During the winter or spring of 1851 I was asked by Mr. Norton, a Whig member of the legislature from Allegany County, New York, who had been to Washington and came back an administration man, if I did not want to go abroad, adding that Mr. Fillmore would, he thought, offer me a mission if it was known that I would accept it. I replied that I had work enough at home, and thought no more about it until a week or ten days afterward, when Governor Hunt surprised me with the same question, and entered into a long and friendly conversation with me on the subject. Governor Hunt himself, though always conservative, and very desirous to preserve harmony in our party, did not approve of the extreme concessions which it was evident Mr. Fillmore, Mr. Clay, and Mr. Webster were urging. He informed me that he did not, however, desire me to leave the " Evening Journal," although he was authorized to say that if I accepted the mission, and desired to retire from business, Mr. John T. Bush, of Erie, would purchase my interest in the " Evening Journal." I understood Governor Hunt to say that Mr. Joseph B. Varnum, a Whig member of the legislature from the city of New York, who had just returned from Washington, was authorized by Mr. Fillmore to request Governor Hunt to make this effort to avert a rupture in the Whig party in our State. I felt it to be my duty to decline both propositions.

I passed the winter of 1869 at Aiken, in South Carolina, finding among other invalids there the Hon. Hugh Maxwell, of New York, a gentleman whom I had known for many years, and for whose character and talents I entertained a high respect. We had had, however, but a slight personal acquaintance, and very little personal intercourse. I found him a gentleman of high cultivation, and, although at an advanced age, indulging all the social and literary habits and tastes for which he had been distinguished in earlier life. The friendships formed during the winter at Aiken, prominent among which is that with Mr. Maxwell, are among the pleasant recollections of an agreeable winter. At one of our evening communions, Mr. Maxwell inquired if in the early part of Mr. Fillmore's administration I had been offered a foreign mission, and upon my replying affirmatively, he inquired if I knew where and how the idea of sending me abroad originated. I replied substantially, but briefly, as before written. He then informed me that my earnest and reiterated attacks upon President Fillmore's administration created much uneasiness among the conservative Whigs of the city ; that, after reflecting upon the subject and conversing with leading Whigs, he invited several of them to his room in the custom house (Mr. M. was then collector of the port), where, after free consultation, it was agreed that the danger to the administration from the hostility of the " Albany Evening

Journal" rendered it imperative that its management should be changed, and that the surest way of accomplishing this object would be to send its editor abroad; and that he, Mr. M., was requested to write to President Fillmore fully on the subject; that he immediately informed Mr. Fillmore by letter of the result of this conversation, urging him to offer me a mission, that being, in the judgment of his New York friends, the only way of disposing of the troublesome and dangerous man; that Mr. Fillmore replied promptly to his letter, thanking him for his suggestion, saying that it would afford him great pleasure to offer me a foreign mission, first as a suitable recognition of my services to the Whig cause, and next on account of the long and pleasant personal, political, and social relations that had existed between us. Mr. Maxwell then remarked that his principal object in recalling this incident was to show me that Mr. Fillmore not only remembered old friendships, but had based his offer of a mission to me upon better grounds than those suggested by his friends in New York.

In the autumn of 1851 I went to Europe (accompanied by a daughter who has made six passages across the Atlantic with me), visiting with great interest Vienna and Naples, but only as a private citizen. Our government was then represented in Austria by the Hon. Mr. McCurdy of Connecticut, and by the Hon. Mr. Morris at Naples, to both of whom we were indebted for marked attentions. I refer to this European tour now merely to relate an incident which shows that, by one of those chances that occur very seldom, as a stranger I was admitted to an imperial ceremony from which, had I been the diplomatic representative of my country, I should have been excluded.

The Emperor of Russia arrived at Vienna on a visit to the Emperor of Austria on a Saturday afternoon. We went, with a large crowd, to witness at the railway station the reception of one emperor by another. Early on Sunday morning I suggested to the ladies of our party (Mrs. and Miss Hunter of Rochester, and Mrs. W. H. DeWitt of Albany), that by repairing to the palace we might get another glimpse of their majesties while they were going from the palace to the chapel. The probability of this, however, was so slight that no one but my daughter accompanied me. As we approached the palace we fell into what Dr. Johnson calls "a stream of life" running in that direction. The approach to the palace stairway was densely crowded. Immediately before us were a lady and gentleman, to make room for whom the crowd struggling backwards opened a passage. We followed until we reached the foot of the stairway, where sentinels were stationed. After ascending a few steps the lady, who had observed us behind them, spoke to the gentleman, who immediately turned and directed the orderly to pass us. Following them, we were ushered into an immense ante-room filled with marshals, generals, and staff officers of the imperial army, whose magnificent uniforms were resplendent with decorations. Passing through this chamber we came to another, in which were the diplomatic corps with their families in full court dress. Here my progress was arrested for a reason which, as the usher civilly explained it in German, I did not understand. But the gentleman, to whose courtesy we were so far indebted, turned and informed me that my frock-coat excluded me from an apartment graced by ladies, but that my daughter could pass with them. I remained, therefore, in the room occupied by the marshals, etc., for fifteen or twenty minutes, when folding doors were thrown open and the two emperors, followed by the imperial family, passed through these anterooms to the chapel. The highest dignitaries only, military and diplomatic, were invited to this ceremony. The exception was an unknown American citizen with his daughter, who were, in the remarkable way that I have indicated, admitted to that honor. The lady referred to very kindly named the most distinguished ladies and gentlemen to my daughter, and in this way relieved the embarrassment of her position. In the evening of the same day, while taking tea with Mr. McCurdy, our good fortune in having a quiet look at the emperors in the palace was spoken of, exciting first the incredulity and then the surprise of our minister, who, on inquiring why we did not meet him there, replied that our government being represented only by a chargé d'affaires he was not invited ; but the question how we got there remained as much a wonder as that of the "fly in amber."

On the following day, Monday, the Emperor Francis Joseph gave his imperial brother of Russia a review. To see this we started early that our carriage might have an advantageous position, which fortunately, by the promptness and intelligence of our coachman, we secured.   Over forty thousand troops were in line.   At ten A. M. precisely the two emperors, with a magnificently mounted suite, dashed out of the palace yard into the field.   While the line was passing in review, a barouche and four with the empress mother and three other ladies drove into the field.   In that barouche we recognized and exchanged recognitions with the lady by whom we were so highly favored the previous day.   And, on inquiry, we ascertained that she was a cousin of the emperor, residing with her husband, who was governor of the castle near Prague which the ex-emperor on his abdication selected as his home.

In the summer of 1861 a retired merchant of New York called upon me to say that he and other merchants were anxious to obtain a consular appointment for an old and meritorious book-keeper, who for more than thirty years had kept the books of one of our largest and most respectable commercial houses. The book-keeper came to New York from England when he was quite a young man, and now in his old age was anxious to " go home to roost."   In other words, he desired to pass the remainder of his life in England, so that he might finally sleep where his fathers slept.   He was represented to me as a most deserving man, and who, as a book-keeper, was endowed with all the habits and virtues which distinguished Tim Linkinwater. The house he had served so long and faithfully, and other merchants who knew him, were particularly anxious to gratify the old book-keeper.   I was then on my way to Washington, and took the application and testimonials, promising to do the best I could for him.   While at breakfast the next morning with the Secretary of State I made the application, and before I had half completed the enumeration of the old book-keeper's merits, Mr. Seward requested his son Frederick, the assistant secretary, to find a place for him.   I went to the department with Frederick, and in looking over his consular register carefully, his eye finally rested upon Falmouth, where upon examination he found that the consul was an Englishman, and had held the office more than twenty years.   It was decided, therefore, that one Englishman should give place to another, that other being an Americanized Englishman.   I reported this determination to the Secretary, who immediately sent my friend's name to the President ; and when the messenger returned with Mr. Lincoln's approval, Mr. Hunter, the chief clerk, was directed to fill up the commission and obtain the President's signature in time for me to take it to New York that afternoon. Between four and five o'clock P. M. I went to Mr. Hunter for the commission, which lay before him on his desk. He rose somewhat deliberately (as is his manner), took the commission in his hand and delivered it to me without speaking, but with evident reluctance. I said: "Is it all right, Mr. Hunter?" He replied: "I have obeyed orders." "But," I added, "you do not seem pleased. Is there anything wrong about the appointment?" "I have nothing to say about the appointment, but I have never discharged a duty since I came into the department with so much regret." He said: "The first commission that I filled out when I came into this office twenty-six years ago was for Mr. Fox, our consul at Falmouth, who succeeded his then recently deceased father, who received his appointment from President Washington. The consular accounts of Mr. Fox are as neatly and accurately kept as those of General Washington during the Revolution. I think he is the best consul in the service of the government. You will judge, therefore, whether the removal of such a consul is not calculated to occasion regret." When he finished, while he stood looking at me with his pen in his hand, I deliberately tore the commission into strips, threw them into the waste-paper basket, and left the department for the cars. When I explained in New York what had occurred at Washington it was approved, not only by the gentleman who had asked me to interest myself, but by the applicant himself.

CHAPTER LXII.

1860–1861.

ABRAHAM LINCOLN. — HIS NOMINATION. — VISIT TO SPRINGFIELD. — THE CABINET. — DAVIS AND SWETT. — MR. LINCOLN'S STORIES. — THE NEW YORK COLLECTORSHIP. — OFFICE SEEKING. — VICE-PRESIDENT HAMLIN. — J. A. GILMER.

IMMEDIATELY after the nomination of Mr. Lincoln for President, at Chicago, in the summer of 1860, while annoyed and dejected at the defeat of Governor Seward, as I was preparing to shake the dust of the city from my feet, Messrs. David Davis (now a judge of the Supreme Court of the United States) and Leonard Swett called at my room. These gentlemen, warm friends and zealous supporters of Mr. Lincoln, had contributed more than all others to his nomination. After his name was presented as a candidate for President, and received with favor by the citizens of Illinois, Messrs. Davis and Swett visited Indiana, Ohio, Pennsylvania, and Maryland, for the purpose of commending Mr. Lincoln to the favorable consideration of prominent men in those States. They now called to converse with me about the approaching canvass. I informed them very frankly that I was so greatly disappointed at the result of the action of the convention as to be unable to think or talk on the subject ; that I was going to pass a few days upon the prairies of Iowa, and that by the time I reached Albany I should be prepared to do my duty for the Republican cause and for its nominees. They then urged me to return home *via* Springfield, where we could talk over the canvass with Mr. Lincoln, saying that they would either join me at Bloomington, where they resided, or meet me at Springfield.

After passing with a few friends a pleasant week in traveling through Iowa, I repaired to Springfield. There I found Messrs. Davis and Swett with Mr. Lincoln. I had supposed, until we now met, that I had never seen Mr. Lincoln, having forgotten that in the fall of 1848, when he took the stump in

New England, he called upon me at Albany, and that we went to see Mr. Fillmore, who was then the Whig candidate for Vice-President. We entered immediately upon the question which deeply concerned the welfare of the country, and which had an especial interest for Mr. Lincoln. We discussed freely the prospects of success, assuming that all or nearly all the slave States would be against us. The issues had already been made, and could neither be changed nor modified; but there was much to be considered in regard to the manner of conducting the campaign, and in relation to States that were safe without effort, to those which required attention, and to others that were sure to be vigorously contested. Viewing these questions in their various aspects, I found Mr. Lincoln sagacious and practical. He displayed throughout the conversation so much good sense, such intuitive knowledge of human nature, and such familiarity with the virtues and infirmities of politicians, that I became impressed very favorably with his fitness for the duties which he was not unlikely to be called upon to discharge. This conversation lasted some five hours, and when the train arrived in which we were to depart I rose all the better prepared to " go to work with a will " in favor of Mr. Lincoln's election, as the interview had inspired me with confidence in his capacity and integrity.

In December of that year, and after the electoral colleges had shown a large majority for Mr. Lincoln, I was invited to visit him at Springfield, where I again met my friends Davis and Swett. Mr. Lincoln, although manifestly gratified with his election, foresaw and appreciated the dangers which threatened the safety both of the government and of the Union. But while Mr. Lincoln never underestimated the difficulties which surrounded him, his nature was so elastic, and his temperament so cheerful, that he always seemed at ease and undisturbed. The day I left Albany, the " Evening Journal " contained an editorial foreshadowing secession and rebellion; an editorial which had for its object the holding of the border slave States in the Union, so that the boundaries and strength of the rebellion might be narrowed and weakened. It maintained that radical abolitionists were playing into the hands of disunion leaders, and that both would become responsible for the civil war into which we were drifting. It comprehended the horrors of such a conflict, and implored the Northern people to keep themselves clearly in the right, so that when the shock came impartial nations would see and say that the rebellion was without justification or excuse. That editorial drew the line between radical and conservative Republicans, and continued as an issue before the people during the war. It was written under a conviction of its necessity in preventing a disastrous division of the Northern people. I believed then, as I know now, that but for the conservative sentiment awakened in the Republican party the North would have been fatally divided. I believed then, as I know now, that by insisting that the war was prosecuted to maintain the government and preserve the Union, the Democratic masses, with some of their leaders, would remain loyal ; while, on the other hand, if the whole Republican party proclaimed it a war for the abolition of slavery, a united South would prove too strong for a divided North.

The much-dreaded conflict came, and although more fearful than was or could have been apprehended, resulted auspiciously for our government and Union. The radicalism which occasioned the editorial from which the foregoing extracts are taken, grew stronger and more aggressive as the war progressed. While the abolition masses were among the first to enter and the last to leave the army, their leaders who remained at home were viciously hostile to the administration. Indeed, they carried their hostility to the extent of attempting, by a third-party nomination at Cleveland, to defeat Mr. Lincoln's reëlection.

This article reached Springfield by the evening mail. After reading it very attentively, Mr. Lincoln said, " This is a heavy broadside. You have opened your fire at a critical moment, aiming at friends and foes alike. It will do some good or much mischief. Will the Republicans of New York sustain you in this view of the question ? " I replied, "that I had acted upon my own sense of what was wise for our cause ; that I should be denounced in most of the Republican journals; that enlightened politicians who entertained similar views would hesitate to express them, and that it would largely impair, if it did not wholly destroy, my influence in the Republican party ; but that, notwithstanding these consequences, I should unflinchingly persevere in the course I had marked out, with a clear and firm conviction that in doing so, aided by a small minority of Republican journals, with here and there a conservative statesman, we should keep the North united in prosecuting a war which, in preserving the government and Union, would overwhelm and destroy rebellion and slavery." Mr. Lincoln replied, "that these views, views which had not occurred to him, opened a new channel for his thoughts, and that while he should watch the progress of popular sentiment, he hoped to find my apprehensions unfounded." He added, "that while there were some loud threats and much muttering in the cotton States, he hoped that by wisdom and forbearance the danger of serious trouble might be averted, as such dangers had been in former times."

And after this subject had been talked up, and over, and out, Mr. Lincoln remarked, smiling, "that he supposed I had had some experience in cabinet-making; that he had a job on hand, and as he had never learned that trade, he was disposed to avail himself of the suggestions of friends." Taking up his figure, I replied, "that though never a boss cabinet-maker, I had as a journeyman been occasionally consulted about State cabinets, and that although President Taylor once talked with me about reforming his cabinet, I had never been concerned in or presumed to meddle with the formation of an original Federal cabinet, and that he was the first President elect I had ever seen." The question thus opened became the subject of conversation, at intervals, during that and the following day. I say at intervals, because many hours were consumed in talking of the public men connected with former administrations, interspersed, illustrated, and seasoned pleasantly with Mr. Lincoln's stories, anecdotes, etc. And here I feel called upon to vindicate Mr. Lincoln, as far as my opportunities and observation go, from the frequent imputation of telling indelicate and ribald stories. I saw much of him during his whole presidential term, with familiar friends and alone, when he talked without restraint, but I never heard him use a profane or indecent word, or tell a story that might not be repeated in the presence of ladies.

Mr. Lincoln observed that "the making of a cabinet, now that he had it to do, was by no means as easy as he had supposed; that he had, even before the result of the election was known, assuming the probability of success, fixed upon the two leading members of his cabinet, but that in looking about for suitable men to fill the other departments, he had been much

embarrassed, partly from his want of acquaintance with the
prominent men of the day, and partly, he believed, that while
the population of the country had immensely increased, really
great men were scarcer than they used to be." He then inquired whether I had any suggestions of a general character affecting the selection of a cabinet to make. I replied that, along
with the question of ability, integrity, and experience, he ought,
in the selection of his cabinet, to find men whose firmness and
courage fitted them for the revolutionary ordeal which was
about to test the strength of our government; and that in my
judgment it was desirable that at least two members of his cabinet should be selected from slave-holding States. He inquired
whether, in the emergency which I so much feared, they could
be trusted, adding that he did not quite like to hear Southern
journals and Southern speakers insisting that there must be no
" coercion ; " that while he had no disposition to coerce anybody, yet after he had taken an oath to execute the laws, he
should not care to see them violated. I remarked that there
were Union men in Maryland, Virginia, North Carolina, and
Tennessee, for whose loyalty, under the most trying circumstances and in any event, I would vouch. " Would you rely on
such men if their States should secede ? " " Yes, sir ; the men
whom I have in my mind can always be relied on." " Well,"
said Mr. Lincoln, " let us have the names of your white crows,
such ones as you think fit for the cabinet." I then named
Henry Winter Davis of Maryland, John M. Botts of Virginia,
John A. Gilmer of North Carolina, and Bailey Peyton of Tennessee. As the conversation progressed, Mr. Lincoln remarked
that he intended to invite Governor Seward to take the State,
and Governor Chase the Treasury Department, remarking that,
aside from their long experience in public affairs, and their eminent fitness, they were prominently before the people and the
convention as competitors for the presidency, each having higher
claims than his own for the place which he was to occupy. On
naming Gideon Welles as the gentleman he thought of as the
representative of New England in the cabinet, I remarked that
I thought he could find several New England gentlemen whose
selection for a place in his cabinet would be more acceptable to
the people of New England. " But," said Mr. Lincoln, " we
must remember that the Republican party is constituted of two

elements, and that we must have men of Democratic as well as of Whig antecedents in the cabinet."

Acquiescing in this view the subject was passed over. And then Mr. Lincoln remarked that Judge Blair had been suggested. I inquired, "What Judge Blair?" and was answered, "Judge Montgomery Blair." "Has he been suggested by any one except his father, Francis P. Blair, Sr.?" "Your question," said Mr. Lincoln, "reminds me of a story," and he proceeded with infinite humor to tell a story, which I would repeat if I did not fear that its spirit and effect would be lost. I finally remarked that if we were legislating on the question, I should move to strike out the name of Montgomery Blair and insert that of Henry Winter Davis. Mr. Lincoln laughingly replied, "Davis has been posting you up on this question. He came from Maryland and has got Davis on the brain. Maryland must, I think, be like New Hampshire, a good State to move from." And then he told a story of a witness in a neighboring county, who, on being asked his age, replied, "Sixty." Being satisfied that he was much older, the judge repeated the question, and on receiving the same answer, admonished the witness, saying that the court knew him to be much older than sixty. "Oh," said the witness, "you're thinking about that fifteen year that I lived down on the eastern shore of Maryland; that was so much lost time and don't count." This story, I perceived, was thrown in to give the conversation a new direction. It was very evident that the selection of Montgomery Blair was a fixed fact; and although I subsequently ascertained the reasons and influences that controlled the selection of other members of the cabinet, I never did find out how Mr. Blair got there.

General Cameron's name was next introduced, and in reference to him and upon the peculiarities and characteristics of Pennsylvania statesmen we had a long conversation. In reply to a question of Mr. Lincoln's, I said that I had personally known General Cameron for twenty-five years; that for the last ten years I had seen a good deal of him; that whenever I had met him at Washington or elsewhere he had treated me with much kindness, inspiring me with friendly feeling. "But you do not," said Mr. Lincoln, "say what you think about him for the cabinet." On that subject I replied that I was embar-

rassed; that Mr. Cameron during a long and stirring political
life had made warm friends and bitter enemies; that while his
appointment would gratify his personal friends, it would offend
his opponents, among whom were many of the leading and influential Republicans of that State; that I was, as I had already
stated, in view of an impending rebellion, anxious that Mr. Lincoln should have the support of not only a strong cabinet, but
one which would command the confidence of the people.   We
continued to canvass General Cameron in this spirit for a long
time, Mr. Lincoln evidently sharing in the embarrassment which
I had expressed, and manifesting, I thought, a desire that I
should fully indorse General Cameron.   I told him that if it
were a personal question I should not hesitate to do so, for that
I liked General Cameron, and entertained no doubt of his regard
for me, but that as I was not sure that his appointment would
give strength to the administration I must leave the matter with
himself.   "But," said Mr. Lincoln, "Pennsylvania, any more
than New York or Ohio, cannot be overlooked.   Her strong Republican vote, not less than her numerical importance, entitles
her to a representative in the cabinet.   Who is stronger or
better than General Cameron?"   To this question I was unprepared for a reply, for among General Cameron's friends there
was no one eminently qualified, and it would have been equally
unjust and unwise to take an opponent, and finally General
Cameron's case was passed over, but neither decided nor dismissed.

I now renewed my suggestion about having the slave States
represented in the cabinet.   "But," said Mr. Lincoln, "you
object to Judge Blair, who resides in a slave State."   "I object
to Judge Blair because he represents nobody, he has no following, and because his appointment would be obnoxious to the
Union men of Maryland; and that, as I believe, while he can
look into Maryland, he actually resides in the District of Columbia."   "Very well," said Mr. Lincoln, "I will now give you
the name of a gentleman who not only resides in a slave State,
but who is emphatically a representative man.   What objection
have you to Edward Bates of Missouri?"   "None, not a
shadow or a shade of an objection.   That is a selection, as Mr.
Webster might have said, 'eminently fit to be made.'   The
political record of Mr. Bates is proverbially consistent.   He was

a reliable Whig member of Congress from the State of Missouri thirty years ago; he was the able and popular president of the great River and Harbor Improvement Convention at Chicago twenty years ago; his high personal and professional character, his habits of industry, his equable temper, and his inalienable devotion to the government and Union, fit and qualify him in my judgment admirably for a cabinet minister.''

Mr. Lincoln said in talking of Mr. Bates: "I am reminded of the advice which Mr. Barton, a distinguished lawyer of St. Louis, gave to a client thirty or forty years ago. A young man from Pittsburgh, Pa., stopped at the hotel in St. Louis, and immediately placed a package of money in deposit with the branch bank of the United States; after which, and during the day, he made several investments and drew several checks. On the following morning a person called on him to say that he was wanted at the bank, where, as he entered, he found several gentlemen in conversation, one of whom informed him that they had received information of a robbery of the bank from which the money he had deposited had been taken, and that, though delicate and unpleasant, it was deemed proper to inquire who he was, and whether he came honestly in possession of so large a sum of money. The young man replied that he was the son of a wealthy and well-known citizen of Pittsburgh, but that he had no acquaintances in St. Louis and was unable to identify himself. The bank men thought, under the circumstance, it was their duty to retain the money until they could be satisfied that he was the honest owner of it. Finding himself in a tight place the landlord advised the young man (whose name I think was Anderson) to employ counsel, and recommended him to Squire Barton, the law partner of the famous Colonel Thomas H. Benton. He found Squire Barton at his office, over a store, in his shirt sleeves, who listened attentively and without speaking until the whole case was laid before him, and then taking the young man to an open window said, 'That's a pretty large amount of money for a stranger to carry around with him. There've been a good many robberies lately. 'T isn't an honest way of getting a living, but some people don't find that out till they've tried it. If you're the son of General Anderson, as I hope you are, and didn't steal that money, my advice is that you face the music, and I will stand by you; but if, as I strongly suspect, you were tempted, and that money is n't honestly yours, I advise you (pointing in the direction indicated) to make tracks for that tall timber, and to put the Mississippi between you and these bank fellows as soon as you can find a crossing.' 'And how much shall I pay you for your advice?' inquired his client. 'If you intend to *hook it*, $5. If you remain and prove yourself an honest lad, nothing.' "

It was now settled that Governor Seward was to be Secretary of State, Governor Chase, Secretary of the Treasury, and Mr. Bates the Attorney General. I was satisfied that Mr. Lincoln intended to give Mr. Welles one of the other places in the cabinet; that he was strongly inclined to give another place to Mr. Blair, and that his mind was not quite clear in regard to General Cameron. Only one place, therefore, remained open, and that, it was understood, was to be given to Indiana; but whether it was to be Caleb B. Smith or Colonel Lane was undetermined. I inquired whether, in the shape which the question was taking, it was just or wise to concede so many seats in the cabinet to the Democratic element in the Republican party. He replied that as a Whig he thought he could afford to be liberal to a section of the Republican party without whose votes he could not have been elected. I admitted the justice and wisdom of this, adding that in arranging and adjusting questions of place and patronage in our State we had acted in that spirit, but that I doubted both the justice and the wisdom, in inaugurating his administration, of giving to a minority of the Republican party a majority in his cabinet. I added that the national convention indicated unmistakably the sentiment of its constituency by nominating for president a candidate with Whig antecedents, while its nominee for vice-president had been for many years a Democratic representative in Congress. "But," said Mr. Lincoln, "why do you assume that we are giving that section of our party a majority in the cabinet?" I replied that if Messrs. Chase, Cameron, Welles, and Blair should be designated, the cabinet would stand four to three. "You seem to forget that *I* expect to be there; and counting me as one, you see how nicely the cabinet would be balanced and ballasted. Besides," said Mr. L., "in talking of General Cameron you admitted that his political status was unexceptionable. I suppose we could say of General Cameron, without offence, that he is 'not Democrat enough to hurt him.' I remember that people used to say, without disturbing my self-respect, that I was not lawyer enough to hurt me." I admitted that I had no political objection to General Cameron, who, I was quite sure, would forget whether applicants for appointment had been Whig or Democrat. I then renewed the suggestion relating to North Carolina or Tennessee, earnestly pressing its importance. Messrs. Davis and Swett united with me in these views. Mr. Lincoln met us with strong counter views, the force of which we were constrained to admit. " If," said Mr. L., " contrary to our hopes, North Carolina and Tennessee should secede, could their men remain in the cabinet? Or, if they remained, of what use would they be to the government?" We, however, continued to press our point, until Mr. Lincoln yielded so far as to say that he would write a letter to the Hon. John A. Gilmer, then a member of Congress from North Carolina, briefly stating his views of the duty of the government in reference to important questions then pending, and inviting him, if those views met his approval, to accept a seat in the cabinet.

" Now," said Mr. Lincoln, " if Mr. Gilmer should come in, somebody must stay out, and that other somebody must be either Judge Blair or Mr. Bates." Messrs. Davis, Swett, and myself exclaimed against dropping Mr. Bates; and so Mr. Lincoln left us to infer that if Mr. Gilmer came in Mr. Blair would be excluded. Before the subject was finally dismissed, I recurred to the navy, not, as I remarked, with any expectation of changing the programme, but to suggest that if Mr. Lincoln, when on his way to Washington, would stop long enough in New York, Philadelphia, or Baltimore to select an attractive figure-head, to be adorned with an elaborate wig and luxuriant whiskers, and transfer it from the prow of a ship to the entrance of the Navy Department, it would, in my opinion, be quite as serviceable as his secretary, and less expensive. " Oh," said Mr. Lincoln, " ' wooden midshipmen ' answer very well in novels, but we must have a live secretary of the navy." In this way, the conversation being alternately earnest and playful, two days passed very pleasantly.

I wish it were possible to give in Mr. Lincoln's amusing but quaint manner the many stories, anecdotes, and witticisms, with which he interlarded and enlivened what, with almost any of his predecessors in the high office of president, would have been a grave, dry consultation. The great merit of Mr. Lincoln's stories, like Captain Bunsby's opinion, " lays in the application of it." They always and exactly suited the occasion and the subject, and none to which I ever listened were far-fetched or pointless. I will attempt, however, to repeat but one of them. If I have an especial fondness for any particular luxury, it manifests itself in a remarkable way when properly-made December sausages are placed before me. While at breakfast, Mr. Davis noticing that after having been bountifully served with sausages, Oliver Twist like I wanted some more, said, " You seem fond of our Chicago sausages." To which I responded affirmatively, adding that I thought the article might be relied on where pork was cheaper than dogs. " That," said Mr. Lincoln, " reminds me of what occurred down at Joliet, where a popular grocer supplied all the villagers with sausages. One Saturday evening, when his grocery was filled with customers, for whom he and his boys were busily engaged in weighing sausages, a neighbor, with whom he had had a violent quarrel that day, came into the grocery, made his way up to the counter, holding two enormous dead cats by the tail, which he deliberately threw on the counter, saying, ' This makes seven to-day. I 'll call round on Monday and get my money for them.' "

In the course of our conversations Mr. Lincoln remarked that it was particularly pleasant to him to reflect that he was coming into office unembarrassed by promises. He owed, he supposed, his exemption from importunities to the circumstance that his name as a candidate was but a short time before the people, and that only a few sanguine friends anticipated the possibility of his nomination. " I have not," said he, " promised an office to any man, nor have I, but in a single instance, mentally committed myself to an appointment ; and as that relates to an important office in your State, I have concluded to mention it to you, — under strict injunctions of secrecy, however. If I am not induced by public considerations to change my purpose, Hiram Barney will be collector of the port of New York." I supposed that Mr. Lincoln, in thus frankly avowing his friendship for Mr. Barney, intended to draw me out. I remarked that until I met him at the Chicago convention my acquaintance with Mr. Barney was very slight ; but that after the convention adjourned Mr. Barney joined us (my daughter and a lady friend) in an excursion down the Mississippi and through Iowa, and that my impressions of him personally and politically were favorable, and that I believed he would make an acceptable collector. I added that if it were true, as I had heard, that the reply of an extensive and well-known mercantile firm in New York during an exciting crisis, to Southern merchants, who threatened to withdraw their patronage on account of its opposition to slavery, namely, "We offer our goods, not our principles, for sale," originated with Mr. Barney, it entitled him to any office he asked for. "He has not," said Mr. Lincoln, "asked for this or any other office, nor does he know of my intention."

And now, as I was preparing to depart, Mr. Lincoln said: "Some gentlemen, who have been quite nervous about the object of your visit here, would be surprised, if not incredulous, were I to tell them that during the two days we have passed together you have made no application, suggestion, or allusion to appointments." I replied that nothing of that nature had been upon my mind, and that I was much more concerned about the welfare of the country and the successful working of his administration than about matters which would come to perplex all upon whom responsibilities rested, but which it would be both premature and indelicate to obtrude upon him now. "This," said Mr. Lincoln, "is undoubtedly a proper view of the question, and yet so much were you misunderstood that I have received telegrams from prominent Republicans warning me against your efforts to forestall important appointments in your State. Other gentlemen who have visited me since the election have expressed similar apprehensions; but I have remarked that while our friends were extremely sensitive in relation to your designs, they brought along an axe or two of their own to be ground." I told Mr. Lincoln that I had been a great many years actively engaged in political affairs; that I had been associated in conventions, state and national, with friends whose wishes in reference to candidates had generally been gratified; that I had never asked for, or intimated a desire for a promise or a committal, directly or indirectly, of any description, of any candidate, from a president to a justice of the peace, antecedent to his nomination and election; that I had been in consultation with Governors Clinton, Seward, Young,

Fish, Hunt, Clark, King, and Morgan, after their election and before their inauguration, under circumstances similar to those which had rendered my present visit a duty and a pleasure; but that I entertained too high a sense of the honor which the confidence of distinguished statesmen in high public position conferred, to annoy them or stultify myself by thrusting before them unseasonably mere questions of office, — questions that would unavoidably come in due time to engross their thoughts and perplex their judgment.

A year or two after this visit, President Lincoln, while talking with me about the peculiarities of his cabinet, said that immediately after his election, thinking that the Vice-President, from his high character and long experience, was entitled to a voice in the cabinet, the selection of the New England man was conceded to him, and that Mr. Hamlin named " Father Welles." I then informed Mr. Lincoln that there was a precedent for the consideration he had shown for Vice-President Hamlin; that General Taylor, immediately after his election to the presidency, wrote a letter to the Vice-President elect, in which, after expressing his gratification in being associated with a gentleman of large experience in the civil service of the government, on whom he could rely for information and advice, he indicated his desire that the Vice-President should act as an ex-officio member of his cabinet. But when General Taylor reached Washington he ascertained that his views in this respect were impracticable, if not unconstitutional.

It is proper to add, before closing this chapter, that Mr. Lincoln made me the bearer of his letter to Mr. Gilmer, with which I repaired to Washington. It being an open letter, Mr. Gilmer, after reading it attentively, entered into a frank conversation with me upon the subject which was exciting profound interest and anxiety in and out of Congress. He said that he entirely approved of the views of Mr. Lincoln on that question, and that he was gratified with the confidence reposed in him; but that before replying to it he deemed it proper to confer with members of Congress from Southern States, who, like himself, were opposed to secession. Soon afterward the " Border State proposition " was rejected by the House of Representatives. Under these circumstances, hopeless of keeping North Carolina in the Union, Mr. Gilmer declined the offer of a seat in the cabinet.

CHAPTER LXIII.

1861.

The "Herald" and the War. — James Gordon Bennett. — From Washington to Washington Heights. — A Powerful Ally.

At the breaking out of the Rebellion the sympathies of the "Herald" were with the South, or, at least, its marked hostility to the administration not only induced that opinion, but had the effect of encouraging rebels and strengthening the rebel cause. The "Daily News" also sympathized even more unequivocally with the rebels. Fernando Wood, then mayor of New York city, with many prominent citizens, entertained kindred sympathies and sentiments. All this created a strong popular feeling among the great mass of the people, who manifested their loyalty by displaying the Stars and Stripes not only upon public buildings, but from the windows or housetops of private mansions. The "Herald" was called upon to display the American flag, and upon its refusal or neglect to do so violence was threatened by a tumultuous gathering, which, however, was dispersed without committing any overt act.

Meantime the "Herald," by its large circulation in Europe, was creating a dangerous public sentiment abroad. Our representatives in England, France, Belgium, etc., regarded the influence of the "Herald" upon the public mind of Europe with apprehension.

That circumstance, added to our disasters during the early months of the war, induced President Lincoln to bring the subject before his cabinet. It was deemed important, if possible, to change the course of the "Herald" upon the question of secession and rebellion; but how this was to be accomplished was a question of much difficulty. It was agreed that an earnest appeal must be made to Mr. Bennett. Several gentlemen were named (myself among the number) for this delicate mission. The Secretary of State remarked that my relations with

Mr. Bennett were such as to insure the failure of the object contemplated, but it was finally determined that I should be summoned to Washington by telegraph. On my arrival, while at breakfast with Secretary Seward, I was informed of the business in hand. Calling after breakfast upon President Lincoln he remarked, in his peculiar way, that he understood I had had "considerable experience in belling cats," and with this introduction proceeded to say that, in view especially of the influence the "Herald" was exerting in Europe, he deemed it of the greatest importance that Mr. Bennett should be satisfied that the course of the "Herald" was endangering the government and Union, adding his belief that if Mr. Bennett could be brought to see things in that light he would change his course. While appreciating the importance of the mission, I assured Mr. Lincoln that I was the last person in the country to be selected for such a duty, but he insisted that I should make the trial, and I departed on the first train for New York.

My acquaintance with Mr. Bennett commenced in 1827, when he was the Washington reporter of the "New York Enquirer," then conducted by the late M. M. Noah. I was in Washington several weeks during the session of Congress for the purpose of adjusting then existing political complications which, as I hoped, might result in the election of Mr. Henry Clay for president. Mr. Bennett, in his letters to the "Enquirer," attributed acts to Mr. Clay which, in the then excited state of the public mind, defeated the hopes and efforts of his friends. It is not now necessary to recall the past in this connection. Out of those charges grew a conflict between Mr. Bennett and myself which entirely separated us politically, personally, and socially, for more than thirty years, during which time, although living much together at the Astor House, we had not spoken. Notwithstanding this embarrassment, remembering that General Miller, when asked if he could take a British battery at Lundy's Lane, replied that he would "try," I determined to face my enemy. Upon my arrival in New York I called upon my friend Richard Schell, between whom and Mr. Bennett I knew that intimate relations existed. Mr. Schell readily undertook to arrange an interview, and in a couple of hours afterward called at the Astor House with a message from Mr. Bennett inviting me to dinner that afternoon. In stepping out of the cars at the Washington Heights Station I met Mr. Bennett, who had gone out in the same train. After a cordial greeting we were driven in his carriage to his mansion on the Heights. We then walked for half an hour about the grounds, when a servant came and announced dinner. The dinner was a quiet one, during which, until the fruit was served, we held general conversation. I then frankly informed him of the object of my visit, closing with the remark that Mr. Lincoln deemed it more important to secure the "Herald's" support than to obtain a victory in the field. Mr. Bennett replied that the abolitionists, aided by Whig members of Congress, had provoked a war, of the danger of which he had been warning the country for years, and that now, when they were reaping what they had sown, they had no right to call upon him to help them out of a difficulty that they had deliberately brought upon themselves. I listened without interruption for ten minutes to a bitter denunciation of Greeley, Garrison, Seward, Sumner, Giddings, Phillips, and myself, as having, by irritating and exasperating the South, brought the war upon the country. I then, in reply, without denying or attempting to explain any of his positions, stated the whole question from our standpoint. I informed him of facts and circumstances within my knowledge, showing conclusively the deliberate design of severing the Union to prevent California from coming into it as a free State. I gave him the then unknown particulars of an interview of Messrs. Toombs, Stephens, and Clingman, members of Congress from Georgia and North Carolina, with General Taylor. The object of that interview was to induce General Taylor, a Southern man and slave-holder, to veto the bill permitting California to enter the Union as a free State. It was a stormy interview, with threats of disunion on one hand and of hanging on the other. The facts were communicated to Senator Hamlin of Maine, and myself, within ten minutes after the interview closed. Jefferson Davis, General Taylor's son-in-law, though not present was, as General Taylor believed, the master spirit in the movement. General Taylor's death and the compromise measures under the auspices of his successor, Mr. Fillmore, bridged over rebellion for the time being. I then called Mr. Bennett's attention to the condition of things in 1860, when the results of the census disclosed the fact of an unmistakable

numerical and political ascendency of freedom over slavery.
This ascendency crushed the Southern hope of extending slavery
into free territory, that having been the object of the repeal of
the Missouri compromise and the only national issue then pending. I then reverted to the Democratic National Convention of
1860, startling Mr. Bennett with the assumption that that convention was deliberately demoralized by its leaders for the purpose of throwing the government into our hands, and thus
furnishing the pretext desired for secession. I claimed that the
harmonious nomination of an available candidate would have
insured the success of the Democratic ticket, but that the convention was broken up by leading Southern men, into whose
hands General Butler and Caleb Cushing played. Two Democratic candidates for president were placed in the field, with the
knowledge and for the purpose of giving the election to Mr.
Lincoln, and then, before a word was spoken or an act performed by the incoming administration, a pre-determined course
of secession and rebellion was entered upon.

No one knew better than Mr. Bennett the truth, the force,
and the effect of the facts I presented, but his mind had been
so absorbed in his idea of the pernicious character of abolition
that he had entirely lost sight of the real causes of the rebellion.
He reflected a few minutes, and then changed the conversation
to an incident which occurred in Dublin in 1843, at an O'Connell meeting which both of us attended, though at that time not
on speaking terms. In parting Mr. Bennett cordially invited
me to visit him at his office or house as often as I found it convenient. Nothing was then said in regard to the future course
of the "Herald," but that journal came promptly to the support
of the government, and remained earnest and outspoken against
the rebellion.

It was charged that Mr. Bennett's changed course was occasioned by the mob which surrounded his office, and it was also
charged that the "Herald" had been bought up by the administration. Both of these accusations were utterly unfounded.
Up to the time of my interview with Mr. Bennett, several weeks
after the threatened violence, there was no change in the course
of the "Herald," nor was one word spoken, suggested, or intimated in our conversation conveying the idea of personal interest or advancement. My appeal was made to Mr. Bennett's

judgment, and to his sense of duty as an influential journalist to the government and Union. That appeal, direct and simple, was successful. The President and Secretary of State, when informed of the result of my mission, were much relieved and gratified. Mr. Lincoln frequently expressed to me his desire in some way to acknowledge his sense of obligation to Mr. Bennett, and some two years afterward, when the French mission was open, the President authorized Mr. Wakeman, then surveyor of the port, to offer it to Mr. Bennett, which, however, he declined. Our personal and social relations being thus reëstablished, they continued throughout his life.

CHAPTER LXIV.

1865.

PRESIDENT LINCOLN'S CABINET. — CHANGES IN 1865. — GOVERNOR MOR-
GAN. — MR. McCULLOCH. — MR. FESSENDEN.

IN the winter of 1865 I received a note from President Lincoln asking me to come to Washington. Immediately after my
arrival I called at the White House, and although early, several
persons were waiting to see the President. Mr. Lincoln requested me to call at an hour indicated, when I found him
alone. He commenced the conversation by saying: "You will
remember that after the result of the late presidential election
was known, I told you that I expected to have more influence
with the President now that he had got a new lease. You and
your friends thought that they were severely tried during my
first four years. I did not say much about it then, but intended,
if circumstances were favorable, to even up the account. I
shall have Mr. Fessenden's resignation of the Treasury Department on Monday. Now, if you had the vacancy to fill, whose
name would you send to the Senate?"

I replied that, although wholly unprepared for such a question, yet I was not unprepared with a name that I would suggest for his consideration. I then mentioned Governor Morgan
as, in my judgment, a suitable man for the place, provided it
would answer to give the two leading places in his cabinet to the
State of New York.

"I anticipated this name," said Mr. Lincoln; "and even if
I had not intended to consult your wishes I should have felt
quite safe in trusting the matter to your judgment. I can
afford to give Governor Morgan the Treasury, even though Mr.
Seward has the State Department, because the Governor can be
confirmed, and the people will sustain the appointment. But,"
he added, "this could not be done if a word or a whisper of it
gets out. Can you and I keep the secret?" He then inquired

if there was any doubt of Governor Morgan's acceptance. I told him I thought not; that he had been a capable and successful merchant; that he had shown great executive and financial ability as governor of our State; and that I could not doubt of his acceptance of a department in which he could render much greater service to his country. And, after some further conversation, Mr. Lincoln allowed me to suggest — in the strictest confidence and in general terms — to Governor Morgan that a contingency might happen in which he would be called to the discharge of other duties.

On the way to the cars I stopped at Governor Morgan's house, and, after very earnest injunctions of secrecy, made the suggestion in terms so vague and general as to leave the Governor wholly in the dark as to the nature of the duties referred to, and as to my authority to make the suggestion.

It was understood between Mr. Lincoln and myself that I should hasten home, and, without disclosing or intimating the possibility of a vacancy in the United States Senate, do whatever might be done, with the knowledge I possessed, to give the proper direction to the question of filling Governor Morgan's place in the Senate.

On my arrival at Albany I had not a little curious conversation with Governor Fenton, without whose coöperation it would have been impossible to move satisfactorily. I found that the gentlemen toward whom attention would naturally be drawn for such a position resided in the western part of the State. I suggested Lieutenant-Governor Selden or Judge J. C. Smith as available, but I soon discovered that the Governor, like some of his predecessors, had aspirations for the United States Senate when the time and opportunity should arrive. We then talked with less restraint of candidates in other portions of the State, and I left him with the belief that, should it become necessary to act, we could agree upon a suitable candidate. I now, however, with a better knowledge of his tactics, am confident that had Governor Morgan accepted the Treasury Department, Governor Fenton would have been a candidate for the vacancy.

When the time came for Mr. Lincoln to supply the vacancy occasioned by the resignation of Mr. Fessenden, he took the Senate and the country by surprise in the nomination of Governor Morgan, who, so entirely had I failed to prepare him for the event, was quite as much surprised as his colleagues. Governor Morgan, as soon as he could leave his seat, went over to the White House, and informed the President that he must decline the appointment. He consented, however, to leave the matter over two or three days, giving both himself and the President time for consideration. I returned immediately to Washington, and after a long interview with Governor Morgan, was constrained to report his persistent declination to the President. I failed, however, as I then and now believe, to ascertain what were Governor Morgan's real reasons for refusing the Treasury Department. Upon reporting that failure to Mr. Lincoln, he said: "That is very awkward, but we must look elsewhere for a secretary. Who is your next man?" I replied that I was too much mortified by this miss-fire to try again. Mr. Lincoln said: "I am disappointed, for I thought Governor Morgan would be willing to help us 'run the machine;' but I had two other men in my mind. What do you say to Mr. McCulloch or Mr. Hooper?" I replied that I had a high appreciation of the character and services of both gentlemen, but that I was personally almost unknown to them; that Mr. McCulloch had been brought to Washington by Secretary Chase, and might be fairly supposed to have imbibed his views and impressions; and that I had no reason to believe that Mr. Hooper sympathized with Governor Seward or his friends. Mr. Lincoln laughingly remarked that he supposed I could not forget how Massachusetts disappointed me at Chicago; adding, it was hard for Governor Seward to be crowded out by a new man. And then he renewed his request for me to name a man. I then said: "Why not call Mr. Adams home?" "I have thought of that, too," said Mr. Lincoln, "but will it do to have so long an interregnum?" I remarked that I thought Mr. Chandler, the assistant secretary, capable and trustworthy. "True," said Mr. Lincoln, "we know that here; but will it do to let the finance department, on which so much depends, be run by deputy?" I then spoke of Senator Foster. "An excellent man," said Mr. Lincoln, "and one whom I would readily appoint, if Connecticut were large enough to be entitled to two members of the cabinet." I finally suggested Mr. Hamlin. "Hamlin," said Mr. Lincoln, "has the Senate on the brain, and nothing more or less will cure him." And then I gave it up;

and Mr. Lincoln said: " Let us fall back on Mr. McCulloch, who now seems most available," adding that he would hold the question open for two or three days, giving me time to confer as freely and frequently as I desired with that gentleman.

I found myself not a little embarrassed on my way, one Sunday morning, to the residence of Mr. McCulloch. The idea of establishing relations with that gentleman " on compulsion" seemed like seeking knowledge under difficulties. These difficulties, however, disappeared by degrees as our conversation proceeded. There were two elements in the character of Mr. McCulloch on which, *per se*, I was disposed to rely. He had Scotch blood in his veins, and had been in politics a Whig.

This may be a proper occasion to say that during my whole political life, in all similar conversations in reference to important political interests, I never asked or intimated a desire to receive, directly or indirectly, anything in the shape of a pledge or a promise ; nor have I ever, in reference to such things, regarded a man from whom such pledges or promises were required or who was capable of giving them, worthy of confidence or respect. After Mr. Lincoln's first election as president he invited me to Springfield, where I passed two days with him in free consultation about the great questions upon which he would be called to act. Mr. Lincoln was frank and unrestrained, evidently inviting corresponding frankness and freedom on my part. His cabinet, his inaugural, his policy, etc., etc., were fully discussed, and when I was about to take my leave Mr. Lincoln inquired playfully if I had n't forgotten something, adding, after a moment's pause, " You have not asked for any offices." I replied that when the proper time arrived I should probably, like hosts of other friends, ask for such favors. " But," said Mr. Lincoln, " you have the reputation of taking time by the forelock. I was warned to be on my guard against you ; and the joke of the matter is, that those who gave the warning are after offices themselves, while you have avoided the subject."

But, going back to Mr. McCulloch — my interviews with that gentleman, if protracted, were made so by his intelligent, right-minded, and straightforward expression of views and opinions. If, in going to Mr. McCulloch, I had something of the feeling of "Toots" in calling on "Captain Cuttle" for the "favor of his friendship," I left him with a strong feeling of regard and confidence, and so reported to Mr. Lincoln, who immediately sent his name to the Senate — a step which neither Mr. Lincoln nor the people have had any occasion to regret. On the contrary, Mr. McCulloch proved himself an enlightened, independent, and upright Secretary of the Treasury. To the friends whom I represented he was just and faithful. To myself, who was frequently compelled to occupy his time and attention, he was uniformly courteous and patient, always granting what was proper and in his power to grant, and never refusing without a good reason and in a friendly spirit. All my recollections of Mr. McCulloch in his department — the only place I am sorry to say that I ever met him — are pleasant ones.

CHAPTER LXV.

1833–1877.

In speaking of such a large-hearted man as Moses H. Grinnell I could not be brief. That gentleman's influence, always bright and genial, was seen and felt throughout the city for nearly half a century. Of his intelligence, enterprise, and integrity as a merchant nothing need be said, for these elements of character stand out conspicuously. His liberality and enthusiasm in all good works, in all generous enterprises, and in all patriotic movements, inspired the sympathy and coöperation of others. There was irresistible magnetism in his voice and manner. All hearts and all purses responded to his appeals, — appeals only made when he had first contributed largely. Though devoting much time to public enterprises, to political duties, to social life, and to healthful relaxations, his business was never neglected. He was a thorough merchant, to be found always during business hours where business called him. Mr. Grinnell lived in New York's palmiest days of bountiful, yet refined hospitalities. He was a member of the Hone and Kent clubs, the intellectual and social odors of which linger pleasantly in the memory of their few survivors. Among the gentlemen to be met habitually at the table of Mr. Grinnell forty years ago were Washington Irving, Philip Hone, Chancellor Kent, Richard M. Blatchford, Simeon Draper, Robert B. Minturn, J. Prescott Hall, Charles H. Russell, George Curtis (the father of George William Curtis), Edward Curtis, William H. Aspinwall, Ogden Hoffman, Charles A. Stetson, Roswell Colt, John Ward, James Watson Webb, Dr. John W. Francis,

Charles King, Samuel B. Ruggles, and James Bowen. Ten
years later came William M. Evarts, John Jacob Astor, Isaac
Bell, Edward Minturn, William Kent, Marshall O. Roberts, and
Benjamin F. Silliman. As occasional guests at the same table
I have met John Quincy Adams, Daniel Webster, Edward
Everett, William H. Seward, Gulian C. Verplanck, Hugh Maxwell, General Scott, Commodore Perry, Governor John Davis
of Massachusetts, Governor Kent of Maine, and many other
prominent men. My acquaintance with Mr. Grinnell commenced in 1833. He was then a Democrat, but had taken no
active part in politics. Most of his intimate acquaintances
were Whigs, and upon the organization of the old Republican
and Clintonian parties under the Whig banner, Mr. Grinnell
espoused that cause, becoming and remaining a zealous, efficient, and influential Whig. He was a delegate to the Whig
State Convention of 1834. Passing over the period of his service in Congress, from 1839 to 1841, it is interesting to note
how near Mr. Grinnell came to becoming governor of this State.
In 1856, after a consultation between some of his political
friends, Mr. Grinnell was agreed upon as the candidate for
governor. A few weeks before the convention assembled, Mr.
R. M. Blatchford called with me to confer with Mr. Grinnell upon the subject of his candidacy. Although evidently
gratified with the offer of a nomination that was sure to result
in an election, he said that his acceptance would depend upon
his partner, Mr. Robert B. Minturn, by whose advice he guided
himself in important matters. Mr. Minturn, upon whom we
immediately called, said that Mr. Grinnell's services were essential to the interests of the house, and he could not consent
to his withdrawal, even temporarily, from the business. When
Mr. Minturn's objections were stated to him, Mr. Grinnell
promptly and cheerfully declined the nomination. The late
John A. King was then nominated and elected, beating Amasa
J. Parker, and becoming the first Republican governor of New
York State, the power which the Whig party had previously
held being transferred to the new Republican party, by whom
also E. D. Morgan was elected governor in 1858.

The political influence, wielded quietly but effectively for
many years by Mr. Grinnell, is illustrated by the manner in
which Washington Irving was appointed minister to the court

of Madrid, an appointment to which the literary world owes the pleasure it derives from Irving's "History of Mahomet and his Successors." While Mr. Webster was Secretary of State, I dined with him in Washington one night, Mr. Grinnell, Mr. R. M. Blatchford, and Mr. Simeon Draper also being guests. At the dessert Mr. Grinnell told Mr. Webster that Washington Irving, while writing his "History of Columbus," found it necessary to have access to the archives in Madrid, and that his friends had concluded to ask for his appointment as consul to that city. After a slight pause, Mr. Webster said: "Do I understand you, Mr. Grinnell, to say that you ask for Washington Irving's appointment as consul to Madrid?" Mr. Grinnell responded affirmatively, when Mr. Webster, with great emphasis, asked, "And why not minister to Spain?" But little more was said. Mr. Grinnell returned to New York, rejoicing in the appointment of his literary friend as minister to Spain. Such a thing as this pleased Mr. Grinnell thoroughly. He was so large-hearted that he desired to make everybody happy; he was generous to the last degree. Unlike many men situated in life as he was, he did not contribute to hospital or asylum funds at stated intervals only, but gave in charity every day. In fact he was always giving either money or assistance of other kinds to the needy. Mr. Minturn was like him in this respect, — indeed, no better man ever lived in New York than Robert B. Minturn. I have often had occasion to ask both gentlemen for free passages in their vessels, either for foreigners who were unfortunate here and wished to return home, or for the needy relatives abroad of men who were struggling onward in this country. Many of these people by becoming good citizens fully repaid me for my efforts, and Messrs. Grinnell and Minturn for their charity. A case in point I remember very well. On a cold, blustering night, thirty or more years ago, I was stopped in one of the streets of Albany by a lad of about thirteen years of age. He asked for employment, and his manner impressed me favorably. His story was that he had come from Ireland to seek an uncle whom he could not find. He was destitute, and wanted work. I took him home with me, and, as he said he desired to learn a trade, I procured him employment as an apprentice to a builder named Stewart. Favorable reports of his conduct were given me from time to time, and at the end of three years his employer surrendered his indentures and paid him as a journeyman. Before that event, however, he came to me for aid to bring his mother and sister from Ireland. I applied to Mr. Grinnell, and, as usual, he gave them free passages. A few years after he became a journeyman, the young man went with his mother and sister to the West. In 1860 myself and daughter were in Keokuk, Iowa. We wanted to see the place, and sent for a carriage. Upon going to the vehicle we found in it my quondam protégé. It was his private carriage, and he had come to the hotel to take us out in it. He had settled in Keokuk after leaving Albany, and had become a well-to-do master builder, supporting his mother and sister in good circumstances. He was grateful not alone to me but also to Mr. Grinnell, who he knew had assisted him in his youth.

Mr. Grinnell was also very much attached to the persons connected with him in business as employees. He looked after their interests carefully, and whenever one of them died he cared for his family like a father. He was interested in the Children's Aid Society and the industrial schools of this city, and he, Isaac Bell, James Bowen, Owen W. Brennan, and James B. Nicholson composed the best board of charity commissioners New York has ever had.

I first met Henry S. Sanford in Paris in 1852, just after Louis Napoleon's *coup d'état.* The American minister, Mr. Rives, refused to recognize the new master of the Tuileries, and American residents and visitors would have been put to much annoyance by the absence of any official relations between their representative and the French government, had not Mr. Sanford, who was secretary of legation, possessed the tact to remove the difficulty by making his personal acquaintance with the leading men of the new empire serve, instead of diplomatic formalities, in providing for his countrymen the privileges they desired.

I have known Mr. Sanford well, I may say very well, ever since. While I was abroad during the Rebellion, I had occasion to know the value of his services. Mr. Sanford was in Paris on his way to Brussels before our new minister, Mr. Dayton, arrived, and his exertions in behalf of the Union cause at a critical moment, when the French government and people were hostile to us, were of great value. Everything needed to be done abroad at that time. We wanted arms, clothing, and all kinds of military supplies. Mr. Sanford was exceedingly zealous to serve the government, and often anticipated his instructions in his desire to be useful. While at Brussels he frequently crossed the path of persons who were acting as agents for the United States in making purchases, and who were eager chiefly to make money for themselves. His interference with their projects provoked their hostility. With another class of agents, whose sole motive was to serve their country, Mr. Sanford cordially coöperated. As an example of the latter class I might mention Mr. George Schuyler, of this city, who was sent abroad to buy arms, and who as a thoroughly honest man appreciated Mr. Sanford's exertions, and worked in accord with him. Mr. Sanford's great activity, resulting from his temperament and his enthusiasm for the Union cause, was sometimes mistaken for officiousness. It offended Mr. Adams, and to some extent annoyed Mr. Dayton. It is not true, however, that Mr. Dayton was angry with Mr. Sanford. I was in Paris after the Trent affair was terminated, and the danger of war with England averted. Mentioning to Mr. Dayton that I meant to make a trip in Belgium and Holland with my daughter, he said he would take a holiday and go with me. We set off together, and when we had reached Brussels we all went to Mr. Sanford's house and spent three agreeable days there. Of course Mr. Dayton would not have accepted Mr. Sanford's hospitality if he had not been upon good terms with him.

If the people knew how important was the work which Mr. Sanford enabled us to accomplish, they would feel that they owed him a great deal of gratitude.

There is a lesson in the shifting fortunes of that remarkable man, Andrew Johnson, which may be read advantageously. There is inherent strength, if not intrinsic worth, in the character of a man who, after sinking out of sight covered with obloquy, not only rises to the surface but resumes his position as a senator in Congress. I cannot bring myself to regret Andrew Johnson's return. First, I remember, with lively gratitude, his brave devotion to the government and Union from the beginning to the end of the Rebellion. When other Southern senators advocated secession and threatened disunion, Andrew Johnson rebuked and denounced them. When the overt act of rebellion was committed, he pronounced treason a crime, invoking the punishment due to traitors.

I was a good deal with Vice-President Johnson, in company with the late Preston King, immediately after the assassination of President Lincoln. I know that his first solicitude was to ascertain and carry out the policy of Mr. Lincoln. I know that he went to the White House with that determination. He inherited the political hostilities which had already assumed formidable proportions in the Senate against Mr. Lincoln, but unfortunately he did not inherit Mr. Lincoln's temper or tact. Before President Johnson had uttered one syllable, or had done one act subjecting him to the just censure of Republicans, he was assailed by Senators Sumner, Wade, Chandler, etc., and denounced in leading Republican journals. At that crisis I had anxious interviews with him, and while he did not conceal his sense of the injustice of these assaults, he avowed and re-iterated his determination to "fight the question .out in the Republican party." Subsequently, and on several occasions, I had earnest conversations with him in relation to his views and policies, and I am free to say that I left him on those occasions with a high sense of his ability and wisdom, and with unwaver-ing confidence in his integrity and patriotism. And yet that wise man, for such, under the guidance of judgment and rea-son, he really was, during the progress of events was bereft of both, and became the victim of passion and unreason. I met him at Albany while "swinging round the circle," and endeav-ored in a brief interview to show him that men, in a popular sense, were like flies, and that more of them could be caught with honey than with vinegar. In other words, I suggested that, when during his tour he was called upon by his constit-uents for speeches, instead of "hitting out right and left" against Congress, Congress not being there to reply, he might find objects and works of improvement and progress to admire and commend, in which his audience would be interested. I urged that speeches consisting of Orator Choate's "glittering generalities" would prove more acceptable to his hearers and far safer for himself than all the anathemas he could fulminate against his enemies.

But he was aggressive and belligerent to a degree that rendered him insensible to considerations of prudence and those common-sense qualities which, under other auspices, were marked traits of his character. And thus he proceeded on his evil mission through many States, dealing blows right and left, which neither hit nor harmed anybody but himself and his friends.

Returning to Washington, the spirit of antagonism intensified, he became the victim of a delusion which provoked and precipitated his impeachment. And yet, when his trial came, nothing was proved to require or justify his conviction. He was impeached as men are not unfrequently indicted, upon a general but vague popular idea that they have been guilty of something and ought to be punished. And so President Johnson, serving out his accidental term, exasperating his enemies and mortifying his friends, passed into a retirement from which no one supposed he would ever emerge. Nor could any common man have dug himself out of a pit so deep and dark as that into which he had fallen. Striking upon this rock his political fortunes were wrecked. But underlying his infirmities of temper there were strong redeeming traits of character, — traits which, in the estimation of the people, fitted him for public usefulness. And this conviction — a conviction of which the people of Tennessee themselves were scarcely conscious — furnishes a solution to the problem of his most unexpected return to public life. I cannot regard this apparently capricious result in a simply amusing or ludicrous aspect. It is suggestive and significant.

The death of the late Sir Henry Holland occurred soon after his return from Russia and Italy. His illness must have been a brief one. He started, as will be seen by the following letter, upon his annual summer tour in good health and spirits : —

No. 72 BROOK STREET, LONDON, *July* 17, 1873.

MY DEAR FRIEND, — I cannot feel satisfied to leave London for my annual voyage without exchanging a few lines of friendship with you, asking you to tell me of yourself, of your daughter, and all in whom you are interested. The accounts I have received of you have been good, and therefore welcome to me. But they have been only general reports, and I shall be glad to have them confirmed from yourself.

I do not seek to make this a letter of news. The newspapers furnish you with all such information, political and social. All that I need say for the moment is, that we have just gone through a course of multitudinous and splendid entertainments to this Persian sovereign. He has excited here an amount of interest far beyond what is due either to personal merits or political importance. But the old name of Persia brought up again in the person of an Oriental prince, moved the mind of the multitude, ignorant of the many dynasties which have ruled and oppressed the country since the days of its ancient sovereigns, and of the miserable and barren remnant which modern Persia forms of the ancient Persian empire. I have been present at several of the fêtes given to him, and am fully sated with the sight.

To say a word about myself. My plan for the autumn is to go by St. Petersburg and Moscow to Nijni-Novgorod (at the time of the great fair there), and then returning to England to take my second son (your friend) with me to Rome and Naples, which he has not yet visited. I have been pressed much to visit the United States once more, but this I fear I must decline, though if my strength were maintained I should be sorely tempted to make a dash at the Yellowstone River, when the communication with it is fairly opened. To talk even of these things at eighty-five is, however, a piece of unwarrantable rashness.

Pray give my affectionate remembrances to Miss Weed, and send me a good account of her health. And say something for me also to my young friend at Albany, now grown into a full lady. Farewell my dear Mr. Weed. Yours affectionately,   H. HOLLAND.

I do not leave London until the first of August, so that I may perchance hear from you or Miss Weed before my departure. I must not forget to say that I received your interesting paper on the Junius question.

If you see my excellent friend Evarts, pray tell him of my earnest wish to hear from him, if at any time amidst his multitudinous business he can spare time for a few lines.

To one who has for many years not only been privileged to enjoy the society, but has profited largely by the professional experience and wisdom of Sir Henry Holland, this sudden bereavement fell heavily. Presumptuous as it was when both had so nearly reached the end of the journey of life, I looked fondly forward to future communion with this cherished friend. It had been arranged that we should visit California together in 1872, but circumstances which he could not control disappointed that expectation. It will be seen, however, from his letter, that notwithstanding his advanced age the project was not abandoned. Recent discoveries on the Yellowstone River had attracted his attention and strengthened his desire to see the only portion of the United States he had not visited.

During the Rebellion Sir Henry was among the comparatively few distinguished Englishmen who not only sympathized with the North but who rendered good services to our government. Of these services I hope to speak at another time. But for the high sense he entertained of the obligations of professional reticence, I should have long since been permitted to reveal a conversation between the queen and her physician that would have occasioned grateful and enduring regard for her majesty in the hearts of all patriotic Americans.

In this connection, with the keen remembrance of those dark days in London, the subject never recurs without exciting a strong desire to recognize with thankfulness services rendered our government and Union by the Duke of Argyle, Milner Gibson, Monckton Milnes (now Lord Houghton), Mr. Cobden, John Bright, Sir J. Emerson Tennant, the Rev. Newman Hall, the Rev. William Arthur, the Earl of Shaftesbury, Sir Roundell Palmer, Messrs. Forster, Kinnaird, Torrens, Stansfield, Bazley, Baxter, Potter, White, Smith, and others in and out of Parliament.

CHAPTER LXVI.

1861–1880.

1861. — HAVING shown when and why I declined foreign missions, it seems proper that I should follow up the narrative with an event of more recent occurrence. I will now, therefore, relate when, and how, and under what peculiar circumstances I did finally go abroad in a semi-official character.

Late in October, 1861, it was deemed important by the administration that some gentlemen of intelligence and experience, possessing a good knowledge of all the circumstances which preceded and occasioned the Rebellion, should be sent abroad to disabuse the public mind, especially in England and France, where numerous and active agents of secession and rebellion had long been at work in quarters too ready to accept versions unfavorable to the North. Simultaneously I arrived at Washington, and was informed by the Secretary of State that the late Edward Everett of Boston, and Archbishop Hughes of New York, J. P. Kennedy of Baltimore, and Bishop McIlvaine of Ohio had been invited to accept this mission, but that he was embarrassed by the declension of Messrs. Everett and Kennedy. Mr. Everett, having formerly been our minister at the Court of St. James, did not feel at liberty to accept an unofficial position ; Mr. Kennedy did not feel able to abandon his business and go abroad without compensation. The four gentlemen thus selected were informed by the Secretary of State that their actual expenses only would be paid. The Secretary then asked me to suggest two suitable persons to supply these vacancies. I named Mr. Winthrop of Boston and Mr. Ewing of Ohio. He thought well of both, and said he would immediately suggest their names to the President and cabinet. Archbishop Hughes, Bishop McIlvaine, and Secretary Chase were to dine that day with Secretary Seward. I told him that I would drop in after his guests had left in the evening. I called at nine o'clock and found the Archbishop, who had been informed that I was expected, waiting for me. And now I learned, greatly to my surprise and regret, that the Archbishop had declined. Of the four gentlemen designated Bishop McIlvaine alone had accepted. The Secretary, after I came in, resumed the conversation and renewedly urged the Archbishop to accept. But he persisted in his declination, repeating, as I inferred, the reasons previously given for declining. The conversation was interrupted by a servant who ushered Baron von Gerolt, the Prussian minister, into the parlor. The Secretary seated himself with the baron upon a sofa in the ante-room, and I took advantage of the interruption to urge the Archbishop with great earnestness to withdraw his declination. He reiterated his reasons for declining. I told him that I had already listened attentively to all he had said, and that while I knew he always had good and sufficient reasons for whatever he did or declined to do, he had not yet chosen to state them ; and that while I did not seek to know more than he thought proper to avow, I must again appeal to him as a loyal citizen, devoted to the Union, and capable of rendering great service at a crisis of imminent danger, not to persist in his refusal unless his reasons for doing so 'were insurmountable. After a long pause he placed his hand upon my shoulder, and, in his impressive manner and clear, distinct voice, said, "Will you go with me?" I replied, "I have once enjoyed the great happiness of a voyage to Europe in your company, and of a tour through Ireland, England, and France under your protection. It was a privilege and a pleasure which I shall never forget. I would cheerfully go with you now as your secretary or your valet, if that would give to the government the benefit of your services." And here the conversation rested until Baron von Gerolt took his leave. When Governor Seward returned the Archbishop rose and said, "Governor, I have changed my mind, and will accept the appointment with this condition, that he," placing his hand again upon my shoulder, "goes with me as a colleague. And as you want us to sail next Wednesday, I shall leave for New York by the first train in the morning. I lodge at the convent at Georgetown, and I will now take my leave. So good-night and good-by." I accompanied the Archbishop to his carriage where, after he was seated, he said with a significant gesture, " This programme is not to be changed."

Returning to the parlor I found Secretary Seward, as I anticipated, embarrassed and depressed. No explanation was needed. His position in the cabinet and with Congress was giving him and his friends much annoyance. He was charged by radical members of both, and by the radical press, with a want of energy and courage, although in point of fact he had been steadily and zealously in favor of the largest army and the largest appropriations of money for war purposes from the beginning. The country was rife with personal slanders against him ; leading senators were determined to drive him out of the cabinet. For wisdom and firmness in counsel and hard mental and physical labor day and night, he was all but literally stoned and scourged. Altogether, his position was one of extreme embarrassment. I was much more obnoxious to the same class of Republicans. Three members of the cabinet (Messrs. Chase, Welles, and Blair), together with several distinguished members of Congress, were politically and personally my enemies. Secretary Chase had fair reasons for his hostility, for I had strenuously and steadily opposed him in his aspirations for the presidency. Leading radical journals were bitterly hostile to me. I had incurred the displeasure of these classes early in the Rebellion by insisting that there was a strong loyal sentiment in Western Virginia, Eastern Tennessee, and throughout North Carolina, — a sentiment which, if cherished and protected, would narrow the boundaries of rebellion. I had sustained what was known as the " Border State proposition " in Congress, — a proposition which, if adopted, would have gone far to divide and weaken the South ; and, worse than all, I had maintained from the beginning that the war ought to be prosecuted for the maintenance of the government and the preservation of the Union, holding and declaring at the same time that slavery would be deservedly destroyed as the only adequate penalty and punishment for a wanton and wicked rebellion against the best form of government in the world. Perhaps no other man, who had enjoyed for thirty years or more so largely the confidence of his party, had ever become so suddenly obnoxious to the ruling sentiment of that party. Secretary Seward, therefore, apprehended, as he had abundant reasons for apprehending, that in superadding my offenses to his own responsibilities, they would inevitably sink him. I felt this keenly, and determined to return to New York and relieve him by persuading the Archbishop to go without me. The Secretary informed me that he should be in New York on the following Monday morning, two days before the time fixed for the departure of the commissioners. I remained in Washington attending to other duties till the afternoon of the next day, but had no further conversation with the Secretary on that subject. On my arrival at Albany I found the following letter from the Archbishop : —

New York, October 29, 1861.

My dear Mr. Weed, — I cannot " condescend " to appoint you to either of the offices which you so humbly suggested in a whisper the other evening at Washington. But I do hereby appoint you, with or without the consent of the Senate, to be my friend (as you always have been) and my companion in our brief visit to Europe.

The more I reflect upon the subject the more I am convinced that, whether successful or not, the purpose is marked, in actual circumstances, by large, enlightened, and very wise statesmanship.

I have engaged a state-room for you next to my own on the Africa, which sails on the 6th proximo.

We shall have time enough to talk on the way about matters and things.   I remain, very sincerely,

Your obedient servant,
John, Archbishop of New York.

I returned to New York on Monday morning, prepared for either contingency. I found the Archbishop inflexible, and after he frankly explained to me his reasons for insisting upon my accompanying him, I did not feel at liberty to disappoint him. Secretary Seward came on from Washington on the Sunday night train, and immediately after breakfast the Archbishop called upon him at the Astor House, as did Mr. R. M. Blatchford and the late Mr. R. B. Minturn, to whom, with myself, the Secretary read his instructions and then handed them to the Archbishop, with which he took his leave. Mr. Minturn then quite warmly expressed his gratification upon my appointment, to which Secretary Seward replied, " Mr. Weed goes abroad as a volunteer, and at his own expense." Mr. Minturn at first regarded this as a joke, but, upon learning that the Secretary was in earnest, he left the room abruptly. I turned the conversation for a few minutes, and then left also. I found Mr. Minturn walking in the hall in front of my door, more than usually disturbed. He followed me into my room, and handed me a check for $1,000, remarking that I would find a credit at Baring Brothers, in London, to meet my expenses, as long as the interests of the country required me to remain there. Mr. Blatchford, when left alone with the Secretary, made some inquiries which disturbed him so much that he came down and protested against my leaving the country under circumstances so humiliating. Meantime Mr. Seward departed by a special train for Washington. I realized painfully the perplexities of my position. Between my promise to the Archbishop, the rebuff of the Secretary, and a reasonable degree of self-respect, it was difficult to determine what I ought to do. I did not doubt that when the fact that I was to go abroad in a highly important and confidential capacity became known at Washington, a storm would be raised which would constrain the Secretary to disavow the appointment, as he might do with justice and truth, for, as I have already stated, it was demanded by Archbishop Hughes as the condition upon which he himself consented to go. I remarked to Mr. Blatchford that Mr. Seward had been so often assailed, and so long held responsible for all my alleged shortcomings, that he had become impatient and nervous, so much so that it needed only this feather to break the camel's back. Mr. Blatchford, however, was not appeased, and immediately sat down in my room and wrote, if I may judge by his excited manner, a very earnest letter to the Secretary. This letter was mailed immediately, and reached Governor Seward while at breakfast the next morning. A few hours afterward Mr. Blatchford received a telegram from the Secretary, informing him that my credentials would reach New York by special messenger in time for the steamer. This changed the whole aspect of the question, and proved quite as gratifying to my friends Blatchford and Minturn as to myself.

In due time my letter to Earl Russell, accrediting me unofficially to the English government, to the Hon. Charles Francis Adams, our minister to England, to Hon. William L. Dayton, our minister to France, and to the Prince Napoleon, were received. They were couched in language as strong and generous as confidence and friendship could inspire. The cloud, therefore, which lowered for a few days over me revealed its silver lining, and I departed, resolved, under the auspices of a kind Providence, in which I trusted, not to disappoint the expectations of my friends. How far I was successful in this resolution, and what occurred during the eventful and trying period of my sojourn in England and France, will constitute other chapters in this narrative. It is sufficient for my present purpose to say that I was greatly and strangely favored by circumstances. The doors of princes and of potentates were opened for me in unexpected and unusual ways. The steamer which followed us, arriving out two days after we landed, brought intelligence of the taking of Messrs. Mason and Slidell from under the British flag. This occasioned throughout England a universal and indignant war-cry. On the following day, breaking through all the usual forms of diplomacy, through an accidental channel I was tendered an audience by Earl Russell at Pembroke Lodge, Richmond Hill, his country residence, and subsequently was received by the Duke of Argyll, Milnor Gibson, Count de Morny, and other distinguished officials in London and Paris, as a representative of my country, without ever having an opportunity, with a single exception, of presenting my letters of instruction. From Prince Napoleon, to whom I delivered Governor Seward's letter, I received marked attentions. The Prince, differing widely and boldly from the Emperor, was a warm friend of our government, and sought occasions to serve us. Our foreign ministers in London, Paris, and Brussels received me with a cordiality and treated me with a consideration which is pleasantly and gratefully remembered. The letters to Earl Russell, etc., etc., not having been delivered, are now preserved as souvenirs for my descendants.

The Trent affair agitated England greatly. Her people were angrily excited, and their government profoundly anxious for a peaceful solution of the difficulty. Meantime, as there were but two steamers a month in the winter, and no cable, information was waited for impatiently. Our friends were disappointed and alarmed by the ominous reticence of the Secretary of State, and under this pressure I wrote him a letter, expressing regret that he did not keep Mr. Adams privately advised of the progress and probabilities of that all-absorbing question, to which I received the following reply : —

WASHINGTON, *March* 7, 1862.

MY DEAR WEED, — I thought I had as much industry as anybody around me, and with it a little versatility. But I know nobody, and never did know that one man who could do all you seem to think I neglect to do, as well as all the labor I actually perform. You knew when you left here how much I had to do outside of my own proper department, how little time official consultations and audiences leave me to work at all. But all this seems now forgotten, and you insist that I should have written private notes to Mr. Adams while the Trent affair was pending. How unreasonable ! Our first knowledge that the British government proposed to make it a question of offense or insult, and so of war, reached me on a Thursday. The Thursday following I ascertained how this government would act upon it, and the reply went from my hands the same day.

I am under the necessity of consulting the temper of parties and people on this side of the water quite as much as the temper of parties and people in England. If I had been as tame as you think would have been wise in my treatment of affairs with that country, I should have had no standing in my own. I am willing to let my treatment of the British nation go on record with the treatment of this nation by the British ministry, and abide the world's judgment of the question on which side justice, forbearance, and courtesy have been exercised.

I shall seem just as much reserved in this as in other letters. I know of things intended to be done, and expected to be done, but I cannot certainly know that they will be successfully done, much less how soon. If I promise them, and promise them speedily, and the agents relied upon fail, I shall be reproached for false prophecies, as I was last summer.

I hope Harriet has recovered. Indeed, if things are half as well in England as it seems to me here that they ought to be, I trust that you have given her the benefit of the Italian spring.

Everybody writes me that you have done everything well, and that your services have been exceedingly useful. I rejoice in your success, and congratulate you upon having deserved and gained the confidence of the wise and good at home and abroad, by labors devoted to the salvation of the Union, with so much manifestly resting upon you.　　　　Faithfully yours,

WILLIAM H. SEWARD.

THURLOW WEED, ESQ., London.

In 1862, while in London, I was sitting at the Legation with Mr. Moran, its secretary, when a plain, elderly gentleman, in modernized Quaker costume, came in and was introduced to me as Mr. Fox, our consul at Falmouth. Before he left the room to see our minister, Mr. Adams, I asked him if he knew how near he came to losing his official head a year ago. In replying that he had no such knowledge, he added that he understood that he had had some narrow escapes in former times, but that since the Rebellion broke out he had been so busy in trying to show his countrymen that in a war to extend and strengthen slavery their sympathies should be with the North, that he had not thought about being removed. He then added that it was not so much for the emolument as for the pleasure of serving the American government that he desired to retain the office which his father received from George Washington. He was evidently much gratified at the incident I related, and invited me very cordially to visit him.

CHAPTER LXVII.

1861–1880.

1861–1862. — During the darkest days of the Rebellion the danger of war with France and England was most imminent. Antecedents and traditions led us to hope for sympathy in France, and to apprehend hostility in England. So far as the French government was concerned that hope was utterly disappointed. Nor did the friendly feeling which we looked for among the French people exist. With one exception the Emperor and those associated with him in the government were against us. That exception was the Prince Napoleon. He was our firm friend, and for that reason was out of favor. In England the commercial cities, the capitalists, and as a rule the aristocracy, were against us. In the manufacturing districts we had friends whose representatives in Parliament stood by us faithfully on all questions. But the Trent affair occurring at a most critical moment united "all England" in a cry for war. Our firmest friends in and out of Parliament were dismayed. All felt and said that unless the Confederate commissioners, Mason and Slidell, were released, war was inevitable. While that question was pending Messrs. Cobden, Bright, Forster, Kinnaird, and other members of Parliament were powerless and speechless. Our ministerial friends, the Duke of Argyll and Milnor Gibson, were paralyzed.

At that most critical moment Mr. M'Cullagh Torrens rendered us services which entitle him to the affection and grati-

tude of the American people. I was introduced to him the
morning after my arrival in London, early in December, 1861,
by Mr. Peabody, at whose bank a large number of panic-struck
Americans had assembled. Mr. Torrens, when I retired, met me
at the door of the banking-house, remarking that my arrival in
London was opportune, and that I must see Earl Russell immediately. I replied that our minister, Mr. Adams (then the
right man in the right place), would present me to the minister
as soon as practicable. "That will not do," rejoined Mr. Torrens. "Time presses; you must see the Earl to-morrow;" adding that he would arrange an audience and inform me of the
time and place that evening. I was surprised at the warm interest manifested by an Englishman and a stranger, and doubtful of the propriety of anticipating the kind intentions of Mr.
Adams; but that gentleman relieved my doubts on this point
by advising me to avail myself of Mr. Torrens' timely offer.

I dined that day with the late Sir J. Emerson Tennent, meeting a large and what proved to be a war party of gentlemen,
among whom was the colonel of a regiment which was to leave
London the next morning to embark at Liverpool for Canada.
The colonel was toasted, and in response made a brief but exciting war speech, dwelling with much effect upon the duty of
Englishmen to resent the insults to their flag. I was seated at
the table next to Lord Clarence Paget, of the admiralty, who
informed me that their preparations for war were active and
formidable, and that for the first time since 1815 they were
working double-handed, night and day, in the dock-yards. Returning from dinner to my hotel in Hanover Square I found
Mr. Torrens, who directed me to leave London the next morning at eleven o'clock, and drive to Pembroke Lodge, Richmond
Hill, Earl Russell's country seat.

I found the minister quite alone, and was courteously received. Conversation for the first ten or fifteen minutes was
embarrassed by an evident determination on the part of the
minister to ignore all other questions until the honor of England should be satisfied by the surrender of Mason and Slidell.
Gradually, however, the restraint passed away, and his lordship
explained the circumstances which led to the Queen's proclamation giving belligerent rights to the rebel States. It was evident that even if his sympathies were not with the South, he

had come to the conclusion that we were the aggressors. I endeavored to correct that impression by calling his attention to two or three undeniable facts upon which the whole merits of the question turned. After an hour and a half lunch was announced, and the conversation became general.

In the drawing-room, after the Earl had conversed aside with Lady Russell for a few minutes, thanking him for the time he had spared me, I was taking leave, when Lady Russell interposed, saying, "You must not go without seeing the lodge grounds," in walking through which her ladyship pointed out the various objects and localities with which history had made me familiar. In the course of our walk she remarked that ladies of course knew nothing of state secrets, but that they had ears, and sometimes heard things which might not have been intended for them ; adding, that it would probably relieve my anxiety to know that in our difficulties the sympathies of the Queen were with our government; that her majesty remembered the attentions extended to her son, the Prince of Wales, and would do everything in her power to prevent a rupture with America.

With this gleam of hope I returned well satisfied with my visit to Pembroke Lodge, and grateful to Mr. Torrens for the prompt and thoughtful service he had rendered. But that gentleman was not content with one good turn. He was constantly at work in our cause. The "Daily News," next to "The Times," was the most influential journal in England. The "News" espoused our cause boldly and warmly. Many of its best and ablest American articles were written by Mr. Torrens.

Some weeks after Parliament met there was a vacancy for Finsbury; Mr. Torrens, a member of the previous Parliament, had not been returned. He now offered for Finsbury and was chosen, when his sphere of usefulness was much enlarged. His efforts in behalf of our government and Union, in and out of Parliament, were constant, and continued until the war was over.

While waiting with intense solicitude for the decision of our government upon the demand of England for the surrender of Mason and Slidell, I received from the Hon. Arthur Kinnaird, M. P., in the strictest confidence, positive evidence that the Queen had, at the right moment, caused the dispatch demanding the surrender of Mason and Slidell to be so far modified in language and spirit as to render a compliance with it less difficult to our government. Several days after receiving this information, confirming the assurance kindly given me by Lady Russell, I received additional and conclusive evidence from another high source. Since the illness of Prince Albert, the late honored and lamented Sir Henry Holland had made daily visits to Windsor. We saw him every evening either with Mr. and Mrs. Adams at the legation or at our own lodgings. To the question, whether the Queen said anything about our troubles, he replied that her majesty was too much absorbed in her own to talk or think about public matters.

Some days after the information received from Mr. Kinnaird Sir Henry came to us in buoyant spirits, saying that he now had pleasant news. The Queen, he said, had that day asked if there was serious danger of war with America, receiving in reply an assurance from the court physician that war could only be averted by the act of the American government. The Queen then informed Sir Henry and his medical associate what occurred between her majesty, Lord Palmerston, and Prince Albert, when the dispatch demanding the surrender of Mason and Slidell was brought to Windsor for approval. This statement not only confirmed the material facts communicated by Mr. Kinnaird, but superadded minute and interesting details.

This information, however, like that imparted by Mr. Kinnaird, was given under strict injunctions of secrecy. But the death of Lord Palmerston removing one seal of secrecy, and anxious that our people should know how much they were indebted to the Queen of England, I wrote to Mr. Kinnaird, asking his permission to make a full revelation of the facts within my knowledge. That gentleman communicated with Mr. Gladstone, the successor of Lord Palmerston. Mr. Kinnaird's reply to my letter, an extract from which I feel at liberty to publish, will show that the question encountered another obstacle.

[From the Hon. A. Kinnaird to Thurlow Weed.]

2 PALL MALL, EAST, *December* 22, 1870.

DEAR MR. WEED, — I am sorry I have been so long in answering your letter, but I lost no time in communicating with Mr. Gladstone. At first he only sent me an answer through his secretary saying that he would inquire, as he was not aware of the fact. I have at last received a very full answer from him, a copy of which I inclose confidentially. I cannot agree with him as to a verbal correction not being of the greatest importance, for a person may inadvertently express a thing in a way which might appear insulting or distrustful, when even the slightest alteration in the wording might completely change its aspect. Of course, under the circumstances, it will be impossible to make any official use of Gladstone's communication. But it must rest with you to decide whether you will refer to the matter as resting upon your own memory of what you heard when you were in England at the time of the war. I do trust that there will never be any alteration in the friendly relations between the two countries, and that you will succeed in getting your government to terminate the Alabama controversy, as in England there is a full disposition to do so. Remember me most kindly to Miss Weed and all our mutual friends.

Yours very truly,   A. KINNAIRD.

There can be no impropriety in saying that Mr. Gladstone assumed that whatever passes between the Queen and her cabinet ministers, while a question is under consideration, is in its nature confidential. I am constrained, therefore, to act upon Mr. Kinnaird's suggestion in affirming as I do, on trustworthy information, that on three occasions, during the first year of the Rebellion, Queen Victoria contributed essentially to the preservation of peace between this country and England. On two occasions her majesty discountenanced suggestions from the French government which meant war.

The first was a proposition for the joint intervention of France and England, the object being a recognition of the Confederate government. The next was the introduction into Parliament, after an interview by the mover with the French Emperor, of a resolution repudiating our blockade. The popular feeling in England was so strongly in favor of the Confederate States that our friends in Parliament and in the cabinet, but for the conviction that their course was tacitly approved by their sovereign, would have found themselves unable to successfully resist those hostile measures.

When the dispatch demanding the surrender of Mason and Slidell was read by Lord Palmerston to the Queen, and the consequences of a refusal were explained, her majesty was startled and distressed at the idea of war with America. Taking the dispatch to the Prince Consort, who, then in his last illness, was sitting in his apartment, the Queen asked him to read it, saying that she thought the language and spirit were harsh and peremptory. The Prince, concurring in opinion with her majesty, subjected the dispatch to erasures and interlineations, in which amended form it was returned to the premier. In relating this incident to Sir Henry Holland, the Queen added, "That was the last time the Prince used his pen." Not quite sure that Mr. Kinnaird, in his letter, intended to permit me to state how he obtained the information relating to the modification of Lord Palmerston's dispatch, I am constrained to withhold an interesting incident, without, however, relinquishing the hope of bringing it out at another time and in another form.

[This hope was realized in 1880, as will be seen by the following extracts from "The Life of the Prince Consort," by Theodore Martin, published in that year: —]

Next day (30th of November), after the cabinet meeting, Lord John Russell forwarded to the Queen the drafts of the various dispatches which were to be sent to Lord Lyons. They reached Windsor Castle in the evening, and doubtless occupied much of the Prince's thoughts in the long hours of the winter morning, when he found sleep impossible. Ill as he was, in accordance with his accustomed habit he rose at seven, and before eight he had finished and brought to the Queen the draft of a memorandum on the subject of these dispatches. "He could eat no breakfast," is the entry in her majesty's "Diary," "and looked very wretched. But still he was well enough on getting up to make a draft for me to write to Lord Russell in correction of his draft to Lord Lyons, sent to me yesterday, which Albert did not approve." When he brought it to the Queen, he told her he could scarcely hold his pen while writing it. Traces of his weakness are visible in the hand-writing, and may be perceived in the annexed fac-simile, even by those who are not familiar with his autograph. This fac-simile has a special value as representing the last political memorandum written by the Prince, while at the same time inferior to none of them, as will presently be seen, in the importance of its results. . . .

All these considerations had no doubt their weight in determining the decision of the United States government. But they would probably have failed to sway it into compliance with the British demands, but for the temperate and conciliatory tone in which, thanks to the Prince, the views of the government had been conveyed. Mr. Seward told Lord Lyons, before the copy of the dispatch was placed in his hands, that "everything depended upon the wording of it," and begged, as a personal favor, to be allowed to read it before it was communicated to him officially. In compliance with this request, it was sent to him under a cover marked "private and confidential." The effect was instantaneous. "Almost immediately afterwards," Lord Lyons says, in a private dispatch to Lord John Russell (19th of December, 1861), "he came here. He told me he was pleased to find that the dispatch was courteous and friendly, — not dictatorial nor menacing." "His task of reconciling his government to a pacific course — no easy one — was thus greatly simplified, and on the 26th he announced in an elaborate dispatch, much of which was obviously written to reconcile the more fiery portion of the American public to the unpalatable concession, that Captain Wilkes had acted without instructions, and that the four persons taken from the Trent should be cheerfully liberated." This welcome intelligence reached London on the 9th of January, 1862. It was communicated the same day to the Queen (who was then at Osborn). In her reply her majesty said: " Lord Palmerston cannot but look on this peaceful issue of the American quarrel as greatly owing to her beloved Prince, who wrote the observations upon the draft to Lord Lyons, in which Lord Palmerston so entirely concurred. It was the last thing he ever wrote ! "

We are informed by the Right Honorable W. E. Forster, who knew Mr. Thurlow Weed at this time, that he was sent over as an accredited, though not an official, agent of the United States government, to watch over their interests, and to do his best to neutralize English sympathy with the South. Some tidings of what had been done by the sovereign in modifying Lord John Russell's dispatch seem to have reached Mr. Weed, and in December, 1874, when Mr. Forster was in New York, he was told by Mr. Weed that the alterations had done much to preserve peace. That gentleman regarded the fact as of so much importance that being himself unable to attend a public reception given by politicians of all parties to Mr. Forster, he wrote a letter to be read to the meeting in which the following passage occurs: " While you are recognizing the claims of the eminent British statesman to our regard, I am sure that you will cheerfully, gratefully, and with a profound sense of obligation, remember the action of the Queen on a question of momentous importance. When Lord Palmerston went to the Queen with a dispatch demanding from our government the surrender of Mason and Slidell, her majesty, absorbed by solicitude for the health of the Prince, had heard little of the Trent affair, and was startled and shocked at the idea of war with America. Not liking the peremptory language and defiant speech of the dispatch, the Queen took it to the apartment of the Prince Consort, who used the pen for the last time in modifying the language and tone of the demand."

The enthusiasm which the reading of this letter excited showed, Mr. Forster writes, the American estimate of the Queen's and Prince's wise kindness at a most anxious crisis.

Our war with the Confederate States, as we now know and realize, was formidable enough in all its aspects and consequences, without the aggravations of a simultaneous conflict with England and France. The French Emperor was unquestionably in favor of the Confederate States, and desired to aid them even at the expense of a war with our government. His point was that France needed cotton. The Emperor said to Archbishop Hughes what his brother, the Count de Morny, repeated to me, that when the French people were out of employment the government was expected to furnish them with bread; that cotton was essential to the welfare of France, and that for this reason the French government was justified in urging either the recognition of the Confederate government or the abandonment of our blockade. He sought and expected the coöperation of England, a large majority of whose citizens were with him in sentiment and sympathy. But that national calamity was averted by the firm, enlightened, steady, and wise course of eminent and influential English friends of our government and Union, to all of whom my sense of gratitude is measured by the value of the services rendered.

CHAPTER LXVIII.

1861–1880.

1861–1865. — ON the ninth day of November, 1861, I left New York for Havre in the steamer Arago, and was fortunate enough to meet on shipboard Lieutenant-General Winfield Scott, who contemplated passing the winter in the south of France.

General Scott, whose wife was in Paris, having informed the President that he desired to go abroad, was invited to act with our commission. Archbishop Hughes and Bishop McIlvaine departed in a Cunard steamer. We had a rough fifteen days' voyage. Passengers, as usual, beguiled the time at whist. General Scott, Colonel Winthrop of New Orleans, Mr. Green, a retired merchant of New York, and myself, made a table for the voyage. After the first day, instead of " cutting " as usual for partners, Messrs. Winthrop and Green played constantly against the General and myself. I mention this circumstance for the purpose of surprising gentlemen who, as whist players, knew General Scott so long and so well, with the additional circumstance that during the whole voyage the General's equanimity was undisturbed — that not a word of reproof, nor even an impatient gesture, was heard or observed.

One evening after our rubber I said to the General: " There is one question I have often wished to ask you, but have been restrained by the fear that it might be improper." The General drew himself up and said in his emphatic manner : " Sir, you are incapable of asking an improper question." I said : " You are very kind; but if my inquiry is indiscreet I am sure you will allow it to pass unanswered." " I hear you, sir," he replied. " Well then, General, did anything remarkable happen to you on the morning of the Battle of Chippewa?" After a brief but impressive silence he said : " Yes, sir, something did happen to me, something very remarkable. I will now for the third time in my life repeat the story : —

" The fourth day of July, 1814, was one of extreme heat. On that day my brigade skirmished with a British force, commanded by General Riall, from an early hour in the morning till late in the afternoon. We had driven the enemy down the river some twelve miles to Street's Creek, near Chippewa, where we encamped for the night, our army occupying the west, while that of the enemy was encamped on the east side of the creek. After our tents had been pitched I observed a flag borne by a man in peasant's dress approaching my marquee. He brought a letter from a lady who occupied a large mansion on the opposite side of the creek, informing me that she was the wife of a member of Parliament who was then at Quebec; that her children, servants, and a young lady friend were alone with her in the house; that General Riall had placed a sentinel before her door; and that she ventured, with great doubts of the propriety of the request, to ask that I would place a sentinel upon the bridge to protect her against stragglers from our camp. I assured the messenger that the lady's request should be complied with. Early the next morning the same messenger, bearing a white flag, reappeared with a note from the same lady, thank-. ing me for the protection she had enjoyed, adding that in acknowledgment of my civilities she begged that I would, with such members of my staff as I chose to bring with me, accept the hospitalities of her house at a breakfast which had been prepared with considerable attention and was quite ready. Acting upon an impulse which I have never been able to analyze or comprehend, I called two of my aids, Lieutenants Worth and Watts, and returned with the messenger to the mansion already indicated.

" We met our hostess at the door, who ushered us into the dining-room, where breakfast awaited us, and where the young lady previously referred to was already seated by the coffee urn, our hostess asking to be excused for a few minutes, and the young lady immediately served our coffee. Before we had broken our fast Lieutenant Watts rose from the table to get his bandana (that being before the days of napkins), which he had left in his cap on a side-table by the window, glancing through

which he saw Indians approaching the house on one side, and
red-coats approaching it on the other, with an evident purpose
of surrounding it and us, — and instantly exclaimed : 'General,
we are betrayed!' Springing from the table and clearing the
house I saw our danger, and remembering Lord Chesterfield
had said, 'Whatever it is proper to do it is proper to do well,'
and as we had to run, and my legs were longer than those of
my companions, I soon outstripped them. As we made our
escape we were fired at, but got across the bridge in safety.

"I felt so much shame and mortification at having so nearly
fallen into a trap, that I could scarcely fix my mind upon the
duties which now demanded my undivided attention. I knew
that I had committed a great indiscretion in accepting the singular invitation, and that if any disaster resulted from it I
richly deserved to lose both my commission and my character.
I constantly found myself wondering whether the lady really
intended to betray us, or whether we had been accidentally observed. The question would recur even amidst the excitement
of battle. Fortunately my presence and services in the field
were not required until Generals Porter and Ripley had been
engaged at intervals for several hours, so that when my brigade,
with Towson's artillery, were ordered to cross Street's Creek,
my nerves and confidence had become measurably quieted and
restored. I need not describe the Battle of Chippewa. That
belongs to and is part of the history of our country. It is sufficient to say that at the close of the day we were masters of the
position, and that our arms were in no way discredited. The
British army had fallen back leaving their wounded in our possession. The mansion which I had visited in the morning was
the largest house near, and to that the wounded officers in both
armies were carried for surgical treatment. As soon as I could
leave the field I went over to look after my wounded. I found
the English officers lying on the first floor, and our own on the
floor above. I saw in the lower room the young lady whom I
had met in the morning at the breakfast-table, her white dress
all sprinkled with blood. She had been attending to the British wounded. On the second floor, just as I was turning into
the room where our officers were, I met my hostess.

"One glance at her was quite sufficient to answer the question which I had been asking myself all day. She *had* intended

to betray me, and nothing but the accident of my aid rising for his handkerchief saved us from capture.

"Years afterward, in reflecting upon this incident, I was led to doubt whether I had not misconstrued her startled manner as I suddenly encountered her. That unexpected meeting would have occasioned embarrassment in either contingency; and it is so difficult to believe a lady of cultivation and refinement capable of such an act that I am now, nearly half a century after the event, disposed to give my hostess the benefit of that doubt."

"And now, sir," added the General, "this is the third time in my life I have told this story. I do not remember to have been spoken to before on that subject for many years." He looked at me, and seemed to be considering with himself a few moments, and then said: "Remembering your intimacy with General Worth, I need not inquire how you came to a knowledge of our secret."

"Well, General," I replied, "I have kept the secret faithfully for more than forty years, always hoping to obtain your own version of what struck me as a most remarkable incident in your military life."

We then chatted pleasantly about other incidents of the war of 1812. On remarking that when I saw him in September, 1812 — then a major of artillery — he was at once the tallest and the slenderest person I had ever seen, he replied: "Yes, sir; you recall a physical fact which to those who see me now must appear incredible, yet I remember that in those days soldiers drew irreverent comparisons between their commanding officer and a ramrod or a bean-pole."

Our passage was a protracted one, during which I had long and frequent conversations with General Scott, from whom I derived much valuable information. He was, though physically infirm, in full possession of his intellectual faculties.

We encountered heavy gales during the first eight days of the voyage. Several of our passengers, including Colonel Scott, a son-in-law of the veteran General, were secessionists. These, with one exception, were indisposed to associate with Union people. The exception was Colonel Winthrop of New Orleans, with whom I had formed an agreeable acquaintance at Florence in Italy in 1852. On our arrival at Southampton, where the English mails were left, an incident occurred which occasioned much excitement and some uneasiness. As we were passing up Southampton Water just before sunrise a steamer appeared about a mile astern. When our anchor was cast that steamer in passing displayed Confederate colors, and proved to be the Nashville, by which the Harvey Birch and other Union vessels had just been captured and burnt. All was immediately astir on the Arago, all expecting an attack from the Nashville as soon as we got out of neutral water. General Scott, erect and looking an inch or two higher than usual, asked Captain Lines what means of defense he had. Thirty muskets and two cannons were found to be available. The crew, and such passengers as were qualified for duty, were promptly formed upon the forward deck where the business of drilling commenced. Meantime our secession passengers were unable to conceal their gratification at the prospect of falling into the hands of friends. But that General Scott would have regarded it as a desertion, I am not sure that I should not have deemed it a duty to go on shore instead of remaining on board the Arago. Just as we were heaving up the anchor, however, all anxiety about the Nashville was relieved. An agent came on board with the information that the Nashville had put into Southampton for repairs and was going into the dry dock. Defensive operations ceased and the voyage was resumed without apprehension. We remained a day at Havre for the purpose of accompanying General Scott to Paris. The steamer which followed us from America brought the news of the taking of Messrs. Mason and Slidell, the Confederate commissioners, from the British vessel. This aroused a storm of official and popular indignation throughout England, with which the French press, if not the French government, sympathized. The Hon. Mr. Dayton invited Lieutenant-General Scott, Archbishop Hughes, Mr. John Bigelow (then our consul at Paris), and myself to his house for consultation. General Scott, then suffering from a fresh attack of gout, was unable to attend. In the hope of allaying the excitement which the capture of Messrs. Mason and Slidell had occasioned, it was deemed important that a letter from General Scott should immediately appear in the French and English journals. We all knew, however, that the General, then suffering acute pain and his hand much swollen, was physically, at least, incapacitated.

All knew how fastidiously careful the General was of his literary reputation, and how difficult it would be to induce him to adopt a line or sentence not written by himself. But the emergency was so great that an effort had to be made, and the delicate and difficult duty of "belling the cat" was put upon me. Receiving my instructions in regard to the points to be presented in the proposed letter I repaired, not without many misgivings, to the Hotel Westminster, where I found the General suffering from rheumatic gout. He was much excited by the threats of war, and had already made up his mind to return home in the steamer which brought us to France, saying that "old and infirm as he was, if England was to seize her opportunity to make war upon us, he could not, with his sense of duty and honor, remain abroad." He said that in the event of war England would make the city of New York her first point of attack; that, in view of the importance of protecting our great commercial metropolis in such an emergency, he had matured a plan of operations insuring its safety; and that, if too infirm to take the field, he could and would save the city of New York.

After listening attentively to my message, he said that he concurred in the importance of the suggestion, and would promptly act upon it if it were not a physical impossibility. I replied that, knowing how severely he was suffering, nothing but a matter which deeply concerned the welfare of a country that he had served so long and faithfully could have induced me to have preferred such a request; that on my way from the legation it had occurred to me that if I could obtain from him in conversation his views of the points to be submitted, and an idea of the spirit and temper which the subject and occasion would inspire, they might be written out and submitted to him for revisal and correction. To this suggestion he cheerfully assented, and I took my leave, promising to return with the draft of the letter as soon as it could be prepared.

Meantime, in my absence, Mr. Bigelow had been at work diligently preparing a letter — a letter which, three hours afterward, I handed to General Scott, who read it first with absorbing interest and again with critical attention. After expressing his warm approval of every sentiment and his admiration of its style and tone, he attached his large, bold autograph to the letter without making the slightest change even in the punctuation, in regard to which he was known to be particularly tenacious and sensitive. I returned to the legation, where my friends were as much surprised as delighted with the success of an enterprise which they had deemed almost impossible. I departed immediately for London, and on the following day General Scott's letter appeared in the "Times," "News," "Star," and "Telegraph." Mr. Bigelow prepared copies for the leading journals of Paris. It was accepted abroad and at home as an able and well-timed appeal to the judgment, reason, and good sense of both countries, and reflects equal credit upon the ability of Mr. Bigelow and the patriotism of General Scott.

General Scott entered the army of the United States as a captain of artillery in 1808. His name became illustrious as early as 1814, while his subsequent career in our Florida, Black Hawk, and Mexican wars served to brighten and freshen the laurels won in early life. I remember, immediately after the conquest of Mexico, to have listened, with several other gentlemen at the Astor House, to a most interesting account of the various battles that occurred between Vera Cruz and Mexico from my friend Kendall, editor of the "New Orleans Picayune," who was attached to General Scott's staff. In the course of this narrative he spoke of General Scott from two stand-points. When the army was in repose, and some of the officers inclined to relax their discipline, and others to "lay around loose," General Scott was as strict and vigilant as when preparing for battle. Officers were required at all times to wear their uniforms and side-arms. This occasioned annoyance, and they not unfrequently applied the epithet of "Old Fuss and Feathers" to the commanding general. But, added Mr. Kendall, on all occasions of difficulty and danger all thoughts and eyes were turned toward headquarters. In preparing for battle, and while the conflict lasted, not only the orders but the gestures of General Scott were as anxiously listened to and observed as they were promptly and cheerfully obeyed. In battle, confidence in the wisdom of their general inspired officers and soldiers alike, and rendered the army invincible. Those who laughed at him while the sun was shining turned to him for safety amid the thunders and lightning of battle. When we arrived at the capital, and General Scott announced his purpose to ride with his staff in full uniform through the principal streets of the city of the Montezumas, the generals of his army, fearing that he would be fired upon by persons in concealment, urged him, unavailingly, however, to desist. Mr. Kendall added that that ride through the conquered capital of Mexico was a most imposing and impressive military pageant; General Scott, splendidly mounted, a few feet in front of the staff, with his towering person and tall plume attracting and reflecting back the rays of a bright sun, being the "observed of all observers."

Of the political episodes of General Scott's life I may have occasion to speak in another chapter. Meantime it may be proper to say here that while, during the last six or seven years, other friends have frequently suggested and occasionally urged me to work up into a book the material, personal and political, which during a long and somewhat eventful life in subordinate positions had been accumulating, I had not finally decided to do so until stimulated by the following letter : —

New York, *April* 21, 1865.

Dear Sir, — I read a little faster than I recovered vision. Your very interesting letters from Europe will deserve a place in every American library. This is my candid judgment, independent of the frequent mention in the book, with honor, of my name. Two paragraphs near the close of the book, describing your first entrance into New York, remind me of Franklin's entrance into Philadelphia, and excite the hope that you may favor the world with a full autobiography. I cannot expect to live long enough to read the work, but you can give it the power of exciting thousands of smart boys to conquer difficulties in careers of distinguished usefulness.

With greatest esteem, yours truly,

Winfield Scott.

Thurlow Weed.